What readers are saying about this book...

"Perhaps the best book out there..." Y.D. IL

"Had all the facts and explanations I required." R.E. MI

"Very, very good and informative, I'm also impressed with the disk and Tempest." D.F. CA

"Excellent reference! Easy to understand and find information." R.T. MI

"This is the best book I've read." P.M. WA

"Best DOS book I've seen..." S.J. CA

"A very practical guide and reference for using MS-DOS." P.C. Colombia

"...Excellent, compared to all existing ones I've tried out." J.L. NY

"Your books are absolutely excellent, informative and attractive." C.F. MI

What readers are saying about Tempest...

"An absolutely wonderful product. The word needs to get out on this software." M.R. WA

"Great program, worth far more than it sells for." O.L. CA

"Excellent program for DOS users and terrific software value." V.G. FL

"Tempest graphic shell is very easy to use..." C.M. IL

"Excellent program for the price." H.A. MI

"Excellent software... indicates a lot of thought and very careful design has gone into its production." A.J. Australia

SPECIAL EDITION

Includes Tempest- The Graphical Shell Software for DOS 6.0

DOS 6.0
COMPLETE

Special Edition Includes
Tempest Graphical Shell
Software for DOS 6.0

by
Manfred Tornsdorf
and
Helmut Tornsdorf

Abacus
A Data Becker Book

Copyright © 1993   Abacus
                            5370 52nd Street, S.E.
                            Grand Rapids, MI 49512

Copyright © 1993   DATA BECKER GmbH
                            Merowingerstrasse 30
                            4000 Duesseldorf, Germany

Editors: Robbin Markley, Louise Benzer,
                            Scott Slaughter, Gene Traas,
                            George Miller, Jim D'Haem, Tony
                            Greer, Al Wier

ISBN 1-55755-182-0

Printed in U.S.A.
11 10 9 8 7 6 5 4 3 2 1

Foreword - Special Edition

For a limited time, **Tempest**, the graphic shell for MS-DOS 6.0 is included with **DOS 6.0 Complete - Special Edition**.

Tempest is a graphical Program Manager and Shell for all DOS computers. It's the graphic shell alternative to DOS 6.0's DOSSHELL. Using pull-down menus, dialog boxes and windows, **Tempest** makes working with DOS 6.0 easier than ever. All DOS commands are executed with just a click of your mouse button. Whether you need to move files, rename directories or launch programs, you'll find **Tempest** is the answer to easier computing.

TEMPEST is a complete independent software package included with this Special Edition of **DOS 6.0 Complete**. The complete TEMPEST manual is included as the last section of this book.

Foreword

MS-DOS 6.0 expands upon and improves the earlier versions of the operating system for IBM compatible personal computers. For the first time, MS-DOS comes supplied with all the essential utilities for an operating system in a more powerful, easier to operate format. MS-DOS 6.0 provides several solutions to your problems. Also, it has become the best DOS for Windows, offering performance features that haven't been realized by any other version of DOS.

This close symbiosis with Windows enables you to run the two systems alongside each other both better and more easily. Therefore, we have emphasized this close relationship between DOS and Windows throughout this book.

For a long time now, users haven't even been getting the most out of the earlier versions of DOS. We want to keep this from happening when you use the new, powerful MS-DOS 6.0. We would like to offer you a book that is not only complete, with detailed coverage of all the aspects of MS-DOS 6.0, but also guarantee you a good overview of the book at all times, through the clear structure of the book. The numerous practical examples, combined with the tips and tricks, save you unnecessary experimentation and allow you to benefit from years of experience. To provide you with easy access to this book, we have done the following:

- Quick **Overviews** before each chapter: All good books are also written for readers in a hurry (i.e., they don't force the reader to struggle through 50 pages when a brief overview on two pages will also do the trick).

- The comprehensive **Glossary** of important terms in MS-DOS 6.0 prevents you from having to memorize all the terms. For example, you can find out quickly what a term having to do with memory management means.

- Our **Index** will also help you find information quickly. This index not only combines many index entries under the main concepts, it also marks the main location in the book with a page reference. That means you'll always be able to find the page where the term or topic is discussed in great detail.

We hope that this book comes as close as possible to your needs and expectations. If you have any suggestions or ideas of your own, we would be happy to hear from you.

About this book

DOS 6.0 Complete is a combination of an introduction and reference guide to MS-DOS 6.0 for beginners and advanced users. We'll learn the ins and outs of this new operating system. During your initial learning sessions, you'll need information about the functions and commands of the operating system. Once you have some experience with MS-DOS 6.0, you won't need a reference for the syntax and explanation of commands.

The reference section

The MS-DOS commands are listed alphabetically and described in Syntax, Options and Description sections. Certain characters and notations used in these sections have the following meaning:

[]   Parameters enclosed in square brackets are optional.

| Alternative parameters are separated by a vertical bar. Only one of the parameters separated by a vertical bar can be entered in the command.

path   Specifies the hierarchical order of the directories separated by a backslash.

filename
          Specifies the name of the file and may include an extension.

pathname
          Specifies the path followed by the filename.

*   Any character or combination of characters may be replaced by an asterisk (*). This wildcard character can be located in any position of the filename or extension, but wildcards are permitted only when explicitly noted.

?   Any single character may be replaced by a question mark (?). This wildcard character can be located in any position of the filename or extension, but wildcards are permitted only when explicitly noted.

Options are listed after each command's Syntax for easy reference.

The Tempest section

TEMPEST is a complete independent software package included with this Special Edition of **DOS 6.0 Complete**. The complete TEMPEST software manual is bound as the last section of this book.

Tempest provides a graphical Program Manager and Shell for MS-DOS 6.0. Tempest makes working with MS-DOS 6.0 easier than ever by using pull-down menus, dialog boxes and windows. **Tempest** can do even more for you. You can create your own customized environment by designing your desktop with the built-in versatile Icon Editor. **Tempest** also includes a convenient text editor and two integrated screen savers, preventing programs from burning an image into your monitor by blanking the screen during inactive periods. Whether you need to move files, rename directories or launch programs, you'll find **Tempest** is the answer to easier computing.

Icons used in this book

In this book you'll see a number of icons, which will help you locate information quickly:

The "Warning" icon indicates the possibility of errors and other problems. Read the accompanying paragraph before invoking the command or function.

The "Error" icon indicates typical errors that may occur. Reading the accompanying paragraph may help you avoid these errors. If an error does occur, this text often lists a solution to the problem.

The "Note" icon provides additional information about the current topic, or refer you to other locations where you can find more information.

 The "Hint" icon indicates tips and tricks for using the corresponding command or function.

Getting the most out of *DOS 6.0 Complete*

- If you're new to MS-DOS 6.0, read Chapter 1, "Introduction to MS-DOS". If you still haven't installed MS-DOS 6.0, you'll find the necessary information in your MS-DOS 6.0 User's Manual.

- If you need information about a new subject, refer to the specific section of *DOS 6.0 Complete* that describes that particular subject. All the basic information is located there. Note any references and turn to the reference section for additional information.

- To find the important options of a command, with which you're familiar, skim the appropriate chapter. Pay attention to the corresponding captions.

- If you're familiar with a basic subject, but need special details, use the reference section. This section contains an overview that can be used to quickly find the necessary information. In addition, the comprehensive index also helps you locate information quickly.

Different versions of DOS

DOS 6.0 Complete covers both MS-DOS and the IBM version called PC-DOS. Since IBM is a licensed version of MS-DOS, the differences between the two versions are insignificant. In the following sections we'll refer only to MS-DOS. Any differences will be pointed out in the appropriate sections.

The Companion Diskette

The companion diskette has two subdirectories, TEMPEST and DOS6CPLT. The Tempest files are located in the TEMPEST directory and the DOS6CPLT directory contains the listings for batch, COM and EXE files discussed in this book. See the last section in this book for information on TEMPEST.

The INSTALL program on the companion diskette can be used to install the files of the companion diskette. Simply insert the companion diskette in your drive and type INSTALL, then follow the instructions displayed on your screen. More information is contained in the README.TXT file located on the companion diskette.

The DOS6CPLT directory has two subdirectories:
- The BASIC directory contains the QBasic program listings from Chapter 17 (Using QBasic).
- The TOOLS directory contains a group of new, ready-to-run programs to streamline your sessions with DOS.

We hope that this book comes as close as possible to your needs and expectations.

Helmut Tornsdorf, Manfred Tornsdorf and company

Table of Contents

Chapter

Introduction To MS-DOS

In this chapter we'll briefly discuss the history of MS-DOS and introduce the new features of the latest version, MS-DOS 6.0. Following an explanation of the most important changes in Version 6.0, you'll find a table summarizing the available MS-DOS commands. Any differences between older versions of DOS and Version 6.0 are indicated for each command. So, you can quickly determine whether any DOS commands have been added or changed.

The information in this chapter serves two purposes. If you're using an earlier version of MS-DOS, you can determine whether upgrading to the new version is worth the cost and effort. Also, you can quickly learn what you need to know in order to use the new and improved features of MS-DOS 6.0.

Certain commands are no longer included with DOS 6.0. However, the MS-DOS upgrade program will not remove these commands during installation. If any of these commands are needed, you can order a Supplemental Disk from Microsoft that contains these commands. The following commands are:

- ASSIGN
- BACKUP
- COMP
- EDLIN
- EXE2BIN
- GRAFTABL
- JOIN
- MIRROR
- RECOVER

1.1   Basic Functions of MS-DOS

MS-DOS is an operating system that provides your computer with important basic functions. It serves as a link not only between the user and the PC, but also between the application program and available hardware. By handling the differences between various hardware devices, MS-DOS makes your PC compatible with numerous peripherals.

The main purpose of the operating system is to ensure that your computer can operate, or actually "cooperate" with the entire computer system. Data transfer between the computer and peripheral devices must be carefully organized and controlled. The operating system coordinates this data transfer so that your computer operates in harmony with various peripherals, from the input devices (keyboard, mouse, joystick, lightpen, etc.) to data storage media, screen and printer. The operating system also ensures smooth data transfer between the processor and memory.

The operating system's second task, which is illustrated in the lower portion of the following figure, is ensuring that all the available types of devices can be used. With the help of the operating system and special programs called drivers, many types of disk drives, monitors, and printers, for example, can work with your computer. The operating system "smoothes out" the differences among these hardware devices, providing a common (device-independent) interface for application programs.

The following diagram illustrates the basic tasks of an operating system:

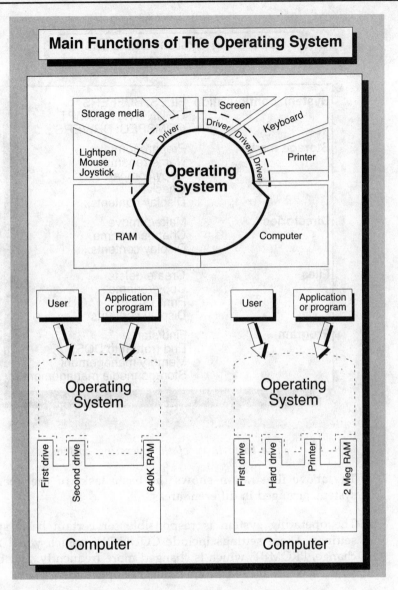

Basic functions of the operating system

```
                    ┌─────────────────────────────────────┐
                    │   Operating System Basic Tasks      │
                    └─────────────────────────────────────┘

   System configuration   FILES; BUFFERS
                          COUNTRY; PROMPT
                          COMSPEC; DRIVERS ....

   Storage media          Prepare/format
                          Name/rename
                          Copy/compare
                          Check
                          Display contents....

   Directories            Make/remove
                          Change/rename
                          Display contents....

   Files                  Create/delete
                          Copy/rename
                          Print
                          Display contents

   Program                Find/start
                          End (return to DOS)
                          Memory management
                          Storage media management
```

The basic tasks of the operating system

The above illustration shows the basic tasks of the operating system, arranged in different areas.

The operating system is responsible for certain basic system settings. These settings include COUNTRY, which you'll rarely change, PROMPT, which is changed more frequently, and FILES, which specifies the maximum number of open FILES.

As the name "DOS" (Disk Operating System) indicates, one of the operating system's most important responsibilities is disk handling. These functions include formatting diskettes, listing directory contents, etc.

Directories are used to access the files on disks (hard drives and diskettes) and help keep large disks organized. You can use the operating system to create and delete directories, change the current directory, and list a directory's contents.

Files contain the results of your work with your computer. You can use the operating system to create, copy, rename, delete, and otherwise manipulate files.

Some files contain executable programs. The operating system locates these files, activates them, and ensures that it is available to perform additional operations once these programs end.

1.2   History of MS-DOS

MS-DOS was introduced along with the first IBM PC. This PC had from 16 to 64K of main memory and used single sided diskettes with 160K capacity. MS-DOS 1.0, which was included with these PCs, had fewer commands and options than the latest versions of MS-DOS.

MS-DOS Version 1.1 was introduced shortly after this. It was able to support 320K of memory and also increased the storage capacity of diskettes (up to 320K) by using both sides of the diskette (double sided).

In 1983, the IBM PC/XT (XT is an abbreviation for eXTended), with a 10 Meg hard drive, appeared on the market. This hard drive could store 10 million characters.

So that users could manage the larger number of files, an option, that allowed users to create subdirectories, was added to MS-DOS. This meant that, instead of using one directory to store numerous files, you could store related information in various subdirectories of the directory. This is similar to the drawers of a desk; the desk represents a directory and the drawers represent the subdirectories. This new version of MS-DOS was Version 2.0. In this version, you could specify a search path for MS-DOS commands and programs by using the PATH command.

Version 2.0 was also better able to support new devices and peripherals. The new version had new commands for configuring the computer (DEVICE for adding additional utility programs, BUFFERS and FILES for adapting to different storage media) and a special driver called ANSI.SYS for extending the screen and keyboard control system.

In 1984 developers added the option of customizing MS-DOS for different countries. To do this, Version 2.1 contained a program called COUNTRY.SYS. In the same year, MS-DOS was translated into several languages and licensed to many personal computer manufacturers. As a result of this, Version 2.11 became widely distributed.

Next came the development of the successor to the PC/XT, the new PC/AT (known as the AT today). This new computer was not only faster, but could also manage more than 640K of memory and included a hard drive and a disk drive with 1.2 Meg capacity. In 1984, MS-DOS 3.0 was released as a temporary solution for use with the AT, with support for the new disk drives and hard drives. In the same year, Version 3.1 was introduced. This version provided network capabilities, simulated drives, and keyboard adaptation to special characters (such as accents in foreign languages).

With MS-DOS 3.1, for the first time it was possible to use extended memory for the AT. MS-DOS 3.1 included the driver VDISK.SYS, which could use a part of the main memory or extended memory for file storage (RAM disk).

In 1986, Version 3.2 provided support for the new 3 1/2 inch disk drives with 720K storage capacity. The configuration command, DRIVPARM, allowed users to change the parameters of drives. The new APPEND command not only made it possible to find commands in any directory (see PATH), but also allowed users to define a search path for files. MS-DOS finally had a command for copying files that included subdirectories and had special options for data backup (XCOPY).

The most widely-used version of MS-DOS, Version 3.3, was introduced in 1987. It allowed users to adapt to country-specific characters that could be displayed on the screen and printed on IBM printers. You could also use CALL to call other batch files, from a batch file, as subroutines. Also, the new configuration command FASTOPEN enabled users to find subdirectories and files quickly.

Many believed that MS-DOS would be eliminated by its successor, the multitasking operating system OS/2. However, OS/2 required a lot of memory (a minimum of 2 Meg) and an extremely fast computer. Since memory was rather expensive at the time (1 Meg was about $500; today it's about $50), in 1988 MS-DOS Version 4.0 was introduced. This version's most important innovations were:

- For the first time, a graphical user interface was available with the DOS Shell. You could operate this interface with pull-down menus, a mouse or the keyboard.

- The 32 Meg limit for hard drives was eliminated. Hard drives could now be up to 2 gigabytes (2048 Meg) in size.

- EMM386.EXE and XMA2EMS.SYS enabled users to manage expanded memory; some MS-DOS commands could also use this memory.

- Installation went smoothly, was menu-driven, and automatically created the necessary system files AUTOEXEC.BAT and CONFIG.SYS.

1.3 A Major Improvement: MS-DOS 5.0

After Digital Research developed DR DOS 5.0, a very powerful and user-friendly competitor to MS-DOS, it was obvious that MS-DOS needed additional improvements. As a result, MS-DOS 5.0 was introduced in the summer of 1991.

Installation

The MS-DOS 5.0 installation is extremely simple. Actually, there are two versions of MS-DOS 5.0. One version is used if MS-DOS has never been installed on the computer and the other version is used when you're upgrading from an earlier MS-DOS version. The upgrade version automatically stores all of the important data on the hard drive onto a backup diskette. This diskette is used to restore this data if problems occur during the installation. Also, instead of being overwritten, existing versions of DOS are backed up to a special directory. You don't even have to boot MS-DOS 5.0 for the installation. You can also start the installation program (SETUP) from other versions of DOS.

MS-DOS 5.0 doesn't require a lot of memory

Many users want to use the new features and improvements of Version 5.0 but think that it will require so much memory that there won't be enough memory left for their applications. However, if you own an AT with at least 1 Meg of memory, you don't have to worry. With the extended memory manager, HIMEM.SYS, MS-DOS 5.0 uses the first 64K of extended memory (high memory), leaving about 50K more main memory for application programs. If you start MS-DOS without any drivers ("bare"), about 623K will be available for programs. With the required base settings of BUFFERS=25 and FILES=25, almost 615K will still be free.

This option requires at least an AT with free extended memory and the appropriate lines in the CONFIG.SYS file. The installation procedure automatically inserts these lines in CONFIG.SYS. You need a minimum of an AT with the 80286 processor in order to use extended memory. This memory is outside the limits of a PC based on the 8086/8088.

All important MS-DOS commands include a reference to the version being used. For example, you cannot start with MS-DOS 5.0 and then use commands unique to MS-DOS 6.0. However, MS-DOS is upwardly compatible in all other instances. So, you can simply install the new MS-DOS 6.0 and continue working with all your programs and files.

The revised DOS Shell

MS-DOS 5.0 features a completely revised DOS Shell. Many of the elements of the MS-DOS 5.0 Shell are similar to those found in Windows. The Program Manager is different from the "Start Programs" screen of Version 4.01. Most importantly, the new MS-DOS Shell operates according to SAA (System Application Architecture) standards. So, to run a program, you can press [Alt]+[F]+[R]. Or, you can select a program from the Main group of the program list area.

The DOS Shell of Version 5.0 also has many other improvements. Along with colors, users can set different graphics modes. It's also possible to divide different tasks, since you can finally create new groups (subgroups) within program groups. This allows you to create specific user shells.

In addition to the program list area, which appears in the lower half of the window, the DOS Shell also contains the file list area, which appears in the upper half. The file list area displays the directory tree on the left and the files in the current directory on the right. You can divide the screen in half to show two directories and their files. This makes it easier to copy and move files. It's also possible to assign certain file extensions to programs and to start the proper program automatically when selecting a file with one of these extensions.

The file list area is very similar to the Microsoft Windows File Manager. A plus sign (+) next to a directory in the tree indicates that the directory contains subdirectories. Click on the plus sign with the mouse to display these subdirectories. Select the directory again to close the subdirectories.

Multitasking in the DOS Shell

MS-DOS 5.0 is still a single-user, single-program operating system. However, with the Task Swapper in the MS-DOS Shell, you can easily run more than one program simultaneously. When you activate the appropriate menu item in the MS-DOS Shell, the program list opens one area for active programs. Then if you start a program from the MS-DOS Shell, you can press Ctrl+Alt to switch to the next program and press Ctrl+Esc to return to the MS-DOS Shell. The current program is "frozen" and saved on the hard drive. In the MS-DOS Shell, the program appears in the list of active programs. By doing this, you can start several programs and switch between them.

QBasic

MS-DOS versions up to 4.01 included GW-BASIC. However, the QBasic interpreter is included with MS-DOS 5.0. With QBasic, you can easily develop programs because the editor also supports a mouse. If you're familiar with BASIC, a powerful, user-friendly programming language, and want to create EXE files, you can use QuickBASIC 4.5 or the new Visual Basic for DOS to compile QBasic programs.

New Full Screen Editor

The line-oriented editor, EDLIN, from previous versions of DOS has been replaced by MS-DOS Editor in MS-DOS 5.0. This is a full screen editor similar to the QBasic editor.

Help included

The MS-DOS commands include an integrated help system, which you can activate with the /? switch. This help screen is available for both the external commands and the resident commands stored in the command interpreter. For example, to access information about the DIR command, type:

```
DIR /?
```

With this help system, you can easily access information without having to look through manuals. The HELP command displays a list of the commands for which MS-DOS 5.0 provides a help screen.

Simplifying input and programming macros with DOSKEY

The new DOSKEY command lets you re-activate previously entered command lines and edit them with the cursor keys. So, if you make a mistake while typing a long command line, you don't have type the entire line again.

DOSKEY also contains a "built-in batch language" that you can use to assign complex command sequences to a single command. Microsoft refers to these command sequences as macros. These macros are similar to batch files (you can even pass parameters). The main advantage of using macros is that if you assign the name of an internal MS-DOS, such as DIR, to one of these macros, the macro is called first. Therefore, your own version of the command is executed before the original. This lets you customize MS-DOS according to your preferences.

Data security with UNFORMAT, UNDELETE and MIRROR

A series of new commands expands MS-DOS 5.0's data security capabilities. Because of changes made in FORMAT procedures, you can use the UNFORMAT command to restore a hard drive or diskette that was accidentally formatted. You can recover deleted files with the UNDELETE command. If you do this immediately after deleting the file, it is almost always successful. If you also use the MIRROR command (on supplemental disk from Microsoft), which saves the File Allocation Table, you'll have almost complete data protection.

1.4   Why a New MS-DOS 6.0?

As you can see from our description of the innovations of MS-DOS 5.0, this version was clearly an important improvement over other DOS versions. So you are probably wondering whether a new version of MS-DOS is needed, especially with the existence of Windows and OS/2.

However, Microsoft believes updating DOS is important. A major reason Microsoft continues to develop MS-DOS is that DOS is the operating standard for the PC. So, when this standard is improved, millions of PC users benefit.

Also, Windows is still an operating system add-on that relies on the basic functions of MS-DOS. So, increasing MS-DOS's performance also increases the performance of Windows.

MS-DOS 6.0 in brief

Before presenting the new features of MS-DOS 6.0 in detail, we want to give you a quick overview:

- MS-DOS works even more closely with Windows. Certain drivers have been optimized and important programs are included in both MS-DOS and Windows versions.

- MS-DOS 6.0 has a powerful help system that lets you search for and print out information.

- MS-DOS 6.0 offers improved data security, with programs for virus detection, backups and recovery of deleted files. Since these collaborate closely with the other MS-DOS functions and are also available as Windows versions, they will quickly evolve into a standard.

- MS-DOS can effectively double your valuable hard drive space by automatically compressing data.

- MS-DOS 6.0 includes a defragmentation program to reorganize your hard drive, where files tend to become scattered and fragmented over time. Defragmenting can speed up hard drive access and allow larger permanent swap files for Windows.

- MS-DOS 6.0 can automatically optimize main memory with MEMMAKER. Better drivers for extended memory also make more memory available for MS-DOS and Windows.

- A new hard drive cache (SMARTDRV.EXE) offers improved performance with Windows and compressed hard drives.

- MS-DOS 6.0 offers flexibility in the AUTOEXEC.BAT and CONFIG.SYS files, as well as the option to ignore bad system files for "emergency" starting.

All improvements and extensions preserve maximum compatibility to existing versions of MS-DOS and DOS programs. According to Microsoft's claim, MS-DOS 6.0 is 100% compatible with previous versions.

MS-DOS and Windows

MS-DOS 6.0 improves upon the already impressive collaboration between MS-DOS 5.0 and Windows 3.1. In some respects, MS-DOS and Windows are so well dovetailed that using a "different" operating system or interface may severely impair performance.

Better memory management

MS-DOS 6.0 improves the allocation of available memory, leaving more memory free for application programs. These improvements are carefully tuned to Windows memory requirements, so that both program packages profit from them with neither one encroaching on the other.

For many users who were formerly not managing options and parameters to the best advantage, the available memory will increase drastically with MS-DOS 6.0. The new version includes a powerful utility called MEMMAKER that handles memory optimization automatically.

Workgroup Client

If your computer has a network card installed, it can easily be connected to one or more Windows for Workgroups computers, Windows NT computers or a LAN Manager Server.

You then have easy access (controllable by passwords) to the hard drives and directories of Windows for Workgroups computers. Access control can also be exercised from other programs via a memory-resident pop-up program.

Using a network printer in a Windows for Workgroups network is equally easy. This not only solves many problems associated with printing to different printers, but also saves the cost of purchasing additional printers or complicated printer switches.

Windows backup programs included for data security

MS-DOS 6.0 includes a robust assortment of programs for ensuring data security. Most have already proven their worth as popular products of well-known utilities developers.

One great advantage of the data security features is that the same programs work in both DOS and Windows. This way, a hard drive backed up from Windows can be restored from within DOS. Program operations and interfaces are also the same when scanning for viruses and recovering deleted files.

The only difference is that the Windows programs use the Windows display capabilities, while the DOS programs use the SAA interface.

Windows-compatible hard drive compression

A hard drive compression program is of little value unless it is 100% safe and works well with Windows. The MS-DOS 6.0 "hard drive doubler" works with Microsoft's MRCI (Microsoft Realtime Compression Interface), This means that the compression technique is thoroughly integrated and will not interfere with any DOS commands or Windows processing.

Windows-compatible cache program

The cache program SMARTDRV is also designed for seamless integration with Windows. SMARTDRV can cache hard drives and diskette drives, including disk write accesses. As a result, drastic increases in access speed can be achieved.

SMARTDRV can also lend memory to Windows to help alleviate bottlenecks. A special Windows application called SMARTMON lets you monitor the caching process. You can use the information so obtained to optimize cache settings.

Choice of system configuration

Another useful feature for working with Windows is the ability to add menus and options to the AUTOEXEC.BAT and CONFIG.SYS system files. This is good news for users who previously had to get along with compromises in system file settings, or who used different variants for DOS and Windows and copied them over as needed. Now you can choose from multiple configurations in the MS-DOS start phase.

This makes it easy to use the optimal configuration for MS-DOS or Windows according to your needs.

Convenient data security

Protecting valuable data is increasingly vital to PC users. MS-DOS 6.0 offers clear advances in data security, as seen in the following areas:

Computer virus protection

MS-DOS 6.0 offers effective protection against computer viruses through an anti-virus program for MS-DOS and Windows. Besides checking both hard drives and diskettes for stored viruses, the program also scans memory to provide active protection against any viruses and their attempts at destruction.

Powerful backup

Backing up your hard drive is fast and easy with MS-DOS 6.0. The Windows variant of the backup program can even run as a background application. Users with little or no experience can expect to perform trouble-free backups with ease.

The use of special hardware capabilities makes the backup program very fast, and the number of diskettes required is considerably reduced by data compression techniques.

Easy file recovery with Undelete

Already in MS-DOS 5.0, a program was available for the recovery of deleted files. The program, however, required a good working knowledge of DOS and could not be run from within Windows. In MS-DOS 6.0, Undelete is more powerful and easier to use. Files are actually stored in a hidden directory for a time rather than immediately deleted. This provides better protection against accidental data loss, especially with network drives. The Windows version of Undelete also lets you restore files from within Windows.

Improved hard drive usage

Along with data security, great value is placed on the efficient utilization of hard drive space. MS-DOS 6.0 offers several aids for efficient disk usage:

DoubleSpace

Despite constantly increasing hard drive capacities, program requirements for disk space seem to increase even faster. For this reason, finding enough disk space continues to be a concern for many users. MS-DOS 6.0 includes a special program that effectively doubles the storage capacity of an existing hard drive. In most cases, the compression technique that accomplishes this is barely noticeable to the user. Whether or not there is an impact on overall performance depends mostly on the speed of the drive itself. For slower disk drives, compression coupled with caching and defragmentation (see below) can actually improve access time.

Microsoft is likely to set a standard with its integrated compression software DoubleSpace. The danger of compatibility problems or data loss is then drastically reduced compared to compression programs of other developers.

The compression program is very user friendly, requires no special procedures to use, and can also compress diskettes and removable hard drives. Installation is so safe that, if interrupted by a power loss, the procedure can simply be restarted and will continue without problems. The program can also recognize disks that have been compressed by Stacker. Optimal compatibility with Windows, the MS-DOS 6.0 defragmenter DEFRAG and the cache program SMARTDRV is guaranteed.

SMARTDRV

MS-DOS 5.0 included the cache program SMARTDRV to speed up access on slower hard drives. In MS-DOS 6.0, this program is considerably more powerful and user friendly. MS-DOS automatically sets up the program during installation and also enables caching for write accesses, clearly enhancing overall performance. When SMARTDRV is used in conjunction with DoubleSpace, the improvement is even greater, since compression permits greater quantities of data to be cached. Also, SMARTDRV works smartly with Windows. It can lend space to Windows, and a utility called SMARTMON can be used from within Windows to monitor and control SMARTDRV.

DEFRAG

A disk tends to become fragmented with repeated use. As files are created, changed and deleted, gaps develop in the data, so that instead of covering a contiguous area it is scattered in disconnected pieces. This requires more frequent disk access and can slow performance considerably.

MS-DOS 6.0 has a utility called DEFRAG that can restore order to your disk. Unlike similar utilities from other vendors, DEFRAG is integrated by MS-DOS 6.0 to work trouble-free with SMARTDRV and DoubleSpace and can even support and enhance their performance.

Memory optimization

Version 5.0 of MS-DOS brought significant improvements in memory availability. Many computers that previously had 450K - 520K free for application programs could increase this to 580K - 610K under MS-DOS 6.0.

MEMMAKER

Unfortunately, taking advantage of these improvements was not always easy. Many users were reluctant to use the available techniques because of their intricate nature and the complicated control parameters required to implement them. Some mistakes could even hang the system and make it impossible to restart the computer.

In MS-DOS 6.0 a special utility called MEMMAKER makes memory management safe and easy. You no longer have to worry about disabling your computer by choosing the wrong settings.

MS-DOS 6.0 uses more special resources for memory management and can be optimized explicitly for Windows. Complete compatibility with all MS-DOS programs that use high or extended memory can be expected.

Improved EMM386

The EMM386.EXE memory manager has been improved and expanded. It gives more high memory to TSR programs and device drivers and can manage both extended and expanded memory in a single pool, eliminating the need for prechecking of memory type. The result is more available memory for application programs.

Memory management information

The user has better access to the details of memory management. MS-DOS 6.0 includes a special diagnostic program called MSD (MicroSoft Diagnostic), that provides information about particular regions of memory and device drivers. The MS-DOS command MEM also has additional options that extend the amount of information available to the user.

Improved operating system functions

Besides the many enhancements to the user interface and typical user tasks, MS-DOS 6.0 offers notable improvements for the system manager and advanced DOS user as well:

Safer installation

Installation of MS-DOS 6.0 is so safe that you can even restart your computer during installation and then continue the process or restore the system to its former status. The same is true for conversion of Stacker-compressed drives.

The installation process addresses all the major system components. Optimal settings are generated for available memory, and disk compression and caching can be implemented with flexibility and ease.

MS-DOS 6.0 network extension, available from Microsoft, simplifies network (Windows for Workgroups, Windows NT, or

LAN Manager) connection by automatically recognizing an existing network card and performing the appropriate setup. An installed OS/2 will also be recognized and taken into consideration.

Variable boot options

MS-DOS 6.0 makes it possible to include flexible configurations for booting in the system files AUTOEXEC.BAT and CONFIG.SYS. Then depending on your particular purpose, you can specify which configuration should be used for startup.

Safer starting

Many users had major problems after modifying their systems because the AUTOEXEC.BAT or CONFIG.SYS files were improperly changed. Such problems could even prevent the computer from starting.

MS-DOS 6.0 provides the ability to perform an "emergency" boot by ignoring both of these system files. Press the F5 key. Alternatively, you can request an interactive mode in which you confirm or skip the commands in the system files line by line.

Complete on-line documentation

Besides the help previously available for individual commands, MS-DOS 6.0 includes a free-standing utility that provides menu-controlled documentation on all MS-DOS commands, complete with examples of their use. The documentation can also be printed.

INTERLINK for desktops and laptops

Even without special network hardware, MS-DOS 6.0 permits easy data exchange between two PCs with a null-modem cable. This feature is of interest primarily to laptop or notebook users, who frequently need to exchange or update data with a second computer.

1.5   New Commands and Extensions

Command	Function	DOS 5.0	DOS 6.0
ANSI.SYS	Expand screen/kybd support	X	F11 and F12 now supported
APPEND	Searchpath for files	X	No change
ASSIGN	Change drive assignment	X	Can be found on supplemental disk
ATTRIB	File attributes	X	No change
BACKUP	Data backup	X	Can be found on supplemental disk
BREAK	Test/change break condition	X	No change
BUFFERS	Set buffer count	X	No change
CALL	Call subroutine	X	No change
CHCP	Show/add code page	X	No change
CD/CHDIR	Change directory	X	No change
CHKDSK	Check diskette/hard drive	X	No change
CHKSTATE	Device driver for MEMMAKER	O	New, used only by MEMMAKER
CHOICE	Options in batch files	O	New, enables better programming
CLS	Clear screen	X	No change
COMMAND	Start command interpreter	X	/K: Name of file to be executed
COMMENT	Add comment	X	No change
COMP	Compare files	X	Can be found on supplemental disk
COMSPEC	Environment variable for command interpreter	X	No change
COPY	Copy	X	No change
COUNTRY	Set country-specific DOS	X	New code pages
CTTY	Change standard input/output device	X	No change
DATE	Date input/output	X	No change
DBLSPACE	Hard drive doubler	O	New, increases hard drive capacity
DBLSPACE .SYS	Driver for DoubleSpace	O	New, used only by DBLSPACE.SYS
DEBUG	Call machine-language monitor	X	No change
DEFRAG	Optimize disk	O	New, optimizes disk storage
DEL	Delete files	X	No change
DELOLDOS	Delete old DOS version	X	No change

Command	Function	DOS 5.0	DOS 6.0
DELTREE	Delete directories	O	New, deletes DIR trees
DEVICE	Install device driver	X	No change
DEVICEHIGH	Device driver in upper memory	X	Permits specifying memory where device driver is to be loaded
DIR	Directory contents	X	Sorting also allowed by compression rate
DISKCOMP	Compare diskettes	X	No change
DISKCOPY	Copy diskettes	X	No change
DISPLAY.SYS	Device driver	X	New code pages
DOS	Use of extended memory	X	No change
DOSHELP	DOS help overview	O	New, previously HELP
DOSKEY	Input/keyboard utility	X	No change
DOSSHELL	Call DOS Shell	X	No change
DRIVER.SYS	Device driver	X	No change
DRIVPARM	Set drive parameters	X	No change
ECHO	Message display on/off	X	No change
EDIT	Full screen editor	X	No change
EDLIN	Load line editor	X	Can be found on supplemental disk
EGA.SYS	EGA screen driver	X	No change
EMM386.EXE	Expanded Memory Manager	X	No change
EMM386.EXE	Device driver	X	New parameters
ERASE	Delete files	X	No change
EXE2BIN	Convert EXE to COM files	X	Can be found on supplemental disk
EXIT	Exit command interpreter	X	No change
EXPAND	Expand compressed files	X	No change
FASTOPEN	Fast file open	X	Storing of additional options possible
FC	Compare files	X	No change
FCBS	Set number of FCBs	X	No change
FDISK	Partition hard drive	X	No change
FILES	Max number of open files	X	No change
FIND	Find character string	X	No change
FOR	Command repetition	X	No change
FORMAT	Format disk	X	No change
GOTO	Jump in batch files	X	No change
GRAFTABL	Load graphics character set	X	Can be found on supplemental disk
GRAPHICS	Load graphics print program	X	No change

Command	Function	DOS 5.0	DOS 6.0
HELP	MS-DOS help	X	New, revised. Calls program from which further help is available on each command.
HIMEM.SYS	Device driver	X	New parameters
IF	Conditional cmd execution	X	No change
INCLUDE	Computer configuration	O	New, permits sub-program calls in CONFIG.SYS
INSTALL	Load internal programs	X	No change
INTERLNK	Redirects requests in the network	O	New, controls network connection via cable
INTERLNK .EXE	Device driver	O	Driver for network connection via cable
INTERSRV	Start server	O	Specifies server computer in cable network
JOIN	Assign path to drive	X	Can be found on supplemental disk
KEYB	Select keyboard layout	X	New code pages
KEYBOARD .SYS	Device driver	X	New code pages
LABEL	Name/rename diskette or hard drive	X	No change
LASTDRIVE	Set number of drives	X	No change
LOADFIX	Fix program loading problems	X	No change
LOADHIGH	Load program in upper memory	X	Permits specifying of area where program is to be loaded
MAIL	Network communications	O	New, controls communication in a network
MD/MKDIR	Make directory	X	No change
MEM	Memory allocation	X	New parameters
MEMMAKER	Memory optimization	O	New program, optimizes memory
MENUCOLOR	Computer configuration	O	New, sets the color of the main menu in the CONFIG.SYS
MEMDEFAULT	Computer configuration	O	New, sets the default menu in the CONFIG.SYS
MENUITEM	Computer configuration	O	New, specifies items in the main menu of CONFIG.SYS

Command	Function	DOS 5.0	DOS 6.0
MICRO	Network message	O	Controls type of network message
MIRROR	Save system information	X	Can be found on supplemental disk
MODE	Screen/keyboard	X	No change
MODE LPTn = COMn	Redirect printer output	X	No change
MODE COMn	Configure serial port	X	New PARITY switches
MODE LPTn	Set parallel printer port	X	No change
MODE ... CODEPAGE ...	Character set tables	X	New code pages
MORE	Page by page display	X	No change
MOVE	Move files	O	New, enables moving files and directories
MSAVE	Virus protection	O	New, program for detecting and eliminating viruses
MSBACKUP	Data backup	O	New, menu driven program for backup and restoring data
MSD	Computer information	O	New, displays hardware information
MSHERC	Hercules graphics	X	Can be found on supplemental disk
NLSFUNC	Loads country-specific information	X	No change
NUMLOCK	Sets NumLock	O	NumLock key
PATH	Define path	X	No change
PAUSE	Interrupts processing	X	No change
POWER	Reduces power consumption	O	New, ideal for notebooks and laptops
POWER.EXE	Device driver	O	New, only necessary for POWER
PRINT	Printer setup	X	No change
PRINT	Set print files	X	No change
PRINTER .SYS	Device driver	X	No longer present
PROMPT	Define prompt character	X	No change
QBASIC	Start program editor	X	New start parameters
RAMDRIVE .SYS	Install RAM disk	X	No change
RD/RMDIR	Remove directory	X	No change
RECOVER	Restores files	X	No longer present
REM	Define comment line	X	No change
RENAME	Rename files	X	No change

Command	Function	DOS 5.0	DOS 6.0
REPLACE	Replace files	X	No change
RESTORE	Restores files	X	Only for restoring backups made with MS-DOS 3.3 to 5.0
SET	Define environment variable	X	No change
SETUP	Install MS-DOS	X	No great changes
SETVER	Change DOS version	X	No change
SHARE	File sharing	X	No change
SHELL	Loads command interpreter	X	No change
SHIFT	Changes position of variables	X	No change
SIZER.EXE	Device driver	O	New, only used by MEMMAKER
SMARTDRV .SYS	Device driver	X	New switches
SORT	Sort data	X	No change
STACKS	Memory for interrupts	X	No change
SUBMENU	Computer configuration	O	New, defines startup menu in the CONFIG.SYS
SUBST	Associates a path with a drive identifier	X	No change
SWITCHES	Enhanced keyboard	X	New switches
SYS	Copies system files	X	No change
TIME	Shows time/sets system clock	X	No change
TREE	Shows directories	X	No change
TRUENAME	Determine path	X	No change
TYPE	Display file contents	X	No change
UNDELETE	Undelete deleted files	X	New switches, Mirror integrated
UNFORMAT	Undoes format	X	No change
VER	Checks version	X	No change
VERIFY	Verifies disk write operations	X	No change
VSAFE	Virus protection program	O	New, continuously checks the computer for viruses
VOL	Volume label and serial number	X	No change
XCOPY	Copies files	X	No change

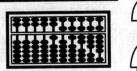

2

Working With MS-DOS 6.0

Here we'll show you the basics of working with MS-DOS. We'll show you how to start and exit DOS, enter and work with DOS commands and start applications.

2.1 Installing MS-DOS 6.0

You must install the MS-DOS operating system before using it for the first time. Before starting the installation process, make copies of the MS-DOS diskettes.

The OEM Version

An OEM version of MS-DOS 6.0 is available only on new PCs. This version's installation process is simpler than the upgrade's installation routine because it doesn't contain provisions for saving an older version of DOS or for handling existing AUTOEXEC.BAT and CONFIG.SYS files.

The Upgrade Version

MS-DOS is already installed on most of the personal computers purchased today. It's usually up to the user to upgrade from an existing version of MS-DOS (2.11 or later) to a newer release. For this reason, we'll discuss installing the upgrade version of MS-DOS in the following section. Information about installing the OEM version is located in Section 2.1.2.

2.1.1   Installing the Upgrade Version

Special installation options

When you start the installation program SETUP, you can use certain special parameters to modify the installation process according to your needs:

/B   Specifies a black/white display instead of a color display.

/E   Installs the utility programs for MS-DOS and Windows versions.

/F   To install MS-DOS on diskettes instead of on a hard drive, activate SETUP with the /F parameter. This is valid for the upgrade version only.

/G   Does not create UNINSTALL disk and doesn't prompt you when you need to upgrade your network.

/I   This parameter prevents automatic hardware settings that may lead to incompatibility problems.

/M   If your boot partition (active partition) has insufficient free space for the complete installation of MS-DOS 6.0 (2.8 Meg), use this parameter to select the minimal installation (about 512K).

/Q   This parameter unpacks files from the MS-DOS installation diskettes and copies them to the hard drive.

/U   This switch is used for incompatible hard drive partitions where normal installation isn't possible. This includes, for example, hard drives that operate with the utility programs Speedstor or DiskManager.

☞   MS-DOS 6.0 includes a special file called INFO.TXT, which contains information about compatibility problems. This file is usually located in your DOS directory. To display this file, use the text editor EDIT.

Why install?

The MS-DOS installation process performs two important tasks. First this process unpacks the files on the installation diskettes and copies them to the hard drive. Then MS-DOS is customized for your particular computer configuration. This is very important for using the operating system and the computer effectively. Today there are numerous configurations, ranging from a PC/XT with one floppy drive, 512K of memory and a monochrome Hercules graphics adapter to a 486 with several megabytes of memory and over 100 Meg of hard drive space.

MS-DOS can recognize some configuration elements automatically. For others, you may have to enter information or make corrections. However, the installation process is simple and easy to use. If you need help, on-line help is available for the various entries that are needed.

Installation requirements

If an earlier version of MS-DOS is already installed on your hard drive, backup the entire hard drive before installing MS-DOS 6.0. Under certain circumstances, all existing data may be destroyed. Also, the hard drive must be prepared for recording data before MS-DOS is installed.

- The hard drive must be formatted into tracks and sectors with a process called "hard" or "low-level" formatting. The computer manufacturer or dealer usually does this because this process requires detailed technical information about the hard drive.

- The hard drive must be divided into one or more sections called partitions. The need for partitioning arose as a result of the 32 Meg maximum disk size available to earlier versions of MS-DOS. As larger drives appeared, they were partitioned and handled as multiple hard drives, each of which could contain a maximum of 32 Meg of data.

- MS-DOS 6.0 can manage hard drives of up to 2,048 Meg without partitioning. However, at least one partition must be defined. The computer dealer usually does this before selling the computer.

- The hard drive must be prepared for recording data (formatted). During the formatting process, the operating system checks the entire hard drive and creates all the necessary management information for recording data. This means that any existing data is erased.

If you use the SETUP program to install MS-DOS, it automatically checks the hard drive for the appropriate requirements.

☞   If there isn't enough free space available on the hard
drive, the SETUP program informs you of this. Then you
have three options:

• Quit the install program.

• Install MS-DOS 6.0 on diskettes.

• Restart SETUP with the /M parameter to create a minimal
configuration of MS-DOS 6.0 on your hard drive (512K). This
option is useful for systems with only a small DOS partition C:
(e.g., 1 Meg).

Important keys

During installation, several windows, in which you can determine
the desired settings, appear. The following keys can be used:

[F1]   Displays help information for the current screen in a
separate section of the screen. This information can be
scrolled with the [↑] and [↓] keys. Pressing [Esc] removes
the help text and resumes the installation process.

[↑]/[↓]   These two cursor keys activate the various options and
settings. The currently selected option is clearly
highlighted.

[Tab]   Switches between different input areas.

[Enter]   Confirms the settings on a screen and resumes installation.

[Esc]   Displays the previous screen. You can use this key to move
"backwards" through the installation and change a
previously selected setting.

[F3]   Aborts the installation process after a security prompt.

Preparing for the installation

Before installing MS-DOS 6.0, be sure you have two blank
diskettes ready for storing information necessary to revert to your
current version of DOS in case of problems. Label these diskettes
UNINSTALL #1 and UNINSTALL #2. The install program SETUP
prompts you to insert the diskettes in drive A: when needed. Ensure
that they are properly formatted for this drive. Data from your
old version of MS-DOS, including the File Allocation Table and

the directory of the hard drive, on which you're installing the new version, will be saved on these diskettes. Sometimes only one uninstall diskette is needed.

   Since the recovery diskettes contain start files, you must use drive A: for them.

Write-protect the original MS-DOS 6.0 diskettes and make a backup copy of each one using DISKCOPY. Use the backup diskettes to perform the installation.

Installing with the SETUP program

MS-DOS Version 6.0 has its own installation program, which automatically executes a menu-controlled installation from the diskettes to your hard drive. You should always install MS-DOS using this program, since it also decompresses the files, which are on the diskettes in compressed form.

```
Microsoft MS-DOS 6 Setup
========================

  During Setup, you will need to provide and label one
or two floppy disks. Each disk can be unformatted or newly
formatted and must work in drive A. (If you use 360K disks,
you may need two disks; otherwise, you need only one disk.)
Label the disk(s) as follows:


                    UNINSTALL #1
                    UNINSTALL #2 (if needed)
  Setup saves some of your original DOS files on the
UNINSTALL disk(s), and others on your hard disk in a
directory named OLD_DOS.x. With these files, you can restore
your original DOS if necessary.
When you finish labeling your UNINSTALL disk(s), press ENTER
to continue Setup.

ENTER=Continue  F1=Help  F3=Exit
```

The Start Screen

Insert "DISKETTE 1" into drive A: and type the command SETUP. The SETUP program checks your PC's configuration, then displays a greeting and some information about itself. Press the function key F1 to display help information, press F3 to exit SETUP, or Enter to continue the installation.

   Even if you have a hard drive, you can direct the installation to diskettes by calling SETUP with the /F parameter.

After pressing ⎡Enter⎤ a message, indicating that you should have the UNINSTALL diskette(s) ready, appears.

SETUP then displays the configuration it has determined for your PC:

```
DOS version    : MS-DOS
MS-DOS path    : C:\DOS
Display type   : Hercules
```

And the following line is displayed:

```
Settings are correct.
```

If the settings aren't correct, use the ⎡↑⎤ and ⎡↓⎤ keys to select the entry to be changed and to display the other options for this entry. Use the ⎡↑⎤ and ⎡↓⎤ keys again to select the appropriate option for your system, and press ⎡Enter⎤ to confirm your selection. Then move the cursor to the statement: "Settings are correct" and press ⎡Enter⎤.

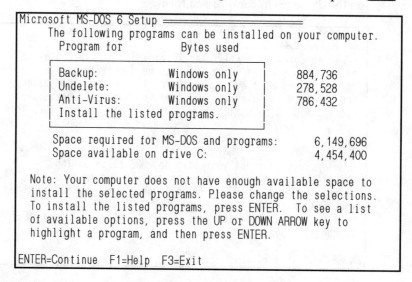

```
Microsoft MS-DOS 6 Setup ════════════════════════════
       The following programs can be installed on your computer.
       Program for          Bytes used

      | Backup:           Windows only    |   884,736
      | Undelete:         Windows only    |   278,528
      | Anti-Virus:       Windows only    |   786,432
      | Install the listed programs.      |

       Space required for MS-DOS and programs:    6,149,696
       Space available on drive C:                4,454,400

   Note: Your computer does not have enough available space to
   install the selected programs. Please change the selections.
   To install the listed programs, press ENTER.  To see a list
   of available options, press the UP or DOWN ARROW key to
   highlight a program, and then press ENTER.

ENTER=Continue  F1=Help  F3=Exit
```

The Tools selection screen

The next screen asks whether you want to install the tools for BACKUP, UNDELETE and the virus protection program. You must indicate whether these tools should be used by MS-DOS, Windows, neither or both. Again, use the ⎡↑⎤ and ⎡↓⎤ keys to view the options and make selections; then press ⎡Enter⎤ to confirm your selections.

Move the cursor to the line "Install the listed programs" and press ⎡Enter⎤. If you've requested installation for Windows, the next screen asks you for the Windows path.

On the next screen, press $\boxed{Y}$ to begin the installation (you cannot stop this process once it begins) or exit SETUP with $\boxed{F3}$. When you press $\boxed{Y}$, SETUP starts unpacking files and copying them to the hard drive. Then you'll be asked to insert a diskette for UNINSTALL #1 into drive A: and press $\boxed{Enter}$. If the diskette isn't formatted, you're asked to select a diskette capacity for formatting.

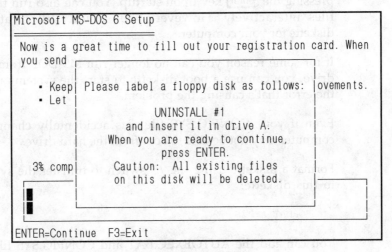

```
Microsoft MS-DOS 6 Setup

Now is a great time to fill out your registration card. When
you send ┌──────────────────────────────────────────────────┐
         │                                                  │
  • Keep │ Please label a floppy disk as follows: │ovements. │
  • Let  │                                                  │
         │                 UNINSTALL #1                     │
         │             and insert it in drive A.            │
         │          When you are ready to continue,         │
         │                  press ENTER.                    │
  3% comp│          Caution:  All existing files            │
         │            on this disk will be deleted.         ├──────
         │                                                  │
 █       │                                                  │
 █       │                                                  │
         └──────────────────────────────────────────────────┘

ENTER=Continue  F3=Exit
```

The UNINSTALL-Recovery

After the UNINSTALL disks are created, you must insert Diskette 1 again and the remaining files are copied. You'll be prompted to insert diskettes as needed (the number of diskettes depends on their size). When all files have been copied to the hard drive, SETUP prompts you to remove the last diskette from the drive and press $\boxed{Enter}$. The PC performs a warm boot (reset) to start MS-DOS 6.0.

During installation, your old DOS version is saved in the OLD_DOS 1 directory. If you won't be removing MS-DOS 6.0 from the hard drive, you can delete this directory with the DELOLDOS command. However, you shouldn't delete MS-DOS 6.0 because you may lose data.

Problems during the installation

If the installation aborts and you must restart your PC, place the UNINSTALL #1 (recovery) diskette in the drive and press $\boxed{Enter}$. A message, indicating that the installation process wasn't completed, appears. Then you can either continue the installation or restore the old MS-DOS version.

First try to continue the installation. If this doesn't work, you must restore the old version and then contact your computer dealer for help.

Preparing a boot diskette

In MS-DOS 6.0, you can avoid running the CONFIG.SYS file by pressing the ⌜Enter⌟ key upon startup. You can also run the system files interactively. However, you should still create a boot diskette for your computer.

If for some reason you can no longer run MS-DOS from the hard drive, you can use a boot diskette to start the system and correct the error that's causing the problem.

Even if your CONFIG.SYS file was accidentally changed, your computer may not be able to boot from the hard drive.

Format a diskette using the /S switch to transfer the system files to this diskette:

```
FORMAT A: /S
```

You can add the AUTOEXEC.BAT and CONFIG.SYS files to this diskette, along with a few DOS commands and help files. Remember to include the most important commands, such as SYS, FORMAT1, DISKCOPY, UNDELETE, UNFORMAT and CHKDSK.

Quick steps for installing MS-DOS 6.0 on the hard drive

- Prepare backup diskette(s) UNINSTALL #1 (and #2) for restoring old version of DOS.
- Insert MS-DOS diskette marked "DISKETTE 1".
- Type SETUP and ⌜Enter⌟.
- Confirm computer configuration (if correct).
- Select Tools settings.
- Start the installation process.
- Insert UNINSTALL #1 (and #2) at prompt.
- Reinsert first installation diskette.
- Insert remaining diskettes.
- Remove last diskette and reboot.

2.1.2 Installing the OEM Version

The version of MS-DOS 6.0 that you receive when you purchase a new computer is called the OEM (Original Equipment Manufacturer) version. Since it's the first operating system installed on your computer, the OEM version doesn't include some of the functions found in the upgrade version.

An older version of DOS doesn't exist

Unlike with the upgrade version of MS-DOS 6.0, an older version of DOS doesn't have to be saved. Therefore, UNINSTALL diskettes aren't needed for restoring the older version. Also, the DELOLDOS command isn't included because a previous version of DOS doesn't have to be saved in the /OLD_DOS 1 directory.

If your computer dealer has already installed an operating system (e.g., MS-DOS 5.0) on the new computer, installing the OEM version of MS-DOS 6.0 will rename the old \DOS directory and replace it with MS-DOS 6.0.

Initial system configuration

Although the upgrade version identifies and modifies existing system configuration information (especially the settings in the CONFIG.SYS and AUTOEXEC.BAT files), the OEM version creates completely new system files. If these files already exist, they are renamed CONFIG.OLD and AUTOEXEC.OLD.

Also, you must specify the desired country setting during installation to obtain the correct date/time format and keyboard layout.

Installation details

- Insert "Diskette 1" into disk drive A: and switch on the computer.

- The computer boots from disk drive A: and automatically activates the installation program SETUP.

You can use the following keys:

F1	Displays detailed information about each step of the installation process.
F3	Terminates the SETUP program.
Enter	Continues the installation.

- The next screen displays the default settings for the current date/time format, country, keyboard layout and storage medium (in our example, the hard drive) that will be used to install MS-DOS 6.0.

- Verify the settings and make any necessary changes.

- Press (Enter) and again select the desired entries. You now have a choice of installing on the hard drive or on diskettes.

- The next screen shows the C:\DOS directory, in which MS-DOS 6.0 is usually installed. You can accept the default directory or change it. If you want the MS-DOS Shell to open automatically at startup, also accept the next default setting. Otherwise, change this setting to NO.

- If a DOS partition wasn't created on your computer, the SETUP program now asks whether you want to:

  1. Reserve the entire free hard drive space for MS-DOS.
  2. Reserve part of the free hard drive space for MS-DOS.
  3. Don't reserve any of the free hard drive space for MS-DOS.

- If you choose the first option, the hard drive is configured as a single active DOS partition and immediately formatted.

- The second option activates the hard drive installation program FDISK, which lets you specify the size of the partition.

- If you select the third option, you don't want to install MS-DOS 6.0 on the hard drive. In this case, SETUP installs MS-DOS on diskettes.

☞   If this screen appears during the installation and you don't have much computer knowledge, choose option 1. In order to use FDISK and partition a hard drive, you need some experience with operating systems.

- The actual installation is now performed.

- You'll be prompted to change diskettes at the appropriate times.

- When the installation is complete, remove all diskettes from the drives and press (Enter). Your computer reboots under the new operating system MS-DOS 6.0.

- The CONFIG.SYS and AUTOEXEC.BAT system files are created automatically during the installation. If there are old system files that now have the ".OLD" ending, you can transfer any desired settings into the new system files. Otherwise, you can easily use the few settings in the current files.

For information on optimizing the system files, refer to Chapter 15 "Optimizing AUTOEXEC.BAT and CONFIG.SYS".

2.2 Setting up MS-DOS

Basically, MS-DOS 6.0 is customized to your computer when you install it using the SETUP program. Installation is very easy and is controlled by menus. Most users will never run into installation problems. However, SETUP cannot handle all of the options during installation or perform any kind of fine tuning. So you cannot make all of the adjustments during installation.

Also, you might want to use some of MS-DOS' special features to optimize your system's performance or to change the current settings for later use. For example, if you change the equipment on your computer (additional memory, larger hard drive, different monitor, mouse etc.), then the operating system must be adapted to the new hardware.

You can adapt MS-DOS to the hardware (and your requirements) at any time by changing two system files. Most of the necessary commands are stored in either the AUTOEXEC.BAT or CONFIG.SYS file.

Make changes carefully

Be very careful when making changes to either the AUTOEXEC.BAT or CONFIG.SYS files because mistakes can lead to serious problems. For example, your computer may not be able to find programs or the keyboard might not be able to produce the characters you want.

Mistakes in the CONFIG.SYS file could prevent the computer from starting (booting) successfully. If this happens the computer won't be able to operate and you may not be able to correct the mistake very easily.

You should always create a bootable backup floppy diskette before making changes to the AUTOEXEC.BAT or CONFIG.SYS files. You can then use this diskette to start your system and correct any mistakes in the files.

Setting up the AUTOEXEC.BAT file

The AUTOEXEC.BAT file contains MS-DOS commands that are automatically processed when the computer boots. This automates the starting sequence and saves time because the commands don't have to be typed at the keyboard.

An AUTOEXEC.BAT file is automatically created when you install MS-DOS. The following explanations will help you understand the contents of a typical AUTOEXEC.BAT file.

Making MS-DOS commands always available

If you installed MS-DOS in a subdirectory on your hard drive, use the PATH command to ensure that these commands can be executed at any time. For example, if MS-DOS is in the DOS subdirectory on the C: hard drive, then your AUTOEXEC.BAT should contain the following line:

```
PATH C:\DOS
```

 Some application programs work properly only if the directory containing the program files is included in the search path for commands. For example, Microsoft Word 6.0 is such a program. If you haven't specified a path for the WORD directory, you won't be able to use the thesaurus.

Making data files always available

Just as the PATH command lets you use commands from any directory, the APPEND command lets you access data (non-executable) files from any directory. This is important for many MS-DOS device drivers and programs that work with OVL (overlay) files. To access data files in the DOC directory on drive C: from any directory, without adding a path specification, add the following command line:

```
APPEND C:\DOC
```

Using foreign character sets

The KEYB command is used to adapt MS-DOS to foreign character sets. For example, to change to the U.K. keyboard, which will replace the # sign with the £ sign, the AUTOEXEC.BAT file should contain the following line:

```
KEYB UK,437,C:\DOS\KEYBOARD.SYS
```

 In some cases, the KEYB command is already installed in the CONFIG.SYS with the MS-DOS 6.0 SETUP command. Under these circumstances you don't necessarily need the line in the AUTOEXEC.BAT.

You should be aware of the advantages of using the INSTALL command in the CONFIG.SYS file. Using the INSTALL command in the CONFIG.SYS file allows you to load memory resident programs into memory before the AUTOEXEC.BAT file is processed. The CONFIG.SYS is processed only once at the beginning of the boot process. But the AUTOEXEC.BAT file can be processed (even accidentally) more than once. However, running the AUTOEXEC.BAT file more than once may result in error messages with certain MS-DOS commands (PRINT /D or FASTOPEN /X). If you load these commands using INSTALL from the CONFIG.SYS file, you won't accidentally try to run these commands again while the computer is running.

Specify the location of the command interpreter

When certain application programs are started, they overwrite part of the COMMAND.COM program in memory. Therefore when the application program ends COMMAND.COM must be reloaded. So that MS-DOS knows where on the hard drive to find the command interpreter the following is in the AUTOEXEC.BAT:

```
SET COMSPEC=C:\COMMAND.COM
```

 Enter the complete path for the COMMAND.COM.

For example, if COMMAND.COM is in the DOS subdirectory of your hard drive, the following command line should be in the AUTOEXEC.BAT file:

```
SET COMSPEC=C:\DOS\COMMAND.COM
```

You also need to insert the SHELL command in the CONFIG.SYS.

Set the system prompt

Use the PROMPT command to define the appearance of the MS-DOS system or ready prompt. It's a good idea to specify a system prompt that displays the current directory in the AUTOEXEC.BAT:

```
PROMPT $P$G
```

Set the break option

Use the MS-DOS BREAK command to determine when the Ctrl + C key combination for aborting a command can be used. Add the following line to your AUTOEXEC.BAT file to switch on the break option when accessing a diskette or hard drive:

```
BREAK ON
```

This option is especially important when using application programs and commands that require intensive diskette or hard drive access.

Allow screen printouts in graphics mode

When a color or graphics card adapter is used, the MS-DOS GRAPHICS command enables you to print a graphics display screen. Add the following line to your AUTOEXEC.BAT file:

```
GRAPHICS
```

Display special characters in graphics mode

In order to use the expanded ASCII characters 128 to 255 in graphics mode, use the GRAFTABL command (which is located on the Supplemental disk from Microsoft) to load a table of these characters in the memory. This command increases the size of MS-DOS that is resident in memory. It also enables you to use character sets for different countries.

```
GRAFTABL
```

Set a character set table

After preparing all of the devices to be used with character set tables (character sets are stored in Codepages), you can activate the new character set with CHCP. CHCP stands for CHange CodePage. The following command lines adapt the screen of an EGA card and the keyboard to the multilingual international table:

```
MODE CON CP PREP=((850) C:\DOS\EGA.CPI)
KEYB UK,850,C:\DOS\KEYBOARD.SYS
CHCP 850
```

You only need to install a character set if you require special characters.

Set a temporary directory

Certain MS-DOS commands create temporary files. For example, this happens when more than one command is combined with the pipe symbol "|". Older versions of MS-DOS would place these temporary files in the root directory or in the current directory, deleting them at the end of the command line.

MS-DOS, Windows and many other applications create temporary files. Since these temporary files can be annoying, a temporary directory can be set up. To do this, you first set up an environment variable named TEMP, which supplies the directory name. For example, if you have a directory named C:\DOSTEMP and want to use it as a temporary directory, your AUTOEXEC.BAT should contain the following command line:

```
SET TEMP=C:\DOSTEMP
```

 Unlike MS-DOS, many other programs (such as Microsoft Word 6.0) use TMP instead of TEMP to set a temporary working directory. For these types of temporary files, you would define the directory as follows:

```
SET TMP=C:\DOSTEMP
```

Increase the amount of conventional memory

If your computer uses an 80386 or 80486 microprocessor and has more than 640K of memory, the amount of conventional memory available for application programs may be increased by loading memory resident programs into additional memory. Most systems have 384K of additional memory, which is usually set aside for the operating system.

Some portions of this additional memory, called upper memory blocks (UMB), are left unused. Usually these UMB's aren't available for running device drivers or applications. However, if you run the EMM386 memory manager, you can access these UMB's.

In order to load device drivers and other programs into UMB's, the DEVICEHIGH or LOADHIGH command must be used to install these drivers and programs from the AUTOEXEC.BAT file. To load the code pages for the United Kingdom keyboard driver into an upper memory block of reserved memory instead of conventional memory, use the following command line:

```
LOADHIGH KEYB UK,,C:\DOS\KEYBOARD.SYS
```

Example

A simple AUTOEXEC.BAT for MS-DOS in the DOS subdirectory of the C: hard drive might look as follows:

```
PATH C:\DOS
C:\DOS\KEYB UK,437,C:\DOS\KEYBOARD.SYS
SET COMSPEC=C:\DOS\COMMAND.COM
BREAK ON
PROMPT $P$G
SET TEMP=C:\TMP
```

More Hints

If your computer doesn't have a battery operated clock, include the following lines in your AUTOEXEC.BAT:

```
DATE
TIME
```

Your computer will prompt you to enter the date and the time whenever you start or reboot your system. This will ensure that the date and time stamp for your files are always current.

In order to print files from the MS-DOS Shell, you must use the MS-DOS PRINT command with the /D switch before calling the MS-DOS Shell. Otherwise the menu command for printing won't print. The /D switch defines a device for the print queue for printing files. Use the following command line in your AUTOEXEC.BAT:

```
PRINT /D:LPT1:
```

This initializes the print queue through the first parallel port. However, this uses a portion of your computer's conventional memory area. So you should only use this option when you need to print in the MS-DOS Shell.

Load the MS-DOS Shell automatically when you start the computer

To install and run the MS-DOS Shell from the AUTOEXEC.BAT, simply use the DOSSHELL command. This command should be the last command in the AUTOEXEC.BAT file. Otherwise, any commands which follow may not be activated.

Setting up the CONFIG.SYS file

The following commands and options apply only to the CONFIG.SYS file. In the following examples, we assume that MS-DOS is installed in the C:\DOS directory of the hard drive. If this isn't the name of your DOS directory, change the examples to the actual name of your DOS directory.

The explanations are intended to help you understand the commands in the CONFIG.SYS. When you install MS-DOS, the CONFIG.SYS file is created automatically and the installation procedure adapts it to your computer.

Adjust the date and currency format

Use the COUNTRY command to adapt MS-DOS to the date and currency format of a country. For example, use the following setting for the United Kingdom:

```
COUNTRY=044,437,C:\DOS\COUNTRY.SYS
```

The computer will display the date and time in the format used in the United Kingdom.

Optimize access to disk drives

The BUFFERS statement can be used to speed up access to diskettes and hard drives. With a system that has 640K conventional memory and a hard drive, type the following in the CONFIG.SYS file:

```
BUFFERS=20
```

If you use the special driver program SMARTDRV.SYS to speed up access, use the setting BUFFERS=30 for BUFFERS. Higher settings not only waste valuable memory, but could actually reduce the speed of your computer.

Set the number of files opened simultaneously

Many application programs may require more than the 8 files that are provided by the default settings for MS-DOS. This number can be increased with the FILES command. For example, you could include the following line in your CONFIG.SYS file:

```
FILES=20
```

You may need even more files for some database programs. Check the program's manual or increase the value if an error message appears.

Set the number of logical disk drives

By default, MS-DOS can manage 5 disk drives lettered A-E. To define more disk drives, use LASTDRIVE. You might use this command if your hard drive has multiple partitions or you redefine disk drives. To use 8 disk drives lettered A to H, type the following command line in the AUTOEXEC.BAT:

```
LASTDRIVE=H
```

Define a command interpreter

Usually MS-DOS loads the COMMAND.COM program from the root directory of the current disk drive as a command interpreter. You specify an alternate path or filename with SHELL. If the command interpreter is in the DOS subdirectory, use the following line:

```
SHELL=C:\DOS\COMMAND.COM /P
```

 The path and the name of the command interpreter you specify must be the same as those specified by COMSPEC in the AUTOEXEC.BAT file. Make sure you specify the /P switch. This switch makes COMMAND.COM permanent. You can't quit the command interpreter by entering Exit.

Determine the size of the system environment

MS-DOS stores important information in an area called the system environment. You can increase the amount of memory reserved for the environment variables with the SHELL command. Since 512 bytes of system environment is enough for most applications, change the size in the CONFIG.SYS file as follows:

```
SHELL=C:\DOS\COMMAND.COM /P /E:512
```

 Be sure that you specify the /P switch; otherwise when you re-start the computer it won't run the AUTOEXEC.BAT system file. Specifying this switch also guarantees that the command interpreter is permanently installed in memory and that you can't exit from the command interpreter.

Allow for additional functions for your screen and keyboard

A special driver program, called ANSI.SYS, can be used to change the keyboard and the type of screen output. ANSI.SYS is loaded by using the DEVICE command. Install ANSI.SYS by using the following line in CONFIG.SYS:

```
DEVICE=C:\DOS\ANSI.SYS
```

Accelerate access to files

FASTOPEN speeds up the access of files that are used often. This is especially useful for database programs. Insert the following command line:

```
INSTALL=C:\DOS\FASTOPEN.EXE C:=100
```

Use additional memory

MS-DOS can directly manage only 640K of memory as conventional memory. If your computer has more memory, certain application programs can use the additional memory as Expanded Memory. The EMM386.EXE memory driver is used to manage the extended memory. The MEMMAKER program can set this up automatically for your system.

MS-DOS can use extended memory (Extended Memory) as a RAM disk. Use the RAMDRIVE.SYS device driver (refer to, "Use memory as an additional disk drive"). You can also use extended memory to speed up access to your hard drive by activating the SMARTDRV cache program from the CONFIG.SYS file. SMARTDRV is also a device driver.

 Use the MEM command to see if your computer has extended memory. The information that's displayed may look similar to the following:

```
 655360 bytes total conventional memory
 655360 bytes available to MS-DOS
 564160 largest executable program size

1441792 bytes total contiguous extended memory
      0 bytes available contiguous extended memory
 589824 bytes available XMS memory
        MS-DOS resident in High Memory Area
```

Total memory refers to the amount of conventional memory that MS-DOS can directly use, while the "largest executable program size" indicates how much memory is available when working with commands and programs. We'll discuss extended memory in more detail in the following section.

Special memory features

Installing and using more than 640K isn't always easy. Usually it requires a knowledge of memory management. Until now, distinguishing between conventional memory, extended memory and expanded memory was very complicated, which obviously made it difficult to use.

Although total memory management is more efficient and safer with MS-DOS 6.0, it's not easy to achieve an "optimum" installation of extended memory.

The following features can be used with the CONFIG.SYS:

• Before MS-DOS 6.0, extended memory was used mainly through the system call 15 (INT 15). However, this often caused multiple programs to collide, resulting in a system crash. Now a special driver program called HIMEM.SYS is used to manage extended memory.

• HIMEM.SYS also prepares a special memory area called High Memory. Under certain circumstances, MS-DOS can use this memory, thus increasing the amount of available conventional memory. To do this, you must activate HIMEM with the DEVICE command in CONFIG.SYS. You must also use the DOS=HIGH switch in the CONFIG.SYS.

• You can also load driver programs (RAM disk, SMARTDRV, mouse drivers etc.) in a special memory area (Upper Memory) to increase the conventional memory available for programs. Use the UMB setting after the DOS= switch. To use both High Memory and Upper Memory in MS-DOS, include the following command line in CONFIG.SYS:

```
DOS=HIGH,UMB
```

Use memory as an additional disk drive

You can speed up access to diskettes by using part of the conventional memory as a RAM drive instead of a mechanical disk drive. Use the RAMDRIVE.SYS device driver to do this.

Insert this line in the CONFIG.SYS file:

```
DEVICE=C:\DOS\RAMDRIVE.SYS
```

Unlike the SMARTDRV program for temporary storage of hard drive contents, the RAMDRIVE program uses extended memory. So you must reserve memory using HIMEM.

After defining a RAM drive, the next time you boot your computer, a new disk drive will be available. This drive will have a capacity of 64K and can contain 64 files or directories. The computer displays an informational message when you start your computer. Unfortunately, since the memory for the RAM disk comes from conventional memory, memory hungry applications may not have enough memory to run.

 In PC-DOS the driver is called VDISK.SYS instead of RAMDRIVE.SYS.

If your computer has extended memory, you can use it for the RAM disk. This takes some of the burden off of conventional memory. Insert the /E switch in the command line. Many ATs with 1 Meg of total memory have 384K of extended memory. To use this extended memory for a RAM disk, include the following command line in CONFIG.SYS instead of the one above:

```
DEVICE=C:\DOS\RAMDRIVE.SYS 384 /E
```

Expanded memory can also be used for a RAM disk. Use /A as a switch. If you have 1024K of expanded memory, you can use it as an additional disk drive with the following command line:

```
DEVICE=C:\DOS\RAMDRIVE.SYS 1024 /A
```

Accelerate access to hard drives

If your computer has enough extended or expanded memory, you can speed up access to your hard drive by using the SMARTDRV.SYS cache program. The parameters following the SMARTDRV command specify how much extended memory to use for temporary storage. If an amount isn't specified, a value of 256K is used. In order to install 1024K of extended memory for temporarily storing data, type the following command line in the CONFIG.SYS:

```
DEVICE=SMARTDRV.SYS 1024
```

Extended memory uses the MS-DOS 6.0 SMARTDRV program which uses an XMS driver. So, before using SMARTDRV you must install the HIMEM.SYS driver.

If you use available expanded memory instead of extended memory, use the /A switch. The line above would then read:

```
DEVICE=SMARTDRV.SYS 1024 /A
```

Define additional disk drives

MS-DOS recognizes all disk drives that are properly installed. To change the defined size of a disk drive, use the DRIVER.SYS device driver.

For example, if you have a 3.5 inch 1.44 Meg drive as drive B:, you can define this drive to also act like a 720K capacity drive rather than a 1.44 Meg capacity drive, change CONFIG.SYS to include the following line:

```
DEVICE=C:\DOS\DRIVER.SYS /D:1 /F:2 /H:2 /S:9 /T:80
```

The next time your computer is warm started, MS-DOS will report an additional loaded driver, indicating the disk drive letter to specify when you want to use disk drive B: as a 720K disk drive. Normally disk drive B: will remain a 1.44 Meg disk drive named B:. When you access the new drive, it will act like a 720K drive.

If the DRIVER.SYS file isn't in the root directory, specify the complete path.

Example

A sample CONFIG.SYS file for MS-DOS located in the root directory of the C: (hard) drive should look similar to the following:

```
DEVICE=C:\DOS\HIMEM.SYS
DOS=HIGH,UMB
DEVICE=C:\DOS\ANSI.SYS
COUNTRY=044,,C:\DOS\COUNTRY.SYS
FILES=20
BUFFERS=20
SHELL=C:\COMMAND.COM /P /E:500
INSTALL=C:\DOS\FASTOPEN.EXE C:=100
```

Use Upper Memory

If your computer has extended memory available as Upper Memory, you can also load driver programs (extension .SYS) into this special memory area. This provides more conventional memory for application programs. You can use the DEVICEHIGH command in place of DEVICE:

```
DEVICEHIGH=C:\DOS\ANSI.SYS
```

If your computer doesn't have Upper Memory or there isn't enough room, the computer automatically loads the driver in the conventional area (Conventional memory up to 640K).

2.3 Starting MS-DOS

Although you can run MS-DOS 6.0 from a floppy diskette after installing it, you might have problems with some commands. Use the SETUP installation program and install MS-DOS so that it can be adapted to your computer. If you haven't installed MS-DOS 6.0 yet, do so now.

The methods for starting MS-DOS vary depending on your computer and the kind of installation.

  If your computer is switched on and you want to re-start it, you don't have to switch off the computer. Simply press [Ctrl] + [Alt] + [Del] (warm start). This so-called warm start saves wear and tear on the power supply and monitor of your computer.

Starting MS-DOS from a diskette

You'll need a system diskette to boot your computer. This diskette must have been previously formatted with the /S switch of the FORMAT command and will contain the MS-DOS files and commands. For example, the diskette should include the AUTOEXEC.BAT and CONFIG.SYS files we discussed in the previous section.

Insert the system diskette

Insert the system diskette into drive A: and close the disk drive door (if you have one).

  If you're not sure which of your disk drives is labeled A, don't insert a diskette. Instead, see which disk drive light goes on first. Usually this is drive A:. Otherwise, refer to your computer manual.

Switching on your computer

Switch on your monitor, then switch on the computer. The screen will display various messages, depending on the kind of computer you have.

If your computer doesn't have a battery operated clock, you're prompted to enter the date and the time. The screen displays the default values and the notation for making the entries. Enter the date and the time (don't forget to press (Enter) after each entry). If you press (Enter) without making entries the default values for the date and the time will remain.

Computer ready for operation

Your computer is ready for operation and you can begin entering commands when the system prompt appears on the screen:

        A:\>_

     Even if MS-DOS is installed on your hard drive, you should still make a system diskette and keep it available. Sometimes it may be impossible to start MS-DOS from your hard drive, which would obviously prevent you from using your computer. For example, this could happen if mistakes were made while changing the CONFIG.SYS file. Your computer would fail when you try to start it.

Special features about entering commands

When booting your computer from a system diskette, you could have some problems working with your computer. This usually occurs if your hard drive contains all of the MS-DOS commands. The commands exist, but the computer can't find them.

If you start MS-DOS from a diskette and the commands are on the hard drive, define a search path on the directory with the commands. For example, if the DOS directory on the hard drive is C:\DOS, use the following line to create your search path:

        PATH C:\DOS

Instead of defining a search path, you can type the complete path in front of any MS-DOS command. For example, to format a diskette in drive A: type the command line:

        C:\DOS\FORMAT A:

If your computer doesn't have a hard drive, you'll have problems working with MS-DOS because all of the MS-DOS commands do not fit on a single diskette. Instead, they are stored on several diskettes.

So copy the commands you use most often to your system diskette. Then copy the remaining commands to other diskettes. If the message "Bad command or filename" appears and you typed the command correctly, insert the diskette containing the command.

Starting MS-DOS from the hard drive

Fortunately, if you have a hard drive, you won't need a diskette to start the computer. However, remember to remove any diskettes from drive A: before attempting to boot your computer. MS-DOS will only start from the hard drive if a diskette isn't in disk drive A:

Switch on your computer

Always switch on the monitor first before switching on your computer. As your computer starts you'll see different messages on the screen, depending on the kind of computer you have.

Enter the date and the time

If your computer doesn't have a battery operated clock, you'll be prompted to enter the date and the time. The screen displays the preset values and notation for entering the date and time. Enter the date and the time, pressing (Enter) after each entry. If you press (Enter) without making any entries, the default values will remain.

Computer ready for operation

Your computer is ready for operation when the system prompt appears on the screen followed by the cursor:

```
C:\>_
```

Now you can enter commands. If you've set up your system to start the MS-DOS Shell to start automatically, instead of seeing the system prompt, you'll be in the MS-DOS Shell. You can either start the command interpreter from the MS-DOS Shell with the "Command Prompt" program item or exit the MS-DOS Shell and remove it from memory by pressing (F3).

Quitting

If you aren't running an application program and the computer is displaying the system prompt, your computer may be switched off at any time. However, remove all diskettes from the disk drives before switching off your computer.

Before switching off your computer, you should quit the application programs properly. Turning off the power to your computer while running an application program could cause loss of valuable data. You should also secure the heads of your hard drive before switching off the computer. Many hard drive manufacturers supply a PARK program with their software. This program, which isn't part of MS-DOS, moves the heads of the hard drive to a shock-protected position.

If you're in the MS-DOS Shell, before switching off your computer exit the MS-DOS Shell by pressing F3 and secure your hard drive by using PARK. This is especially important if you've started programs, from the MS-DOS Shell, that you still haven't quit. The MS-DOS Shell stores information in temporary files. If you don't exit from the MS-DOS Shell properly, these temporary files won't be deleted correctly when you've completed your work.

2.4   Using the Keyboard

The keyboard of a computer is similar to a typewriter keyboard, except for some additional keys which are used for computer related functions.

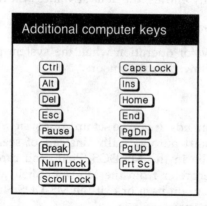

Special functions of keys in MS-DOS

Enter
After typing a command, pressing this key causes the computer to execute the command. It's usually larger than the letter keys and located on the right side of the keyboard.

Spacebar
This is the wide key at the bottom of the keyboard.

Backspace
Correction key, also called the Backspace key. This key is usually found above the Enter key with an arrow pointing to the left. You can use this key to delete the character before the cursor. Continue pressing the Backspace key to delete additional characters until there are no characters in front of the cursor.

← → ↑ ↓
Although these cursor keys can move the cursor anywhere on the screen in application programs, they don't have many functions within MS-DOS. However, MS-DOS 6.0 includes a special auxiliary program called DOSKEY to simplify entering and changing command lines, especially when working with frequently used DOS commands.

Ctrl
Special key for producing control key combinations.

Control key combinations

Ctrl + S
Pauses the output of data to the screen. Press any key or Ctrl + S again to continue displaying data on the screen.

Ctrl + C
Interrupts a command and returns to the system prompt.

Ctrl + Alt + Del
Re-starts your computer (executes a warm boot).

☞ When you execute a warm boot, all of the data in the conventional memory area of the computer is lost.

Ctrl Prt Sc
Switches output to the printer on or off.

Keyboard shortcuts for the command line

To simplify your work at the command line, you can use one of the special function keys or editing keys. Additional keys are available to edit a command line if you use DOSKEY. These functions are discussed in detail in Section 2.6.

F1   Pressing F1 copies the template of the previous command, one character at a time, to the current cursor position. Pressing F1 repeatedly will copy the entire template.

F2   Retypes characters from the template up to a matching character. The matching character is specified by pressing its key after pressing F2.

F3   Copies any remaining characters in the template. For example, typing DIR *.BAK and pressing Enter will display all files with the .BAK extension in the current directory. Typing DEL and pressing F3 will type the remainder of the command into the command line: DEL *.BAK. Pressing F3 when the cursor is at the beginning of a new command line will retype the complete template.

F4   Skips over characters in the template up to a matching character, without copying the characters to the command line. The matching character is specified by pressing its key after pressing F4.

Del   Erases the character at the cursor position and moves forward one character in the template.

Ins   Switches between the insert and overstrike modes. In the insert mode, new characters are inserted without typing over the previously entered characters. Move the cursor with the left and right cursor control keys.

Backspace
        Erases the character in front of the cursor on the command line and moves forward one position in the template.

2.5   Entering and Repeating Command Lines

When you type at the system prompt, MS-DOS saves a copy of the last line that you typed in a temporary location called a *template*. To save you the trouble of retyping long command lines, you can redisplay (recall) this command line, change it if you wish and execute it a second time.

Entering and correcting new command lines

A command line is entered after the system prompt. You can type a command in either uppercase or lowercase - commands are not case sensitive. The (Backspace) key can be used to delete the character to the left of the cursor so that you can correct a typing error. MS-DOS copies the command line to a temporary storage location, called the template, and executes it as soon as you press (Enter). The template saves only the last command line entered.

Repeating a command line

If the cursor is located at the start of a command line, press (F3) to display the previous command. The previous command is copied from the template to the current command line and the cursor is placed at the end of the command line. Press (Enter) to execute the command again.

The following examples are techniques for editing the command line.

Example 1

Suppose that you want to display all of the files in the DOS directory that have the .EXE extension. Instead of typing:

```
DIR C:\DOS\*.EXE
```

you accidentally type the following command line:

```
DIR C:\DOS\*.EYE
```

Press the (Backspace) key twice to delete the last two characters. Then enter the correct characters (XE) and execute the command line by pressing (Enter).

Example 2

Suppose that you want to copy all of the files, with the .DOC extension, from A\DOC\PRIVATE to a hard drive, but you accidentally type the following line:

```
COP A:\DOC\PRIVATE\*.DOC C:
```

After pressing (Enter), the error message "Bad command or filename" appears. Since this line is still in the template, you can correct it. Press (F1) three times to display the first three correct characters "COP".

Then press (Ins) to change to insert mode. Type (Y) to insert the correction at the current position and then copy the rest of the line

from the template to the current command line by pressing F3.
Press Enter to execute the correct command line.

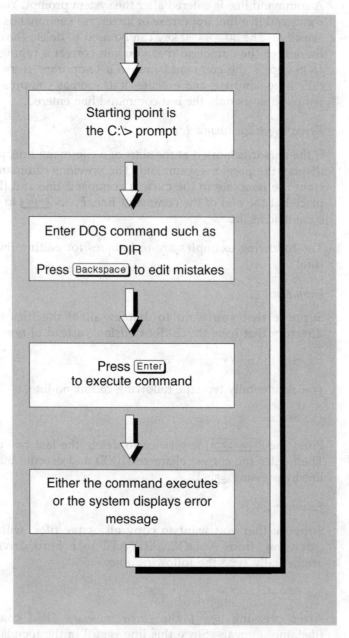

Starting point is
the C:\> prompt

Enter DOS command such as
DIR
Press Backspace to edit mistakes

Press Enter
to execute command

Either the command executes
or the system displays error
message

Entering and changing commands at the system prompt
(C:\>)

2.6 Entering and Correcting Commands with DOSKEY

As many users know, it can become very time-consuming to enter and correct commands in MS-DOS. However, MS-DOS 6.0 has a utility command called DOSKEY, which simplifies using the DOS command line. This program is loaded into the computer's memory when you start your computer. DOSKEY also lets you create batch files and macros easily and can even replace external and internal MS-DOS commands with modified versions.

Running DOSKEY

DOSKEY is a TSR-Program (Terminate and Stay Resident Program), which means that after being used the first time, the program remains in memory until the computer is restarted. This command can be entered without any parameters or other specifications. After calling it from the command line or from an AUTOEXEC.BAT file, your computer will load DOSKEY and display the message "DOSKey installed". Although this program uses approximately 4K of memory, its versatility and usefulness are worth it.

DOSKEY lets you use the cursor keys to recall, edit and/or re-execute commands that have been stored in a special 1024 character "history" buffer. (The size of the history buffer may be changed, which we'll explain later.) Several parameters and switches can be used to control the way DOSKEY works.

Insert or overstrike mode

DOSKEY simplifies editing the command line. After it is installed, you can use the ⬅ and ➡ cursor keys to move the cursor or press the ⌈Del⌋ key to erase characters. Depending on the input mode, either insert new characters at the current cursor position or type over existing characters. These are the switches for setting insert or overstrike modes:

/INSERT As its default setting, DOSKEY automatically uses insert mode to edit commands. Press the ⌈Ins⌋ key to switch between insert and overstrike mode.

/OVERSTRIKE
Installs overstrike mode when DOSKEY is installed in memory. So characters entered in this mode replace any existing characters at the current cursor position.

As with other command switches, you specify the switch after typing the command name (e.g., DOSKEY /OVERSTRIKE).

Changing the size of the line buffer

DOSKEY stores command lines in a special history buffer, which by default is 1024 characters in length. When this memory area is full, the oldest lines are removed to make room for new lines. In most cases, you'll find that a 1024 character history buffer is sufficient for storing command lines. However, macros are also stored in this buffer. So if you use macros, consider increasing the size of the buffer.

/BUFSIZE=

> Specifies the size of the buffer for command lines and macros. By default DOSKEY reserves 1024 bytes of memory for this. Once DOSKEY is installed you can only change this parameter with /REINSTALL.

/REINSTALL

> Installs another copy of DOSKEY in conventional memory. This is needed, for example, to change the size of the history buffer with /BUFSIZE. However, for every new copy you lose about 4K of memory.

Displaying the history buffer lines and macros

Command lines and macros stored in the DOSKEY history buffer can be displayed on the screen. By re-directing this information, you can also print lists to the printer or create batch files.

/MACROS

> Displays a list of all of DOSKEY macros that are currently defined. The macros are displayed in the format Name=Commands. By using the redirection symbol ">", the macro list can be sent to the printer or a file.

/HISTORY

> Displays a list of all of the commands stored in the DOSKEY history buffer. By using the redirection symbol ">", the macro list may be sent to the printer or a file. Also, by redirecting this list to a file and appending the .BAT extension, a batch file may be created.

You can also display the history buffers contents by pressing F7. DOSKEY displays each command line with a line number. By pressing the F9 key and entering a line number you can recall a specific line for editing or re-execution.

Editing the current command line

As we mentioned earlier, the command lines are stored in the history buffer. Pressing the ↑ and ↓ cursor keys will scroll the stored command lines.

The current line can be edited by using the ← and → cursor keys to move the cursor within the line. Use the Del key to erase characters. If you enter the wrong character, simply type over it with the correct character (with overstrike mode switched on). To insert characters that are missing, switch to insert mode (if it isn't already on) by pressing Ins and insert the desired character in the current cursor position.

You can also start DOSKEY directly in insert mode by using the /INSERT switch. Notice how the cursor changes appearance when you switch to insert mode. Press Ins again to switch the cursor back to normal.

To move the cursor to the beginning or end of a command line, use the Home and End keys respectively. The cursor can be moved from word to word by holding down the Ctrl key while pressing the ← or → cursor keys. Pressing Ctrl + End deletes all of the characters from the current cursor position to the end of the line. Ctrl + Home can be used to delete all of the characters from the current cursor position to the beginning of the line. The rest of the line remains unchanged.

Repeating a command line

To display the preceding line in the history buffer, press the ↑ key. If you've just started DOSKEY and haven't entered any commands, nothing will happen because DOSKEY hasn't stored any lines yet.

 After you call DOSKEY you can't use the editing options of the function keys. For example, press F3 to edit the last entered command line. Other special keys are defined; these are discussed later in this chapter.

PgUp displays the first stored line and PgDn displays the last stored line in the history buffer.

Search and display options for command lines

If you lose track of the contents of the history buffer, press F7 for a complete list of all of the lines. The lines in the list will be numbered. An example may look similar to the following:

```
1: dir
2: cd dos
3: dir *.exe
4: cd..
```

If more than 24 lines are in the command buffer, the following message appears:

```
-- More --
```

To continue the display, press any key.

You can then edit or execute a specific line without having to repeatedly press the ↑ or ↓ cursor keys. To do this press the F9 key. The screen displays the prompt "Line number". Then, type the line number of the desired command.

In the previous example, to execute the command line "DIR *.EXE" again, first press F9, then enter three for the third line and press Enter. The line appears as the current command line. Edit or execute it again by pressing Enter.

The following is a method for retrieving a command line that was already entered. Simply type the beginning of the line. For example, type the following command lines and press Enter after each line.

```
...
COPY C:\DOS\*.COM A:
DIR A:
CHKDSK A:
```

Suppose that you want to copy the COM files, which were just copied onto a diskette in drive A:, to another diskette. This means that you'll be using the command line "COPY..." a second time. Simply enter a part of the line and press F8. For example, type CO and press F8. DOSKEY searches for the first appropriate line and displays it on the command line for editing or execution. For our example, simply type:

```
CO F8
```

If the command you wanted wasn't displayed, you may have used COPY to copy a different file earlier. Simply press F8 again. DOSKEY will then search for the next appropriate line.

Creating batch files automatically

A batch file is a text file containing a series of MS-DOS commands. They are often used to simplify repetitive or complicated tasks. When you type the name of a batch file at the system prompt, MS-DOS executes the lines stored, just as if you typed them at the keyboard - except that you didn't have to type them.

For many DOS users, batch files are a mystery. Although they are aware of batch files, they're hesitant to use them because they equate creating batch files with "programming". So they think working with batch files is too complicated.

DOSKEY makes it easy to create batch files. DOSKEY stores lines in its buffer similar to a batch file. However, you cannot run these lines one after the other except when pressing the ↑ and ↓ cursor keys to recall the appropriate commands. The following is a simple procedure for creating a batch file from commands that are directly entered at the keyboard:

1. Press Alt + F7 to clear the contents of the history buffer.

2. Then enter the MS-DOS command lines in the usual way. DOSKEY records them in the command buffer as DOS executes the commands.

3. To create a batch file called WORK.BAT from these executed command lines, type the following command line:

```
DOSKEY /HISTORY >WORK.BAT
```

This causes DOSKEY to write all of the lines, without line numbers, to a file named WORK.BAT. Since you're redirecting the contents of the history buffer to the WORK.BAT file, your batch file is almost complete. However, there is one little catch. DOSKEY also recorded the last command (the command line for creating the batch file: "DOSKEY /HISTORY >WORK.BAT") and included it in the WORK.BAT file. This command must be removed with an editor.

You can use EDIT, the MS-DOS editor to "fix" this batch file. To fix WORK.BAT type:

```
EDIT WORK.BAT
```

Now delete the last line ("DOSKEY /HISTORY >WORK.BAT")
and save the finished batch file.

 If you discover that you'd like to create a batch file from
the history buffer but didn't first clear the contents by
pressing [Alt] + [F7], then you can still use this method.
Type:

```
DOSKEY /HISTORY >FILE.BAT
```

Edit the file FILE.BAT, delete any unnecessary command
lines and save the results.

Working with macros

Besides saving commands in the history buffer and providing a
flexible way to recall, edit and execute DOS commands, DOSKEY
also lets you create and execute macros. A macro is like a simple
batch file. Creating a macro is giving a name to a series of
commands. To do this, use a notation similar to the one for defining
environment variables using SET. First, enter the name of the
macro followed by an equal sign. Following the equal sign, enter
the series of commands that are to be performed. DOSKEY can
distinguish a macro definition from a command by the = sign. Type
the command line as follows:

```
DOSKEY NAME=Commands
```

Separate commands by using the character sequence $T.
Parameters can be passed in a macro, as with batch files. Instead
of using %1 to %9, use $1 to $9 as parameters specified from the
command line.

$* stands for the entire parameter specification, including all
special characters (spaces etc.) entered on the command line. If you
enter more than one parameter, you can address all of the
parameters at once with $*.

Suppose that you want to sort a directory by filenames, but you
don't want to enter the parameters /O:n every time you want to use
this command. Simply define a macro named DIRS with the
appropriate command line:

```
DOSKEY DIRS=DIR /O:n
```

Now, when you need a sorted directory, simply use the new "command" DIRS. By doing this you've created a new MS-DOS macro.

The following is an example of how you could define a macro named DISK for formatting and checking a diskette:

```
DOSKEY DISK=FORMAT A: $T CHKDSK A:
```

Passing parameters in macros

Similar to batch files, you can pass parameters to DOSKEY macros by using $1, $2, etc. Suppose that we want to expand our example, DISK, so that either drive A: or B: can be selected. To do this, we must replace A: with a parameter as shown below.

```
DOSKEY DISK=FORMAT $1 $T CHKDSK $1
```

Now you can start the macro using drive A: by specifying the disk drive identifier as a parameter:

```
DISK A:
```

You can use more than one parameter by using $2, $3, etc. The parameter $* contains a complete list of parameter specifications. When you specify three parameters after a macro name, they are available separately as $1, $2 and $3. However, all three, including the spaces in between, are in the parameter $*.

Replacing internal MS-DOS commands

You can also replace internal MS-DOS commands with DOSKEY macros. DOSKEY always checks its list of macro names before executing a DOS command. If it finds a matching name in its list, DOSKEY executes the macro. If it doesn't find a matching name, DOSKEY passes the command onto the DOS command interpreter which will then execute the command.

As a test, define a macro named DIR and give it an entirely different function, as below:

```
DOSKEY DIR=ECHO DIR is forbidden...
```

Then enter the MS-DOS DIR command from the command line. Instead of seeing the current directory on the screen, you'll see the message defined in our macro.

In this way, MS-DOS 6.0 can be used to adapt normal MS-DOS commands to your own needs. Prior to MS-DOS 4.0, this could only be accomplished by using batch files.

If you wanted DIR to always display files by page, you can define a macro as follows:

```
DOSKEY DIR=DIR /P $1 $2 $3
```

When DIR is called without any other parameters, DOSKEY substitutes the character sequence DIR /P. If another parameter is specified after DIR, $1 is replaced by this parameter. DOSKEY changes "DIR C:\DOS" to "DIR /P C:\DOS". You can specify up to three parameters in this definition of the DIR macro.

    If you define a "replacement" macro, you can still execute the "real" DOS command by beginning the command line with a space. In this case, DOSKEY does not substitute the macro, so the true DOS command is executed.

Using special characters in macros

Certain characters have a special meaning in command lines. These characters are immediately analyzed by the command interpreter and understood as commands. The two characters "<" and ">" for redirecting input and output as well as the pipe symbol "|" for linking commands are among these special characters. If you entered these characters directly in a macro definition, the command interpreter would not understand them. In macros, these special characters are defined differently:

$L   Redirects the input, similar to <.

$G   Redirects output to a file or a device. A double GG produces the character sequence >>, which directs output to an existing file.

$B   This is the pipe symbol in DOSKEY macros, similar to "|".

To create a macro that sends a directory to the printer, use the following macro definition:

```
DOSKEY PRINTDIR=DIR $G LPT1:
```

By using parameters, you can even create a macro named "Print", which produces a command line to send the output to the printer:

```
DOSKEY PRINT=$1 $2 $3 $4 $5 $G LPT1:
```

In order for the computer to display all of the EXE files in the DOS directory in five columns using DIR, use the command line "DIR C:\DOS*.EXE /W". To have the computer send the results to the printer instead, use the PRINT macro previously defined.

```
PRINT DIR C:\DOS\*.EXE /W
```

 When you use DOSKEY remember that it is closely connected to the keyboard and the command interpreter. The macros you created with DOSKEY won't work in a word processor or in a database program. You won't be able to use them in batch files.

Using macro definitions

After you start learning to use macros to speed up and simplify your work, you may become disappointed the next time you start your computer. You'll find that all of your macro definitions are gone and must be re-entered. Obviously, this is time-consuming and defeats the purpose of creating macros - making your work easier.

Although you cannot use DOSKEY macros in batch files, batch files can be used to define DOSKEY macros. For example, to have the PRINT and DIR macros automatically created and available every time you start your computer, type the following command lines in AUTOEXEC.BAT:

```
DOSKEY PRINT=$1 $2 $3 $4 $5 $G LPT1:
DOSKEY DIR=DIR /P $1 $2 $3
```

Alternatively, you can create a special batch file, called MACRO.BAT, which contains all macros you want to use. To activate the macros, call the batch file by entering MACRO from the command line. It doesn't matter whether or not DOSKEY has already been installed.

If you've defined several new macros that you want to keep, use the /MACROS switch so that you don't have to create the MACRO.BAT definition file. Redirect the display of the available macros to a file and then enter the command word DOSKEY prior to each command with an editor.

For example, do this if the MACRO.BAT file hasn't been created and you want to store the existing macro definitions. Start the editor with:

```
EDIT MACRO.BAT
```

For our example macros, the contents of the file would look like the following:

```
DOSKEY PRINT=$1 $2 $3 $4 $5 $G LPT1:
DOSKEY DIR=DIR /P $1 $2 $3
```

Make certain to insert "DOSKEY " at the beginning of each line.

This procedure will write all of the macro definitions into the specified file (MACRO.BAT). The only thing missing is the DOSKEY command. After saving the file and exiting the editor, use these macros by calling the batch file to install them.

DOSKEY editing keys summary

The following is a summary of the DOSKEY key commands:

↑	Provides the previously issued command in the buffer.
↓	Provides the command in the buffer following the displayed command.
←	Moves the cursor one character left.
→	Moves the cursor one character right.
Del	Erases the character to the left of the cursor.
Ins	Shifts back and forth between insert and overstrike mode.
Backspace	Erases the character to the left of the cursor.
PgUp	Makes the first command in the buffer available on the command line.
PgDn	Makes the last entered (most recently used) command available.
Home	Places the cursor at the beginning of the line.
End	Places the cursor at the end of the line.
Esc	Removes the current command line from the screen.
Ctrl + ←	Moves the cursor one word to the left.

Ctrl + →
Moves the cursor one word to the right.

Ctrl + Home
Erases all characters (left of the cursor) in the current line to the beginning of the line.

Ctrl + End
Erases all characters (right of the cursor) in the current line to the end of the line.

F7 Displays all of the stored command lines.

Alt + F7
Deletes all of the stored command lines.

F8 Calls a stored line by entering the first letters of a previously used command and pressing F8 . DOSKEY searches for the first appropriate line and displays it on the command line for execution or editing.

F9 Specifies a command by the line number in the buffer.

F10 Displays all stored macros.

Alt + F10
Deletes all stored macros.

Special macro characters

$L Redirects the input, similar to <.

$G Redirects output to a file or a device. A double GG produces the character sequence >>, which directs output to an existing file.

$B This is the pipe symbol in DOSKEY macros, similar to "|".

$T This character is used to separate commands in a macro.

$1-9 Batch parameters, similar to the %1-9 characters in batch files.

$* This represents all the parameters on the command line.

$$ Represents the dollar sign ($) character.

Quitting DOSKEY

You can't quit DOSKEY like other programs because it permanently remains in the memory of the computer. You can install a new copy with DOSKEY /REINSTALL, but you can't exit any of the copies. To quit DOSKEY and remove it from memory, reboot your computer.

2.7   Using DOS Commands and Files

When you type a command at the prompt, you are asking MS-DOS to perform a simple task for you. You may be asking it to display information or you may be asking it to adjust one or more of its operating settings. In this section, we'll describe some of the characteristics about the DOS commands.

All about commands

In MS-DOS the first entry in a command line is called a command. A space must follow the command. Anything typed after the space is called a parameter(s). This is why commands must be separated on the command line by a space. MS-DOS doesn't differentiate between uppercase and lowercase characters. For example, you can type "FORMAT", "Format" or "format"; for any of these, MS-DOS will execute the FORMAT command.

If you aren't running DOSKEY, leading spaces don't have any affect on the command. So it doesn't matter whether you enter "FORMAT A:" or "   FORMAT A:". However, if you created a DOSKEY macro named FORMAT, entering a space at the beginning of the command line would cause the MS-DOS command FORMAT, not the macro FORMAT, to be executed.

Executing commands from any directory

Some MS-DOS commands are in the computer's memory at all times and can be executed immediately. These are called built-in or internal commands. Other MS-DOS commands are first loaded from diskette or the hard drive before they can be executed. These are called external commands. This technique of storing seldom used commands on disk and loading them when needed leaves more room in the computer's conventional memory. Since every command that is stored in memory takes up space, it wouldn't be possible to fit all MS-DOS commands in conventional memory (640K).

When you type an external command at the prompt, MS-DOS searches for it in the current directory of the current drive. If these commands are all contained in the DOS directory, then this procedure will work only if the current directory is the DOS directory. Of course, this isn't always practical especially if you're using a hard drive.

One way to "tell" DOS where, on the hard drive, to find the external command is to specify its path. The path is the drive identifier and the directory where the external command is stored. For example, to use the FORMAT command, which is in the C:\DOS directory, type the following:

```
C:\DOS\FORMAT
```

Having to specify the path for each MS-DOS command quickly becomes cumbersome and annoying. One way to avoid this inconvenience is by using the PATH command.

```
PATH C:\DOS
```

The PATH command tells MS-DOS to search for commands first in the current directory. If it can't find the command there, then it searches for this command in the C:\DOS directory.

So now you can use the FORMAT command from any directory by simply typing the name of the command; the path specification isn't necessary.

You can also tell DOS to search other directories to find commands. Simply use the PATH command and specify these other directories separated by semicolons:

```
PATH C:\DOS;C:\PROGRAM
```

Now MS-DOS searches first in the current directory, then the C:\DOS directory and finally the C:\PROGRAM directory to find a command.

Since the search path specified from the command line is only valid for the current work session, you can put a PATH command in the AUTOEXEC.BAT file. Remember that the search path is always set to the current directory when your computer is first booted. This is why many users put a PATH command in their AUTOEXEC.BAT file.

   The PATH command is only used to specify search paths for finding commands.

In this book, we use only the command names when executing the commands. If the command isn't in your current directory and you haven't defined a search path for the directory containing the command, you must enter the complete path to the command (the disk drive and directory specifications).

How commands are processed

Most often, you'll enter a command at the keyboard. A part of MS-DOS, called the command interpreter, receives it and first checks whether the command is one of the built-in/internal commands, such as DATE, TIME, etc. If it isn't, the command interpreter first searches in the current directory for an existing program with the .COM extension (especially external DOS commands).

Then the command interpreter searches the current directory for files with the extensions .EXE and .BAT. After this, the search continues with the directories specified by PATH. DOS always searches for commands in this order: COM, EXE and BAT.

If the command interpreter doesn't find an executable file after searching the last directory in the path, the screen displays the message: "Bad command or filename".

The next illustration shows an example of different directories in a path.

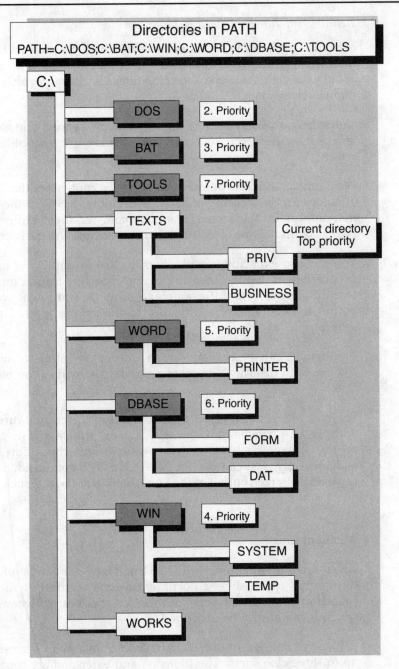

An example of using the PATH command

Defining input/output devices for commands

Many MS-DOS commands communicate with the user as they're performing their functions. Sometimes they display information about what they are doing and sometimes they prompt you to enter more information.

Unless you explicitly change them, commands expect you to enter information from the keyboard and display information on the screen.

For example, the DIR command displays the contents of the current directory on the screen. Similarly, many other MS-DOS messages may appear on the screen. If a command requires confirmation before continuing, you confirm the operation by using the keyboard.

You can also explicitly specify other devices for input and output. It's possible to "redirect" the output and messages from commands to a different device (for example, a printer). You might want to output the contents of a directory to the printer instead of the screen.

Commands can pass their screen output as input to another command. In this way, several commands can divide a complicated task.

For example, you can display the contents of the current directory with the DIR command. Ordinarily, this information is displayed on the screen. However, if you want to sort this information alphabetically, you can use the MS-DOS SORT command. So you can pass the screen output of the DIR command to SORT, such as:

```
DIR|SORT
```

All about files

On a storage medium, MS-DOS manages all kinds of data (programs, spreadsheets, documents, etc.) as files. A file is a collection of data that belongs together and has a filename, by which it can clearly be identified.

A filename consists of one to eight characters and an extension of up to three characters. The filename and extension are separated by a period. For example, a typical filename is:

```
LETTER.DOC
```

If you enter a filename that has more than eight characters, MS-DOS only uses the first eight characters. For example, if you entered "MICROSOFT.CORP" as your filename, MS-DOS will shorten it to "MICROSOF.COR".

 When you display a directory with DIR, the screen doesn't display the period used to separate the name and the extension. Instead, there is space between the name and the extension.

Searching for files

Most users use MS-DOS commands to manipulate or view data files. When using a command that refers to a file, enter the full filename and extension. For example, to display the contents of a file named LETTER.DOC on the screen, use this command:

```
TYPE LETTER.DOC
```

Here the TYPE command searches the current directory to find the file LETTER.DOC. But you can specify an alternate directory to search by using a pathname. For example, if the file LETTER.DOC is in the C:\DOC directory, you can use the following:

```
TYPE C:\DOC\LETTER.DOC
```

You might have another file with the same name in a different directory, say C:\DOC. Then you'll specify that directory:

```
TYPE C:\TEXTS\LETTER.DOC
```

Rather than specifying the path for the file in each command, you can use the APPEND command to set the search path for the files. For example, if you want to always search for data files in the C:\DOC directory you can use:

```
APPEND C:\DOC
```

Now you can use the TYPE command to display the contents of any file in the C:\DOC directory without having to specify the path of the data file.

 The APPEND command can only specify search paths for data files. Use the PATH command to define search paths for commands and programs.

If the file isn't in the current directory and there is no path defined for the directory with APPEND, the disk drive and the path specification for the file must be specified.

Be careful when using APPEND. Normally, you should use the complete path of the file instead of APPEND for two reasons:

1. You may get strange results, especially when editing files with application programs. For example, the word processor Microsoft Word 6.0 ignores the search path set with APPEND. Instead, Word 6.0 looks for a specified file in the current directory.

2. You may have problems using APPEND in MS-DOS. While you can display the contents of a file in the file search path easily (TYPE), you cannot delete or copy the file. To delete or copy a file, the directory must be specified explicitly.

Filename naming conventions

As we mentioned earlier, a filename consists of the actual filename, which can have a maximum of eight characters, and an extension of up to three characters. Imbedded spaces aren't allowed. The extension identifies the type of file. Some extensions in MS-DOS are fixed (COM and EXE for executable program files and BAT for batch files), while others have become defacto standards (TXT for text files, DOC for word processor documents, etc.).

All of the letters from A to Z, the numbers 0 to 9 and certain special characters, such as !#$%()&-_, are permitted in filenames. Lowercase letters are automatically converted to uppercase letters.

Characters that aren't allowed in filenames are +=:;.,<>/\ and the space character. The space character is used to separate entries and to separate commands from any additional entries (parameters). Many commands require additional information for correct execution. For example, the FORMAT command won't perform its task of preparing a diskette for storing information unless you at least specify the disk drive as a parameter. The FORMAT command and the disk drive identifier are separated by a space.

Besides these characters, certain groups of characters are reserved for special purposes. Therefore they cannot be used as filenames.

Among these are the device names: CON, AUX, COM1, COM2, PRN, LPT1, LPT2, LPT3, NUL.

Specifying more than one file with wildcards

You can execute some MS-DOS commands and use more than one file at a time by using substitute characters (wildcard). These special characters enable you to omit one or more characters from a filename:

*   Substitutes for the rest of the filename or its extension.

?   Substitutes for a single character in the filename or its extension.

Wildcards, which simplify working with several files, are required to execute some tasks.

Wildcards have two very important jobs in MS-DOS:

- They can be used to indicate several files. For example, copy all of the files, with the .EXE extension, from the C:\DOS directory without using a wildcard. In order to do this, you would have to determine all of the filenames and then enter a command line with the MS-DOS COPY command for each file. It's a lot easier if you use a wildcard to copy all of the files with the .EXE extension: *.EXE.

- Wildcards are also useful if you want to filter information. Suppose that you're looking on the hard drive for a file named LETTER.TXT. You could use DIR LETTER.TXT to search for the file; by entering the /S switch you would include the subdirectories in your search as well. If you didn't know the exact name of the file you were looking for, you obviously wouldn't want to go through LETTER.TXT, LETTER1.TXT, LETTERS.TXT etc. It's much easier to type the part of the filename that you do know and use a wildcard for the rest: LETTER*.TXT.

The "*" character in filenames or extensions indicates that the remainder of the filename or its extension can be any combination of characters. Any character you type after the "*" is ignored.

Examples

A*.EXE   All filenames beginning with A and ending with the .EXE extension (APPEND.EXE, ATTRIB.EXE).

M??ER.TXT

> All files with 5 letters in the filename and the .TXT extension. The first letter is M and the last two letters are ER (MEIER.TXT MAYER.TXT, MEYER.TXT).

LETTER.*   Files named LETTER that have any extension.

INVOICE.*

> All files named INVOICE that have any extension (INVOICE.TXT, INVOICE.DOC, INVOICE.SIK etc.).

.   All files.

Use wildcard characters carefully when referring to more than one file. The command could affect files that you really didn't want to include, especially when you're deleting files. Therefore, first use DIR to display the files that should be included. For example, if you want to delete all of the files in a directory that begin with the letter A, simply type:

```
DIR A*.*
```

This displays the names of all of the files that meet your selection criteria. When you're certain that the file specification is correct and that you no longer need any of the files, type:

```
DEL A*.*
```

Naturally you'll want to be careful when you type a command such as the previous one. You may end up deleting files that you didn't intend to delete.

Unfortunately, not all MS-DOS commands work with wildcard characters. For example, the TYPE command will only display the contents of a specific file on the screen. Entering TYPE *.TXT won't display the contents of all of the text files.

In many cases you can write a batch file to accomplish the same tasks as using wildcards. You could also use another command with wildcards that will have the same effect.

For example, we already mentioned that TYPE *.BAT will not display all of the BAT files in the current directory. But you can use a variation of the COPY command to accomplish the same thing. Here you can copy all of the BAT files to the screen (called CON: for the console device) using this:

```
COPY *.BAT CON
```

2.8   Working with Disk Drives and Hard Drives

This section discusses some things you should remember when working with disk drives and hard drives.

5 1/4 inch disk drives

There are two kinds of 5 1/4 inch disk drives. One model can store up to 360K of data. A high capacity model can store up to 1.2 Meg of data.

To use a diskette, insert it in the disk drive and close the drive door. The disk drive is then ready for operation.

To remove a diskette from a disk drive, lift the door lever and pull out the diskette. You should immediately place the diskette in its paper jacket (sleeve) to prevent it from getting dirty or being touched through the opening, which exposes the media itself. To protect diskettes from being accidently deleted or modified, cover the notch on the side of the diskette with tape. This is usually referred to as write protecting the disk.

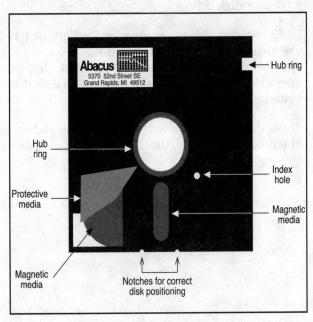

The main parts of a 5 1/4 inch diskette

You should protect diskettes from high temperatures as well as electromagnetic fields. Leaving a diskette in your car on a sunny day could destroy it and your data. If you leave a diskette near magnets or transformers, such as those found in computer monitors, your data may also be destroyed.

 You can write to both sides of a diskette without having to remove it from the disk drive and turning it over. The disk drive is capable of writing on both sides of the diskette.

360K disk drives

DSDD diskettes (Double Sided, Double Density) are used to store up to 360K of data.

1.2 Meg disk drives

DSHD diskettes (Double Sided, High Density) are used to store up to 1.2 Meg of data. You can also read, write and format 360K diskettes with a 1.2 Meg disk drive. The disk drive automatically recognizes when a 360K diskette is inserted. To format a 360K diskette in a 1.2 Meg disk drive, use a special switch (/4) as a parameter for the MS-DOS FORMAT command.

3 1/2 inch disk drives

3 1/2 inch disk drives can store either 720K or 1.44 Meg of data. To use a diskette, first insert it into the drive. It clicks into position and the eject button pops out. The disk drive is then ready for operation. To remove a diskette from the disk drive, press the eject button.

These diskettes can be write protected by sliding the write protect notch on the side of the diskette so that you can see thru the opening.

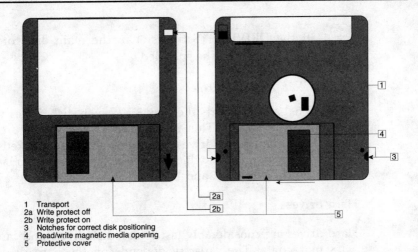

1   Transport
2a Write protect off
2b Write protect on
3   Notches for correct disk positioning
4   Read/write magnetic media opening
5   Protective cover

The main parts of a 3 1/2 inch diskette

 To protect the data on a 3 1/2 inch diskette from being deleted or overwritten, slide the plastic write protect notch so that you can see through the hole.

720K disk drives

DSDD diskettes (Double Sided, Double Density), are used to store up to 720K of data.

1.44 Meg disk drives

DSHD (Double Sided, High Density) diskettes are used to store up to 1.44 Meg of data. You can also read, write and format 720K diskettes with a 1.44 Meg drive. If you're going to use the disk drive only for diskettes with 720K, use the DEVICE=DRIVER.SYS command in the CONFIG.SYS with the optional parameters or the SETUP program for your computer (NOT the MS-DOS SETUP program).

For example, to use the second disk drive B: with 720K instead of 1.44 Meg, you must type the following line into the CONFIG.SYS:

```
DEVICE=DRIVER.SYS /d:1 /f:2 /H:2 /S:9 /T:80
```

The next time you start your computer, MS-DOS will display the drive identifier that you can use as a 720K drive. Drive identifier B: remains a 1.44 Meg drive, but the new identifier acts like a 720K drive. You won't have to enter any switches with the FORMAT command to format 720K diskettes on the new drive.

If the DRIVER.SYS file isn't in the main directory, the entire path must be specified.

The new 2.88 Meg disk drives

MS-DOS 6.0 also supports the new 3 1/2 inch disk drives with a capacity of 2.88 Meg. This is twice as much as the previous capacity. The new disk drives needed for 2.88 Meg diskettes are downwardly compatible, which means that they can also be used with diskettes with 720K and 1.44 Meg.

Hard drives

Hard drives are considerably faster than disk drives and can hold a lot more data. The capacity depends on the hard drive; the minimum is generally 20 Meg or 30 Meg.

Differences from diskettes

Hard drives differ from diskettes in the following ways:

- While a diskette spins in the disk drive at a rate of 300 revolutions per minute, the storage medium in a hard drive spins at 3600 revolutions per minute. The higher speed (twelve times higher) makes it possible for the hard drive to read and write data much faster.

- The number of tracks and sectors per storage medium is increased significantly. Also, the distance between the read/write head and the storage medium is much smaller. This accounts for the higher storage capacity.

- A hard drive doesn't consist of one disk spinning. Hard drives are made up of stacks of 2 to 6 disks, with two read/write heads for each disk. All disks in the stack spin simultaneously. This also accounts for the higher storage capacity.

Hard drives are sensitive to shock. Sometimes computer systems are delivered with a PARK command. PARK moves the heads of the hard drive to a special "Safe" position. Before you move your computer you should run the PARK program. Since MS-DOS itself does not have this program, you should use the program that is supplied by the manufacturer of your hard drive.

Using a hard drive: Special features

Most commands that can be used with a diskette also work on a hard drive. The commands DISKCOPY and DISKCOMP for copying and comparing diskettes are exceptions. You cannot use these commands on a hard drive.

Unfortunately a hard drive cannot be write protected like a diskette. In a sense, the data on a hard drive is "unprotected". However, instead of write protect, certain precautions can be taken to protect the data on a hard drive. Files can be given a special attribute that protects the file from being accidentally destroyed or changed (write protect attribute).

2.9   Starting Application Programs

Application programs can be started at the command line, just like other MS-DOS commands.

Loading application programs from a diskette

To run a program from a diskette, insert the diskette that contains the application program in drive A: and make this disk drive the current drive by typing:

A: (Enter)

Now enter the name of the application program and press (Enter).

 If you don't know the name of the program, use the DIR command to display all of the files on the diskette. Executable files have .EXE, .COM or .BAT extensions. For example, you can use "DIR *.COM" to display all of the COM files. Program names are often abbreviated with two letters. For example, the filename for Multiplan is abbreviated as "MP".

Starting applications from the hard drive

If you define a search path for the directory of the application with the PATH command, you can start the application by entering the name of the program.

If you didn't define a path, you can make the hard drive the current drive by typing:

C: (Enter)

Then use CD and the name of the directory to change to the directory of the application program:

```
CD Directory_name Enter
```

Start the application by entering the name of the application program. For example, if the word processor Word 6.0 is in the WORD directory on the hard drive, select the directory by entering CD \WORD. If you're currently in the main directory, you won't need to enter the backslash; instead enter CD WORD.

With MS-DOS commands you can specify the entire path of the program. So, you don't have to change directories. For example, the Word word processor, which is stored in the C:\WORD directory, can be started from any directory by typing the following command line:

```
C:\WORD\WORD
```

 Some programs expect that you'll run them from their own directory (the program directory must be the current directory). You can solve this problem easily with a batch file, in which one of the commands changes to the appropriate directory and the next command starts the program. (Refer to the hints in this book.) For example, to start Word from the WORD directory, create the WORD.BAT batch file:

```
C:
CD C:\WORD
WORD %1 %2 %3
```

If you place this batch file in a directory which is in the search path (for example, in the directory of other DOS commands), then you can run the word processor.

2.10 Help in the Command Interpreter

MS-DOS 6.0 contains a powerful help system for working with the command interpreter. This help system is divided into two parts: One part contains a brief overview of all available MS-DOS commands and the second part contains detailed explanations of each command.

Help for all commands

To display an overview of all the MS-DOS commands, simply type the FASTHELP command without any parameters. You can page through the information that's displayed.

```
FASTHELP
```

Press any key to move to the next page. To stop displaying help text, press Ctrl+C.

To obtain detailed information about a specific MS-DOS command, enter the name of the command after the FASTHELP command. For example, for information about the FORMAT command, type:

```
FASTHELP FORMAT
```

The new help text for FASTHELP is located in the DOSHELP.HLP file in the DOS commands directory. You can read and modify this file by using the text editor EDIT. However, don't change the structure of this file and keep the commands in alphabetical order.

 You can display the same help information by typing the /? switch when you call the MS-DOS command (see below).

Detailed information about individual commands: On-line help

To obtain detailed information about any MS-DOS command, activate the command with the /? switch. You can also access this information by entering the name of the command, as a parameter, after the HELP command.

The help text for the MS-DOS commands in Version 6.0 has a special format. After a few lines explaining the command's function, there is a blank line and then the syntax of the command, an explanation of the individual parameters, and, in some cases, additional comments. A help screen may look similar to the following:

```
Copies the contents of one diskette to another diskette.

DISKCOPY [drive1: [drive2:]] [/1] [/V]

   /1   Copies only the first side of a diskette.
   /V   Verifies the correctness of the copy.

Both diskettes must have the same density.
The same drive can be used for drive 1 and drive 2.
```

Help system

In MS-DOS 6.0 you can use the HELP command to access information about all the available DOS commands. The MS-DOS help system provides an explanation of the command, examples of how the command can be used, and additional comments.

Help system

When the program starts, a screen appears listing all the commands. Select the desired command with the cursor keys and press Enter. Information about the command appears. To access additional information, select **Notes** and press Enter. Select **Examples** and press Enter to see examples of how the command can be used.

Press Alt+C to return to the overview. You can page forward through all the help screens by continually pressing Alt+N. To page backward, press Alt+B.

To exit the help system, press Alt+F X or select **File/Exit**.

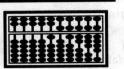

Storage Devices

When using your computer, it's important to distinguish between data that's located in the computer's working memory (called main memory or RAM) and data that's located on storage media. The data stored in the computer's memory are lost when you switch off the computer. So, a permanent way of storing data is needed. To do this, you must use storage media.

Storage media, especially diskettes, can also be used to transfer data from one computer to another. For example, you can copy a document from your computer's memory to a diskette and then give the diskette to a co-worker. This person can then work with the document on his/her own computer.

3.1   Overview

We'll start with some information about the two main types of storage media: Diskettes (also called floppy diskettes) and hard drives. We'll use the term "disk" when referring to both of these media.

Handling disks properly

Do not expose diskettes to excessive heat.

Protect hard drives from vibrations or movement during operation.

Keep disks away from magnetic fields. Don't place diskettes on or near transformers or power supplies.

Differences between hard drives and diskettes

Diskettes are available in two sizes and various capacities. The main difference between hard drives and diskettes is that hard drives have a much larger capacity and are faster. MS-DOS tries to handle all storage media in the same way. However, for technical reasons, certain commands apply only to diskettes (DISKCOPY) or hard drives (FDISK).

Formatting diskettes

When you purchase a diskette, you receive a storage medium that's coated with magnetic material. Before you can use the diskette, it must be formatted. The formatting process prepares a diskette for use by checking it for defects and dividing it into management units. MS-DOS normally performs a quick format if a diskette was previously formatted at the requested density. In addition, it stores certain recovery information, which usually enables you to salvage your data if you accidentally format a diskette.

Formatting hard drives

Before it can be used to store data, a hard drive must be divided (configured) into one or more partitions with the FDISK command. MS-DOS partitions are also formatted at this time.

Creating a system (start) diskette

To create a system diskette, use the SYS command and specify the letter of the target drive.

Naming a disk

You can assign an electronic label to a disk after it's formatted. You can also use the LABEL command to do this. This label is displayed along with the contents or it can be accessed directly with the VOL command.

Displaying the contents of a disk

The DIR command displays the contents of the current directory. The TREE command displays the directory structure, which shows how the directories are related. This provides the complete path information that's needed to access the desired data.

Copying diskettes

To make a copy of a diskette, use the DISKCOPY command. For 1.2 Meg diskettes, the copying process occurs in several steps. When you need to swap diskettes, MS-DOS displays a message informing you of this.

Comparing diskettes

Use the DISKCOMP command to compare two diskettes. Similar to DISKCOPY, for 1.2 Meg diskettes this process involves several steps. When needed, MS-DOS prompts you to swap diskettes.

Checking disks

The CHKDSK command is used to check a disk for structural defects. Any defects that are found are automatically fixed if the /F parameter is specified.

Virtual drives

Virtual drives provide options for storing and working with data that exceed the possibilities offered by your computer's peripheral hardware. With this feature, you can simulate a disk drive or directory that isn't actually present. A RAM disk, which is extremely fast, is a virtual drive. However, its contents are lost when you switch off the computer.

Disk processing commands

DISKCOPY (D), DISKCOMP (D), FORMAT, FDISK (H), CHKDSK, MSBACKUP, RESTORE, SUBST, LABEL, SYS, UNFORMAT, VOL (D)=Diskette (drives) only, (H)=Hard drives only

3.2 Working with Storage Media

When handling disks, be very careful. Any damage to a diskette, such as mechanical damage, excessive heat, and magnetic fields, can cause data loss. Hard drives are better protected than diskettes (floppies) because the actual storage medium is hermetically sealed. However, even hard drives are sensitive to movement.

Remember the following when handling disks:

* Always store 5 1/4 inch diskettes in their envelopes (sleeves).

* Never touch the magnetic surface of a diskette.

* Do not bend diskettes; apply as little pressure to them as possible.

* Use only felt pens or pencils to write on diskettes. It's better to first write on the label, then apply the label to the diskette.

- Do not expose diskettes to temperatures over 120 degrees Fahrenheit (about 50 degrees Celsius). Leaving a diskette in your car during a hot summer day may damage the media.

- Keep diskettes and hard drives away from electromagnetic fields. Don't place diskettes on or next to the monitor or near transformers or power supplies.

- Protect hard drives from vibrations; ensure that the computer is safely positioned on a sturdy desk or table.

- Never switch off the computer when your hard drive or diskette is being used. Disk drives and most hard drives have indicator lights that are lit during read/write accesses.

3.3   Different Storage Devices

Since the first personal computer was introduced, diskettes have been continually improved. Therefore, there are several kinds of diskettes and methods of storage available. There are two physical sizes of disk drives, each with different capacities.

5 1/4 inch disk drives

These disk drives are for the 5 1/4 inch diskettes, which are made of flexible plastic.

360K diskettes

These diskettes have become almost obsolete. Since they are used only in PC/XTs, which are no longer sold, only owners of older PCs need them. These diskettes can hold 360K of data and are labeled DSDD (Double Sided/Double Density) diskettes. These designations aren't used today because Single Sided and Single Density diskettes are no longer used. If you need 360K diskettes, you can refer to them as PC/XT diskettes.

1.2 Meg diskettes

A standard AT computer has a 1.2 Meg disk drive, capable of storing 1,200,000 characters of data. This higher storage capacity is possible because of a higher recording density and special diskettes. The magnetic data tracks on these diskettes are twice as close together as on a PC/XT diskette. These higher density diskettes are identified as DSHD (Double Sided High Density). They are also referred to as AT diskettes. It's difficult to determine whether a diskette can store 360K or 1.2 Meg by simply looking at it.

A 5 1/4 inch disk drive

Although a high density diskette can be inserted into a PC/XT system, you won't be able to read or write to the diskette. However, an AT can read XT (low density) diskettes and can even format them by using a special parameter of the FORMAT command. In this case, the disk drive only writes on every other data track to create the 360K capacity.

If you're using an AT, you should have a supply of both types of diskettes. Since most programs are still available on low density diskettes, you can use the less expensive low density diskettes to make backup copies.

Flexible diskettes can be damaged easily

There are two disadvantages to using 5 1/4 inch disk drives. They are rather large and take up a lot of space in the computer cabinet (which is always getting smaller). Also, the floppy diskettes are relatively unprotected. Since the inner magnetic surface that stores the data is exposed in several places, it can be easily damaged. These floppy diskettes can also be accidentally bent. The smaller 3 1/2 inch diskette was developed to solve these problems.

3 1/2 inch disk drives

These drives use the 3 1/2 inch diskettes, which are made of hard plastic. The magnetic inner surface is hidden by a metal slide (write protect hole) that remains closed until the diskette is placed in the disk drive. Removing the diskette from the drive closes the slide. These diskettes are well-protected from damage and dirt. For example, you can safely carry 3 1/2 inch diskettes in your shirt pocket.

3 1/2 inch disk drives also vary in storage capacity. A PC/XT drive can write 720K on DS/DD (Double Density) diskettes. The AT can write 1.44 Meg on special DS/HD (High Density) diskettes. High density diskettes are now the standard.

A 1.44 Meg disk drive can also read and use diskettes with a lower capacity. So, if you buy a 1.44 Meg disk drive, which is slightly more expensive, you can still use 720K diskettes.

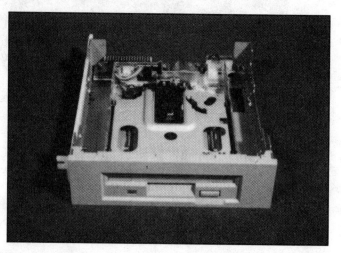

A 3 1/2 inch disk drive

3 1/2 inch disk drives for portable computers and laptops

The small 3 1/2 inch disk drive is used in almost all portable and laptop computers, where size is critical.

The new 2.88 Meg diskettes

A new generation of 3 1/2 inch disk drives and diskettes has recently been introduced. Because of an innovation in the magnetic coating process, 2.88 Meg can be stored on a single diskette, which is double the previous maximum. The new drive is downwardly compatible (i.e., it's also capable of processing diskettes at capacities of 720K or 1.44 Meg).

The new drives and diskettes are still rather expensive, but will become less expensive as they become more widely used. However, MS-DOS 6.0 is capable of handling the new higher density.

About hard drives

Until about 1987, the inexpensive PC/XTs generally had two diskette drives. Today, most personal computers automatically come with a hard drive. A built-in hard drive offers the following advantages:

Advantages of hard drives

- A hard drive can hold a tremendous amount of data. As you obtain more and larger programs, your disk space requirements increase dramatically.

- Hard drives are much faster than disk drives. The increased speed is especially noticeable when you work with some of the more complex programs or with large amounts of data.

Inside a hard drive

Disadvantages of hard drives

- When a hard drive becomes full, you can't simply replace it with a new one. The storage medium is built into the drive itself. Since the inside of a hard drive must be protected from dust, it's hermetically sealed. Therefore, when the disk is full, you must select some files to delete or copy to diskettes.

- Hard drives are sensitive to movement. A PC with a hard drive shouldn't be moved while it's operating. Almost all computers now have an autopark function. When the computer is switched off, this feature places the read/write heads in a special position so that any vibrations won't cause damage.

3.4   Formatting Diskettes

Data can be written only to storage media that has been previously "prepared" or formatted. This applies to hard drives as well as the various kinds of floppy diskettes. One exception is the RAM disk, which can store data after you start its driver program from the CONFIG.SYS file.

When you purchase a diskette, you receive a storage medium that's coated with magnetic material. Before you can use the diskette, it must be formatted. Formatting a diskette divides it into tracks which are further divided into sectors. MS-DOS uses these sectors to store "chunks" of data. MS-DOS also creates special reserved areas on the media for managing the stored information, similar to a root directory. The MS-DOS FORMAT command is used to format diskettes.

Preparing a diskette: Formatting with FORMAT

Dividing the diskette into tracks and sectors and preparing information for managing the diskette take place during formatting. All media must be formatted before it can be used.

   You can now buy preformatted diskettes. This is helpful when you need a new diskette but don't have time to format it.

During formatting, MS-DOS checks the diskette for defective areas and marks these bad areas so that they aren't used later to store data.

The following figure shows the various formatting options for diskettes. With older DOS versions, the formatting process remagnetized the entire surface of the diskette. However, now the exiting format can be preserved when possible (i.e., when the diskette was previously formatted to the same density). In this case, MS-DOS simply checks for any defects and then recreates the system (data management) area.

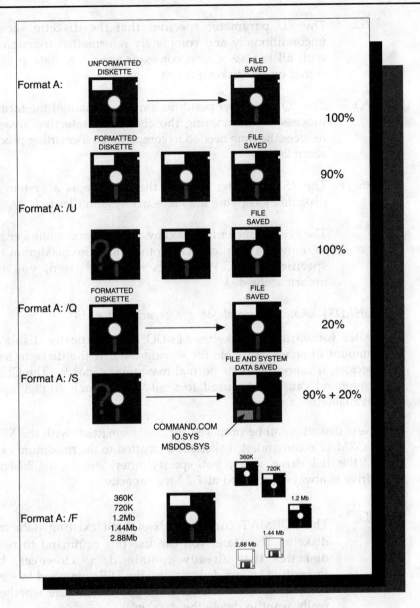

UNFORMATTED DISKETTE

FILE SAVED

Format A:

100%

FORMATTED DISKETTE

FILE SAVED

Format A: /U

90%

FILE SAVED

Format A: /Q

100%

FORMATTED DISKETTE

FILE SAVED

Format A: /S

20%

FILE AND SYSTEM DATA SAVED

90% + 20%

COMMAND.COM
IO.SYS
MSDOS.SYS

360K

720K

1.2 Mb

360K
720K
1.2Mb
1.44Mb
2.88Mb

1.44 Mb

2.88 Mb

Format A: /F

Diskette formatting options

/U: The /U parameter specifies that the diskette should be unconditionally and completely reformatted (remagnetized) with all the associated consequences. Any data previously stored on the diskette is lost.

/Q: The /Q parameter performs a quick version of the formatting process by eliminating the check for defective areas. This reduces the time needed to complete the formatting process by about 20%.

/S: /F: The /S parameter formats the diskette as a system (boot) diskette by copying the necessary system files to it.

        The /F: parameter followed by an appropriate number is used to request a size (capacity) other than the maximum for the specified drive. When this option is used, you cannot unformat the disk.

CHKDSK shows the total storage capacity of a disk

After formatting a diskette, MS-DOS automatically displays the amount of space available for storing data. If the diskette has bad sectors, it cannot hold its normal maximum capacity. The CHKDSK command can also be used to verify how much storage space is available on a diskette.

New diskettes can be prepared for use (formatted) with the MS-DOS FORMAT command. A diskette is formatted to the maximum capacity of the disk drive, unless you specify otherwise. So, a 1.2 Meg disk drive is always formatted at 1.2 Meg capacity.

    The FORMAT command deletes all existing data from a diskette. Therefore, you can use this command to reformat diskettes that already contain data. However, before formatting such a diskette, use the DIR command to view the contents of the diskette. Then you can decide whether you really want to delete the data on it.

UNFORMAT

FORMAT provides protection from accidental formatting and loss of data. Sometimes, even without using MIRROR, it's possible to recover data that was lost when formatting a diskette or hard drive. You can do this by using the UNFORMAT command.

Special features of formatting

FORMAT can be used only on a real disk drive

Formatting a diskette is a mechanical and magnetic process. So you can only use the FORMAT command on disk drives that have the corresponding mechanism and electronic circuitry. This means that you cannot specify a pseudo disk drive defined by SUBST or a drive in another computer on a network. Likewise, you cannot use FORMAT to prepare a RAM disk (a pseudo disk drive in main memory). Instead, a RAM disk is "installed" when you define it to MS-DOS.

FORMAT prompts you to insert the diskette to be formatted and to confirm your action by pressing (Enter). If you don't have a hard drive, you have the option of starting the command from the DOS diskette and then inserting the diskette to be formatted in the same drive.

 A very useful feature of MS-DOS 6.0 is its ability to preserve existing files when formatting, so that they can be recovered, if necessary.

The entire diskette isn't automatically deleted by the formatting process. Instead, if the diskette is already formatted, usually only the system areas (root directory and File Allocation Table) are recreated. The old system information can be saved on the diskette and, if necessary, later used to restore it to its previous condition.

This isn't possible, however, if the diskette is formatted to a different density. When you change densities, FORMAT warns you that a subsequent UNFORMAT won't be allowed.

Formatting various disk drives types

When formatting diskettes, you must distinguish between different disk drive types and their capacities. If a capacity isn't specified, MS-DOS formats a diskette at the maximum capacity of the drive.

360K disk drive (5 1/4 inch)

A 360K drive (XT drive) uses double sided, double density (DSDD) diskettes. When you use the MS-DOS FORMAT command to prepare these diskettes on a 360K disk drive, you don't have to specify any additional parameters.

```
FORMAT driveid
```

For example, to format a diskette in drive A: (first disk drive), use the following command line:

```
FORMAT A:
```

The FORMAT command then prompts you to insert the diskette to be formatted. After you press (Enter), formatting begins, displaying the progress on the screen. Finally, MS-DOS prompts you to enter a volume label for the diskette. You can enter a label containing up to eleven characters or simply press (Enter) to skip this option:

☞   You cannot use high density (1.2 Meg) diskettes in a 360K disk drive. With this type of drive, you cannot increase data security by using the higher density.

1.2 Meg disk drive (5 1/4 inch)

A 1.2 Meg disk drive (also called an AT drive because it first appeared with ATs) is a high capacity version of a 360K disk drive. It can store more than three times as much data as a 360K diskette. However, special DS (double sided, high density) diskettes are needed.

To format a high density diskette in a high density drive, use FORMAT without adding any parameters:

```
FORMAT driveid
```

For example, to format a high density disk in drive A:, use the following command line:

```
FORMAT A:
```

Normally when a disk drive is used, it automatically recognizes the capacity of the inserted diskette. However, this doesn't happen when you format a diskette. By default, a 1.2 Meg disk drive formats a diskette at the highest possible capacity (1.2 Meg). To override this default, enter the /F switch, a colon and the desired capacity after the command and the disk drive specification. In our example, this would be :360.

The parameter: /F:360 or /4

To format a 360K diskette in a 1.2 Meg disk drive, use the following command line:

```
FORMAT A: /F:360
```

You can also use the /4 parameter to do this. To remember this switch, remember that a 360K diskette has only about 1/4 of the capacity of a 1.2 Meg diskette. So another way to format a diskette with a 360K capacity is:

```
FORMAT A: /4
```

If you don't enter the switch (/4 or /F:360) when formatting a double density diskette, the disk drive will try to format it at a higher capacity than is allowed. This takes longer because errors always occur. Also, the diskette will have unusable (defective) sectors and corrupted data.

Actually, you can bypass the /F or /4 switches by using a feature of MS-DOS that lets you set up multiple drive identifiers for the same disk drive. This means that one physical drive can have two logical identifiers.

☞ A special driver program called DRIVER.SYS must be used with this option. A line in the CONFIG.SYS file references this program and passes the appropriate data to it. A definition line similar to the following is required:

```
DEVICE=C:\DOS\DRIVER.SYS /D:0 /F:0
```

The instructions have the following meanings:

DEVICE=C:\DOS\DRIVER.SYS

This starts the driver program. You may have to specify a different directory path instead of C:\DOS.

/D:0   Specifies the disk drive to be used.
        0=Drive A:, 1=Drive B:.

/F:0   Specifies the type of disk drive.
        0=360K, 1=1.2M, 2=720K, 7=1.44M, 9=2.88M.

The next time you boot the computer, the driver program will display a message similar to the following (instead of D:, another disk drive identifier may appear):

```
Loaded external device driver for drive D:
```

Now you can address drive A: as a 1.2 Meg disk drive and address the same disk drive under the label D: as a 360K disk drive. On drive D:, you won't need to add "/F:360" when you format a 360K diskette. It's the same physical disk drive, but it can be addressed by two different drive identifiers A: and D:.

Problems exchanging data between ATs and PCs

One reason 1.2 Meg disk drives are popular is that they can also access 360K diskettes. However, few people realize that compatibility can only be guaranteed when reading 360K diskettes. There is no guarantee that you can write to them error free.

You may think that a PC can read data written by an AT as long as the diskette was formatted on the PC. However, the opposite of this is true. In order for a PC drive to read a diskette written by an AT, the PC drive should not have formatted the diskette or written to it.

720K disk drive (3 1/2 inch)

Three and one-half inch disk drives are standard for all laptop computers and for many of the newer desktop computers. These drives are more sturdy than 5 1/4 inch disk drives. Even though these drives have advantages, most computers still use 5 1/4 inch disk drives.

The smaller 3 1/2 inch diskettes are constructed differently from its 5 1/4 inch counterpart. The diskette case is made of sturdy plastic and, instead of a hole in the middle, it has a small circular metal piece that spins the media. The read/write slot is protected by a metal slide. The slide opens automatically when you insert the diskette into the drive and closes when you remove the diskette from the drive.

The 3 1/2 inch diskettes are a lot sturdier and less susceptible to physical damage than 5 1/4 inch diskettes. You must protect 5 1/4 inch diskettes from dust, humidity and touch. Although 3 1/2 disks can also be damaged by water or dust, they are better protected due to their sturdy cases. As you can see, 3 1/2 inch diskettes have several advantages.

When you buy 720K 3 1/2 inch diskettes, they should be double sided (DS) double density (DD).

You can format 720K diskettes without specifying any additional parameters:

```
FORMAT driveid
```

If you use a 3 1/2 inch disk drive with 720K capacity as your second disk drive (B:), use the following command to prepare your diskette:

```
FORMAT B:
```

1.44 Meg disk drive (3 1/2 inch)

This drive is similar to the 1.2 Meg disk drive; it can be used at the 1.44 Meg high capacity or the 720K standard capacity (double density).

To prepare a 3 1/2 inch high density diskette for data (1.44 Meg), type the following command for disk drive B:

```
FORMAT B:'
```

Since high density (HD) 1.44 Meg diskettes are fairly expensive (about $20 for 10), you may choose to use the less expensive, standard DSDD diskettes which can be used to store up to 720K of data. Then you can format them using one of the following ways:

Option 1:

With MS-DOS Version 6.0 the procedure for formatting a double density disk is easy. Simply enter /F:720 after the drive identifier when you format the diskette. This tells your 1.44 Meg disk drive to format the diskette at 720K capacity:

```
FORMAT B: /F:720
```

Option 2:

If you forget the extra parameter, an error message appears. You can redefine your drive's capacity under a second logical identifier, just as we discussed for a 1.2 Meg disk drive. To do this, insert a special line in your CONFIG.SYS file. To redefine drive A: from 1.44 Meg to 720K, use the following line:

```
DEVICE=C:\DOS\DRIVER.SYS /D:0 /F:2
```

If the second disk drive (B:) on your computer is the 3 1/2 inch drive, replace "D:0" with "D:1". The next time you start your computer the DRIVER.SYS program will display a message telling you which drive identifier (letter) you can use as a 720K disk drive. Remember that the original disk drive identifier (letter) for use with 1.44 Meg diskettes is still valid.

DOS indicates the drive identifiers at startup

For example, if you installed a hard drive on your computer, it will have drive letter C:. The DRIVER.SYS program then assigns the newly defined disk drive the letter D:.

If you installed the 3 1/2 inch disk drive as a second disk drive (B:), you can still format 1.44 Meg diskettes with the following:

```
FORMAT B:
```

When you want to create a 720K diskette, simply use your new drive identifier (drive D:):

```
FORMAT D:
```

The drive automatically recognizes lower density (DD) diskettes

Similar to 1.2 Meg diskettes, 1.44 Meg diskettes must also meet certain quality requirements. DS (double sided, high density) should appear on the label. Although a 1.44 Meg disk drive recognizes lower density diskettes (DD) by a notch in the case (similar to a write protect notch), it cannot format them at 1.44 Meg.

It's only a matter of time before 3 1/2 inch diskettes with 1.44 Meg memory capacity becomes popular. After all, they're not much more expensive than 720K diskettes. If you buy an AT and want to use a 3 1/2 inch disk drive, we recommend that you also buy a 1.44 Meg disk drive.

2.88 Meg disk drive (3 1/2 inch)

MS-DOS 6.0 is prepared for the new 3 1/2 inch diskettes and disk drives with 2.88 Meg capacity. The capacity is doubled compared to the 1.44 Meg disk drives. This is done by doubling the sectors per track from 18 to 36.

MS-DOS automatically recognizes the capacity

Since MS-DOS automatically recognizes the capacity, special preparations aren't necessary in order to use diskettes with lower capacities in this type of disk drive.

To format 720K diskettes, use /F:720 as a switch. To format 1.44 Meg diskettes use either one of these switches: /F:1.44 or /F:1440.

Formatting differences

New, unformatted diskettes are magnetic surfaces that don't contain any information. The initial formatting process divides the medium into tracks and sectors. The diskette is also checked for readability

(VERIFY) and then the necessary system areas (boot sector, root directory, and File Allocation Table) are created.

Formatting no longer deletes everything without a directive

If you reformat a diskette but don't change the density, the diskette doesn't have to be redivided into tracks and sectors. This part of the formatting process used to cause serious problems if you accidentally formatted the diskette because any existing data was destroyed. Now existing data is protected. So, what happens depends on the diskette's condition:

- If the diskette isn't formatted yet, MS-DOS detects this and formats it at the maximum capacity of the disk drive. Obviously, data isn't lost because an unformatted diskette can't contain any readable data.

- If an already formatted diskette is being reformatted at the same capacity, MS-DOS performs only the VERIFY function and updates the system areas. Since the data area isn't disturbed, it writes a copy of the old system areas as a hidden file. This file can be used to UNFORMAT the diskette if necessary.

- If an already formatted diskette is being reformatted at a different capacity, MS-DOS must re-establish the tracks and sectors. So, any existing data are destroyed. You must confirm a warning message reminding you that UNFORMAT won't be possible.

☞ Saving the old system areas for UNFORMAT occupies space on the diskette. If enough space isn't available, the information won't be saved and you won't be able to undo the formatting. A 1.2 Meg diskette needs about 12K free before reformatting.

The outline shows the basic procedures for safely formatting a diskette and then recovering the data.

DOS saves the old system area as a hidden file on the diskette and creates a new system area. Now if you store data on the diskette, the old system area is overwritten and the old data, while still present, is no longer salvageable.

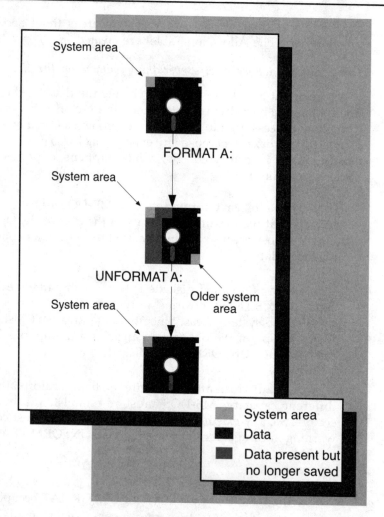

Safe formatting and data recovery

With UNFORMAT, the new system area is deleted and replaced with the old copy that was saved. Now the data has been restored and is again "visible".

Formatting diskettes quickly

On a diskette that has been formatted, MS-DOS has checked the entire medium for readability and created the system areas. Any defective portions of the diskette are marked and excluded from the File Allocation Table so they won't be used to store data. This is why the amount of free space isn't identical on every empty (newly formatted) diskette.

MS-DOS checks the medium

When a diskette is reformatted, MS-DOS checks for defects (VERIFY) and then, based on this check, recreates the system area. Although this process is faster than the initial formatting, it's still time-consuming (about a minute for a 1.2 Meg diskette).

A diskette doesn't have to be checked for readability continually. For example, if you're using FORMAT only to free some space on the diskette without deleting files, you may want to skip the verify procedure. (This is especially useful when you have subdirectories.) MS-DOS provides a quick format procedure. Simply use the following line to activate this option:

```
FORMAT driveid /Q
```

The parameter /Q for "quick format"

Quick formatting takes only about 12 seconds for a 1.2 Meg diskette, because MS-DOS simply saves the old system areas for a possible UNFORMAT and create the new ones.

To free up a formatted 1.2 Meg diskette in drive A:, for example, use the following command:

```
FORMAT A: /Q
```

 Quick formatting cannot be used when changing the density, because new tracks and sectors must be written.

Quick formatting is a convenient way to reuse a diskette that contains files, in several directories, that you no longer need. So, you don't have to delete each file individually with the DEL and RD commands.

Formatting and deleting diskettes

Sometimes you may not want your data to be recoverable. With unconditional formatting, the data is safely deleted so that no one can see or restore the data.

All data on the diskette is completely overwritten with /U

MS-DOS can reformat the diskette into tracks and sectors, which completely overwrites all existing data. The surface of the diskette is also checked for defects (verified). To perform an unconditional format, use the /U parameter.

```
FORMAT driveid /U
```

To perform an unconditional format on a diskette in drive A:, use the following:

```
FORMAT A: /U
```

 Quick formatting (/Q) and unconditional formatting (/U) cannot be performed simultaneously because quick formatting simply updates the system areas without deleting data. Use the /U option carefully since it's impossible to recover the data once it's unconditionally deleted.

Assigning a volume label and serial number to a diskette

After formatting, MS-DOS automatically prompts you for a name, an "electronic label" of sorts for the diskette. If you don't wish to label it at this time, just press [Enter].

 Later you can use the LABEL command to assign or change a volume label. The DIR command displays the label before the root directory.

A diskette name (label) can contain up to eleven characters

The volume label you choose for your diskette can have a maximum of 11 characters and can (unlike filenames) contain spaces. You should use this method of "electronic diskette labelling" to give your diskettes meaningful names. So instead of displaying the individual files stored on the diskette, you can use a simple command (VOL) to determine what kind of information the diskette contains.

MS-DOS 6.0 doesn't use the volume labels of diskettes to distinguish between different diskettes. Instead, a volume serial number, which is automatically placed on a diskette when it's formatted, is used. This number consists of 8 hexadecimal digits. MS-DOS can use this volume serial number to determine when you've changed diskettes.

MS-DOS displays the volume label, volume serial number and other information after formatting a diskette. The DIR command also displays this information:

```
Volume in drive A is WORKDISK
Volume number: 3120-11E0
Directory of A:\
```

In this example the volume label is WORKDISK and the volume serial number is 3120-11E0.

 You can also check the current volume label and serial number by using the VOL command.

Special formatting switches

You can use /1 (only 360K disk drive) to format only one side of a diskette (180K), /8 to format a diskette with 8 instead of 9 sectors and /B to format a diskette with room reserved for the operating system (boot) files. Although users seldom use these options, they are available for compatibility with earlier versions of DOS.

The following table provides an overview of the various disk drives and capacities. It also provides the specifications used with the FORMAT command:

Disk drive	Capacity	Tracks	Sectors	FORMAT: Switch
5 1/4 inch	160K	40	8	/1/8 (only PC-drive)
	180K	40	9	/1 (only PC-drive)
	320K	40	8	/8 (only PC-drive)
	360K	40	9	(on AT: /F:360)
	1.2 Meg	80	15	(only AT)
3 1/2 inch	720K	80	9	(1.44 Meg: /F:720)
	1.44 Meg	80	18	(only AT)
	2.88 Meg	80	36	(new disk drives)

Different capacities and parameters possible when using FORMAT

Information about a formatted diskette

After you finish formatting and entering a name for the diskette, information about the storage device is displayed:

```
C:\>format a: /s
Insert new diskette for drive A:
and press ENTER when ready...

Checking existing disk format
Formatting 1.2M
Format complete
System transferred

Volume label (11 characters, ENTER for none)? WORK DISK

   1213952 bytes total disk space
    117760 bytes used by system
   1096192 bytes available on disk

       512 bytes in each allocation unit
      2141 allocation units available on disk

Volume Serial Number is 2928-12DD

Format another (Y/N)?
```

Diskette information after formatting

These lines have the following meanings:

total disk space:
>   Total storage capacity of diskette.

used by system:
>   Space taken up by system files (if present).

in bad sectors:
>   Space not available because of defects (if present).

bytes available on disk:
>   Space available to store data.

bytes in each allocation unit:
>   Smallest storage unit on the diskette; even if a file only contains one character, it takes up at least the space of one allocation unit.

allocation units available on disk:
>   Number of available allocation units.

volume serial number:

MS-DOS labels each new diskette with a serial number so that it can determine when you change diskettes.

☞ If the error message "Parameters not supported by drive" appears, the parameters you specified cannot be used on this disk drive (e.g., /1 on ATs or 3 1/2 inch disk drives).

☞ If the error message "Invalid medium or track 0 defective" appears, you either tried to format a diskette at a capacity too high for it (1.2 Meg) or you cannot format the system track. In the first case, use /4 for 360K. In the second case, use the diskette only for data (do not use /S).

Automatic formatting

There are a few situations in which MS-DOS automatically formats a diskette without requiring you to use the FORMAT command:

* When you use the DISKCOPY command to copy a diskette, MS-DOS automatically formats the diskette if you haven't already done so. Except for the volume serial number, the duplicate copy is identical to the source diskette. Therefore, MS-DOS automatically formats it with the correct capacity. If this isn't possible (because the source diskette was formatted for 1.2 Meg and the target diskette isn't high density (HD)), MS-DOS aborts the DISKCOPY command with an error message.

Automatic formatting with MSBACKUP

* When you use the MSBACKUP command to copy data, MS-DOS also automatically formats diskettes if you haven't already done so. The MSBACKUP command lets you select the capacity that should be used for the target diskettes.

3.5 Formatting Hard Drives

Just as a floppy diskette must be formatted, so must a hard drive be prepared before it can be used to store data. Preparing the hard drive consists of dividing the hard drive into one or more areas (partitions) and formatting.

Many PCs are sold with preformatted and partitioned hard drives. So, you can skip this procedure if you don't want to change the partitioning.

Dividing the hard drive into partitions

Since hard drives can hold much more data than diskettes, you can use a hard drive for more than one operating system. In order to allow for multiple operating systems and because there are different ways of managing a hard drive, MS-DOS lets you divide a hard drive into multiple partitions.

A partition is an arbitrary number of related tracks on the hard drive. For example, on a 400 track hard drive, tracks 0 to 300 might represent one partition and tracks 301 to 400 a second partition. Partitioning allows for different operating systems to use separate parts of the hard drive and manage their data in different ways.

You can divide a hard drive into a total of four partitions. Therefore, it's possible to have up to four different operating systems on one drive. The hard drive partitioning information is stored in the first sector of the hard drive, which is called the partition sector.

The partition sector data is extremely important to the functioning of the entire hard drive. If it's destroyed, you'll lose all your data. To prevent this from happening, the MIRROR command saves a copy of the partition sector. Then, if the sector is damaged, UNFORMAT can use the saved copy to recover the lost data.

Why partitions are used

Up through Version 3.2 of MS-DOS, a hard drive could only have one MS-DOS partition, and this had a maximum size of 32 Meg. If you used a 40 Meg hard drive, these early versions of MS-DOS could not access the remaining 8 Meg.

Dividing the second partition into logical drives

Starting with MS-DOS 3.3, two partitions could be defined on a hard drive, with the first or primary partition having a maximum capacity of 32 Meg. Even with an additional 32 Meg for the second, or extended partition, the DOS maximum manageable hard drive capacity was limited to 64 Meg. But 64 Meg was too limiting for some users. For this reason, it's now possible to subdivide the second, extended partition even further, into logical disk drives.

A logical disk drive can contain up to 32 Meg of data. You can add as many logical disk drives as there are identifiers (drive letters) available for disk drives (depending on the total capacity of the hard drive). Since MS-DOS supports a total of 26 disk drive identifiers from A: to Z:, a hard drive can have a maximum of 26 logical disk drives (25 + primary partition), which enables it to manage 832 Meg of hard drive capacity. Since the first two disk drive letters are usually reserved for disk drives A: and B:, practically speaking there are 24 hard drives possible, yielding a maximum capacity of 768 Meg.

The 32 Meg limitation is removed

Starting with MS-DOS 4.0, a partition (or logical disk drive) is no longer limited to 32 Meg. This partition can now be up to 2048 Meg (2 Gigabytes). For compatibility, at least one partition is still needed on the hard drive (the active or bootable partition). MS-DOS 6.0 can also work with several smaller partitions.

The primary partition is required for DOS

In order to work with MS-DOS, you must have a primary DOS partition installed on the hard drive. You can also install and use an extended DOS partition. MS-DOS can be started from a primary DOS partition, just as it can be started from a system diskette. The partition must contain the operating system. So, when you format the hard drive, specify the /S switch.

Although MS-DOS 6.0 can manage almost any size hard drive without dividing it into partitions, you may want to consider multiple partitions under the following conditions:

- If you occasionally work with another version of DOS, such as MS-DOS 3.3. Previous to MS-DOS 3.3, the maximum size for a partition was 32 Meg.

- If you want to use another operating system instead of MS-DOS (e.g. UNIX or OS/2) you must divide the hard drive into more than one partition. First install MS-DOS on one part of your hard drive and prepare the other part with the command that corresponds to the other operating system.

- If the directory or the File Allocation Table (FAT) is destroyed, you lose only the data in the partition that was destroyed. This is another good reason to divide a large hard drive into several smaller partitions.

A hard drive has only one "primary DOS partition"

A hard drive can only have one "primary DOS partition". If the entire capacity for this partition isn't used, you can only use the rest under MS-DOS for storing data if it is defined as an extended DOS partition. Then you'll define "logical" disk drives in the extended DOS partition. In other words, you must assign disk drive identifiers to the logical drives in the extended /DOS partition.

FDISK command

To divide the hard drive into partitions, use the FDISK command. A menu with four or five options is displayed. Option 5 appears only if more than one hard drive is installed in your computer. To select an option, type the corresponding number and press ⎡Enter⎦. To return to the previous menu, press ⎡Esc⎦. In the main menu, pressing ⎡Esc⎦ terminates the FDISK command. If you already changed the partition data, reboot the computer with an MS-DOS system diskette.

  If you use FDISK to make changes to the hard drive partitions and your hard drive is already installed and formatted, you should write down the names of all the logical disk drives. FDISK prompts you to enter the logical drive letter before it deletes each logical disk drive. Use the VOL command to determine the logical drive letter for each drive.

You can specify the size of a partition either in megabytes or percentages. If you enter a numerical value, FDISK interprets this as a value in megabytes. To enter a percentage, type a percentage symbol (%) after the number.

  All of the data on a hard drive will be lost when partitions are changed. So, make a backup diskette for the data that must be saved. Also, you'll need a boot diskette to restart your computer after partitioning because the operating system will also be deleted.

You should follow certain steps when configuring a hard drive into partitions and logical drives. First we'll provide an overview of these steps and then we'll present some examples to show you how to use these steps.

Creating a partition

- Creating a primary DOS partition

- Creating an extended DOS partition

- Creating a logical drive

Deleting a partition

- Deleting all logical drives

- Deleting the extended DOS partition

- Deleting the primary DOS partition

Creating a primary DOS partition for the entire hard drive

The easiest way to prepare a hard drive for working with MS-DOS is to create a single partition for starting the computer (primary partition).

 Changing partitions with FDISK (even when you're creating a primary DOS partition) deletes all of the data on the hard drive.

To create a partition choose option 1 for "Create DOS partition or logical disk drive" and press (Enter). Then enter 1 to "Create a primary DOS partition" and press (Enter) again.

 If a primary DOS partition already exists, FDISK displays an error message and won't allow another primary DOS partition. In this case, you must first delete the existing primary partition with option 3 of the menu before creating a new one.

```
                            Create Primary DOS Partition
          Current fixed disk drive: 1

          Do you wish to use the maximum available size for a Primary
          DOS Partition
          and make the partition active (Y/N).....................? [Y]












          Press Esc to return to FDISK Options
```

Create primary DOS partition

To the above prompt, answer by typing Y and pressing Enter. This
causes MS-DOS to treat the entire hard drive as a single partition.
Since no further partitions are possible, FDISK ends.

```
          System will now restart

          Insert DOS system diskette in drive A:
          Press any key when ready . . .
```

Reboot after partitioning

Reboot after partitioning

Insert the first installation diskette in the disk drive and press Enter.
The computer then automatically reboots and continues the
installation program.

You still won't be able to store any data on a hard drive prepared in this way. The hard drive must first be formatted. MS-DOS determines if the drive has been formatted during installation and automatically formats the hard drive if necessary.

Creating a primary DOS partition (partitioning the hard drive)

MS-DOS 6.0 can use hard drives with practically unlimited capacity as a single partition identified by a single drive identifier. But it's usually best to divide it into several smaller drives. One reason for dividing the hard drive into partitions of up to 32 Meg is to preserve compatibility to earlier versions of DOS and to make managing data easier.

To specify part of the hard drive as a "primary partition", choose option 1 "Create DOS partition" in the main menu of FDISK and press Enter. If your hard drive already has a primary partition, it must be removed beforehand. Select option 1 again and press Enter. Answer the prompt for the maximum size of the DOS partition with N and press Enter.

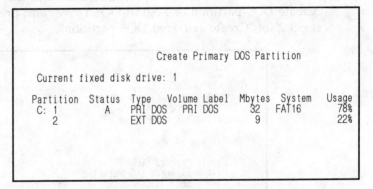

```
                        Create Primary DOS Partition

       Current fixed disk drive: 1

       Partition  Status  Type     Volume Label  Mbytes  System   Usage
       C: 1         A     PRI DOS   PRI DOS        32     FAT16     78%
          2               EXT DOS                   9               22%
```

Specifying a portion of the hard drive as a primary partition

The screen displays the total size and available size in percentages. The actual size displayed depends on your particular hard drive. Enter the desired size in megabytes (numbers only) or in percentages (numbers followed by percentages). Any errors can be corrected by pressing the Backspace key and retyping the corrections. Press Enter when your entry is complete.

FDISK displays important data for the new partition

FDISK then displays the new partition and the corresponding statistical information. First the disk drive letter is displayed; the next number is the partition number. This is followed by the type of partition (PRI DOS for primary DOS partitions and EXT DOS for extended DOS partitions). The volume label and size of the partition then follow.

After creating the primary partition, you can create extended DOS partitions. Press [Esc] to return to the main menu of FDISK.

 You can't boot from the hard drive when you create a primary DOS partition. You must first specify which partition is to be the active partition by using option 2 of the menu.

Creating an extended DOS partition

If you create a primary DOS partition and don't specify the total capacity of the hard drive, you can define an extended DOS partition. If you don't define an extended DOS partition, you won't be able to use the rest of the hard drive. You must create "logical" disk drives in the partition before the extended DOS partition is assigned a disk drive letter.

To define an extended DOS partition, enter 1 in the main menu for "Create DOS partition or Logical DOS Drive" and press [Enter]. Then select 2 for "Create extended DOS partition".

```
                    Create DOS Partition or Logical DOS Drive

        Current fixed disk drive: 1

        Choose one of the following:

        1. Create Primary DOS Partition
        2. Create Extended DOS Partition
        3. Create Logical DOS Drive(s) in the Extended DOS Partition



        Enter choice: [1]



        Press Esc to return to FDISK Options
```

Select 2 to create an extended DOS partition

FDISK displays the current status of the hard drive with the defined primary DOS partition. If you want to use all of the hard drive for MS-DOS, assign the rest of the hard drive to the extended DOS partition. Otherwise, the rest of the hard drive can't be used in DOS because MS-DOS cannot manage more than two partitions (one primary and one extended). If you want to use another operating system on the hard drive (UNIX, OS/2) in addition to MS-DOS, leave enough space on the hard drive to run the other operating system.

You can enter the size of the extended DOS partition either in megabytes or as a percentage. FDISK automatically calculates the rest of the hard drive for the extended DOS partition. Use the ⌜Backspace⌝ key to delete any mistakes in your entry. Press ⌜Enter⌝ after completing your entry; FDISK displays the message "Extended DOS partition created". The screen displays the current division of the hard drive:

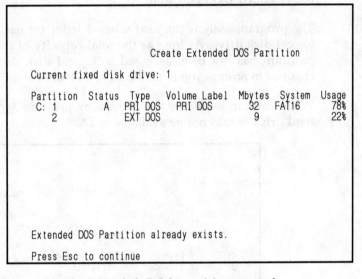

```
                   Create Extended DOS Partition
Current fixed disk drive: 1

Partition Status  Type  Volume Label  Mbytes System Usage
  C: 1       A   PRI DOS   PRI DOS       32   FAT16   78%
     2           EXT DOS                  9           22%




Extended DOS Partition already exists.

Press Esc to continue
```

Extended DOS partition created

After you press ⌜Esc⌝, FDISK asks you to define logical disk drives for the extended DOS partition.

Defining logical disk drives in the extended DOS partition

Before you can use the space in the extended DOS partition, you must first define one or more logical disk drives. To do this, choose option 1 "Create DOS partition" in the FDISK main menu. Then choose option 3 to define logical disk drives.

 When you create an extended DOS partition, FDISK automatically activates this menu option.

Capacity of extended partition in percent

The screen displays the total size of the extended DOS partition and the amount available in megabytes. Instead of the entire hard drive, the percentage only refers to the size of the extended partition. If there aren't any existing logical disk drives, the screen displays a message (showing 100% available capacity) that tells you this.

FDISK shows the new configuration of the extended DOS partition

If there are already logical disk drives defined, FDISK will let you know by displaying the identifiers of these logical drives. Now you can enter the size for the logical disk drives, specifying the capacity in megabytes or percentages. FDISK then displays the new division of the extended DOS partition.

The program assigns the next unused letter for each newly defined logical disk drive. As long as the total capacity of the extended DOS partition has not been assigned to logical disk drives, FDISK will continue to prompt you to define more disk drives.

While you can terminate this process by pressing Esc, the rest of the hard drive would not be available to DOS.

```
                   Create DOS Partition or Logical DOS Drive

       Current fixed disk drive: 1

       Choose one of the following:

       1. Create Primary DOS Partition
       2. Create Extended DOS Partition
       3. Create Logical DOS Drive(s) in the Extended DOS Partition




       Enter choice: [1]




       Press Esc to return to FDISK Options
```

Defining logical disk drives

```
           Create Logical DOS Drive(s) in the Extended DOS Partition
  Drv Volume Label  Mbytes  System   Usage
  D:  EXTENDED          9   FAT12    100%




















           All available space in the Extended DOS Partition
           is assigned to logical drives.
           Press Esc to continue
```

Logical disk drive in the extended DOS partition

 If you want to retain the ability for DOS 3.3 and earlier to access the data in one of these partitions, you must assign only a maximum capacity of 32 Meg for the logical disk drives.

If the total capacity has already been allocated, FDISK displays the current division. Use Esc to return to the main menu.

 Logical disk drives are sections of the hard drive that you can address using their own disk drive identifiers. When you create logical disk drives, you're dividing your hard drive into multiple disk drives.

Remember the disk drive letters of these logical disk drives. You'll use these disk drive letters later to access the different parts of the hard drive.

Setting the active partition

Use menu option 2 to specify the active DOS partition. Start MS-DOS from this partition, just as you would from a system diskette. The active partition must contain the DOS operating system.

 If there isn't an active partition, FDISK informs you of this and indicates that you cannot boot the computer from the hard drive.

```
                              Set Active Partition
            Current fixed disk drive: 1

            Partition  Status  Type   Volume Label  Mbytes  System   Usage
               C: 1       A    PRI DOS  PRI DOS        32    FAT16     78%
                  2            EXT DOS                   9              22%




            The only startable partition on Drive 1 is already set active.

            Press Esc to continue
```

Setting the active partition

After choosing this option, you must enter the number of the desired partition and press Enter. If a hard drive only has MS-DOS partitions, you can only select the primary DOS partition. After you set the active partition, the program displays the current status of the hard drive. Return to the main menu by pressing Esc.

    If the entire hard drive is set up for MS-DOS or if there is only one DOS partition defined as the active partition, FDISK displays an error message. Return to the main menu by pressing Esc.

Deleting a primary DOS partition

When you delete the primary DOS partition, the data on the partition will be lost. You cannot recover this data, even if you immediately recreate a primary partition of the same size.

    You can only delete a primary DOS partition if there is no longer an extended DOS partition.

Select option 3 (Delete DOS partition or logical disk drive) in the FDISK main menu. Then activate option one, in the submenu, for deleting a primary DOS partition. A security prompt is displayed. Confirm by pressing Y.

```
                    Delete DOS Partition or Logical DOS Drive

    Current fixed disk drive: 1

    Choose one of the following:

    1.   Delete Primary DOS Partition
    2.   Delete Extended DOS Partition
    3.   Delete Logical DOS Drive(s) in the Extended DOS Partition
    4.   Delete Non-DOS Partition



    Enter choice: [ ]




    Press Esc to return to FDISK Options
```

Deleting the primary DOS partition

The message "Primary DOS partition deleted" appears and the screen displays the new status of the hard drive.

```
                        Delete Primary DOS Partition

    Current fixed disk drive: 1

    Partition  Status  Type    Volume Label  Mbytes  System  Usage
    C: 1         A     PRI DOS   PRI DOS        32    FAT16    78%
       2               EXT DOS                   9             22%



    Total disk space is   41 Mbytes (1 Mbyte = 1048576 bytes)




    Cannot delete Primary DOS Partition on drive 1
    when an Extended DOS Partition exists.
    Press Esc to continue
```

Primary DOS partition deleted

Press [Esc] to return to the main menu of FDISK. Be careful when you press [Esc] because pressing this key too many times aborts FDISK. If this happens you must reboot the computer.

Deleting an extended DOS partition

```
                   Delete DOS Partition or Logical DOS Drive

Current fixed disk drive: 1

Choose one of the following:

   1.  Delete Primary DOS Partition
   2.  Delete Extended DOS Partition
   3.  Delete Logical DOS Drive(s) in the Extended DOS Partition
   4.  Delete Non-DOS Partition



Enter choice: [ ]




Press Esc to return to FDISK Options
```

Deleting an extended DOS partition

Use option 3 in the main menu and option 2, in the submenu, for deleting an extended DOS partition. The screen displays a security prompt. Confirm this prompt by pressing Ⓨ. Press Ⓔsc to return to the main menu.

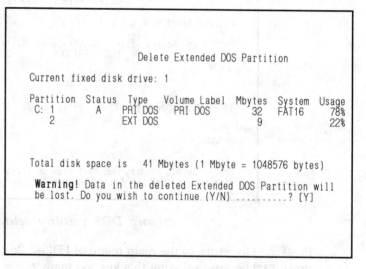

```
                        Delete Extended DOS Partition

Current fixed disk drive: 1

Partition  Status  Type    Volume Label  Mbytes  System  Usage
   C: 1      A     PRI DOS   PRI DOS        32    FAT16    78%
      2            EXT DOS                   9             22%



Total disk space is   41 Mbytes (1 Mbyte = 1048576 bytes)

Warning! Data in the deleted Extended DOS Partition will
be lost. Do you wish to continue (Y/N) ..........? [Y]
```

Extended DOS Partition deleted

You can only delete an extended DOS partition if there aren't any logical disk drives in the DOS partition. If there are logical disk drives, first they must be deleted.

Deleting logical disk drives in extended DOS partitions

When you choose option 3 in the main menu and then option 3 "Delete a logical disk drive in extended partition" in the submenu, the screen displays all of the defined logical disk drives. You can either specify the disk drive letters or return to the main menu by pressing Esc. After you enter the disk drive letter, the program prompts you for the volume label. Enter the volume name, which can be set with the MS-DOS VOL command. If the disk drive doesn't have a name, simply press Enter.

```
Delete Logical DOS Drive(s) in the Extended DOS Partition

Drv Volume Label  Mbytes  System  Usage
D:  EXTENDED          9   FAT12    100%




        Total Extended DOS Partition size is    9 Mbytes (1 MByte =
                                                 1048576 bytes)

        WARNING! Data in a deleted Logical DOS Drive will be lost.
        What drive do you want to delete....................? [ ]


        Press Esc to return to FDISK Options
```

Deleting a logical disk drive

After you respond to the obligatory warning prompt, the drive definition appears with the status "deleted". Once the last logical drive in the extended DOS partition has been deleted, the screen indicates that no drives are defined. At this point the capacity of the extended DOS partition cannot be used. Use Esc to return to the main menu.

Displaying the partition data

You can display the current division of your hard drive at any time. To do this, choose menu option 4 "Display Partition Information" in the main menu of FDISK.

```
                              Display Partition Information
    Current fixed disk drive: 1

    Partition Status  Type   Volume Label  Mbytes  System  Usage
     C: 1        A   PRI DOS PRI DOS          32    FAT16    78%
        2            EXT DOS                   9             22%



    Total disk space is   41 Mbytes (1 Mbyte = 1048576 bytes)


    The Extended DOS Partition contains Logical DOS Drives.
    Do you want to display the logical drive information
    (Y/N)......?[Y]



    Press Esc to return to FDISK Options
```

Displayed partition information

The screen displays information about the primary DOS partition
and any extended DOS partition. If there are also logical disk drives,
a prompt appears on the screen. To set the division of the extended
DOS partition into logical disk drives, press (Enter). The screen
displays the same information when you create or delete logical disk
drives. Press (Esc) to return to the main menu of FDISK.

Ending partitioning

To stop partitioning and exit FDISK, press (Esc) in the main menu.
FDISK will prompt you to insert a system diskette into drive A: if you
changed the partitions. Press any key and the computer
automatically reboots.

     If changes weren't made to the partitions, the computer won't
        have to be rebooted. Press (Esc); the command interpreter's
        system prompt appears. This happens if you were simply
        looking at the partition information.

Changing the partitioning

Although the dealer usually makes the first division of your hard
drive, you may often need to change the partitioning. In the following
section we'll provide examples and reasons for changing the
partitioning.

Reasons for changing the partitioning

There are several reasons for changing the partitioning of a hard drive. For example, perhaps you've always worked with MS-DOS and managed your entire hard drive as one large partition. Now you want to use a different operating system. You can divide the drive into two partitions, so that part of it can be used with a different operating system.

Sometimes it's easier to organize and save your data under separate disk drive identifiers. This means that you must partition your hard drive accordingly.

Even if your hard drive was configured into two partitions by your computer dealer, perhaps you're not satisfied with the sizes. For example, instead of two 50 Meg partitions, you may want one partition that's 90 Meg and another that's 10 Meg.

Limitations and problems

When you change the size of the partitions, the least that you'll have to do is to delete two disk drives. The most that you'll have to do is to delete all existing disk drives. Since all of the data stored on these drives is lost, you should first backup the data on the hard drive.

The following examples describe the most common changes in the partitioning, along with the results for the data stored there. We assume that the hard drive has a 100 Meg capacity.

Example 1

You originally divided the hard drive into two partitions of 50 Meg each. Now you want to use the entire drive as one partition.

Solution

Both partitions must be deleted and a new primary partition must be created with the total capacity. By doing this, all of the data on the entire hard drive is lost. Using FDISK, first delete the logical disk drive in the extended DOS partition, then delete the partition. Now you can remove the primary DOS partition. Finally, choose 1 for creating a primary DOS partition twice and answer each prompt for the maximum size of the DOS partition by pressing Y and Enter.

You'll need to reboot the computer. Since you destroyed the contents of the entire hard drive, your computer will no longer boot from the hard drive. Place a boot diskette that contains MS-DOS 6.0 into the disk drive. Now you'll need to reformat the hard drive. You should also copy the system onto the hard drive (using the FORMAT command with the /S switch).

Example 2

You have a hard drive with a primary partition (50 Meg) and an extended partition (50 Meg). The extended partition has two logical disk drives with 25 Meg each. You want to combine both of these logical drives into one logical disk drive with 50 Meg.

Solution

Delete both logical disk drives in the extended partition. You don't have to make any changes to the primary or the extended partition. Define a new disk drive in the extended partition using all 50 Meg. Since you don't have to change the primary partition, its contents remain intact. You'll lose the contents of both logical disk drives.

Example 3

You have a hard drive with a primary and an extended partition, each 50 Meg. You want to change the division so that the primary partition is 90 Meg and the extended partition is 10 Meg.

Solution

Remove the extended and the primary partition by deleting the logical disk drives in the extended DOS partition. Then remove the extended DOS partition and then the primary DOS partition.

Define a new primary partition with 90 Meg and an extended partition with the remaining 10 Meg. Now create the logical disk drive in the extended partition. Deleting both partitions causes all of the data on the hard drive to be lost. Ensure that the primary partition is the "active" one. Reformat both disk drives (the primary partition and the logical drive). Format the primary partition with the system (FORMAT /S).

Formatting the hard drive

You can format a hard drive with the FORMAT command after you use FDISK to divide it into one or more partitions. FORMAT identifies any defects on the hard drive and marks these areas so that they're not used later. FORMAT also deletes all existing data on the hard drive.

Sometimes you may want to reformat your hard drive without changing the partitioning. For example, if you're going to take your computer to the repair shop and want to remove sensitive data from the drive, you should format the hard drive. Or perhaps a software error has caused serious defects in the structure of the data on the drive and it can no longer be repaired with CHKDSK. In these instances, you can reformat the hard drive without using FDISK.

 If the hard drive is divided into several partitions and logical disk drives, you must format each individually using the FORMAT command. When formatting, specify the disk drive letter. Format the primary disk drive with the /S switch to copy the system files from the system diskette to the hard drive. You can then boot your computer from this disk drive.

 You can also use the MS-DOS Shell to format your hard drive with the group of Disk Utilities programs. Start FORMAT. You can then enter any parameters for the FORMAT command. The following section describes these parameters. Be careful: If you try to format the hard drive with the operating system from the MS-DOS Shell, you will definitely have problems. This process deletes all of the files of the MS-DOS Shell and all MS-DOS commands in general.

Formatting the hard drive with system files

When you format the primary DOS partition, you should transfer the system files so that you can boot your PC from the hard drive. The system files are the hidden files IO.SYS and MSDOS.SYS and the command interpreter COMMAND.COM on your disk. If you don't transfer the system files when you format drive C:, you won't be able to boot the computer from the hard drive. Use the /S switch to transfer the system files to your hard drive:

```
FORMAT driveid /S Enter
```

After typing this, if the operating system (including the hidden files) still isn't on the hard drive and there isn't a system diskette with these files in drive A:, the FORMAT command prompts you to place a DOS diskette in drive A: and confirm by pressing Enter.

To continue with the formatting process, answer the security prompt by pressing Y. When the formatting is completed, specify a volume label or the hard drive. The volume label can have a maximum of 11 characters and can contain spaces. A clear label provides added protection against accidental formatting in the future because the volume label must be specified. To skip the label, press Enter.

The screen displays the total memory and available memory:

total disk space:	Total storage capacity of the hard drive or partition.
used by system:	Occupied by system files.
in bad sectors:	Space not available because of defects (if present).
bytes available on disk:	Space available to store data.

 Since the hard drive contains the operating system, it uses part (approximately 70K) of the hard drive, which cannot be used for storing data. MS-DOS often indicates this as: "in hidden files".

Formatting other hard drive partitions

If the hard drive contains an extended DOS partition with logical disk drive(s), you must also FORMAT them:

```
FORMAT driveid
```

To proceed with formatting, answer the security prompt that appears by pressing Y. When formatting is completed, enter a volume name for the drive. (Press Enter to skip this option.) The screen then displays the total storage capacity for the drive.

 Since you can start MS-DOS only from the primary DOS partition, you don't have to transfer the system files to these other logical drives. Therefore, the message "used by system" doesn't appear on the screen. MS-DOS 6.0 automatically gives the drive a serial number, just like a diskette. As with a diskette, this number is displayed with the DIR command.

Creating a system diskette

Occasionally you may need to start (boot) your computer from a diskette. Perhaps you can't boot from the hard drive or you just want to try a new AUTOEXEC.BAT or CONFIG.SYS file from a diskette. To do any of these things, the diskette must be formatted as a system diskette.

It's especially important to have a good system diskette when you're experimenting with changes to your CONFIG.SYS or AUTOEXEC.BAT files. Some of the changes made to these files may result in a problem booting your computer. Unless you have a bootable system diskette, it's impossible to use the computer to correct these changes.

Formatting diskettes as system diskettes: the /S parameter

When you're formatting a new diskette and want to copy the operating system onto the diskette, use the /S switch. This switch copies two hidden files and the command interpreter COMMAND.COM onto your diskette. This leaves a little less storage space on the diskette. If you don't have MS-DOS installed correctly on your hard drive, you will have to insert a system diskette (boot diskette) into drive A:. Use the first MS-DOS installation diskette.

```
FORMAT driveid /S
```

To format a diskette in drive A: as a system diskette, use the following command line:

```
FORMAT A: /S
```

 If the diskette has a lower capacity than the disk drive you're using, you must specify the correct capacity using the /F: switch. To format a double density diskette for storing data and the system files on a 1.2 Meg disk drive, type:

```
FORMAT A: /S /F:360
```

Creating a system diskette with SYS

If you want to boot your computer from a normal diskette that already contains data, you must copy the system files to it. However, you cannot use the COPY command to do this because it can't place the system files in their proper place at the beginning of the root directory. You must use the SYS command to do this.

Ensure that there is enough space on the diskette for the files to be copied. SYS copies the two system files and the COMMAND.COM file to the diskette in the specified drive.

To make the formatted diskette in drive A: a system diskette by copying the system files and COMMAND.COM to it, type:

```
SYS A:
```

Starting the computer with a system diskette

You can start the computer from a diskette prepared in this way.
Simply insert the diskette into drive A: and switch on the computer.

CONFIG.SYS and AUTOEXEC.BAT are part of a successful startup

After MS-DOS 6.0 is installed, your computer will be initialized
differently. This occurs because of several settings that are made
automatically from CONFIG.SYS and AUTOEXEC.BAT at startup.
You should create both of these files on the new system diskette. Also
copy the driver programs and the necessary MS-DOS commands to
this diskette.

 If a diskette that isn't formatted as a system diskette is in
drive A: when you start the computer, MS-DOS displays an
error message and prompts you to insert a system diskette and
press any key. If you accidentally left a diskette in a disk
drive and want to start from the hard drive, simply remove
this diskette and press any key. Otherwise, exchange the
data diskette for a system diskette.

3.6   Labeling Storage Media

MS-DOS allows you to assign a volume label your storage media.
Many DOS commands identify the media by its volume label.

 If a hard drive is divided into several partitions and logical
disk drives, you can give each partition/logical disk drive a
different volume label.

Labeling a storage media

Use the LABEL command to give a volume label to a storage media:

```
LABEL driveid
```

The screen displays the previous volume label of the storage media.
You can enter a new volume label with a maximum of 11 characters.
Unlike filenames, a volume label name can contain imbedded spaces.
However, the following characters cannot be used:

```
<          less than
>          greater than
+          plus
=          equal
,          comma
;          semicolon
:          colon
.          period
*          asterisk
?          question mark
(          open parenthesis
)          close parenthesis
[          open bracket
]          close bracket
/          slash
\          backslash
```

If you don't specify a driveid, LABEL uses the current disk drive. When you enter the LABEL command you can specify the new volume label of the storage device directly after the colon:

```
LABEL A:vollabel
```

Deleting the name of a storage media

To delete a volume label, use the LABEL command again but press [Enter] without typing a new label. Answer the prompt that follows by pressing [Y].

Asking for names

You can use the VOL command at any time to determine the volume label of a storage media:

```
VOL
```

If you don't specify a disk drive, VOL automatically displays the volume label of the current disk drive. To determine the volume label of the diskette in drive A:, use the command:

```
VOL A:
```

In addition to the volume label, the screen also displays a volume serial number consisting of eight (two pair of four hexadecimal) digits. MS-DOS 6.0 automatically assigns this volume serial number when the media is formatted. Even if two storage devices have the same name, this number is used to identify a storage device:

```
VOL C:

Volume in disk drive C: is DR_C
Volume Serial Number is 3817-13CC
```

Storage media formatted with MS-DOS 3.3 and earlier don't have a volume serial number.

The volume label and volume serial number of a diskette or hard drive are displayed when you use the DIR command to view the contents of the storage media.

3.7 Displaying the Contents

A storage media can contain files and/or directories. A file is a group of data, such as a letter or spreadsheet information. Files appear in the disk directory as separate entries, which contain the filename, extension, file size and the date the file was created. Files contain stored data.

A subdirectory is an arbitrary collection of files that can be identified by a separate name. A directory collects the names of these separate files under a single name. By removing the individual filenames from the main directory (root directory) a SUB directory helps maintain order in the storage device.

```
QBASIC    HLP    130581  12-13-90    4:09a
RAMDRIVE  SYS      5783  12-13-90    4:09a
README    TXT     16945  02-14-91   11:57a
RECOVER   EXE      9098  12-13-90    4:09a
REMLINE   BAS     12314  12-13-90    4:09a
REPLACE   EXE     19554  12-13-90    4:09a
RESTORE   EXE     38054  12-13-90    4:09a
SETVER    EXE      9162  12-13-90    4:09a
SHARE     EXE     10768  12-13-90    4:09a
SHELL     CLR      4406  10-06-88   12:00a
SHELL     HLP     66527  10-06-88   12:00a
SHELL     MEU      4588  10-06-88   12:00a
SMARTDRV  SYS      8005  12-13-90    4:09a
SORT      EXE      6618  12-13-90    4:09a
SUBST     EXE     18350  12-13-90    4:09a
SYS       COM     13200  12-13-90    4:09a
TREE      COM      6764  12-13-90    4:09a
UMB       TXT     27574  12-13-90    4:09a
UNDELETE  EXE     13666  12-13-90    4:09a
UNFORMAT  COM     17680  12-13-90    4:09a
XCOPY     EXE     15624  12-13-90    4:09a
        101 file(s)    2514793 bytes
                       6684672 bytes free

C:\DOS>
```

Disk directory

Setting the current storage device

Many MS-DOS commands affect the current storage media or the current disk drive, unless otherwise specified. To activate another disk drive, enter the disk drive identifier (letter plus colon):

X:

A: and B: are usually disk drives and C: represents the first hard
drive. To make your hard drive the current drive, type the letter
followed by a colon:

C:⟨Enter⟩

Use the PROMPT command to automatically display the current
drive in a system prompt:

PROMPT $N

We recommend using "PG" as your system prompt because it causes
the screen to display the current drive and current directory:

PROMPT PG

If your hard drive (C:) is the current drive, the system prompt would
look like the following:

C:\>

Displaying the contents of a directory

Use the DIR command to display the contents of the directory on the
storage media. Typing DIR without parameters displays the contents
of the current directory.

DIR

The following is an example of how the screen would look if the root
directory of the hard drive is the current directory:

```
Volume in drive C: is DR_C
Volume Serial Number is 3817-13CC
Directory of C:\

DOS            <DIR>       08-08-90   12:42
CONFIG   SYS       228     04-29-91   15:09
ANSI     SYS      9029     03-22-91    5:00
COMMAND  COM     52925     02-12-93    6:00
DRIVER   SYS      5409     03-22-91   12:00
MOUSE    SYS     31687     12-12-89   16:49
CONFIG   BAK       245     08-07-90   14:25
AUTOEXEC BAK       224     08-07-90   14:25
AUTOEXEC BAT       221     08-07-90   15:10
TEXTS          <DIR>       08-08-90   13:00
TOOLS          <DIR>       08-08-90   13:00
WORD           <DIR>       08-08-90   13:14
        12 File(s)       78134 bytes
                       7190528 bytes free
```

The beginning of the display shows general information about the storage device (volume label, volume serial number and the name of the directory being displayed). Next, a list of existing files and subdirectories in the root directory is displayed. You can identify a file because there will be a number representing the file size in front of the date.

Subdirectories are indicated by the characters <DIR>. In the second to last line, DIR displays the total number of files and subdirectories and the amount of storage space occupied by the files, and in the last line the amount of unused storage space available on the drive.

To display the contents of a subdirectory, specify the name of the directory and, if necessary, the complete path:

```
DIR directoryname
```

This form of the DIR command has the same meaning as:

```
DIR directoryname\*.*
```

If the current directory is the root directory, you can use the following command to display the contents of C:\DOS:

```
DIR DOS
```

To display the contents of C:\DOS from any directory of the hard drive, use the complete path of the directory, as in the following command:

```
DIR C:\DOS
```

To pause the screen display, press Ctrl + S. Press any key to continue displaying the directory. The optional /P switch can be used to pause the screen output automatically after each page (screen). Again, press any key to continue the display. To display the C:\DOS directory page by page, use this form:

```
DIR C:\DOS /P
```

After displaying a page, the DIR command stops and waits for you to press a key.

Displaying all of the directories of a storage media

Use the TREE command to display all of the directories of a storage media. This command displays only the directories; files aren't displayed. The output appears in a tree structure:

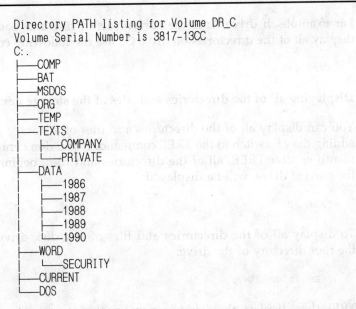

```
Directory PATH listing for Volume DR_C
Volume Serial Number is 3817-13CC
C:.
├───COMP
├───BAT
├───MSDOS
├───ORG
├───TEMP
├───TEXTS
│       ├───COMPANY
│       └───PRIVATE
├───DATA
│   ├───1986
│   ├───1987
│   ├───1988
│   ├───1989
│   └───1990
├───WORD
│       └───SECURITY
├───CURRENT
└───DOS
```

The TREE command presents a graphic picture of the organization of a disk drive by directory. This option is especially valuable for changing directories when you don't know the path of the directory to which you want to change. In our example, to see the contents of the 1986 directory, first move to the Data directory.

The deeper a directory is within the directory structure, the farther it is indented to the right. If you don't specify a directory after the TREE command, all of the directories of the current drive, beginning with the current directory, are displayed:

```
TREE
```

If C:\DATA is the current directory, TREE displays only this directory and its subdirectories:

```
Directory PATH listing for Volume DR_C
Volume Serial Number is 3817-13CC
C:\DATA
├───1986
├───1987
├───1988
├───1989
└───1990
```

To display all of the directories of the current disk drive, specify this as follows:

```
TREE driveid\
```

For example, if drive A: is the current disk drive and you want to display all of the directories on drive C:, use the following command:

```
TREE C:\
```

Displaying all of the directories and files of the storage device

You can display all of the directories and files of a storage device by adding the /F switch to the TREE command. If you don't enter a drive identifier after TREE, all of the directories and files, beginning with the current drive, will be displayed:

```
TREE /F
```

To display all of the directories and files of any disk drive, specify the root directory of the drive:

```
TREE driveid\ /F
```

TREE then displays the directory name within the tree structure and the files of the directory below it:

```
Directory PATH listing for Volume DR_C
Volume Serial Number is 3817-13CC
C:.
|     CONFIG.SYS
|     ANSI.SYS
|     COMMAND.COM
|     DRIVER.SYS
|     MOUSE.SYS
|     CONFIG.BAK
|     AUTOEXEC.BAK
|     AUTOEXEC.BAT
|
├───COM
|         MEYER01.DOC
|         MEYER02.DOC
|         MEYER01.BAK
|         MEYER02.BAK
|         INVOICE.STY
```

Since there is so much information, more than one screen page may be needed to display the entire list. You can pause the display after each page by using the MORE filter. To continue the display, press any key.

For example, to display all of the files on drive C: page by page, use the following command:

```
TREE C: /F | MORE
```

The pipe symbol (|) links two commands together: the TREE and MORE commands. If a pipe symbol isn't on your keyboard, hold down the Alt key and enter the digits 1 2 4 on the numeric keypad (to the right of the keyboard).

 If you use the MORE filter, it takes a few seconds before the files are displayed on the screen.

3.8 Copying Diskettes

DISKCOPY can duplicate the entire contents of a diskette to another diskette. The duplicate will have the same format as the source diskette. When the disk is copied, any data on the target diskette is lost. So it's a good idea to write protect the source diskette so that you don't accidentally lose the data by inserting the source diskette into the disk drive at the wrong time. Since DISKCOPY requires you to swap the source and target disk several times, it's easy to lose track of which disk should be in the drive at any given time.

Use DIR to examine the directory of the target diskette before you duplicate the diskette so that you can be sure that you don't overwrite important data.

If the target diskette hasn't been formatted, DISKCOPY automatically formats it for you. After you insert the target diskette, a message informs you of the formatting process. DISKCOPY takes longer using an unformatted target disk.

 The target diskette is automatically formatted with the same storage capacity as the source diskette. However, the computer must be capable of doing this. You cannot copy an HD diskette with 1.2 Meg onto a DD diskette. DISKCOPY will realize that it cannot attain the desired capacity on the target diskette and abort with an error message. Also the disk drives must be of the same type. You cannot copy a 5 1/4 inch diskette onto a 3 1/2 inch diskette.

After you insert the source diskette, DISKCOPY displays a message about the diskette's format:

```
Copying 80 tracks
15 sectors per track, 2 side(s)
```

In the previous example, the source diskette is a 5 1/4 inch diskette with 1.2 Meg capacity.

Unlike the COPY and XCOPY commands, DISKCOPY creates an identical copy of the source diskette. So instead of just the data, you're also transferring the relative location of the data on the diskette. This means that the data on the copy is arranged in the same way as the source diskette.

That's why DISKCOPY is the best command to use for making backup copies of irreplaceable diskettes. For example, you should use DISKCOPY to make backup copies of all of the diskettes included with a program.

    In contrast to earlier versions of DOS, source and target diskettes aren't 100 percent identical. DISKCOPY automatically gives the target diskette a new volume serial number. In spite of this, MS-DOS 6.0 treats both diskettes as though they were identical; the DISKCOMP command for comparing diskettes won't find any differences in MS-DOS 6.0. Comparisons in other versions of DOS will indicate a difference on side 0, track 0, since this is where the volume serial number is stored.

You can only make a copy if the target diskette is free of defects. If the target diskette cannot be formatted completely and correctly, the copying process aborts after the message "Formatting While Copying" appears. The following error message appears:

```
Drive types or diskette types
not compatible
```

In this case, use a different diskette for your target diskette and retry the operation. Although you could continue using the defective diskette by formatting it with FORMAT, a message, informing you that there are X number of bytes in defective sectors, appears. These defective sectors are automatically excluded from data storage.

DISKCOPY always copies the entire diskette, regardless of the amount of data stored on it. The process takes just as long when the diskette is completely blank (but formatted). You cannot copy an unformatted diskette. If you're copying only a few small files it might be better to use the COPY command instead of DISKCOPY.

Since DISKCOPY produces a duplicate of the source diskette, it also preserves the relative location of data on the diskette when copying. Even though this can be an advantage at times, it's usually a disadvantage because the longer you work with a diskette, the worse the distribution of the data becomes. When this happens the data becomes fragmented. MS-DOS can process data faster when it is stored contiguously. Copying the files with COPY or XCOPY onto a blank diskette provides an ideal arrangement of your files. So it's better to copy data by files instead of using DISKCOPY whenever possible.

Copying with a single disk drive

When you copy a diskette with a single disk drive, you must insert the source and target diskettes alternately into the same disk drive. Be very careful not to mix up the source and target diskettes.

If your computer doesn't have a hard drive, you'll need to insert the MS-DOS diskette containing the DISKCOPY command into the disk drive before you can type the command. DISKCOPY is an external command:

```
DISKCOPY A: A:
```

Next, insert the source diskette into drive A: and press a key. After a few seconds, you'll be prompted to insert the target diskette into drive A: and press a key. Depending on the available main memory and capacity of the diskette, DISKCOPY will prompt you to insert the source and target diskettes into drive A: several times. When the process is finished, DISKCOPY asks whether you need to copy another diskette. Answer either by pressing Ⓨ or if you don't want to copy another diskette, press Ⓝ.

If you start DISKCOPY from a disk drive, you don't have to specify the drive for the source and the target. The current drive is automatically used.

 Don't start DISKCOPY from within an application program. You won't have a lot of main memory available and you'll have to swap diskettes more often. It's a lot quicker to exit the application program and reload the program after you finish copying.

Copying with two disk drives

When you copy a diskette with two disk drives, you won't have to swap the source and target diskettes. However, if the computer doesn't have a hard drive you must insert the appropriate MS-DOS diskette before using DISKCOPY so that the computer can load the DISKCOPY command:

```
DISKCOPY A: B:
```

Insert the source diskette into disk drive A: and the target diskette into disk drive B: and press any key. When the copying process is finished, DISKCOPY prompts you to copy another diskette. Press Ⓨ to confirm or Ⓝ if you don't want to copy.

If the target diskette isn't formatted, the computer automatically formats it with the correct capacity.

Unfortunately, DISKCOPY doesn't support making multiple copies of the same diskette. To create two copies of one diskette, the computer must read the data from the source diskette twice. DISKCOPY also doesn't support extended memory. So even if you have 2 Meg in your PC, you will still need to swap the source diskette and the target diskette at least three times.

Verifying when you copy diskettes

If you want to be absolutely certain that the data on the copied diskette is identical and free of defects, you can specify the /V switch (for verify). To copy a diskette in drive A: and have the program automatically verify the process, use the command:

```
DISKCOPY A: A: /V
```

Since using this switch slows down the process considerably, you may choose to use it only for copying crucial data.

3.9   Comparing Diskettes

Use the DISKCOMP command to verify whether two diskettes have the same contents. The disks should have identical formats. For example, a 5 1/4 inch diskette cannot be compared with a 3 1/2 inch diskette. The command doesn't affect the contents of the diskettes. DISKCOMP doesn't simply check for the same contents, it also checks for the identical relative location of data on both diskettes. So DISKCOMP is mainly suited for checking diskettes copied by DISKCOPY. If you used COPY or XCOPY to copy the data onto another diskette, DISKCOMP will find many differences, which are caused by the rearrangement of the data. In these instances, use COMP to compare the files.

DISKCOMP can only compare diskettes with the same format and capacity. If the format is different, DISKCOMP terminates, after you insert the second diskette, with the message:

```
Drive types or diskette types
not compatible

Compare process ended

Compare another diskette (Y/N)?
```

Use COMP to compare files if the diskettes have different formats.

 When comparing files, DISKCOMP doesn't compare the different volume numbers. So a comparison of storage devices copied by DISKCOPY will be positive, while earlier versions of DOS (such as MS-DOS 3.3) will display messages indicating differences.

Single disk drive

Comparing is basically the same as copying a diskette with DISKCOPY. If there isn't a hard drive, you must insert the correct MS-DOS diskette before calling DISKCOMP because it is also an external command:

```
DISKCOMP A: A:
```

Next, insert the first diskette in drive A: and press any key. DISKCOMP automatically determines the format of the diskette and displays it on the screen. Depending on the amount of available main memory and the capacity of the diskette, DISKCOMP will prompt you to insert both diskettes into drive A: several times.

If both diskettes are identical, the following message appears:

```
Compare ok
```

If the diskettes aren't identical, DISKCOMP displays the differing elements found during the comparison, for example:

```
Compare error on
side 0, track 0

Compare error on
side 1, track 0
```

After the process is completed, DISKCOMP prompts you to compare more diskettes. Press Y to confirm or N if you don't need to compare anymore diskettes.

If you start DISKCOMP from a disk drive, you won't have to specify the drive. The program automatically uses the current drive.

With DISKCOMP you don't have to change 1.2 Meg diskettes as often as you do with DISKCOPY. On computers with 640K main memory and typical configuration, you must insert the source and target diskette three times for DISKCOPY and only twice for DISKCOMP. The reason for this is that DISKCOPY can only read from the source and write to the target. DISKCOMP can read more data for the comparison and then compare it with the former source diskette, after comparing it with the target diskette.

Two disk drives

Comparing diskettes on a PC with two similar size disk drives is also similar to copying a diskette:

```
DISKCOMP A: B:
```

Insert the first diskette into drive A:, insert the second diskette into drive B: and press any key. DISKCOMP then displays information about the comparison and gives you the option of comparing two more diskettes.

3.10 Checking Storage Media

Checking your storage media is an important and necessary process. If there are errors or defects on the media, you may not be able to use the data.

It's not easy to determine whether a disk is defective. Bad sectors can result in losing data that may have taken days or weeks to compile. So if potential errors and problems on a storage media are discovered early, it's less likely that damage will occur. In this section, we'll discuss the ways to check media for defects. You should do this regularly.

Checking disks with CHKDSK

Use the external command CHKDSK to check a disk for defects and display information about the disk. This command can be used in various ways to check the structure of the data on a disk. CHKDSK recognizes the following errors:

- Portions of files are no longer allocated to the file.

- Files have invalid allocations.

- The same parts of the disk are allocated to more than one file at the same time.

- Access to parts of a directory is no longer possible.

- The File Allocation Table (FAT) is defective.

- Directory is defective.

- Parts of the disk can no longer be read correctly.

CHKDSK /F can also fix errors

Fortunately for users, CHKDSK not only recognizes errors, but in many cases repairs them. Since attempting to repair a defective storage medium can cause further changes to its contents, you must specify the /F switch. Without this switch, CHKDSK only checks for and displays errors on the screen.

You cannot call CHKDSK with the /F switch from the MS-DOS Shell or from a program started with the Task Swapper.

Information about capacity and existing files/directories

To examine a disk for errors, activate CHKDSK with the appropriate drive identifier:

```
CHKDSK driveid
```

If you don't specify a drive, the contents of the current drive are examined. If no errors are detected on the drive, CHKDSK displays information similar to the following:

```
Volume LW_C          created 12.04.1989 12:06
Volume Serial Number is: 3817-13CC

21309440 bytes total disk space
   73728 bytes in 3 hidden files
   49152 bytes in 19 directories
13963264 bytes in 697 user files
   40960 bytes in bad sectors
 7182336 bytes available on disk

    2048 bytes in each allocation unit
   10405 total allocation units on disk
    3507 available allocation units on disk

  655360 total bytes memory
  537632 bytes free
```

The items have the following meanings:

- The maximum capacity on this drive.

- Number of files that are hidden from most MS-DOS commands and usually aren't accessible to the user. You can only display hidden files with special auxiliary programs or the MS-DOS Shell. The system files for starting the computer from this drive (IO.SYS and MSDOS.SYS) are hidden files.

- Number of directories and storage space MS-DOS requires for managing directories (shown only if present).

- Number of "normal" files, programs and storage space used.

- Space on the disk that cannot be used because of defects.

- Space still available for files and directories.

The information about the allocation units provides an explanation of the smallest storage units that MS-DOS can use to store data. 360K and 720K diskettes have 1024 bytes per allocation unit while 1.2 Meg and 1.44 Meg diskettes have only 512 bytes per allocation unit. Hard drives have allocation units containing either 2048 bytes or a multiple of 2048. A file always takes up at least one allocation unit.

Finally CHKDSK displays the amount of memory in the computer and the amount of memory that is available for user programs. This information refers to the computer itself instead of to the disk.

Information about errors on the disk

If CHKDSK detects errors on the disk, it displays them. The program compares the File Allocation Table (FAT) to the existing files and directories. CHKDSK reports any differences as errors.

CHKDSK reports lost allocation units

Any files on the disk that you can no longer access with MS-DOS are indicated. Then CHKDSK displays the number of allocation units (clusters) that are affected (lost allocation units) and the number of files (chains) that can no longer be accessed. If the allocation of clusters within a file is destroyed, CHKDSK may report more than one chain. The following is an example of what a lost allocation unit on a diskette might look like if you used CHKDSK without additional parameters:

```
Volume WORK       created 03.02.1990 16.54
Volume Serial Number is: 3916-17FC
Errors found, F parameter not specified.
Corrections will not be written to disk.

   1 lost allocation unit found in 1 chains.
     1024 bytes disk space would be freed

  362496 bytes total disk space
    1024 bytes in 1 user file
    1024 bytes in 1 restored file
  360448 bytes available on disk

    1024 bytes in each allocation unit
     354 total allocation units on disk
     352 available allocation units on disk

  655360 total bytes memory
  537632 byte free
```

 At the beginning a warning message tells us that CHKDSK will not make corrections to errors it finds because you didn't specify the /F switch. Next it tells us that it has found 1 lost allocation unit in a chain. The prompt to convert the chains to files has no effect since the corrections are not written to the disk.

If you run CHKDSK and find lost allocation units, you should run it again with the /F switch. This converts the lost chains to files.

 Use CHKDSK regularly to check important diskettes and your hard drive for potential errors. You cannot call CHKDSK with the /F switch when the MS-DOS Shell or Windows is active. CHKDSK will display an error message.

Viewing the checking process

To get a better idea of where the error occurred, you can display the checking as it progresses:

```
CHKDSK driveid /V
```

For example, to check a diskette in drive A: and display specific information as it checks the diskette, use the command:

```
CHKDSK A: /V
```

Since the information may be extensive, you can redirect the messages from CHKDSK to a file or a printer. This produces a written error report. For example, to check all of the hard drive (C:) and output all of the information to the printer, use the following command line:

    CHKDSK C: /V >PRN

Unfortunately CHKDSK doesn't have an option that lets you automatically stop screen output after every page and continue by pressing a key. To check the entire hard drive and display the information on the screen page by page, it's necessary to include the MORE command by using the following command line:

    CHKDSK C: /V | MORE

 If your keyboard doesn't have the "|" character, you can reproduce it by holding down [Alt] and pressing [1], [2], [4] on the numeric keypad.

If an error appears, you'll immediately know which directory or files are affected. You can save unaffected files to diskettes.

Correcting errors on a disk

When you discover errors on disks, you should correct them as soon as possible. However, before doing this, save all of the information on the media to prevent an even greater loss of data. If you're working with a floppy diskette, use DISKCOPY to create a backup copy. On a hard drive, use the MSBACKUP command. Then use CHKDSK with /F to correct the errors.

Correcting errors in the data structure

The /F switch tells CHKDSK to fix the errors on the disk wherever possible. You can choose to convert lost allocation units to files or have CHKDSK release them for further use.

In the first case, CHKDSK creates a file in the root directory named FILE????.CHK, where ???? is a consecutive number, beginning with 0000. If the lost data are ASCII files, you can display them with TYPE and possibly rebuild them.

If only garbage characters appear on the screen, it's probably a program file. You can use the file manager of the MS-DOS Shell or a special utility program (such as Norton Utilities or BeckerTools) to display the contents of the file. This might help you determine what the original file was.

HELP SCANDISK

Lost allocation units are created when a program creates a file on the storage device, but doesn't finish the process properly because an error occurred. For example, this could occur during a power failure.

 Always determine the position and kind of error (CHKDSK /V) before using /F to make corrections. This indicates which files and directories are in danger. Then you can check them with CHKDSK after repairing the error and replace them with backup copies if necessary.

Making corrections with special utilities programs

Although CHKDSK is useful for correcting errors, it may not be able to correct serious problems. If this happens you'll need to purchase a special utility program that is more powerful. The "Diskdoctor" from Norton Utilities or the "BeckerTools Recover" program from Abacus may help in salvaging damaged data.

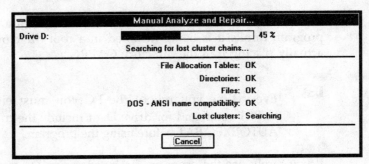

BeckerTools Recover program finds and corrects disk errors

3.11 Redirecting Drive Access

With MS-DOS, it's possible to create pseudo disk drives and access these drives via an existing directory. Each reference to this "new" disk drive is actually a reference to the directory. This technique can be used, for example, to install programs, which usually must be installed only in a root directory, in a subdirectory.

The SUBST command assigns an existing directory to a drive letter, for which no real drive actually exists.

Defining the substitution

With the following line

```
SUBST driveid directory
```

every access to the drive must be redirected to the specified directory.

 The drive definition requires a valid identifier. You may have to increase the number of possible drives with the LASTDRIVE command in the CONFIG.SYS file.

 Suppose that a program must be installed in the root directory but you would rather install it in the subdirectory C:\PRG on the hard drive. You don't currently have a D: drive. Use the following command line to set up a new drive D:

```
SUBST D: C:\PRG
```

Now you can enter

```
D:
```

to switch to the new drive and install the program. Although the program thinks it is being installed in a root directory, MS-DOS is actually placing it in the directory C:\PRG.

 Every time you reboot the PC you must either enter the SUBST command for drive D: or include the command line in AUTOEXEC.BAT before using the program.

If you rarely use the program that needs drive D:, create a batch file that sets up the drive with SUBST when it starts and removes it again when it ends.

Removing the assignment

To remove an assignment, specify the redirected drive with the /D switch:

```
SUBST driveid /D
```

You cannot do this if the redirected drive is the current drive in MS-DOS. Also, you shouldn't remove the assignment if there are application programs using this drive.

Displaying the assignment

To display all redirected drives and their directories, use the SUBST command without any parameters:

```
SUBST
```

For the previous example, the display should look like this:

```
D: => C:\PRG
```

Avoiding long path specifications

You can use SUBST to replace long path specifications with shorter ones. This saves entering complex path specifications. For example, if you don't have a drive D: and you frequently work with the directory C:\DATA\TEXTS\PRIVATE, you can make your work a lot easier by making this directory into a pseudo drive:

```
SUBST D: C:\DATA\TEXT\PRIVAT
```

Now when you want to use the directory C:\DATA\ TEXT\PRIVAT, simply enter D:. The allocation may be cancelled by using the following command line:

```
SUBST D: /D
```

This only works if the directory C:\DATA\TEXT\PRIVAT (that is D:) isn't the current directory.

Limitations

You cannot use the following commands for drives that you redirect to a directory using SUBST:

```
MSBACKUP
RESTORE
FORMAT
SYS
FDISK
CHKDSK
RECOVER
LABEL
DISKCOPY
DISKCOMP
```

3.12 Overview of Advanced Options

In this section we'll provide an overview of some of the programs MS-DOS provides for working with disks. Since these programs are complicated, we'll discuss them only briefly here. These programs are discussed in detail elsewhere in this book.

Optimizing data storage

If it ever seems like your hard drive is slowing down as time goes on, it probably is. Hard drives become slower as more data is placed on them. The more often data is deleted and new data files are created, the more apparent the problem will become. To understand this completely, you need to know a little about how MS-DOS stores data on a hard drive.

If the hard drive is empty, MS-DOS stores data contiguously. This means that MS-DOS writes data on a track of the hard drive until it is full, then starts storing data on the next track.

Since a hard drive usually has at least two disks with two read/write heads each for the top and the bottom, MS-DOS can write on four tracks before the read/write head must be moved. These tracks, which can be processed without moving the heads, are called "cylinders".

On a typical disk drive with 17 sectors per track you can fit 17 * 512 or 8,704 bytes on a track. So 34,816 bytes can be stored on the four tracks of a cylinder. Since the computer can read or write to a file with 34K without having to move the read/write heads, the process is very fast.

Also, it's ideal if files are distributed consecutively on the disk sectors. When this occurs, the heads don't have to be moved several times, which results in a pause while the heads "seek" a new position.

Files become fragmented over time

Files are constantly being deleted and saved on the hard drive. Even within the same file changes can be made to the text and saved. When a file is deleted, empty regions develop on the hard drive. Later these regions are used again to store data. If the newly saved files are bigger than the amount of free, contiguous space, the file is scattered over different places on the hard drive.

When the computer reads or writes to these files, the head must be moved to new tracks continuously, so that it can read or write other parts of the file. This causes performance to degrade considerably.

This process can be difficult if a hard drive is almost full. In this case there are only several small areas in which MS-DOS can distribute the files. For this reason you should never fill your hard drive to more than 90% of its capacity.

Consolidating files with DEFRAG

MS-DOS contains a special program that can organize the files on your hard drive optimally. This program, called DEFRAG, is a disk optimizer.

If you use DEFRAG to optimize a full 80 Meg hard drive, the program takes a long time to run. Although this process doesn't require any input from the user, the computer still cannot be used to perform other tasks, even if it's capable of multitasking.

Preparations and prerequisites for optimizing

You shouldn't optimize your hard drive until you've performed a complete backup. This is important because software or hardware errors or accidents during optimization may cause data loss.

Remember that the optimization process drastically changes the internal data storage structure of your hard drive. The internal directory structure is changed, the File Allocation Table is continually updated, and much of the data is read and rewritten to a different place on the disk. If this process is interrupted before the program is finished, the integrity of the data is lost. Because the optimization program is so complicated, other programs, Windows applications, or TSRs cannot run until it's finished.

Before using a disk optimizer, check the disk for errors and correct them if possible. You can do this with the CHKDSK command.

More details about using the DEFRAG command can be found in Section 14.5.

Increasing the hard drive capacity

MS-DOS also provides a program that can increase the capacity of your hard drive. This program, also called a disk-doubler, compresses data when it's stored and automatically decompresses it again when it's read.

Such programs are becoming more important as applications and the documents they process become larger. Today even a 100 Meg disk can quickly become full.

The MS-DOS compression program is called DoubleSpace. Its data compression technique lets you pack more data onto your hard drive, which increases its capacity.

You should familiarize yourself with this program before using it. For more information about this program, refer to Section 14.8.

Chapter

Order Through Directories

In this chapter we'll present a general overview of hard drives and diskettes.

Every hard drive or diskette has at least one directory, called the root directory. By convention, the root directory is identified by the backslash symbol (\). The directory currently in use is indicated, after the drive identifier and the backslash symbol.

The system prompt is displayed after you start your computer. In the following example, the current directory is in the root directory of Drive C:.

```
C:\>
```

If you insert a diskette in disk drive A: and change the current drive to drive A:, the system prompt displays:

```
A:\>
```

 A colon, backslash and the greater than symbol are displayed after the drive letter because MS-DOS presets this in the AUTOEXEC.BAT using the PROMPT PG statement during installation. This can be changed to suit your needs.

Why use directories?

Directories are mainly used when working with hard drives. If only the root directory exists, then MS-DOS always stores all files in the root directory. Since hard drives usually have a very high storage capacity, an unwieldy number of files might accumulate in the root directory. Obviously this makes it difficult to keep track of files.

What is more, you can only store a specific number of files on a hard drive or diskette before dividing it up into subdirectories. Once you reach this number, your PC will give you a memory error message, even though there could still be a lot of memory on the hard drive or diskette.

To avoid confusion in your root directory, MS-DOS lets you define and work with subdirectories, which help you better manage the files.

Directories can be compared to drawers in a desk. One drawer can be used to store personal letters and another could store business letters. The drawer containing the business letters could also be subdivided into a section containing letters concerning financial matters and a section containing letters regarding your legal matters.

Directories on diskettes, and especially on your hard drive, serve the same purpose as the drawers in a desk.

What are directories?

Directories are "logical", which means that they are manageable parts of a storage device. You can structure or organize a storage device by arranging or placing a collection of files in a named "drawer" or directory. The named "drawer" is similar to the label on an office file cabinet - it describes what is inside the drawer.

You will probably choose to store files that belong together in a particular directory on your hard drive. For example, you could put all of your personal letters in a directory called PERSONAL. By doing this, you can easily locate and backup files that belong together. Also, you might choose to place files that belong to a certain application program in one directory.

Since the application program will often require different files, placing all of the necessary files for a particular application program in one directory guarantees that the program will be able to easily find them. Often when you install these programs, you will be prompted to place the files belonging to the program in a particular directory. The installation program will automatically create this directory.

Another advantage of directories is that you can have files with the same name in different directories. This wouldn't be possible if you only worked with the root directory.

For example, you could have a directory containing tax information (TAXES90, TAXES91, etc.) with a file called MILEAGE in each directory. In the MILEAGE file you could keep track of your travel expenses for different years.

4.1   Overview

The following are some guidelines for working with directories.

Importance of directories

Today's PCs with hard drives are impossible to manage without directories. Directories create order, separate different data and programs and make it possible to quickly find and edit data.

Directory fundamentals

Directories, like files, have names but they usually don't have an extension. Each drive has a root directory, which can contain other directories and files. This forms a typical tree structure. The path specification describes the route to a specific directory, beginning at the root directory. From there, the path specification provides the name of the next subdirectory after a backslash (C:\TEXTS\LETTERS\1992).

In the current drive, there is also a current directory, in which MS-DOS searches for all data and programs. To use data and programs from other directories, you must use the complete path specification from the root directory.

Changing directories

In this chapter, we'll discuss working with directories using the options of the command area. A separate chapter covers working with directories using the MS-DOS Shell.

To change to a different directory, use CD (Change Directory). You can use the full path specification (CD C:\DOS) or just specify the directory to which you're changing (CD LETTERS for a directory called LETTERS in the current directory). Use CD.. to move up one directory in the tree structure. CD \ always takes you to the root directory.

Creating and deleting directories

To create a directory in the current directory, use MD (Make Directory). The directory name cannot already exist in the current directory (cannot be a filename either). Use RD (Remove Directory) to remove a directory that no longer contains any files or subdirectories. When creating or removing directories, you can work in any directory, as long as you use the complete path specification, starting from the root directory.

Renaming directories

To rename a directory, create the new directory first, then copy all the files from the old directory to the new directory. Next, delete all the files in the old directory. Once you've done this, you can remove the directory. It's easier to rename directories in the MS-DOS Shell, since you can simply give the directory a new name.

Search path for programs and files

Since MS-DOS automatically searches the current directory for commands and files, commands in other directories require the proper path specification. For example, to format a diskette from C:\DATA, you must enter C:\DOS\FORMAT A:. Instead of using such complicated specifications, you can also define one or more directories that MS-DOS automatically searches. Use PATH for commands and APPEND (with a few restrictions) for files. You should at least define the directory of MS-DOS commands with PATH C:\DOS. The OEM version of MS-DOS already contains this path specification; the update installation does not.

Displaying directories and their contents

Use DIR to display the contents of a directory. To include all subdirectories, add the /S switch to the command. Use TREE to display the directory structure on the screen.

Copying directories

Use COPY *.* to copy the contents of a directory. To include all subdirectories, use XCOPY *.* /S.

Directory as pseudo drive

Use SUBST to assign a drive letter to a subdirectory. This enables you to replace long path specifications with short drive letters.

4.2   MS-DOS and Subdirectories

As we previously mentioned, each hard drive or diskette has a root directory. This root directory is always the highest level directory on every hard drive or diskette.

You can organize the files or the drive by creating new subdirectories of the root. These subdirectories can, themselves, contain other subdirectories, and so on. Here's a directory listing for a drive that contains two subdirectories called DOS and APPS as well as individual files. Notice that the listing is for the root directory of the C: drive - indicated by C:\.

```
Volume in drive C is 386
Volume Serial Number is 163B-4567
Directory of C:\

DOS          <DIR>        10-12-90    1:18p
APPS         <DIR>        10-12-90    3:20p
AUTOEXEC BAT       294    02-03-91    8:36a
COMMAND  COM     47845    03-22-91    5:10a
CONFIG   SYS       122    02-15-91   11:41a
```

Directory structure

The above listing is an example of a directory structure of drive C:. At the top is the root directory. On the hard drive this directory contains only the most important system files, such as the AUTOEXEC.BAT, CONFIG.SYS and the COMMAND.COM command interpreter.

The example also shows two subdirectories: one containing the external DOS commands and programs of the operating system and another containing application programs. For example, this subdirectory might contain the database program dBASE IV and the word processing program Word.

Many users choose to store programs in a subdirectory separately from the data which they use. For example, this data might be stored in a subdirectory called C:\DATA\DB and C:\DATA\DOC.

  You can use the MS-DOS Shell or the TREE command to display the structure of your hard drive.

Directory names

When assigning names to directories, remember that the names can't be longer than eight characters. The characters used for filenames are also valid for directory names.

All alphanumeric characters can be used. The letters from A to Z, the numerals 0 to 9 as well as the following special characters can be used for directory names:

```
!        exclamation point
#        number sign
$        dollar sign
%        percent sign
(        open parenthesis
)        close parenthesis
&        and
-        minus
_        underline
```

When lowercase letters are entered, DOS automatically converts them to uppercase letters.

The following characters cannot be used in directory names:

```
+        plus
=        equal
:        colon
;        semicolon
.        period
,        comma
*        asterisk
<        less than
>        greater than
/        slash
\        backslash
```

Imbedded spaces cannot be used because a space is used to separate parameters which would confuse DOS.

 The period character isn't entirely prohibited because it is used to separate the name and its extension.

In addition to these individual characters, some groups of characters are prohibited because they have special names (device names). Among these are: CON, AUX, COM1, COM2, PRN, LPT1, LPT2, LPT3, NUL, which are all device names.

Although directory names can also have extensions (e.g., DOCUMENT.DOC), they are rarely used with directories. There are various reasons why you shouldn't use extensions with directories. For example:

- You should ensure that a directory with an extension doesn't contain a file with the same name as the directory. Since files usually have an extension, you can avoid this problem by not adding an extension to a directory name.

- When you change to a directory you must always specify the complete name. So it's a lot easier to do this if you use shorter names (without extensions).

The directory names "." and ".."

When viewing the contents of a subdirectory, you'll also see two entries, which appear before the other subdirectories, that contain one and two periods. In its internal management of directories, MS-DOS manages these two additional directory names with the following meanings:

.   The period always refers to the current directory in MS-DOS. This entry is needed for the internal management of the directories.

..   The two periods always refer to the directory immediately above the current directory. MS-DOS also uses this entry for internal management.

 Later you'll see that you can use CD .. to move to the next highest directory.

Using directory names

If you have a lot of nested directories on your hard drive or diskette, you must be able to refer to them easily.

In MS-DOS, the entire name of any directory is composed of the path specification to the directory and the actual directory name. The path specification includes the names of directories to the specified directory, starting with the root directory. Directories are separated by a backslash character (\); path specifications can contain up to 63 characters.

For example, if the PERSONAL directory is a subdirectory of the TEXTS directory, the path specification would look like the following:

```
\TEXTS\PERSONAL
```

The backslash, which represents the root directory, is first. It's followed by the names of the directories down to the last directory. Each directory name is separated by a backslash. These specifications always refer to the current storage device (diskette or hard drive).

To refer to a directory from a different storage device as the current directory, specify the drive letter at the beginning of the path specification. This type of path specification looks like the following:

```
A:\TEXTS\LETTERS
```

Since you always identify drives with a colon, remember to enter a colon after the drive letter.

    In the MS-DOS Shell the pathname of the current directory is always specified in the line directly above the drive line. If you ever need a path specification but don't remember what it looks like, you can display it in the MS-DOS Shell.

```
File Options View Tree Help  Menu bar

C:\DOS    ◄─────────────  Path specification

[A:]   [B:]   [C:]   [D:]   [E:]   Drive icons
```

The path specification in the MS-DOS Shell

The current directory

When MS-DOS works with directories, it manages a current directory for each drive. This is always the last directory you selected from the corresponding directory. As a rule, when you begin working at the computer, the current directory is the root directory.

The MS-DOS Shell works a little differently. You must always define the drive to which your specifications refer. MS-DOS doesn't manage a current directory for every drive. So, regardless of the drive, the current directory in the MS-DOS Shell is always the root directory.

When changing drives, the current directory in the command interpreter is always reset, unless you specify another directory.

If the C:\DOS directory is the current directory, you can switch to drive A:, by typing:

```
A: Enter
```

To return to drive C:, type:

```
C: Enter
```

This switches you back to the C:\DOS directory.

Unless you specify otherwise, MS-DOS commands always affect the files in the current directory. To use a command on any other directory, you must specify the entire name of the directory for the parameters in the command.

Use this kind of directory management carefully. Be especially careful when editing data on a different storage device than the current one or transferring data between different storage devices (copying). For example, to copy all of the files on the current directory of the hard drive to a diskette, use the following command:

```
COPY *.* A:
```

MS-DOS copies the files into the current directory of the diskette instead of to the root directory. To copy to the root directory, the line should appear as follows:

```
COPY *.* A:\
```

To display the current directory of a storage device, use the CD command and specify the drive, whose current directory you want to display, after the command. For example, to display the current directory of drive A:, type the following:

```
CD A:
```

How many directories are possible?

Even though all the other directories can have an almost unlimited number of entries, the root directory has a limited number of entries. The reason for this is that the root directory always begins at the same disk location and has a fixed length which limits the number of entries that may follow. Subdirectories, on the other hand, can have an almost unlimited length, similar to files.

The root directory allows only a specific number of entries. Files and directories are both considered entries. The highest number of valid entries depends on the type of storage device. The following table shows the maximum number of entries possible in the root directory of different storage devices:

Storage device	Maximum number of entries
180K diskette	63
360K diskette	111
720K diskette	111
1.44 Meg diskette	223
1.2 Meg diskette	223
Hard drive	511

4.3   Setting up a Directory

To create a new directory, use the MD (Make Directory) command. Type the name for the new directory after the command. Remember that directory names, similar to files, can only be eight characters long and that not all characters are allowed. Press [Enter] to confirm the name you've entered. To create a new directory, type the following:

```
MD directory_name
```

Creating a directory as a subdirectory in the current directory

To create a subdirectory, type the name of the new directory after MD. This new directory is always a subdirectory of the current directory. For example, if you're located in the C:\DOC directory and type the following command:

```
MD LETTERS
```

the LETTERS directory would be created as a subdirectory of the DOC directory. The pathname of the subdirectory is as follows:

```
C:\DOC\LETTERS
```

Creating a new subdirectory for any directory

To create a subdirectory for another directory besides the current one, simply specify the path of this directory to your new directory name. To create a subdirectory named PERSONAL for the DOC directory, from any directory, type the command line:

```
MD C:\DOC\PERSONAL
```

Remember that only one directory at a time can be created with a single command. If you wanted to create a sub-subdirectory for a subdirectory, the first subdirectory must already exist.

Suppose that you want to create a directory, named TEST1, that will be a subdirectory of the TEST directory. You would use the command:

```
MD C:\TEST\TEST1
```

This will only work if the TEST directory already exists. Again, you can only create one directory at a time with the MD command.

Directory names

MS-DOS manages directories similar to the way it manages files. So you cannot use a name for your subdirectory that has already been given to a file in the current directory. For example, you can't set up a subdirectory named PERSONAL in C:\DOC if this directory already contains a file named PERSONAL. However, you can avoid this problem by using extensions for files, and not for directories.

Also, remember which characters cannot be used in directory names.

Directories on diskettes

You can also set up directories on diskettes. However, it isn't as important to set up directories on diskettes as it is on hard drives because of the smaller number of possible files. To set up a directory on a diskette, either make the disk drive the current drive and create the directory with the following command:

```
MD directory_name
```

Or enter the command for creating a new directory directly from the current drive by adding the drive, where you want to create the directory, to the command:

```
MD A:\DOC
```

Automatic directories

Some programs automatically set up directories during installation. Usually when you install programs, you're prompted to enter the directory, in which you want to store the program files. If this directory doesn't exist on your storage device, the program automatically creates it during installation. Often programs also set up subdirectories for these directories. In these subdirectories, the installation programs place files that contain examples for the program or certain other necessary files. Some programs also set up directories for backup copies of files (e.g., Microsoft Works).

4.4 Choosing a Directory

When entering a command or working with a specific file, MS-DOS automatically looks for the command or file in the root directory if no other path is specified. If the command or file isn't in the current directory, MS-DOS displays the following error message:

```
Bad command or file name
```

In this case, make the directory containing the file the current directory. In the next few paragraphs we'll show you various ways to change directories.

Changing to any directory

To execute a command or find a file, make the directory, which contains the command or file, the current directory. Use the CD (Change Directory) command to do this. After the CD command, enter the name of the directory you want to make the current directory. The command line always has the following structure:

```
CD directory
```

To change to any subdirectory (i.e., to make it the current directory), you must always specify the entire path.

Changing to a lower directory

To change to a directory that is a subdirectory of the current directory, simply specify the name of the subdirectory after the CD command.

If you're currently in the DOC directory and want to change to the PERSONAL subdirectory, simply type:

```
CD PERSONAL
```

When used this way, the CD command always moves you to the directory (if it exists) one level lower than the current directory.

Changing to a higher directory

The entire directory name doesn't have to be specified in order to move to a directory one level higher than the current one. Since MS-DOS always marks the higher directory with "..", you can type:

```
CD ..
```

 Remember that the parameter ".." is a result of MS-DOS setting up two special directories in each subdirectory, "." and "..". The first one "." represents the current directory while the second one ".." represents the next highest directory. So ".." can be used to move one level higher in the directory structure. The root directory doesn't have this special ".." directory because it's already the highest directory.

Changing to the root directory

Since MS-DOS always assigns the name "\" to the root directory, you can select the root directory of the current drive by typing:

```
CD \
```

 MS-DOS marks a current directory for every existing drive. When you change to another drive, the last directory you selected automatically becomes the current one.

You can't specify the root directory of a storage device by only using the drive label. You must specify the root directory with the drive label and a backslash symbol (\).

Displaying the current directory

To display the name of the current directory, type CD without using any additional parameters.

You can also display the current directories of other drives by typing the drive letter after the CD command:

```
CD A:
```

This information is especially important when working with data from a storage device other than the current one. For example, the following command displays the contents of the current directory of the diskette in A:

```
DIR A:
```

However, this isn't necessarily the contents of the root directory of A:. To display the contents of the root directory, type:

```
DIR A:\
```

Displaying the directory with PROMPT

To always display the current drive and directory on the screen, change the system prompt with the PROMPT command. To do this, type the following command line:

```
PROMPT $P$G
```

 When you install MS-DOS 6.0, this system prompt is automatically set up and included in the AUTOEXEC.BAT file.

$P represents the "current directory of the current drive" and $G represents the "greater than symbol" (>). The screen displays the current directory with a greater than symbol as the system prompt.

Other options are also available for changing the display of the system prompt using PROMPT. See "The MS-DOS 6.0 Commands" chapter for the options of the PROMPT command.

 Make sure this command line is in your AUTOEXEC.BAT file so that you don't have to type the PROMPT command to change your system prompt each time you start your computer.

4.5   Search Paths for Commands and Files

When you type a command or batch file name at the system
prompt, MS-DOS searches for the command or batch file in the
current directory. If the command or batch file isn't in the current
directory, MS-DOS displays the error message:

```
Bad command or filename
```

You can, of course, precede the command or batch file name by a
path if you know where these files are located, and MS-DOS can
then execute them. But it becomes very tedious to have to type the
entire pathname or change to a specific directory in order to
execute a command. It would make life much easier if you were
able to use these commands and batch files from any directory.

The PATH command provides such a way. When you define a
search path with PATH, MS-DOS automatically searches the
directories listed in the search path for commands and batch files.

Search paths for programs

MS-DOS considers all files with the extensions COM, EXE or BAT
to be programs. The external MS-DOS commands are examples of
these program files.

To call these commands and other program files from any
directory, use the PATH command to define a search path.

   Frequently, the PATH command is inserted into the
AUTOEXEC.BAT file to define the search path. By doing
this, you won't have to re-enter the search path every
time you boot your computer.

Creating a search path

To put a directory in the search path, enter the directory name
after the PATH statement. It's important to enter the entire
pathname. Enter the drive identifier as well as the directory
name.

The command line for creating a search path looks like the
following:

```
PATH directory_name
```

Since the program files that are used most often are usually in different directories, you can include several directories in the search path. Each directory name is separated by a semicolon.

There are two different ways of defining the search path:

```
PATH directory1;directory2;directory3
```

or

```
PATH=directory1;directory2;directory3
```

To add a directory to an existing search path, you must specify all of the previously defined directory names, in addition to the new one. If you don't the previously defined paths will no longer be valid.

In the following example we'll define a search path that makes the MS-DOS commands, the program files of Word and dBASE IV available.

You'll be able to call MS-DOS commands from any directory and start the Word and dBASE IV programs from any directory. The command line for defining this search path looks like this:

```
PATH = C:\DOS;C:\WORD;C:\DBASE4
```

Displaying the search path

If you type PATH without any parameters, the screen displays the previously defined search path:

```
PATH
```

 Some applications use OVL files, which are overlay files. These are parts of a program that aren't kept in memory at the same time. For these applications, the PATH command will not correctly search for the OVL files.

If this happens, use APPEND to create a search path for the OVL files. Most programs automatically prevent this kind of problem.

Sequence of search

When you type a command at the system prompt, MS-DOS first searches for the command in the current directory. If you don't specify an extension, MS-DOS looks for files with the following extensions in this order: .COM, .EXE and .BAT.

If MS-DOS finds a COM file with the name you entered, it runs the program or command. Otherwise it searches for an EXE file and runs it if found. If it doesn't find one, it looks for a BAT file with the corresponding name, etc.

If there are two files in a directory with the same name, but with the extensions .COM and .BAT, MS-DOS will run the COM file.

 You can change the sequence of the search by entering the extension after the command. MS-DOS then looks for a command with the specified extension. To start a batch file named FORMAT.BAT in the directory of the MS-DOS commands instead of the MS-DOS FORMAT.COM command, specify the extension .BAT:

```
FORMAT.BAT
```

When MS-DOS searches beyond the current directory for files, it searches the directories in the sequence specified in the search path. This is why the MS-DOS directory is usually specified in the search path first. This enables you to find the MS-DOS commands quickly.

When program files with the same name are located in different directories, MS-DOS always finds the file in the directory that was first specified in the search path.

The diagram on the next page demonstrates what happens when a command is entered after a search path has been defined with PATH.

First, MS-DOS looks for a command or a program file in the current directory (in our example: C:\PROG\WORD, see diagram). The sequence COM, EXE and BAT is used for the search.

Next, MS-DOS searches in the first directory specified in the path definition (C:\DOS). Following this, other directories are searched in the sequence specified in the path.

The longer the path specification (i.e. the more directories that are specified in the search path), the longer it takes MS-DOS to search for the command you specify.

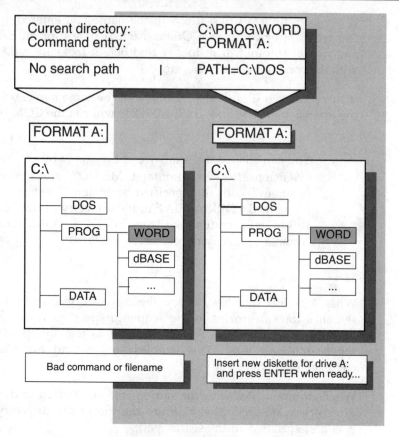

Meaning and function of PATH

Length of a search path

Defining a long search path will slow down MS-DOS. This happens because MS-DOS sequentially searches all of the directories in the search path in the specified sequence. So, it can take a while for MS-DOS to find the program you want, especially if it's in the last directory of the search path. If MS-DOS doesn't find the program, it displays the error message:

```
Bad command or file name
```

Which directories should be included in the search path?

As previously mentioned, you shouldn't include too many directories in the search path. In the next few sections we'll give you some hints on which directories to include in your search path and which ones to omit. We'll also discuss how you can start programs without including them in the search path.

It's not necessary to define a search path for directories with only one program file, such as directories with files for application programs. Usually it's better to create a batch file that calls the program.

For example, to start the Works program from any directory without specifying the C:\WORKS directory in the search path, use COPY CON, the EDITOR or a word processor to create the following batch file, named WORKS.BAT, in the DOS directory:

```
C:\WORKS\WORKS %1 %2 %3
```

 For more information about passing parameters, read the chapter on batch files.

If you create batch files this way but the programs aren't working properly, perhaps they shouldn't be included in the search path. Instead, try to solve this problem in a different way.

One option is to create another batch file that first changes the current directory to the directory containing the program files, and then calls the program.

For example, suppose that you want to be able to run the word processing program Word from any directory but don't want to include the Word directory in the search path. Create the following batch file in the DOS directory:

```
CD C:\WORD
WORD %1
```

You can also create a directory to store all of your batch files. This directory is then added to the search path ahead of the directory containing the MS-DOS commands. By doing this you can "replace" MS-DOS commands with batch commands using the same name. This lets you adapt MS-DOS commands to your own requirements.

For example, you could prevent MS-DOS from formatting your hard drive by creating a batch file, named FORMAT.BAT, that always calls FORMAT with the A: parameter. You must keep this file (FORMAT.BAT) in the BAT directory so that MS-DOS finds and runs it before it finds the FORMAT.COM program file in the DOS directory. Again, the BAT directory should be defined in the search path ahead of the MS-DOS commands directory.

Deleting search paths

To delete the defined search path, enter a semicolon after the MS-DOS PATH command:

```
PATH ;
```

   The space after the command is not absolutely necessary.

Remember that this command cancels the previously defined search path.

If you define a new search path that doesn't contain the directory of external (transient) MS-DOS commands, these commands will no longer be available for use. MS-DOS will display the error message:

```
Bad command or file name
```

Specify the complete path of MS-DOS commands or define a new search path that includes the directory of the commands.

Remember that every new definition of a search path cancels all previously defined search paths.

Search paths for files

Use the APPEND command to create, delete and display search paths for data files. This command applies only to files that aren't program files (files that don't have the extensions .COM, .EXE or .BAT).

You should only use APPEND when programs prompt you to do so. You may have trouble working with files found by APPEND. For example, instead of saving a file in the directory from which it was opened, APPEND saves it in the current directory. The old version of the file will still be in the original directory and the newer version will be in the current directory. Obviously this can lead to confusion and potential loss of data.

Creating a search path for data files

To define a directory as a search path for data files, specify it using the APPEND command. As with the PATH command, the drive can be specified as well as the entire directory name. There are two ways to define such a search path:

```
APPEND directory
```

or

```
APPEND=directory
```

To use APPEND to define a search path for several directories, specify the directory names separating each with a semicolon:

```
APPEND Directory1;Directory2;Directory3
```

or

```
APPEND=Directory1;Directory2;Directory3
```

The following is an example of a search path for two different text directories:

```
APPEND=C:\DOC\PERSONAL;C:\DOC\BUSINESS
```

Always define the complete search path when you use APPEND. Each time you call APPEND, the previous search paths are cancelled.

Deleting a search path

To delete a search path for data files type APPEND followed by a semicolon:

```
APPEND ;
```

☞ The space after the command is not absolutely necessary.

Displaying a search path

Typing APPEND without parameters displays the previously defined search path:

```
APPEND
```

Using APPEND for the first time

The first time you use the APPEND command, you can use the /E switch. This creates an environment variable name APPEND in which the appended search path is stored. Saving the appended search path in an environment variable has two advantages: you can extend the appended search path with a batch file and a program can easily determine the appended search path.

Search paths for both commands and data files

One form of the APPEND command can be used to define a search path for commands as well as data files. This form of the APPEND command is a substitute for the PATH command.

Defining a common search path for programs and data files

Use the APPEND command's /X:ON switch to define a search path for both commands and data files. For example, if your word processing program and the document files that you edit with the word processor are found in a directory named WP, use this command:

```
APPEND C:\WP /X:ON
```

Then, both the word processing program and the documents can be accessed from any directory.

To turn off the command search path, use the /X:OFF switch. When you turn off the command search, APPEND continues to use the search path for opening data files.

Finding files regardless of the path specification

Let's say that you are using an application to process a file named LETTER.TXT that you believe is in the C:\DOC directory. You might specify the filename preceded by the path: C:\DOC\LETTER.TXT. If you are mistaken and LETTER.TXT is in the DATA directory, not in the DOC directory, then your application will not find your file.

If you use the APPEND command with the /PATH:ON switch, MS-DOS will first look for the DOC directory for your file. If it isn't there it will look for the file in the appended search path. For example, if this command were used:

```
APPEND C:\DATA /PATH:ON
```

then the above application would be able to find the LETTER.DOC data file.

Use the /PATH:OFF switch to cancel this option.

4.6   Displaying and Printing the Directory

Use the DIR command to display the contents of directories. This will provide information about the directory.

Regardless of how DIR is started, the contents of the directory are always displayed. This directory has the following structure and provides the following information:

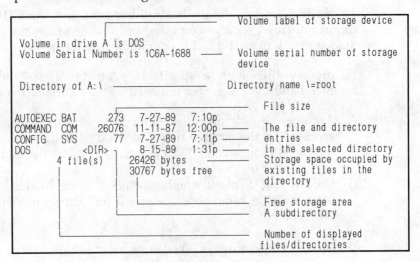

```
                                              Volume label of storage device
         ┌─────────────────────┐
  Volume in drive A is DOS
  Volume Serial Number is 1C6A-1688 ──────  Volume serial number of storage
                                              device

  Directory of A:\ ─────────────────────  Directory name \=root
                                     ┌────  File size
  AUTOEXEC BAT      273   7-27-89   7:10p
  COMMAND  COM    26076  11-11-87  12:00p ──────  The file and directory
  CONFIG   SYS       77   7-27-89   7:11p ──────  entries
  DOS          <DIR>      8-15-89   1:31p ──────  in the selected directory
          4 file(s)   26426 bytes ──────────  Storage space occupied by
                      30767 bytes free         existing files in the
                                                directory

                                              Free storage area
                                              A subdirectory

                                              Number of displayed
                                              files/directories
```

Directory contents

MS-DOS provides the following information about the storage device and the directory:

Volume label of storage device
  11 character volume label from FORMAT or LABEL.

Volume serial number of storage device
  8 digit hexadecimal number used by MS-DOS to determine when a diskette is changed.

Directory   Path specification of the displayed directory.

Entries   Filename, file size, creation date, creation time.

Number files
  Number of entries in this directory listing.

Storage space occupied by files
  The amount of storage space occupied by all files in this directory listing.

Unused storage area
> The amount of unused storage space remaining on the storage device.

Displaying files with certain archiving attributes

If a directory contains hidden or system files, they are not normally displayed in a directory listing.

To see if a storage device has hidden files, use the CHKDSK command. However, this command only provides the number of hidden files; it doesn't provide the number of system files.

To display files with a specific file attribute, use the DIR command and the /A: switch followed by the attribute character.

A   Archive flag displays whether or not a file has been archived. If the archive flag is deleted, the file is secure. If the file is changed, MS-DOS automatically sets the flag.

H   Hidden flag displays whether or not a file is hidden. While some MS-DOS commands work with and display hidden files, others do not.

D   Directory flag displays whether or not it is a directory.

R   Read-Only flag displays whether or not a file is write protected.

S   System flag displays whether or not a file is a system file. Some special programs treat system files differently (for example, the hard drive optimizer SD.EXE of Norton Utilities).

You can also precede the file attribute with a minus sign to display only the files that don't have the indicated attribute.

Example

To display all files that don't have the archive flag set, type:

```
DIR /A:-A
```

Use the following command line to display only system files in the root directory of the hard drive:

```
DIR C:\ /A:S
```

You can also display the various file attributes in the MS-DOS Shell. For more information on how to do this, refer to the chapter on the MS-DOS Shell.

Display order

DIR normally displays the files and directories in the order in which they were created. If you delete an entry in this directory, MS-DOS considers the space previously occupied by this entry available for a new entry. When a new entry is inserted into the directory, it uses the space occupied by the deleted file. Once MS-DOS has filled all of these "gaps", it places new entries at the end. As you can see, the entries are not very orderly.

Sorting the contents of a directory

Using the DIR command /O: switch, you can display the directory contents in one of several different orders. Here are the codes to use to reorder the directory listing:

C   Displays by compression ratio (smallest to largest).

D   Displays the files sorted according to date and time.

E   Displays the files sorted alphabetically according to file extension.

G   Displays the directories first, then the files.

N   Displays the files alphabetically sorted according to the filenames.

S   Displays the files sorted according to the size of the file.

_   To reverse the sorting sequence, precede the code with a minus sign.

Example

In your C:\DOC directory you're looking for the last text file that was created. However, you can't remember the filename. Use this command line:

```
DIR C:\DOC\*.DOC /O:D
```

You'll see a listing of all of the DOC files, sorted by date, with the last edited file listed last.

Displaying the contents of the current directory

Display the contents of the current directory by typing DIR. All of the information about the current directory will appear.

Displaying the contents of any directory

To display the contents of any directory, enter the name of the directory after the DIR command. If the directory is on a different storage device than the current one, specify the drive identifier (letter):

```
DIR Directory_name
```

Use the following command line to display the contents of the DOS directory from any directory on your hard drive:

```
DIR \DOS
```

Display the contents of the root directory of drive A: from any drive by typing:

```
DIR A:\
```

Contents of a subordinate directory

Display the contents of a directory that is one level lower than (directly subordinate to) the current directory by entering the name of this directory after DIR. You don't have to specify the entire pathname.

For example, to examine the contents of the PERSONAL directory, which is a subdirectory of DOC, type the following command line from the DOC directory:

```
DIR PERSONAL
```

Contents of the "." and ".." directories

Each subdirectory contains two additional directory entries named "." and "..", which MS-DOS requires for directory management. The "." represents the current directory and the ".." represents the next highest directory. Test this from within a subdirectory by typing both of the following command lines one after the other:

```
DIR .
DIR ..
```

The first command line displays the same information you would have seen if you had entered only DIR (the current directory). The second command line displays the contents of the next highest directory. Use exactly the same parameter to change to the next highest directory.

```
CD..
```

Displaying the directory contents one page at a time

When you use the DIR command and there are a lot of entries in a directory, the contents of the directory might scroll by faster than you can read them. This happens because there are more files than will fit on the screen at the same time. Only the last files in the directory will remain on the screen.

To prevent the screen from scrolling by, use the /P switch. MS-DOS then displays one screen page of the directory at a time and waits for a key press before displaying the next page. The command line is as follows:

```
DIR Directory /P
```

Displaying the contents in five columns

Occasionally you may want to display the entries of a directory on a single screen so that you can get a general overview of the contents. MS-DOS provides a way to do this.

Use DIR's /W switch. This lists the entries on the screen in five columns. To display the directory in columns, use the following command line:

```
DIR Directory /W
```

```
Volume in drive C is MS-DOS_6
Volume Serial Number is 1A61-5AC5
Directory of C:\DOS
[.]              [..]              DBLSPACE.BIN     FORMAT.COM       NLSFUNC.EXE
COUNTRY.SYS      KEYB.COM          KEYBOARD.SYS     ANSI.SYS         ATTRIB.EXE
CHKDSK.EXE       EDIT.COM          EXPAND.EXE       MORE.COM         MSD.EXE
QBASIC.EXE       RESTORE.EXE       SYS.COM          UNFORMAT.COM     NETWORKS.TXT
README.TXT       DEBUG.EXE         FDISK.EXE        DOSSHELL.VID     DOSSHELL.GRB
CHOICE.COM       DEFRAG.EXE        DEFRAG.HLP       DOSSWAP.EXE      EGA.CPI
EGA.SYS          HIMEM.SYS         MEM.EXE          XCOPY.EXE        DELTREE.EXE
MOVE.EXE         RAMDRIVE.SYS      SMARTDRV.EXE     DISPLAY.SYS      DOSHELP.HLP
DOSSHELL.COM     DOSSHELL.EXE      FASTHELP.EXE     EDIT.HLP         FASTOPEN.EXE
HELP.HLP         HELP.COM          MODE.COM         POWER.EXE        PRINT.EXE
QBASIC.HLP       SHARE.EXE         SETVER.EXE       APPEND.EXE       DELOLDOS.EXE
DISKCOMP.COM     DISKCOPY.COM      DRIVER.SYS       FC.EXE           FIND.EXE
GRAPHICS.COM     GRAPHICS.PRO      LABEL.EXE        SMARTMON.EXE     SMARTMON.HLP
SORT.EXE         LOADFIX.COM       MWBACKUP.EXE     MWBACKUP.HLP     REPLACE.EXE
SUBST.EXE        TREE.COM          DOSKEY.COM       MOUSE.COM        VFINTD.386
MWBACKF.DLL      MWBACKR.DLL       MSBACKUP.EXE     MSBACKUP.OVL     MSBACKFB.OVL
MSBACKFR.OVL     CHKSTATE.SYS      UNDELETE.EXE     MWUNDEL.EXE      MWUNDEL.HLP
MWGRAFIC.DLL     MSBACKUP.HLP      WNTOOLS.GRP      MSBACKDB.OVL     MSBACKDR.OVL
MSBCONFG.OVL     MSBCONFG.HLP      MEMMAKER.HLP     DBLSPACE.EXE     MEMMAKER.INF
INTERLNK.EXE     INTERSVR.EXE      MSCDEX.EXE       DBLSPACE.HLP     DBLSPACE.INF
DBLSPACE.SYS     DBLWIN.HLP        DOSSHELL.HLP     EMM386.EXE       MEMMAKER.EXE
SIZER.EXE        MONOUMB.386       MSTOOLS.DLL      MSAV.EXE         MSAV.HLP
MSAVHELP.OVL     MSAVIRUS.LST      VSAFE.COM        MWAVDOSL.DLL     MWAVDRVL.DLL
MWAVDLG.DLL      MWAVSCAN.DLL      MWAV.EXE         MWAVABSI.DLL     MWAV.HLP
MWAVSOS.DLL      MWAVMGR.DLL       MWAVTSR.EXE      COMMAND.COM      AUTOEXEC.UMB
CONFIG.UMB       MEMMAKER.STS      DOSSHELL.INI
     128 file(s)        5862982 bytes
                        2981888 bytes free
```

Contents of directory displayed in 5 columns by DIR/W

Contents of directory without additional information

To display only the names of your files and directories, use the /B switch. When this switch is used, no other information is displayed on the screen.

Selecting files with substitute characters

DIR is suitable for checking whether specific files are in specific directories or for searching for files whose name you've forgotten.

For example, suppose that you wrote a letter with a word processor but you can't remember the name you saved the letter under. All you can remember is that the filename starts with "B". You could find the file by displaying the directory in which you saved it, but it would take a lot of time because there are so many files to check. It would be a lot faster to display only the files that start with "B". In order to do this, MS-DOS provides the wildcard.

Wildcards are characters that can represent any character or character sequence within a filename.

MS-DOS provides two wildcards (placeholders) that can be used to select certain files:

*   Represents any remainder of a filename or extension.

?   Represents a single character in a filename or its extension.

Special features of wildcards

You can use wildcards for filenames and their extensions. MS-DOS manages both of these as independent regions.

If you use the asterisk as your wildcard, MS-DOS ignores all the characters entered after it. So you should use the asterisk only at the end of your search entry (filename or file extension).

For example, defining the following search entry isn't very useful:

```
DIR *WORK.TXT
```

MS-DOS responds to this command line by finding all files with the .TXT extension.

However, you can place the question mark anywhere in the filename or extension because it always represents only one character.

When you use the asterisk or the question mark at the end of the filename or extension, it can also represent a single character that is missing.

The following are a few examples of how you can utilize wildcards.

If you would like to display all files that start with the characters LETTER, use the following command line:

```
DIR LETTER*.*
```

The screen displays all files with the filename LETTER. In this case the wildcard can also represent a nonexistent character. This always occurs when you specify the wildcard as the last character in the filename or extension. So it doesn't matter if you use "*" or "?".

To display all files with the .BAT file extension that begin with the letter "B", use the command line:

```
DIR B*.BAT
```

You could use one of the two following command lines to display all of the files in the C:\BAT directory with either the .BAT or .BAK extension:

```
DIR C:\BAT\*.BA?
DIR C:\BAT\*.BA*
```

 The DIR command treats filenames and wildcards somewhat differently than the other MS-DOS commands. If the actual filename or extension isn't present, DIR automatically uses the asterisk "*". So DIR without any additional parameters is the same as DIR *.*.

If you want DIR to display only files without extensions, you must type the actual filename with a period at the end:

```
DIR name.
```

Since directory names usually don't have an extension, you can use this command line to display all of the subdirectories of the current or specified directories.

```
DIR *.
```

Displaying files in subdirectories

To display files in the subdirectories of the current directory, enter the /S switch after DIR.

Example

To display all of the text files within all subdirectories in the C:\DOC directory, use the following command line:

```
DIR C:\DOC\*.TXT /S
```

You can use this variation to search for a specific file anywhere on your hard drive. For example, if you want to know in which directory the file BOOK.DOC is located, type the following command from the root directory of the hard drive:

```
DIR BOOK.DOC /S
```

The screen will display all directories that contain this file.

Defining DIR default switches

You can specify switches for the DIR command to use by default if they aren't overridden. The DIRCMD environment variable is used to set these defaults. For example, if you always want to view the directory contents a page at a time type:

```
SET DIRCMD=/P
```

Now typing only DIR actually defaults to DIR /P since the DIRCMD environment variable contains the switches for the DIR command.

To display the directory sorted by date, set the DIRCMD environment variable by using the following command line:

```
SET DIRCMD=/O:D
```

Wildcards can also be used to determine which files to display. If you want the DIR command to display only text files with the .TXT extension, set the environment variable DIRCMD by using the following:

```
SET DIRCMD=*.TXT
```

 When setting this variable, remember that DIR will only display files specified by the switches. If the DIRCMD variable was set as described above and you display the contents of a directory with DIR before calling the DELETE command, not all of the files in the directory will be displayed. You may accidentally delete files.

To remove this definition of the DIR command, specify the DIRCMD variable without any definition, similar to the following:

```
SET DIRCMD=
```

 You can define this environment variable in the AUTOEXEC.BAT file. For example, you may want to display the directory page by page.

Printing a directory

Occasionally you might want a printout of a directory. This means that you must send the contents of the directory to an attached printer.

To print a directory, simply redirect the output of the DIR command to your printer. Use the following command line for LPT1 and substitute the appropriate parameter for your printer:

```
DIR >LPT1
```

4.7   Displaying and Printing all Directories

The TREE command displays a graphic overview of the directories on a storage device.

Displaying all of the directories of the current storage device

The TREE command can also be used to display all of the directories of the current storage device. Remember that this command only displays directories and their subdirectories, not the files contained within. Subdirectories are always indented so that you can distinguish them from higher level directories. To display the structure of the current storage device, type the following:

```
TREE \
```

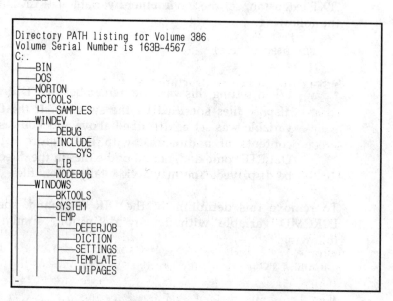

```
Directory PATH listing for Volume 386
Volume Serial Number is 163B-4567
C:.
├───BIN
├───DOS
├───NORTON
├───PCTOOLS
│   └───SAMPLES
├───WINDEV
│   ├───DEBUG
│   ├───INCLUDE
│   │   └───SYS
│   ├───LIB
│   └───NODEBUG
├───WINDOWS
│   ├───BKTOOLS
│   ├───SYSTEM
│   └───TEMP
│       ├───DEFERJOB
│       ├───DICTION
│       ├───SETTINGS
│       ├───TEMPLATE
│       └───UUIPAGES
─
```

An example listing of the TREE command

Displaying all of the directories of any storage device

To display the structure of a different drive than the current one, specify this after the command. The command line would look like this:

```
TREE drive
```

TREE then displays only the directories beneath the current directory of the specified drive. To display all directories, enter the backslash for the root directory, for example:

```
TREE C:\
```

The directory structure of any subdirectory

If you enter a directory after TREE, the structure of this directory will be displayed. You'll see an overview of the existing subdirectories.

If you have a subdirectory named DOC and want to display its structure, type the following command line:

```
TREE \DOC
```

Displaying directories and files

If you want to display the files of these directories, type the /F switch after TREE. For the DOC directory your entry would look as follows:

```
TREE \DOC /F
```

Display the directory structure faster

To speed up the TREE command, type the /A switch. Instead of the extended character set, ASCII characters will be used for the screen display. This simplifies the graphic display.

Displaying the directory structure page by page

If you call TREE for an extensive directory structure, the information will scroll past the screen so quickly that you'll only be able to look at the last page. To prevent this from happening, enter the MORE filter after the command. Separate this from the command by using a pipe symbol (|). This causes the screen to display its output page by page. Press a key to move to the next page. The command looks like the following:

```
TREE | MORE
```

 To create the pipe symbol (|) on international keyboards, press:

> Alt + 1 2 4

To display all of the directories and files of drive C: page by page, use the following command line:

```
TREE C:\ | MORE /F
```

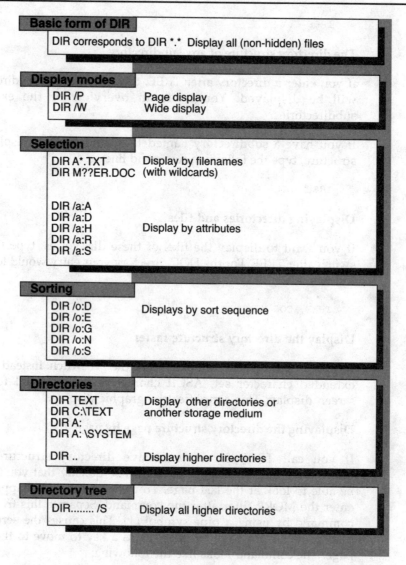

Basic form of DIR

DIR corresponds to DIR *.* Display all (non-hidden) files

Display modes

DIR /P   Page display
DIR /W   Wide display

Selection

DIR A*.TXT   Display by filenames
DIR M??ER.DOC   (with wildcards)

DIR /a:A
DIR /a:D
DIR /a:H   Display by attributes
DIR /a:R
DIR /a:S

Sorting

DIR /o:D
DIR /o:E
DIR /o:G   Displays by sort sequence
DIR /o:N
DIR /o:S

Directories

DIR TEXT   Display other directories or
DIR C:\TEXT   another storage medium
DIR A:
DIR A: \SYSTEM

DIR ..   Display higher directories

Directory tree

DIR........ /S   Display all higher directories

Different methods of displaying the directory

Redirecting output of the directory structure to a file

If you want to place comments next to the directory structure and then print, collect the displayed directories in a file and edit them with a word processing program. Use the following command line:

```
TREE Drive >Dir.txt
```

In our example, the information is redirected to the DIR.TXT file of the current directory.

 When you redirect the screen output to a file, don't use the MORE filter. You won't be able to see anything on the screen but you will still have to press (Enter) several times before the MS-DOS system prompt returns.

Printing all of the directories of a storage device

You can also print a directory structure by redirecting the screen output to the printer. All of the options mentioned for TREE can be used:

```
TREE >LPT1
```

For LPT1, enter the appropriate parameter for your printer.

4.8   Renaming Directories

You cannot simply use the RENAME command to rename directories because this command only applies to files. To rename a directory simply use the MOVE command (new in MS-DOS 6.0).

Renaming directories with the MS-DOS Shell

It's considerably easier to rename a directory with the MS-DOS Shell. Mark the directory you want to rename by placing the cursor on this directory and pressing (Enter).

Then press (Alt) to go to the menu and use the cursor keys and (Enter) to choose the **File** menu. Once there, choose the **Rename** command and press (Enter).

Enter your new name for the directory in the dialog box after "New Name" and confirm by pressing (Enter). It doesn't matter whether or not the directory has subdirectories.

4.9   Removing Directories

The easiest way to remove an unnecessary directory and all files and subdirectories is to use the DELTREE command (new in MS-DOS 6.0). Simply type:

```
DELTREE Directory
```

The system will ask you to confirm the deletion by pressing "y" or "n". By doing this, all files and subdirectories will be deleted.

Another method of removing a directory is to use the RD command. Enter the name of the directory to delete after the command and press Enter. The command line for deleting a directory must have the following structure:

```
RD Directory_name
```

Remember that you can only remove directories when they are empty (i.e., when they no longer contain any files or subdirectories). MS-DOS considers a directory to be empty when it only contains the entries "." and "..".

To remove a subdirectory of the current directory, specify the name of the subdirectory after the RD command. If you want to delete a directory from any other directory, specify the entire path of the directory to be removed, similar to setting up subdirectories. The command line should look as follows:

```
RD C:\DOC\BUSINESS
```

Use this line to remove the BUSINESS subdirectory from the DOC directory. Remember that the directory must be empty before you can delete it.

   You cannot remove a directory if it's the current directory or if you used SUBST to redirect a drive to this directory.

What do I do if the directory isn't empty?

If you try to remove a directory but an error message appears on the screen, the directory probably isn't empty. Display the contents of the directory with:

```
DIR Directory_name
```

If there are still files in the directory, make it the current directory and delete the existing files with the following command:

```
DEL *.*
```

If the directory you want to remove still has subdirectories, remove them with RD. After deleting the existing files and directories, use DIR to look at the contents of the directory. If you still see files displayed on the screen, these files are write protected.

Deleting write protected files

Write protected files have the Read-Only file attribute assigned to them. So DEL cannot be used to delete these files. In order to delete these files, remove the Read-Only file attribute with the ATTRIB command. Call the command, specify -R (for remove Read-Only file attribute) and then the name of the file. The command line should look as follows:

```
ATTRIB -R TEST.TXT
```

After removing the Read-Only file attribute, use DEL to delete the file.

The directory seems to be empty

When you use DIR to display the directory, it no longer shows any files in the directory. If you still can't delete it, then it only seems to be empty. There are probably still some hidden files or files with the system file attribute.

To test this, use DIR to display all hidden and system files. Type:

```
DIR *.* /A:H
DIR *.* /A:S
```

If the screen displays files, change their file attributes. Use the ATTRIB command to do this. The command lines for removing the file attributes look like the following:

For hidden files:

```
ATTRIB -H filename
```

For system files:

```
ATTRIB -S filename
```

You can also use the MS-DOS Shell to check for hidden or system files. The MS-DOS Shell lists hidden and system files when it displays the contents of a directory. Look at the file attributes by calling the **File Display Options** command, and activating the **Display hidden/system files** command in the **Options** menu. Use the **Show Information** command from the **Options** menu to display the attributes of every marked file.

Hidden files have the file attribute "H" and system files have "S". To remove these file attributes, use the **Change Attributes** command from the **File** menu.

After removing the file attributes, use DEL to delete the files. The directory must be empty. Make the next highest directory the current one and delete the subordinate directory with the following command:

```
RD Directory name
```

4.10 Turning a Directory into a Pseudo Drive

The SUBST command is used to substitute a drive identifier for a directory. Rather than referencing to a directory, you can use the drive letter to refer to the contents of the directory.

This method will allow you to use programs that are set up for a system with two disk drives and adapt them to a hard drive system with only one disk drive. The second drive (which really doesn't exist) is created by turning a directory into a pseudo drive.

Defining the assignment

Use the command:

```
SUBST drive directory
```

to redirect each access from the drive to the specified directory.

To use this command, MS-DOS must recognize the drive identifier as a valid one. If necessary, use the LASTDRIVE command to increase the number of drives possible in the CONFIG.SYS file.

Here's an example:

```
SUBST B: C:\EXCEL\XLS
```

In this example, drive identifier B: is defined as an alternative way of referencing the contents of the directory C:\EXCEL\XLS. Now the following two commands produce the same results:

```
DIR C:\EXCEL\XLS
```

and

```
DIR B:
```

In other words, all references to B: are actually redirected to C:\EXCEL\XLS.

By defining directories as pseudo drives, you can avoid entering awkward path specifications. For example, if you don't have a drive D: and you often work with the C:\DATA\DOC\PERSONAL directory, then you can make this directory into a pseudo drive:

```
SUBST D: C:\DATA\DOC\PERSONAL
```

To copy a file named LETTER1.TXT from drive A: to the PERSONAL directory, simply type this short command line:

```
COPY A:\LETTER1.TXT D:
```

Removing the assignment

To remove an assignment, specify the redirected drive with the /D switch:

```
SUBST Drive /D
```

You won't be able to do this if the redirected drive is the current drive in MS-DOS. You also shouldn't cancel the assignment as long as application programs are working with this drive.

Example

For our pseudo drive D:, the following command line is used to cancel the assignment:

```
SUBST D: /D
```

Displaying the assignment

Entering SUBST without any parameters displays all redirected drives with their directories:

```
SUBST
```

Displaying the actual name of the drive

You can use the TRUENAME command to display the real name (the original directory name) of the pseudo drive.

To do this, simply type the command along with the drive whose true name you want to display:

```
TRUENAME drive
```

The screen then displays the correct name of the directory.

If you redirected the C:\TEMP directory to D:, type the following:

```
TRUENAME D:
```

The screen then displays the original name of the pseudo drive:

```
C:\TEMP
```

 You can always use the TRUENAME command to check whether or not drives are redirected. This command always displays the original name.

C h a p t e r

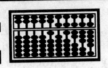

Handling Files

Files are groups of data that belong together. A file may be a program file, a group of commands, a text document, graphical or numerical data. A filename is used to identify the data.

Certain commands are no longer included with DOS 6.0. However, the MS-DOS upgrade program will not remove these commands during installation. If any of these commands are needed, you can order a Supplemental Disk from Microsoft that contains these commands. The following commands mentioned in this chapter are:

- COMP
- EDLIN

5.1   Overview

The following are some guidelines for working with files.

What are files?

Files are groups of data that belong together. A file may be a program file, a group of commands, a text document, graphical or numerical data. A filename is used to identify the data.

Structure of filenames

Filenames consist of letters and numerals. A filename has an eight character name and a three character extension, which indicates the contents of the file. The name and the extension are separated by a period (e.g., LETTER15.DOC). The same filename cannot be used twice in a directory.

Using wildcards to specify more than one file

By using wildcards, you can address several files simultaneously with an MS-DOS command. A question mark "?" represents any character and an asterisk "*" represents the rest of the name or extension. For example, COPY M??ER.DOC copies the documents MOYER.DOC, MEYER.DOC and MAYER.DOC, while COPY LETTER*.* copies LETTER15.DOC, LETTER1.DOC and LETTER44.BAK. However, with many application programs, you can edit only single files. So you cannot use wildcards in these instances.

Creating files

Actually, MS-DOS was intended to be an operating system for managing data, instead of for creating data. Usually, application programs create files. For example, a word processor creates letters and a draw program creates image files. However, in MS-DOS you can also create and make changes to simple text documents with EDLIN (on Supplemental Disk from Microsoft) or EDIT. You can also redirect screen output of commands to a file by specifying the redirect character ">" and then the filename. Then you could use an editor, such as EDIT, to edit the data.

You can change the name of a file at any time with REN.

Copying files

The COPY command copies files. To include copies in subdirectories, use XCOPY /S.

 COPY and XCOPY overwrite files in the target directory when their filenames are identical to the file that's being copied.

Comparing files

Use COMP (on Supplemental Disk from Microsoft) to compare files character by character. For text files, use FC to compare the files line by line.

Displaying file contents

TYPE displays the contents of a file on the screen. However, you shouldn't use this command with certain files, such as program files. In such cases, it's better to use the MS-DOS Shell because the Shell automatically switches to "Hex mode", which displays the file contents as characters and ASCII values.

Printing files

To print a file, use COPY File LPT1 to "copy" the file to the printer. However, the computer cannot be used until the entire file is sent to the printer. So, instead of using this method, set up a waiting queue with PRINT /D:LPT1 and use PRINT File to print one or more files "in the background". PRINT supervises the print job. You can use the computer for other tasks while PRINT is printing.

Deleting files

Use DEL to delete files. The command DEL *.* deletes all the files in a directory after a security prompt. Instead of immediately deleting the files, MS-DOS simply frees the space used for the file. Usually you can recover deleted files with the UNDELETE command.

File attributes

Along with their filename and contents, files also have special attributes for management purposes. You can display these attributes and make changes to them with the ATTRIB command. For example, after each change to a file, MS-DOS sets the archive flag, indicating that the current version of the file hasn't been saved yet. Use the write protect flag to protect a file from being deleted or overwritten. Files with a set hidden flag are no longer included in the directory display. The system flag prevents a file from being moved to a different location on the hard drive or diskette.

Checking files

To check a file for readability, copy it to the NUL dummy device. Use CHKDSK to determine whether a file is saved contiguously on the hard drive/diskette.

Searching for files and file contents

Add the /S switch to DIR to search the entire hard drive or diskette for a file. For example, to search the entire hard drive for a file called ACCT.DOC, use DIR C:\ACCT.DOC /S. You can also search for file contents with FIND. By using wildcards and /S, you can have FIND search several files and subdirectories. If FIND should disregard case (upper or lowercase), specify /U. To search all files on the hard drive for "Meyer", use FIND /S "Meyer" C:*.*.

5.2   Naming Files

Every file must have a name. In this section we'll present some guidelines for assigning filenames.

Possible filenames

A filename consists of a name, which can contain up to eight characters, and an extension. The filename extension can contain up to three characters.

All alphanumeric characters (letters from A to Z, the numbers from 0 to 9 as well as some special characters) can be used in filenames.

```
!   HELLO!.TXT
#   TEXT#.TXT
$   SALARY$.DBF
%   TAXES%.DBF
(   (TEST.TXT
)   (TEST).WKS
&   90&91.DBF
-   LETTER-1.TXT
_   MEYER_90.TXT
```

Lowercase letters are automatically converted to uppercase letters.

The following characters cannot be used in filenames:

+	plus
=	equal
:	colon
;	semicolon
.	period
,	comma
*	asterisk
<	less than
>	greater than
/	slash
\	backslash

The space character also cannot be used because it is used as a separator between elements of commands (parameters). For example, FORMAT A: /4.

☞   The period separates the filename from its extension.

Along with these single characters, there are also groups of characters which cannot be used for filenames. Among these are:

CON, AUX, COM1, COM2, PRN, LPT1, LPT2, LPT3, NUL. All of these names are significant to DOS because they are names of devices.

The file extension

Certain file extensions have a fixed meaning in MS-DOS. The most important extensions are:

.SYS   Used for system files.

.COM   Used for MS-DOS command files. COM files are linked to a specific starting address and are generally smaller than comparable EXE files.

.EXE   Used for MS-DOS executable files or application programs.

.BAT   Used for batch files.

.BAK   Used for backup copies that are automatically created by some text editors and word processors.

Other extensions are commonly used as a result of being assigned by significant user programs, such as Word, WordPerfect and WinWord. For example:

.TXT   For text files (in EDIT).

.DOC   For document files (Word, WordPerfect or WinWord).

.DBF   dBASE database files.

.BAS   For BASIC programs.

.PAS   Turbo Pascal files.

.TMP   Used for temporary files, which are used by application programs to store data briefly. Usually, temporary files are automatically deleted. However, if a program isn't ended properly (e.g., you switch off the computer while you're still working with a program), these temporary files aren't deleted and occupy disk space.

.WKS   Lotus 1-2-3 file spreadsheet files.

.WK1   Lotus 1-2-3 file spreadsheet files.

.XLS   Excel spreadsheet files.

Specifying more than one file using wildcards

To address more than one file with an MS-DOS command, wildcards can be used. Use wildcards to specify one or more characters:

*   Replaces all characters following the asterisk in filenames or extensions.

?   Replaces any single character in a filename or its extension. If the question mark is placed at the end of a filename, it can represent any character or no character.

The "*" character in filenames or extensions determines that the rest of the characters in the filename or extension can be any character. So if you enter another character after "*", it will be ignored.

Examples

    A*.EXE

The example above specifies all files whose names start with A and have the .EXE extension (APPEND.EXE, ATTRIB.EXE).

    M??ER.TXT

This example applies to all files beginning with M and ending with ER that have 5 letters in the filename and the .TXT extension (MEIER.TXT MAYER.TXT, MEYER.TXT).

    .

The above example specifies all files.

    F*T.COM

The previous example refers to all files beginning with F that have the .COM extension. The character T is ignored because it follows the "*" wildcard. This example could be used to address FORMAT.COM, FDISK.COM.

    S???.*

This example specifies all files with names that begin with S and have no more than four characters. The extension could be anything (SORT.EXE or SYS.COM).

Wildcards can only be used with existing files. If you're creating a new file, you won't be able to use "*" or "?".

5.3 Creating Files

Files are either automatically created by programs or they're created by users. In this section we'll present the MS-DOS commands that are used to create files.

Files automatically created by MS-DOS

Application programs usually store data in files. Some MS-DOS commands also create files. The following are some of the commands that create files:

SETUP   Installs MS-DOS and automatically creates the AUTOEXEC.BAT and CONFIG.SYS files.

MSBACKUP
     Creates data and control files on backup diskettes. An optional parameter can be used to create a log file.

CHKDSK   Finds areas on a storage medium that aren't linked with files or are designated as unused, and converts these areas to files.

EDLIN   Makes backup copies of edited text files.

MSAV   Microsoft 's Anti-Virus program can create a report (RPT) file that lists all of the files checked for viruses.

Creating text files with MS-DOS

Text files may be created in MS-DOS with COPY CON, the optional EDLIN program or the MS-DOS Editor program.

Use COPY CON to create text files

The COPY CON command copies keyboard entries to a file. To create a file, type the following command line:

```
COPY CON Filename
```

Then enter lines of text using the keyboard. End each line by pressing (Enter). A line can contain up to 127 characters. To end the process and save the file, press either (Ctrl) + (Z) or (F6) and (Enter).

If you enter a name that already exists, the new file overwrites the older file and the contents of the old file are lost.

Text files with EDLIN

 Remember, you can purchase a Supplemental Disk from Microsoft to get the EDLIN command, if needed.

Start EDLIN by entering the command and the name of the file to be created. An asterisk appears on the screen indicating that you're in the command mode of EDLIN. Enter Ⓘ to move to input mode.

Now enter any text. Each line may contain up to 253 characters. Press Enter to move to the next line. To exit insert mode, press Ctrl + Ⓩ when the cursor is in an empty line. This will return you to the command mode. To save the file press Ⓔ and Enter.

Creating files with EDIT

Enter EDIT to start the MS-DOS Editor. The MS-DOS Editor will load. After pressing Esc to clear the welcome dialog box, you can create and edit text files.

Enter your text and press Enter to move to the next line.

To save the file, press Alt + Ⓕ to choose the **File** menu. Move the cursor to the **Save as** command and press Enter. Enter your filename in the area that appears. Press Enter again to save the file.

To exit the editor, press Alt + Ⓕ and then move the cursor to the **Exit** command.

 For more information about working with the MS-DOS Editor, refer to Chapter 8.

Creating files by redirecting a command

There is another way to create files in MS-DOS. Ordinarily MS-DOS commands display information on the screen. However, the output of an MS-DOS command can be redirected to a file. You can use ">" to create a file for the output of a command.

Use the following command line to write all of the output of a command to a file instead of the screen:

```
Command >File
```

You can use any required parameters after the command. MS-DOS creates a file and redirects all screen output of the command to this file. Any existing file with the same name will be overwritten.

Certain commands cannot be redirected. Instead of displaying information to the standard output device (usually the screen), these commands use a special error output device.

Some programs write information directly to the video (screen) memory. The output from these programs also cannot be redirected to a file.

 If you're developing programs with Turbo Pascal and want to arrange the screen output in such a way that it can be redirected to a file, you cannot use the CRT unit. Without this unit the screen display of the program uses the standard output device and can be redirected.

Example

Suppose that you want to print the contents of a directory and you also want to include some explanatory notes about the individual files. You could use the word processor EDIT or EDLIN to create a file containing a list of all the files in the directory.

However, it's much easier to create the file by redirecting the DIR command to a file and then editing the file.

To create this file, change to the desired directory (CD) and type the following command line:

```
DIR > CONTENTS.TXT
```

You can edit the file with either the MS-DOS Editor or EDLIN and then print it.

 Be careful when redirecting commands to a file from a batch file. You can redirect direct commands, DIR > NUL. But you cannot redirect a batch file that handles certain commands. For example, you can't use DIRS.BAT > NUL to redirect a batch file named DIRS.BAT.

5.4   Copying Files

Copying files is important when working with your computer. When you copy files, the source files are preserved in their original location. For example, you could copy files from a hard drive onto a diskette, either for a backup or to copy the data onto another computer.

You can also copy files that only need to be changed slightly. If you only need to make a few changes to a document, it's easier to copy a file and edit it than to create a new file. This can be done with text files. For example, you can do this when you need to send the same letter to several people.

Various MS-DOS commands can be used to copy files. This chapter explains these options.

Copying files from a directory - COPY

The COPY command can be used to copy one or more files from a directory.

Copying files

To copy a file from the current directory to another directory, both the source file and the target directory must be specified.

```
COPY File1 Directory
```

This method of copying produces a copy of the source file in the specified directory. The copy has the same name as the original. After the computer is finished copying the file, MS-DOS indicates how many files were copied and the ready prompt reappears on the screen.

To copy a file from a directory other than the current directory, the entire path and the filename must be specified.

If a target directory isn't specified, MS-DOS uses the current directory as its target. If the file to be copied is also in the current directory and a new name for the new file hasn't been specified, MS-DOS reports an error because a file cannot be copied onto itself. In place of a target directory, specify a new filename.

Examples

If you want to copy the file INVOICE.TXT from the current directory onto a diskette in drive A:, type the following:

```
COPY INVOICE.TXT A:
```

Suppose that you want to copy the MS-DOS FORMAT command from the C:\DOS directory into the current directory. (The DOS directory cannot be the current directory; otherwise you'll receive an error message, since you would try to copy the file onto itself.) Since you want to copy to the current directory, you don't have to specify the name of the target directory:

```
COPY C:\DOS\FORMAT.COM
```

Use the following command to copy all MS-DOS commands, with the COM extension, from the DOS directory to the directory C:\PROGRAMS:

```
COPY C:\DOS\*.COM C:\PROGRAMS
```

 If the target directory doesn't exist, MS-DOS will display a corresponding error message.

Example

Suppose that you want to copy the file LETTER1.TXT from the current directory to the directory A:\DATA. However, the directory DATA doesn't exist. MS-DOS copies the file LETTER1.TXT to the main directory of drive A: under the filename DATA.

```
COPY LETTER1.TXT A:\DATA
```

Copying more than one file

Wildcards can be used to specify the filename for the source. MS-DOS will copy all files with matching filenames.

For example, copy all text files from the current directory onto a diskette in drive A: to provide a backup of your files. Do this by typing the following command:

```
COPY *.TXT A:
```

You might run into a problem if you wanted to create backups of files in the current directory and keep them in the current directory. Suppose that you have the following files in the current directory:

```
COMP01.TXT
COMP01.BAK
COMP02.TXT
```

You don't remember which files were located in the directory and now you want to back up all the files beginning with the letters COMP, use the following command:

```
COPY COMP*.* COMP*.BAK
```

The following message appears on the screen:

```
COMP01.TXT
COMP01.BAK
File cannot be copied onto itself
     1 File(s) copied
```

MS-DOS copied COMP01.TXT correctly, then tried to copy COMP01.BAK to COMP01.BAK. Since this is impossible, MS-DOS aborts the process with an error message and indicates that it could copy only one file (COMP01.TXT). To avoid this mistake, use the following (correct) command line:

```
COPY COMP*.TXT COMP*.BAK
```

 Using the COPY command can be dangerous because it overwrites an existing file in the target without asking you to confirm it. So use DIR to check whether there are any existing files in the target. This problem can be avoided by using the XCOPY command with the /P switch. You can also prevent files from being overwritten by copying files in the MS-DOS Shell.

Copying and checking files

The /V switch causes MS-DOS to verify the copies, which means that it tests whether the original file is identical to the copied file. Verifying files helps you determine whether any errors occurred during the copying process. The command line for verifying the copy operation looks similar to the following:

```
COPY File1 Directory /V
```

Using the verify option will ensure that the original file and the copied file are identical and will protect against any errors during a copy operation.

Copying files and changing filenames

By specifying a filename as the target, you can give files new names when they're copied. This is also the only sensible way to copy files within a directory:

```
COPY File1 File2
```

Wildcards can be used for both the source and the target. MS-DOS copies all files with the appropriate filename and changes the filename according to the default in File2. Here are a few examples:

Make a copy of all files with names beginning with the letter A, but change the first letter (A) of the filename to the letter B in the copy. Use the following command line:

```
COPY A*.* B*.*
```

Copy all files with the .TXT extension from the current directory to the main directory of drive A: and change the filename extension to .BAK by using the following command line:

```
COPY *.TXT A:\*.BAK
```

Select only those files you want to copy

When using wildcards, unwanted files might be copied accidentally. This problem can be solved by doing the following:

• Before copying, use the DIR command with exactly the same filenames as the ones to be copied. This ensures that you know which files will be affected by the copying process.

ASCII and binary file options

Use the /B and /A switches to make changes on files while copying them. The switches remain valid until another switch cancels them:

These two switches determine how end of file marks (Ctrl + Z = ASCII 26) are treated during the copy process. The end of file marks (EOF (End of File)) are used to determine when the end of a file has been reached by commands for pure text files (ASCII files). For programs or specially structured files from application programs, MS-DOS doesn't determine the end of the file by the end of file character, but determines the file size from the directory.

/A After the source file: file up to end of file mark (Ctrl + Z = ASCII 26) is copied; data following the end of file mark is ignored.

/A After the target file: adds an end of file mark to the end of the target file.

/B After the source file: end of file mark is ignored; command copies file including all end of file marks.

/B After the target file: no end of file mark at the end of the file.

The abbreviation /A represents ASCII and /B represents binary. When you use /A, MS-DOS treats the files like ASCII files that always end with Ctrl + Z. Since binary files can contain any characters, the character with the ASCII code 26 cannot signal the end of file.

Appending files

Another option when copying files is to combine several files into one file. This can be accomplished by specifying several files instead of a single source file. Separate the filenames with an addition symbol (+).

```
COPY File1+File2+File3 Total_file
```

Several files can also be combined into one file by using wildcards for the source and specifying a single filename as the target file. MS-DOS copies all files with the appropriate filenames to the new file.

If a name for the target file isn't specified, MS-DOS uses the name of the first source file. The original contents of this file are lost. MS-DOS displays a message on the screen informing you of this.

The /A and /B switches can be used when copying several files into one file. These switches produce the effects previously described.

Copying files from more than one directory - XCOPY

The XCOPY command is used to copy files from a directory and its subdirectories.

This command is ideal for backing up a directory and its subdirectories onto a diskette. The advantage, compared to MSBACKUP, is that the files on the copied diskette are directly addressable from DOS.

The disadvantage of using XCOPY is that the number of files you can copy depends on the available space on the target storage medium.

Copying files

To copy the files of a directory with all of its subdirectories, use the following command:

```
XCOPY Source Target /S
```

The /S switch ensures that the files of the subdirectories are also copied. The structure of the directory is preserved when this method of copying is used. Files from subdirectories are copied into the correct subdirectory. If necessary, the directories are automatically created. When this method of copying is used, only the subdirectories that contain files are copied.

If the /S switch isn't specified, the command only affects files from the current directory.

The following paragraphs provide a more thorough explanation of the terms source and target when the /S switch is specified:

Source If a filename is specified as the source, XCOPY copies this file from the current directory as well as any files with this name from the existing subdirectories. Wildcards can be used. If this option of XCOPY isn't wanted, specify the file by using the exact pathname.

If a disk drive or a directory is specified as the source, XCOPY copies all files as well as the subdirectories and their contents.

Target If a disk drive or a directory is specified as the target, the files are copied to that directory. If the source contains files in subdirectories, the subdirectories are also used in the target and, if necessary, MS-DOS creates them. If a target isn't specified, XCOPY uses the current directory.

If a filename is used for the target, MS-DOS renames the files as it copies. Wildcards can be used.

If wildcards are used to select more than one file as the source, only one name is specified as the target. If there aren't any subdirectories with this name, you will be prompted to make the target unit either a directory or a file. If you specify the target unit as a directory, it will be created as a subdirectory of the current directory. If you specify the target unit as a file, only the last of the source files will be copied to the new file.

The following are a few more examples of working with XCOPY.

The following command line copies all files with the .TXT extension from the hard drive to a target diskette in drive A:. The command also sets up all of the necessary subdirectories on the target diskette.

```
XCOPY C:\*.TXT A:\ /S
```

The next command line copies the entire contents of the diskette in drive A: including any subdirectories to the DISKETTE directory of the hard drive:

```
XCOPY A:\ C:\DISKETTE /S
```

XCOPY Switches

Different switches can be specified to control the way XCOPY works. For example, switches can be set to select only certain files to be copied or even to control the copying process itself.

/A   Copies only files that have been created or changed since the last copying process (archive flag is set). The archive flag doesn't change.

/D:MM-DD-YY
            Copies only files that have been changed since the specified date.

/E   Creates subdirectories in the target even though they might be empty.

/M   Copies only files that have changed or have been created since the last copying process (archive flag is set). The archive flag is reset.

/P   Gives a prompt for each file to be copied. Enter Ⓨ to copy.

/S   This switch must be set to copy subdirectories.

/V   Verifies the files in the target after the copying process.

/W   Requires a key press before the copy process will begin. This allows you to start XCOPY from the MS-DOS diskette and insert another diskette as your source.

Example

To copy all of the files and subdirectories, from the DATA directory, that have been created or changed since the last backup, to a diskette and designate them as saved by clearing the archive bit, use the following command line:

```
XCOPY C:\DATA\*.* A: /S /M
```

5.5   Comparing Files

MS-DOS provides two commands for comparing files: COMP (on the Supplemental Disk from Microsoft) and FC. The COMP command only compares files of the same length while the FC command compares files of any length. The number of lines, in the files to compare, can be specified with COMP by setting the /N switch. It may then be used to compare files of different length.

   Remember, you can purchase a Supplemental Disk from Microsoft to get the COMP command, if needed.

The results of the comparison operation may be displayed in hexadecimal format or as characters by setting the /D (display in hexadecimal format) or /A (display as ASCII characters) switches.

In either case, information about any existing differences will be provided. The default setting (no parameter set) displays the differences as hexadecimal.

Comparing files of the same size

Use COMP (on the Supplemental Disk from Microsoft) to compare two files of equal length. The following is the command line for this comparison:

```
COMP File1 File2
```

Path specifications and wildcards can be used for the names of File1 and File2. If only a path specification is entered for File2, MS-DOS will search this directory for a file with the same name as File1.

If File1 and/or File2 aren't specified (simply enter COMP), the command will ask for the required information with a series of prompts.

If COMP finds any differences, they are displayed in bytes. A message, similar to the following, appears:

```
Compare error at OFFSET 0
file1 = 48
file2 = 68
```

OFFSET displays the offset to the mismatched bytes. Next, the differing bytes in File1 and File2 are displayed as hexadecimal values.

In the previous example, the first mismatch was found at the first character in the file (OFFSET=0); File1 has a hexadecimal value of 48 and File2 has a hexadecimal value of 68 at this location.

The /L switch is used to display the line number of the different file instead of the offset to the mismatched file.

When comparing with COMP, there is usually a difference between upper and lowercase letters. When the /C switch is specified, the differences between upper and lowercase letters are ignored.

After ten mismatches, COMP stops the comparison for the selected files and displays the following message:

```
10 Mismatches - ending compare
```

After all of the specified files have been compared, answer the prompt by pressing Y to select more files for comparison.

If differences between the files aren't found, the command displays the following message:

```
Files compare OK

Compare more files (Y/N)?
```

When earlier versions of COMP were used to compare programs (binary files) instead of text files, the following message was displayed:

```
EOF Mark not found
```

EOF is an abbreviation for End Of File. MS-DOS uses the character with ASCII code 26 (Ctrl + Z) as an end of file mark for text files. Unlike text files, the size of binary files must be obtained from the directory.

After completing a comparison, the following prompt appears on the screen:

```
Compare more files (Y/N)?
```

Answer Y; you're prompted to enter the names of additional files to compare.

Comparing files of different sizes

Use the FC command to compare files that are different sizes. Set the /B switch so that a binary comparison is performed. FC compares the files byte by byte. The command line is as follows:

```
FC File1 File2 /B
```

FC then displays the differences in hexadecimal notation:

```
Address Value1 Value2
```

It's best to compare only files whose contents are almost identical. As soon as a different character is found in a pair of files, error messages will be displayed. Here's an example of what can happen:

File1 contains the text:

```
HELLO, how are you?
```

File2 contains the text:

```
HELLO how are you?
```

FC displays the following messages:

```
C:\>fc /b file1.txt file2.txt
Comparing files FILE1.TXT and FILE2.TXT
00000005: 2C 20
00000006: 20 68
00000007: 68 6F
00000008: 6F 77
00000009: 77 20
0000000A: 20 61
0000000B: 61 72
0000000C: 72 65
0000000D: 65 20
0000000E: 20 79
0000000F: 79 6F
00000010: 6F 75
00000011: 75 3F
00000012: 3F 0D
00000013: 0D 0A
00000014: 0A 0D
00000015: 0D 0A
FC: FILE1.TXT longer than FILE2.TXT

C:\>
```

The only difference in the two files is that File2 is missing a comma. FC begins reporting differences at this point.

COMP can also be used to compare files of varying lengths. Specify the /N switch followed by an equal sign and the number of the lines to be compared. The COMP command displays the differences and the line numbers in which the differences occur.

Comparing two files

The syntax for using the FC command is:

```
FC File1 File2
```

Path specifications can be set for the files but wildcards cannot be used for specifying filenames. Only two files can be compared at a time.

Example

When Microsoft Word is installed, the installation program indicates that AUTOEXEC.BAT has been changed and the original file has been renamed to AUTOEXEC.OLD. To ensure that important lines aren't omitted, check both files for differences and changes. Although you can use an editor program to examine both files, FC is faster and easier.

New file: AUTOEXEC.BAT

```
@ECHO OFF
SET COMSPEC=C:\DOS\COMMAND.COM
SET TMP=C:\TMP
VERIFY OFF
BREAK ON
PATH   C:\DOS;C:\WORD
C:\DOS\KEYB UK,,C:\DOS\KEYBOARD.SYS
PROMPT $P$G
@ECHO ON
```

Old file: AUTOEXEC.OLD

```
@ECHO OFF
SET COMSPEC=C:\DOS\COMMAND.COM
SET TMP=C:\TMP
VERIFY OFF
BREAK ON
PATH   C:\DOS
C:\DOS\KEYB UK,,C:\DOS\KEYBOARD.SYS
PROMPT $P$G
@ECHO ON
```

The following command line compares both files:

```
FC AUTOEXEC.BAT AUTOEXEC.OLD
```

FC displays the section that has been changed:

```
***** AUTOEXEC.BAT
BREAK ON
PATH C:\DOS;C:\WORD
C:\DOS\KEYB UK,,C:\DOS\KEYBOARD.SYS
***** AUTOEXEC.OLD
BREAK ON
PATH C:\DOS
C:\DOS\KEYB UK,,C:\DOS\KEYBOARD.SYS
*****
```

If the specified files are different, FC tries to synchronize them. This means that it tries to find identical lines.

FC has a 100 line buffer for this purpose. If there are more than 100 lines that are different, FC ends the comparison and displays a message on the screen.

Even though there are a lot of differences between the files, you can continue the comparison by specifying the size of the line buffer. Use the /LB switch (line buffer) and specify the number of lines after the parameter.

At least two lines must match in order for FC to recognize the following partition of the files as identical. Use the /X switch to set the value which specifies the number of identical lines for a match.

To compare files without displaying the longer sections of the files that are different, use the /A switch:

```
FC File1 File2 /A
```

By using periods, FC will identify the lines of a file that are different:

```
***** File1
Last identical line
...
First identical line
***** File2
Last identical line
...
First identical line
```

Comparing files regardless of case

Use the /C switch to ignore the differences in the case of letters (upper and lowercase) when comparing files.

```
FC File1 File2 /C
```

FC converts lowercase letters into uppercase letters.

Comparison displaying the line numbers

The /N switch displays line numbers for differences found in files.

```
FC File1 File2 /N
```

For example, if the fifth line is different, the screen displays the following:

```
***** File1
    4:  Last identical line
    5:  Different line
    6:  First identical line
***** A:File2
    4:  Last identical line
    5:  Different line
    6:  First identical line
```

Special switches

The following is a table of all the switches that can be used with the file comparison commands. The switches for the COMP command (on the Supplemental Disk from Microsoft) are:

/A   Display differences as ASCII characters. This is only useful for comparing files that consist of printable characters.

/D   Display differences as ASCII codes in the decimal numerical system. A table of the ASCII codes for all characters is included in the Appendices.

/L   Specifies the line numbers containing differences. Instead of the line number, the command specifies the position of the character in the entire file.

/N:XXX   Determines that the command only compares the first XXX lines of both files. In files, the location of differences is indicated by line numbers. This switch also enables you to compare files of different length. Without using this switch, COMP will abort immediately when files are different lengths.

/C   If /C is specified, the command will ignore differences in uppercase/lowercase letters when comparing files. Usually differences in the case of letters leads to comparison errors.

The following switches are available for FC:

/A	Abbreviates the output, the first line is displayed, then the different regions in the files are marked "..." and finally the last line is output.
/B	Forces a binary comparison.
/C	Comparison regardless of upper/lowercase letters.
/L	Compares files as ASCII text.
/Lbxx	Sets maximum consecutive mismatches in xx lines.
/N	Displays line numbers during ASCII comparison.
/T	Tab characters aren't converted to spaces. Usually FC expands tab characters by spaces to the next tab stop.
/W	Compresses tab characters and spaces.
/nn	Sets the number of identical lines that must match after a mismatch. In order for the files to be considered identical, FC must find nn identical lines in both files after the mismatched area.

5.6 Viewing File Contents

Although ASCII files can be displayed on the screen, binary files will only display a small part of the file before special characters appear along with warning beeps. Even files prepared by programs, such as databases and word processors, contain characters which will create problems if displayed on the screen. Files can be viewed more easily by using the MS-DOS Shell, which will be explained later in this chapter.

Viewing a file

The TYPE command can be used to display files on the screen:

```
TYPE Filename
```

To pause a screen display, press Ctrl + S and to continue the display press the Spacebar or Ctrl Q.

The MORE filter can be used with the TYPE command by using the pipe symbol (|). The screen pauses after every screen page and then continues with the next page after any key is pressed.

Viewing one or more files

To display one or more ASCII files on the screen, use the following:

```
COPY File CON
```

Similar to the COPY command, wildcards can be used for filenames. MS-DOS displays the filename at the beginning of each file.

To display all of the batch files (files with the .BAT extension) in the current directory, on the screen, use the following command line:

```
COPY *.BAT CON
```

If more than one page is displayed, you can stop the display by pressing Ctrl + S. To set a page by page display, use the following command line:

```
COPY *.BAT CON | MORE
```

Viewing files with the MS-DOS Shell

The **View File Contents** command in the **File** menu can be used from the MS-DOS Shell to examine the contents of a file. If text files are displayed, the text is displayed in ASCII mode. MS-DOS Shell automatically uses HEX mode for program files and other non-ASCII text files.

By selecting options from the **Display** menu, files can be displayed in either HEX or ASCII mode.

5.7   Printing Files

Files can be printed directly or placed in a print queue. Using a print queue enables you to continue working with your computer while files are printed in the background.

  Files can be printed with the MS-DOS Shell by marking the files to be printed and selecting the **Print** command from the **File** menu. However, before this can be done, the printer must be initialized with the PRINT /D switch.

Printing files directly

To print one or more files directly, use COPY to copy the files to the printer port:

```
COPY File LPT1
```

Substitute the proper printer port if your printer isn't connected to LPT1. If necessary, configure the port. The filenames for the files that will be printed can also contain the path specifications. Wildcards can also be used to select more than one file.

Setting up a print queue for the printer

With PRINT, the print queue can be set up for the printing process. Although this allows you to continue working in MS-DOS, using a print queue will also slow down your PC slightly.

The print queue is defined the first time PRINT is called. While PRINT is using the print queue, the printer cannot be accessed with any other command.

Setting up the print queue

The first time PRINT is called, the print queue can be set up and the printer connection defined:

```
PRINT /D:LPT1
```

(Substitute the proper port if your printer isn't connected to LPT1. If necessary, configure the port as explained in the section on the Serial Port.)

If the /D switch isn't included, PRINT prompts you for the printer connection.

Defining the number of files and buffer size

Set the maximum number of files in the print queue and the size of the buffer the first time PRINT is called.

```
PRINT /D:LPT1 /Q:Number /B:Buffer
```

/Q:Number

If the number of files to be printed isn't specified, PRINT uses a default value of 10. The value for the number of files in the print queue can be between 1 and 32.

/B:Buffer This switch allows you to set the size of the print buffer. The default value is 512 bytes. Generally, larger buffers allow the PRINT command to execute faster.

Determining waiting times

The first time PRINT is called you can define how much time is available for printing a character, how long PRINT waits for the printer and the amount of time PRINT can use for printing.

/M:Print time

> Sets the number of time units available for printing a character. The default value is 2, but a value between 1 and 255 can be used.

/U:Waiting time

> Determines how long PRINT waits before the printer can receive another character. The default value is 1, but a value between 1 and 255 can be used.

/S:ratio   Sets the time ratio for the background process. The default value is 8, but a value between 1 and 255 can be used. When using the default value, there is eight times as much available time for working with the command interpreter as there is for the printing process. The higher the value, the more rapidly the PC reacts and the more slowly the printer prints.

You should experiment with the value for the ratio and set it so that you can work without being interrupted and the printing process will continue. Since printers vary in speed, there is no general value.

Changing the print queue

New files can be added and existing files can be deleted from the print queue. The list of files in the print queue can be displayed and the entire print queue can be deleted.

Adding a file to the print queue

To add a file to the print queue, simply specify the filename after the PRINT command:

```
PRINT Filename
```

Several files can be specified by separating each filename with spaces. Also, wildcards can be used for selecting and printing several files. This method can be used to add additional files to the print queue while PRINT is busy printing files.

Deleting files from the print queue

Files can be removed from the print queue by specifying the filename and the /C switch:

```
PRINT Filename /C
```

The /C switch affects the specified filename and all of the subsequent filenames in the print queue. For example, three files can be removed from the print queue as follows:

```
PRINT File1 /C File2 File3
```

 Using /C only removes the files from the print queue (from the print list); it doesn't delete them from the storage medium.

Adding files to the print queue and resuming printing

The /P switch adds the preceding filename and all subsequent filenames to the print queue:

```
PRINT Filename /P
```

The /P and /C switches can be combined in a single command line, which allows you to add and remove files simultaneously.

Example

The following command line removes the file WARNING.TXT from the print queue and adds the INVOICE.TXT file:

```
PRINT Warning.txt /C INVOICE.TXT /P
```

Deleting all files from the print queue

The /T switch is used to delete all files from the print queue and abort the printing process:

```
PRINT /T
```

5.8 Deleting Files

MS-DOS provides the DEL (Delete) and ERASE commands for deleting files. Since these commands are identical, we'll refer only to the DEL command in our explanations. However, remember that the ERASE command works the same way as the DEL command.

The DEL command

The DEL command can be used to delete one or more files from a storage medium.

```
DEL Filename
```

If a filename is specified, the command removes only the specified file. Path specifications can be used if the file isn't in the current directory.

Wildcards ("*" and "?") can be used to delete more than one file at the same time. However, if the /P switch isn't specified, the command deletes all of the files without displaying a security prompt.

Deleting all files in a directory

The wildcard *.* can be used to delete all of the files in either the current directory or a specified directory. In this case, the command will use a security prompt, which checks whether or not all of the files should be deleted. Enter Y for "Yes" to delete all of the files. Enter N for "No" to end the delete process.

The contents of an entire directory can be deleted by using the DEL command from a higher directory. For example, if you want to delete all of the files in the PERSONAL directory, which is a subdirectory of TEXTS, type the following if TEXTS is the current directory:

```
DEL PERSONAL
```

After a security prompt, the command deletes all of the files but leaves system, hidden and read-only files.

To delete the contents of any directory, specify the entire path. After a security prompt, the command will remove all of the files in the directory.

Special features for using wildcards

Always check which files will be affected by the deletion by using the DIR command. This is especially important when using wildcards because DEL will erase files without using additional security prompts.

For example, type:

```
DIR *.BAK
```

and then type:

```
DEL *.BAK
```

Prompt before deleting each file

The /P switch can be used to determine which files should be deleted. When this switch is specified, the screen displays each filename and a prompt before deleting the files. To delete the file press Y or to skip the file press N.

Undoing deletion of files

DEL doesn't remove the file from the storage medium. Instead, the first letter of the filename is replaced with the hex value E5. This marks the file as deleted and the space occupied by the file is made available for further use.

Recovering a single file

If no other files have been stored on the storage medium, the UNDELETE command can be used to recover the deleted file. To recover a deleted file, call UNDELETE with the filename of the deleted file. For example, the following command line would be used to recover an accidentally deleted TEST.TXT file:

```
UNDELETE TEST.TXT
```

The command will ask whether you really want to undo the deletion of the file. Answer the prompt with Y for "Yes". Then you're prompted to enter the first character of the filename. In our example this would be "T". MS-DOS then responds with a message indicating whether or not the file can be restored.

Recovering several files

Eventually you may accidentally delete several files in a directory. You can undo the deletion by calling UNDELETE, in the directory which contained the deleted files, and answering a prompt for each file. To recover a file, enter the first letter of the filename. After finishing this process, MS-DOS indicates whether or not the file was recovered.

 Always retrieve accidentally deleted files immediately. If any other files are saved, MS-DOS may overwrite the file(s) that were deleted. Once a file has been overwritten, it can no longer be recovered.

5.9   Renaming Files

Files within a directory can be renamed with the REN (RENAME) command. After a file is renamed, it's no longer available under its old name:

```
REN Oldfile Newfile
```

Oldfile   This parameter is the current filename. The name can include a path specification and a disk drive label. Wildcards ("*" and "?") can also be used.

Newfile   This parameter is the new filename. It cannot contain any path specifications. In other words, it must remain in the same directory. Any characters of the filename defined by wildcards remain unchanged.

If a file with the new filename already exists in the current directory, MS-DOS displays an error message:

```
Duplicate file name or file not found
```

Either select a new name for the file or use COPY.

Example

The following command line renames the file AUTOEXEC.OLD to AUTOEXEC.BAT. In order for the command to be successful, there shouldn't be an AUTOEXEC.BAT in the directory:

```
REN AUTOEXEC.OLD AUTOEXEC.BAT
```

To rename all files beginning with the characters LETTER so that the new filenames begin with COMP, use the following command line:

```
REN LETTER*.* COMP*.*
```

5.10 Special Features of Files

MS-DOS stores special information (attributes) about every file. The ATTRIB command can be used to display and change this information.

Changing the write protect flag

The write protect flag determines whether or not a file can be changed or deleted. Use the ATTRIB command to set or delete this file attribute.

Protecting a file from being changed

To protect a file from being deleted or changed, use the command:

```
ATTRIB +R Filename
```

This file can no longer be deleted with DEL. Also, this file can't be specified as a target for the COPY command (it can't be overwritten by COPY). If you try to delete or copy to the file, MS-DOS displays the error message, "Access denied".

When specifying the filename, wildcards can be used to set the write protect flag.

Clearing the write protect flag

Use the following command to delete or change a file:

```
ATTRIB -R Filename
```

Setting and clearing the write protect flag in subdirectories

The /S switch can be set to process all of the specified files and associated subdirectories in the current or specified directory:

```
ATTRIB +R Filename /S
```

If the filename doesn't have a path specification, the command affects the current directory and any subdirectories.

Changing the archive flag

ATTRIB can also be used to set or clear the archive flag. A set flag means that the specified file has been changed or created since the last backup. If a file has this attribute set, you should create a backup copy as soon as possible. MS-DOS changes the archive flag automatically.

The archive flag can also be used for selecting files to use with the XCOPY, MSBACKUP and RESTORE commands.

Marking a file as changed

To mark a file as changed, use:

```
ATTRIB +A Filename
```

Wildcards can be used in the filename. Using wildcards enables you to change the attributes of several files simultaneously.

The command sets the archive flag of a file. The file still hasn't been changed; it is only marked as changed.

MS-DOS automatically sets the archive flag whenever files are created or changed. Sometimes it's helpful to set the flag later. For example, you may want to back up (even if it wasn't changed) or edit the file.

Marking a file as backed up

To mark a file as backed up, use the following command:

```
ATTRIB -A Filename
```

The command clears the archive flag of the file. This doesn't back up the file. Instead, the file only appears to have been backed up with the XCOPY, MSBACKUP and RESTORE commands (if you use the appropriate parameters with the commands). These commands may be configured to ignore files that have the archive flag cleared.

When changes are made to a file, MS-DOS automatically sets the archive flag.

If you've changed files and don't want to back them up, clear the archive bit for these files before performing a backup.

Example

Several files, which are located in the C:\DOC directory, have been edited. Make a backup copy of these files to create a special print file called PRINT.TXT. The PRINT.TXT file doesn't need to be backed up. The following command line can be used to exclude PRINT.TXT from the backup:

```
ATTRIB -A PRINT.TXT
```

Now the remainder of the changed files can be backed up by typing the following command line:

```
XCOPY *.TXT A: /M
```

The /M switch used with XCOPY, determines that only files with set archive flags should be backed up. The command marks the files as backed up (XCOPY automatically resets the archive flag).

Changing the archive flag for files in several directories

The /S switch allows you to change the attributes of the specified files in the current or specified directory and any subdirectories:

```
ATTRIB +A Filename /S
```

This command line sets the archive flag for all of the corresponding files, including files in any subdirectories.

```
ATTRIB -A Filename /S
```

The previous command line clears the archive flag for all corresponding files, including files in any subdirectories.

If the filename doesn't include a path specification, the command affects the current directory and any subdirectories. If a path specification is included, the command affects the directory specified in the command line.

Changing the hidden attribute

The hidden attribute marks a file as hidden. This means that the DIR command no longer displays the filename and the file cannot be removed by using DEL. However, there is a way to display files with this hidden attribute set. Call DIR as shown in the following command line:

```
DIR /A:H
```

Setting the hidden attribute

To set a file as hidden, use the following command:

```
ATTRIB +H Filename
```

Wildcards can be used in the filename.

Clearing the hidden attribute

The following command is used to clear the hidden file attribute and allows you to handle the file as any normal file.

```
ATTRIB -H Filename
```

This command clears the hidden attribute, allowing you to use the DIR and DEL commands.

Changing the hidden attribute for files in several directories

By using the /S switch, specified files in the current directory and any subdirectories can be affected.

```
ATTRIB +H Filename /S
```

The command line shown above sets the hidden attribute for all corresponding files, including files in any subdirectories.

```
ATTRIB -H Filename /S
```

This command line deletes the hidden attribute for all corresponding files in the current directory and any files in subdirectories.

If the filename specification doesn't include a path specification, the command affects the current directory and any associated subdirectories. If a path specification is included, the command affects only the specified directory.

Changing the system attribute

The system attribute marks files as system files. Certain programs treat system files differently. For example, the BeckerTools Compress program for optimizing hard drives considers system files as unmovable.

Setting the system attribute

To mark a file as a system file, use the command:

```
ATTRIB +S Filename
```

Wildcards can be used in filenames.

Clearing the system attribute

The following command line clears the system attribute, which allows the file to be handled as a normal file.

```
ATTRIB -S Filename
```

Changing the system attribute for files in several directories

The /S switch allows you to edit all of the specified files in a directory and its associated subdirectories:

```
ATTRIB +S Filename /S
```

The above command line sets the system attribute for all files in the current directory and any files in any associated subdirectories.

```
ATTRIB -S Filename /S
```

This command line clears the system attribute for all files in the current directory and any files in any associated subdirectories.

If the specified filename doesn't include a path specification, the command affects the current directory and all of its subdirectories. Otherwise the command affects only the specified directory.

Displaying file attributes

To display the file attributes of one or more files, use the ATTRIB command with the filename only, as shown below:

```
ATTRIB Filename
```

Wildcards can also be used in filenames. Use the /S switch in the command line to display the attributes of files in the subdirectories.

5.11 Checking Files

In this section we'll discuss ways to check the integrity of files. When this is done, files are checked for readability and for optimum distribution on the storage medium.

Checking files for readability

You should occasionally check files for readability. For example, suppose that some files have been copied onto a diskette. When the DIR command is used, the filenames are displayed. However, when you try to access the files, an error message appears.

This could be either a nuisance or a fatal error, especially if you were planning to copy these files onto someone else's computer. So, you should check the files on the diskette for readability.

The COPY command will check a file for readability. If MS-DOS cannot read parts of the file correctly, it automatically displays an error message. The fastest, most effective way to check file integrity is by using the dummy device NUL, as shown in the following command line:

```
COPY File NUL
```

Wildcards can be used when specifying the filename.

The previous command line copies the file to "nothing". The copying process itself is executed. However, since the copying process is extremely fast, no files are actually created.

If MS-DOS is no longer able to read a file correctly, use the RECOVER command to recover the file. Additional information about this command will be provided in later sections.

Checking files for optimum distribution on the storage medium

If it ever seems like your hard drive is slowing down as time goes on, it probably is. Hard drives become slower as more data is placed on them. The more often data is deleted and new data files are created, the more apparent the problem will become. To understand this completely, you need to know a little about how MS-DOS stores data on a hard drive.

If the hard drive is empty, MS-DOS stores data contiguously. This means that MS-DOS writes data on a track of the hard drive until it is full, then starts storing data on the next track.

Since a hard drive usually has at least two disks with two read/write heads each for the top and the bottom, MS-DOS can write on four tracks before the read/write head must be moved. These tracks, which can be processed without moving the heads, are called "cylinders".

On a typical disk drive with 17 sectors per track you can fit 17 * 512 or 8,704 bytes on a track. So 34,816 bytes can be stored on the four tracks of a cylinder. Since the computer can read or write to a file with 34K without having to move the read/write heads, the process is very fast.

Also, it's ideal if files are distributed consecutively on the disk sectors. When this occurs, the heads don't have to be moved several times, which causes waiting times while the heads "seek" a new position.

File Fragmentation

Files are constantly being deleted and saved on the hard drive. Even within the same file changes can be made to the text and saved. When a file is deleted, empty regions develop on the hard drive. Later these regions are used again to store data. If the newly saved files are bigger than the amount of free, contiguous space, the file is scattered over different places on the hard drive.

When the computer reads or writes to these files, the head must be moved to new tracks continuously, so that it can read or write other parts of the file. This causes performance to degrade considerably.

This process can be difficult if a hard drive is almost full. In this case there are only several small areas in which MS-DOS can distribute the files. For this reason you should never fill your hard drive to more than 90% of its capacity.

Checking files for contiguity

Naturally, the less your files are fragmented over the storage medium, the faster MS-DOS can read them. MS-DOS reads files faster when they're saved contiguously.

To check the distribution of a file on a storage medium, use the following command line:

```
CHKDSK File
```

CHKDSK displays the usual information about the storage medium and the memory of your computer and indicates whether or not the file is contiguous:

```
All specified file(s) are contiguous
```

The previous message indicates that the specified file is optimally allocated.

```
File contains XX non-contiguous blocks
```

Instead of being allocated contiguously on the diskette, the specified file consists of XX fragments.

Wildcards can be used for filenames.

Combining files in DOS

If the storage medium contains many fragmented files, the DEFRAG command can be used to allocate them contiguously. Use the MSBACKUP command to make a security copy of your entire hard drive. After a backup copy has been made, use DEFRAG to defragment your files. Do not use this command from within Windows.

5.12 Searching for Files

File searches can be performed with either DIR or CHKDSK.

Searching for files in a directory

To search for files in a directory, enter the filename along with DIR. If the file isn't in the current directory, specify the drive and directory as well.

Searching for files on the entire storage medium

Use DIR from the root directory to search for files on the entire storage medium. After the command enter the name of the file you're searching for and the optional /S switch. The /S switch specifies that the command will search for all subdirectories.

```
DIR FILENAME /S
```

5.13 Searching Contents of Files

The FIND command can be used to search one or more files for a specified text string.

Displaying lines containing a specified search text

Use the following command line to display all of the lines of a file that contain a certain search text:

```
FIND "Search text" File
```

FIND displays the name of the file and all of the lines in the file containing the search text:

Example

To search the AUTOEXEC.BAT for the term ECHO, use the following line:

```
FIND "ECHO" AUTOEXEC.BAT
```

Depending on the contents of your AUTOEXEC.BAT file, the following information is displayed:

```
---------- AUTOEXEC.BAT
@ECHO OFF
@ECHO ON
```

The search text must be enclosed in quotation marks. If the character sequence for the search is already enclosed in quotation marks, a double set of quotation marks must be used. The FIND command is case sensitive, which means that it is affected by upper and lowercase letters. If the /I switch is specified, the case of the letters (uppercase or lowercase) will be ignored.

To search more than one file, enter each filename separated by a space:

```
FIND "Search text" File1 File2 File3
```

Special options for searching

By specifying optional switches it's possible to utilize other features:

/C Displays only the number of lines containing the search text.

/N
    Displays the line number in front of each line containing the search text.

/V Reverses the search condition. Displays only lines that don't contain the search text.

/I Ignores the case of letters (upper and lowercase).

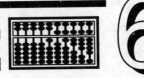

6

Application Programs

Whether you realize it or not, application programs rely on MS-DOS to perform many of their tasks. For example, to format a diskette, a word processor will call on the services of MS-DOS rather than perform this function itself.

While it may appear that the word processor is formatting the diskettes, in reality MS-DOS is in charge of the formatting.

Before you buy an application program, you should make sure which version of the operating system is required. Usually an application is designed to work with several MS-DOS versions.

Since operating systems are usually "upward compatible" a minimum version of MS-DOS may be required for that application. This means that the application will usually work correctly with higher versions of MS-DOS. So an application that requires MS-DOS 2.2 or higher will also work with MS-DOS 3.3, 4.0, 5.0 and 6.0.

However, there are exceptions to this rule. Some special utilities or tools often depend on specific internal functions of the operating system. For example, a utility program might work with MS-DOS 3.3, but not with MS-DOS 6.0. If you're not sure which version is required, ask your computer dealer or the manufacturer of the program.

The following figure shows the relationship of the operating system and an application program. It demonstrates the most important and basic link between the user's idea or task and the finished product. Cooperation between the operating system and the application program is extremely important.

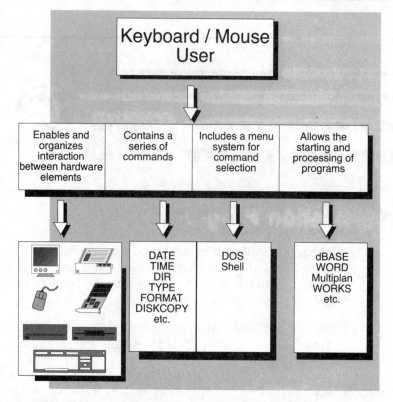

The operating system is important to how your computer is used

When a user begins to work on a task, he/she has an idea of how to complete it. The user is already using many of the diverse capabilities of the operating system when the computer is switched on and the application program is started.

Using the services of the operating system, an application program (such as a word processor) is used to produce the desired end result (for example, a letter).

When working with files, application programs usually use many of the internal functions of the operating system (DOS). For example, to copy a document file to a diskette or back up your hard drive, the application program calls on the various functions of DOS to perform these.

6.1 Overview

The following is a listing of the important rules and information for working with application programs. These are the programs you use to perform daily tasks (e.g., word processor, database, spreadsheet, etc.). MS-DOS is important to these programs because they cannot even start up without the operating system. Also, the conditions and rules of the operating system also apply to the application programs (rules for hard drives/diskettes, directories, files).

Installing programs

If possible, use the installation programs included with the application for installation. Also, install the programs in their own subdirectories. Do not copy several programs into one directory, and never copy them to the root directory or the DOS directory. Installation programs are also important because they adapt an application program to the peripherals connected to the computer. So, you shouldn't simply copy the files to your computer.

Changing the system files

Most installation programs automatically make changes to the AUTOEXEC.BAT and CONFIG.SYS. While expanding the search path in the AUTOEXEC.BAT with PATH is usually an important change, other changes may interfere with the operation of other programs. For this reason, always back up the system files before installing programs and then compare them with the new system files to determine whether there are any unwanted changes.

Starting programs

You can start a program by typing its name at the DOS prompt and pressing [Enter]. The program must either be in the current directory or the program directory must be listed in the search path with PATH.

Starting programs with parameters

Many programs allow you to specify additional information (parameters) when you start the program. For example, you can specify the name of the file you are editing when you start a word processing program. The MS-DOS Shell lets you associate files with programs. Then you can double-click the file to start the associated application program with the file as its parameter.

Exiting programs

Unless a program has crashed, you should exit the program by using the proper shutdown procedure. If you simply switch off the computer to quit the program, you could lose data.

6.2   Installing Programs

Most application programs are distributed on floppy diskettes. These programs usually contain many files on several diskettes. To use an application program, these files must be copied into a specific directory on your hard drive. This is the only way to control and maintain programs. We advise that you avoid keeping several different programs in a single directory.

Copying files isn't always enough

Computer systems vary greatly in hardware and performance. Some systems use different types of graphics adapters (CGA, EGA, VGA, Hercules, etc.) and may or may not include a hard drive or mouse or other hardware.

Many application programs must be adapted or customized to the specific hardware components of your particular computer system. So, simply copying all of the files from the diskettes onto your hard drive may not be enough. Many application programs must be *installed* before they will operate properly.

Interactive installation programs

Most application programs include special installation programs. These programs copy and configure the files on your hard drive. Some installation programs only tell you what they are doing and prompt you to change diskettes. Other installation programs work with you. This means that the installation program prompts you for various information so that it can determine the specifications required for optimum performance with your computer system.

Why use installation programs?

In many cases it's important that the application program determine which graphics adapter (graphics card) your computer uses. This is especially important for graphics programs. You may also have to answer questions about the operation of your mouse (mouse type, serial, bus, etc.), the kind and model of your printer or other accessories and the configuration of your computer. The application program records the information and adapts itself to function properly with your system. This information is usually stored in a special file created during the installation process. If this file is missing, your application program either won't run or the program will crash, which causes loss of data.

Installation programs are also necessary for another reason. Some applications are saved on the diskette in a special compressed form to save space. The information is compressed by using special techniques. These files are sometimes called "packed" files.

The advantage of packed files is that more data can be stored on a diskette. However, these files require a program to "unpack" the files to their original size. Installation programs perform this function automatically during the installation process. For example, the files on your MS-DOS 6.0 diskettes were compressed before being placed on the diskettes and uncompressed when installed to your hard drive. It would be difficult and time-consuming for users to unpack these files by hand.

Before installing a program, always make backup copies of the original diskettes and use the backup copies for installation. Also, be sure to write protect the original diskettes before making the copies. This will insure that the original diskettes aren't destroyed by a copying error.

Installing an application

If the application program you want to install comes on several diskettes, one of the diskettes is usually labelled "Start disk", "Installation" or something similar. The installation program, if included with the application, is usually on this diskette. The most common names for installation programs are INSTALL or SETUP. You can use DIR to display the existing files and programs or type:

```
DIR *.EXE

DIR *.COM

DIR *.BAT
```

to display all of the executable files and determine the name of the installation program. You can also refer to the program's user manual for instructions on installing the application. The installation instructions are usually located in a chapter near the front of the manual or in a separate booklet packaged with the program.

Using a batch file can simplify searching for executable programs on your disks. The following batch program, SHOWPRG.BAT, displays all of the executable files, in the current directory, with the extensions .COM, .EXE or .BAT. The batch file displays the programs in alphabetical order and page by page:

```
@ECHO OFF
REM SHOWPRG - Display all programs
IF EXIST *.EXE DIR *.EXE  >FP.TMP
IF EXIST *.COM DIR *.COM  >>FP.TMP
IF EXIST *.BAT DIR *.BAT  >>FP.TMP
FIND <FP.TMP /V "e" | SORT | MORE
IF EXIST FP.TMP DEL FP.TMP
ECHO ON
```

Save this batch file in a directory that has been specified in your search path. This lets you start the batch file from any directory. To display all of the programs on a diskette in drive A:, set A: as the current drive and call the batch program:

```
A:
SHOWPRG
```

 A special temporary file, called FP.TMP, is stored on the diskette of the current drive. So, the diskette can't be write protected and enough space must remain on the diskette to store FP.TMP. In order to use write protected diskettes, replace FP.TMP with C:\FP.TMP in the batch file. This will always store FP.TMP in the root directory of your hard drive.

The previous version of SHOWPRG.BAT lists all executable files in alphabetical order. Frequently, users prefer to have the files displayed in a different order. For example, the files can be listed by extension (.COM, .EXE or .BAT) with as many files on the screen as possible. To do this, modify SHOWPRG.BAT as shown below:

```
@ECHO OFF
IF EXIST *.EXE DIR *.EXE /W >FP.TMP
IF EXIST *.COM DIR *.COM /W >>FP.TMP
IF EXIST *.BAT DIR *.BAT /W >>FP.TMP
FIND <FP.TMP /V "e" | MORE
IF EXIST FP.TMP DEL FP.TMP
ECHO ON
```

 If you don't want to write to a floppy diskette, simply replace FP.TMP with C:\FP.TMP in the batch file.

This version of the batch program displays all the executable files in five columns on the screen. First the EXE files are displayed, followed by the COM files and finally the BAT files. MS-DOS follows this sequence when it searches for executable files. This version also excludes all of the information about the storage device, which provides more space for the files. The following is an example of what the display could look like:

```
APPEND   EXE    ATTRIB   EXE    EXE2BIN  EXE    FASTOPEN EXE    FC          EXE
FDISK    EXE    ILESYS   EXE    FIND     EXE    GWBASIC  EXE    FSFUNC      EXE
JOIN     EXE    LINK     EXE    MEM      EXE    NLSFUNC  EXE    REPLACE     EXE
SHELLC   EXE    SELECT   EXE    SHARE    EXE    SORT     EXE    SUBST       EXE
XCOPY    EXE


ASSIGN   COM    BACKUP   COM    CHKDSK   COM    COMMAND  COM    COMP        COM
DEBUG    COM    DISKCOMP COM    DISKCOPY COM    DOSEDIT  COM    EDLIN       COM
FORMAT   COM    GRAFTABL COM    GRAPHICS COM    KEYB     COM    MODE        COM
MORE     COM    MOUSE    COM    PRINT    COM    RECOVER  COM    RESTORE     COM
SHELLB   COM    SYS      COM    WHERE    COM    FDISK    COM    LABEL       COM
SELECT   COM    TREE     COM


WORK   BAT    SHELLTXT BAT    WORD   BAT    AUTOEXEC BAT    DOS-SHELL BAT
```

The executable files

Sometimes a file called README (or something similar) is located on one of the diskettes (usually on diskette no. 1). These files contain information that was not included in the manual. Perhaps it has information that was inadvertently omitted when the manual was printed. Sometimes you'll find information about the installation program in a README file. So you should always read this file before beginning the installation.

README files are text files that can be read with an editor or a word processor. If you don't have either of these programs on your computer, you can read this information file by using the TYPE command. However, entering TYPE README.DOC will cause the entire contents of the file to race over the screen. It's easier to read the file if you add the MORE command. (You can create the pipe symbol by pressing [Alt] + [1] + [2] + [4], if your keyboard does not have this character.) The command is as follows:

```
TYPE README.DOC | MORE
```

If the file doesn't have an extension (.DOC, .TXT), you don't need to enter one. Whenever the text fills the screen, the output stops until a key is pressed. After pressing a key, the next page of text is displayed.

With MS-DOS 6.0, reading files is even easier. You can use the MS-DOS Editor program, EDIT, to display files. Type the following command:

```
EDIT README.DOC
```

The file will be loaded and you can use the cursor keys and the PgUp and PgDn keys to scroll through the document. You can even print the document by selecting the **Print** command from the **File** menu.

Installing application programs properly

There are several factors to consider when installing application programs. By experimenting, you could probably install programs onto your hard drive without using the installation programs. However, this method could eventually lead to problems. One of your programs might suddenly stop working and you won't know what caused the problem. The following are a few simple rules for installing application programs.

Directories for program files

Always use the installation program supplied with your application software. This will ensure that the software is installed correctly and that maximum performance will be achieved. However, if you want to install application programs by hand (without the supplied installation program), always copy the files of these programs into their own subdirectories. For example, there would be a separate directory for Microsoft Word, a separate directory for dBASE, etc. Usually installation programs also create new directories and copy the files of an application program into them.

Separating the different programs and their files isn't the only reason new directories are created. Files of the same name can be used by different programs. So if the programs aren't in different directories, files can be overwritten each time you copy new program files onto your disk.

Also, if you decide to delete a program from your hard drive, you won't be able to determine which files belong to that particular application program. So placing all files in a common directory can eventually cause many problems.

Directories for data files

You should also create a separate directory for all of the files created by an application program. This will provide a better overview of the contents of your hard drive and will simplify backing up the data on your hard drive.

Since the files that the application program needs in order to operate usually aren't changed after installation, you only need to back up the contents of this directory once. The data that the application program processes, on the other hand, needs to be backed up at regular intervals. If the data is stored in a special directory, the backup process can be quicker, easier and more accurate.

If you use one application program to work on several types of data, you should store the data in their own subdirectories. This makes it easier to find files of the same type.

Although all files in a directory must have different names, files in different directories can have the same name. For example, if you do your taxes on your computer, you can set up a directory for each year and use the same filenames (STATE.TXT, FEDERAL.TXT, LOCAL.TXT).

Calling programs and data in one command

Many application programs allow you to specify which data file is to be loaded when the program is started. The application program starts and opens the data file. So you don't have to wait for the program to start before specifying which file to use.

To make the directory containing the data files the current directory for the application program, change to the data directory before starting the program and call the application program. Remember that the MS-DOS PATH command must be used to set the search path for the directory containing the program files.

The complete path to the program can also be specified. For example, to start Microsoft Works from the C:\WORKS directory, you would type:

```
C:\WORKS\WORKS
```

Obviously, you could also create a batch file, called WORKS.BAT, that would contain the above command line for starting Works.

The path to the program directory

If the application program is installed on your hard drive in its own subdirectory, the PATH command can be used to include this directory in the search path. Then you can start the program from any directory. If your search path for MS-DOS commands is C:\DOS, to include the Microsoft Word word processor in the search path, expand the PATH line in AUTOEXEC.BAT.

```
PATH C:\DOS;C:\WORD
```

If you used the Microsoft Word installation program, the search path is set and AUTOEXEC.BAT is modified during the installation process.

   Avoid too many program directories in the search path. First, an MS-DOS command line can contain a maximum of only 127 characters. Since the complete search path must be specified, the entire path specification can be up to 122 characters long. Second, when a command is entered, MS-DOS searches the entire search path for the command. So the longer this search path is, the longer it takes MS-DOS to search it.

Only the programs that are required (dBASE IV, Word 5.0 etc.) or programs that are constantly used should be included in the search path. Instead, you can use a batch file to start programs that aren't used as often. By using a batch file, you don't have to change directories (see below). If you use the MS-DOS Shell, you could make the appropriate entries for these programs in the program list, which we'll explain later. This will let you start these programs easily.

The start batch solution

Creating a batch file that can call a program and load a file is easy. You don't even have to know a lot about batch programming. Simply create a one line ASCII file (a text file without formatting) that contains the complete path for starting the program and one or more variables for the names of files to be opened. These variables are used to pass the parameters from the batch file to the program.

Create a batch file called W.BAT for calling Word and place it in a directory which has been defined by PATH (for instance, the BAT directory discussed earlier). Use an editor program (Word or the MS-DOS Editor) to type the following line, then save it as an ASCII file:

```
C:\WORD\WORD %1 %2 %3
```

To start Microsoft Word to edit the LETTER.DOC file in the current directory (C:\DOC), type:

```
W LETTER
```

Avoiding problems during installation

As we previously mentioned, most application programs contain installation utilities. However, even with these programs, you can still encounter problems. By taking a few precautions, you'll be able to avoid most of these problems.

Automatically changing the start and configuration files

Some programs automatically modify AUTOEXEC.BAT and CONFIG.SYS during installation. Commands in these files, which the application program needs in order to function properly, are inserted in these files. Depending on the installation program, the original versions of AUTOEXEC.BAT and CONFIG.SYS are saved with new extensions (.SAV or .OLD, for example). Since you can't be certain whether you will still have copies of the original files after installation, use COPY to back up these files onto a diskette before running the installation program.

Use The MS-DOS 6.0 Commands chapter, and Appendix A, Device Drivers (the reference lists all of the MS-DOS commands that can appear in the AUTOEXEC.BAT or the CONFIG.SYS), to check the changes or refer to Section 2.2 "Setting up MS-DOS", which provides a short description of all the important elements of these files.

Many installation programs make changes to three settings:

- They extend the search paths for commands (PATH) to the directory, in which the new application is installed.

- They check the BUFFERS parameter for a minimum value and, if necessary, increase this value. Although this speeds up access to the hard drive, it decreases the amount of memory proportionally. If you install a new application program and a previous one no longer functions correctly or an error message indicating that there isn't enough memory is displayed, the reason may be due to an increase in BUFFERS.

- They check the FILES parameter for a minimum value and, if necessary, increase the value. This sets the number of files that can be used simultaneously by MS-DOS. While in many cases the value 20 is sufficient, some programs (databases, for example) require a larger value. Although increasing the value for FILES results in less memory, don't undo the change the installation program has made.

Besides these changes, which generally don't affect other programs, there are changes that can cause problems.

Early versions of GEM (Graphics Environment Manager) automatically create a search path (SET COMSPEC) for the command interpreter. This can lead to problems if COMMAND.COM isn't in the specified directory. After quitting some programs you may receive the error message "Invalid command interpreter". If this happens, you'll have to reboot your computer. To solve this you can either undo the change or correct the GEM.BAT file, which changes the system variables.

Keeping older program versions

If you have an application program on your hard drive and purchase a new version of this program, don't replace the early version of the application program with the new one immediately. Install the new version so that both are available for a transitional period. Sometimes new versions of a program won't work with files that were created with earlier versions of the same program.

When installing a new version, use a new directory with a meaningful name. For example, if you have been using Microsoft Word 4.0, stored in the C:\WORD directory, and want to switch to Microsoft Word 5.0, install the new version of Word in a directory called C:\WORD5.

Some installation programs specify the name for the new directory. So you aren't able to change the name during installation. Because of this, you should change the name of the directory containing the earlier version before starting the installation program. This fools the installation program and prevents all of the old files from being overwritten.

Installing the new version in addition to the earlier one can help you avoid some potential problems:

• Sometimes the new version of the program can't use all of the data from the earlier version. If this happens, use the older version to process this data.

• The driver program supplied with the new program for the screen or printer could cause problems with your hardware. For example, you may have a full page monitor and a special driver program for the early version of the program. The new version might not be able to use this special driver.

- Some programs can only be installed once and have to be "deinstalled" onto diskettes with a special program before installing them on another computer. If a new version of the program is installed in the directory containing the early version, it overwrites important information and the old version can no longer be used (dBASE III plus).

Check your hard drive for the necessary storage space

When you install a new version of a program in addition to an earlier version, there may not be enough space on your hard drive. When this happens the installation program might terminate unsuccessfully. The program may also abort with a message, indicating that the hard drive is full. So remember that not all installation programs check for sufficient disk space on the storage device before starting.

 The amount of storage space remaining on the device is displayed at the end of the DIR command display.

There should be enough space on the hard drive to copy all of the installation diskettes onto the hard drive. For example, if an application program is distributed on twelve 360K diskettes, you'll need at least 4.3 Meg of memory. If you don't have enough room on the hard drive, use XCOPY or MSBACKUP to move rarely used data to diskettes. First back up this data to a diskette, then delete the data from the hard drive.

 Some programs require much more space on the hard drive than indicated by the number of distribution diskettes. One reason for this is that many programs come in packed formats. During installation, the files are automatically unpacked which therefore requires more space. Also, some programs require additional storage space on the hard drive. For example, Windows 3.1 uses the hard drive to store temporary data.

6.3   The Command Interpreter

Application programs can be started just like MS-DOS commands. For this, the computer must display the system prompt.

Loading application programs from a diskette

Insert the diskette containing the application program in drive A: and make this drive the current drive by typing:

```
A:
```

Enter the name of the application program and press Enter.

If the application program was installed on diskettes, usually a start or program diskette must be inserted to start the program.

Some applications are started from a batch file. For example, Ventura Publisher is started using VP.BAT. Use the following command to check whether this batch file is on the diskette:

```
DIR *.BAT
```

 Some programs are loaded entirely in the computer's memory in such a way that you can replace the program diskette with a data diskette. If this isn't the case, insert the data diskette in the second drive (if you have one). Don't save data on the program diskette because there usually isn't enough unused disk space and you could also destroy the application program through an error.

Starting application programs from the hard drive

If PATH defines a path for the directory of the application or a batch file, the application can be started from any directory.

If a path wasn't defined, you must make the hard drive the current drive:

```
C:
```

Use the Change Directory command CD to specify the name of the directory in which the application program is located:

```
CD Directory
```

The application can then be started by typing the program name.

Many programs aren't started directly. Instead they use a supplied batch file, such as VP.BAT for Ventura Publisher. You can use the following command to check for this batch file in the directory of the program:

```
DIR *.BAT
```

Overlay files

Instead of being completely loaded in memory, some application programs use OVL files, which are loaded as needed. To start these application programs from any other directory, sometimes you may need to use the MS-DOS APPEND command, which sets a search path for programs and files. If this special search path isn't defined, the application program might not be able to load the OVL files and will end with an error message (and possible loss of data).

For example, to set a search path for program and OVL files for dBASE in the C:\DBASE directory, insert the following line in the AUTOEXEC.BAT:

```
APPEND C:\DBASE /X:ON
```

Searching for programs or files

If an application program is installed on the hard drive but you can't remember the name of the directory, use the new options of DIR to search the hard drive for the program file. If you can remember the name or part of the filename used to start the program, use DIR with the part you remember to search the entire hard drive. You can also substitute wildcards (* and ?) for the unknown parts of the name.

First use the CD\ command to change to the root directory of the storage device to search. The /S switch instructs DIR to include all subdirectories in the search. If you're currently in the root directory and include all subdirectories in the search, the entire storage device is searched. The command looks like this:

```
DIR Filename.extension /S
```

DIR displays information about the directory where the file was found as well as all the information usually displayed about a file.

Searching for programs: the easy way

You can create a batch file that will search the entire storage device for files. For simplicity's sake, name this file

WHERE.BAT. By using this batch file, you don't have to change to the root directory and type DIR along with the /S switch. For example, if you type WHERE MOUSE.*, DIR will display all of the files called MOUSE, along with a line indicating in which directory the file is located. The following is the WHERE.BAT batch:

```
@REM WHERE.BAT Section 6.3
@REM Batch for searching the current drive for a file
@ECHO OFF
IF "%1" == "" GOTO SYNTAX
CD\
DIR %1 /S
GOTO End
:Syntax
ECHO Correct syntax is: WHERE FILENAME.EXT
:End
ECHO ON
```

If hard drive C: isn't the current drive, make it the current drive before using WHERE.

If you don't remember the name of the directory, in which the word processing program Word is stored and you're also not sure whether the program file is called WORD.EXE or WORD.COM, search for it by using WORD.*. Type the following:

```
WHERE WORD.*
```

The batch file searches the entire drive and displays the directory, in which each file was found. For this example with Word, the screen display should look like the following:

```
Volume in drive C is 80MB386
 Volume Serial Number is F1F2-F3F4
Directory of C:\WORD5
WORD     EXE    637103 01-09-89   10:20a
WORD     PIF       369 11-11-89   11:11a
        2 file(s)     637472 bytes
Total files listed:
        2 file(s)     637472 bytes
                     34726784 bytes free
```

The program file is called WORD.EXE and is stored in the C:\WORD5 directory.

6.4   Starting Programs from the MS-DOS Shell

You can also start programs from the MS-DOS Shell. Using the MS-DOS Shell, there are three ways to start programs that are just as convenient as starting programs from the command line.

- Select a program from the main list.

- Select a program file or a file associated with the program from a file list.

- Select the **Run** command from the **File** menu.

The program list

If you use a particular program frequently, you should include it in the program list in either the Main group or create a new program list. These groups are displayed at the bottom of the default MS-DOS Shell screen.

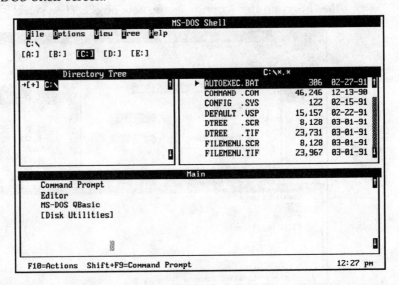

The Main group of the MS-DOS Shell is in the lower part of the window

Select the Main group either by clicking the left mouse button or by pressing the ⌞Tab⌟ key until the first item (Command Prompt) is highlighted. Now you're ready to add a new item to the program list in the Main group.

To add a program to the main list, activate the **File** menu and select the **New** command.

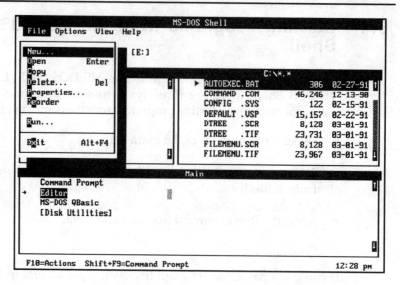

Selecting New from the File menu

A dialog box is displayed for defining a new program object. Select the "Program Item" option as the new object. Then select OK.

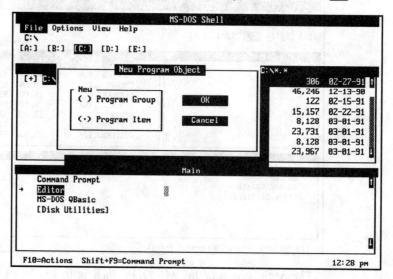

Selecting Program Item from New Program Object

Another dialog box is displayed in which you can enter the appropriate information about the file. You'll need to enter the program item to be displayed in the Main group, the command needed to start the program, the start up directory, any application shortcut key, which can be used as a "hot key" to instantly switch to the program, an optional password for access to the program and other options.

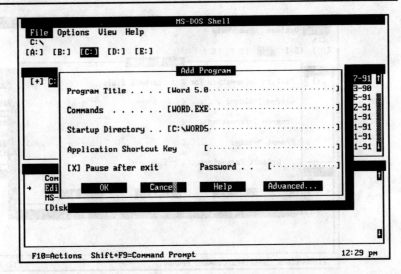

Adding a program to the Main group in the MS-DOS Shell

• The Program title text box corresponds to the name of the program as it should appear in the program list. In the above example, the program title is Word 5.0.

The Commands text box is needed to start the program. This can be the name of the program or a batch file. To start Word in the C:\WORD directory, enter C:\WORD. Just as parameters can be specified in a batch file, parameters can be passed to start a program and load a document. The command in the preceding example could be written as:

```
C:\WORD\WORD %1
```

Press (Enter) or click on "OK" with the mouse to complete the definition of the program. Next you'll be prompted to supply information that will be used when the program is called.

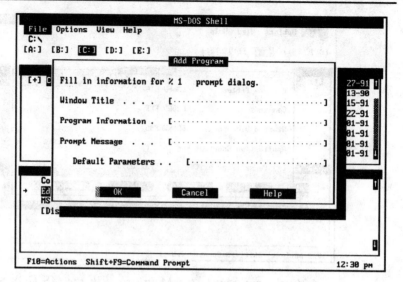

Program Item Properties dialog box

If the parameter "%1" was specified during the definition of
the program, an additional screen appears for defining specific
parameters prior to executing the program.

Enter the required information or press Enter to ignore this
prompt.

After the program has been installed on the program list as
previously described, it can be started by selecting it from the
Main group with either the mouse or the cursor keys.

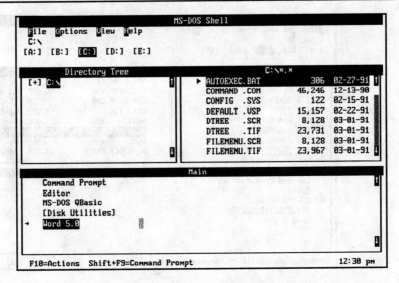

MS-DOS Shell with Word 5.0 installed as part of the Main group

The file list

Any executable program can be started from the file list, which is located on the right side of the screen. Locate the program by selecting the drive, directory and any subdirectory in the appropriate Shell areas, then, in the right area, select the program file to start.

This program file must have either a .COM, .EXE or .BAT extension. To start the program file, press Enter or use the mouse to double-click on the filename.

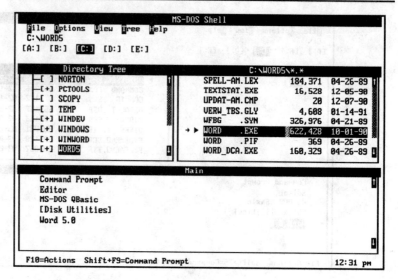

*Preparing to start WORD.EXE from the MS-DOS Shell file
list*

 Don't start TSR (Terminate and Stay Resident) programs
from the MS-DOS Shell.

The following section explains the steps for starting a program
from the file list in greater detail.

Selecting a drive

Use `Tab` to move the selection highlight in the MS-DOS Shell to
the drive icons or use the mouse pointer to point to the letter of the
required drive and press the left mouse button.

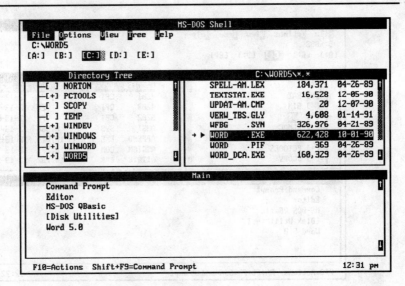

Positioning the cursor to select drive C:

Use the cursor keys to highlight the required drive. To activate this drive, press (Enter) or double-click on it with the mouse button.

The tree structure of the directories in the selected drive appears in the left area of the MS-DOS Shell, as previously shown.

Selecting a directory

Use (Tab) to activate the left area or click on the Directory Tree area with the mouse. Using either the cursor keys or the mouse to highlight (select) the required directory. The names of files stored in this directory are displayed in alphabetical order in the right area.

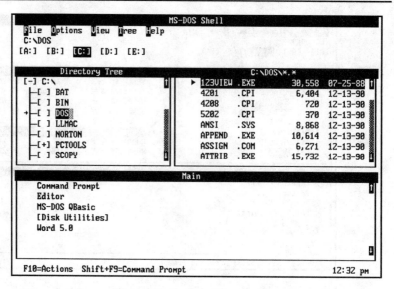

Note the arrow displayed next to the DOS directory in the Directory Tree and DOS files in the file list (right area)

Selecting (marking) a file and starting it

Use ⌈Tab⌋ to switch to the right area or select it with the mouse pointer. Select the program file to run (COM, EXE, BAT) by using the ⌈↑⌋ and ⌈↓⌋ cursor keys to move by line, the ⌈PgUp⌋ and ⌈PgDn⌋ keys to move by page or by pointing with the mouse pointer. Pressing ⌈Home⌋ moves to the top of the file list. Pressing ⌈End⌋ moves to the end of the file list.

If you're using the mouse, you can click both direction arrows on the scroll bar to scroll the contents of the file list. Clicking in the grey field enables you to jump to the next screen within the file list.

You can select the file to be run by using the ⌈↑⌋ and ⌈↓⌋ cursor keys and stopping at the desired file. The filename appears as inverse text (highlighted), which indicates that the file is marked. The program can be started by pressing ⌈Enter⌋.

If you're using a mouse, select a file by clicking the left mouse button. Double-click the left mouse button to start the program.

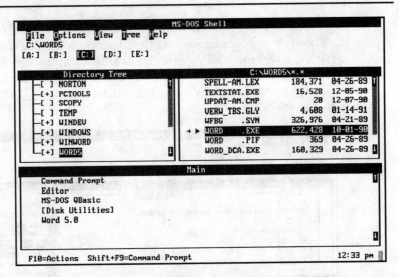

WORD.EXE in the file list is selected; pressing (Enter) *will run this program*

Searching for a file and starting it

The MS-DOS Shell simplifies searching the entire storage device for a file. Open the **File** menu and activate **Search**.

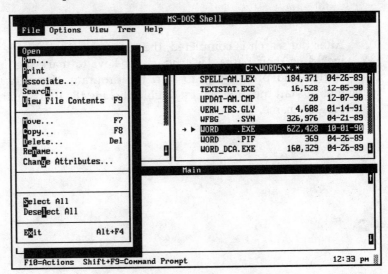

The File menu in MS-DOS Shell

After selecting the **Search** command, a dialog box, similar to the
one shown below, appears. Enter the filename you're looking for or
a partial filename along with wildcards (* and ?). Select the
"Search entire disk" item either by pressing the [Tab] key to move
the cursor to the line or by using the mouse. Press [Enter] or use the
mouse to select [OK].

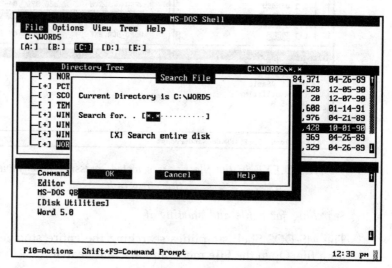

MS-DOS Shell Search dialog box

After the search is completed, the screen displays the files found,
including their paths. Use the cursor keys to mark the line to be
started and press [Enter] to start the program. If you're using a
mouse, start the program by double-clicking the line containing the
program name.

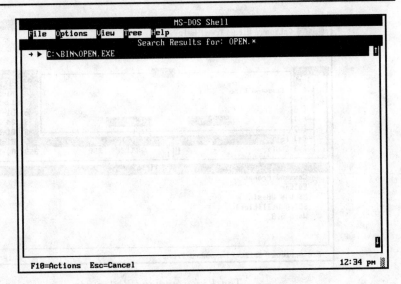

The results of searching for OPEN.*

Using RUN to start a program

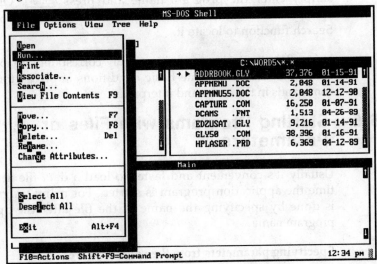

Selecting the Run... command from the File menu

The third way to start a program from the MS-DOS Shell is by using the **Run...** command from the **File** menu. When this command is activated, a dialog box appears which allows you to enter the name of the program you want to start.

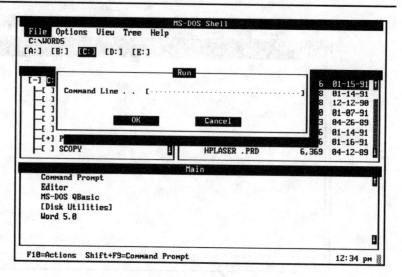

The Run command dialog box

If the program is in a directory that has been defined by PATH, simply enter the program name and press (Enter). Otherwise, specify the entire path. If the path is unknown, use the **File Search** function to locate it.

Using **Run** to start a program roughly corresponds to executing a command line. The same basic conditions apply as for entering commands in the command interpreter.

6.5 Starting Programs with Files or Parameters

Usually it's convenient and faster to load a data file at the same time the application program is started. For many programs, this is done by specifying the name of the file after the application program name.

Specifying parameters from the command area

With most application programs you can specify the data file you want to edit as part of the command line for starting a program. If you're using one directory for data files and a separate directory for the application program, change to the data directory before starting the program. The directory that contains the program file must have been defined as part of the search path set by PATH. As an alternative, you could use a batch file for starting the program.

Often other parameters can be specified when calling a program. These parameters influence the way the program works. For example, starting the Microsoft Word word processor with the /L switch starts Word and loads the file which you last edited.

The /RUN switch in QBasic, which is part of MS-DOS 6.0, runs a QBasic program without having to access the QBasic menus to load and run the QBasic program. Specify the name of the program in the command line:

```
QBASIC /RUN CASTLE
```

Parameters and filenames can also be used with the MS-DOS Shell.

Specifying parameters from the program list of the MS-DOS Shell

In order to pass parameters to an application program from the MS-DOS Shell, you must add the program to a program list and define the program line to include a dialog box ("%1") when the program is called.

Although this sounds somewhat complicated, it's actually quite easy. First select the program list area (located at the bottom of the screen). Press the Tab key or use the mouse to make this the current area. Then select the **New** command from the **File** menu.

We briefly discussed this in Section 6.4 and additional information can be found in the chapter on the MS-DOS Shell. Two parameters can be specified by using two dialog boxes ("%1" and "%2") after the name of the command.

Opening files and programs from the file list

Although additional parameters can't be specified when starting a program from the MS-DOS Shell file list, an interesting and useful option is available when you open files with this list. File extensions can be defined as being "associated" with a specific application program.

When you associate files and an application, you are specifying that any file with a particular extension is to be used with a specific application. For example, you can associate all files having the .TXT extension with the MS-DOS EDIT command. Then when you select a TXT file and open it, the MS-DOS Editor is used to edit that file.

To associate all files with the .TXT extension with EDIT, select the DOS directory in the file list and highlight the EDIT.COM program. Then select the **Associate** command in the **File** menu. In the dialog box, enter the file extensions that should be associated with the program in the line labeled "Extensions". In this example, type TXT. Pressing (Enter) completes the association. Note that multiple file extensions can be associated with a single program.

Even though twenty extensions can be associated with a program file, a specific extension can be associated with only one program. For example, .TXT can be associated with the MS-DOS Editor (the EDIT command) but it can't also be associated with Microsoft Word 5.0.

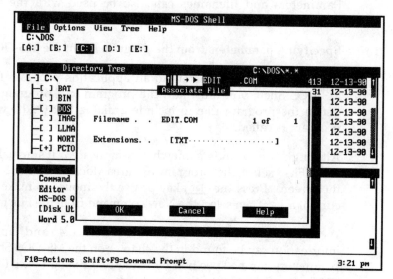

The Associate File dialog box

Now when you activate a file, with the .TXT extension, in the file list by pressing (Enter) or by double-clicking the mouse button, EDIT is automatically called with the file so that you can edit the file.

You could also associate the .BAT extension with the EDIT program. This would enable you to make changes in the AUTOEXEC.BAT or any batch file, very easily. Simply double-click on the batch file in the file list and it automatically loads into EDIT.

6.6 Quitting Programs

Most programs have a special command for exiting the program. Refer to the program's user manual for specific instructions. If the application program requires a large amount of memory, a part of the command interpreter is removed from the memory. The command interpreter must later be reloaded into memory when you exit from such a program.

Never switch off the computer without first exiting the application program properly. If you just switch off the computer, you may lose some of your data. If there is a power failure while using a program or if the computer seems to be dead (no response to the keyboard, etc.), restart the computer and use CHKDSK /F to check the hard drive or diskette for any possible problems.

If you're using MS-DOS from a hard drive and you're still prompted to insert a diskette with COMMAND.COM when you exit an application program, then you can use the following command that tells DOS where on the hard drive to find the command interpreter. If the COMMAND.COM file is in the root directory, the command line looks like the following:

```
SET COMSPEC=C:\COMMAND.COM
```

If the command interpreter is in a subdirectory of the hard drive, enter the complete path. Of course, you can insert this command into your AUTOEXEC.BAT file.

Quitting the MS-DOS Shell

Never exit the MS-DOS Shell by simply switching off your computer. Quit the MS-DOS Shell by pressing Alt + F4 or F3 to ensure that there are no more programs in the list of active programs (the Task Switcher, which will be discussed later) and all of the settings of the MS-DOS Shell have been saved to the MS-DOS Shell INI file.

The MS-DOS Shell INI file (DOSSHELL.INI) contains information about changes and preferences you've selected for the MS-DOS Shell. Simply switching off your computer won't save any of these settings. So this information will be lost.

6.7 Avoiding Problems with Programs

By taking simple precautions, you can avoid potential problems with application programs. The following are the most important features and precautions to keep in mind.

Backing up data

Plan for safe guarding your data while you're installing a new application program on your hard drive. Install the program in it's own subdirectory and set up another subdirectory for storing the data created with the application program. After it's installed, it's not as easy to change the way in which the data is stored.

Setting the time and the date

If your computer doesn't have a real time clock, add the MS-DOS DATE and TIME commands to your AUTOEXEC.BAT file and enter the current values when starting your computer. The date and time stamps will help you determine which version of a file is most recent. Users frequently create several versions of a basic document and then aren't able to tell them apart. So the date and time of a file stored in the directory can be very helpful.

As we previously explained, you can also use the XCOPY, MSBACKUP and RESTORE commands to back up and restore data created before or after a certain date. This makes protecting your data easier because you can be much more selective about which files are backed up.

Many users don't back up their data because it seems inconvenient and tedious to spend time doing a back up. However, by storing your data in specific subdirectories, and following a few simple procedures, the amount of time spent backing up data can be reduced to a few minutes.

Separating programs and data

Create directories for application programs and their associated data. This saves time and energy when backing up data. Usually an installed program only needs to be backed up once because the program can be reinstalled from the original diskettes. However, since the data that's created is often changed, it needs to be backed up at regular intervals.

You should also divide data among several directories and ensure that a directory doesn't contain more data than will fit on a single diskette. This enables you to perform backups quickly and easily. Simply use the COPY command to back up data from each directory onto a diskette.

Choosing filenames

If the application program doesn't automatically assign filenames or extensions (.DOC for document files from a word processor), be sure that you choose filenames that match. This will enable you to use COPY or XCOPY with wildcards in order to copy all of the data that belong together.

Example 1

Suppose that you have spent time creating illustrations, tables and texts for a report. The files all have different filename extensions since each application program creates a different file type. Create a separate directory for all of the files associated with the report so that all of the data can be backed up easily.

If for some reason this can't be done, start each filename with the same characters (e.g., REP for report). Then all of the files on the entire hard drive that are associated with the report can be backed up to diskettes with a simple command:

```
BACKUP C:\REP*.* A: /S
```

Example 2

If you work primarily with a word processor and all of your text files have the .DOC extension, you can back them up like this:

- If the files will all fit on a diskette, type:

```
XCOPY *.DOC A: /S
```

- To backup all of the text files on the hard drive, even if all of the files won't fit on a single diskette, use the following command:

```
BACKUP C:\*.TXT A: /S
```

The /S switch specifies that the command applies to all of the subdirectories.

If you've created so much data for a project that backing up the entire directory is too complicated (requiring several diskettes) and the data that has been changed doesn't exceed the capacity of a single diskette, create a special batch file that only backs up the data that has been changed. Place this special PCX-DOC.BAT batch file in the same directory as the data.

For example, the PCX-DOC.BAT file could copy all files with the
.DOC extension and all illustrations with the .PCX extension onto
a diskette:

```
@ECHO OFF
ECHO Back up data to a diskette
ECHO Please insert diskette and press any key
PAUSE
COPY *.DOC A:
COPY *.PCX A:
ECHO Data backed up
ECHO ON
```

If all of the data won't fit on one diskette, use PCX-DOC2.BAT
listed below, which uses XCOPY with the /M switch to copy only
the files, that have changed, onto multiple diskettes:

```
@ECHO OFF
ECHO Back up data to a diskette
ECHO Please insert text diskette and press any key
PAUSE
XCOPY *.DOC A: /M
ECHO Please insert illustration diskette and
ECHO press any key
PAUSE
XCOPY *.PCX A: /M
ECHO Data backed up
ECHO ON
```

You can find more information about backing up data in the
corresponding chapter of this book. Remember that dividing the
disk into specific directories and arranging data properly can
make data security and working with application programs much
easier.

Avoiding problems with certain MS-DOS commands

Certain MS-DOS commands are more prone to problems than
others. Here are a few areas to watch out for:

Problems with APPEND

APPEND lets MS-DOS use a file even if it's not in the current
directory without having to specify the entire path of that file.

Not all application programs nor even all MS-DOS commands
(such as COPY, DEL or RENAME) can use the APPEND command.
Some application programs are unable to process files that aren't
in the current directory. For example, Microsoft Word 5.0 does not
recognize the settings of the APPEND command.

Some application programs may also have problems with files in the search path. Although the program can read the file correctly, the file is saved in the current directory, not the original directory. If you notice an application program having these problems, don't use APPEND.

In general, APPEND shouldn't be used on directories with data that is processed. You can use APPEND for directories that contain the help files for a program (help texts, spell checker etc.).

Example

Your current directory is C:\PROG1 and you use APPEND to set a search path to the C:\DATA1 directory. This directory (C:\DATA1) contains the LETTER.DOC file. Start an application that uses the LETTER.DOC without specifying a path. Because APPEND was set, MS-DOS finds the file and loads it. However, when you save the file, the original version remains unchanged in the C:\DATA1 directory and a new modified version is saved in the C:\PRG1 directory. Not only have you wasted storage space, but since there are several versions of this file, you may accidentally work with an older version of the file rather than the newest version.

Problems with FASTOPEN

FASTOPEN speeds up access to the data on your hard drive by returning the physical disk location of files on the hard drive in memory. When a file is opened multiple times, its location is already in memory and therefore need not be retrieved from the hard drive again. This technique greatly speeds up retrieval of data from the file whenever applications use these files frequently.

Because of this technique, you may have problems with programs that change the location of a file on the hard drive (programs for hard drive optimization, such as SD.EXE from Norton Utilities, COMPRESS.EXE from PC Tools and BeckerTools Compress from Abacus). Don't use FASTOPEN while using these or similar programs. If different programs collide, it will not only crash your computer, but can also cause considerable loss of data.

Special features of TSR programs

Terminate and Stay Resident programs remain in the memory of the computer after being run. Usually you can activate this type of program by pressing a "hot" key.

Many driver programs (e.g., mouse drivers such as MOUSE.COM) are also kept in the memory after being started. You may encounter several problems when working with these kinds of programs:

Memory space

Each TSR or driver program reduces the amount of available memory in the computer. This can prevent large application programs from running or reduce the amount of available memory for processing data.

Sequence of programs

TSR programs change important information in the memory of your computer. These changes can cause problems, especially when you're using multiple TSR programs. Do not assign identical hot keys (key press combinations for activating a TSR program). Refer to the TSR's documentation pertaining to the sequence in which TSR's should be started.

Unfortunately, many software developers insist their TSR be started first. However, this can't always be done, specially if more than one TSR has this same requirement. You may have to experiment to find out which sequence of programs can work.

Hotkeys

Also remember that you can't use a key combination which calls a TSR program in any other application program. Doing this interferes with important program functions. For example, if a TSR program uses [Alt] + [F] to start, this key combination can't be used in Microsoft Word because it always activates the TSR program. Many TSR programs allow you to choose any key combination for starting when you install the program. Use this option to avoid conflicts with application programs.

Don't start TSR programs from within application programs

Many application programs let you use an MS-DOS command from within the application itself. When using Microsoft Word 5.0, for example, you can use the LIBRARY RUN command to execute an MS-DOS command. However, this command should never be used to install TSR programs.

For example, if you forgot to start the mouse driver for your word processor, quit the word processing program using the command for quitting, start the driver program and start the word processor again. Otherwise, you might have problems with memory management. You might not be able to start any other program after quitting the word processor.

TSR programs in the MS-DOS Shell

You should remember some special features when working with the MS-DOS Shell. If you want to use a TSR program for your entire work session, start it before starting the MS-DOS Shell. For example, if you need to use the editing and macro capabilities of DOSKEY (supplied with MS-DOS 6.0), start DOSKEY in your AUTOEXEC.BAT file before starting the MS-DOS Shell.

Everything we've discussed about starting TSR programs from application programs also applies to the MS-DOS Shell. Using [Shift] + [F9] or selecting MS-DOS Command Prompt leaves the MS-DOS Shell and goes to the command interpreter. Don't use this option to install TSR programs.

For example, if you forgot to start PRINT, press [Alt] + [F4] to quit the MS-DOS Shell, start PRINT and then call the MS-DOS Shell a second time. Starting PRINT from within the MS-DOS Shell could cause problems with memory management. You might not be able to start any other programs after leaving the MS-DOS Shell.

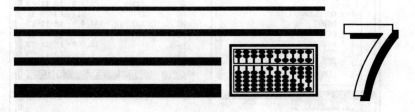

Chapter

7

The MS-DOS Shell

The Shell is an alternate way of working with DOS. Instead of having to type commands at the system prompt, the Shell lets you select the desired commands and programs from pull-down menus.

SAA Interface

The Shell was first introduced in DOS in Version 4.0. For MS-DOS 5.0 and 6.0, the appearance and operation of the Shell has changed to conform to the SAA (System Application Architecture) standard.

The SAA standard was designed to create a user interface that is both uniform and user-friendly. This can significantly decrease the time needed to learn how to use different programs. The SAA standard also contains guidelines for exchanging data, which makes it easier to share data between different programs.

Simple operation with the mouse

The Shell lets you use the most important operating system commands and applications by using an easy-to-operate menu system. It's especially easy to use the Shell if you have a mouse attached to your computer. This makes it even easier to move, select and use the various commands. You'll find that using the mouse simplifies your work with DOS.

Customizing the MS-DOS Shell

The Shell is very versatile. You can use the Shell as it comes from Microsoft or you can adapt it to fit your own needs by integrating new groups and programs.

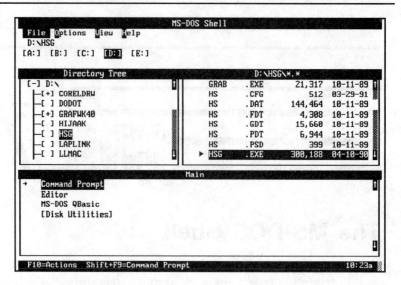

The MS-DOS Shell

The Shell is designed for two very different types of users. It helps novice users operate a computer and use DOS without completely understanding complicated commands and the command interpreter.

It also lets experienced users set up a computer that is custom-made to their individual needs. The Shell has many options for customizing the user interface that exceed the capabilities of other user interfaces.

7.1   Overview

The MS-DOS Shell is the graphical user interface of MS-DOS. It provides users with an alternative to the line oriented interface of the COMMAND.COM command interpreter.

Starting the MS-DOS Shell

To start the MS-DOS Shell, enter DOSSHELL. If you want the MS-DOS Shell to load automatically each time you start the computer, add this command to the AUTOEXEC.BAT.

The MS-DOS Shell screen layout

The menu bar is located at the top of the screen; the drive icons are located below the menu bar. The rest of the screen is divided into an area for the File Manager, which is used for working with files, hard drives/diskettes and directories, and an area for the Program Manager, from where you can easily start programs.

Working with menus

Use the mouse or press [Alt] to activate the menus at the top of the screen. Within the menus, move the highlight with the cursor keys and press [Enter] to make a selection.

Working with windows

Press [Tab] to change to the windows of the File Manager, the Program Manager or to change to the drive icons. If you are working with the mouse, simply click on the desired element.

Dialog boxes and check boxes

Press [Tab] to select the check boxes in the dialog box. Use the [Spacebar] to enable and disable the check boxes.

Selecting a drive

To make a new drive active for the File Manager, keep pressing [Tab] until the drive line is highlighted, use the cursor keys to select the desired drive and press [Enter]. With the mouse, simply click on the desired drive.

Changing directories

In the "Directory Tree" display of the directories, you can highlight directories with the cursor keys; the MS-DOS Shell immediately displays the files in the directory. After selecting a directory, use [+] and [-] to show or hide subdirectories.

Selecting files

Use the cursor keys to select files and press [Shift]. To select more than one file, hold down the [Ctrl] key while selecting. To select multiple non-consecutive files, press [Shift], choose the file with the cursor keys and press [Ctrl]. With the mouse, click on the file to select it. To select several consecutive files, hold down [Shift] and click on the last file in the group. With the mouse, press [Shift] and click on files to select multiple non-consecutive files.

File operations

To perform file operations like copying, deleting, opening and renaming files, select the files and then choose the command from the File menu.

Working with groups

Groups in the MS-DOS Shell are like directories for combining data and keeping them organized.

Groups in the Program Manager are enclosed in brackets. To select a group, use the cursor keys to move the highlight to the group and then press [Enter]. To create a new group, choose New from the File menu.

Working with programs

MS-DOS Shell programs are different from application programs, because they contain only information about the program, instead of the actual program. Start a program from the Program Manager by selecting it and pressing [Enter]. To add a new program, choose the New command from the File menu.

Working with several programs

You can start several programs in the Program Manager of the MS-DOS Shell. To do this, select Enable Task Swapper in the Options menu. Press [+] to switch between different running programs. Press [+] to return to the MS-DOS Shell.

Associating files with programs

You can associate specific file extensions with a program so that you can start up a file and its program at the same time. To do this, select the file, choose Associate from the File menu and specify the program in the dialog box. Then you can start the file by selecting it and pressing [Enter] or by double-clicking the file with the mouse. The file starts along with the program associated with it.

7.2 Advantages of the MS-DOS Shell

The MS-DOS Shell gives the user a predefined way to "talk" to MS-DOS. Since the Shell graphically presents file, directory and program information on the screen, it can organize and simplify the routine computing tasks that the user needs to perform.

How does the Shell simplify a user's work? Let's use a short example - making a copy of a file. To perform this task from the command line you might type:

```
COPY myfile.txt newfile.txt
```

Of course this isn't a very difficult task to perform. But in order to type the previous command to perform this simple task, we had to know several things:

- The name and spelling of the command - Copy

- That the name of the source file must be typed after the command

- The exact spelling of the source file - myfile.txt

- That the name of the target file must be typed after the source filename

- The exact spelling of the target file - newfile.txt

- That a space must be inserted between the source and target filename

However, by using the Shell you can easily select the file from a list and select the task from a pull-down menu. This is easier because you don't have to memorize the command name and syntax.

Installing the MS-DOS Shell

When you install MS-DOS 6.0 on your hard drive, you copy four files that are required by the Shell. These files are: DOSSHELL.EXE, which is a program file; DOSSHELL.HLP, which is an information file to teach you about using the Shell; DOSSHELL.VID, which contains hardware information for the Shell; DOSSHELL.INI, which contains configuration data for the Shell. You won't be able to run the Shell unless all of these files were installed during installation.

7.2.1   MS-DOS Shell Basics

The MS-DOS Shell simplifies two important areas of personal computing:

- Managing files and directories

- Running programs

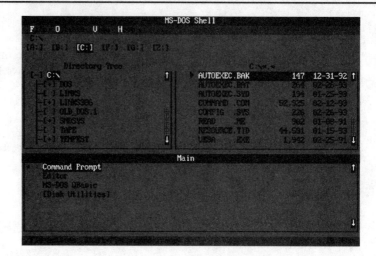

The MS-DOS Shell

Managing files and directories with the MS-DOS Shell

The Shell simplifies your work with files and directories. The Shell file list and Directory Tree areas present the directory and filenames of a floppy diskette or hard drive in one of several *views*.

By selecting one of the commands in the **View** menu, you can increase or decrease the amount of information on the screen. This decreases the amount of "clutter" on the screen. You can easily create and change directories or copy, compare, delete and rename files, for example.

Running programs from the MS-DOS Shell

The Shell also lets you start programs. The Shell's program list area displays all of the programs you can select and start. To start a program, select it using the cursor keys and press (Enter) or double-click the mouse button.

You can also group programs. When programs are grouped, the group name appears in the list rather than the names of the individual programs. Selecting the group displays the names of all programs belonging to this group. By using this method, you can organize the programs on your disk more effectively.

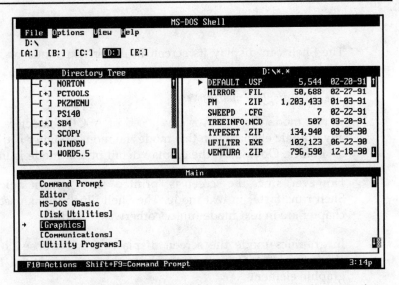

Program groups have been added to the program list area for user convenience

7.2.2   Opening the MS-DOS Shell

When you start the Shell with the DOSSHELL command, the screen that's displayed is quite different from the usual command line and system prompt. By pressing a few keys or by moving the mouse around and clicking, you can perform many operations without typing the DOS commands.

Using the mouse

It's very easy to operate the MS-DOS Shell with the mouse. Moving the mouse on your desk causes the mouse pointer to move on the screen. This lets you position the mouse pointer (a small rectangular block or arrow) over different commands, groups or items.

Pressing down the left mouse button selects a command. This is called "clicking". Pressing the mouse button twice is called "double-clicking".

Unlike selecting a command from the keyboard, double-clicking activates a command. Depending on the command, this action can have several effects.

The MS-DOS Shell Screen

The Shell can display its screen in either text mode or graphics mode.

The two display modes

In text mode the screen is composed of ASCII characters without any graphic elements. In this mode the mouse pointer is displayed as a block. Obviously, the display detail in text mode is limited.

However, since the screen is "printed" or re-drawn quickly, the Shell runs faster in text mode. The Shell illustrations used in this chapter are in text mode (unless otherwise noted).

In graphics mode the screen display isn't composed of ASCII characters, but of individual pixels that are combined to make graphic elements.

Symbols that appear as brackets or letters in text mode are displayed as icons or small pictures in graphics mode.

In graphics mode the mouse pointer is displayed as a small diagonal arrow that changes in appearance under certain conditions. Although graphics mode gives you greater detail, the speed of the display is slower than in text mode.

The following illustration shows the MS-DOS Shell in graphics mode. Although this display differs slightly from the display in text mode, closer examination reveals that it contains the same basic information.

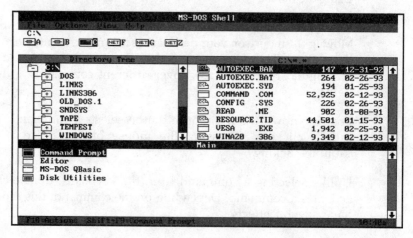

The MS-DOS Shell in graphics mode

The screen layout

Some parts of the MS-DOS Shell screen appear the same, whether you're using the Shell's text or graphics mode. For example, the top screen line always displays "MS-DOS Shell".

The menu bar

The menu bar is the second line of the screen. It contains the title of the menus. These titles vary depending on whether the view is set for the file list area, Directory Tree area or program list area.

When you select one of the menus, you will "pull down" a list of commands beneath that menu title (hence, the term pull-down menus).

To activate the menu bar, press [Alt] or [F10]. To select or pull-down one of the menus, press the letter of the underlined character in the menu title. Alternatively, you can press the [←] or [→] cursor keys to highlight the desired menu title and then press [Enter]. To select one of the menus with the mouse, click on the menu title.

The title bar

Each area has its own title bar, which contains the title (the subject) of the area. For example, if the view is set to program list, the title bar contains the name of the active group. In the following example, the title bar contains "Main". This is the default group.

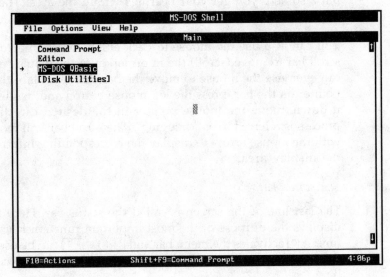

The MS-DOS Shell displaying only the program list area

The title bar displays the words "Directory Tree" above the area of the screen that displays the names of the subdirectories. Above the area of the screen that displays the file list, the title bar contains the full path of the current directory.

If more than one area of the screen is displayed, you can switch between the two areas by pressing the (Tab) key. To select one of the areas with the mouse, move the mouse pointer to the title bar of the desired area and click.

The scroll bars

Each area of the Shell has a vertical grey bar along its right border, which contains a direction arrow pointing up and down. This is the scroll bar. If an area contains more information than will fit in the area, a grey slider bar appears in the scroll bar.

The slider bar indicates the relative position of the information that is displayed. If the slider bar is positioned at the top of the scroll bar, then the top portion of the information is being displayed. If the bar is in the middle of the scroll bar, you are seeing the middle portion of the information and if it appears at the bottom of the scroll bar, the end of the information is displayed.

To move the contents of the area, press the (↑) and (↓) cursor keys or the (PgUp) and (PgDn) keys. Notice that the scroll bar moves as you press the keys. Scroll bars not only help you move within an area, but also help you get your bearings within the area. They are an important component of the SAA concept.

You can also use the mouse to click either direction arrow of the scroll bar to move (scroll) the information in the display area. You can even use the mouse to move the bar directly. Place the mouse pointer on the bar, press the left mouse button and, while holding it down, move the mouse pointer in the desired direction. This process is referred to as "dragging". The scroll bar will move along with the mouse arrow to display the corresponding information in the display area.

The status bar

The last line of the screen is called the status bar. Here the Shell displays the purpose of the most important function keys and the time. (F10) activates the menu bar and (Shift) + (F9) can be used to exit the MS-DOS Shell to enter commands on the MS-DOS command line.

You can later return to the MS-DOS Shell by typing "EXIT". The right corner of the status bar displays the current time or system time. Occasionally messages and prompts also appear on this line (e.g., "Insert diskette in drive B: and press any key").

7.3 MS-DOS Shell Fundamentals

Since the MS-DOS Shell is based on the SAA standard, the individual work areas operate in similar ways. So we'll only summarize the basic processes.

7.3.1 Working in an area

As we mentioned in the introduction, after starting the MS-DOS Shell, the file list area, the Directory Tree area and the program list area are displayed. The logical drives of your PC are displayed between the menu bar and the title bars of the file list area and Directory Tree area.

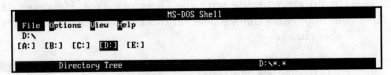

List of logical drives in the MS-DOS Shell

The logical drives

This line is referred to as the "drive icons" and is always on the screen when **Program/File List** from the **View** menu is selected. By selecting the drive you can decide which storage media contents will be displayed by the Directory Tree area. When the MS-DOS Shell is started, the drive icons are displayed as the first area.

To select a new drive, use the → and ← keys to select the appropriate icon and activate it with the Spacebar or by pressing Enter. You can also change the active drive by pressing Ctrl + drive letter. For example, press Ctrl + A to change the current drive to drive A:. Pressing Ctrl + C changes the current drive to drive C:.

The mouse can be used to click directly on the desired drive icon to activate it and to display its Directory Tree and file list areas.

Double-clicking the left mouse button while pointing to a drive icon causes the file information to be read again. This is useful after you've changed a diskette in the selected drive. You can also force the selected drive to be re-read from the keyboard by selecting the drive icon and pressing Enter.

Changing areas with Tab

After selecting the desired drive, use Tab to change to the next area. Each time Tab is pressed the active area changes from right to left and from top to bottom. Pressing Shift + Tab changes the areas in reverse order. This enables you to move the selection cursor to the desired area very quickly.

Using the mouse is an even faster way to activate an area. Point to the title bar of an area and click the left mouse button. You can also click any item within the area to activate that area. This process also selects the item within the area. However, you may not want to select this item.

When changing from either the Directory Tree area or file list area to the program list area (or vice versa), the entries in the menu bar are changed. The program list area doesn't have the **Tree** menu for working with the Directory Tree. However, this is the most obvious change. The various menu commands and their effects also change.

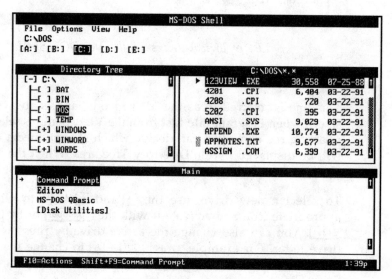

MS-DOS Shell with the program list area activated

7.3.2 Using the pull-down menus

The menu bar contains the names of the pull-down menus. A menu contains a list of commands that can be selected and activated.

Pressing ⟨Alt⟩ or ⟨F10⟩ activates the menu bar from the keyboard.

You can tell that the menu bar is activated because "File" appears in inverse video (the background changes color). Also, each title in the menu bar either has its first letter underlined (graphics mode), has a colored mark (text mode in color) or has a selection cursor (monochrome text mode).

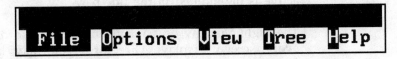

Menu bar activated in low resolution text mode

There are different methods for opening one of these pull-down menus and accessing the desired command.

Selecting a menu with the cursor key

After the menu bar is activated, the ⟨→⟩ and ⟨←⟩ cursor keys can be used to select the desired menu. Then use the ⟨↑⟩ or ⟨↓⟩ cursor keys to open the menu.

When the menu opens, use the ⟨↑⟩ or ⟨↓⟩ cursor keys to select one of the commands. Press ⟨Enter⟩ to activate a command.

Selecting a menu with the letter keys

Another, faster option for selecting a menu consists of pressing the letter keys. Just press the first letter in the name and the pull-down menu will open. You can also use the letter keys to select commands.

After opening the menu, press the highlighted letter of the activated command to perform the function.

Selecting a menu with the mouse

Another way to select a menu is by using the mouse. Click on the desired menu title to open the pull-down menu. You can also click on each command in the open menu.

You can determine whether a command can be activated by its appearance on the screen. Depending on the setting of the screen (graphics or text) and the color (color or monochrome), the commands that cannot be activated are either invisible or dimmed (have a colored or grey background).

We'll discuss how to use the **Colors...** and **Display...** commands of the **Options** menu later in this chapter.

 The menu titles and commands change when you switch among the file list area, Directory Tree area and the program list area. Usually, the area that is currently active is highlighted in the title bar.

The highlight may occasionally be difficult to detect in every screen display. Therefore, you may have to experiment before you determine whether the area is currently active. Usually the cursor keys can be used to move the selection cursor within the area.

For example, as you can see in the following picture, the **File** menu has five activated commands when the Directory Tree area is active. You cannot activate a command such as **Print** or **View File Contents** because these commands are dimmed.

```
┌─────────────────────────────────┐
│  File  Options  View  Tre       │
│ ┌───────────────────────────┐   │
│ │ Open                      │   │
│ │ Run...                    │   │
│ │                           │   │
│ │ Search...                 │   │
│ │                           │   │
│ │                           │   │
│ │                           │   │
│ │                           │   │
│ │                           │   │
│ │ Create Directory...       │   │
│ │                           │   │
│ │                           │   │
│ │ Exit              Alt+F4  │   │
│ └───────────────────────────┘   │
└─────────────────────────────────┘
```

File menu with Directory
Tree area active

However, when you activate the file list area (by pressing Tab) until the area is highlighted), many more commands are active in the **File** menu:

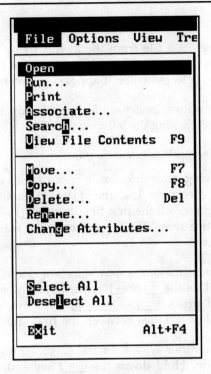

File menu with file list area active

7.3.3 Selecting files and other elements

The commands of the pull-down menus (especially those of the
File menu) only work when you use them on an element such as a
group, a program, a directory or a file. So you must select one of
these elements before the command is activated. For example, to
copy a file, you must first select the file.

Selecting files

Use either the cursor keys or the mouse to select the directory in
the left area of the screen (the Directory Tree area). Notice that
as you select different directories, files in that directory appear in
the file list area (right area of the screen).

Use [Tab] to switch to the file list area, where you can select files to
be edited. Use either the [↑] or [↓] cursor keys or the mouse and the
scroll bar to select the file.

Selecting one file

You can select a file from the keyboard by using the ⬆ and ⬇ cursor keys to move the selection cursor to the desired file. A filename is selected when it appears in inverse video.

With the mouse, select a file by pointing to it with the mouse pointer and clicking the left mouse button.

Selecting several consecutive files

The following procedure can be used to select several consecutive files in a directory. Use the ⬆ or ⬇ cursor keys to place the selection cursor on the first file. Press (Shift) + (F8) to switch on add mode (notice that "ADD" appears in the status bar at the bottom of the screen).

In add mode, making a new selection doesn't cancel the previous selection. Use the ⬆ or ⬇ cursor keys to select the last file in the series and press (Shift) + (Spacebar). This extends the selection to include all of the files between the first and the last file.

There is another way to mark several files when add mode is switched on. Hold down the (Shift) key and press ⬆ or ⬇. This moves the selection through the list, automatically selecting each file that it touches.

When add mode is switched on, you can cancel a selection by pressing the (Spacebar) to select the file a second time. The (Spacebar) works like a switch that switches back and forth between the two states.

 Selecting several files in the MS-DOS Shell is similar to using wildcards in the command line. Although the only way to handle several files from the command line is if they have the same name (BOOK.* or *.EXE), the MS-DOS Shell is much more flexible. The files can be displayed in different ways. However, the displayed sequence of files in the MS-DOS Shell can be specified alphabetically, according to file extension, etc. This assures that the desired files appear together.

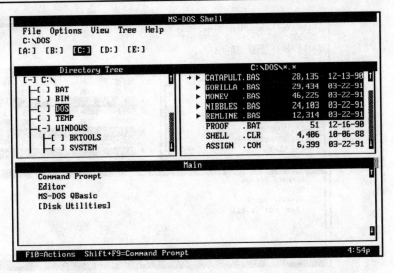

Several consecutive files selected in the file list area

Press Shift + F8 again to switch off add mode. The status bar changes back to its original configuration.

To select multiple files with the mouse, click the first file, hold down the Shift key, click the last file and release Shift. This selects the first and last file, in addition to all files in between. To cancel the selection of the last file, hold down the Shift key and click the scroll bar.

Selecting multiple non-consecutive files

Use the ↑ or ↓ cursor keys to select the first file. Press Shift + F8 to activate add mode. Use the cursor keys again to choose the next file and press the Spacebar to select it. Continue this process until all desired files are selected. To cancel the selection of a file, use the cursor keys to select it and press the Spacebar again.

Press Shift + F8 to switch add mode off again.

If you are using a mouse, click on the first file to select it. Then hold down the Ctrl key and point and click on the next file to select it. Continue until all of the necessary files have been selected. Release Ctrl. To move within the area, you can also hold down Ctrl and click the scroll bar.

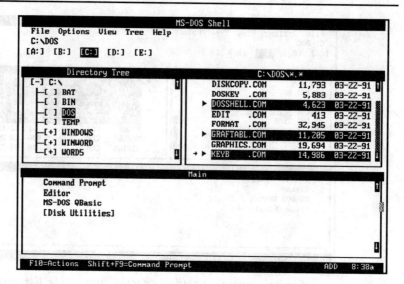

Several non-consecutive files selected in the file list area

Selecting groups and programs

There's an even easier way to select files. You can select groups of files or programs defined in the program list area. Use either the ⬆ or ⬇ cursor keys or click the mouse once to select the group or program. You can also use the commands from the pull-down menu.

To start a program, either press Enter or double-click on the program name in the file list or program list areas. Double-clicking on a group in the program list area causes the contents of the group to be displayed.

Each group has a menu command called Main, which can be used to return to the main group. Pressing Esc moves one level higher within nested groups.

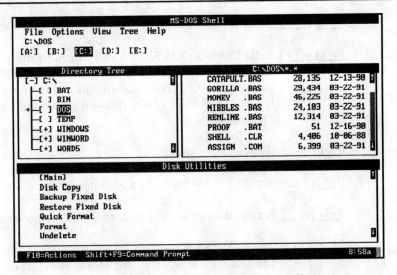

The Disk Utilities group open in the program list area; note the command [Main] for returning to the top level

How the keyboard operates in the MS-DOS Shell

The following is an overview of the functions provided by the keyboard in the MS-DOS Shell:

Enter	Activates a selected command, starts a selected program or confirms an entry. When a drive icon is selected, pressing Enter reads the directory structure of the drive again.
Esc	Use this key to terminate a selected menu or a dialog box. If you are in a group, pressing Esc takes you to the next highest group.
Alt	Activates the menu bar.
F1	Use this key to call for help in the MS-DOS Shell. The MS-DOS Shell displays the help screen of the currently selected command.
F2	Pressing F2 copies programs to another group.
F3	Pressing F3 exits the MS-DOS Shell and returns to the MS-DOS command line at the system prompt.
Alt + F4	Leaves the MS-DOS Shell and returns to the command line of MS-DOS.

Shift + F8   Switches add mode on and off for selecting files.

Shift + F9   Exits the MS-DOS Shell and returns to the command line of MS-DOS; the MS-DOS Shell remains resident in the background of the conventional memory. Typing the MS-DOS EXIT command will return you to the MS-DOS Shell.

F10   Activates the menu bar.

PgUp   Scrolls the contents of an area up a page at a time.

PgDn   Scrolls the contents of an area down a page at a time.

Spacebar   The Spacebar is used to select or unselect files in the file list area when the add mode is switched on. If a dialog box is active, certain options can be switched on and off with the Spacebar. If the drive icon area is active, the Spacebar can be used to switch to another drive.

Tab   Use Tab to move between areas of the MS-DOS Shell. If a dialog box is active, press Tab to move to the next dialog item. Shift + Tab moves the cursor to the previous item.

7.4   Working with Groups and Programs

DOS 6.0 makes it easy to run programs from the MS-DOS Shell. When you use the **View** menu to select either the **Program/File List** or the **Program List** command, the Shell displays groups and programs in the program list area. By grouping programs you can set up a computer that even inexperienced users are able to operate easily.

7.4.1   Groups and programs

A group is a set of one or more programs. You can arbitrarily "collect" programs into a group and then later view the contents of the group, select one of the programs from the list and then run it. By combining similar programs into groups, you can organize the MS-DOS Shell.

When you install DOS 6.0, you automatically set up a group called Main. When you select **Program/File List** or **Program List** from the **View** menu, the Main screen will look as follows:

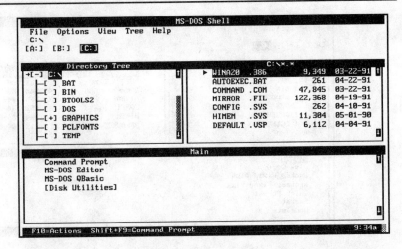

The program list showing the entries of the Main group

Notice that the group name is in the title bar of the program list area. You can see from the list that this group contains four entries: Command Prompt, Editor, MS-DOS QBasic and [Disk Utilities].

Since the first three entries are programs, they're listed without brackets. They are the command line system prompt (which isn't really a program but a way to enter a DOS command from the Shell), the MS-DOS Editor program EDIT and the QBasic programming language.

Since the last entry is enclosed within brackets, it must be the name of another group. This group is called the Disk Utilities group.

All you need to do to run a program is to select a program entry. When a program is run, the MS-DOS Shell "goes to sleep" and the selected program is started. You interact with the program just as if you had started it from the DOS command line. When you exit from that program, you return to the MS-DOS Shell which then "wakes up" again.

If you select a group entry, then the contents of that group are displayed in the program list area. So if you select the [Disk Utilities] group, you would see the following on the screen:

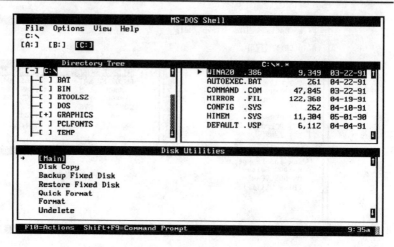

*The program list showing the entries of the Disk Utilities
group*

Again notice that the group name "Disk Utilities" appears in the
title bar. The programs in the Disk Utilities group are used for
maintaining the files on your disk. Running these programs is an
alternate way of performing file and disk operations using
commands that you type at the command prompt.

You'll see an entry for the Main group at the top of the list. By
selecting Main, you can move back to the next highest group.

7.4.2   Starting programs

It's very easy to start programs from the program list area. Use the
⬆ or ⬇ cursor keys to select the desired program entry and press
Enter.

Selecting and running a program is even easier with a mouse. Move
the mouse pointer to the program entry and double-click the left
mouse button.

The program icon

In the graphics mode of the MS-DOS Shell program, entries are
displayed with an icon to the left of the entry. This icon resembles
a box with a horizontal line near the top. A group entry will have
an icon with six small rectangles within the icon.

In text mode, groups in the program list are enclosed in brackets, as
the following shows:

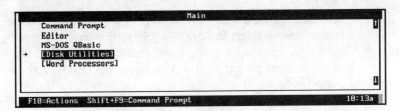

Groups are enclosed in brackets when MS-DOS Shell is in text mode

A dialog box appears if a program requires one or more parameters to start. Type the required information in the text box and press ⌜Enter⌝.

For example, both the MS-DOS Editor and MS-DOS QBasic ask you to enter a filename.

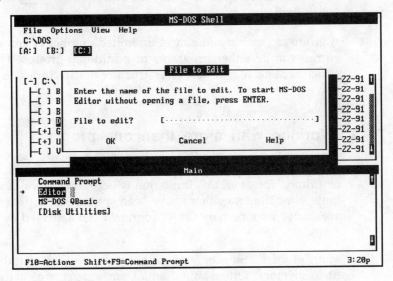

The MS-DOS Editor dialog box

7.4.3 Selecting groups

A menu line containing a group of programs is called a program group.

The group icon

In graphics mode, a group appears as an icon to the left of the group name. The icon is a rectangle with six small rectangles inside. In text mode, a group appears with its name in brackets.

Selecting a group is as easy as starting a program. Use the ⬆ or ⬇ cursor keys to select the desired program group and press (Enter). It's even easier to start a group with a mouse. Move the mouse pointer to the desired program group and double-click with the left mouse button.

After a group is selected, the screen displays the contents of the group. The title bar changes from Main to the name of the selected group (for example, Disk Utilities). Each program group display has a line, at the top of the menu, that contains the name of the next higher group.

If the next higher group is the Main group, then "Main" is displayed. Pressing (Esc) or double-clicking on the top line of each group takes you to the next higher group level. The ⬆ or (PgUp) keys can also be used to select the entry. Press (Enter) to activate your selection.

A group can include an almost unlimited number of entries. These entries can be either programs or additional groups. The group structure slightly resembles the structure of directories on the hard drive.

7.4.4 Working with more than one program

MS-DOS was originally designed to work with only one program at a time. However, this limitation is becoming more flexible. For quite some time now there have been special utility programs that are loaded into memory (TSR programs) and activated by pressing a key.

Many of these TSR programs are becoming so large that they won't fit in memory. Often only a small portion remains active in the computer while the main part of the program is loaded from a floppy diskette or hard drive when needed. MS-DOS 6.0 provides the convenience of using multiple programs.

The MS-DOS Shell lets you start more than one program and then lets you switch back and forth between the programs, without exiting from the active program, to restart the next one. There is still only one program in the memory. The other programs are *swapped out* or temporarily stored on the hard drive.

Although this method isn't as fast or convenient as a full multitasking operating system (e.g., Windows or DeskView), it does make some tasks easier.

The Task Swapper

The Task Swapper lets you switch between programs using the MS-DOS Shell. It keeps track of all of the current settings of the active program and temporarily stores the information on the hard drive when you switch to another program or back to the MS-DOS Shell.

This means everything the program has stored in the conventional memory area is temporarily saved on the hard drive as a hidden file. Your hard drive must have sufficient unused storage space available for the information.

Also, the hard drive should have at least several megabytes free. If you have a couple of large programs running (such as word processors, graphics programs or databases), each data block to be stored could be up to 640K in size.

If there isn't enough free space on your hard drive, the Task Swapper beeps to let you know that it cannot store this information.

The list of active programs

To use the Task Swapper, first you must enable it. Select the **Options** menu either with the mouse or by pressing [Alt] followed by [O]. Then select **Enable Task Swapper**.

A fourth area will open at the lower right section of the screen called Active Task List.

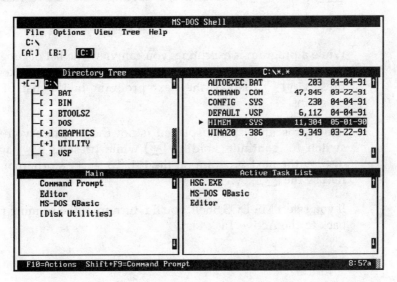

The MS-DOS Shell with Task Swapper enabled

When the Task Swapper is switched on, the program list area is vertically divided into two areas. The area on the left displays the list of programs in the current group and the area on the right displays the list of active (stored) programs. When first activated, the Active Task List will be empty.

Switching from one program to the next

When Task Swapper is enabled, each program started from the program list or file list areas is automatically entered in the list of active programs. To switch between programs, press Alt + Esc.

If only one program has been started, pressing Alt + Esc will return you to the MS-DOS Shell without quitting the program.

Any other program can be started from the MS-DOS Shell. Pressing Alt + Esc always takes you to the next program in the list of active programs. To return immediately to the MS-DOS Shell, without exiting any running programs, press Ctrl + Esc.

Another method for adding programs to the Active Task List is to hold down the Shift key while double-clicking on the program name with the left mouse button. Alternatively, use the cursor keys to select the program, then hold down the Shift key while pressing Enter to select the program.

This enters the name on the Active Task List. However, the program is not executed immediately. To load and run any program on the Active Task List, select the program from the list and press Enter. Press Tab, if necessary, to highlight the Active Task List.

An easier way to switch between programs

While a program is executing, you can view the list of programs in the Active Task List by pressing and holding the Alt key. Then press Tab to display the next program in the list of active programs.

If the program name displayed is not the program you want to switch to, continue holding Alt while pressing Tab again to display the next program on the list. To select a program, simply release the Alt key.

If you select MS-DOS Shell, you'll return from the running program back to the Active Task List.

Returning to the MS-DOS Shell

Pressing Ctrl + Esc takes you from a running program back to the MS-DOS Shell. You can activate another program from the list of active programs any time you want.

Using key combinations to switch between programs

Application shortcut keys can be assigned for even easier switching. The shortcut keys assigned must use the key combination of Ctrl + letter key, Shift + letter key or Alt + letter key.

Also, the program must have been assigned to the program list area as a program item either at the Main area or as part of a program group.

Specifying an application shortcut key

For example, we want to define Ctrl+E the shortcut key for the MS-DOS Editor (called Editor in the program list area). To define an application shortcut key for the MS-DOS Editor, switch to the program list area and select Editor.

Next, activate the **File** menu and select the **Properties...** command. This opens the Program Item Properties dialog box. It displays the name, the command to execute the program (with any optional parameters), the startup directory and any defined application shortcut key and password.

Press Tab (or use the mouse pointer) to move the cursor to the Application Shortcut Key text box. Specify the desired key combination by pressing and holding Ctrl or Shift or Alt while pressing a letter key. In this example, we're using Ctrl+E as the shortcut key. So, hold down Ctrl and press E.

The Application Shortcut Key text box should now display CTRL+E as shown in the following:

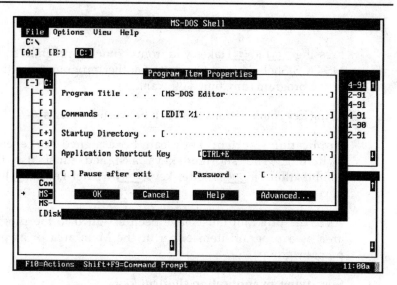

The Program Item Properties dialog box

Select the OK command button either by pressing the Tab key until the cursor is located at the button and pressing Enter or by using the mouse to point and click on the OK button.

Notice in the Commands text box that EDIT %1 is listed. If a % (indicating a parameter) is listed in the Commands text box, a second Program Item Properties dialog box is displayed requesting information for the parameter.

The MS-DOS Editor will prompt the user to enter a filename every time the program is started because of the %1 parameter in the command line. We'll discuss installing programs with parameters later in this section.

Since we're only interested in defining shortcut keys here, press Enter to accept the second Program Item Properties dialog box.

Press Shift+Enter to add the MS-DOS Editor to the Active Task List. If the File to Edit dialog box appears, press Enter. Again, at this time we're only interested in defining the shortcut keys for the MS-DOS Editor.

Next we want to define Ctrl+Q as a shortcut key for MS-DOS QBasic. Switch to the program list area and use the cursor keys to select MS-DOS QBasic.

Next, activate the **File** menu and select the **Properties...** command. As with the MS-DOS Editor example, the Program Item Properties dialog box opens.

Press [Tab] (or use the mouse pointer) to move the cursor to the Application Shortcut Key text box. We want to define [Ctrl]+[Q] as the shortcut key for MS-DOS QBasic. Hold down [Ctrl] and press [Q].

Select the [OK] command button either by pressing the [Tab] key until the cursor is located at the button and pressing [Enter] or by using the mouse to point and click on the [OK] button.

Press [Enter] to accept any additional dialog boxes which may appear, similar to the dialog boxes for defining the MS-DOS Editor shortcut keys above. Press [Shift]+[Enter] to add the MS-DOS QBasic to the Active Task List.

Now the Active Task List should appear like this:

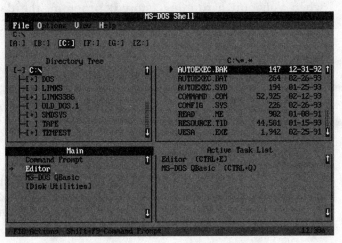

The shortcut keys appear with the program name in the Active Task List

Reserve Shortcut Keys

The following key combinations are not available:

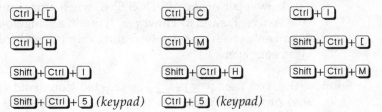

[Ctrl]+[I]   [Ctrl]+[C]   [Ctrl]+[I]

[Ctrl]+[H]   [Ctrl]+[M]   [Shift]+[Ctrl]+[I]

[Shift]+[Ctrl]+[I]   [Shift]+[Ctrl]+[H]   [Shift]+[Ctrl]+[M]

[Shift]+[Ctrl]+[5] *(keypad)*   [Ctrl]+[5] *(keypad)*

Removing a program from the list

An active program is removed from the list by quitting the program. After quitting the program, you will return to the MS-DOS Shell. The name of the program will no longer appear in the Active Task List.

Another way to remove a program from the list of active programs is to delete a selected program name. Use the **Delete...** command from the **File** menu. The program name can also be removed by selecting the program name from the Active Task List and pressing the key.

This only deletes the program name from the Active Task List and not the hard drive or disk drive. A warning message indicates that when you quit a running (stored) program, the data that the program used but did not store, may be irretrievably lost.

 You should only use Delete (or DEL) to remove a program from the list of active programs when absolutely necessary. This doesn't delete the hidden file, which contains data about the program, from the hard drive.

Quitting Task Swapper

The Task Swapper can only be switched off when all of the programs in the list have been quit properly. To close the Task Swapper, use the **Options** menu and either click **Enable Task Swapper** once or press Enter to de-activate it.

The Active Task List area will disappear. The MS-DOS Shell also may not be closed by using **Exit** or the Alt + F4 key combination when any programs remain in the Task Swapper.

The MS-DOS Shell prevents you from quitting either the Task Swapper or the MS-DOS Shell when a program is on the Active Task List. However, there is a dangerous way you can bypass this safety feature: Simply switching off your computer.

Suppose that you used Shift + F9 or selected Command Prompt from the program list area to leave the MS-DOS Shell temporarily. After executing commands from the MS-DOS command line you could easily forget that the MS-DOS Shell, with its stored files, is still running.

You might even switch off your computer. Now those hidden storage files, which occupy an enormous amount of memory, are still on your hard drive. Before switching off your computer, enter the EXIT command to check whether the MS-DOS Shell is still running.

7.4.5   Special features for more than one program

When you use the Task Swapper, there are a number of special features to consider. The following is a brief list of some simple rules that will help you avoid serious problems.

The meaning of the XXXXDOSC.BAT file

When you start a program from the MS-DOS Shell, a file called XXXXDOSC.BAT is automatically created.

 Each of the four "X"s represents a hexadecimal number (0-F). This number is used so that there aren't any files with the same filenames. An example filename might read 8435DOSC.BAT.

This batch file contains everything that is needed to start the selected program. For example, this file contains the line that you entered when defining a new program as a command line. After you exit the program correctly, the XXXXDOSC.BAT file is automatically deleted.

 You should never delete or change these BAT files. Deleting these files could lead to problems with the MS-DOS Shell. It's also best to create a special directory for temporary files (e.g., C:\TEMP) and set a special environment variable called TEMP in the AUTOEXEC.BAT:

```
SET TEMP=C:\TEMP
```

This causes the MS-DOS Shell to place all temporary files (including the special XXXXDOSC.BAT file) in this directory.

When is it possible to switch between programs?

You can only use the Task Swapper to switch between different programs in the Active Task List after the XXXXDOSC.BAT file is finished running. For example, if the command line for a program is:

```
WORD TEXT1.DOC | COPY TEXT1.DOC A: | DIR
```

you cannot switch while editing in Word. While you are using Word, the batch file hasn't finished running.

Use caution when deleting files

When using the Task Swapper, be especially careful when deleting files. The MS-DOS Shell has to place parts of memory in temporary storage on the hard drive by creating special files. These files use the .TMP extension and begin with the character sequence "~WO".

While you are working with the MS-DOS Shell, do not delete, change or rename these files. If you do make changes to these files, you won't be able to switch between programs. Also, your computer will probably crash and all of the unsaved data from the applications currently running will be lost.

There has to be room to switch

In order to use the Task Swapping option, there must be sufficient free space on your hard drive. If there isn't enough room to store programs and their data on the hard drive, you won't be able to switch.

The speed required for switching between programs can be increased considerably by using a faster hard drive. Another option is to optimize your system for speed by using the available utilities provided with MS-DOS 6.0, such as SMARTDRV.SYS and FASTOPEN.EXE.

Updating the contents of the MS-DOS Shell

 If you used a program and changed the contents of the drive and then returned to the MS-DOS Shell, you'll notice that the Directory Tree/file list area hasn't recorded the changed data. This is normal for all changes to files and directories that are caused by programs run from the program list area.

To update the display of the current status of all of the files in a drive, double-click the drive icon or select the drive icon and press [Enter]. An alternative is to select the **Refresh** command in the **View** menu.

Use caution with programs that note the data location from storage media

When working and switching between several programs, be careful when selecting programs to run.

All programs that use the location of data on a storage media (floppy diskette or hard drive) are forbidden. So, you cannot start a program for optimizing and clearing the hard drive from the MS-DOS Shell and then switch to the MS-DOS Shell or another program. When you want to work on the system, leave the MS-DOS Shell (Alt + F4) and start the program from the command line.

 Since commands, such as FASTOPEN, and programs, such as cache programs, assume that they are running alone in the PC, they use information about the absolute storage locations. Therefore, these types of programs cannot run from the MS-DOS Shell. You must install them before starting the MS-DOS Shell for the first time.

7.4.6 Installing and changing programs

One important feature of the Program list is that the program list area can be customized. This makes it easier for you to run applications.

Adding a program item

To add a new program item, first switch to the program list area and then activate **New...** from the **File** menu. A dialog box will ask whether you want to set up a new program (Program Item, which is the default setting) or a new group (Program Group).

After pressing Enter or clicking OK, the Add Program dialog box appears. This dialog box lets you enter important program information.

 The two dialog boxes for setting up a program are also used for changing a program item.

Changing a program item

Before a program item can be changed, it must be selected with either the mouse or the cursor keys. The properties of the selected program item can be changed by activating **Properties...** from the **File** menu. This command opens the Program Item Properties dialog box, in which you can enter the program definitions.

Program Title

In the Program Title text box, type the name of the program as it should be displayed in the program list. This name will serve as the identifier for starting the program. The title can contain up to 23 characters. Select a clear and logical name. To move to the next text box, press ⌈Tab⌋.

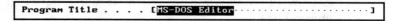

Program Title . . . . [MS-DOS Editor·····················]

The Program Title text box from the Program Item Properties dialog box

Commands

The next text box is labeled Commands. Enter the command that normally would be entered at the system prompt on the MS-DOS command line to run the program.

For example, if you have the program Word installed in the directory C:\WORD and used PATH to define a path to this directory, you only need to enter WORD. If the path isn't defined, you must enter the complete command, including the path: C:\WORD\WORD. Up to 255 characters can be used.

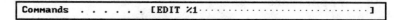

Commands . . . . . . [EDIT %1·····················]

The Commands text box from the Program Item Properties dialog box

Additional commands can be specified, batch files can be run and replaceable parameters can be included as part of the command line.

The MS-DOS Shell executes each command in the order it appears in the Commands text box. If more than one command is entered, the additional commands must be separated by a semicolon (;). Each semicolon must have one or more spaces on each side of it.

Batch files can be run by including the CALL command in the command line. For example, to run a batch file named INIT.BAT prior to running a program and a batch file called CLEANUP.BAT after the program ends, type the following command line:

```
CALL INIT ; PROGRAM ; CLEANUP
```

The commands must be separated by a space, semicolon and another space. The programs will not run correctly if the spaces are omitted.

Using Parameters

Parameters are additional information given to a program when it is started. For example, when the MS-DOS Editor or MS-DOS QBasic are started from the program list area, a dialog box will request the name of an optional file to load. You can enter a filename here and it will load as soon as the program starts.

This additional information (the filename to load) is passed in a variable. Many programs, such as Word, can use optional parameters in this way.

To enter optional parameters in a dialog box every time a program is run from the program list, enter a replaceable parameter in the Commands text box of the Program Item Parameters dialog box. Replaceable parameters are entered as a percentage sign (%) followed by a number from 1 through 9.

In the previous illustration, the MS-DOS Editor will prompt the user to enter a filename every time the program is started because of the command line:

```
EDIT %1
```

Including Replaceable Parameters

To include a replaceable parameter with a program item, first select the item from the program list area, then open the **File** menu and choose **Properties....** The Program Item Parameters dialog box will appear.

Use the ⌨Tab key or the mouse to activate the Commands text box. Enter the command to execute the program, followed by the necessary replaceable parameters. Enter each parameter as %1, %2, %3, etc., and select the ⌨OK button.

Startup Directory

```
Startup Directory . . [C:\DOC............................]
```

*The Startup Directory text box from the Program Item
Properties dialog box*

In the Startup Directory text box, you can specify which directory becomes the current directory before the program starts. For example, if you store all of your word processing documents created by Word in the C:\DOC directory, enter this directory here. When Word is run from the program list area, C:\DOC will become the current directory.

Application Shortcut Key

```
┌─────────────────────────────────────────────────────────────┐
│  Application Shortcut Key      [CTRL+E·····················] │
└─────────────────────────────────────────────────────────────┘
```

Application shortcut key text box in the Program Item Properties dialog box

This text box lets you combine Ctrl, Alt, Shift and another key (e.g., a letter) to a program. This assignment allows you to change directly from the Task Swapper to the program.

To enter the key code in this text box, hold down the Ctrl, Alt or Shift key and press a letter, number or function key. The MS-DOS Shell then enters the key combination pressed in this text box. (You cannot use the numbers 0 - 9 with Shift. Pressing Shift turns the numbers into special characters.)

Pause after exit

If you used Tab or the mouse to move to this check box, you can press the Spacebar or click on Pause after exit to place an [X] inside the brackets, which switches this feature on or off.

The X signifies that the MS-DOS Shell will wait for you to press any key before returning to the MS-DOS Shell screen after exiting the program. If there is no X, the feature is switched off and the MS-DOS Shell screen reappears immediately after you leave a program.

You may not want to clear the screen and open the MS-DOS Shell immediately after exiting a program because some programs (like the MS-DOS commands DIR, CHKDSK and MEM) display information on the screen as they end. Calling the MS-DOS Shell immediately will prevent you from reading the screen before the Shell reappears.

Password

If you enter a password, containing one to eight characters, in the Password text box before the program is started, you will be prompted for a password. The keystrokes entered for a password are not displayed on the screen.

You cannot make changes, copy or delete this program item until
the correct password is entered. This option of the MS-DOS Shell
is case sensitive, which means that it recognizes the difference
between upper and lowercase characters.

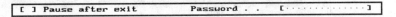

Pause after exit and Password items of the Program Item
Properties dialog box

O K

Pressing (OK) (use (Tab) or the mouse to select it and confirm by
pressing (Enter) or clicking the left mouse button on it) accepts the
settings you've made as correct.

The command buttons in the Program Item Properties dialog
box

Cancel

Pressing (Cancel) will cancel all of the settings and all of the
previously entered data in this dialog box will be lost.

Help

Selecting (Help) displays the MS-DOS Shell help screen for the
Program Item Properties dialog box.

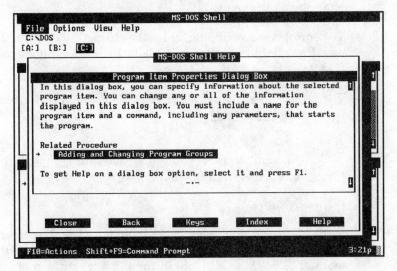

The Program Item Properties help screen

Advanced...

Selecting the [Advanced...] button displays a new dialog box where you can make advanced settings.

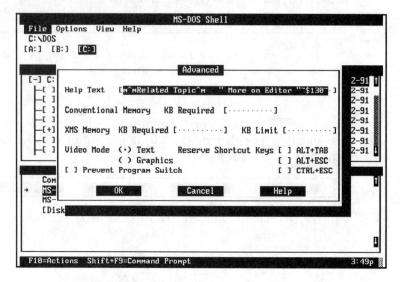

The Advanced Mode dialog box

Help Text

The Help Text text box lets you define a string of explanatory text that will appear when you select a program and call the **Help** menu by pressing [F1]. Up to 478 characters can be entered and word wrapping is automatic.

To control word wrapping, enter the characters "^M" anywhere a new line should begin. Enter blank lines by typing "^M" twice (^M^M).

The caret "^" is usually available as a key on your keyboard, if it is not, press [Alt] + [9] [4].

 Remember that you must activate [Num Lock] to enter characters from the numeric keypad.

Conventional Memory KB Required

In the Conventional Memory KB Required text box, enter the amount of memory that the program requires according to the user's manual. The MS-DOS Shell then makes this memory area available.

Example

The word processing program Word has a 638K EXE file. The MS-DOS Shell cannot release that much memory. According to the Word manual, the required (minimum) memory space amounts to 384K. This is the value that must be entered.

If you don't know the required amount, leave this text box empty. The MS-DOS Shell will determine the required memory. If you enter a value that is larger than the amount of memory space that the MS-DOS Shell can release, an error message will inform you of this when you try to start the program. So you won't be able to start the program.

XMS Memory KB Required

In the XMS Memory KB Required text box, enter the desired XMS memory space in kilobytes. In the KB Limit text box, enter the highest amount of XMS Memory available on your system. XMS is a special method of managing and controlling extended memory. If the Task Swapper isn't activated, the XMS memory specifications are ignored.

For most programs it's best to leave this text box blank. The time for switching to and from a program increases significantly when XMS memory is specified.

The entries in the XMS memory text boxes determine how programs will use extended memory. In the first text box (XMS Memory KB Required) you must determine the minimum amount of XMS memory that must be available in order to start a program.

In most cases, you should enter 0 so that the presence of extended memory doesn't influence starting the program. If a program requires a specific amount of XMS memory to run properly, enter this amount in the KB Required text box.

Cache programs, which require a certain amount of XMS memory for temporarily storing data, are an example. If a cache program uses conventional memory instead of XMS memory, starting the program could be disastrous because conventional memory is suddenly decreased drastically. Use this text box to prevent a program from starting with conventional memory.

 Entering any value other than 0 delays the start process for the program.

The KB Limit text box enables you to set the maximum amount of XMS memory that can be used for the program. This option is useful for programs that always use all of extended memory. When working with more than one program (with the Task Swapper), usually you shouldn't use extended memory. You can prevent a program from using XMS memory by entering a zero in this text box.

Video Mode

The Video Mode options are used to determine whether the program runs in text mode or graphics mode. To select graphics mode either click or use the [Spacebar] to activate the Graphics option. If Text is selected and you switch to graphics mode while the program is running, the Task Swapper might not switch. You must also activate Graphics for programs that only run in graphics mode.

Graphics mode requires more memory than text mode. Whenever possible, programs should be set up to run in text mode, especially if you are using a high-resolution graphics monitor (VGA, EGA or monochrome).

Reserve Shortcut Keys

The three key combinations in the Reserve Shortcut Keys check boxes ([Alt]+[Tab], [Alt]+[Esc] and [Ctrl]+[Esc]) are necessary for switching active programs with the Task Swapper.

However, some programs require one or more of these key combinations for their own internal functions. If your application uses these key combinations, you cannot use them with the Task Swapper.

Use either the [Spacebar] or click between the brackets with the mouse pointer to prevent these key combinations from being used with the Task Swapper.

If an X is displayed in the brackets, the key combination won't affect the Task Swapper. If all three key combinations are selected, the program cannot work with the Task Swapper.

Prevent Program Switch

Selecting the Prevent Program Switch check box and placing an X in the brackets prevents switching from this program. To exit the program you must return to the MS-DOS Shell.

OK

Selecting [OK] (use [Tab] to go to [OK], then press [Enter] or click with
the mouse) accepts the settings as correct.

Cancel

Selecting [Cancel] ignores all of the settings in the dialog box. Any
entries previously made are lost.

Help

Calls the appropriate pages of the MS-DOS Shell help screen.

Tips for creating a new program

When adding a new program to the program list area, you may
want to enter one or more MS-DOS commands. First use the [Tab]
key to move to the program list area. Then select **New...** from the
File menu. Press [Enter] to accept the default, Program Item.

The Add Program dialog box appears. Type the name of the
program in the Program Title text box and press [Enter].

Then type the command in the Commands text box. If you enter
more than one command, be sure that you separate each command
with a space, semicolon and another space.

If the program is located in a specific directory, you can enter that
directory in the Startup Directory text box. Also, if desired, enter a
shortcut key in the Application Shortcut Key text box and a
password in the Password text box.

If an X doesn't appear in the Pause after exit check box, the
command will return automatically to MS-DOS Shell. Otherwise,
the command will wait until you press a key to return to MS-DOS
Shell.

Then use the cursor keys to move the selection cursor to the program
name. Press [Enter]. The program then executes the commands you
entered in the Commands text box.

When the command has executed, the message:

```
Press any key to return to MS-DOS Shell . . . .
```

will appear if the Pause after exit check box was activated.

The command line can be used to start batch files as well as COM
or EXE programs. Since batch files can be almost any length, the

limitations in the length of the command lines in the MS-DOS Shell no longer apply.

For example, a file called WORK.BAT could be created in the DOS directory and called from the command line. However, a batch file cannot be called directly in an MS-DOS Shell command line. In other words, you cannot type:

```
WORK.BAT
```

Your batch file will end at the completion of WORK.BAT and none of the remaining command elements in the command line will be executed. Instead, use CALL. For example, to call the WORK.BAT batch file for the example above, use the following command line:

```
CALL WORK.BAT
```

The commands in program lines in the MS-DOS Shell work like batch files and are subject to the same rules.

You can also use other elements of batch programming in command lines of the MS-DOS Shell (e.g., IF). The batch file:

```
IF EXIST MS-DOS Shell.BAT TYPE MS-DOS Shell.BAT
ECHO End of program
PAUSE
```

corresponds to the following command line in the MS-DOS Shell:

```
IF EXIST MS-DOS Shell.BAT TYPE MS-DOS Shell.BAT ; ECHO
End of program ; PAUSE
```

 The commands must be separated by a space, semicolon and another space. The programs will not run correctly if the spaces are omitted.

7.4.7 Installing programs with parameters

If a program requires one or more parameters to run, a dialog box for entering the proper parameters appears on the screen after you select the program item. The MS-DOS Editor and MS-DOS QBasic, both of which are part of MS-DOS 6.0 and installed in the MS-DOS Shell, have these dialog boxes.

You can specify the file to edit in the dialog box of the editor and specify which BASIC file to read in the dialog box of QBasic.

You can install a word processing program so that when you call the program, you can specify, in a dialog box, the file that should be loaded with the word processing program.

Enter "%1" ("%2", "%3", through "%9" are also valid) to start a program with one or more parameters. Enter "%1" after the program name in the Commands text box of the Program Item Properties dialog box.

For example, to start Word with a dialog box for parameters, enter "WORD %1" or "C:\WORD\WORD %1" after "Commands".

```
┌─────────────────────── Add Program ───────────────────────┐
│                                                           │
│  Program Title . . . . [MS Word 5.5·················]      │
│                                                           │
│  Commands  . . . . . . [C:\WORD\WORD %1·············]      │
│                                                           │
│  Startup Directory . . [·························]         │
│                                                           │
│  Application Shortcut Key    [····················]       │
│                                                           │
│  [X] Pause after exit    Password . . [············]      │
│                                                           │
│     OK         Cancel        Help       Advanced...       │
└───────────────────────────────────────────────────────────┘
```

Installing Word 5.5 to start with a dialog box for entering a filename

The parameter window

For each variable (%n) entered in the command line, the MS-DOS Shell displays a parameter window when the program item is selected.

When creating the program item, enter information in the dialog box to customize the dialog box which will be displayed for your program item.

```
┌─────────────────────────────────────────────────────────┐
│                  ▐ Program Item Properties ▌              │
│                                                           │
│   Fill in information for % 1   prompt dialog.            │
│                                                           │
│   Window Title  . . . .   [▛MS-Word 5.5·················] │
│                                                           │
│   Program Information .   [You may enter the name of a file ] │
│                                                           │
│   Prompt Message  . . .   [File to edit?···············]  │
│                                                           │
│      Default Parameters . .   [······················]   │
│                                                           │
│                                                           │
│      ▐  OK  ▌        ▐  Cancel  ▌        ▐  Help  ▌        │
│                                                           │
└─────────────────────────────────────────────────────────┘
```

*The dialog box for entering information about additional
parameters*

When entering a "%1" after a command in the Commands text box
when creating or changing a command line and selecting (OK), you'll
see a dialog box like the previous one. It lets you add additional
information about the parameter.

The top line indicates with which parameter this dialog box is
associated. This is useful when multiple parameters are passed to
a program item.

Enter the title of the window in the Window Title text box. In the
figure above, "MS-WORD 5.5" was entered for the Window Title.
Other text could have been used. This text can contain up to 22
characters.

Program Information

The Program Information text box usually contains information on
the parameter to be entered. This information can be two lines
with up to 50 characters each.

Prompt Message

The Prompt Message text box allows you to specify a prompt. This
prompt is displayed in front of the input line in the parameter
window. The text of the system prompt can be up to 17 characters
long.

Default Parameters

The Default Parameters text box can contain a default parameter
which is displayed in the input line when the parameter window
appears. This default parameter can be accepted by pressing (Enter)
or can be edited. The text of the default parameter can be up to 19
characters long.

Either click (OK) or press (Enter) to accept the entries. Select Cancel if you don't want to accept the entries. If you specified more than one parameter in the Command text box, the setting options for the next parameter window appear.

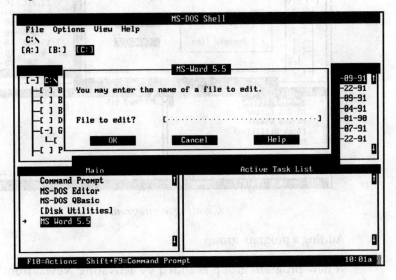

Starting MS-Word 5.5 from the Program Item list displays this dialog box

7.4.8 Installing program groups

As mentioned earlier, programs can also be combined into groups and added to the program list area as group lines. The following setup screen appears when you either create or change a group. The Title text box must be specified, the Help Text and Password text boxes are optional.

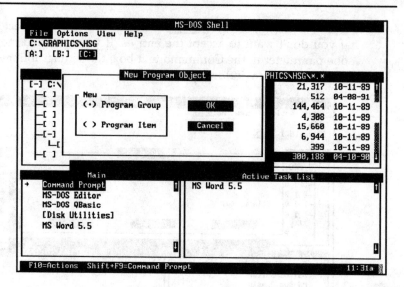

Creating a program group

Adding a program group

A new program group is added by activating **New...** from the **File** menu. A dialog box appears in which you can select either the Program Group option or the Program Item option. The default setting is Program Item.

Press the ⬆ cursor key or click Program Group with the mouse to select "group". Then either press (Enter) or click (OK). Then the Add Group dialog box appears. You can now define the new program group.

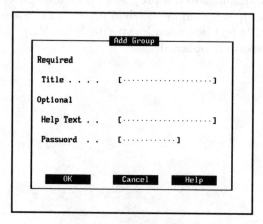

Add Group dialog box

Changing a program group

The following procedure can be used to make changes to an existing program group. First, use the mouse or the cursor key to select the program group to be changed. Then activate **Properties...** from the **File** menu. The Program Group Properties dialog box is displayed as shown below. This dialog box has the same setting options as the Add Group dialog box except that the old values are already in the lines.

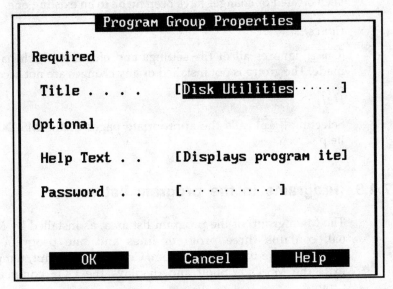

Changing a program group

Title

Enter the text, which will be displayed as the menu entry for the program group, in the Title text box. The title can contain up to 23 characters. For example, to set up a group that contains several word processing programs, the text entry could be "Word processors". Press ⌷Tab⌷ to move to the next text box, Help Text.

Help Text

The Help Text text box enables you to enter information about the group. Press ⌷Tab⌷ again to move to the next text box.

Password

By specifying a password you can control who has access to this group. The MS-DOS Shell always asks for this password. When the password is entered, the screen display only shows an asterisk. This is a safety feature that prevents others from seeing your password as you enter it.

The MS-DOS Shell password protection option is case sensitive. In other words, it recognizes the difference between upper and lowercase characters.

Save

Selecting OK (use Tab or the mouse to move to OK, then press Enter or click on it) accepts the settings as entered. A new group has now been created or changes have been made to an existing one.

Cancel

Cancel ignores all of the settings and changes which have been made. The group is not installed or any changes are not accepted.

Help

Selecting Help calls the appropriate pages of the MS-DOS Shell help screen.

7.4.9 Programs in the program list area

The Main group of the program list area, as installed by MS-DOS 6.0, contains three program lines and one program group. Activating the top program item, Command Prompt, temporarily exits the MS-DOS Shell and displays the DOS command line prompt.

The second entry starts the MS-DOS Editor. The third line (MS-DOS QBasic) starts a new version of the BASIC programming language. Activating the fourth line opens the DOS Utilities group, which contains additional programs.

The following sections provide an explanation of the program lines as well as the program group.

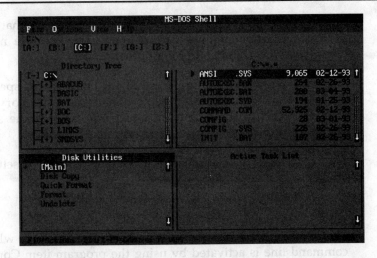

The Disk Utilities program group

The MS-DOS Command Prompt

The MS-DOS Command Prompt can be used to leave the MS-DOS Shell temporarily and start a new command interpreter (COMMAND.COM).

COMMAND.COM is usually stored in the root directory of the hard drive or diskette from which your computer is booted. COMMAND.COM provides an interface between the user and the computer by taking input from the keyboard and acting on this input.

Some commands, such as DIR, are recognized by COMMAND.COM and executed under the functions of the MS-DOS operating system. Other commands are interpreted as program names.

The corresponding programs are loaded from the hard drive or floppy diskette. After running a program, COMMAND.COM regains control of the computer and waits for new input.

To return to the MS-DOS Shell, type EXIT. The command interpreter can also be called by pressing (Shift) + (F9) from the MS-DOS Shell.

 COMMAND.COM starts with the smallest environment if you activate Command Prompt or press (Shift) + (F9). The environment is a special memory space containing basic settings for working with MS-DOS. For example, it contains the settings for the appearance of the system prompt or the current search path.

To call commands or programs from the command line that require a larger environment, use **Properties...** from the **File** menu to change the DOS command prompt program item.

When the Program Item Properties dialog box appears, specify the /E: switch to increase the environment memory after "COMMAND" in the Commands text box. Specify the size for environment memory in bytes following the /E: switch.

The following is an example of the Commands text box setting the environment memory for 512 bytes:

```
COMMAND /E:512
```

This increased environment memory is only available when the command line is activated by using the program item Command Prompt. The key combination (Shift) + (F9) starts COMMAND.COM with the minimum amount of environment memory (160 bytes).

The MS-DOS Editor

Selecting the MS-DOS Editor starts the editor supplied with MS-DOS 6.0. After activating this program item, a dialog box will request the name of the file to be edited.

Refer to Chapter 8 for more information on the MS-DOS Editor.

MS-DOS QBasic

Activating the MS-DOS QBasic program item starts QBasic. After activating this program item, a dialog box will request the name of the file to be edited.

Refer to Chapter 17 for more information on QBasic.

The Disk Utilities

After installing MS-DOS 6.0, the Disk Utilities group is the only group available in the Main group of the program list area. When this item is selected, a new list of commands is displayed. The name "Disk Utilities" appears in the title bar.

The top line is a program group named Main. When Main is selected or (Esc) is pressed, you will return to the Main group (the top level).

Disk Copy

Disk Copy is used to copy diskettes. First select a source drive and a target drive. The default setting specifies A: as the source drive and B: as the target drive. These settings can be changed. After confirming your choices by pressing (Enter), the MS-DOS DISKCOPY command is executed.

MS Anti-Virus

Use the MS Anti-Virus program to detect and remove computer viruses from your floppy diskettes and hard drives.

MSBACKUP

Use the MSBACKUP program item to make a backup of your hard drive. The default setting is to backup all of the files and subdirectories on drive C:. The setting for the target drive is A:. These settings can be changed.

Quick Format

The Quick Format program item enables you to format diskettes in a few seconds. The program uses the FORMAT command with the /Q switch. The default setting is for drive A:, although you can change to another drive.

Format

Use the Format program item to format diskettes or fixed disks. The program uses the FORMAT command. The default setting is for drive A:, although you can change to another drive.

Undelete

The Undelete program item is used to recover deleted files. The MS-DOS UNDELETE command is called. The default setting uses the /LIST switch.

7.4.10 Protecting groups and programs

The MS-DOS Shell makes using MS-DOS a lot easier. One interesting feature of the MS-DOS Shell is an option to prevent users from accessing certain commands. This feature can be used to prevent data changes or destruction.

The following sections explain the different methods the MS-DOS Shell provides for protecting data.

Password

One easy method of protection is to install passwords for programs and program groups. When creating new program items or groups or making changes to existing programs or groups, enter a password in the Password text box of the Program Item Properties or Program Group Properties dialog box.

After a password is installed, the correct password must be entered before a group or program item can be activated from the MS-DOS Shell.

For example, all Utility programs can be protected as a group by assigning them to a group and then assigning the group a password.

A more practical example is to assign a password to the FORMAT command. This will prevent anyone who doesn't know the password from using FORMAT.

To remove the password, simply delete the expression from the appropriate line of the Properties dialog box. However, before you can make any changes, you must enter the password to gain access to the dialog box.

Unfortunately, a password offers only limited protection. All of the information about a group is stored in the DOSSHELL.INI file. The password is stored in an encrypted form. Also, someone could gain access to the protected file(s) by discovering the password.

7.5   Working with Files and Directories

Before MS-DOS 6.0, the only easy methods available for working with files were supplied by third party developers. However, the Directory Tree/file list area of the MS-DOS Shell provides an easy solution to most of your file handling tasks.

The Directory Tree/file list area can be used to edit files, directories, diskettes and hard drives. These areas of the MS-DOS Shell can be used to create, rename, copy, compare and delete files. These are only some of the commands that are available.

7.5.1   The screen of the Directory Tree/file list area

The **View** menu on the menu bar lets you display the Directory Tree/file list area as either one or two lists or display both the Directory Tree/file list area and the program list area on the screen simultaneously.

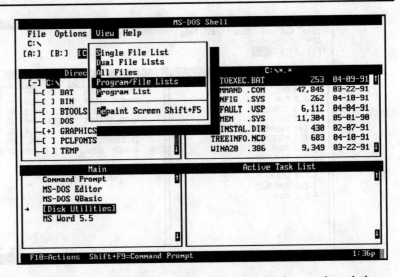

*The View menu lets you customize the display modes of the
MS-DOS Shell*

If you choose **Single File List**, the Directory Tree/file list area
fills the entire screen with one file list. The left side of the screen
displays the Directory Tree while the right side of the screen
displays the file list of the selected directory.

If **Dual File Lists** is selected, the Directory Tree/file list area is
divided horizontally on the screen. This lets you display the
contents and structure of two drives. The Directory Tree area is
located on the left and the file list area of the current directory is
on the right.

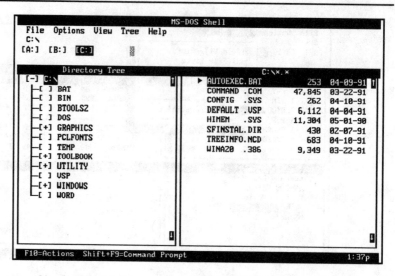

Single File List command from the View menu displays directories and files

The drive icons can be used to select which drive should be displayed. You can display two different drives or different directories on the same drive, as the following shows.

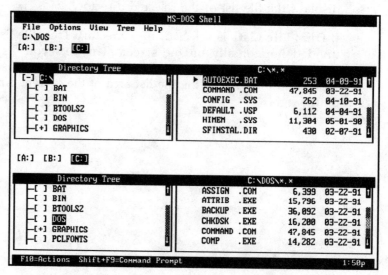

Dual File Lists can display both the root directory and the DOS directory of C:

7.6   The MS-DOS Shell Menus

This section contains an explanation of the menu bar functions. The contents of the menu bar change, depending on whether the program list area or the Directory Tree/file list area is active.

The **Tree** menu is displayed in the Directory Tree/file list area. The remaining menus, **Options**, **View** and **Help** are identical in both the program list area and the Directory Tree/file list area. The **File** menu for the program list area and the **File** menu for the Directory Tree/file list area are discussed separately.

7.6.1   The File menu for the program list area

The **File** menu for the program list area is used to create, change, start, copy or delete files. You can leave the MS-DOS Shell or run programs and MS-DOS commands from the command line. The following sections explain the individual commands of the program list area.

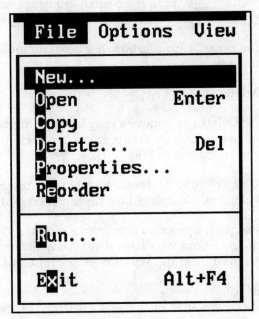

The File menu for the program list area

New...

Use **New...** to add a new program group to the program list area or to add a new program item to the current group. When **New...** is

selected, a dialog box offers you a choice between creating a new
program item or a new program group.

Open

Selecting **Open** starts a selected program (from the program list) or
opens a selected group. This command corresponds to pressing (Enter)
or double-clicking a command with the mouse.

Copy

Use **Copy** to copy a selected program item from one group to
another group. All of the option settings of this program item are
retained. The program item copied isn't deleted from the original
group.

After selecting this command, the following message is displayed
on the status bar, at bottom of the screen: "Display the group to
copy to, then press (F2). Press (Esc) to cancel".

Use the cursor keys or the mouse to select the target group and open
it with (Enter). When the desired group appears on the screen, press
(F2) to copy the program item. Pressing (Esc) cancels the operation.

You cannot copy a group. If a program group is selected, **Copy** is
inactive.

Delete...

Use **Delete...** to remove a program item from a program group or to
remove a program group. It can be selected directly from the **File**
menu or by pressing the (Del) key.

After selecting **Delete...** to remove a program item or group, a
dialog box is displayed for confirmation of the delete operation.

Removing a program item from a program group doesn't delete the
program from your hard drive. Only the entry for the program is
removed from the MS-DOS DOSSHELL.INI file.

 Because of the new structure of the MS-DOS Shell - all
groups and programs are in one file (DOSSHELL.INI) - it's
very dangerous to delete a group containing several
program lines or subgroups. The deleted group is
permanently removed, along with all of the entries. When
the DOSSHELL.INI file is changed, a backup copy isn't
made.

Properties...

Use **Properties...** to view existing program lines or group lines. The options are the same as for New. For more information about this item, refer to the sections on installing and changing programs and setting up groups.

Reorder

Use **Reorder** to change the position of a selected program group or program item within the active group. After this command is selected, the following message appears in the bottom screen line: "Select location to move to, then press Enter". Use the mouse or cursor keys to select and position the line containing the title to change. Press Enter to complete the process.

Run...

When **Run...** is activated, a dialog box appears in which you can enter an MS-DOS command or program name. Then press Enter to execute the command or program. After the command or program is completed, a message informs you to press any key to return to the MS-DOS Shell.

 Don't run any TSR programs from the MS-DOS Shell. These types of programs could cause the MS-DOS Shell to crash.

Exit

The last command of the menu is **Exit**. When selected, the MS-DOS Shell terminates without any additional prompt. The MS-DOS Shell can also be ended by typing Alt + F4 or by pressing F3.

7.6.2 The File menu for the file list area

The **File** menu of the Directory Tree/file list area can be used to create, delete, copy and rename files and directories. It can also start programs, view file contents, search for files, assign programs to file groups and more. The following sections explain the different commands of the **File** menu of the Directory Tree/file list area.

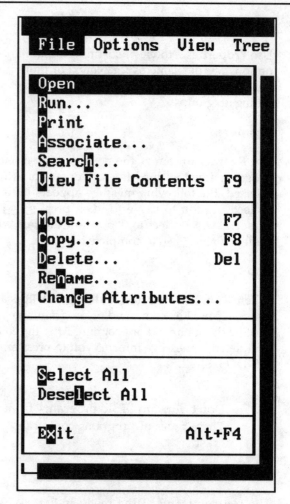

The File menu for the file list area

Open

Use **Open** to start programs. All programs or executable files have
.COM, .EXE and .BAT filename extensions. Attempting to open any
other types of files displays an error message.

   Other file types can be used to start programs when they
are associated with programs. We'll discuss this in more
detail in the section on the **Associate...** menu.

Programs can also be started by selecting the program name from
the file list area and pressing [Enter].

You can also use the mouse to start a program by selecting the filename and double-clicking the left mouse button.

After exiting a program, you are prompted to press any key to return to the MS-DOS Shell.

Run...

When **Run...** is selected, a dialog box, in which you can enter an MS-DOS command or a program name, is displayed. Press Enter to execute the command or program.

After exiting a program, you are prompted to press any key to return to the MS-DOS Shell.

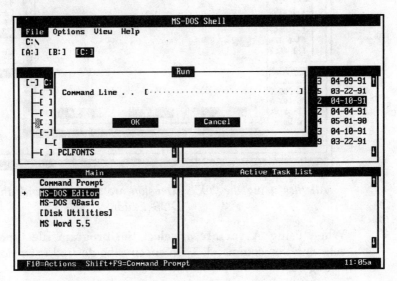

A dialog box for entering the command is displayed when Run... is activated

Print

Use **Print** to print the contents of selected files to an attached printer. The printing operation takes place in the background.

Associate...

The **Associate...** command is used to assign files with a certain extension to a specific program. When a file with the specified extension is opened, the associated program automatically starts.

For example, you could assign all files with the .TXT extension to the MS-DOS Editor program EDIT as shown in the following figure. This means that whenever OPEN (or a double-click) is used to start a file with the .TXT extension, the MS-DOS Shell automatically starts the "associated" program. (In the example, the MS-DOS Editor is started.)

 Files that don't have filename extensions cannot be assigned to an application.

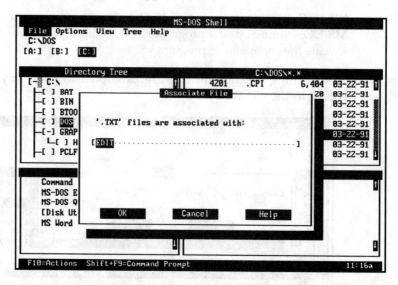

All files using the .TXT extension are associated with the MS-DOS Editor

When using **Associate...**, select the program file type before selecting this command. Then specify the desired extension in the dialog box.

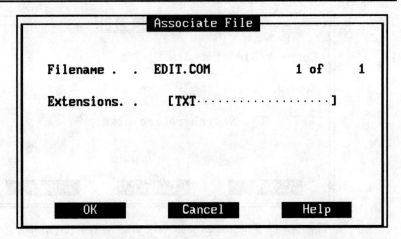

All files with the .TXT extension are assigned to the MS-DOS Editor

If several programs are selected, you will be prompted to associate each program with file types.

 More than one extension for association with a program can be specified. However, each extension can only be assigned to one program. The association can also be set by clicking a file with the desired extension, selecting **Associate...** and then specifying the path and name of the program.

Search...

Eventually you may forget which directory contains a certain file. You can ask the Directory Tree/file list area to search within a directory or on the entire storage medium for files. Select the desired directory and then choose **Search...**. Enter either the entire filename or just part of it in the dialog box that is displayed. Wildcards (* and ?) are accepted.

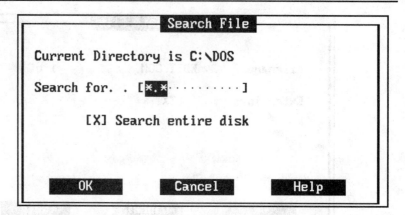

The Search File dialog box lets you search for a specified file or files in either a specified directory or the entire disk

View File Contents

View File Contents displays the contents of a selected file. You can also press the F9 key to activate this command.

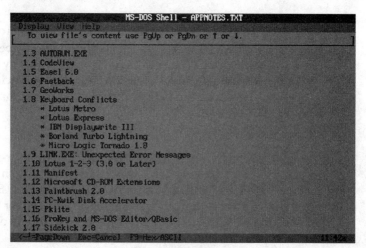

Using View File Contents to display a file as ASCII text

When the file is displayed, pressing F9 switches between ASCII and hexadecimal display modes. Use PgUp and PgDn to scroll through the pages of the file or use ↑ and ↓ to scroll line by line through the file. Press Esc to return to file management.

*Pressing F9 while using View File Contents toggles
between ASCII and hexadecimal display modes*

The top screen line displays the name of the file being viewed. A
new menu bar, containing the **Display**, **View** and **Help** menus, is
also displayed. Use **Display** to switch between ASCII display and
hexadecimal display (or press F9). To exit, use the **View** menu or
press Esc.

It makes sense to display a file in text form only when it consists of
legible ASCII characters. This is the case with files such as
AUTOEXEC.BAT and CONFIG.SYS.

Display a file in hexadecimal format when you want to inspect
program files.

Move...

Move... shifts one or more files to a different directory. This
automatically deletes the files in the original directory. In the
dialog box that appears, the top line displays the filename(s) to
be moved. Specify the target directory in the bottom line.

```
┌──────────────────── Move File ────────────────────┐
│                                                    │
│                                                    │
│   From:    [README.TXT · · · · · · · · · · · · · ] │
│                                                    │
│   To:      [C:\DOS · · · · · · · · · · · · · · · ] │
│                                                    │
│                                                    │
│                                                    │
│     ┌─────────┐      ┌──────────┐     ┌─────────┐  │
│     │   OK    │      │  Cancel  │     │  Help   │  │
│     └─────────┘      └──────────┘     └─────────┘  │
└────────────────────────────────────────────────────┘
```

Enter the source file and the target directory or disk in the Move File dialog box

 Since **Move...** deletes the original file, be very careful when using it.

Move... can also be selected by pressing [F7].

 If only one file is being moved, it can be assigned a new name. Specify the new name in the bottom dialog line after the target directory.

Copy

Copy is used to place a copy of one or more files in a different directory. The original files remain in the original directory.

 When only one file is copied, it can be assigned a new name in the target directory. Specify the new name in the dialog box with the target directory.

Pressing [F8] also can be used to Copy files.

Delete...

Delete... erases all selected files.

 It's possible that the **Select Across Directories** command in the **Options** menu is activated. If this command is selected, a black dot will appear in front of it in the menu. When this command is active, there may be files in other directories that could be deleted.

After selecting the appropriate files, choose **Delete...**. A dialog box appears containing the names of selected files. If all of the selections are correct, select OK. You are then prompted to delete each file (if you set this option earlier in the **Options** menu). Answer Yes to delete a file. You can still exclude files from the deletion by pressing No.

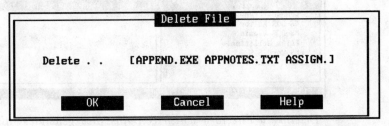

APPEND.EXE, APPNOTES.TXT and ASSIGN.COM selected
for deletion

If you have previously switched off Confirm on Delete from the **Confirmation...** command of the **Options** menu, the confirmation dialog box won't be displayed. The selected files will be immediately deleted.

If you selected a directory instead of a file, the (empty) directory can be deleted after you answer a prompt to confirm your intent. If the directory is not empty, a message, informing you of the error, is displayed.

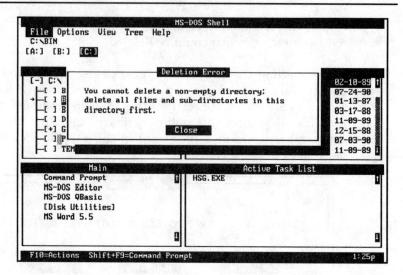

Deleting a directory which contains files generates this error message

Rename...

Rename... assigns a new name to files or directories.

If more than one file is selected, you will be prompted to rename each file. If there is already a file with that name, the MS-DOS Shell does not execute the command.

Remember that none of the files in a directory can be selected if you want to rename a directory.

Change Attributes...

Change Attributes... can be used to change the attribute setting for a file. If more than one file is selected, first you can choose, in a dialog box, whether to change the attributes for all of the files at once or to change the attributes for individual files.

You can specify more than one attribute by selecting the attributes to change with the ⬆ and ⬇ cursor keys and pressing the `Spacebar` to select them or by using the mouse. A mark, which appears to the left of each attribute, indicates whether or not a file attribute is set.

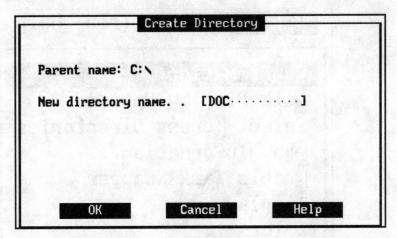

```
┌──────────────┤ Change Attributes ├──────────────┐
│                                                  │
│  File:  AUTOEXEC.BAT                1 of      1  │
│                                                  │
│  To change attribute, select item and press     │
│  the SPACEBAR. Press ENTER when complete.        │
│                                                  │
│     Hidden                                       │
│     System                                       │
│  ▶  Archive                                      │
│     Read only                                    │
│                                                  │
│    ███ OK ███      ██ Cancel ██      ██ Help ██   │
│                                                  │
└──────────────────────────────────────────────────┘
```

The Archive Bit is already set for AUTOEXEC.BAT

Create Directory...

To use the MS-DOS Shell File menu **Create Directory...** command to create a new directory, the Directory Tree area must be active. The new directory is always a subdirectory of the current (selected) directory. The current directory is displayed in the top line of the Create directory dialog box. Specify the name of the new directory in the next line. Use the same method to assign filenames.

```
┌──────────────┤ Create Directory ├──────────────┐
│                                                 │
│                                                 │
│   Parent name: C:\                              │
│                                                 │
│   New directory name. .  [DOC········]          │
│                                                 │
│                                                 │
│                                                 │
│                                                 │
│                                                 │
│    ███ OK ███      ██ Cancel ██      ██ Help ██  │
│                                                 │
└─────────────────────────────────────────────────┘
```

Preparing to create a new directory named DOC using Create Directory

Select All

Use **Select All** to select all of the files of a directory.

Deselect All

Use **Deselect All** to remove all selections from the current directory.

Exit

The last command of the **File** menu is called **Exit**. When you select this command, you leave the MS-DOS Shell without any further prompts. You can also leave the MS-DOS Shell by pressing Alt + F4 or F3.

7.6.3   The Options menu

The first four settings of the **Options** menu affect only the Directory Tree/file list area. They are inactive if only the program list area is displayed. These four commands allow you to control the confirmation for deletes, replacements and mouse operations. They also enable you to set the file display options, switch the selection option for more than one directory on and off and display detailed information on files, directories and drives.

These settings can switch the Task Swapper on and off, select the video display and make different settings for color and monochrome monitors.

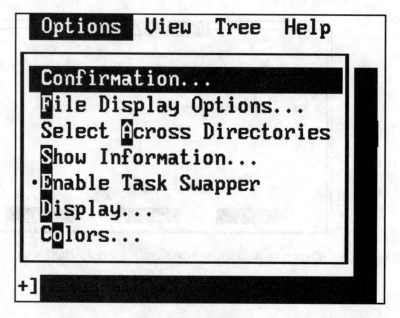

The Options menu

Confirmation...

Use MS-DOS Shell Options menu **Confirmation...** to switch the confirmation prompts on or off. These prompts are dialog boxes that appear on the screen when you want to delete or move a selected entry. You must confirm the operation (delete or move).

The Confirmation dialog box enables you to change three options. If any of these options is activated, an [X] is displayed in front of the option. Select an option by clicking on it or pressing the (Spacebar).

If the first option, Confirm on Delete, is selected, a confirmation prompt appears before every file or directory is deleted.

The second option, Confirm on Replace, requires a confirmation prompt when copying and moving files.

Confirm on Mouse Operation, the third option, displays a confirmation prompt before copying or moving files while holding down the mouse button.

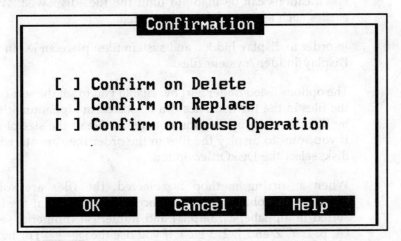

The Confirmation dialog box from the Options menu

File Display Options...

Changes made in MS-DOS Shell Options menu **File Display Options...** affect the way files are displayed in the file list of the Directory Tree/file list area.

```
┌────────────────┤ File Display Options ├────────────────┐
│                                                         │
│  Name:     [*.*··········]                              │
│                                                         │
│                                             Sort by:    │
│                                                         │
│  [ ] Display hidden/system files         (·) Name       │
│                                          ( ) Extension   │
│                                          ( ) Date        │
│  [ ] Descending order                    ( ) Size        │
│                                          ( ) DiskOrder   │
│                                                         │
│         ███ OK ███      ███ Cancel ███     ███ Help ███  │
│                                                         │
└─────────────────────────────────────────────────────────┘
```

Setting the file display options

In the Name: text box you can determine which files in the file list will be displayed. The default setting is *.*. This setting means that all files in the current directory are displayed. Other specifications can be made to limit the files displayed. Wildcard entries such as "*" and "?" are accepted.

In order to display hidden and system files, place an [X] in front of Display hidden/system files.

The options listed under Sort by: enable you to set the sort order for the files in the file list. Files can be sorted in alphanumeric order, by file extension, by creation date of the file or the size of the file. If you want to display the files in the order they are stored on the disk, select the DiskOrder option.

When a sorting method is selected, the files are sorted in "ascending" alphanumeric sequence. This means that the files are sorted in alphabetical (alpha) and numerical (numeric) sequence (A, B, ... Y, Z and 1, 2, 3 etc.). If you use the [Spacebar] or mouse to select the Descending order check box, the files will be displayed in "descending" sequence (Z, Y, ... B, A and 9, 8, 7 etc.).

Select Across Directories

Activating the third command, MS-DOS Shell Options menu **Select Across Directories**, enables you to select files in different directories. With the default settings, any selected file is cleared when you leave the directory where the selection was made.

We recommend switching off this option when deleting files. It's a lot safer when you are only able to select and delete files in the current directory.

Show Information...

Selecting MS-DOS Shell Options menu **Show Information...** displays information about a selected file, the current directory and the current drive.

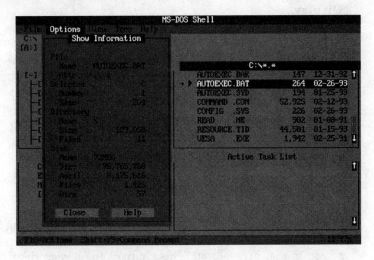

Show Information dialog box with information about the selected file (AUTOEXEC.BAT), the current directory (the root directory) and the current drive (C:)

Show Information... displays the following information:

File displays the name of the selected file and its attributes.

Selected displays the letter of the current drive, and the number and total size of all selected files.

Directory displays the following information about the directory being displayed in the file list. It provides the name of the directory, its total size and the number of files in the directory.

Show Information... displays data about the current drive, including the name of the diskette/fixed disk, its total storage capacity (Size), the available free storage area, the number of files stored and the number of available directories.

Enable Task Swapper

Selecting **Enable Task Swapper** switches the Task Swapper on and off. To activate this command, click once or select it with the cursor key and press Enter. A mark is placed in front of the text to indicate that the Task Swapper is switched on. More detailed information about the Task Swapper is available elsewhere in this book.

Display...

Use **Display...** to choose one of eight screen displays if you have a VGA graphics card. Three options are in text mode and five are in graphics mode:

```
Text       Low Resolution        (25 Lines)
Text       High Resolution 1     (43 Lines)
Text       High Resolution 2     (50 Lines)
Graphics   Low Resolution        (25 Lines)
Graphics   Medium Resolution 1   (30 Lines)
Graphics   Medium Resolution 2   (34 Lines)
Graphics   High Resolution 1     (43 Lines)
Graphics   High Resolution 2     (60 Lines)
```

Use the cursor keys to select the desired option. Selecting Preview enables you to test the screen display. After you've selected a screen mode, press Enter. This changes the screen display to the one selected.

The Hercules monochrome graphics card limits your options. There are two kinds of text resolution with 25 lines each: graphics resolution with 25 lines and graphics resolution with 43 lines.

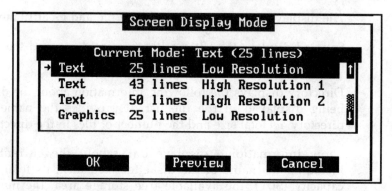

Selecting the screen display mode

Colors...

If you have a color monitor, the **Colors...** command lets you choose from four preset settings. Two of the settings are monochrome and two are color. The Color Scheme dialog box displays the active color scheme in the top dialog line.

Use the ⬆ cursor key to move to the settings. Then use ⬆ and ⬇ to select a setting and press (Enter). This activates the selected color display. If you like the display, accept it by pressing (Enter). If you don't like the display, press (Esc) to activate the previous display.

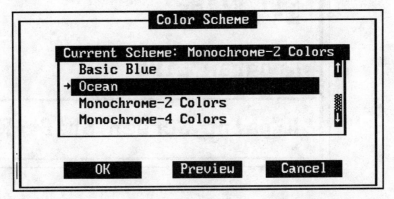

Selecting the color display using Colors from the Options menu

If you don't like the colors that are used, design one according to your preferences. To design your own color scheme, you must edit the DOSSHELL.INI file, in which the color palettes are defined.

 Never edit the DOSSHELL.INI file while the MS-DOS Shell is running. The MS-DOS Shell notes the position of this file's cluster on the storage medium (diskette, hard drive) when it starts and immediately writes all changes to this cluster. Making changes while the MS-DOS Shell is running could lead to data loss and crash the Shell.

7.6.4 The View menu

This menu is used to change the display mode of the MS-DOS Shell. You can choose to display only the program list area or only the Directory Tree/file list area on the screen. You can also display both areas on the screen simultaneously. The **View** menu also has a command for dividing the Directory Tree/file list area into one or two file lists and listing all of the files of a drive in alphanumeric order.

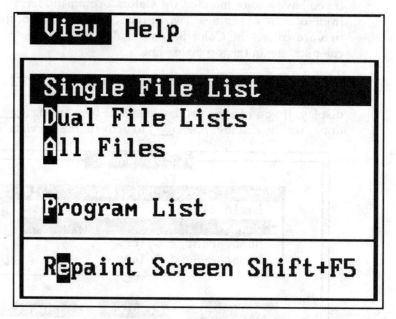

The View menu

Single File List

Select **Single File List** and the Directory Tree/file list area fills the entire screen with a single file list. The left side of the screen displays the Directory Tree while the right side of the screen displays the file list of the selected directory.

Dual File Lists

Dual File Lists divides the Directory Tree/file list area horizontally on the screen. This lets you see the directory structure for two drives on the left side of the screen and the file list of the current directory on the right side of the screen. Use the drive icons to select which drive and file list is displayed. These lists can be two different drives or directories on the same drive.

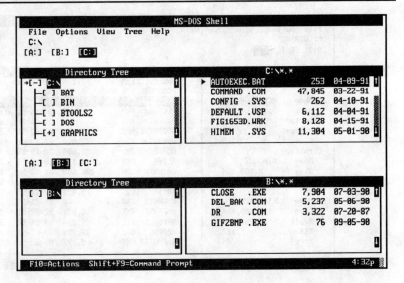

Displaying two file lists

All Files

Select **All Files** to display a list of all of the files in the current drive in alphanumeric order. The directory structure is cancelled. The left side of the screen contains an area with the same information you receive from **Show Information...** of the **Options** menu.

The file list is on the right side of the screen. The information in the left area always refers to the selected file in the right area.

```
                                      MS-DOS Shell
        File  Options  View  Tree  Help
        C:\WINDOWS
        [A:]  [B:]  [C:]

                                                      *.*
                                      ABOUTDLG.FRM       2,920  04-10-91  11:19a
        File                          ACADEMIC.STY       1,536  10-04-90   3:05p
          Name : ACCESSOR.GRP      → ► ACCESSOR.GRP       7,159  04-15-91   2:40p
          Attr : ...a                 ADDFORM .FRM         842  04-10-91  11:20a
        Selected         C            ADDPATH .BAT          62  01-21-91   1:13p
          Number:        1            ADDPATH1.BAT          74  02-02-91   2:02a
          Size :     7,159            ADDRESS .TBK      51,918  02-13-91  12:04p
        Directory                     ALARMS  .TBK      91,054  10-10-90   1:00a
          Name : WINDOWS              ALIEN   .HSG      16,128  10-11-89   8:59a
          Size :  3,503,924           ANIMATE .TBK     206,640  04-03-90   1:00p
          Files:        85            ANIMATE .TBK     178,034  02-11-91   5:40p
        Disk                          ANSI    .SYS       9,029  03-22-91   5:10a
          Name : BIG DISK             ANZBYTE .BAS         460  01-21-91   1:14p
          Size :  105,406,464         ANZBYTE .EXE       6,832  02-03-91   9:58p
          Avail:  61,257,728          APPEALS .STY       1,024  10-04-90   3:05p
          Files:      1,182           APPEND  .EXE      10,774  03-22-91   5:10a
          Dirs :         45           APPNOTES.TXT       9,677  03-22-91   5:10a

        F10=Actions  Shift+F9=Command Prompt                              5:00p
```

Displaying All Files from the View menu of the MS-DOS Shell

Program/File Lists

The **Program/File Lists** command returns the original appearance of the MS-DOS Shell screen. The screen is divided horizontally in the middle, displaying the Directory Tree and the file list area in the top half and the program list area in the bottom half.

Program List

The **Program List** command displays only the program list area.

Repaint Screen

The **Repaint Screen** command redraws the screen but doesn't update the list of files in the program list or file list areas. This command can be selected directly from the menu or by pressing [Shift] + [F5].

Refresh

Refresh rereads the disk and updates the program list area and the file list area to reflect any changes, such as deleted or restored files. Select **Refresh** either from the menu or by pressing the [F5] key.

7.6.5   The Tree menu

This menu is only available when the Directory Tree/file list area is selected. Commands found here are used to open and close the tree structure of the Directory Tree/file list area. This means that the display of the tree structure can be set to show only the root directory or extended far enough to show all of the subdirectories.

If a directory has one or more subdirectories that aren't being displayed due to the display mode, a "+" will be displayed in the icon to the left of the directory name. If all of the subdirectories of a directory are being displayed, you will see a "-" in the icon.

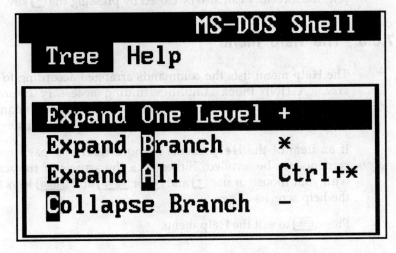

The Tree menu of the MS-DOS Shell

Expand One Level +

Choose **Expand One Level +** to open the selected directory by one level. If this directory has subdirectories, they remain closed. You can only open directories that display a "+" in the directory icon. Pressing the ⊕ key also opens a selected directory.

Expand Branch

Select **Expand Branch** to open the entire selected directory. If this directory has subdirectories containing other subdirectories, all of the directories are displayed. You can only open directories that display a "+" in the directory icon. The branches can also be expanded by pressing the "*" key.

Expand All

Use **Expand All** to open the entire directory structure. This means that every directory will be opened and all subdirectories will be displayed. You can only open directories that display a "+" in the directory icon. Pressing (Ctrl), "+" and "*" from the numeric keypad will also execute this command.

Collapse Branch

Use **Collapse Branch** to close the entire selected directory. You can only close directories that display a "-" in the directory icon. A selected directory can also be closed by pressing the ⊡ key.

7.6.6   The Help menu

The **Help** menu lists the commands arranged according to subject areas. A Help Index simplifies finding necessary information. Help is also subject oriented for the MS-DOS Shell fundamentals, the keyboard, commands, procedures and even help on using Help.

If an item of the **Help** menu is more than one page long, the contents can be scrolled. Either click the arrows of the scroll bar with your mouse or use ⊡ and ⊡ or (PgUp) and (PgDn) keys to scan the help screens.

Press (Esc) to exit the **Help** menu.

*The Help menu for the MS-DOS
Shell*

Index

Select **Index** to view a help screen listing subjects from A to Z.

Keyboard

Select **Keyboard** to learn about the most important keys and key
combinations.

Shell Basics

Select **Shell Basics** to find help about MS-DOS Shell
fundamentals.

Commands

Select **Commands** to find help about MS-DOS Shell commands.

Procedures

Select **Procedures** to find help about MS-DOS Shell procedures.

Using Help

Select **Using Help** to learn about using the help system.

About Shell

Select **About Shell** to display the MS-DOS Shell version number
and the copyright notice.

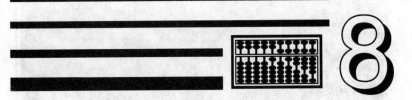

C h a p t e r

8

Using The MS-DOS Editor

The MS-DOS Editor is a full screen editor that lets you create, view and change text files quickly and easily. It's comparable to a simple word processor. You can view a file on the full screen and use the cursor keys to easily change the contents of the file.

Fundamentals

Like the MS-DOS Shell and QBasic, MS-DOS Editor is based on the SAA (System Application Architecture) standard. The editing features of MS-DOS Editor can be used by pressing appropriate keys on the keyboard or by using a mouse.

In this chapter we'll show you how to make your selections at the keyboard. Of course, you can also select the same functions by clicking on the menus with the mouse by pointing and clicking on the appropriate commands.

To start the MS-DOS Editor, type the following and then press Enter:

```
EDIT
```

The following screen appears:

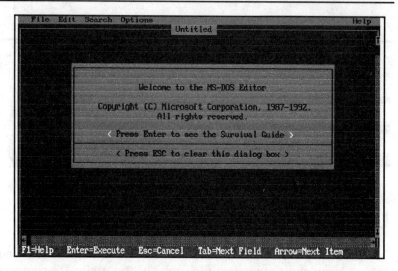

MS-DOS Editor - the full screen editor

You can receive information on the MS-DOS Editor by pressing
(Enter). This opens the Survival Guide help files:

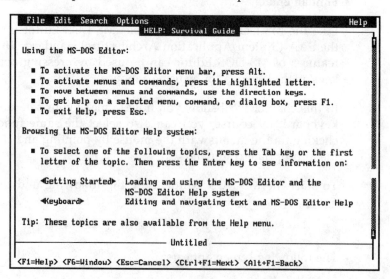

The MS-DOS Editor help files

Alternatively, you can press (Esc) to clear the dialog box.

The menu bar

Press (Alt) to activate the menu bar in the top line of the screen.
When it's active, the first letter of the menu name is highlighted.
To pull down a menu, press the letter corresponding to the menu
name.

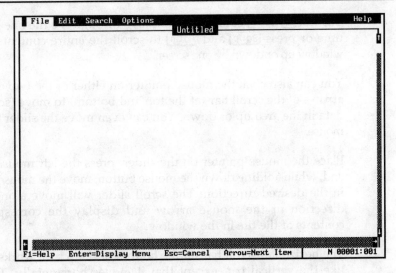

The Edit menu bar activated

You can also use the → and ← cursor keys to choose from among the menus. When the selection cursor covers the desired menu name, press (Enter) to pull down the menu.

If you are using the mouse, point to the desired name in the menu bar and click the left mouse button to pull down the menu. Point and click on the appropriate command to perform the desired function.

The pull-down menus

The pull-down menus contain lists of commands. For each command, one letter is highlighted. To select a command, press the desired highlighted letter. You can also use the ↑ and ↓ cursor keys to select a command. When the selection cursor covers the desired command, press (Enter) to select it.

The scroll bar

On the right margin of the screen is a vertical grey strip with arrows pointing up and down, as seen in the previous figure. This is the scroll bar. Within this strip is a rectangle. This is the scroll slider.

Its position within the scroll bar indicates which section of the file is being displayed. If the slider is at the top of the scroll bar, the start of the file is being displayed. If it is in the middle of the scroll bar, you are seeing the middle portion and if it's at the bottom, the window contains the last part of the file.

Use the ⬆ or ⬇ cursor keys to move through the file one line at a time or press ⎙PgUp⎙ and ⎙PgDn⎙ to scroll the entire contents of the window up or down by one screen.

You can also click the mouse pointer on either of the two direction arrows of the scroll bar (at the top and bottom) to move (scroll) the data in the area up or down. You can even move the slider with the mouse.

Place the mouse pointer on the slider, press the left mouse button and, while holding down the mouse button, move the mouse pointer in the desired direction. The scroll slider will move along in the direction of the mouse arrow and display the corresponding contents of the file in the window.

The horizontal scroll bar on the bottom of the screen works exactly like the vertical bar, except that it moves horizontally. To scroll horizontally, you can also use the key combinations ⎙Ctrl⎙ + ⎙PgDn⎙ to move right and ⎙Ctrl⎙ + ⎙PgUp⎙ to move left.

8.1   Overview

The following is a brief description of the MS-DOS Editor and how it works.

The purpose of the MS-DOS Editor

The MS-DOS Editor is intended for editing simple text files, and making changes to batch or system files. For example, you can use the MS-DOS Editor to change your CONFIG.SYS file or AUTOEXEC.BAT file.

Starting the MS-DOS Editor

Type the following and press ⎙Enter⎙ to run the MS-DOS Editor:

```
EDIT
```

Menu selection

You can activate the menu bar either by using a mouse, or by pressing the ⎙Alt⎙ key. Once a menu title is highlighted using the keyboard, you can move through the menu titles and menu commands using the cursor keys. Pressing ⎙Enter⎙ selects the currently highlighted menu command.

Loading a file

To load a file select the **File** menu and the **Open...** command. In the file selector box which appears, you can select a file, drive or directory.

Saving a file

To save a file select the **File** menu and the **Save As...** command. Enter a filename when the Save As dialog box appears. For any subsequent changes to this file, select the **File** menu and the **Save** command.

Text entry and correction

Type text into the MS-DOS Editor as you would a standard typewriter. The Enter key must be pressed at the end of each line. You can delete characters using the Del key and the Backspace key.

To delete, copy or paste complete passages, press and hold the Shift key and move the cursor to select the passage. See the **Edit** menu for details.

Exiting the MS-DOS Editor

To leave the MS-DOS Editor, select **File/Exit**. If you have been editing a file and have not yet saved that file, the MS-DOS Editor will ask whether you want to save the file.

8.2 Starting the Editor and Loading a File

Since the MS-DOS Editor is a transient program, you must load it from your diskette or hard drive every time. When DOS 6.0 is installed, the EDIT.COM program is installed in the DOS directory.

Since you probably have defined your search path to include the DOS directory, MS-DOS Editor can be started from any directory. If you aren't using a hard drive, you must insert the diskette containing EDIT.COM into the current drive.

 After starting the editor, you may display a help screen (called the Survival Guide). Press Enter to activate the help system; press Esc to go directly to the insert screen of the editor.

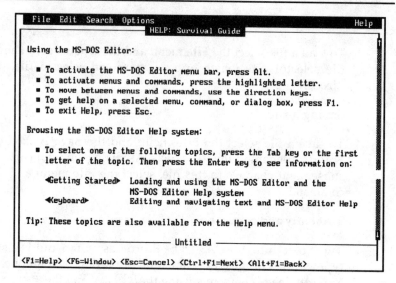

The MS-DOS Editor help system

Starting the MS-DOS Editor

Type the EDIT command to start the editor.

As with all resident and external MS-DOS commands of Version 6.0, when you call the MS-DOS Editor you can specify the /? switch to display a condensed help screen explaining the command syntax.

This help screen displays the various options available when starting the editor.

```
C:\DOS>edit /?
Starts the MS-DOS Editor, which creates and changes ASCII files.

EDIT [[drive:][path]filename] [/B] [/G] [/H] [/NOHI]

  [drive:][path]filename  Specifies the ASCII file to edit.
  /B    Allows use of a monochrome monitor with a color graphics card.
  /G    Provides the fastest update of a CGA screen.
  /H    Displays the maximum number of lines possible for your
        hardware.
  /NOHI Allows the use of a monitor without high-intensity support.

C:\DOS>
```

Entering EDIT /? from the command line

As you can see from the syntax description, you can run the MS-DOS Editor to edit a specific file. For example, to edit an ASCII file named SAMPLE.TXT, you would type:

```
EDIT SAMPLE.TXT
```

If you're using one of the switches listed in the previous screen, enter it after the filename:

```
EDIT SAMPLE.TXT /H
```

In this case, the MS-DOS Editor starts and lets you edit the SAMPLE.TXT file. It will display the contents of the file using the highest number of lines that your graphics display card is capable of displaying.

Loading a file

To load a file into the MS-DOS Editor, select the **File** menu and activate the **Open...** command. A dialog box appears for selecting the file to load.

You can select from the File Name: text box, two list boxes (Files and Dirs/Drives) and three command buttons ([OK], [Cancel] and [Help]).

Use the [Tab] key to move between the boxes and command buttons. The mouse pointer can also be used to select the text box or list boxes.

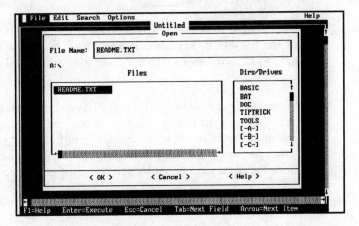

The MS-DOS Editor file selector

The Files list box displays the names of all files with the default filename extension of .TXT. This extension can be changed by typing a different extension in the File Name text box or all files in the selected directory can be displayed by typing *.*.

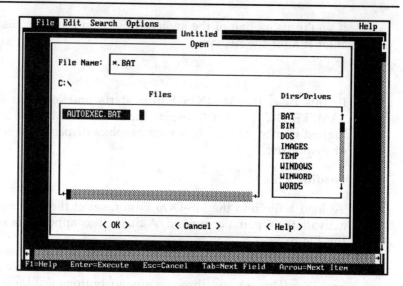

MS-DOS Editor displaying *.BAT files in the root directory of drive C:

Type the filename (either the entire name or with wildcards) in the File Name text box. If a complete filename is entered, select OK; otherwise press Enter.

If the filename is entered with wildcards, the drive and directory for the file can be specified in the Dirs/Drives list box. Use the ↑ and ↓ cursor keys or the mouse and the scroll bar to make a selection.

After the drive and directory have been selected, all files corresponding to the specifications entered in File Name text box appear in the Files list box. Again, use either the ↑ / ↓ or → / ← cursor keys or the mouse and the scroll bar to make your selection. Close the command either by selecting OK or by pressing Enter.

The selected file is then displayed and can be edited on the screen.

Starting with a file

The file to be edited can be specified when MS-DOS Editor is started by typing:

```
EDIT filename
```

MS-DOS Editor then starts and the contents of the file are displayed on the screen. If the EDIT.COM file is in a defined path, then you can change to the directory containing the file to be edited and start MS-DOS Editor. Alternatively, you can start MS-DOS Editor with a file from any directory by specifying the complete path of the file to be edited before the filename. It would look like the following:

```
EDIT D:\PROG\TEST.TXT
```

Creating new files

It's also easy to create a new file using MS-DOS Editor. You have two options. However, be careful when using the second option.

The first, and safer option is to call EDIT followed by the filename of your new file, including the file extension. For example, to create a new file called TEST.TXT, enter EDIT TEST.TXT. If there is no file named TEST.TXT in the current directory, EDIT starts with a blank screen titled TEST.TXT. You can then enter text in the file, select the **File** menu and the **Save** command to store it on the diskette or hard drive.

 This method is safer because if this file (TEST.TXT) already exists in the current directory, EDIT loads it and displays it on the screen. This reminds you that the filename already exists and that you will need to select a different name for your new file. (If you accidentally load a file, open the **File** menu and select **New** to remove the file that was accidentally loaded and display a new area.)

The second method consists of starting the editor without specifying a filename. EDIT then starts displaying an empty screen. After you have entered text, save the contents by opening the **File** menu and selecting the **Save As...** command. Type the filename in the dialog box that appears.

If a file with the same name already exists, a message indicating this will appear on the screen. You can then decide whether you want the contents of the original file to be overwritten by the contents of the new file.

Editing existing files

As previously mentioned, an existing file can be loaded when starting the editor or you can use the **Open...** command from the **File** menu. The file is displayed on the screen for editing.

8.3   Saving a File

One of the most important functions of any editor is saving files.
The MS-DOS Editor saves data in ASCII format. You'll be able to
use many other editors or word processing programs with text files
created by MS-DOS Editor.

Remember that when you save a file in the MS-DOS Editor, a new
file will overwrite a file with the same name that already exists
in the current directory of the hard drive or diskette. The MS-DOS
Editor doesn't make a backup copy of the old file. This means that
there isn't a .BAK file containing the contents of the previous
version of the file. By overwriting an earlier file with the contents
of the new file, you will lose the data.

Saving a new file

To save a new file that doesn't have a name, open the **File** menu
and select the **Save As...** command. The Save As dialog box
appears with the File Name text box and Dirs/Drives list box.
Select the drive and directory, in which the file should be saved,
from the Dirs/Drives list box. Type the filename in the File Name
text box. Finally, press (Enter) or select (OK) to save the file.

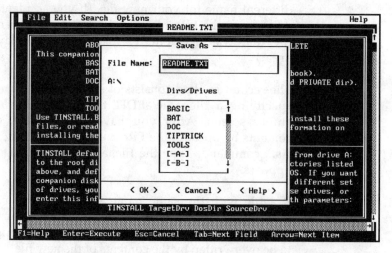

The MS-DOS Editor Save As dialog box

Saving an open file

If you open and edit an existing file or you start EDIT with a
filename, the filename and its directory are already established.
You can save the file by using the **Save** command from the **File**
menu.

You can also change the filename and directory before saving the file. Just open the **File** menu and select the **Save As...** command. Type the filename in the File Name text box. The directory from which the file was loaded or the active directory is selected from the Dirs/Drives list box beneath.

Changing filenames

You can also use the **Save As...** command to save the file with a new name. Type the new filename and press (Enter) or select (OK). The MS-DOS Editor then stores the file on your hard drive or diskette using the new filename and preserving the original file.

Clearing the screen and the main memory

After saving a file, the contents of the file are still displayed on the screen and remain in memory. To create a new file, use the **New** command from the **File** menu. When you activate this command, it clears the contents of the file from memory and the screen.

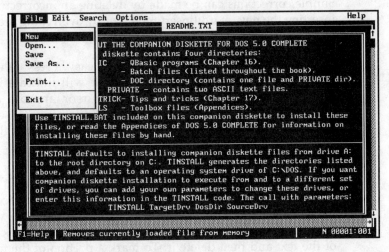

Selecting New from the File menu

Quitting MS-DOS Editor without saving

To quit the editor without saving the file in the memory, select the **Exit** command in the **File** menu.

If you made any changes to the file since the last save, MS-DOS Editor will remind you that you haven't yet saved the contents of the file to disk. Select Yes to save. If you choose No, the file is not saved and you leave the editor.

8.4   Entering and Editing Text

The full screen editor makes it easy to enter text and edit existing text.

Entering text

Use the keyboard to enter text in the editor just as you would use a typewriter. Unlike word processing programs, MS-DOS Editor doesn't automatically make a new line when you reach the end of a line (at 78 characters) on the screen. Instead, it shifts the displayed area farther to the right. The length of a text line is limited to 256 characters. If you reach the end of a line when entering text (at character 256), you'll hear a short warning beep. Press Enter to move to the beginning of the next line.

Inserting and overtyping text

Simple corrections can be made by deleting an incorrect word and inserting the new word (insert mode) or by overtyping the incorrect word with the new word (overtype mode).

Switching between these two modes is easy. Press either Ins or Ctrl + V. The appearance of the cursor will indicate in which mode you're currently located. The cursor appears as a line underneath the letter when MS-DOS Editor is in insert mode. When in overtype mode, the cursor changes to a rectangle the size of a letter.

Making changes in insert mode

In insert mode, first delete the word you want to replace. Do this by positioning the cursor at the start of the incorrect word and pressing Del until the word is deleted. You can also mark a portion of the text and then delete it. To mark a portion of the text, move the cursor to the start of the text and press Shift + → until the desired portion is highlighted. To delete the marked text, press Del.

Making changes in overtype mode

In overtype mode, a character covered by the blinking rectangle is replaced by a new typed character. After each keystroke, the cursor moves one character to the right. When using overtype mode, make sure that the text you're entering doesn't overtype any text that should remain. In case the new text entry is longer than the original text, press Ins (or Ctrl + V) to switch off overtype mode and switch on insert mode.

Deleting parts of text

There are several ways to delete passages of text, ranging from deleting letters, to words, or even entire lines.

Deleting a character with (Backspace)

You can use either the (Backspace) key or press (Ctrl) + (H) to delete a character to the left of the cursor. It doesn't matter whether you are in insert mode or overtype mode.

Deleting a character with (Del)

Use (Del) or press (Ctrl) + (G) to remove the character above the cursor (insert mode) or the character covered by the cursor (overtype mode).

Deleting a word with (Ctrl)+(T)

Press (Ctrl) + (T) to delete a word at a time. This deletes all characters from the current cursor position and then moves to the right to the next space, a special character or a punctuation mark. Special characters such as spaces and punctuation marks are treated as separate words. If the cursor is in the middle of a word, deleting begins from this point and continues to the end of the word.

Deleting a line with (Ctrl)+(Y)

Entire lines can be deleted by pressing (Ctrl) + (Y). The entire line in which the cursor is located is deleted. It doesn't matter where the cursor is in the line. After deleting the line the cursor is positioned at the beginning of the next line.

Deleting a block using (Del) *to delete marked text*

Here's an easy way to delete blocks of text. Mark the block of text to be deleted, hold down the (Shift) key and press the cursor keys ((→), (←), (↑) or (↓)) to move the cursor; then press (Del). MS-DOS Editor displays marked text in inverse video. After marking it, just press (Del).

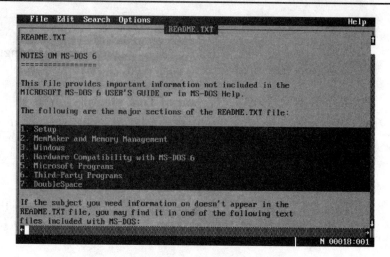

Marking a block of text

Tabs

You can also use tabs in the MS-DOS Editor. Tabs are imaginary stops on the screen. The cursor can be moved to these positions by pressing the (Tab) key. Tabs can be used to place columns of numbers underneath each other or set up tables.

   The MS-DOS Editor doesn't insert ASCII tab characters; instead it inserts the corresponding number of spaces.

Before loading a file, containing tab characters, from a diskette or a hard drive, set the desired number of tab spaces. Do this using the **Display...** command from the **Options** menu. In the Display Options dialog box set the number of spaces between tabs by changing the Tab Stops option. The default setting is 8. Any value between 1 and 99 can be selected.

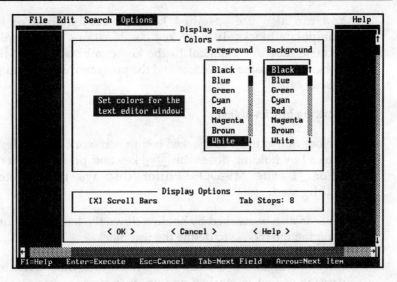

Options/Display... dialog box

8.5   Working with Blocks of Text

Like many other word processors, you can also work with blocks of
text using the MS-Editor. A block is simply a marked passage of
text. In the MS-DOS Editor, working with blocks of text is not
quite as smooth as it is with most word processors, but it is easy.
The MS-DOS Editor manages blocks of text by using a buffer,
which is a reserved area of memory.

After you've defined a block, you manipulate it with the **Edit**
menu.

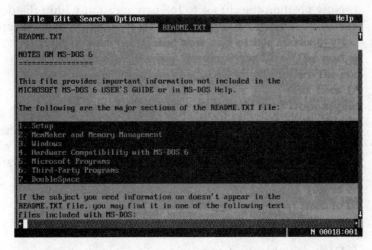

*A block of text defined in the MS-DOS Editor appears as
inverse text*

You can also use specified keys (or combination of keys) to manipulate blocks. If these key combinations seem familiar, it's because they are identical to the key combinations for handling blocks of text using WordStar and the programming language Turbo Pascal.

Marking blocks of text

A block of text must be marked before you work with it. Text can be marked by holding down the [Shift] key and pressing either [→], [←], [↑] or [↓]. The MS-DOS Editor displays marked text as highlighted.

Text can also be marked by holding down the left mouse button and dragging the mouse to define the text block.

Only one block of text can be selected at a time. That is, if one passage of text is marked and another passage has already been marked, the first marked passage will no longer be highlighted.

Moving blocks of text

Moving a block of text within a document is a two-step process. You must first move it to the buffer and then move it from the buffer to the new location in the document.

First mark the passage to be moved. Next select the **Cut** command from the **Edit** menu or press [Shift] + [Del]. This cuts the passage from the document. Although it disappears from the screen, it has moved to the buffer.

Now position the cursor to the new location within the document. Finally, select the **Paste** command from the **Edit** menu or press [Shift] + [Ins]. The passage will reappear in the new location.

Copying blocks of text

Copying a block of text is similar to moving a block.

First mark the passage to be copied. Next select the **Copy** command from the **Edit** menu or press [Ctrl] + [Ins]. Then move the cursor to the appropriate location within the document and select the **Paste** command from the **Edit** menu or press [Shift] + [Ins]. The copied passage will appear in the new location.

Deleting blocks of text

Deleting a block of text is simple. First mark the passage to be deleted. Then select the **Clear** command from the **Edit** menu or press Del. Text which is deleted is not placed in the buffer and cannot be copied, moved or recovered.

Saving a block of text as a file

Occasionally you'll want to save a block of text as a file. You can do this by using the buffer. First mark the passage and copy it to the buffer using the **Copy** command from the **Edit** menu or Ctrl + Ins (or Shift + Del which cuts the passage into the buffer).

Next select the **New** command from the **File** menu to clear the screen. Then select the **Paste** command from the **Edit** menu or press Shift + Ins to paste the contents of the buffer (containing the desired block of text) to the screen.

Finally, select the **Save As...** command from the **File** menu to give this block of text a new filename and save it onto a diskette or hard drive.

Inserting files to text

Just as you can save a block of text separately from an entire document, you can also insert the contents of a file into a different document. The procedure is similar to the description above.

Use the **Open...** command from the **File** menu to load the file from which you want to cut or copy text. Mark the block of text (or the entire document). Next, use either Shift + Del, Ctrl + Ins or select the **Cut** command or **Copy** command from the **Edit** menu to place the text block into the buffer.

Select the **New** command from the **File** menu to clear the screen. Then select the **Open...** command of the **File** menu to load the file into which you want to insert the contents of the buffer.

Place the cursor where you want to insert the text and either press Shift + Ins or select **Paste** from the **Edit** menu to copy the block of text from the buffer into the file.

Cancelling a selection

To cancel a selection (cancel a marked block), simply press any cursor key. The selection will no longer be highlighted.

8.6   Edit Keys

The following table lists the functions of all keys and key combinations.

Simple editor keys

[Esc]	Aborts commands, closes dialog box.
[←]	Moves the cursor one character to the left (also [Ctrl] + [S]).
[→]	Moves the cursor one character to the right (also [Ctrl] + [D]).
[↑]	Moves the cursor one line up (also [Ctrl] + [E]).
[↓]	Moves the cursor one line down (also [Ctrl] + [X]).
[Backspace]	Deletes the character to the left of the cursor (also [Ctrl] + [H]).
[Del]	Deletes character in the current cursor position (also [Ctrl] + [G]).
[Ins]	Switches insert mode on or off (also [Ctrl] + [V]).
[Home]	Cursor jumps to the beginning of the line.
[End]	Cursor jumps to the end of the line.
[PgUp]	Cursor jumps one screen up (also [Ctrl] + [R]).
[PgDn]	Cursor jumps one screen down (also [Ctrl] + [C]).

Extended editor keys

[Ctrl] + [A]	Cursor jumps to previous word.
[Ctrl] + [F]	Cursor jumps to next word.
[Ctrl] + [N]	Rest of the line from current position of the cursor shifts to the next line.
[Ctrl] + [PgUp]	Horizontal scrolling page by page (78 characters to the left).

⌈Ctrl⌉ + ⌈PgDn⌉

Horizontal scrolling page by page (78 characters to the right).

⌈Ctrl⌉ + ⌈Q⌉⌈S⌉

Cursor jumps to beginning of line.

⌈Ctrl⌉ + ⌈Q⌉⌈D⌉

Cursor jumps to end of line.

⌈Ctrl⌉ + ⌈W⌉   Entire screen scrolls one line down. Cursor remains in the same position.

⌈Ctrl⌉ + ⌈Z⌉   Entire screen scrolls one line up. Cursor remains in the same position.

⌈Ctrl⌉ + ⌈T⌉   Deletes the next word.

⌈Ctrl⌉ + ⌈Y⌉   Deletes the line where the cursor is located.

⌈Ctrl⌉ + ⌈K⌉ + ⌈?⌉

Sets a mark; ? stands for a number between 0 and 3. This enables you to mark passages of text while you are working. You can use the ⌈Ctrl⌉⌈Q⌉ + ⌈?⌉, described below, to move the cursor to these marks. The marks aren't displayed and are not saved when you close the file.

⌈Ctrl⌉ + ⌈Q⌉ + ⌈?⌉

Jumps to mark ?. ⌈Ctrl⌉ + ⌈K⌉ + ⌈?⌉ must be used to set the marks before using this key combination (see the previous).

8.7   Moving the Cursor

In this section we'll show you how to move the cursor within the editor. In most cases there are two ways to move the cursor and a way to perform the same action with the mouse. The different keyboard methods are shown in the following table:

Movement	First Method	Second Method
One character right	`→`	`Ctrl` + `D`
One character left	`←`	`Ctrl` + `S`
One line up	`↑`	`Ctrl` + `E`
One line down	`↓`	`Ctrl` + `X`
One word left	`Ctrl` + `←`	`Ctrl` + `A`
One word right	`Ctrl` + `→`	`Ctrl` + `F`
One page up	`PgUp`	`Ctrl` + `R`
One page down	`PgDn`	`Ctrl` + `C`
Beginning of file	`Ctrl` + `Home`	
End of file	`Ctrl` + `End`	
One window left	`Ctrl` + `PgUp`	
One window right	`Ctrl` + `PgDn`	
Beginning of line	`Home`	
End of line	`End`	

8.8   The Edit Menus

Using the letter keys

Press `Alt` to activate the menu bar. Then press the highlighted letter key to pull down the individual menus. Pressing the highlighted letter causes the menu to be opened.

Using the cursor keys

The `↓` and `↑` cursor keys can also be used to open the pull-down menus, while the `→` and `←` cursor keys can be used to select a pull-down menu. Move the area shown in inverse text to the desired command and press `Enter` to execute the command.

Using the mouse

If you are using the mouse, point and click to the desired menu and the pull-down menu will open. You can also activate individual commands by clicking on them with the mouse.

Now we'll explain how the menus are organized and what the commands do.

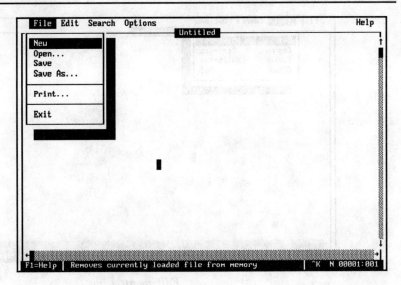

File menu

The File menu

New   Clears the screen and deletes the file contents.

Open...   Use this command to load an existing file from a
                 diskette or hard drive to command memory.

Save   Use this command to save a file which has been
                 previously saved. If you haven't saved a file yet, this
                 command prompts you to enter a filename.

Save As...   Use this command to save a new file. You can also use
                 it to save an existing file with a new name.

Print...   Use this command to print either the entire file or a
                 marked block of text on the printer.

Exit   Use this command to leave the editor and return to the
                 MS-DOS Shell or command line.

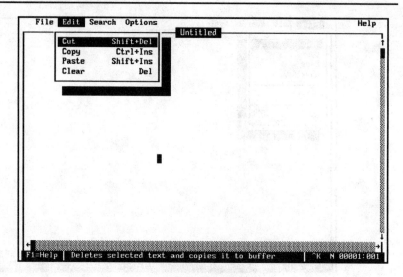

Edit menu

The Edit menu

Cut   Use this command to delete a marked block of text
               from the document and copy it to the buffer.

Copy   Use this command to copy a marked block from the
               document to the buffer.

Paste   Use this command to insert the contents of the buffer
               (block of text) at the position of the cursor in the
               document.

Clear   Use this command to delete a marked block of text.
               The deleted text is not copied to the buffer.

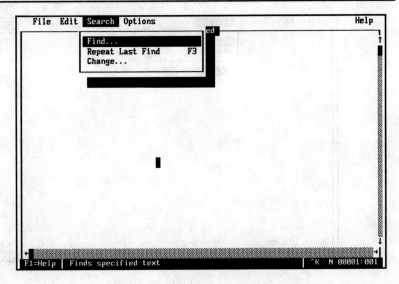

Search menu

The Search menu

Find...   Use this command to search for any character string in the document. You can specify whether to search for upper or lowercase letters, search for the target string as a separate word (and not as a part of another word) as well as the target string itself.

Repeat Last Find

Use this command or press F3 to repeat the last search.

Change...   Use this command to replace any character string in the document with any other string of characters.

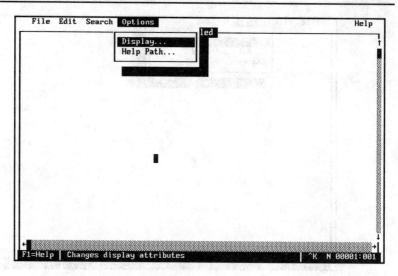

Options menu

The Options menu

Display... Use this command to select the color of the screen background and the color of the font (the foreground), to switch the scroll bar on and off and to set the distance between the tabs.

Help Path...

Use this command to specify the path for the directory containing the EDIT.HLP file.

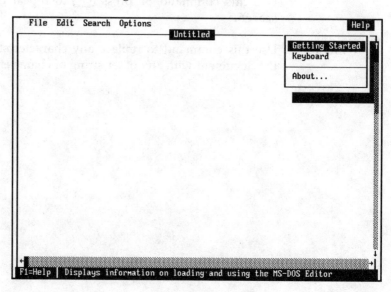

Help menu

The Help menu

Getting Started
   Displays a help screen that explains how to work with the editor.

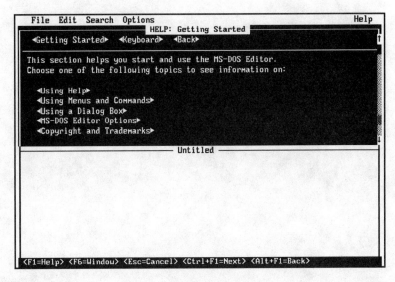

Getting Started help screen

Keyboard Displays a help screen explaining the editing keys and other special keys.

About... This displays information about the copyright and version number of the editor.

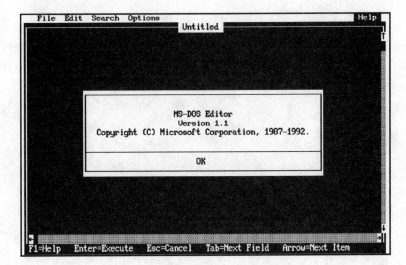

About dialog box

Getting Started

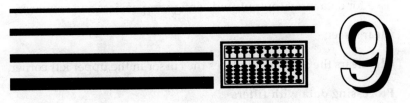

Data Input And Output

This chapter explains how MS-DOS communicates with users - how it inputs and outputs data. As a rule, MS-DOS commands accept your input from the keyboard and output messages to you on the screen.

However, you can change these defaults for any number of reasons. For example, instead of displaying a directory on the screen, you may want a hardcopy printout of it or you may want to sort data alphabetically before displaying them on the screen.

This chapter also discusses different options for adapting MS-DOS to work with your particular hardware. These options include printer access, screen display modes, disk drive formats and storage capacities.

Driver programs

As a rule, MS-DOS uses driver programs to communicate with hardware devices. A driver program is responsible for the direct communication between DOS and a specific device. Some drivers are integral parts of MS-DOS (e.g., disk drive control), while others can be accessed by including them in your CONFIG.SYS file. Since these driver programs come into play very early in the booting procedure, MS-DOS can be freely configured to work with a wide variety of devices.

MS-DOS can also be configured to many country-specific conventions. These include the date and time formats, currency symbol, and the use of special characters and letters on the keyboard. In most cases, MS-DOS will be correctly configured to conform with your local conventions. Any special country configuration is usually not necessary.

9.1   Overview

The following section contains a brief overview of the commands used for data input/output, and configuring devices and countries.

Clear screen

CLS clears the screen and places the cursor in the upper left corner.

Processing data with filters

These special commands can be used to further process existing information. As opposed to other MS-DOS commands, filters can be placed after another command or even after one another using the pipe symbol "|".

Displaying one page at a time

If the information to be displayed by an MS-DOS command will be longer than a single screen page, you can use MORE to stop the display from scrolling after each page is displayed (for example DIR | MORE or TYPE | MORE).

Sorting the display

The SORT filter can be used to sort your information alphabetically (TYPE ADDRFILE.TXT | SORT).

Searching for text (file contents)

FIND can be used to search files or screen output for text strings. For example, to find the ECHO command in the AUTOEXEC.BAT file, you would use FIND "ECHO" AUTOEXEC.BAT. All files on your hard drive created on December 3, 1992 would be located as follows:

```
DIR C:\*.* /S | FIND "12-03-92"
```

Redirecting input

Commands usually receive their input from the keyboard. Many commands (and especially filters) can be instructed to receive their input from a file using the redirect character "<". For example, if the file RETURN.DAT contains a CR/LF (the character that corresponds to ⌈Enter⌉), you can avoid having to press ⌈Enter⌉ after DATE as follows: DATE <RETURN.DAT.

Redirecting output

If you want to save the output of a command, perhaps for additional processing later, you can redirect the output to a file using ">". To send the output from DIR to the file CONTENTS.DAT, use DIR > CONTENTS.DAT. You can send the display of available memory to your printer with MEM > LPT1. You can also cause the output of a command to disappear without being displayed or saved by redirecting it to the null device NUL.

Linking commands

In general, the pipe symbol " | " links two or more commands:

```
COMMAND1  |  COMMAND2
```

COMMAND1 will send its output to COMMAND2 instead of to the screen. COMMAND2 uses the output from COMMAND1 as its input. This can be applied just about anywhere, but it only makes sense when the output of one command creates a meaningful input for another.

Setting up devices with MODE

MODE can be used to set up and configure devices.

MODE LPT1

> Sets up the first printer.

MODE LPT1=COM1

> Redirects the first parallel port to the first serial port.

MODE COM1

> Configures the first serial port with the given parameters.

MODE mode

> Selects a screen display mode.

MODE CON X Y

> Sets the keyboard speed.

MODE CON RATE=32 DELAY=1

> Sets up the fastest possible key repeat rate with the shortest possible delay.

Defining a new drive

The DRIVER.SYS device driver can be used to define a new disk drive. You can use the definition of an existing drive as a pattern, then assign a new drive letter and change the parameters as desired.

Controlling the display with ANSI.SYS

The device driver ANSI.SYS gives you access to special control commands that influence your screen display. These commands can be entered via ESC sequences using the PROMPT command (PROMPT $e[.....).

Setting up the keyboard with ANSI.SYS

ANSI.SYS can also be used to create your own custom keyboard assignments. An ESC sequence can be used to assign a new meaning to just about any key on your keyboard.

Selecting a keyboard layout

The American keyboard is usually the default. The United Kingdom standard keyboard can be selected with KEYB UK.

Date and currency formats

Date and currency formats can be changed to U.K. standards as follows:

```
COUNTRY=044,437,COUNTRY.SYS
```

If you do this, you should also be sure to select the U.K. keyboard (KEYB UK).

Using foreign character sets

The number of special letters required for all languages exceeds the number of available ASCII characters, so it is necessary to work with a selected character set (also referred to as a code page). The character set must be assigned to the keyboard, screen, and printer so that these devices will remain consistent with one another.

    Only in rare cases is setting up a new character set actually worth the trouble it takes.

Keyboard

The United Kingdom character set is prepared using COUNTRY 044, a code page, and the COUNTRY.SYS driver. Code page 437 = USA/Default is recommended. Set the keyboard driver to the same code page:

```
KEYB UK,437
```

Display

Your screen display must also be prepared to use the selected character set using the DISPLAY.SYS driver in the CONFIG.SYS file. For a VGA graphics card:

```
DEVICE=DISPLAY.SYS CON=(EGA,437,1)
```

A line in the AUTOEXEC.BAT file using the MS-DOS MODE command is also needed:

```
MODE CON CP PREP=(437) EGA.CPI
```

Printers

Your printer must also be set up in order to properly print the selected character set. This is also done with a MODE command in AUTOEXEC.BAT:

```
MODE LPT1 CP PREP=(437) 1050.CPI
```

Switching between character sets

In order to switch between character sets, both must first be properly configured. Then the switching function can be activated with NLSFUNC and another code page selected with CHCP.

9.2 Setting Screen Output

The CLS command is used to clear the screen. Type CLS and press Enter and the data on the screen is cleared and the cursor is repositioned to the upper left corner of the screen.

MS-DOS also provides "filters", which are programs that process and change (filter) the screen output of MS-DOS commands. Filters enable you to sort data before it's displayed on the screen and to display information page by page, for example.

MORE (Output information page by page), SORT (Sort information) and FIND (Search for a text) are all MS-DOS filters.

Unless you specify otherwise in the command line, these filters take the information to be processed from the current input device, which is usually the keyboard. The system prompt disappears when these filters are used.

You should know how these filters operate. As you probably already know, a command can be aborted by pressing [Ctrl] + [C]. You can also abort a filter command with [Ctrl] + [C] if you use one of the filters accidentally.

Since MS-DOS sets up a temporary file when you use a filter, there must be sufficient room for the file on the current storage device (normally, your hard drive) or the directory specified by the TEMP environment variable. If there is no TEMP variable and there isn't enough storage space to write the temporary files, MS-DOS displays the message:

```
Intermediate file error during pipe
```

Other error messages may also be displayed for other reasons. For example, the drive might be a diskette that is write protected.

The filter command can still be used if another drive has the sufficient storage space. Make this drive your current drive and start the command from there. MS-DOS always creates the temporary file on the current drive.

Example

The current drive is A: and you want to use the following command to display the contents of the A: drive.

```
DIR | MORE
```

Since there isn't enough room on the diskette for the temporary file, MS-DOS displays an error message. However, there is enough room for the temporary file on a diskette in drive B:. So, type the following:

```
B:
DIR A: | MORE
```

If you have a hard drive and want to avoid this problem permanently, MS-DOS 6.0 gives you the option of always creating these temporary files on a specific drive you select. Do this by defining an environment variable, named TEMP, which contains the complete path of the desired directory. For example, if you have a directory called C:\TMP and you want all temporary MS-

DOS files to be placed in this directory, use the following command line:

```
SET TEMP=C:\TMP
```

If this line is added to your AUTOEXEC.BAT file, this definition is then activated whenever you switch on your computer.

Clearing the screen

To clear the screen and display the defined system prompt, use the CLS command as follows:

```
CLS
```

Using CLS can speed up screen output considerably. If the system prompt is located at the bottom of the screen and you want to display the directory of a disk, MS-DOS has to shift (scroll) the entire contents of the screen to the top for each new line that's displayed. Typing CLS before typing DIR clears the screen so that the display can begin at the top of the screen. This allows DOS to display the first 25 lines without wasting time scrolling the screen.

This technique can be used to speed up lengthy screen output, especially when working with batch files.

Displaying data one page at a time

The MORE filter can be used to display data one page at a time. MORE determines how many lines fit on the screen and then pauses at the end of each screen page. If the screen display has been altered by the MODE command, the MORE filter adjusts accordingly.

Displaying a file page by page

Use the following command to display a file page by page:

```
MORE <File
```

This command is quite useful when displaying lengthy files. Although you could use the TYPE command and press Ctrl + S to pause output to the screen, you might not be able to press Ctrl + S fast enough and thereby lose several lines that scrolled off the screen. When this happens, you must display the file again.

The redirection character "<", which redirects the input, must be used with the MORE command. This redirection indicates that instead of receiving its input from the keyboard, MORE receives input from the specified file.

After one screen page of the file is displayed, a message line appears at the bottom of the screen and MORE waits for a key to be pressed. After you press a key, it continues to display the next page.

You should display a file on the screen page by page only if it's an unformatted text file (an ASCII file). If you display programs or files from applications, strange characters will probably appear on your screen. Text files (ASCII files) and program files (binary files) are handled differently by DOS.

The end of an ASCII file is marked by the special end of file character (ASCII code 26, Ctrl + Z), while binary (program) files can end with any character. Binary files can contain end of file marks within a file.

So if you try to display a binary file on the screen by using TYPE or MORE, MS-DOS will stop when it encounters the first end of file mark. All you'll see on the screen are a few lines of strange characters.

```
C:\>type windows\bktools2.exe
MZw• ñ          ♦ @►||  @  ☺                                    ♦
@►     ►

                    Φ+This program requires Microsoft Windows.
$Z♫
```

Displaying a binary file with TYPE

If the file is very long and you want to stop displaying the file on the screen, press Ctrl + C. This key combination interrupts or aborts all MS-DOS commands.

Example

To display the AUTOEXEC.BAT file page by page, use the command line:

```
MORE <C:\AUTOEXEC.BAT
```

If the file is shorter than a screen page, MS-DOS displays it on the screen without a message from MORE.

The MS-DOS Shell provides an easier way to display the contents of a file. Select the file from the file list then either select **View File Contents** or press F9.

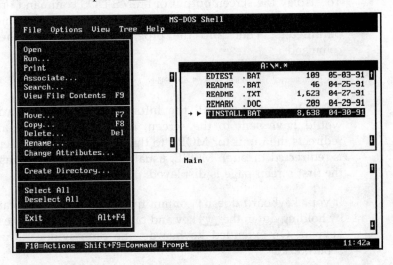

Selecting the file TINSTALL.BAT from the file list and the View File Contents command from the File menu

When you select **View File Contents** (or press F9) a screen similar to the following appears which shows the contents of the selected file.

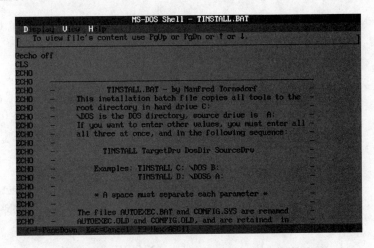

Viewing the contents of the selected file from within the MS-DOS Shell

Displaying the screen output of other MS-DOS commands page by page

To display the screen output of an MS-DOS command one screen page at a time, enter the command with all of the necessary parameters. Then add the pipe symbol "|" and the MORE command:

```
Command parameters | MORE
```

MS-DOS first stores all the information which the command would have sent to the screen, in a temporary file and then redirects the input for MORE to this temporary file. When output is redirected through MORE, usually there is a brief pause before the first screen page is displayed.

If your keyboard doesn't contain the pipe symbol, you can type it by holding down the [Alt] key and pressing [1][2][4] on the numeric keypad. On extended keyboards, the pipe symbol is usually a separate key.

Example

The following command displays all of the files in the C:\DOS directory one screen page at a time:

```
DIR C:\DOS | MORE
```

The following command displays the directory tree on the hard drive C: one screen page at a time:

```
TREE C: | MORE
```

To display all of the files of the hard drive, along with their path specifications, one screen page at a time, type the following command line:

```
CHKDSK C: /V | MORE
```

The MS-DOS DIR command (for displaying a disk directory) has an option to pause the screen after each page is displayed. To do this, enter the /P switch after the command.

If you use /P instead of the MORE filter, the display begins immediately. When the pipe symbol is used, the first command must be completely processed before output to the screen begins. With some commands, this can take a long time.

If more than one filter is used in a command line, be sure that MORE is the last item in the command. If it isn't the last item, MORE will pause its processing after each screen page and the commands after MORE won't receive the information until you press a key.

Displaying the contents of files with TYPEM.BAT

By using the following batch file, you won't have to enter the pipe symbol. This batch file is contained on the companion diskette in the TOOLS directory. This batch file, called TYPEM.BAT, can be used in place of the TYPE command:

```
TYPE %1 | MORE
```

The following file, called TYPEM2.BAT, is a more extensive version of TYPEM.BAT:

```
@ECHO OFF
IF NOT "%1"=="" GOTO Output
ECHO You must enter a filename!
GOTO EndItAll
:Output
TYPE %1 | MORE
:EndItAll
```

Sorted output

The filter SORT is used to display files and screen output sorted alphabetically. The size of the data files is limited to 63K. Larger files will generate an error message.

Displaying sorted files

Use the following command line to display a file in alphabetical sequence:

```
SORT <File
```

SORT looks at all of the characters in a line to determine the sort sequence. When SORT finds a line with the character (Ctrl) + (Z) (ASCII code 26), it considers this the end of file marker and does not read past this line.

SORT isn't case sensitive, which means it doesn't distinguish between uppercase and lowercase letters. Data is sorted according to the sequence 0,1,...9,A,...Z. In general, characters are sorted according to their ASCII codes.

Usually, you'll want to display the output of sorted ASCII files on the screen. However, occasionally you may want to redirect SORT to store its output in a file. This can be accomplished by using the redirection symbol (>). For example, you could type:

```
SORT < NAMES.TXT > SORTED.TXT
```

This command line will sort the file NAMES.TXT and store the results in a file named SORTED.TXT.

Example

Although you're unlikely to want to sort and display your AUTOEXEC batch file, we're using this file in the example because most users include an AUTOEXEC batch file on their system. Type the following command:

```
SORT <C:\AUTOEXEC.BAT
```

Large sorted files can be displayed a page at a time by adding the MORE filter:

```
SORT <C:\AUTOEXEC.BAT | MORE
```

Sorting and displaying the output of other MS-DOS commands

To sort and display the results of other MS-DOS commands, type the command with all necessary parameters and add the pipe symbol " | " followed by the SORT command:

```
Command parameters | SORT
```

MS-DOS writes all screen output from the first command into a temporary file. Then the file is redirected to the input of SORT. There may be a slight delay while the command line is processed because the temporary file must be created and the first command must be completely executed.

Example:

Typing TYPE to display the AUTOEXEC.BAT file and then sorting the display with SORT will produce the same results as the preceding example. The SORT filter processes the screen output of the MS-DOS TYPE command in the following example.

```
TYPE C:\AUTOEXEC.BAT | SORT
```

Special sorting switches

/R   Specifying the /R switch reverses the sorting direction
          (sort order). So when this switch is specified, the sort
          order is from Z to A and from 9 to 0.

/+n   When /+n is specified, SORT begins sorting according to
          characters in the nth column. If this switch isn't specified,
          SORT begins sorting at the first character in each line.

Example: Displaying a disk directory sorted alphabetically

You can use the following command to sort and display all of the
files in the DOS directory:

```
DIR C:\DOS | SORT
```

It's easier to read the data if you display it one screen at a time. To
do this use the following command:

```
DIR C:\DOS | SORT | MORE
```

The filenames and every line displayed by the DIR command,
including the information about the storage device, is sorted
alphabetically.

The DIR command has its own switch for sorting data. The files in
the DOS directory can be sorted by filename and displayed by
using the following command:

```
DIR C:\DOS /O:N
```

To display the data page by page, simply add the /P switch for
page:

```
DIR C:\DOS /O:N /P
```

Example: Disk directory sorted by the filename extension

To sort all of the files in the DOS directory according to file
extension and display them one screen page at a time, use the
following command:

```
DIR C:\DOS | SORT /+10 | MORE
```

MS-DOS 6.0 also lets you accomplish the same result as the
previous command by using a switch with the DIR command.

```
DIR C:\DOS /O:E /P
```

In addition to files, DOS 6.0 also displays subdirectories and additional information about the storage device. The DIR command also sorts these subdirectories and interrupts the display when you use the SORT filter to sort. Use the sorting options of the MS-DOS DIR command for sorting by filename, extension, etc. Only DIR contains these options.

Example: Displaying files sorted according to attributes

In the following example, SORT is very useful because the MS-DOS command ATTRIB doesn't use any special "sorting parameters". The following command displays all of the files in the current directory sorted according to file attributes:

```
ATTRIB *.* | SORT
```

Displaying only lines that contain specific text strings

The FIND command can be used to limit the display to either the lines from the file which contain certain text strings or the lines that don't contain the strings.

Although FIND was case sensitive in previous versions of DOS, MS-DOS 6.0 includes a new switch (/I), which ignores the case of characters.

The following command displays only the lines that contain the search string:

```
Command parameter | FIND "search string"
```

The search string must be enclosed in quotation marks. If the character sequence for which you're searching is already enclosed in quotation marks, type another set of quotation marks ("").

Example

To display all of the files, in the C:\DOS directory, that were created or changed in 1993, use the following command:

```
DIR C:\DOS | FIND "-93"
```

The minus sign (or dash), which is placed in front of 93, is important because it limits the displayed files to those that have the date sequence "xx-xx-93".

The FIND filters help sort and display disk directories without having the data placed on the storage device. You may want to use the following short batch file, DIRSD.BAT, to sort and display directories:

```
@ECHO OFF
DIR %1 | FIND /v "e" | SORT | MORE
```

You can specify a file after DIRSD, DIRSD *.EXE or DIRSD T*.TXT. You could also specify any directory, such as DIRSD C:\DOS. If you don't specify any parameters, the command sorts and displays all of the files in the current directory.

After DIR is called, the "e" eliminates (filters) the information that is usually displayed at the top and bottom of the screen, such as the number of files, bytes used and bytes free information. Only the names of the files and corresponding information will be displayed.

The special /V switch reverses the search condition and only lines that don't contain the search string are displayed. Since all of the files and directories are displayed in capital letters and the disk information lines each contain a lowercase "e", the batch file prevents lines that have an "e" from being displayed.

It's also possible to use the filters one after another. The single command elements are separated by the pipe symbol. The previous example also illustrates the meaning of the term "pipe". The data generated by the DIR command are processed and handled as if they were passing through a pipe before the information is displayed on the screen (after MORE).

 If more than one filter is used in a command line, be sure that MORE is the last item in the command. If it isn't the last item, MORE will stop the "processing line" after every screen page and the commands following MORE won't receive the information until you press a key.

Using FIND to search for files

To search the entire hard drive for a specific file, use the following command:

```
CHKDSK drive /V | FIND "FILENAME"
```

In uppercase letters, specify the filename or the known part of the name. This is necessary because DIR outputs filenames in uppercase letters and the FIND command differentiates between upper and lowercase letters. As explained below, an optional switch, /I, can be used with FIND to ignore the case of characters during the search. The command would be:

```
CHKDSK drive /V | FIND /I "FILENAME"
```

Special search switches

By specifying additional switches with the FIND command, you can use the special switches that are available in the search. Some of these switches are ignored if FIND is used after a command as a filter:

/V   Reverses the search condition; displays only those lines that do not contain the search string.

/C   Displays only the number of lines that contain the search string.

/N   Displays the line number of each line that contains the search string.

/I   This new switch ignores the case of characters in the search string.

Example: Counting the lines of the AUTOEXEC.BAT

To display all the lines in the AUTOEXEC.BAT file with line numbers, use the /N and /V switches and specify a search string that doesn't appear in any line of AUTOEXEC.BAT:

```
FIND /N /V "abcdef" C:\AUTOEXEC.BAT
```

With this command line, FIND counts all of the lines that don't contain the search string. In this example, this is all of the lines in the AUTOEXEC.BAT file.

Example: A better way to sort a disk directory

When the SORT filter is used to sort a disk directory, it also sorts the names of subdirectories and the additional data about the storage device. This information may not be necessary when redirecting the directory to a file. If you don't want this information to appear, use FIND.

The following command line displays and sorts only the files in the current directory by name. (Ensure that there are twelve spaces before the zero.):

```
    DIR | FIND /V "<DIR>" | FIND /V "e" | FIND /V "          0"
    | SORT | MORE
```

To sort the files by extension, use SORT /+10, to sort by file size, use SORT /+13. Let's look at this line in detail:

Explanation

As you can see, this command line is rather complex. When you're working with command lines like this you should create simple batch files that contain the command line or use the DOSKEY command of MS-DOS 6.0.

By using these methods, you won't have to enter the complete line every time you want to use the command or after making a typing error while entering the line.

Each element of the command has the following meanings:

```
    FIND /v "<DIR>"
```

This statement limits the search to only files by excluding lines that contain the search string "<DIR>".

```
    FIND /v "e"
```

Next, FIND is used again to exclude information about the storage device (bytes free, bytes used, etc.). As previously explained, DIR outputs filenames in uppercase letters, while the lines of the additional information each contain at least one lowercase "e" (make sure there are twelve spaces before the zero).

```
    FIND /v "          0"
```

This part of the command looks rather strange. When MS-DOS passes the information from DIR to MORE using FIND and SORT, temporary files are created and then deleted.

These temporary files don't have extensions and are 0 bytes long when the DIR command is used; they are deleted by the DIR command.

```
    SORT
```

The SORT command sorts the data. By specifying /+xxx, the command will sort the files by extension (where xxx = 10) or by file size (where xxx = 13).

```
    MORE
```

MORE displays only one screen page of data at a time. This is very useful with long directories. As explained earlier, MS-DOS waits for you to press a key before displaying the next screen of information.

 When using DIR, you cannot use both MORE and the /P switch to display the output page by page.

Depending on the size of the directory, you may need to press a key a few times to continue the DIR command (if /P is used). When the line is processed, all of the information will quickly scroll by on the screen.

Each time the output from the DIR command completely filled the screen, the message "Press any key to continue..." would be displayed. MS-DOS doesn't pass the information from the first command DIR to FIND until DIR has displayed all of the information.

Display directories sorted alphabetically

The following command line outputs only the subdirectories in alphabetical order. Make sure there are twelve spaces before the zero. It also displays "." and ".." because these symbols represent the current directory and the parent directory:

```
DIR | FIND "<DIR>" | FIND /V "e" | FIND /V "            0"
| SORT | MORE
```

The MS-DOS 6.0 DIR command not only sorts, but can also limit the display to certain kinds of files or directories. There is an easier way to obtain the same results (without the MS-DOS SORT filter):

```
DIR /a:d /o:n /p
```

9.3   Redirecting Input and Output

Usually MS-DOS commands receive their instructions and information from the keyboard and output information to the screen. You can change these defaults when you enter the command for the DOS command.

This is called redirecting the input or output. Redirection can help reduce a lot of tedium and typing in your daily work.

Redirecting input to a file

MS-DOS commands usually receive input from information typed at the keyboard. To change this, use the "<" character to redirect the input.

To direct the input from a file to a command, use the following command:

```
COMMAND <FILENAME
```

Parameters can be specified after the command. The command will then take its input from the specified file and process it as if the input was being typed in from the keyboard.

A command that has had its input redirected to a file receives no information from the keyboard. Complete control is given to the specified file and doesn't return to the keyboard until the command has been completed. The command can't be aborted if the file doesn't contain any characters for ending the command.

If you encounter problems, you must perform a warm boot (press the Ctrl Alt Del keys). Unfortunately, you could lose data when this happens. The special MS-DOS filters are an exception to this rule (MORE, SORT and FIND) because they process a file to the end and then quit.

Input can only be redirected for commands that receive input from the default input device. You cannot redirect the input of commands that read the keyboard directly.

Example: Displaying the date

Every time your computer is started, the current date should be displayed. However, you don't want this to interrupt the execution of your AUTOEXEC.BAT file. So the DATE command must obtain the input it needs (ENTER) from a file so that it can end without changing the date.

Use COPY CON to create a file called ENTER.DAT in the C:\DOS directory. The file should contain only a blank line:

```
COPY CON C:\DOS\ENTER.DAT
```

Press Enter at the beginning of the following line. Press Ctrl + Z at the end of the line and press Enter again. Test the following line and then include it in your AUTOEXEC.BAT file:

```
DATE <C:\DOS\ENTER.DAT
```

The date is displayed and the system prompt immediately appears. The DATE command took input from the ENTER.DAT file.

Example: Displaying the boot sector of a diskette

Input redirection can also be used to control complex processes automatically. The EDLIN editor (on the Supplemental Disk from Microsoft) and the DEBUG program, which is used for finding errors, are ideal candidates for input redirection because they can process more than one line of input.

The following example can be used to display the first sector (boot sector) of a diskette in drive A:. Create an ASCII file using EDLIN or another editor. This file, called BOOT.REC, should contain the following lines:

```
L 0100 0 0 1
D 0100 01FF
Q
```

This file contains the exact commands to instruct DEBUG to load the boot sector into memory, display it on the screen and automatically stop. In order for DEBUG to execute these commands, redirect the input from BOOT.REC to DEBUG:

```
DEBUG <BOOT.REC
```

You could also create a batch file, called SHOWBOOT, which contains the preceding command line.

Redirecting output to a new file

Normally MS-DOS commands display information on the screen. The characters ">" and ">>" can be used to redirect output to a specific device or file.

To write all of the output from a command to a file instead of displaying it on the screen, use the command:

```
COMMAND PARAMETERS >FILENAME
```

Parameters can be specified with the command. MS-DOS creates a file with the specified filename and redirects all output from the command to this file. An existing file with the same name as the specified filename is overwritten.

The output of some commands cannot be redirected because the commands don't output information to the default output device, (the screen). Instead they send their output to a special device for error handling.

For example, some programs write information directly to video memory. You cannot use the redirection character to redirect the screen output of these programs to a file.

Example

If you use Turbo Pascal to develop programs and want to redirect the screen output to a file, don't use the CRT unit in programs. By doing this, the screen output of the program goes to the standard output device and can be redirected. Not using the CRT unit does slow down the speed of output. If you absolutely must use the CRT unit, use the special AssignCrt command in Turbo Pascal.

Example

You want to record the time whenever your computer is switched on. For this example, you'll need the ENTER.DAT file, which was created in the previous section. Add the following line to your AUTOEXEC.BAT:

```
TIME <C:\DOS\ENTER.DAT >TIME.DAT
```

This causes the TIME command to store the current time in the TIME.DAT file every time you boot your computer. This file can be viewed, after restarting your computer, by typing:

```
TYPE TIME.DAT
```

Adding output to an existing file

Occasionally you may want to combine the output of several commands into a single file. The redirection sequence ">>" can be used instead of the ">" character:

```
COMMAND >>FILENAME
```

MS-DOS adds the output of this command to an existing file. If the file doesn't exist yet, MS-DOS creates it.

This method can be used to record how many hours you work on your computer. In a file called TIME.DAT, simply enter the times you start and stop working each day. Add the following command lines to your AUTOEXEC.BAT file or in a batch file named STARTWRK.BAT to record your starting times:

```
ECHO ***** Start **** >>C:\DOS\TIME.DAT
DATE <C:\DOS\ENTER.DAT >>C:\DOS\TIME.DAT
TIME <C:\DOS\ENTER.DAT >>C:\DOS\TIME.DAT
```

These batch files are contained on the companion diskette in the TOOLS directory. At the end of your work session, call another batch file named ENDWRK.BAT before switching off your computer to record your quitting time. This batch file writes the time you stop working into the same file:

```
ECHO ***** End of work **** >>C:\DOS\TIME.DAT
DATE <C:\DOS\ENTER.DAT >>C:\DOS\TIME.DAT
TIME <C:\DOS\ENTER.DAT >>C:\DOS\TIME.DAT
```

Example: Simple directory change

By redirecting additional screen output to a file, you can create new command lines from existing commands and screen output. For example, a batch file that automatically stores the current directory and permits recalling it instantly has the following requirements:

1. A file must be created in the DOS directory that contains only the CD command and a space. (Press the [Shift] key and the [-] key (minus) to create the underscore character in the following command line.)

    ```
    COPY CON C:\DOS\_CD.BAT
    ```

    Press the [Enter] key, then press the keys [C] [D] [Spacebar], [Ctrl] + [Z] and finally [Enter].

2. To extend this batch file so it contains the desired command line, we add the screen output of the CD command to the batch file. For example, if C:\DATA\DOC is the current directory, the command would be:

    ```
    CD >>C:\DOS\_CD.BAT
    ```

Type:

```
CD C:\DOS
```

This command line will switch your current directory to the DOS directory. Use TYPE and the complete pathname to display the _CD.BAT file. It now contains the command, CD and the name of the previous directory (in this example, C:\DATA\DOC). To make C:\DATA\DOC the current directory again, type:

```
_CD
```

By using these lines from batch files, you can use one command to store the current directory and then another command to return to this directory at any time. To make this even easier, recreate the _CD.BAT in your DOS directory and name it to _CD.DAT. This file should only contain the CD command and a space.

Then create another file called NOTE.BAT in your DOS directory. This batch file is contained on the companion diskette in the BAT directory. This file must have the following contents:

```
COPY C:\DOS\_CD.DAT C:\DOS\_CD.BAT
CD >> C:\DOS\_CD.BAT
```

Now, when you want to store the name of the current directory, simply type NOTE. This causes the batch file NOTE.BAT to create another batch file, _CD.BAT, which stores the information for returning to the current directory. Now you can change to any directory and return to the previous directory by typing _CD.

This command can be further expanded by using a variable for the pathname of the directory that should be made current. Type the following lines to create a new batch file, called ACD.BAT, which will automate the entire storing and changing process:

```
ECHO OFF
COPY C:\DOS\_CD.DAT C:\DOS\_CD.BAT
CD>>C:\DOS\_CD.BAT
CD %1
ECHO ON
```

Remember to type Ctrl + Z to save the new batch file. This batch file (ACD.BAT) will automatically store the name of the current directory, change to a new directory and enable you to return to the previous current directory by typing _CD.

Remember that the entire pathname must be specified to change directories. For example, type the following to change from the BAT directory to the DOS directory.

```
ACD C:\DOS
```

Redirecting output to the printer

It's easy to redirect screen output to the printer:

```
Command >LPT1
```

If your printer isn't connected to the first parallel port (LPT1), use the name for the appropriate printer connection.

Example: Printing a disk directory

The following can be used to print the current disk directory:

```
DIR >LPT1
```

Example: Documenting the execution of a command

To copy all of the files in the current directory to a diskette in drive A: and document the backup process by printing it, use the following command line:

```
COPY *.* A: >LPT1
```

Example: Printing a very compact disk directory

To find the contents of a diskette any time, print the disk directory. However, if you want to attach long directories to the diskette sleeve, the standard output can be very long.

The following batch file, PRDIR.BAT, creates the smallest possible printout of the contents of any drive:

```
@ECHO OFF
REM Print compact disk directory to dot matrix printer
MODE LPT1:132,8 > NUL
DIR %1 /W | FIND /V "e" >LPT1
MODE LPT1:80,6 > NUL
ECHO ON
```

This batch file is contained on the companion diskette in the BAT directory. You must pass the drive as a parameter when calling the batch file, as follows:

```
PRDIR A:
```

The batch creates a 5-column disk directory, removing all extra information about the diskette (volume and volume number, free space on the diskette). In addition, the batch switches to the smallest, most narrow font possible. Since the printout is still small enough for floppy diskettes, you can easily attach it to the diskette sleeve.

    This batch file only works with dot matrix printers.

9.4   Linking Commands

Several commands can be linked together so that one command passes its output to the next command, which uses it as input. Use the pipe symbol "|" to separate the commands to be linked.

```
Command1 | Command2 | Command3
```

Command1 receives its input from the keyboard. Then DOS passes the screen output of command1 to command2. Command3 receives the screen output of command2 as its input and the output from command3 is displayed on the screen.

Linking several commands is especially useful when you're using filters.

Input and output can also be redirected. For example, you can take the input for the first command from a file instead of the keyboard or redirect the output of the last command to the printer instead of the screen.

Example

With the following command, the current directory is sorted and displayed one page at a time:

```
DIR | SORT | MORE
```

The next command outputs the current diskette directory to the printer, sorted and one page at a time:

```
DIR | SORT | MORE >LPT1
```

MS-DOS filters are not only used when linking commands. You could also use the output of the ECHO command as input for DEL.

 The next two examples illustrate this. Since the command lines delete data, use them only after carefully considering the results. Be careful you don't accidentally delete useful files.

The following command line deletes the contents of the current directory (except files specified with the ATTRIB command) without prompting you for confirmation. You can use it to delete data within a batch file automatically:

```
ECHO Y | DEL *.*
```

The DEL command receives the necessary confirmation of Ⓨ + Ⓔⁿᵗᵉʳ from the ECHO command.

The following batch file, DELDIR.BAT, removes all files from any specified subdirectory and then removes the subdirectory. This batch file is contained on the companion diskette in the TOOLS directory.

```
ECHO Y | DEL %1
RD %1
```

For example, if the batch file is in the C:\TOOLS directory (specified by the search path for commands) and the C:\SCRAP directory contains files that are no longer needed, the following command line can be used to remove the files and the directory:

```
DELDIR C:\SCRAP
```

The character sequence "%1" allows you to pass parameters that can be used in the batch file.

9.5   Installing a Printer

The MODE command can be used to set the mode of operation of a printer to the parallel port or to redirect the printer output to a serial port. These settings can be changed at any time.

Setting the printer output

The number of characters per line and the line spacing for a parallel printer can be specified.

 These settings only work on IBM or EPSON compatible dot-matrix printers. Many of the setting options can only be used under DOS because applications usually use their own special programs for printers (printer drivers). These programs either reset the DOS settings or completely ignore them.

Setting the number of characters per line

With the MODE command you can increase the number of characters printed in each line from 80 to 132. However, your printer must support a font that is narrow enough to do this. To change the characters per line for a printer connected to the first printer port (LPT1), use the following command:

```
MODE LPT1:132
```

The following command resets the number of characters printed in each line to normal font size (i.e., 80 characters per line):

```
MODE LPT1:80
```

Setting line spacing

MODE can also be used to change line spacing. Type the number of lines per inch after the number of characters:

```
MODE LPT1:Number_of_characters,X
```

For X, specify the value 6 or 8. If you want to change the number of lines without changing the number of characters per line, place a comma in front of the number of lines:

```
MODE LPT1:,X
```

 The default setting is 80 characters and 6 lines per inch.

Many applications (especially word processors) reset the printer. So settings made with MODE are no longer valid.

Redirecting printer output

Data can be redirected from a parallel port to a serial port. Occasionally this must be done if a laser printer can only be connected to the serial port but an application always prints to the first parallel port (LPT1):

```
MODE LPTx=COMy
```

After you specify the number of the parallel port for x and the number of the serial port for y, you'll see a message similar to this.

```
C>mode lpt1:=com1:
Resident portion of MODE loaded
LPT1: rerouted to COM1:
C>
```

Printer LPT1: has been redirected to serial port 1

MODE can also be used to cancel the redirection by typing:

```
MODE LPTx
```

Before redirecting printer output to the serial port, make the proper settings on the serial port, as explained in the following section.

9.6 Setting Serial Ports

The MODE command can be used to specify the settings of the serial port for either printers or other devices (a modem, for example) connected to it:

```
MODE COMx baud,parity,data,stop,retry
```

Baud   Sets a baud rate between 110 and 19200 baud. The following are possible values that can be used for baud:

Setting	Baud Rate
11	110
15	150
30	300
60	600
12	1200
24	2400
48	4800
96	9600
19	19200

The baud rate specifies the speed of data transfer in bits per second. As shown in the previous table, this is a two digit value that specifies the transmission rate in bits per second. To convert this speed (baud rate) to characters (bytes) per second, divide the value by 10. For example, a baud rate of 300 will send approximately 30 characters per second (30 * 8 data bits, 1 parity bit and 1 stop bit).

Parity   Parity is a method to detect data transmission errors. The value can be any of the following:

n	no parity
e	even parity
o	odd parity
m	mark

s	space

The default value is e. Since mark (m) and space (s) refer to TTY printers, they may not be applicable to all computers.

Data bits   This value specifies the number of data bits in a character and may contain a value between 5 and 8. The default value is 7. Not all computers will support a value of 5 or 6. When 7 data bits are specified, 2 stop bits can be selected, as explained below. However, 7 data bits only allow ASCII values of 0-127 to be transferred. The data bits contain the actual ASCII data.

Stop bits   1, 1.5 or 2 signal the end of the character. Not all computers support a value of 1.5; the default setting is 1.

Retry   Specifies the retry action to be taken if a timeout error occurs when attempting to send data to a parallel printer. Using this parameter causes a portion of the MODE command to remain in memory. The following table shows the possible values for retry and a brief description:

e	Return an error from a status check of a busy port.
b	Return "busy" from a status check of a busy port.
p	Continue trying to send data until the printer accepts output.
r	Return "ready" from a status check of a busy port.
n	No retry action. This is the default value.

Don't use any values for retry if you're using a network.

If a comma is used instead of a parameter setting, the most recent settings are used for the omitted parameter.

Examples

The following is an example of how to specify these settings:

```
MODE COM1: 300,n,8,1
```

The baud rate must be specified but all the other parameters are optional. The default setting for the other values are: e,7,1, which means even, 7 data bits and 1 stop bit. A comma can be used for parameters. (Assuming that MODE hasn't been used to change the other parameters previous to this call.)

The following is an example with only the baud rate:

```
MODE COM1:1200
```

This call automatically sets the default parameters to even parity, 7 data bits and 1 stop bit along with 1200 baud.

To set the number of data bits to 8 with the same baud rate, use the following command:

```
MODE COM1:1200,,8
```

9.7   Setting the Display Mode

You can also use a variation of the MODE command to specify the display mode. To use this command, your computer must have an EGA, VGA, CGA or another type of graphics card. You cannot change the settings on computers that use a Hercules Graphics Card.

```
MODE display_adapter
```

Setting the display mode

The following parameters can be used for the mode of display:

mono   Monochrome display, 80 characters per line

40   40 characters per line, color graphics adapter (CGA, EGA, VGA)

80   80 characters per line, color graphics adapter

co40   40 characters per line, color display active, color graphics adapter

co80   80 characters per line, color display active, color graphics adapter

bw40   40 characters per line, color display not active, color graphics adapter

bw80   80 characters per line, color display not active, color
        graphics adapter

 You can only set a mode that is appropriate for the type of
graphics card installed in the computer. MODE can also be
used to switch between several installed graphics cards.
For example, you may do this if you connected more than
one monitor for debugging.

Changing the settings for the display mode is especially useful
when an application changes the mode but doesn't reset the
original mode after you exit the program. For example, if you run
dBASE IV on a computer with an EGA card with 43 lines per
screen, the computer retains this setting even after you quit dBASE
IV. To return to the usual mode of 25 lines per screen, type:

```
MODE CO80
```

If you try to set a mode that the graphics card doesn't support, an
error message similar to the one shown below will be displayed.

```
Function not supported by this computer
```

Setting the number of text lines in the display

You can change the number of lines that DOS displays on the
screen if your computer has an EGA or VGA graphics card. On a
computer with an EGA card, use the following command to set an 80
character color display with 43 lines per screen:

```
MODE CO80,43
```

If the graphics card cannot display the specified number of lines,
the following error message appears:

```
Function not supported by this computer
```

When changing the number of displayed text lines, your computer
requires the extended screen control system. This means that the
ANSI.SYS device driver must be installed by the CONFIG.SYS
file. If ANSI.SYS isn't installed, DOS will display a message
similar to the following:

```
ANSI.SYS must be installed to perform requested function
```

Changing lines and columns in the display

With EGA and VGA graphics cards, you can also change the number of lines that DOS displays without setting the screen mode. Use the command words COLS (columns) and LINES (lines).

The following syntax is used:

```
MODE CON Command_word=Numerical_value
```

Depending on the capacity of the graphics card, either the value 40 or 80 can be used for COLS and the value 25, 43 or 50 can be used for LINES. For a VGA card, use the following command line to set the maximum number of lines in DOS for the screen display:

```
MODE CON LINES=50
```

 The ANSI.SYS device driver must be installed by the CONFIG.SYS file.

9.8 Screen Control System and Keyboard Actions

DOS addresses the screen and keyboard under the common device name of CON. When writing, CON corresponds to the screen; when reading, CON corresponds to the keyboard.

Preparing for screen control and keyboard actions

The device driver ANSI.SYS lets you use special commands for the screen and the keyboard. The CONFIG.SYS file must contain the following command line:

```
DEVICE=ANSI.SYS
```

If the file ANSI.SYS isn't in the root directory, its complete path must be specified. Any new options provided by ANSI.SYS aren't available until you restart the computer.

Since this device driver requires memory, use ANSI.SYS only when absolutely necessary. The memory ANSI.SYS uses will no longer be available to applications.

Sending commands to ANSI.SYS

To use these features of ANSI.SYS, you must send it commands that it understands. You do this by preceding the command with an "escape sequence".

The easiest way to do this is to use a special character sequence ($e[) following the PROMPT command.

DOS automatically converts this to correct escape sequences and passes the commands to ANSI.SYS.

Screen control system with ANSI.SYS

Using ANSI.SYS to extend the screen control system provides many possibilities. For example, you can set the colors for the foreground and the background of the screen as well as change the way characters are displayed. These changes are only valid with DOS. Many applications change these settings when they're activated.

Changing the character display

Use "m" to change the way characters are displayed. The syntax for this change is as follows:

```
PROMPT $e[xm
```

"m" is the actual command for changing the display while "x" represents the desired character attribute:

Value for x	Effect on the character display
0	normal
1	bold
4	underlined (with a color graphics card: change in color)
5	blinking
7	inverted display
8	invisible

Example

To switch the display for all of the subsequent characters to bold font, use the command:

```
PROMPT $e[1m
```

To switch the display back to default font at any time, simply type:

```
PROMPT $e[0m
```

To create the brackets "[" and "]" on international keyboards, press ⟨Alt⟩ + ⟨9⟩ ⟨1⟩ and ⟨Alt⟩ + ⟨9⟩ ⟨3⟩ on the numeric keypad.

 These escape sequences only work if ANSI.SYS has been installed by CONFIG.SYS prior to starting your computer.

The control sequences are sent to ANSI.SYS each time the prompt is displayed. So, if you use the PROMPT line to set bold type, the command sequence is sent each time the prompt is displayed, even though the change has already been made. In many cases this isn't necessary because switching to another text attribute once is sufficient.

In this type of situation it's better to use two separate command lines. The first line contains the control sequence to switch the text attribute and the second line switches on the original prompt message. In the example below, the first line switches on bold text and the second line defines the system prompt as the path and directory, followed by the greater than symbol (>).

```
PROMPT $e[1m
PROMPT $P$G
```

Changing the color of the font

If you have a color monitor and a color graphics adapter, the color of the displayed text can also be changed. Use the same syntax that is used to change the character display but enter a value between 30 and 37 for "x":

Value for x	Effect on the font color
30	black
31	red
32	green
33	yellow
34	blue
35	magenta (violet)
36	cyan (light blue)
37	white

Changing the color of the screen background

To change the color of the screen background, specify a value from the following table for "x" (only for color graphics):

Value for x	Effect on the background color
40	black
41	red
42	green
43	yellow
44	blue
45	magenta (violet)
46	cyan (light blue)
47	white

Samples of font and background color

In order to make several changes to the screen display, separate the individual changes with a semicolon. However, don't place a semicolon in front of the actual command character "m".

The following command changes the font color to red and the background color to blue on computers with a color screen:

```
PROMPT $e[31;44m$P$G
```

To increase the intensity of the displayed characters, change the command to:

```
PROMPT $e[1;31;44m$P$G
```

Changing the definition of the screen display

As we previously explained, the DOS MODE command can be used to set the screen display. Another way to change the display mode is by sending special command sequences to ANSI.SYS. Use the lowercase character "h" as the command code. The syntax for the command is as follows:

```
PROMPT $e[xh
```

"h" is the actual command for changing the display, while "x" sets the screen display according to the following table:

Value for x	Screen display
0	40*25 monochrome
1	40*25 color
2	80*25 monochrome
3	80*25 color
4	320*200 color
5	320*200 monochrome
6	640*200 monochrome
7	Turns on automatic word wrapping. Use 7l to turn it off. If word wrapping is turned off, new characters that you enter overwrite the last character in the screen line.
14	640*200 color
15	640*350 monochrome
16	640*350 color
17	640*480 monochrome
18	640*480 color
19	320*200 color

Example

Use the following commands to set a graphics screen to display 640 * 480 pixels:

```
PROMPT $e[18h
PROMPT $p$g
```

Special features when using batch files

ANSI.SYS receives the control sequences from PROMPT only when ECHO is switched on and at least one system prompt is displayed on the screen. This is especially important for batch files which frequently switch off ECHO.

Example

The following batch file is incorrect and doesn't change the font because ECHO was switched off while the command line "PROMPT $e[1m" was being processed.

```
@ECHO OFF
PROMPT $e[1m
PROMPT $P$G
ECHO ON
```

While ECHO is switched on, the correct system prompt must be displayed with the ESC command for at least one command line. The command line can be blank; so no text is displayed on the screen. The following is the correct version of the batch file, this batch file is contained on the companion diskette in the TOOLS directory under the name FONT.BAT:

```
@REM FONT.BAT Chapter 09
@ECHO OFF
REM ECHO is turned off here
REM These lines are not displayed
REM The REMs below are suppressed by the @ character:
@ECHO ON
@REM Now we send the command line, the line itself
@REM is not displayed yet:
@PROMPT $e[1m

@REM Turn ECHO off again
@ECHO OFF
REM Command sent to ANSI, font switched
PROMPT $P$G
ECHO ON
```

The blank line is important. For each blank line, a system prompt is displayed on the screen. However, since the system prompt consists of an ESC sequence, only a blank line is displayed.

Using ANSI.SYS to program the keyboard

To assign a new character to a key, specify the ASCII code of the key that should be changed after the escape code for the command "$e[". Enter a semicolon followed by the ASCII value of the new key. Then enter "p", which is the command for changing the keyboard layout.

Unlike DOS commands, you must enter the parameter first and then the letter that identifies the command when using the ANSI.SYS driver.

Example: Switching Y and Z

If you want to play a joke on a friend, enter the following two lines on his/her computer when he/she isn't looking (ANSI.SYS must have been installed by CONFIG.SYS):

```
PROMPT $e[121;122p
PROMPT $e[122;121p
```

The first line changes "y" to "z" and the second line changes "z" to "y". Your friend will be thoroughly confused when he/she realizes that this only applies to lowercase letters; the uppercase letters aren't changed.

You need to define a key to ANSI.SYS only once. Set the system prompt back to the original value. After entering the first two PROMPT lines, the system prompt will no longer appear.

```
PROMPT $P$G
```

Cancelling the keyboard definition

To undo this definition, simply type the same command line without the semicolon and without the second ASCII value:

```
PROMPT $e[121p
PROMPT $e[122p
```

The "y" and "z" keys will work normally again.

  Changes to the keyboard layout aren't valid in all programs. Many applications, such as word processors and spreadsheets, have their own defined keyboard layouts. As soon as you exit the application, the redefined keyboard for DOS will be activated again.

Layout of special keys

Programming special keys is more useful than redefining letter keys. Special keys include the function keys and the combination keys Alt, Shift and Ctrl. Since these keys are seldom used, you can safely assign new characters or character sequences to them.

These special keys have number codes that are specified in the definition by a zero and a semicolon in front of the numeral (0;x). For example, to redefine the F2 key to type the backslash "\" character, use the following command:

```
PROMPT $e[0;60;92p
```

  When you change the keyboard layout with ANSI.SYS, the change isn't necessarily valid in all applications. For example, Word 5.0 ignores function keys changed with ANSI.SYS. Word has its own options for defining macros, character strings or commands in function keys.

Using EDLIN to create command files

If you don't like changing the keyboard layout by using PROMPT lines, you can use EDLIN (can be found on the Supplemental Disk from Microsoft) instead. EDLIN can be used to create the files containing the necessary commands for ANSI.SYS. However, this can only be done with EDLIN; word processors such as Word 5.0 or the MS-DOS editor EDIT cannot be used.

In EDLIN, enter the ESC character by typing `Ctrl` + `V` and then the bracket [. To type the control sequence ESC[, press `Ctrl` + `V` [[(press the bracket key twice).

EDLIN is used to create the file BS.DAT. Start EDLIN by typing:

```
EDLIN BS.DAT
```

A line containing the message "New File" is displayed. Then a new line, in which the normal system prompt is replaced with an asterisk, is displayed. Enter a `I` to insert lines in the new file. Enter "`Ctrl` `V` [[0;60;92p" for the command sequence. The line in EDLIN should look like the following ("1:*" represents the current line 1):

```
1:*^V[[0;60;92p
```

Press `Enter` to end the line and enter `Ctrl` + `Z` to leave insert mode. Now press `E` and `Enter` to save the file and quit EDLIN.

```
C:\>edlin bs.dat
New file
*i
        1:*^V[[0;60;92p
        2:*^Z
*e

C:\>
```

The BS.DAT file using EDLIN

To activate this change in the keyboard, the file must be output to the screen. Type:

```
TYPE BS.DAT
```

The screen will display a blank line as ANSI.SYS processes the control sequence. When you press `F2`, the backslash appears on the screen. You can make more changes to the keyboard by entering the command lines in EDLIN. The change is completed when the file is displayed on the screen with TYPE.

Modifying the keyboard with commands and automatic execution

An entire sequence of characters can be assigned to a key. The character sequence must be enclosed in quotation marks. For example, to assign the character sequence "DIR /W" to F1 (code 59), type the following PROMPT line:

```
PROMPT $e[0;59;"DIR /W"p$P$G
```

Press F1; the command appears after the system prompt. To execute the command without having to press Enter, add the ASCII code 13 (Enter) to the command:

```
PROMPT $e[0;59;"DIR /W";13p$P$G
```

Command shortcuts

After you've assigned DOS commands to all of the function keys, you may not be able to remember which key belongs to which command. So you should use the first letter of a command in conjunction with the Alt key. For example, to assign the FORMAT A: command to Alt + F, type the following command line:

```
PROMPT $e[0;33;"FORMAT A:"p
```

 Commands that could destroy data shouldn't be executed automatically. So don't add ASCII code 13 (Enter) to the command line.

Key codes

While the ASCII code can be specified for "normal" keys, special values must be specified for extended keys. These values always start with a zero, followed by a semicolon and the second value. The following table shows these values:

Key	Code	Key	Code
F1	59	Alt+1	120
F2	60	Alt+2	121
F3	61	Alt+3	122
F4	62	Alt+4	123
F5	63	Alt+5	124
F6	64	Alt+6	125
F7	65	Alt+7	126
F8	66	Alt+8	127

Key	Code	Key	Code
F9	67	Alt + 9	128
F10	68	Alt + 0	129
F11	133	Alt + –	130
F12	134	Alt + F1	104
Ins	82	Alt + F2	105
Del	83	Alt + F3	106
Home	71	Alt + F4	107
End	79	Alt + F5	108
Pg Up	73	Alt + F6	109
Pg Dn	81	Alt + F7	110
Alt + A	30	Alt + F8	111
Alt + B	48	Alt + F9	112
Alt + C	46	Alt + F10	113
Alt + D	32	Alt + F11	139
Alt + E	18	Alt + F12	140
Alt + F	33	Shift + F1	84
Alt + G	34	Shift + F2	85
Alt + H	35	Shift + F3	86
Alt + I	23	Shift + F4	87
Alt + J	36	Shift + F5	88
Alt + K	37	Shift + F6	89
Alt + L	38	Shift + F7	90
Alt + M	50	Shift + F8	91
Alt + N	49	Shift + F9	92
Alt + O	24	Shift + F10	93
Alt + P	25	Shift + F11	135
Alt + Q	16	Shift + F12	136
Alt + R	19	Shift + Tab	15
Alt + S	31	Ctrl + F1	94
Alt + T	20	Ctrl + F2	95
Alt + U	22	Ctrl + F3	96
Alt + V	47	Ctrl + F4	97
Alt + W	17	Ctrl + F5	98
Alt + X	45	Ctrl + F6	99
Alt + Y	44	Ctrl + F7	100
Alt + Z	21	Ctrl + F8	101
←	75	Ctrl + F9	102
→	77	Ctrl + F10	103
↑	72	Ctrl + F11	137

Key	Code	Key	Code
↓	80	Ctrl + F12	138
Ctrl + Prt Sc	114	Ctrl + Pg Up	132
Ctrl + ←	115	Ctrl + Pg Dn	118
Ctrl + →	116	Ctrl + End	117
Ctrl + Home	119		

Beginning with DOS 4.0, ANSI.SYS supported extended keyboards (with extra keys such as F11 and F12). These extended keys can be accessed by specifying the /X switch when calling ANSI.SYS:

```
DEVICE=ANSI.SYS /x
```

9.9   Modifying the Keyboard

You can change the settings for the character set and speed of the keyboard.

Selecting the keyboard

The MS-DOS default keyboard is the American keyboard. To install a foreign language keyboard, such as the British keyboard, use the following command line:

```
KEYB UK
```

The abbreviation "UK" sets the British (United Kingdom) keyboard definition. Normally KEYB searches in the current directory for the file with the keyboard definitions named KEYBOARD.SYS. So if the file isn't in the root or current directory, specify the complete path.

```
KEYB UK,,C:\DOS\KEYBOARD.SYS
```

In between the two commas, specify the desired code page. This will prevent problems if the keyboard was set up to work with country specific characters.

The following abbreviations can be used for the various national keyboard definitions:

BE	Belgium
BR	Brazil
CF	Canada (French)
CZ	Czechoslovakia
DK	Denmark
FR	France
HU	Hungary
GR	Germany
IT	Italy
LA	Latin America
NL	Netherlands
NO	Norway
PL	Poland
PO	Portugal
SF	Switzerland (French)
SG	Switzerland (German)
SP	Spain
SV	Sweden
SU	Finland
UK	Great Britain
US	United States
YU	Yugoslavia

 If you must define a special keyboard for your computer, use the KEYB command from your AUTOEXEC.BAT file. It's also possible to install a new keyboard with the CONFIG.SYS file. Use the following line:

```
INSTALL=C:\DOS\KEYB.COM UK
```

Setting the speed of the keyboard

You can use the MODE command to set both the speed and the delay rate of most keyboards. However, not all computers recognize this command function. These settings are only possible on AT class computers with programmable keyboards.

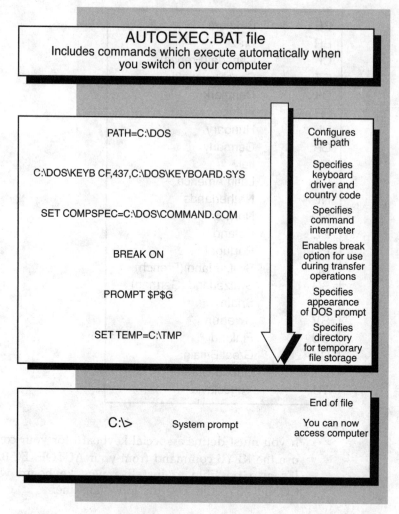

Include keyboard settings in the AUTOEXEC.BAT file

The following is the command line for setting the values:

```
MODE CON Rate=x Delay=y
```

"Rate" defines the key repetition rate, which can be between 1 and 32. The larger the specified value, the faster the cursor moves when a key is held down. Rate=1 repeats the key two times per second, Rate=32 repeats the key approximately 30 times per second.

"Delay" defines the time that passes until the pressed key begins repeating automatically. The values that can be used for delay are 1, 2, 3 and 4, which represent a delay of .25, .50, .75 and 1 second, respectively.

Example

To set a keyboard for the highest possible speed, use the following command:

```
MODE CON Rate=32 Delay=1
```

The keyboard now has a repetition frequency of 30 characters per second and a delay of 1/4th second. The default values are 20 for IBM AT-compatible keyboards and 21 for IBM PS/2-compatible keyboards. The default delay is 2 or 1/2 second. If either value is changed, both must be set.

9.10 Defining New Disk Drives

The DRIVER.SYS device driver can be used to define new disk drives. DOS usually recognizes existing disk drives automatically and installs them accordingly.

Being able to define new disk drives is important because disk drives can be operated in various ways. For example, you can use DRIVER.SYS to define a "logical" drive that makes a 1.2 Meg disk appear to be a 360K drive.

 Unlike earlier versions of DOS, DRIVER.SYS cannot be used for hard drives in DOS 6.0.

Installing a new disk drive

To assign a new drive identifier to an existing disk drive or use an external disk drive, type the following command line in CONFIG.SYS:

```
DEVICE=DRIVER.SYS /D:Number /F:Format
```

For "Number" specify either the number of the existing disk drive or external disk drive. A value of 0 corresponds to the first disk drive (A:), 1 corresponds to the second disk drive (B:), etc.

"Format" specifies the type of disk drive according to the following table:

0	160K, 180K, 320K, 360K
1	1.2 Meg (AT disk drive)
2	720K (3.5 inch disk drive)
7	1.44 Meg (3.5 inch disk drive)
9	2.88 Meg (3.5 inch disk drive)

The definition isn't activated until the computer is restarted. When booting, DOS displays the message:

```
External driver loaded for disk drive X
```

For X the computer assigns the first unused disk drive identifier. For example, if the highest drive letter previously assigned is C (for the hard drive), DOS assigns the letter D. The new logical disk drive can be used under disk drive identifier D:.

Example

You can define an existing AT disk drive A: (1.2 Meg) as a 360K disk drive. To do this, add the following line in CONFIG.SYS:

```
DEVICE=DRIVER.SYS /D:0 /F:0
```

/D:0   Zero indicates that DOS should use disk drive A: for the "new" disk drive.

/F:0   Zero indicates that this new disk drive can be addressed as a 360K disk drive.

For example, if you type the previous command and DOS displays the following message when booting your computer

```
External driver loaded for disk drive D
```

you can use drive D: like a 360K disk drive. You no longer need to use the /4 switch when you format 360K diskettes.

Don't be surprised if you see the following two identical lines in the CONFIG.SYS of an AT:

```
DEVICE=DRIVER.SYS /D:0 /F:0
DEVICE=DRIVER.SYS /D:0 /F:0
```

Both command lines define a new 360K disk drive (because of /F:0) based on the existing drive A: (defined by /D:0). This computer could have two new disk drives, D: and E:, that automatically format diskettes at 360K.

Installing and defining a disk drive

When DRIVER.SYS is used to define a disk drive, you can not only define the capacity of the drive (within limitations), but also specify additional parameters, such as the number of tracks and sectors.

To use an existing disk drive under a new label with different settings, add the following line to CONFIG.SYS:

```
DEVICE=DRIVER.SYS /D:Number Parameter
```

The following switches can be used (in combinations) if they are supported by the disk drive:

/C   This switch checks whether the diskette lever is open or closed. This enables DOS to determine when you change diskettes. (Use this with AT disk drives.)

/F:Format   Define the type of device here. Instead of "Format", enter the values from the previous table.

/H:Heads   Define the number of read or write/heads supported by the disk drive here. You can set from 1 to 99 heads; the default setting is 2.

/S:Sectors Define the number of sectors per track here. This number depends on the disk drive. You can set from 1 to 99 sectors; the default value is 9.

/T:Tracks   Define the number of tracks per page here. This number depends on the disk drive. You can set values from 1 to 999; the default value is 80.

The following table lists possible combinations for the switches:

Disk drive	/F	/T	/S	/H	Comment
360K	0	40	9	2	from PC/XT
720K	2	80	9	2	from PC/XT
1.2 Meg	1	80	15	2	from AT
1.44 Meg	7	80	18	2	from AT
2.88 Meg	7	80	36	2	special disk drive

9.11 Setting the Date and Currency

DOS can be adapted to the specific requirements of the different countries. For example, you can adapt it to a country's date, time and currency symbol. It's also possible to use country specific characters.

A special driver program is installed through the CONFIG.SYS file to adapt the date, time, decimal separators and currency symbols to different countries. In order to do this, add the following line to your CONFIG.SYS file:

```
COUNTRY=xxx,,COUNTRY.SYS
```

If the COUNTRY.SYS file isn't in the root directory, specify the entire path.

Enter the proper country code, which is displayed in the second column of the following table. For example, you would enter "044" for the United Kingdom. The default settings for DOS install "001", which is the code for the USA.

The country code is taken from the international telephone area codes of the different countries.

Land	Code	Date	Time	Dec.	Tsd.	Code Pg
USA	001	M-D-Y	ST:M:S.HS	.	,	437
French.Can.	002	Y-M-D	ST:M:S,HS	,	,	863
Latin Am.	003	D/M/Y	ST:M:S.HS	.	,	437
Netherl.	031	D-M-Y	ST:M:S,HS	,	.	437
Belgium	032	D/M/Y	ST:M:S,HS	.	,	437
France	033	D/M/Y	ST:M:S,HS	,		437
Spain	034	D/M/Y	ST:M:S,HS	,	.	437
Italy	039	D/M/Y	ST:M:S,HS	,	.	437
Switzerland	041	D.M.Y	ST.M.S.HS	.	,	437
UK	044	D-M-Y	ST:M:S.HS	.	,	437
Denmark	045	D/M/Y	ST.M.S,HS	,	.	865
Sweden	046	Y-M-D	ST.M.S,HS	,	.	437
Norway	047	D/M/Y	ST.M.S,HS	,	.	865
Germany	049	D.M.Y	ST.M.S,HS	,	.	437
Intern.	061	D-M-Y	ST:M:S.HS	.	,	437
Portugal	351	D/M/Y	ST:M:S,HS	,	.	860
Hungary	036	Y-M-D	ST:M:S,HS	,	.	852
Yugoslavia	038	Y-M-D	ST:M:S,HS	,	.	852
Czech.	042	Y-M-D	ST:M:S,HS	,	.	852
Poland	048	Y-M-D	ST:M:S,HS	,	.	852
Brazil	055	D-M-Y	ST:M:S.HS	,	.	437
Finland	358	D.M.Y	ST.M.S,HS	,		437

Example

For the United Kingdom, the CONFIG.SYS file should contain the following command:

```
COUNTRY=044,,COUNTRY.SYS
```

9.12 Country Specific Special Characters

With DOS, the keyboard layout can be adapted to different countries. DOS supports country specific special characters by using code pages (tables of special characters) for the keyboard, screen and printer.

When using different code pages, you must prepare all of your devices according to the manufacturer's specifications. This will ensure that the characters that are printed are the same as those displayed on your screen.

Keyboard

To prepare your keyboard driver to use code pages, type a line similar to the following in your CONFIG.SYS file:

```
COUNTRY=044,Table,COUNTRY.SYS
```

044 is the United Kingdom keyboard layout. If necessary specify COUNTRY.SYS with the complete path. The following parameters can be used for "Table":

437	USA, default
850	multilingual
860	Portugal
863	Canada/France
865	Scandinavian countries

You could use two tables for the United Kingdom (044): 437 and 850.

The following command line is also required for working with code pages. Insert this line in your AUTOEXEC.BAT file:

```
KEYB UK,Table
```

If a value isn't specified for "Table", DOS uses the default table 437.

Depending on the type of installation, DOS could have the following line in your CONFIG.SYS file:

```
INSTALL=C:\DOS\KEYB.COM UK,437
```

This means that DOS was already adapted to the United Kingdom keyboard in the CONFIG.SYS file during installation. So you don't have to enter the line in your AUTOEXEC.BAT file.

Screen

Different code pages can only be used on the screen if the graphics card allows different character displays. Although different code pages can be used with MCGA, EGA and VGA cards, they can't be used with Hercules and CGA cards. Type the following in your CONFIG.SYS file to prepare the screen for code pages:

```
DEVICE=DISPLAY.SYS CON=(Type,Table,Number)
```

If necessary, specify the complete path for DISPLAY.SYS.

Type   EGA for MCGA, EGA and VGA (requires the EGA.CPI file). LCD for LCD screens of portable computers (requires the LCD.CPI file).

Table   Sets the desired code page.

Number   Specifies the number of desired code pages; later you must choose between them (1 for LCD, 2 for EGA).

Example

Suppose DISPLAY.SYS is in the DOS subdirectory of the hard drive, the computer has an EGA card, and you want to use two code pages with the standard table (USA). Type the following in CONFIG.SYS:

```
DEVICE=C:\DOS\DISPLAY.SYS CON=(EGA,437,2)
```

You must then make the following change with the MODE command:

```
MODE CON CP PREP=(Table) Type
```

Specify "Table" and "Type" as previously shown.

Printer

Code pages can be used on the IBM Graphics Printer II (4201) and the Quietwriter III (5202). They can also be used on compatible printers on a parallel port.

Insert the following line in CONFIG.SYS to use code pages for the printer:

```
DEVICE=PRINTER.SYS LPTx=(Type,Table,Number)
```

If necessary, specify the complete path for PRINTER.SYS. Enter the number of the printer port for x.

Type   4201 (requires the 4201.CPI file). 5202 (requires 5202.CPI).

Table   Sets the desired code page (refer to the section about the keyboard).

Number   Specifies the number of code pages; later you must switch between these pages.

After these steps, you still must use the MODE command:

```
MODE LPTx CP PREP=(Table) Type
```

Specify the "Table" and "Type" as previously shown. For x specify the number of your printer port.

Switching code pages

After adding these lines to your CONFIG.SYS file, you can switch between code pages. However, first you must restart your computer so that these changes can be activated.

Before using code pages, DOS must be modified to support the country-specific character set tables. Use the NLSFUNC (National Language Support Functions) command to do this:

```
NLSFUNC
```

Selecting code pages for the keyboard

You can select another character set table by using the following command:

```
KEYB UK,Table
```

If necessary, specify the complete path for KEYBOARD.SYS.

"UK" represents the United Kingdom keyboard layout. The following parameters can be used for "Table":

437	USA, default
850	multilingual
860	Portugal
863	Canada/France
865	Scandinavian countries

Selecting code pages for the screen

To select another screen character set table, you must use two commands:

```
MODE CON CP SELECT=Table
```

"Table" sets the desired code page (see the previous section).

Selecting code pages for the screen in graphics mode

If you're operating your screen in graphics mode, you can display characters with ASCII codes 128 - 255 by using the following command (on the Supplemental Disk from Microsoft):

```
GRAFTABL Table
```

"Table" sets the desired code page (see the previous section).

Use the following command to determine the status of the graphics characters:

```
GRAFTABL /STATUS
```

Selecting code pages for the printer

Use the following command line to select another printer character set table:

```
MODE LPTx CP SELECT=Table
```

"Table" sets the desired code page (see the previous section).

  Avoid switching off a printer when working with code pages (see below).

Setting code pages for all prepared devices

To set a different character set table for all prepared devices, use the CHCP (Change Codepage) command:

```
CHCP Table
```

"Table" sets the desired code page (see the previous section).

If you don't specify any parameters, the command displays the current code page.

Special options for working with code pages

Use the following to obtain information about a device and its defined code page:

```
MODE Device CP /Status
```

"Device" represents the device for which you want information (CON, LPTx). "/Status" can be omitted from the command line.

If device code pages are no longer available, the following reactivates them:

```
MODE Device CODEPAGE REFRESH
```

"Device" represents the device whose character table set you want to reactivate.

 Do this if you switched off the printer while working with code pages.

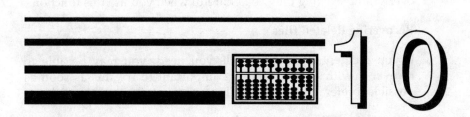

Backing Up And Recovering Data

When everything on your computer is running smoothly, you probably don't think about backing up your work. However, once work that took days or weeks to complete is suddenly destroyed, you'll probably realize that it has been a while since you backed up your work. In this chapter we'll discuss the important topic of data security.

10.1 Overview

First we'll present an overview of the ways MS-DOS 6.0 can help you protect your data.

The principle of data security

The purpose of data security is to protect data from accidental deletion. The most common form of data security is backing up data to diskettes (backup copies).

Backing up a hard drive

With the MS-DOS command MSBACKUP, you can easily back up all the data on your hard drive, if you have enough diskettes. Unlike the BACKUP command of MS-DOS 5.0, MSBACKUP doesn't require complex parameters or preformatted diskettes. Also, a second command (RESTORE) for restoring data isn't needed because MSBACKUP also performs this function.

If you don't need to backup all the data on your hard drive, you can save both time and storage space by saving only parts of it. MSBACKUP lets you select the files you want to save. You can specify all text files, for example, or all files that have been changed since the last backup.

Restoring your data

MSBACKUP also restores your data from the backup diskettes to the hard drive. Restoring data can actually lead to data loss by overwriting existing files, so be careful when you use this function.

Recovering deleted files

If you accidentally delete a file you need, you may be able to recover it with UNDELETE. It's important to try this as soon as possible, preferably before anything else is written on the disk.

Your chances of a successful UNDELETE are improved by running UNDELETE with the /S (Delete Sentry) switch before you delete the file. So the safest solution is to add this line to your AUTOEXEC.BAT file. Even without this precaution, your file may still be recoverable. You should call UNDELETE from the directory where the deleted file was stored.

Reversing disk formatting

If a disk is accidentally formatted, you can usually recover the data on it by immediately running UNFORMAT. As with UNDELETE, it's important to avoid any further writing on the disk before recovery. Since this command can also destroy data, it must be used carefully. UNFORMAT won't work if a disk is too full or if it was reformatted at a different capacity.

Data security limitations

Besides knowing what security measures are available, you should also know the limitations involved in data protection:

- When copying files, you can overwrite and consequently destroy an existing file of the same name on the target disk.

- The destruction of partition data on a hard drive, despite many protective measures, results in the loss of data currently on the disk.

10.2 Why Backup Your Data?

Perhaps you didn't expect to find a chapter containing information on data security in this book. However, if several weeks or months' worth of work is suddenly destroyed, it's comforting to know that you have backup copies. In this chapter we'll show you the safest, easiest ways to back up your valuable data.

Before we begin let's briefly discuss two misconceptions about data security.

Many people believe that the only way to destroy data is by accidentally entering DEL *.* or FORMAT C:. However, since the dangers of using these two commands are well known, the chances of someone accidentally deleting files or formatting a hard drive are relatively small.

Entering DEL *.* destroys only the files in the current or specified directory. The damage can be undone rather easily with special tools, including the MS-DOS UNDELETE command. Most hard drives and versions of DOS allow you to abort FORMAT C:, while the command is running, without experiencing any data loss. Also, in some cases, the UNFORMAT command can be used to recover from an accidental format.

Unfortunately, there are more dangerous threats to your data than these two commands. The following are a few hypothetical examples of how data could be lost.

1. One day your hard drive begins to act strangely. There seems to be a problem with the hard drive controller. Data can be read, but it's impossible to write to the disk.

    Since you need the data urgently, you call your dealer for help. The dealer tells you to bring the computer to the store. In your haste, you forget to park the hard drive before moving it.

    When you arrive, the computer won't operate with the hard drive. Because the disk was subjected to vibration during the trip to your dealer, the read/write head has been damaged.

    Your irreplaceable system information and the information stored on the disk has been permanently destroyed.

2. While working with a word processing program, it suddenly crashes while saving a file. At first, this doesn't seem to be a problem because the program automatically creates BAK files (backup copies of the existing file). However, the next time you boot your computer, it begins to behave strangely and error messages are displayed on the screen.

    As a check, you run CHKDSK which informs you there are over 2,000 lost clusters on your disk. Actually, CHKDSK has found that most of the files on the hard drive are either empty or totally useless, including your word processor's BAK file. You don't have any backup copies on diskettes.

Perhaps these examples will convince you that the data on your hard drive is about as safe as leaving your wallet in an unattended shopping cart at the supermarket.

Quick and easy backup

When the subject of creating hard drive backups is discussed, many users immediately think of inconvenient, tedious processes. However, in most cases there are methods for providing data security that are much faster than the usual method, which involves swapping several backup diskettes.

In the following section we'll discuss different ways you can prevent data loss.

10.3 Overview of the New MSBACKUP Options

With the MSBACKUP program, MS-DOS 6.0 provides a complete program package for backing up, comparing and restoring files.

These file operations were previously performed by commands issued from the DOS command line. With the menu-directed screens of MSBACKUP, you no longer have to remember the exact command syntax and parameters.

The program also offers an extensive help system, which you can access at any time by using F1 or the Help menu.

Configuration

Before using the actual MSBACKUP functions, the program determines how to achieve the best performance and reliability for your configuration. This involves obtaining some screen and mouse settings and performing a preliminary backup called a confidence test.

The program can usually recognize the proper settings for your configuration automatically. You can either accept the settings displayed in the text fields of the configuration menu or change them. Once you define the configuration in this way, you can save it. Then you can skip this step during subsequent backups.

You should always run the confidence test before your first backup. The test, which is completely automated, checks the hardware components of your system to minimize the possibility that errors will occur during the backup. If you unknowingly make backup copies that are defective, you won't be able to restore the data later.

The configuration menu

If you haven't created a configuration file yet and you start MSBACKUP, the configuration menu automatically appears. The program leads you through the steps of defining screen and mouse settings and disk drive information. Normally you can simply accept the data provided by the program.

Keyboard and mouse operation

MSBACKUP can be used with either the keyboard or the mouse.

With the mouse, click any button setting that you want to change; the appropriate list or dialog box opens.

To select an entry from a list, double-click it. Then click the [OK] button to move the entry to the text field. To activate an option, click it once (see also "Selecting files").

If you're using the keyboard, press [Tab] to move to the next text field or button, and [Shift] + [Tab] to move to the previous one. To open a list box, move to the appropriate button and press [Enter] or the [Spacebar].

Use the arrow keys to move to the desired entry, then select it by pressing the [Spacebar]. Then move to the [OK] button and press [Enter] (see also "Selecting files").

Screen and mouse options

The first dialog box that's displayed after starting MSBACKUP shows the screen and mouse settings assumed by the program.

The "Screen Colors:" title button lists what MSBACKUP believes is your graphics adapter. You can click it to open a list of alternate selections and change the entry if desired.

If you have an EGA or VGA graphics card, the "Display Lines:" title button lets you indicate how many lines should be displayed on the screen when MSBACKUP runs.

The "Graphical Display:" title button lets you set the way dialog boxes and the mouse pointer are displayed.

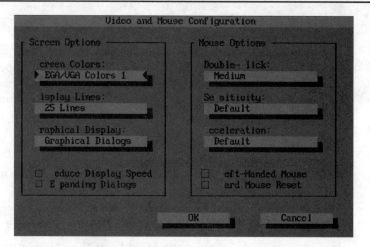

Screen and mouse settings in the configuration menu

If you encounter screen display problems (snow or flickering) with a CGA adapter or other special screen types, you can enable the "Reduce Display Speed" check box. This slows the program down slightly and may improve the screen image.

Enable the "Expanding Dialogs" check box to have dialog boxes appear as though they are expanding to a certain dimension when you open them.

The mouse settings are located on the right side of the first dialog box. These settings include the "Double-click:" title button. Although this is usually set to "Medium", it can be adjusted.

The "Sensitivity:" title button determines how sensitive the mouse pointer is to mouse movement. The "Default" setting accepts the sensitivity you're currently using. "Low" and "High" mean that the mouse pointer moves a shorter or longer distance on the screen, respectively, for a particular movement of the mouse.

The "Acceleration:" field lets you determine whether and to what degree the speed of the mouse pointer will be increased, with respect to mouse movement. The higher the value, the higher the acceleration.

The enabled "Left-Handed Mouse" check box lets you switch mouse buttons for left-handed use.

You shouldn't need to enable the "Hard Mouse Reset" check box unless you have some type of problem with the mouse.

Drive information

When you're finished with the first dialog box, MSBACKUP performs a test to determine whether the fastest and safest method for changing diskettes can be used. This test runs automatically.

Then the correct drive information is requested. Usually the program recognizes this data and makes the appropriate text entries after the test. It's possible to override the backup device selection.

Change any incorrect values by clicking the appropriate drive field and selecting an entry from the list that appears.

You can also click the Auto Config button to have the program make selections automatically.

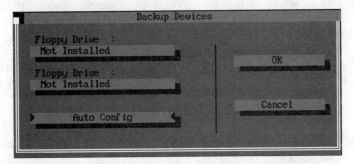

Drive information dialog box

The confidence test

Once you've selected all the necessary settings and any desired options, MSBACKUP performs a test to ensure that all the hardware components are working properly.

The test finds the highest speed setting at which your computer can perform a reliable backup.

First the program determines the fastest processor speed and hard drive access time. Then it executes a test backup of selected files, followed by a compare. Running this test before every backup helps prevent defects in your backup copies.

This test is completely automatic. Simply specify the target drive that should be used for the backup. You can follow progress on the screen as dialog boxes open and the program makes file selections.

You'll need two diskettes for the test. These diskettes can be preformatted and contain data. If they already contain files, you must confirm a security prompt to overwrite them.

Selecting the test backup drive

When the test is finished, a dialog box shows the number of files selected and the storage space and time required by the backup.

Next MSBACKUP compares the files. This process is also completely automatic. When prompted, simply insert the two backup diskettes. The results of the compare will be displayed in a dialog box.

If any errors occurred, the program informs you and reduces the backup speed. The backup process will take longer, but it will be more reliable.

Before actually starting the backup itself, you can finally save the current settings by pressing the [Save] button in the "Configuration" dialog box.

If you press [OK], you can proceed with the backup but the configuration data won't be saved. If you don't save the data, you must repeat the configuration setup the next time you run the program.

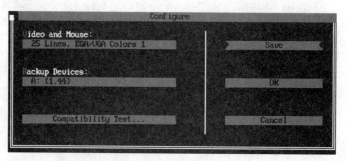

Saving the configuration

The main Backup menu

After determining your configuration, the main Backup menu appears. From here you can branch to one of the three main MSBACKUP functions: Backup, Compare, and Restore. If you select the (Backup) button, a screen similar to the following appears:

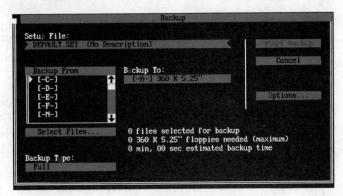

The Backup menu

Selecting drives

The setup file that will be used for the backup appears in the text field at the top of the Backup window. This file provides file selection criteria and other details about the configuration and options you're using. A DEFAULT.SET file is provided.

However, if you already created your own file, its name is displayed instead. If you have more than one setup file, you can click the button to open a list box showing the available files.

The "Backup From" list box shows all the available hard drives (local and network drives) and lets you choose the one you want to backup.

If you want your backup to include all the files on the source drive (this is called a complete backup), simply click the desired drive letter with the right mouse button or select it and press the (Spacebar).

The notation "All Files" will appear to the right of the drive letter. Since this works like a toggle switch, you can repeat the same action to undo it.

If you want to exclude only a few files, use the previous method to select them, then click (Select Files...) and "deselect" those to be skipped (see "Selecting files"). When you use the "Select Files" option, the notation "Some Files" appears to the right of the drive letter.

The "Backup To:" title button indicates the target drive where the backup copies will be made. The default is the one used for the test.

You can change this by opening the list box. Instead of a normal disk drive, it's also possible to specify an MS-DOS drive and path. If you choose this option and click OK, a prompt appears for the path data under the "Backup To:" title button.

This option lets you perform a backup to a directory on your hard drive. Actually any type of media that looks like a DOS drive is permissible. This includes tape drives and network drives.

Backup options

The backup can be performed in several ways.

You can end the backup with a read and compare test to immediately check for any errors that may have occurred. To save storage space, you can also compress the data. However, this can take a little longer than a backup without compression.

You can also protect the backup copies with a password. Since the password is case-sensitive, be sure to note any use of capitalization.

Another option activates a warning before overwriting or formatting backup diskettes.

Depending on the correction information that's stored on the diskettes, it's even possible to repair damaged diskettes.

You can also include old Backup catalog files in the backup. (Refer to the "Catalog files" section for more information.)

Finally, you can request an audible signal when a new diskette is needed or have the program end automatically when the backup is finished.

Choosing backup options

The three backup methods

You can choose from three types of backup methods. They differ in the way they select files and in the amount of time they require. Click the "Backup Type:" option button to display a list of the three methods.

 Remember, regardless of which type of backup you request, the program saves only the files that are selected (see "Selecting files" and "Selecting all files on a drive").

Full backup

A full backup saves every selected file and resets its archive attribute. The archive attribute indicates whether a file is backed up in its present state, because MS-DOS sets this when the file is created or modified.

The first backup you do should be a full backup of all the files on your disk. Since this is the most time-consuming backup method, you may want to use it only occasionally or perhaps only once.

For subsequent backups, you may want to save only those files that were changed or added since a previous backup. There are two ways to do this.

Incremental backup

The incremental backup saves all new files and those that were changed since the last backup. It also resets the archive attribute for each file it saves.

When you perform a second incremental backup, some of the files that were saved on the first one may not be saved again. Only files that were changed or added since the previous (first incremental) backup are saved. This means that over time you'll accumulate a series of backup sets.

To restore files, you must go back to the original backup and restore each incremental set in sequence. So, although this is a quick backup method, restoring files is time-consuming and requires careful file management.

Differential backup

The differential backup saves all new files and those that were changed since the last complete backup. It does not reset the archive attribute.

Since you always save all changes since the last complete backup, you can do periodic differential backups and save only the latest one (in addition to the complete backup).

This backup method is slower than the incremental method, but is also easier and faster to restore.

Selecting files

One of the most important features of a backup program involves selecting the files to be saved. MSBACKUP has an easy-to-use file selection menu that you can open by clicking the [Select Files...] button.

The directory structure of the selected drive appears in tree form on the left side of the screen. The files belonging to the currently selected directory are located on the right side. The selected directory is displayed above the directory window; the storage requirements (sizes) for both the entire drive and the selected files are located below.

A list of files

The buttons at the bottom of the screen help you select and deselect files.

Include and Exclude buttons

With the [Include] and [Exclude] buttons, you can create a list of files to be included or excluded from a backup. Once you've created such a list, the files it specifies are automatically selected each time you do a backup.

If you only want to save a few files, you can use [Include] to place the files in your backup list, without having to select them from a huge display. However, if you want to backup almost all files, [Exclude] lets you quickly specify a few exceptions.

The "Include" and "Exclude" dialog boxes are almost identical in appearance and use. Only their functions are different. You can also open them by selecting a directory from the tree and pressing ⊞ (Include) or ⊟ (Exclude) on the numeric keypad.

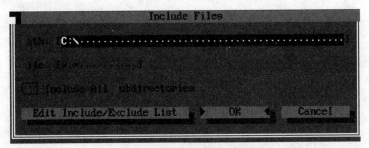

The Include Files dialog box

The selected path appears in the first text field of the dialog box. In the "File:" edit box, you can type the desired filename, using wildcards if desired, as in these examples:

    .

to select all files, or

    *.DOC

to select all files with the .DOC extension. To include subdirectories in your list, enable the "Include/Exclude All Subdirectories" check box.

The files specified in this way are placed in a backup list, which can be stored for subsequent backups. The list can be edited by clicking [Edit Include/Exclude List]. After opening the list, you can select entries and either delete them with the [Del=Delete] button or copy them with the [Ins=Copy] button.

Copying entries is an easy way to add files to a list. Use the [Edit] button to edit an entry. Then a dialog box, which lets you change the path or file specification as desired, appears.

For example, if you had placed .TXT files from a certain directory in your include/exclude list, you can now add files with a different extension.

    Since the contents of your list can be overwritten with the mouse or keyboard in this way, you should be careful not to change the list accidentally.

Sort criteria

Before selecting files, you may want to change the order in which filenames are displayed on the screen. This can make it easier to find the ones you want.

Click the [Display] button to use this feature. You'll see a dialog box that provides various sort options.

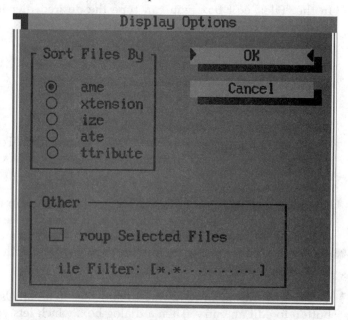

Sort options for files

The available options are "Name", "Extension", "Size", "Date" and "Attribute".

The "Group Selected Files" check box lets you group files with the archive attribute set; these files are candidates for a differential or incremental backup. These files will then be listed first on the file display so you can find and select them easily.

You can also use the "File Filter:" text box to limit the files to be displayed.

To show only .TXT files, for example, type:

```
*.TXT
```

as the filter. To deactivate the filter again, restore the

```
*.*
```

default. The filter is also deactivated (reset to *.*) automatically when you select Display in the backup menu.

☞ Specifying a filter does not undo any file selections you have already made.

Special file selection options

Additional file selection criteria are available by clicking the Special button.

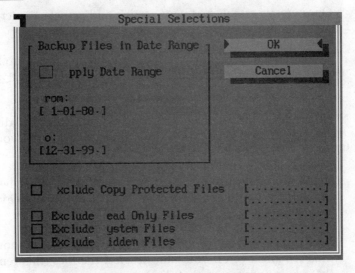

Special file selection options

The "Special" dialog box provides additional ways of limiting the files to be saved. The "Backup Files in Date Range" option, for example, lets you exclude files not created or modified within a certain date range. You specify a "From:" and "To:" date in the following format:

```
mm-dd-yy
```

Specifying a date range does not automatically select the corresponding files. Instead, it simply prevents those files falling outside the range from being displayed (and consequently from being selected). You still must select the files you want to save from the display list.

There are four more special file selection criteria. These let you exclude copy-protected, read-only, system or hidden files. The associated text field accepts up to five filenames, which will then be excluded from the backup.

This exclusion applies to all drives. If you're not sure whether you have any copy-protected files, check your software manuals. Most vendors of copy-protected programs indicate which files cannot be copied.

Files excluded by these criteria are still shown on the file display. However, if you try to select one of them, a dot appears in front of the filename to indicate that the file cannot be selected.

Selecting files

Once you've established your sorting and preselection criteria, you can actually select the files for your backup list.

If you have multiple drives, they are shown on the top line of the work screen. You can use the mouse (or cursor keys and [Spacebar]) to select the drive you want.

In the same way, select the desired directory to display the associated files. If you are in the directory window, you can also select a directory by starting to type its name.

You'll automatically jump to the first directory that begins with the letters you have typed so far. The file display changes accordingly.

Each directory from which you have selected files is shown in red. This remains even if you later deselect the files; this reminds you that you've processed that directory.

Double-clicking a directory (or keyboard selection with the [Spacebar]) automatically selects all its files. An arrow appears in front of the name of any directory whose files are all selected.

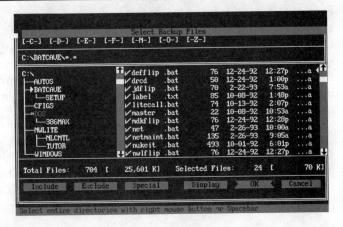

Selecting files

To select several directories as a block, double-click the first one and drag the selection to the last directory.

Use ⎡Tab⎤ or the mouse to switch between the directory window and the file window. In the file window, you can select files or blocks of files the same way you select directories.

Files selected for the backup are indicated with a checkmark in front of the name. Files excluded by special criteria are indicated by a dot if you try to select them, and they will not be saved.

File selection works like a toggle switch. This means that, by using exactly the same methods, you can deselect any file that is currently selected.

Saving your setup

When you've finished making all the file selections for your backup, you can save them in a new setup file. Use the command **File/Save Setup As...** and type a name for the new configuration.

You can create multiple setup files for various types of backups. If you don't specify a name for the current configuration, you'll be asked if you want to save it as DEFAULT.SET when you leave the program.

If you made changes to a previously existing setup file and do not want the changes to be permanent, answer "No" to the confirmation prompt that appears when the program ends.

Starting the backup

Click (OK) to return to the **Backup** menu after completing your file selections. There you will see the number of files selected, the maximum number of diskettes required, and a time estimate for the backup. The (Start Backup) button is now functional. When you click this button the backup begins.

A new menu prompts you to insert the backup diskettes as needed. The lower half of the screen shows information about the backup procedure (elapsed time, compression speed), the expected number of diskettes needed, the number of selected files and file space requirements.

If you insert a diskette that already contains data, the program shows you the contents in a dialog box and asks for permission to overwrite it.

At this point, if you do not want to overwrite the data, you can either switch diskettes or interrupt the backup. Diskettes previously formatted by another backup program will automatically be reformatted by MSBACKUP.

The final status of the backup (number of files, number of diskettes, file space, time, compression factor) is reported when the backup is complete.

Restoring data

If you lose data that was saved with MSBACKUP, this data can easily be restored. Start MSBACKUP and press (Restore) from the main screen to go to the **Restore** menu.

The **Restore** menu looks and functions like the **Backup** menu.

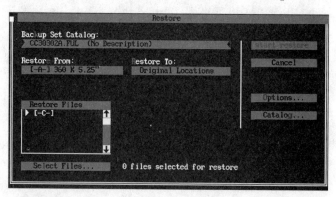

The Restore menu

Catalog files

Doing a backup creates a list of the files and directories saved. This list is called a catalog. The catalog is written both to the hard drive and to the last diskette of the backup set. It is essential for restoring data that has been destroyed.

If the catalog on your hard drive was among the data lost, you can read it in from the last backup diskette. If this is also lost or defective, you can even rebuild the catalog by reading all the other diskettes. Whatever is still readable is placed in the rebuilt catalog, and, therefore, can be restored.

Catalog names have the following extensions:

CAT   Master catalog

FUL   Complete backup catalog

DIF   Differential backup catalog

INC   Incremental backup catalog

A master catalog (*.CAT) contains the same information as all the individual catalogs of a backup series. You can restore data using either the master catalog or the individual catalogs within the series.

The (Catalog...) button lists all the catalogs on your hard drive. If your catalog hasn't been destroyed, you can simply enter the name of the catalog to be restored in the "Backup Set Catalog:" title button.

To do a complete restore, begin with the .FUL backup catalog. Then follow this with any subsequent partial backups. This means either the last differential or all incremental sets in sequence, starting with the oldest (see "Selecting files").

 If you have password protection on a catalog, be sure to use the proper capitalization.

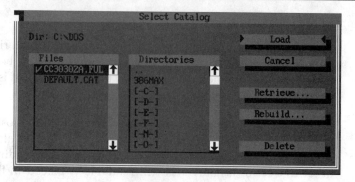

Selecting a catalog

If you have to read in a catalog from a backup diskette, press the
(Retrieve...) button. A dialog box lets you specify the appropriate
drive information.

Then you're prompted to insert the last diskette of the backup set.
Press (Continue) when you are ready to proceed. If the program finds a
catalog on the backup diskette that matches one already on the
hard drive, a warning message asks if you want to overwrite it.

Otherwise, the catalog is copied directly to the appropriate
directory of your hard drive.

If both copies of your catalog have been lost, press the (Build) button
to recreate the catalog. Again, you begin by selecting the drive.
Then you'll see an information screen for showing files and lapse
times, similar to the one displayed during backup.

You're prompted to insert the first diskette of the backup set; then
process for rebuilding the catalog begins. The lower half of the
screen shows the rebuild in progress.

When it's finished, the same information that's shown at the end
of a backup appears.

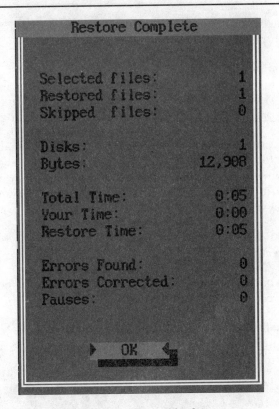

After restoring a backup

Choosing drives

In the "Restore From:" title button, indicate the drive from which you'll read the backup diskettes. Clicking this field opens a list of the available drives.

The "Restore To:" title button works the same way. Here you indicate the drive that should receive the restored data. If you want everything to be restored to the original drive and directory, select the "Original Locations" option.

You can also keep the original directory structure, but restore it to a different drive or under a different path. To do this, select the "Other Drives" option. Then you'll be prompted for the drive or path before the restore begins.

To change only individual directories, select the "Other Directories" option. When this option is active, you'll be prompted for a target directory as each backup (source) directory is restored.

The backup directory is displayed as the default, so you only have to type what you want to relocate or rename.

Restore options

Like Backup, Restore has several basic options available. Press [Options...] to open the "Disk Restore Options" dialog box.

You can check the results of the restore by enabling the "Verify Restore Data (Read and Compare)" check box. The restored data is then compared to the data on the diskettes. Any transfer errors that occur will be recognized immediately. However, this option slows down the restore process.

You can also request confirmation prompts for creating new directories and files or overwriting existing files.

If you enable the "Restore Empty Directories" check box, you can recreate a lost directory structure.

Finally, you can request an audible signal when a new diskette is required or have the program quit automatically when the restore is finished.

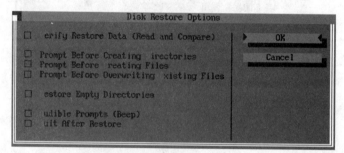

Disk Restore Options

Selecting files

When performing a complete restore, you must be aware of the sequence in which you process a series of backups, so that the most recent version of every file is used. You should start with the full backup.

Then, if you used the differential method to save your files, you can restore only the last differential backup. If you used the incremental method, you must restore all the incremental backups in sequence, beginning with the oldest version.

Although this is the fastest method for creating backups, it's also the most time-consuming and cumbersome method for restoring.

You can also perform file selection in Restore, just as you can in Backup. If you want to restore only certain files, you can go directly to the backup that has the most recent version of the files you want to restore.

In "Restore Files", you can select all files quickly by clicking the drive with the right mouse button, just as in Backup. The notation "All Files" appears to the right of the drive letter. If you want to exclude a few files, you can use this method to select them all, and then use [Select Files...] to deselect them.

Pressing [Select Files...] opens a file selection menu like the one in Backup.

The work area is divided into a directory window and a file window. The only difference between this screen and its counterpart in Backup is in the button set at the bottom of the screen. The [Version] and [Print] buttons replace the [Include] and [Exclude] buttons found in Backup.

[Print] lets you print your catalog.

[Version] can be used only when a master catalog is loaded and there are files in different versions. When this occurs, you can use this command to load a different version.

Files that appear in several versions are preceded by a plus sign (+) in the file display. However, this is only the case when you've loaded a master catalog file.

[Special] gives you control over file selection criteria. These include date range, copy-protected, read-only, hidden and system files (see Backup).

[Options...] lets you sort the file display according to name, extension, size, date and attributes.

To make it easy to find the files that have set archive attributes, these files can appear as a group at the top of the display. You can also use file filters to limit the file display (see Backup).

Mislabeled diskettes

It's easy to label diskettes in the wrong sequence or forget to label them. To determine the number and version of the diskette, use the

DIR command from the DOS prompt to display the file contents. Here's an example:

```
Volume in Drive A is DEFAULT_FUL
Volume Serial Number is 1C04-745C
Directory of A:\
CC00101A.003          135678 01-01-93    10:23a
```

The name of the diskette provides information about the backup configuration that was used (in the previous example, "DEFAULT") and the type of backup (in the previous example, "FUL"). The version number is in the filename given by Backup. It is the fifth character from the left in the eight character name ("1" in our example). The diskette number corresponds to the number in the file extension ("3" in our example).

In addition, you receive information about the size of the file, the date of creation, and the time of the backup.

Starting the restore

When your selections are complete, press [Start Restore]. The restore process runs automatically. Simply insert the proper diskettes as requested, starting with the first one of the set (version) you're currently restoring.

If you accidentally insert the wrong diskette, an error message and a display of the diskette contents appears. Then you can simply replace the wrong diskette with the right one and continue.

Another error message warns you of any defective diskettes.

The lower half of the screen shows status information while the restore is in progress. When it's finished, the final status is shown in a format similar to that of a completed backup. Closing the status window takes you back to the "Disk Restore Options" dialog box or to the main menu, depending on your settings.

Compare

From the main menu, you can run the Compare program to verify the success of a backup or restore. If errors are found, you can immediately repeat the backup or restore process.

It's better to discover potential problems immediately than wait until important data has been irretrievably lost.

The Compare program has the same interface as Restore and you can make your selections as described. When you've selected the files to be compared, press the [Start Compare] button to start.

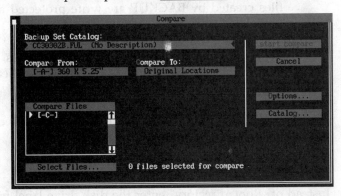

The Compare menu

When you press [Start Compare], the compare process begins and you are prompted to insert the appropriate diskettes as needed.

Progress is shown on the screen. You can see the selected files being compared one after another in the upper portion of the screen. The lower portion of the screen displays the elapsed time, any errors, and the number of diskettes and files processed.

When the compare is finished, the status window shows the final results, including a report of any errors that occurred. After pressing [OK] you'll return to the opening screen of MSBACKUP.

10.4 Backing up the Hard Drive

Backing up data is extremely important when you use a hard drive. Unlike diskettes, DISKCOPY can't be used to make a copy of the hard drive. However, MS-DOS does provide some special commands for backing up the data on your hard drive.

The BACKUP command (found on earlier versions of MS-DOS) can be used to copy the data on your hard drive to diskettes. If the data on your hard drive is destroyed, the RESTORE command (found on earlier versions of MS-DOS, but may be available separately from Microsoft Corporation on their Supplemental Diskette) can restore files from the diskettes.

Why would you want BACKUP and RESTORE if you have MSBACKUP? We'll discuss this in Section 10.6, "Recovering Backup Data of Older DOS Versions."

BACKUP stores the files on diskettes in a special format that can only be used by RESTORE to recover the files. The files created by BACKUP are write protected and cannot be deleted directly.

To use BACKUP diskettes for other purposes, either use FORMAT to format the disks or ATTRIB to clear the files for deletion.

To back up all the data from a hard drive (files, directories and their structure), use the following command line:

```
BACKUP Root_directory Backup_drive /S
```

Instead of "Root_directory" enter the disk drive label followed by a backslash and instead of "Backup_drive" enter the drive that will be used by the backup (A:).

/S   Also include any subdirectories because BACKUP automatically backs up the files in the subdirectories. This preserves the directory structure.

 Beginning with MS-DOS 4.0, the BACKUP command automatically formats diskettes. In earlier versions of DOS (such as MS-DOS 3.3) you must specify the /F switch as an additional switch for the diskettes to be formatted automatically.

Be sure that you have enough blank diskettes for your backup. Use CHKDSK to display how much space the data takes up on the hard drive and then calculate how many diskettes are needed.

If you're using 360K diskettes, base your estimate on 350K of data per diskette, instead of 360K. Since BACKUP places control information on the diskettes, the entire capacity of the diskette isn't available for storing data.

Example

To back up all files from drive C: onto diskettes in drive A:, use the following command line:

```
BACKUP C:\ A: /S
```

MS-DOS prompts you to place the backup diskettes in drive A: and press any key.

BACKUP deletes all of the files in the root directory of
the backup diskettes. If you use the same backup diskettes
for another backup, the previous contents of the diskette
will be lost.

Don't use BACKUP if you have joined or assigned drives or
directories with the MS-DOS commands SUBST, ASSIGN
and JOIN, because this could cause errors. Since these drive
redirections could cause inaccurate backups of your data,
they should be corrected before proceeding.

BACKUP only deletes the existing files in the root directory of the
diskette. Subdirectories and their files on "target diskettes"
remain intact, which decreases the storage capacity for the
backup.

If this is the case, BACKUP will require additional diskettes. You
may want to reformat diskettes containing subdirectories before
using them with the BACKUP command.

Remember to label and number the backup diskettes. If you don't do
this you may have trouble recovering the files with RESTORE.
The backup diskettes must be inserted in the same sequence that
was used when the backup was created.

     If your hard drive is divided into several partitions, a
backup must be performed for each disk drive.

How often should you perform a complete backup?

The time required for a complete backup of a hard drive depends
on the amount of data and the format of the diskette. Fortunately,
it's not necessary to perform a complete backup very often.

Over a period of time you'll make fundamental changes to the
data on your hard drive. For example, you will probably purchase
new programs and install them on your hard drive or replace
existing programs with newer versions. If several months have
passed since the last time you performed a complete backup, you
should back it up again.

Remember, you can always reinstall programs that were installed
since the last backup. So losing data doesn't cause you to lose
programs. However, it's time-consuming to install these programs.

Also, most users set up programs according to their own requirements. So when reinstalling programs you must adapt and set up programs according to the requirements you previously used.

10.5 Restoring all Files

Data loss can occur for many reasons. However, if your data has been backed up, your hard drive can be restored quickly.

Use the RESTORE command to copy your backup diskettes, created by BACKUP, onto your hard drive. The files and directories will be the same as they were at the time the backup was performed. Any changes made since the last backup are lost (unless you saved those changes in some other way).

 When files are restored, data can also be lost if the command overwrites existing files. So don't accidentally increase the amount of damage already done. Fortunately, an optional switch (/N) prevents files from overwriting existing data.

Don't use RESTORE if you have redirected or assigned drives or directories with the MS-DOS SUBST command.

RESTORE places data in the same directory in which it was stored. The command creates exactly the same directory structure that existed when the backup was made. If the directories no longer exist, they are automatically created.

To restore all of the data lost on a backed up storage device without changing any of the existing data, use the following command line:

```
RESTORE Backup_drive Root_directory /S /N
```

In place of "Backup_drive", substitute the drive from which you want to copy back the files. Usually A: is used here.

Instead of "Root_directory", enter the disk drive label followed by a backslash.

/S   Restores files in subdirectories.

/N   Copies only files that don't exist in the target directory. This means that the command doesn't overwrite any files that are still on the hard drive.

Place the backup diskettes in the drive one after the other and press any key. On the screen RESTORE displays the names of all of the restored files.

Example

To copy the data from backup diskettes in drive A: back to drive C:, without overwriting existing files, use the following command line:

```
RESTORE A: C:\ /S /N
```

To restore all files, regardless of whether the files exist on the target drive, use the following command line:

```
RESTORE A: C:\ /S
```

10.6 Recovering Backup Data of Older DOS Versions

Backups made under versions of MS-DOS prior to Version 6.0 cannot be restored using MSBACKUP. MS-DOS 6.0 includes the command RESTORE on the supplement disk for this purpose.

The parameters required by RESTORE can be found in the reference section. However, we recommend replacing older backups with a Version 6.0 backup as soon as possible. MSBACKUP of Version 6.0 provides superior data security.

10.7 FORMAT and DEL or ERASE

Until MS-DOS 4.01, the FORMAT command completely removed the data from floppy diskettes, and created a new system area (root directory, File Allocation Table (FAT)) on hard drives. As a result, the data on a diskette was permanently deleted and the data on the hard drive could no longer be accessed. However, when diskettes are formatted with MS-DOS 6.0, the existing data is no longer overwritten.

The FORMAT command only checks the individual sectors of diskettes and hard drives for readability and then creates a new root directory and a new File Allocation Table for an empty storage device.

When you format a disk, FORMAT stores the existing information. In case of errors, you can unformat the disk using the UNFORMAT command. UNFORMAT restores the files on the storage device.

10.8 Recovering from an Accidental Format

MS-DOS 6.0 formats diskettes and hard drives so that, in case of an emergency, they can be restored with a new command, called UNFORMAT.

More information about preparing diskettes and hard drives can be found in Chapter 3, "Storage Devices".

To undo the formatting of a storage device, call UNFORMAT with the following storage device label:

```
UNFORMAT Disk_drive
```

 Any changes made since the formatting occurred are lost. Since you may not be able to restore the storage device without any defects, only use this option in emergencies. It's best if you use DISKCOPY to create a copy of the diskette or hard drive before using UNFORMAT.

 If the storage device was formatted with the special /U (unconditional format) switch of the FORMAT command or if there wasn't enough space to back up the system information, the restoration may be impossible.

If you accidentally formatted your hard drive (C:), return it to its original state with the command line:

```
UNFORMAT C:
```

UNFORMAT checks the storage device for MIRROR system information backed up with FORMAT. Then UNFORMAT lets you know whether there is any saved system information as well as the time and date the information was saved. UNFORMAT might ask whether it should use the last (L) version or the prior (P) version. Usually the last version (L) should be used.

 If UNFORMAT is used for a disk drive, you're prompted to insert the formatted diskette first.

 Since using UNFORMAT incorrectly can destroy data, the process can be aborted by pressing (Esc). However, before using UNFORMAT remember that this command can cause as much damage as accidentally formatting a storage device.

One interesting option for UNFORMAT is that a test run, which only simulates making the changes to the storage device, can be performed. Since this procedure doesn't actually make any changes, your data isn't in any danger. Use the /TEST switch:

```
UNFORMAT Disk_drive /TEST
```

UNFORMAT switches

/L   Lists every file and subdirectory when used without the /PARTN switch. When used with /PARTN, UNFORMAT displays the partition table of the current drive.

/TEST   Simulates how UNFORMAT would restore the information on the disk without actually performing UNFORMAT.

/P   Sends output to the printer on LPT1:.

10.9 Recovering Files from Defective Storage Media

Occasionally MS-DOS can recover data from defective storage media.

 Tools for creating backups and for recovering data (e.g., PC Tools, Norton Utilities or BeckerTools for Windows), which are more efficient than the tools provided by MS-DOS, are available. So before using the MS-DOS tools, investigate other options.

Buying an extra tool for creating backups is sensible because most backup programs require fewer diskettes and less time than the MS-DOS tools.

The MS-DOS RECOVER command (available separately from Microsoft on their Supplemental Diskette, or on earlier versions of MS-DOS) can be used to recover files containing defective parts (sectors). As much of the file as possible will be recovered.

Before using RECOVER, back up any existing data. RECOVER changes data, which could cause data loss.

Restoring a file

To recover as much of a file as possible, use the command line:

```
RECOVER File
```

RECOVER indicates how much of the file can be recovered.

You should immediately back up the file and check it for readability. For example, if the file contains text, load it in the word processor and determine whether the complete file was recovered or if the file contains strange characters.

The RECOVER command can restore several files simultaneously by using the appropriate wildcards. Use the following command line to recover all of the files in the root directory of drive A:

```
RECOVER A:\*.*
```

Recovering all of the files of a drive

If you can no longer read the root directory of the drive correctly, you won't be able to restore the files as described because RECOVER wouldn't find any files. If this happens, use RECOVER on the drive and try to restore as much as possible:

```
RECOVER Disk_drive
```

After you confirm a security prompt, the command restores as many files as possible. The command renames all of the files as FILEXXXX.REC, assigning them consecutive numbers (XXXX) and placing them in the root directory.

 RECOVER changes the filenames of the specified files and divides defective files into several partial files. To a certain extent, this makes your data useless. So RECOVER should only be used when absolutely necessary. Also, you should always back up existing files.

If files were in subdirectories before you used RECOVER, they are restored to the root directory. The subdirectories are lost and appear as files in the root directory.

Example

A diskette contains the files Text1 to Text4 and the files Data1 to Data4 in a subdirectory called \DATA. CHKDSK provides the following information about the diskette:

```
Volume TEST-360K created 08-22-1990  5:36p
Volume Serial Number is 1629-16E9

   362496 bytes total disk space
     1024 bytes in 1 directory
   189440 bytes in 8 user file(s)
   172032 bytes available on disk

     1024 bytes in each allocation unit
      354 total allocation units on disk
      168 available allocation units on disk

   655360 total bytes memory
   538944 bytes free
```

Suddenly the data on the diskette is no longer available because the directory was destroyed. The DIR command displays the following information:

```
Volume TEST-360K created 08-22-1990  5:36p
Volume number: 1629-16E9


        0 File(s)    172032 bytes free
```

Apparently files no longer exist. However, the low amount of free storage area indicates that the data wasn't deleted. Using RECOVER produces the following results:

```
Volume TEST-360K created 08-22-1990  5:36p
Volume number: 1629-16E9

FILE0001 REC    11776  08-22-90  3:47p
FILE0002 REC    10240  08-22-90  3:47p
FILE0003 REC    92160  08-22-90  3:47p
FILE0004 REC    47104  08-22-90  3:47p
FILE0005 REC     1024  08-22-90  3:47p
FILE0006 REC     6704  08-22-90  3:47p
FILE0007 REC     4672  08-22-90  3:47p
FILE0008 REC     8736  08-22-90  3:47p
FILE0009 REC     5680  08-22-90  3:47p
        9 File(s)     172032 bytes free
```

The files FILE0001.REC to FILE0004.REC are the first four files from the former root directory. FILE0005.REC is the subdirectory DATA, which has been converted to a file, and the files FILE0006.REC to FILE0009.REC were originally in the former DATA subdirectory.

As you can see, the sequence of the files can be used to trace their origin. If you don't know the sequence, the only criterion you can use is the size of the file.

 Since RECOVER restores all of the files to the root directory, which on a 360K diskette can only contain 111 files, it's possible that this limit could be exceeded. RECOVER will abort with a message informing you of this.

On a different storage device, back up the files you've recovered up to this point and delete them from the defective diskette. Then RECOVER can restore more files.

10.10 Optimum Data Security

In this section we'll discuss how you can achieve optimum data security. We'll use three short examples to explain the importance of data security:

1st case

The deadline for turning in your research paper is getting closer. You used a word processor to write your paper. The paper is almost done, the deadline draws near, and all you have to do is print the paper. You're saving the paper in Microsoft Word when your roommate switches on the vacuum cleaner and the power goes out. Word crashes in the middle of saving your research paper, destroying both the text and the backup copy. All you have left is a four week old backup of the hard drive, which contains only the introduction to your paper.

2nd case

A journalist is sitting in a hotel room after a political party convention, typing an article on her notebook computer. The article for Monday's issue in the magazine is almost finished when she realizes she has to back up her work. After typing DIR A: to determine that it's okay to delete the old file on the disk to make room for the article, she types in DEL *.*—destroying the very article she's been writing.

3rd case

A businessman manages all important information and appointments in his electronic appointment calendar and wants to take a quick look at his new business partner's unlisted telephone number.

However, he finds everything has disappeared. He planned on backing up his data, but never got around to it. The telephone number and lots of other important information weren't included in the last backup.

These examples clearly illustrate the importance of backing up data at regular intervals. It's easy to do this if you have a plan for data security. We'll explain this type of plan now, using MSBACKUP and other DOS commands.

This plan may seem more like paranoia than common sense. However, the result (having your data close at hand when disaster strikes) will be worth the time and trouble.

Full backup

The first step is to back up all drives. When you run MSBACKUP, you would select each drive in the "Backup From" list box and configure each drive for "All Files". Make sure that the "Backup Type:" title button lists "Full" for backup type.

The amount of time and diskettes involved in your first full backup will be considerable. For example, our system has three hard drive partitions totalling 240 Meg, which would require 122 3.5 inch high-density diskettes over an 80-minute period of time. However, the time making the full backup will be well-spent if one of your drives becomes corrupted.

Hourly backup

Also, back up the file you're currently processing both on the hard drive and to a diskette at short intervals (e.g., every hour). Often you can use DOS applications (e.g., Word or the MS-DOS Shell) to do this.

It's important to use two backup diskettes. Save to a different diskette each time. Otherwise, you could lose both the source file on the hard drive and the target file on the diskette as you are saving.

Daily backups

At the end of each day, use the MSBACKUP command in incremental backup mode. This backs up all files that you've changed since the last full or incremental backup. Store all daily backups in a safe place for at least a week.

Weekly backup

At the end of the week, use MSBACKUP in differential backup mode. This backs up all files that have changed since the last full backup, plus new files in directories you select.

You should also use at least two different sets of diskettes for weekly backups. By doing this, you can avoid overwriting the most recent weekly backup.

Six month backup

Every few months or after installing several new programs, it's a good idea to perform a full backup of the hard drive using MSBACKUP's full backup mode. Again, use two different sets of backup diskettes. Use set one the first time, set two the next time, etc.

10.11 Virus Protection: Anti-Virus

Information about virus protection

Anyone who works with computers is certainly familiar with the term computer virus. However, not many computer users have a clear picture of computer viruses and the damage they can do, how a virus can sneak into a computer system, or how to prevent viruses.

To protect your computer from computer viruses, you must know what a virus is, why it can be so dangerous, and how it gets into a computer system. You should also know the basic methods of virus protection. That's why we are devoting an entire section of this chapter to this important topic.

What are computer viruses?

Computer viruses are executable programs that reproduce, similar to biological viruses. Once in a computer system, they can spread out over storage devices and in memory. However, this characteristic alone doesn't mean that a program is a virus program. A program isn't a "virus" unless it destroys data or programs. It's the combination of these two characteristics that makes a computer virus so dangerous.

However, even this combination wouldn't be very dangerous, if computer viruses could be located and destroyed. Naturally, programmers of computer viruses want to prevent others from discovering their viruses and destroying them, so they spend a great deal of time programming the viruses and developing ways to destroy data. If you could easily detect and destroy a virus, the purpose of the virus (to do as much damage as possible and multiply as quickly as possible).

Computer viruses can be individual programs that users won't recognize as virus programs immediately (if at all), or they can be connected to or inserted in other programs. When users start these programs, the virus automatically starts along with them and can begin multiplying and destroying data.

When the virus begins running, it can "chop up" stored data, delete or overwrite files, or format entire hard drives. Another popular kind of virus destroys data during backups. Frequently small changes are made to the file, which make the file useless.

Without special tools, such as computer virus detection software, users cannot discover viruses. Since viruses destroy data in various ways and new viruses are always being developed, you must limit the search for viruses to certain characteristics. This makes it difficult to detect newly programmed viruses.

So, you could be working on your word processor and not even know that there is a computer virus in your word processing program. That's why some computer viruses can destroy the entire data contents of a hard drive before the user notices. By then it's often much too late to recover the data. Since infected programs are capable of immediately transmitting computer viruses, data from your computer could infect a friend's computer without him/her even noticing it.

How computer viruses get into a computer

As we mentioned, computer viruses are programs, and programs must be started before they can begin working. This also applies to computer viruses.

A virus cannot do any damage until the program is started. To start a program, it must be copied from a diskette to a computer system or started from the diskette. When you work on a computer, copying files from diskettes is an everyday process that you cannot avoid, but it's the only way a virus can get into your system.

This means that whenever you copy data to your computer, you run the risk of copying a virus along with the data. While this sounds terrible, not all diskettes contain virus programs. However, you should always know exactly where the diskette came from.

Since you can't avoid copying programs and data to your computer, you should consider which storage devices could contain a virus. If you always use original programs and ensure that the diskettes are write-protected, there is no danger of virus infection from diskettes.

However, if you get a program from a friend who got it from another friend, the danger is very great that you are copying a virus onto your computer. Users unwittingly spread viruses in this way, and before the virus is discovered, it can affect a whole chain of PC users.

It's also possible that someone else could copy a virus to your computer. This depends on how important it is for another person to destroy your data and how easy it is for someone to operate your computer. Most PC users don't need to worry about this.

Why are viruses so dangerous?

The most dangerous thing about viruses is that you usually don't notice them until it is too late. By that time, the damage can be substantial. Meanwhile, there are over 600 known virus strains, not to mention the derivative versions and the new viruses that are constantly introduced. As a result, the search for viruses always depends on the latest anti-virus software, which can never be as current as the latest virus.

For example, a program infected with a virus may seem to function perfectly at the beginning, but after a while, more and more defective functions will appear. It will probably take you a long time to discover that this is caused by a virus. By then, the program may have already been corrupted for a long time.

It's even worse when a virus silently destroys data. This can happen so slowly that you won't notice it until six months later. Even if you do make backup copies on a regular basis, it's possible that the backup copies could also be infected.

To protect yourself from total data loss, back up your data at regular intervals. Then write-protect the diskettes and don't make any more changes to them. If you follow this method, you will at least be able to secure the older versions.

In this method, it's important to keep the backup diskettes for a long enough period of time and not use them for the next data backup. Switching between two sets of diskettes works, but it's even better to keep the backup diskettes for an entire year.

Basic protection methods

The best protection from computer viruses consists of not letting them into your system. To do this, carefully monitor every data transfer to your system. However this isn't always easy to do.

You should always have a write-protected, virus-free start diskette available, and you should also write-protect all the other diskettes (always write-protect all the diskettes with important data or programs). The brief time in which you disable the write protection gives the virus only slim chances of multiplying.

Make backup copies at regular intervals, using new diskettes each time. This won't protect you from backup copies, but it will keep the damage to a minimum. Use only copies of original programs.

 Many original programs prompt users to write data about the user onto the original diskette during installation. However, a system infected with a virus will probably contaminate the original diskette. So, use only copies of the original diskette to install programs. Store the original diskettes in a safe place and write-protect them.

You can buy special anti-virus software to scan your diskettes and hard drive for viruses at regular intervals. When the anti-virus program finds a virus, you can remove it by using the appropriate anti-virus program package. MS-DOS 6.0 includes a virus detection program (MSAV) and a virus protection program (VSAFE). See the next page for more information about MSAV and VSAFE.

- Look for virus signatures

- Look for strange changes (EXE, COM, boot block)

- Prevent dangerous system processes (FORMAT)

Scanning for viruses with MSAV

MSAV is a program that scans your hard drive for viruses and removes them. MSAV has a list of 1300 known viruses that you can update periodically.

MSAV can also detect executable programs that have been changed in a way that would indicate unknown virus activity and gives you the opportunity to remove them.

MSAVE also gives you the option of scanning for virus programs that don't appear to have infected a program because you can't see any changes. Such viruses are called stealth viruses and require a special procedure that you can set in MSAV.

The actions performed by MSAV are stored in a file that you can view at any time.

MSAV is easy to operate because it has a menu-driven user interface and runs automatically.

 If your computer is infected with a virus and you must restart it, you must have a virus-free, write protected start diskette.

The MSAV menu

After starting MSAV, a menu, that you can operate easily with the keyboard or the mouse, appears.

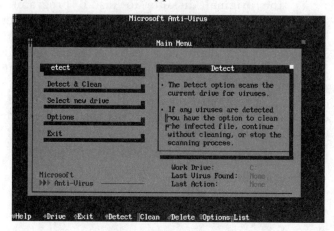

Microsoft Anti-Virus

In the "Express menu" of MSAV, you can choose from five options on the left. A text box on the right describes the function of each option.

Click on the options with the mouse or use ⌈Tab⌋ or a cursor key to highlight an option and then press ⌈Enter⌋.

Press ⌈Esc⌋ to cancel the start of the program. A dialog box appears, in which you are prompted to continue or cancel.

Below the options in the "Express menu", you'll see a graphical display of information about the selected drive and the status of the virus check.

The main menu of MSAV contains the same options available in the "Express menu". You can also call Help by pressing ⌈F1⌋.

Press ⌈F9⌋ or click on "List" to display an alphabetical list of known viruses. There are over 1200 viruses in this list. You can update this list every three months. Contact Microsoft for more information.

Each of these options has a function key assigned to it. Choose "Delete" to remove the checklist files (see the section on "Options").

Click on these options with the mouse or press the function key. To exit MSAV, either click on the close box or press ⌈Alt⌋+⌈F4⌋.

When you exit MSAV, a dialog box prompts you to save the configuration you set in the "Options" menu.

Setting options

Before you begin scanning for viruses, you can make some settings to adapt MSAV to your own requirements. Click on the ⌈Options⌋ button in the main menu or press ⌈F8⌋.

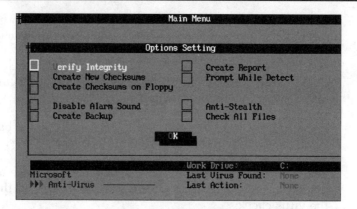

Options in MSAV

If you enable the "Verify Integrity" check box, MSAV looks for changes to executable programs. This helps you detect unknown viruses. By default, this option is enabled.

To use this option, a checklist called CHKLIST.MS must be created by enabling the "Create New Checksums" check box. This file contains information on file size, attributes, date, and time for every program. This information is called checksums.

When you enable the "Create New Checksums" check box, MSAV creates this file when it scans the selected drive. By default this option is enabled. When new files are added to the directory or deleted, MSAV updates the list with the information from the new files.

To delete checksum files, press F7 or click on "Delete". Before MSAV deletes the file, it displays a dialog box that gives you a chance to undo the deletion.

When both the "Create Checksums on Floppy" and "Create New Checksums" check boxes are enabled, you can create a checklist file (CHKLIST.MS) on a diskette. Once the checklist file is created, write-protect the diskette. After that, MSAV will compare files to their checksums, but won't update them any more. This prevents viruses from getting on the diskette.

If the "Create New Checksums" check box is selected for a write-protected diskette, MSAV displays an error message stating that it cannot write to this diskette. Disable the write-protection long enough for MSAV to scan for viruses, then write-protect the diskette again.

Enable the "Disable Alarm Sound" check box to switch off the alarm that sounds when warning messages appear on the screen.

To make backup copies of infected files before removing the virus, enable the "Create Backup" check box. The file is renamed with the VIR extension. Selecting this option can be very dangerous, since the virus in the renamed file isn't removed. Ordinarily, this option shouldn't be activated.

The only time you should activate this option is if you have only one copy of the file and are afraid that the program will no longer work after MSAV cleans it. So, you are willing to risk leaving a virus in the file.

With the "Create Report" check box, you can create a file containing all actions taken by MSAV. This is a text file, named MSAV.RPT, that is saved in ASCII format in the root directory of the selected drive. You'll receive a listing of the viruses detected and removed from the boot sector as well as the total number of scanned files and the file viruses detected and removed. File viruses are the most widespread type of virus.

Enable the "Prompt While Detect" check box to have MSAV display a dialog box whenever it detects a virus. You can then choose to repair the virus, continue scanning without repairing the virus, or stop scanning.

To enable the function for detecting unknown viruses that are in coded form and don't make outward changes to files, enable the "Anti-Stealth" check box.

Finally, you can enable the "Check All Files" check box to have MSAV check all the files for viruses. Otherwise, only files with the extensions EXE, COM, OVL, OVR, BIN, APP and CMD will be checked.

You can save the settings made in the "Options Setting" window when you quit the program. A dialog box appears, in which you can click on the "Save Configuration" check box.

Starting the virus scan

Before you begin scanning for viruses, set the desired drive by clicking the (Select new drive) button or press (F2). MSAV will scan local drives and network drives. When you select this option, a drive line appears beneath the title bar. Click on the desired drive or set it by pressing (Ctrl)+ drive letter.

MSAV automatically begins scanning the directory structure. After that, you can start looking for viruses by clicking either the (Detect) button or the (Detect & Clean) button. You can interrupt or cancel virus scanning at any time by pressing [Esc] and answering the dialog box in the appropriate manner.

Click on [Detect] if you only want to search for viruses. You can still remove the viruses yourself by answering the prompt in the dialog box. The dialog box gives you the option of removing viruses and continuing, continuing without removing, or canceling. Two graphic bars display the progress of the virus scan. The first bar shows the progress of the scan in the entire drive, while the second bar refers to the files in the directory currently being scanned.

When MSAV finds an infected file that has been so severely damaged that it can no longer restore the original state of the file, a dialog box appears, prompting you to delete the file or continue without deleting the file.

When the scan is finished, a window appears with important information about the drives that were checked (hard drives, floppy diskettes), files that were checked, infected and cleaned (COM, EXE and other files), and the scan time.

Viruses Detected and Cleaned			
	Checked	Infected	Cleaned
Hard disks :	1	0	0
Floppy disks :	0	0	0
Total disks :	1	0	0
COM Files :	51	0	0
EXE Files :	117	0	0
Other Files :	418	0	0
Total Files :	586	0	0
Scan Time :	00:00:42		

Viruses Detected and Cleaned

MSAV does a great deal to protect your computer from viruses.

Permanent virus protection with VSAFE

One method of virus protection is to prevent viruses from getting into your computer system in the first place. To do this, you can install the DOS program, VSAFE. This program contains the most important protective mechanisms.

When you install the complete program in your computer system, it checks all the current possibilities viruses have for infiltrating your system and stops them. Some possible virus sources are file operations like formatting, writing to disks and programs that are memory resident. VSAFE not only recognizes such operations, but also, in most cases, is able to stop them.

If you use VSAFE, you have the advantage of virus protection, but it's almost impossible to work efficiently on your computer. For example, suppose that you prevented programs from writing to the hard drive. Then you would no longer be able to save your work.

Therefore, you should decide which protective mechanisms you need the most and which ones will let you work efficiently on your computer. Then set only these options.

VSAFE is a memory-resident program (TSR) that warns you about all the changes it detects that could have been caused by a virus. It provides protection from viruses infiltrating your system.

To load VSAFE into memory and start it up, type the following and press (Enter):

```
VSAFE
```

VSAFE requires 22K of RAM. To start VSAFE each time you boot up your computer, add the appropriate command line to your AUTOEXEC.BAT. Add the entry as close to the start of the system file as possible so you have virus protection before other programs begin running.

Type the following and press (Enter):

```
VSAFE /u
```

to remove VSAFE from memory. The "U" stands for uninstall.

VSAFE options

VSAFE has different options for protecting your computer from viruses. If you enabled all of the options, it could prevent you from working efficiently on your computer. Therefore, you should decide beforehand which of the options you want to activate.

If you start VSAFE without any switches, you can display a list by pressing (Alt) + (V). In the list, press the number key on your keyboard that corresponds to the number of the option you want to switch on or off.

To enable the options as soon as you start VSAFE, use a plus or a minus sign after the numbers to switch an option on or off.

```
VSAFE /[Option[+ | -]...] /NE /NX /AX /CX /N /D /U
```

For each option you select, a warning message appears on your screen when VSAFE executes it. You can choose to cancel or continue the running operation. The options include the following:

1   Warns of low level formatting that completely deletes the hard drive. You should switch on this option because formatting the hard drive is such a rare occurrence and won't disturb you in your daily work on the computer. Only a few viruses destroy data in this manner.

    Default setting: on

2   Protects computer from programs that try to stay resident in memory (TSR). This option can affect your work on the computer, since programs like DOSKEY are also loaded in memory and stay resident in memory. Selecting this option means that you couldn't use any memory resident programs.

    Default setting: off

3   Protects computer from disk write operations. This setting almost completely prevents users from working on the computer since disk write operations are one of the most basic tasks of a computer. We recommend switching on this option only for diskettes suspected of virus infection.

    Default setting: off

4   Checks executable files under DOS. This option improves virus scanning with MSAV and only mildly affects users working on the computer (brief delay).

    Default setting: on

5   Scans the boot sector of a diskette or hard drive for viruses. This option only prevents boot sector viruses.

    Default setting: on

6   Warns of write operations to the boot sector or partition table of a hard drive. This setting leads to problems with the FDISK command, which is used for partitioning hard drives.

    Default setting: on

7   Warns of write operations to the boot sector of a diskette. This setting leads to problems formatting with the /S switch (system diskette).

Default setting: off

8   Prevents programs attempting to make changes to executable files.

Default setting: on

Choose the /NE switch to disable VSAFE in expanded memory; choose the /NX switch to disable VSAFE in extended memory.

Use the /AX or /CX switch to define the hot key combination for calling VSAFE. The "A" represents Alt while the "C" represents Ctrl. The "X" represents the key to be pressed after Alt or Ctrl. To use the hot key combination Alt + T, your switch would read: /AT.

To load the network driver option, use the /N switch. Otherwise, the network redirector cannot be loaded because it attempts to stay resident in memory. The /D switch turns off checksumming.

Running MSAV and VSAFE in Windows

You can also start up MSAV and VSAFE in Windows.

You can link MSAV to any group under Windows as a program. Also, you can use MSAV to scan one or more drives (including network drives) for viruses.

If you link MSAV to Windows, choose the File Properties command to change the command line so that it automatically scans a specific drive. For example, to scan drive D: for viruses every time you start MSAV, make the following entry:

```
MSAV.EXE D:
```

To have MSAV scan more than one drive, enter all the desired drives in the command in sequence after the program name:

```
MSAV.EXE C: D:
```

MSAV will automatically check these drives for viruses after it starts up.

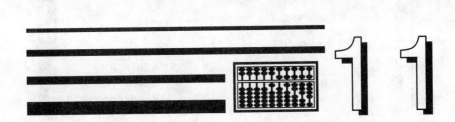

Chapter

11

Batch Files

As you work with DOS you'll find that you're frequently entering several commands in sequence from the keyboard to perform one of your computing tasks. Even when starting a program, you may have to change to the directory where the program files are stored and enter the command for starting the program.

Wouldn't it be easier if you could create a command to call a program from any directory?

DOS has a way to make performing computing tasks easier: batch files. A batch file is an ASCII text file with a .BAT extension. It contains one or more DOS commands, each on its own line. You can think of a batch file as a list of DOS commands.

One batch file that is almost universally used is the AUTOEXEC.BAT file. Starting your computer automatically executes the commands contained in this file.

Batch files can be created with:

- The DOS COPY CON command

- EDLIN (on the Supplemental Disk from Microsoft)

- EDIT

- A word processor, provided the word processor can save text in ASCII format (unformatted text file)

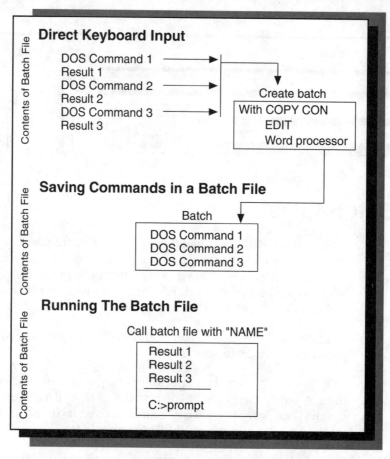

Features and importance of batch programs

The diagram illustrates what batch programs are and what their importance is to MS-DOS users.

At the MS-DOS prompt, you would enter DOS commands from the keyboard (here DOS command 1, DOS command 2 and DOS command 3). For example:

DOS command 1	FORMAT A	Formats a diskette.
DOS command 2	COPY *.* A:	Copies all files from the current directory to the diskette that has just been formatted.
DOS command 3	DIR A:	Displays the results.

However, you can also write these three commands as lines in a text and save them with the BAT extension using one of the options mentioned (COPY CON, EDLIN (on the Supplemental Disk from Microsoft), EDIT, or a word processor that can produce ASCII texts).

Then you can call this text by typing its name (without the BAT extension). MS-DOS then calls the three commands in the file and processes them in sequence. You get the same results you would if you typed each command separately.

11.1 Overview

Here is a brief overview on using batch files to process DOS commands automatically.

What are batch files?

Batch files are lists of DOS command lines that can be started like EXE or COM files. Basically, MS-DOS starts a COM file or an EXE file before searching for a BAT file with the same filename. To prevent MS-DOS from running the COM or EXE file first, specify the filename with the .BAT extension. Use EDIT to create and make changes to batch files.

How to start batch files

To start a batch file, type the filename and press (Enter). However, remember to use CALL to call a batch file from another batch file, otherwise MS-DOS won't continue running the batch file from which you are calling the new batch file. To cancel a batch file, press (Ctrl)+(C), just as you would to cancel a COM or an EXE file.

Overview of special batch commands

ECHO: Output messages and switch off display of command lines.

REM: Insert comments.

IF: Checks for conditions.

GOTO: Go to a line, must begin with :Label.

FOR IN DO:
            Loops in batch files with loop variables.

CALL: Calls another batch file from first batch file.

PAUSE: Interrupts batch file until a key is pressed.

SHIFT: Moves parameters one place to the left.

CHOICE: Prompts user for selection.

Batch files and parameters

You can also add instructions and information to batch files at program start, just like DOS commands and programs. These parameters are separated by at least one space. Within the batch file, you can access the specified parameter with a percentage sign and a number. For example, %1 accesses the first parameter, %2 accesses the second parameter and so on. %0 contains the name of the batch file during the call (without the .BAT extension).

Batch files and environment variables

Within a batch file, you can also access special MS-DOS variables (called environment variables), just as you would from the DOS prompt. Use the convention SET Name=Contents to define environment variables. As an example, for the variable PATH (MS-DOS Search path), use: SET PATH=C:\DOS. Unlike the DOS prompt, in a batch file it's possible to use the contents like variables immediately, by enclosing the variable name in percentage signs. When the batch file is being processed, the variable name enclosed in percentage signs is replaced by the actual value of the variable. Example: ECHO The search path is %PATH%!

Forbidden Characters

Some characters can only be used for special purposes in batch files, but may not be used in comments and screen messages. For example, the "<" and ">" characters for redirecting input and output and the pipe symbol "|" for linking commands may not be used in comments or screen messages.

DOSKEY and batch files

After calling the DOSKEY program, you can begin creating batch files with it. To do this, enter the desired commands in sequence and then redirect the DOSKEY /HISTORY command to a file, which then requires only minor changes.

11.2 Batch Files and Programs

Batch files are similar to DOS programs. Programs are files with the extensions .COM or .EXE. They can be called and executed by typing the name of the program or the name of a startup file from the DOS command line.

While special programs, such as assemblers or compilers, are required for creating COM or EXE files, it's quite easy to create batch files. All the batch files presented in this chapter are on the companion diskette. See the Appendix for more information about the companion diskette.

You can create a simple batch file using the DOS COPY command, the EDLIN (on the Supplemental Disk from Microsoft) editor or the EDIT editor. Each line of the batch file can be a normal DOS command, just as you would type it at the system prompt. Each line is ended by pressing Enter.

DOS recognizes a batch file by its extension. Each batch file must have a filename ending with the .BAT extension. A batch file can contain any resident (memory resident) and external (commands which must be loaded before executing) DOS commands and a few special batch commands.

Batch files can be started just like COM or EXE programs. Type its filename without the extension. DOS runs the commands in the file as though they were entered at the system prompt.

When you type a command at the system prompt MS-DOS searches, in a predefined order, for programs and batch files with the same command name (filename).

First, MS-DOS 6.0 searches for a name defined as a DOSKEY macro. If it finds one, the macro is executed. If it doesn't, DOS checks its list of resident (internal) commands for the same name and executes it if found. Otherwise, DOS assumes that it's an external command or batch file.

The search continues in the current directory. In the order listed below, DOS looks for a file with the same name but having one of these extensions:

- .COM
- .EXE
- .BAT

If it can't find a filename with one of these extensions in the current directory, DOS then searches each directory defined by the search PATH.

So if you type a command, similar to the following, at the system prompt:

TEST [Enter]

1. DOS searches for a macro named TEST.

2. DOS searches for an internal command named TEST.

3. DOS searches the current directory for a file named TEST.COM.

4. DOS searches the current directory for a file named TEST.EXE.

5. DOS searches the current directory for a file named TEST.BAT.

6. DOS searches each directory in the search PATH for a file named TEST.COM, TEST.EXE or TEST.BAT.

If a batch file has the same name as an existing DOS command, the DOS command is executed rather than the batch file.

You can overcome this limitation by specifying the file extension along with the command. For example, if you created a batch file called FORMAT.BAT in the DOS directory and want to call this file instead of the DOS FORMAT.COM command, type:

FORMAT.BAT

This only works with external DOS commands. It can't be used to override an internal DOS command, such as DIR.

Example

If a batch file is named DIR.BAT and you type DIR, DOS will not run the batch file. Rather, it will always run the internal command, DIR.

If a batch file named FORMAT.BAT is stored in the directory of DOS commands and you enter FORMAT, DOS won't run the batch file. It will execute the DOS command FORMAT.COM instead.

However, you can replace all of the external DOS commands with batch files. Just save the batch files in their own directory

(C:\BAT) and specify this directory in the search path ahead of the DOS directory:

```
PATH C:\BAT;C:\DOS
```

You can create a special version of the FORMAT command as a batch file that automatically displays the contents of a diskette before formatting it. This batch file might look like the following batch file called FORMAT1.BAT:

To avoid any confusion with the FORMAT command this batch file is named FORMAT1.BAT on the companion diskette.

```
@ECHO OFF
IF "%1" == "" GOTO error
DIR %1
ECHO Press any key to format disk
ECHO Press CTRL-C to abort
PAUSE
C:\DOS\FORMAT %1 %2 %3 %4
GOTO End
:Error
ECHO You must specify a drive.
:End
ECHO ON
```

Remember if this batch file was named FORMAT.BAT, the batch file directory must be before the DOS directory in the PATH or DOS will find the FORMAT command and not the FORMAT.BAT batch file. The line "C:\DOS\FORMAT %1 %2 %3 %4" must specify the correct path for the DOS FORMAT command. Otherwise the batch file would call itself and not the "real" FORMAT command.

If you run this batch file, and the directory displayed contains files that you don't want to lose, the process can be ended easily when the following message appears:

```
Press any key to continue. . . .
```

The parameter "%1" represents the first parameter passed to the batch file, which is usually the drive label. The parameters "%2" through "%4" represent any other parameters that were specified. The batch file passes these parameters to the DOS FORMAT command. Several requirements must be satisfied in order for this process to run as intended:

- There can't be a macro, defined by DOSKEY, named FORMAT1. If a macro has been defined, type FORMAT1.BAT to run the batch file.

- If the batch file was named FORMAT.BAT, it must be in a directory that has been specified ahead of the DOS directory in the search path.

- If the batch file was named FORMAT.BAT, the current directory cannot be the directory containing the DOS commands. DOS would find the real FORMAT command instead of starting the batch file through the search path. This can be overcome by entering the filename extension as part of the command, FORMAT.BAT.

Be very careful when naming batch files the same name as DOS commands, they may directly affect the operation of other batch files. To avoid any confusion with the FORMAT command the batch file presented in this section is named FORMAT1.BAT on the companion diskette.

11.3 Creating and Running Batch Files

COPY CON, EDLIN (on the Supplemental Disk from Microsoft), EDIT or a word processor can be used to create batch files.

We recommend that you store batch files in their own directory instead of in the DOS directory on a hard drive. If you want to have the batch files available to run at all times, use PATH to set a search path to the directory containing the batch files and enter this directory name before the DOS directory name.

Using COPY CON to create batch files

To create a batch file in the current directory, type the command line shown below:

```
COPY CON FILENAME.BAT
```

Enter each of the command lines at the keyboard. Then press [Enter] after each line. A line can contain up to 127 characters. To complete the process and save the file, enter [Ctrl] + [Z] and press [Enter].

If a file with the specified name already exists, it is overwritten by the new file without any warning. Before using COPY CON to create a file, make sure that the target directory doesn't contain a file that has the same name as the file you are creating.

The COPY CON command is useful for creating small batch files, but there are better ways to create longer batch files. For example, you can only correct the current line when you enter the batch file.

Also, COPY CON cannot be used to change a batch file. If you must change a batch file with COPY CON, the entire batch file must be re-entered.

Using EDLIN to create batch files

It's more convenient to use EDLIN (on the Supplemental Disk from Microsoft) to create a batch file. Although EDLIN is far from the best editor, it still lets you change batch files easily.

Here's a simple example of how to create a batch file with EDLIN.

As with COPY CON, carefully consider the filename for a batch file. In this example, we'll create a batch file that first changes the current directory to the DOC directory and then starts the Microsoft Word word processor from this directory.

We'll call the batch file W.BAT. This will enable you to enter a short command (the W and Enter keys) to start Word.

Start EDLIN with the filename of the file to be created, W and the .BAT file extension, as follows:

```
EDLIN W.BAT
```

 Remember that EDLIN, unlike COPY CON, is a transient DOS program. This means that to start the program, you must either select the directory containing the EDLIN command or the path to the proper directory must have been specified by PATH.

You'll see a message that a new file is being created and you will see an asterisk (*) in the next line. This asterisk indicates that you are in the command mode of EDLIN.

```
Time: 13:33
Date: Mon 03-25-1991
C:\BAT>edlin w.bat
New file
*
```

Entering EDLIN

You can't enter any text in this mode. You can only activate one of the commands of EDLIN. To enter input mode, press I for INSERT and then press Enter.

A new line appears with a 1, colon and an asterisk. You're now in input mode and can type the DOS commands that the batch file will later run. It is important that each DOS command be in its own line.

Press Enter to complete each line and move the cursor to the next line. Let's assume that you keep your document files in a directory named C:\DOC, and that you keep WORD.EXE in the C:\WORD directory. The lines are numbered consecutively. In this example, you would have to type the following commands on the screen:

```
CD C:\DOC Enter
C:\WORD\WORD Enter
```

These are the commands that the batch file will execute.

To save this command sequence as a batch file, first return to command mode by pressing Ctrl + Z or F6 when the cursor is located at the start of a new line. Then press Enter.

The asterisk reappears on the far left side of the screen. This indicates that you're in command mode. Enter E for EXIT and press Enter. The batch file is saved and you are returned to the system prompt of the DOS command line.

Copy the batch file to a directory that is in the search PATH. The batch file can then be started from any directory.

Using EDIT to create batch files

EDIT is probably the best way to create a batch file.

To create a batch file in the current directory with EDIT, start the editor as follows:

```
EDIT FILENAME.BAT Enter
```

Enter EDIT and the name of the batch file to be created. Remember to include the file extension .BAT.

After pressing Enter, the editor screen appears and you can begin typing the lines of the batch file. DOS commands for the batch file must be on separate lines. Press Enter at the end of each line to start a new line.

After entering all of the lines, save the batch file. Press Alt + F to select the **File** menu, then press S to select **Save**. The file is automatically saved under the name you already specified.

You must exit the editor before you can use the batch file. Press Alt + F to return to the **File** menu, then press X to select the **Exit** command. You will return to the system prompt on the DOS command line.

Using a word processor to create batch files

Any word processor that can save files as unformatted ASCII files can also be used to create batch files.

11.4 Using Batch Files

There are various ways to start batch files. A batch file can even be started by another batch file. This section explains the requirements for starting a batch file and provides important information about calling a batch file.

Starting a batch file

Similar to COM and EXE files, a batch file is started by entering its name. The system prompt reappears after the last command in the batch file is executed.

When calling a batch file, remember the following points:

Do not define a macro, using DOSKEY, with the same name as an existing batch file. If a macro has been defined by DOSKEY, you'll have to enter both the filename and the .BAT extension to start the batch file.

• The batch file must be in the current directory or in a directory which is defined in the search path specified by PATH.

- There can't be any COM or EXE files, in the current directory, with the same name. If COM or EXE files with the same name exist, they will be started instead of the batch file.

Requirements for running a batch file

If you start a batch file from a diskette and remove the diskette while the batch file is running, DOS displays a message similar to:

```
Insert disk with batch file
Press any key to continue. . .
```

Replace the diskette with the batch file and press any key.

Running a batch file from within a batch file

Normally if you start a batch file which starts a second batch file, DOS will terminate all batch files and return you to the system prompt of the command line when the last command in the second batch file is completed.

To be able to run a second batch file in the same way you would call a subroutine from BASIC and then continue with the next command in the original batch file, use CALL:

```
CALL FILENAME.BAT
```

DOS executes the called batch file and then runs the next command in the file following the CALL.

Aborting a batch file

A batch file can be stopped at any time by pressing Ctrl + C. The computer will display the prompt:

```
Terminate batch job (Y/N)?
```

Enter Y to abort the batch file. This prompt will not be displayed if the computer is formatting a diskette.

If it takes a long time for DOS to respond to Ctrl + C, use the BREAK ON option in your CONFIG.SYS file. For more information on using BREAK, refer to Chapter 19.

11.5 Displaying and Modifying Batch Files

It's very easy to display, print and modify batch files.

Displaying a batch file

Use the TYPE command to display a batch file on the screen:

```
TYPE FILENAME.BAT
```

If the batch file is longer than one screen page, use Ctrl + S to stop the output. Press any key to continue.

You can also use the following to display a large batch file one page at a time:

```
TYPE FILENAME.BAT | MORE
```

Printing batch files

Use the following to print a batch file to a printer:

```
TYPE FILENAME.BAT >LPT1
```

The greater than character (>) redirects the output to a parallel printer connected to LPT1. If your printer is connected to the first serial port, use COM1 instead of LPT1.

Printing several batch files

You can print several batch files, either directly or in the background. In the second case, you can enter more commands from the system prompt while the batch files are being printed.

Printing several batch files directly

Use the COPY command to print several batch files if the output is redirected to the printer. Use wildcards for the filenames to be printed. If your printer is not connected to the first parallel port, use the proper port identifier in place of LPT1, as shown below. For example, to print all the batch files in the current directory, use the following:

```
COPY *.BAT LPT1
```

The filename and the contents of all the batch files are sent to the printer.

Printing several batch files in the background

You can use the PRINT command to print more than one batch file. Using this method lets you continue working while the files are being printed. To do this, enter the filenames to be printed after the PRINT command, separated by spaces:

```
PRINT FILE1.BAT FILE2.BAT FILE3.BAT
```

You can also use wildcards when specifying the filenames. To print all the files, in the current directory, with the .BAT extension, use the following command line:

```
PRINT *.BAT
```

If several files are selected to be printed, PRINT stores the information in a special list, called the print queue. PRINT enters the specified files in this list and prints them one after the other. There are also special commands for removing files from the print queue.

Before using PRINT for the first time, the port must be set. It's best to do this from the AUTOEXEC.BAT file with the following line:

```
PRINT /D:LPT1
```

As a rule, the print queue can contain no more than ten files. If a wildcard is used, and the filenames apply to more than ten files, the excess files won't be printed. The /Q switch specified with PRINT can be used to increase the maximum number of files the print queue can hold.

    More information about PRINT can be found in Chapter 19.

Editing a batch file

Using the MS-DOS Editor to modify a batch file

Modifying batch files with the MS-DOS Editor (EDIT) is probably the easiest method you'll find. Start EDIT with the name of the batch file to be changed as a parameter.

```
EDIT FILENAME
```

The EDIT screen will appear, displaying the contents of the batch file. Use the cursor keys to move the cursor to the text to be changed.

To insert characters into the batch file, simply type them at the desired location.

Use DEL to remove characters beneath the cursor.

To insert a new line in a batch file, place the cursor at the end of the line immediately before the point the new line should be inserted and press (Enter). A new blank line is inserted. Type the new commands in the new line.

To save a batch file after making changes, press (Alt) + (F) to select the **File** menu and then press (S) for **Save**. The file is automatically saved under its original filename.

To save the modified batch file under a different name, press (Alt) + (F) to select the **File** menu and then press (A) for **Save As**. Enter a new name for the file in the dialog box. After pressing (Enter), the file is saved under the new name.

You must exit from the MS-DOS Editor to test a modified file. Press (Alt) + (F) for the **File** menu and then press (X) for **Exit**.

11.6 Batch File Commands

All DOS commands can be used in batch files. In addition, there are a few special commands that are used exclusively for batch file programming.

Displaying a message

The ECHO command has two different jobs.

Messages can be displayed using ECHO:

```
ECHO Message
```

Here, "message" can contain any text, including spaces. However, there are some characters with special meanings that are not allowed.

Setting the screen to display all command lines

ECHO can be used to determine whether or not DOS displays the command lines of the batch file before executing the commands.

```
ECHO ON
```

This command causes all command lines that follow it to be displayed on the screen. To switch off displaying all command lines, type:

```
ECHO OFF
```

Typing ECHO without any parameters displays the current status.

Suppressing the screen display of a single command line

You can also suppress the display of a single command when ECHO is switched on. Place the "@" character in front of the command line.

```
@COMMAND LINE
```

Even if you use ECHO OFF to switch off the display of the command lines, the first command line still appears on the screen. Use "@" to prevent the first command line from being displayed. Place the "@" character at the beginning of the first line:

```
@ECHO OFF
REM The rest of the batch file follows
```

Example

Here's an example of how ECHO works.

We want to create a batch file that makes the directory containing text files (we'll call this directory DOC) the current directory and display the directory page by page. This batch file is called TEXTDIR.BAT. It is on the companion diskette in the BAT directory.

Here's what the batch file looks like:

```
CD \DOC
DIR /P
```

This batch file displays its command lines on the screen. To prevent this display, insert the following lines in the batch file:

```
@ECHO OFF
CD \DOC
DIR /P
ECHO ON
```

These lines prevent any lines following ECHO OFF from being displayed on the screen.

 Placing "@" in front of ECHO OFF prevents this line from being displayed on the screen as well.

At the end of a batch file, always remember to set ECHO back to ON. In some situations the system prompt might not appear on the screen after a batch file. This could be confusing.

The following example demonstrates a different way to use ECHO to display a screen message.

Make the following changes to the batch file we just created:

```
@ECHO OFF
ECHO Selects the DOC directory and displays the
directory
CD \DOC
DIR /P
ECHO ON
```

When this batch file, called TEXTDIR2.BAT, is run you will see the following line displayed on the screen:

```
Selects the DOC directory and displays the contents
```

ECHO can be used to display relevant information as a batch file is run. This information becomes even more important as you create larger batch files. ECHO can be used to display messages explaining what is happening in a large batch file.

Comments in batch files

The REM command can be used to insert comments into a batch file. DOS does not execute these lines. REM commands can be used by the batch file creator to document the way in which the batch file will operate. A comment line always has the following form:

```
REM Comment
```

Comment lines are especially useful in long batch files; they give you a general idea of the operation of the batch file. You can use comment lines to mark subroutines, etc. This helps you find your place when revising the batch file.

Here's an example of using the REM command.

We want to create a batch file that always displays the current directory sorted according to filenames. We'll call this batch file DIRSORT, and will include a comment line so when we revise it later, we will immediately know what the batch file does.

```
@ECHO OFF
REM   ┌─────────────────────────────────────────┐
REM   ║ Batch for displaying a sorted directory ║
REM   └─────────────────────────────────────────┘
DIR /O:N
ECHO ON
```

The following characters can be used to make a frame around comments:

[Alt]+[2][0][1] ┌ = [Alt]+[2][0][5] ┬ [Alt]+[2][0][3] ┐ [Alt]+[1][8][7]

[Alt]+[1][8][6] ║   ║ [Alt]+[1][8][6]

[Alt]+[2][0][4] ╟   ╫ [Alt]+[2][0][6] ╢ [Alt]+[1][8][5]

[Alt]+[1][8][6] ║   ║ [Alt]+[1][8][6]

[Alt]+[2][0][0] ╚ = [Alt]+[2][0][5] ╩ [Alt]+[2][0][2] ╝ [Alt]+[1][8][8]

When this batch file is called, the comment lines won't be displayed. In fact, unless you use the TYPE command to display the batch file on the screen, you won't see them again until you revise the batch file.

Testing conditions in batch files

The IF command lets you check for different conditions as a batch file is run. If a condition is satisfied, the rest of the line following the condition is executed. Otherwise, the execution skips to the next line.

Comparing character sequences

The following line can be used to compare two character strings:

```
IF CHARACTER_STRING1==CHARACTER_STRING2 COMMAND
```

If both character strings are identical, the command is executed; otherwise the command is skipped and the next command line is executed.

The IF comparisons are not limited to character strings. Parameters and environment variables that have been passed to the batch file can also be compared.

Most of the time you'll be comparing a parameter or an environment variable within the batch file, such as:

```
IF %COMSPEC%==C:\COMMAND.COM ECHO OK
```

When making such a comparison, the parameter or the environment variable may not exist. In this example, if the variable COMSPEC doesn't exist, the following line would be displayed:

```
IF ==C:\COMMAND.COM ECHO OK
```

This line generates an error message because there is nothing to compare on the left side of the equal sign. A simple solution to this problem consists of adding a character on both sides so the correct syntax is assured:

```
IF %COMSPEC%!==C:\COMMAND.COM! ECHO OK
```

If the COMSPEC variable contains the desired contents, then a correct comparison is still ensured:

```
IF C:\COMMAND.COM!==C:\COMMAND.COM! ECHO OK
```

However, if the variable is not present, at least DOS finds something to compare on both sides of the equal sign; so it doesn't generate a syntax error message:

```
IF !==C:\COMMAND.COM! ECHO OK
```

Another common method consists of adding two quotation marks on both sides of the comparison:

```
IF "%COMSPEC%"=="C:\COMMAND.COM" ECHO OK
```

This also prevents a syntax error when a variable isn't present.

 DOS differentiates between upper and lowercase letters when comparing text strings.

Checking whether a file exists

Use the key word EXIST in a batch file to check whether a file exists:

```
IF EXIST FILE COMMAND
```

In the preceding command line, if the file exists, the batch file executes the command; otherwise it will skip to the next command line.

Example

To determine whether the system file AUTOEXEC.BAT exists in the root directory of the hard drive and make a backup copy of it, use the following command line:

```
IF EXIST C:\AUTOEXEC.BAT COPY C:\AUTOEXEC.BAT
C:\AUTOEXEC.BAK
```

You can also use EXIST to check whether directories or drives exist.

To check whether a directory exists, use:

```
IF EXIST \NAME\NUL COMMAND
```

To check whether a specific directory exists before displaying the directory, type:

```
IF EXIST \TEMP\NUL DIR \TEMP
```

To determine whether a drive exists, use:

```
IF EXIST DRIVE_LETTER:\NUL Command
```

To check whether a drive exists before attempting to copy to it, type:

```
IF EXIST A:\NUL COPY AUTOEXEC.BAT A:
```

Checking the return value of programs

Upon completion, a program can supply a return value. This value is ordinarily used to signal an error that occurs while the program is running.

Many DOS commands supply a return value other than 0 when an error occurs. This variable, ERRORLEVEL, can be used to check the return value from within a batch file. ERRORLEVEL 0 means that an error was not found.

The syntax for a command to check the ERRORLEVEL is:

```
IF ERRORLEVEL NUMBER COMMAND
```

If the return value is greater than or equal to a specified number, the command is executed; otherwise it skips to the next command line.

The following is a more detailed explanation of what ERRORLEVEL means and what it does.

The meaning and purpose of ERRORLEVEL

When a command is entered after the system prompt and a mistake occurs when the command is being executed, an error message is displayed. At that point you can correct the command or eliminate the cause of the error.

But what can you do when there are a series of command lines within a batch file that automatically run? Checking ERRORLEVEL is only a partial solution.

What is an ERRORLEVEL?

An ERRORLEVEL is the return value - a report on the success or failure of a program. We'll explain later in this chapter how a program supplies such a value. For now you need to know that each program started by DOS, and even each DOS command, can report a return value between 0 and 255.

Usually programs are started by the command interpreter, which receives the return value, but doesn't display it. On the other hand, if you call the program from within a batch file, the command interpreter notes the returned value and saves it in the variable ERRORLEVEL.

Asking for an ERRORLEVEL

You can determine an ERRORLEVEL only from within a batch file. Many DOS commands supply a return value other than 0 if an error occurs. If an ERRORLEVEL of 0 is returned, it means no error has occurred.

As we mentioned earlier, the syntax of a line that you can use to determine the ERRORLEVEL in a batch file looks like this:

```
IF ERRORLEVEL NUMBER COMMAND
```

If the return value is greater than or equal to a specified number, the command is executed; otherwise it skips to the next command line. Unfortunately you cannot check for a specific value, but only for a minimum value. This makes it difficult to be precise when responding to the error level.

Example

The following batch file, called &FORMAT.BAT, formats a diskette in drive A:. If an error occurs during this process, or if you abort the process by pressing [Ctrl] + [C], the batch file displays a message.

```
@ECHO OFF
FORMAT A:
IF ERRORLEVEL 1 GOTO error
GOTO end
:error
ECHO.
ECHO Formatting not successful!!!
:End
ECHO ON
```

In this example, after the batch file calls FORMAT, it checks if there is an ERRORLEVEL greater than 1 (in other words, whether an error has occurred). The batch file doesn't examine the return value more closely.

What information is provided by ERRORLEVELs

ERRORLEVEL was made a part of DOS for error checking. Three basic conditions apply:

- ERRORLEVEL 0 means: no error found.

- ERRORLEVEL > 0 means: error found.

- There is no set meaning for a special value. Instead this depends on the DOS command. However, the higher the return value, the more serious the error.

ERRORLEVEL with MSBACKUP

To fully understand the meanings of the different return values, you must examine the commands more closely. For example, the DOS MSBACKUP command could return the following values:

0   No error, data backup successful.

1   No files found for backup.

3   Aborted by user ([Ctrl] + [C] or abort after errors in accessing file).

4   Wrong parameters (wrong path for source directory or an invalid option specified when calling the command).

As you can see, the seriousness of the error increases with the value of the number returned. So ERRORLEVEL 1 is more of a warning than a "real" error.

In order to respond to an error condition and take appropriate action within a batch file, check for the highest possible value first.

The following batch file, called FORMATA.BAT, is a simple example of error checking following a FORMAT command:

```
ECHO OFF
FORMAT A:
IF ERRORLEVEL 4 GOTO error4
IF ERRORLEVEL 3 GOTO error3
ECHO No error, formatting successful
GOTO End
:error4
ECHO Illegal drive or parameter. Possible problems with diskette.
GOTO End
:error3
ECHO Formatting terminated by CTRL + C
GOTO End
:End
ECHO ON
```

You should check the ERRORLEVEL whenever possible when calling a program from a batch file.

Also, check for possible errors immediately after starting the program. ERRORLEVEL may be changed by other DOS commands. DOS only saves one ERRORLEVEL at a time. As soon as a new command changes the return value, the previous value is lost.

ERRORLEVEL in DOS commands

Not all DOS commands return error values and each command uses only certain values. Also, different versions of DOS use different return values. You may need to experiment a little.

The following table shows the ERRORLEVEL of some DOS commands along with short explanations. This is only a partial list.

ATTRIB
1   wrong parameter or file not found
3   abort

DISKCOMP
1   invalid drive, wrong syntax
2   terminated by user

DISKCOPY
1   invalid drive, wrong syntax
2   abort

FASTOPEN
1   wrong parameter

FIND
2   wrong parameter

FORMAT
3   abort
4   error found (wrong name specified for diskette, hard drive)

JOIN (on the Supplemental Disk from Microsoft)
1   invalid parameter

LABEL
1   drive not available/invalid

MODE
1   wrong parameter

RESTORE
1   no files found
3   aborted by user
4   source contains no backup data, invalid parameters

SUBST
1   invalid parameter

XCOPY
2   abort
4   invalid number of parameters, invalid path

How do you determine the ERRORLEVEL for commands

It is not easy to determine all the possible ERRORLEVELs for a command because you have to produce the error first and then ask for the ERRORLEVEL.

Although some DOS manuals do have information about the return values for the different errors, the information isn't always complete.

The following batch file, ERROR.BAT, will help you determine as many of the return values as possible (up to the value of 10 for a DOS command).

```
ECHO OFF
%1 %2 %3 %4 %5 %6 %7 %8 %9
ECHO.
IF ERRORLEVEL 10 ECHO 10
IF ERRORLEVEL 9 ECHO 9
IF ERRORLEVEL 8 ECHO 8
IF ERRORLEVEL 7 ECHO 7
IF ERRORLEVEL 6 ECHO 6
IF ERRORLEVEL 5 ECHO 5
IF ERRORLEVEL 4 ECHO 4
IF ERRORLEVEL 3 ECHO 3
IF ERRORLEVEL 2 ECHO 2
IF ERRORLEVEL 1 ECHO 1
ECHO ON
```

Now, to try a command, just enter ERROR in front of the command line. With this method, you can test the different conditions and get the return value for each one. For example, to determine which errors the DOS FIND command returns when you use the wrong syntax, use the following command line:

```
ERROR FIND F
```

As a result, the following is displayed:

```
FIND: Parameter format not correct

2
1
```

So we see that when no target drive is specified, the FIND command returns an ERRORLEVEL of 2.

First, the normal error message for FIND is displayed, then the ERRORLEVEL. Because we intentionally kept the batch file simple, the lowest values are also displayed.

Reversing the condition

The keyword NOT can be used to reverse the three possible conditions.

```
IF NOT CHARACTER_STRING1==CHARACTER_STRING2 COMMAND
```

If the character strings are not equal, command will be executed; otherwise it skips to the next command line.

 If you use parameters or environment variables within such a comparison, use quotation marks on both sides to avoid syntax errors if the variables are not displayed.

```
IF NOT EXIST File Command
```

If the file is not present, command is executed; otherwise it skips to the next command line.

```
IF NOT ERRORLEVEL NUMBER COMMAND
```

If the return value is not greater than or equal to the specified number, the command is executed; otherwise the next command line is executed.

Example

```
ECHO OFF
IF NOT EXIST C:\AUTOEXEC.BAT ECHO System file not
present!
REM Rest of the batch file
```

It's a good idea to use GOTO if you want to execute several commands in response to one condition being met.

Jumping over command lines

Usually, the individual command lines in a batch file are executed one after the other. Sometimes it's necessary to jump over command lines and continue execution at a different place in the batch file. This is done by defining a label and using GOTO to have DOS continue at the label.

The label must be at the beginning of a line and must start with a colon. The label can be up to eight characters long. If a longer label is used, DOS ignores all characters after the eighth one. A typical GOTO command would look like the following:

```
GOTO Label
   :
   :
   :
:Label
```

When DOS encounters a GOTO command, execution branches to the specified line with the label and continues at the command in the following line. The rest of the line with the label is ignored.

It doesn't matter whether you define the label before or after GOTO. In any case, DOS branches to the specified label even if it precedes the GOTO command within the batch file.

Don't use any special characters as part of the name of a label. These characters could cause problems with running the command correctly. Spaces are permitted.

Example

Frequently, GOTO is used in a conditional command. The following batch file, called &GOTO.BAT, displays a message if no parameters are specified when it is called:

```
ECHO OFF
IF "%1"=="" GOTO Syntax
ECHO All clear
GOTO End
:Syntax
ECHO You must specify a parameter!
:End
ECHO ON
```

The first line of this batch file checks whether a parameter was specified. If no parameter was specified and if "%1" is not present (it's equal to ""), the rest of the line is executed.

Then the batch jumps directly to the label "Syntax" and displays the message "You must specify a parameter!". If a parameter was specified, the batch skips the rest of the line (GOTO Syntax is not executed) and continues with the next line.

Using GOTO and IF provides you with the option of asking questions and having other commands depend on the responses to the questions.

Looping in batch files

The FOR command can be used in loops to have parts of a batch file execute several times.

```
FOR %%V in (list) DO COMMAND %%V
```

%%V   This variable "V" (placeholder) accepts all the values from the list, one after the other.

(list)   Specifies the list of files, to which you want the command to apply. You can list each file individually (File1 File2 File3) or by using a wildcard (*.TXT). In the first case, the variable "V" contains File1 File2 File3, in the second case it contains all available files with the .TXT extension.

COMMAND

> After DO, specify the command to be performed for each value in List. Only one command can be used.

 You can also use the parameters of the batch file "%0" to "%9" (see below) or environment variables.

Like many other batch commands, FOR can be used outside of batch files, directly from the system prompt. When FOR is used from the system prompt, only one % sign is used with the variable.

The FOR command cannot be nested. This means that you cannot have another loop with FOR within a loop.

To run more than one DOS command within a loop, use CALL to call a new batch file.

Example

The following batch file displays all files with the .BAT extension on the screen:

```
FOR %%V IN (*.BAT) DO TYPE %%V
```

To run this line from the system prompt, type:

```
FOR %V IN (*.BAT) DO TYPE %V
```

 Only the .BAT files in the current directory are displayed.

The following batch file searches all files with the .DOC extension, in the current directory, for the character sequence "DOS".

```
FOR %%V IN (*.DOC) DO FIND "DOS" %%V
```

The following example displays the names of all COM or EXE files in the current directory:

```
FOR %%V IN (*.COM *.EXE) DO ECHO %%V
```

Calling batch files from batch files

As we mentioned, CALL can be used to run other batch files as subroutines:

```
CALL FILE
```

If DOS encounters this command, it starts the batch file specified in the command line. After the called batch file is complete, DOS continues execution with the command line after CALL. Parameters can be passed to the called batch file:

```
CALL FILE PARAMETER
```

Example

Suppose you have a batch file, named TYPEM.BAT, that displays a specified file on the screen page by page:

```
TYPE %1 | MORE
```

 For "%1" DOS uses the first parameter specified. Usually this is a specified filename.

To have this batch file display the contents of C:\AUTOEXEC.BAT file, type the following command after the system prompt:

```
TYPEM C:\AUTOEXEC.BAT
```

You can also specify the parameter C:\AUTOEXEC.BAT when calling another batch file from within a batch file:

```
CALL TYPEM C:\AUTOEXEC.BAT
```

 You can start a batch file, such as TYPEM.BAT, without using CALL by specifying the name. In this case the batch file would not be executed as a subroutine, and the entire batch file process would end when the secondary batch file (such as TYPEM.BAT) was completed.

The following is another practical use for CALL.

You already know how to apply one command to several variables using FOR...DO. When using FOR...DO you can only use a single command within the loop.

This is where CALL is useful. For example, to use more than one command on several files, use the FOR...DO loop and CALL after DO to call a new batch file containing the commands you want to use on the files. This will cause the commands to be executed.

```
FOR %%a IN (AUTOEXEC.BAT CONFIG.SYS) DO TYPE %%a
```

This line in a batch file displays the AUTOEXEC.BAT and
CONFIG.SYS files on the screen. To copy the files onto a diskette
as well, the batch needs to execute a few more program lines.
However, by using CALL, you can call a new batch file that does
this for you. Change the first batch file to:

```
FOR %%a IN (AUTOEXEC.BAT CONFIG.SYS) DO CALL Command %%a
```

The COMMAND.BAT file would include the lines:

```
TYPE %1
COPY %1 A:
```

PAUSE

PAUSE lets you interrupt the execution of a batch file. The batch
will stop and wait until a key is pressed. PAUSE recognizes Ctrl +
C to terminate the batch file. Using PAUSE provides new
possibilities for batch programming.

When the PAUSE command is used, the following message is
displayed:

```
Press any key to continue . . .
```

After pressing a key, DOS continues executing the batch file with
the next command line.

 Text can be entered after the PAUSE command, but DOS
won't display it on the screen as it does with ECHO.

Example

The following is an example of a batch file that deletes all files
with the .BAK extension. PAUSE allows you to decide whether
the files should be deleted. Using one of the methods we
previously discussed, create the following batch file called
DELBAK.BAT:

```
@ECHO OFF
ECHO All files in the current directory with
ECHO the .BAK extension will be deleted.
ECHO To cancel, press CTRL+C
PAUSE
DEL *.BAK
ECHO ON
```

When this batch file is started, the screen display indicates
what's going to happen (the delete operation) and how to cancel it

(press Ctrl + C). If you press the Ctrl + C key combination, the batch file terminates and you are returned to the DOS system prompt. The files with the .BAK extension won't be deleted in this case.

To delete all the files with .BAK extensions, press any key and the batch file will continue running, executing the following lines. Since this example actually deletes files, use it carefully. It's best to try it out first on a practice diskette, especially if you are uncomfortable with using the file.

SHIFT

Parameters can be passed to a batch file. Parameters are passed in special variables "%1" through "%9". You can use SHIFT to change the contents of these replaceable variables:

```
SHIFT
```

DOS shifts the existing parameters one place to the left. When SHIFT is used, "%1" receives the contents of "%2", "%2" receives the contents of "%3", etc. If you specified a tenth parameter, it is now in "%9". The contents of "%0" are lost. Before the first Shift, "%0" contains the name of the batch file.

Example

The following batch file, &GCOPY.BAT (group copy) copies all of the files or file groups that were specified onto a diskette in drive A:. To do this, all of the specified files are shifted to the parameter "%1" by the SHIFT command. The batch file ends when "%1" no longer contains any files:

```
@ECHO OFF
:Start
IF "%1"=="" GOTO EndItAll
COPY %1 A:
SHIFT
GOTO Start
:EndItAll
ECHO ON
```

To copy all files with the .TXT and .BAK extensions, use the following command line to call the batch file:

```
&GCOPY *.TXT *.BAK
```

When first called, "%1" contains the TXT parameter and "%2" contains the BAK parameter. After the SHIFT is encountered the first time, "%2" is empty and "%1" contains .BAK. When the batch file executes SHIFT the second time, "%1" is empty and the batch file ends by jumping to the label EndItAll.

CHOICE

CHOICE prompts you to make a choice in a batch program. A specified prompt will be displayed so the user can choose from a specified set of keys. This command can only be used in batch programs.

To include CHOICE in a batch file , use the following command line in the batch file:

```
choice /c:ync Yes, No, or Continue
```

Once CHOICE is activated, the user will see "Yes, No, or Continue [Y,N,C]?"

11.7 Batch Files and Parameters

One special advantage of batch files is that you can design them rather generally and then enter additional information as parameters when you call them.

When writing a batch file program, variables are indicated as a percentage sign followed by a number between 1 and 9. This means that nine parameters can be specified.

%0   Contains the name of the batch file as specified in the command line that calls the batch.

%1   Contains the first parameter.

%2   Contains the second parameter.

.

.   Contains the third through eighth parameter.

.

%9   Contains the ninth parameter.

You can also access additional parameters by using SHIFT to shift the parameter list (see previous section).

The parameters "%0" to "%9" are replaced by the contents of each variable before the command line is executed. This will let you check for correct usage by displaying the information when ECHO is switched on (with ECHO ON).

To check whether a parameter has been specified, use IF to check the variable contents:

```
IF "%1"=="" COMMAND
```

If nothing has been stored in "%1" then the parameter is unused and the command is executed. You can use GOTO to branch to the end of the batch file.

DOS always places values in the variables in sequence. So if the variable "%2" is empty, then "%3" and all subsequent variables are also empty.

When writing a batch file that uses parameters, make sure that you specify the exact number of parameters before the batch file is started.

If there aren't enough parameters specified, the batch file usually cannot perform its task correctly. Specifying too many parameters can also cause problems.

The following example, DELD.BAT, demonstrates how to determine the proper number of parameters. The batch file deletes a directory that has been passed as a parameter, but first checks that exactly one parameter was specified.

Otherwise, the batch displays the proper syntax on the screen:

```
@ECHO OFF
REM DELD.BAT deletes the contents of a directory
REM and removes the directory.
REM The directory cannot contain any subdirectories.
IF "%1"=="" GOTO Syntax
IF NOT "%2"=="" GOTO Syntax
ECHO Directory %1 being deleted.
IF EXIST %1\*.* DEL %1\*.*
RD %1
GOTO EndItAll
:Syntax
ECHO Syntax Error!
ECHO DELD.BAT removes a directory
ECHO Call: DELD Directory
ECHO Example DELD DATA
:EndItAll
ECHO ON
```

First the batch file checks if a parameter exists. If no parameter has been specified, the batch process ends and displays the correct syntax.

If the first parameter (%1) has been specified, a check is made for more than one parameter. If more than one parameter has been specified, the batch file again branches to display the proper syntax.

The batch file will display "Directory %1 being deleted" if the proper syntax was entered. DOS replaces "%1" with the specified parameter.

Before the batch uses RD to remove the directory, it must be certain there aren't any more files in the directory. The batch file uses the IF EXIST statement for this check. If any files are present, DEL is used to delete them. Because of the wildcards used in the specification (*.*), DEL automatically displays a security prompt.

After all files have been removed, RD can remove the directory. If the specified directory doesn't exist, RD displays an error message.

Solving batch file problems involving parameters

Sometimes batch file parameters can be troublesome.

The parameters "%0" to "%9" are replaced by the contents of the parameters specified in the command line before it is executed. DOS replaces "%1" with the contents of the first specified parameter. If ECHO is switched on, you can check the command lines for the replaced variables as they are displayed on the screen.

Displaying programs

The following batch file, SHOWPRG.BAT, demonstrates the flexibility of the options for using parameters in batch files. It shows all of the executable programs for a specified filename. The filename can be specified with either wildcards or with the complete filename in the sequence that DOS executes them (.COM, .EXE or .BAT).

```
@ECHO OFF
ECHO %0 shows all specified programs
FOR %%a in (%1.com, %1.exe, %1.bat) DO ECHO %%a
@ECHO ON
```

To find out whether there is more than one FORMAT command with different extensions in the current directory, type:

```
SHOWPRG FORMAT
```

Path specifications and wildcards are allowed. All DOS commands beginning with the letter "F" can be displayed by typing the following command line:

```
SHOWPRG C:\DOS\F*
```

This line should display the following:

```
C:\DOS\FDISK.EXE
C:\DOS\FORMAT.COM
C:\DOS\FASTOPEN.EXE
C:\DOS\FIND.EXE
```

11.8 Batch Files and Environment Variables

In addition to the variables "%0" to "%9", environment variables can be examined or used in batch files.

Using environment variables

To use an environment variable, enclose the variable name in percentage signs:

```
%Variable%
```

DOS replaces this with the current contents of the environment variable before executing the command line. If the environment variable has not been defined, nothing is inserted.

One method for checking whether an environment variable has been defined is to use IF to check whether the variable has any contents:

```
IF NOT "%Variable%" == "" Command
```

If the environment variable has not been defined, the batch file executes the command which follows in the command line. For example, the command could display an error message or jump to the end of the batch file.

Example: Extending a path

The following batch file, &ADDPATH.BAT, adds another directory to the existing search path. The DOS PATH command cannot be used to do this. All directories for the search path must be specified at one time in the command line:

```
@ECHO OFF
IF "%1"== "" GOTO EndItAll
PATH %PATH%;%1
:EndItAll
```

```
PATH
@ECHO ON
```

For example, to add C:\WORD to the existing search path, call the batch file with:

```
&ADDPATH C:\WORD
```

The batch adds the new directory (WORD) to the existing path specification and then displays the new search paths.

Defining an environment variable

The following command can be used to define environment variables in batch files:

```
SET Variable=Contents
```

Instead of environment variables, specify the name of the variable; enter the desired contents for the variable after the equal sign. You can even use spaces for the contents of the variable.

Use SET without entering any parameters to display all defined environment variables.

Example

Suppose that you want to place the name of a user in a variable. Simply type the following after the system prompt:

```
SET User=Meyer
```

You are not limited to defining environment variables from batch files. They can also be defined from the system prompt. However, you can only use the contents of environment variables within batch files.

For example, to store the name of the batch file that is currently being executed in a variable, use the following line in the batch file:

```
SET Batchname=%0
```

To display the name of the last batch file that was executed, use the following command line:

```
SET | FIND "Batchname"
```

First SET determines all defined variables, then FIND looks for the line with the desired variable name. Remember that FIND is case sensitive. This means that CASE differentiates between upper and lowercase letters. Variable names are stored by DOS as uppercase letters.

11.9 Forbidden Characters In Batch Files

There are some characters that you either cannot use or that are not easy to use. These characters are:

%   DOS uses this character to identify the parameters "%1" to "%9". To use this character in text and display it with ECHO, it must be entered twice (%%).

<   You use the less than character "<" to redirect the input from the keyboard to a new device or file. You cannot use this character in batch files.

>   This character redirects the output to a device other than the standard output (the screen) and cannot be used in batch files.

| You use this character (pipe symbol) to pass the output of a program to a different program. This character is also forbidden for other uses in batch files.

If you want to display the characters "<", ">" or "|" from a batch file, write the screen output to a separate file and use the following command to copy it onto the screen:

```
COPY FILE CON
```

11.10 DOSKEY and Batch Files

You can use the DOSKEY utility to create macros, which in many ways are identical to simple batch files. DOSKEY can also be used to build batch files almost automatically. We'll discuss both of these uses for DOSKEY.

Using DOSKEY to create batch files

DOSKEY can be used to create batch files almost automatically.

First DOSKEY must be installed into memory. If you do not already have it installed, type:

```
DOSKEY  Enter
```

From this point on, DOSKEY saves all of the command lines entered (up to the limits of the history buffer). These command lines can later be executed again. To display all of the lines in the history buffer, type:

    DOSKEY /HISTORY

An even easier way to display all of the previous commands is to press [F7]. Any of the commands in the history buffer are listed, just as they would appear in a batch file.

You can use this list to create a batch file with DOSKEY.

To create a batch file based on these previously entered command lines, use the following procedure:

1. Press [Alt] + [F7] to clear all of the commands in the history buffer.

2. Type the DOS command lines at the keyboard the way you ordinarily do. DOSKEY stores these commands in the history buffer as it executes each command for you.

3. To create a batch file, called WORK.BAT, from the history buffer, type the following command line:

    DOSKEY /HISTORY >WORK.BAT

This redirects the contents of the history buffer to a file named WORK.BAT. This *almost* creates your batch file. DOSKEY also records the last command line entered (the command line for creating the batch file: "DOSKEY /HISTORY >WORK.BAT") and writes it to the batch file. Use an editor to remove this line. You can use EDIT:

    EDIT WORK.BAT

Delete the last line and save the completed batch file.

Sometimes you will enter a series of commands and later realize that you could have created a batch file from these lines to simplify your work. Since you didn't use [Alt] + [F7] to clear the history buffer before you started entering commands, other unwanted commands are also stored there. You can still write the history buffer to a file:

    DOSKEY /HISTORY >FILE.BAT

Start EDIT, delete the unwanted command lines and save the file again. Don't forget to remove the last line which created FILE.BAT.

Using DOSKEY to create macros - "mini batch files"

Besides making it very convenient to enter, edit and execute commands at the system prompt, the DOSKEY utility also lets you define *macros*. A macro is an abbreviation for a series of DOS commands. Instead of typing each command at the keyboard, you type the abbreviation and DOS performs each of the commands defined by the macro. In effect, a macro is similar to a batch file. However, a macro cannot contain all of the special batch file commands which make batch file programming so powerful.

To define a macro, use the following syntax:

```
DOSKEY MACRONAME=COMMAND_LIST
```

As an example, let's define a macro that displays the names and paths, in alphabetical order, of all the BAT files in the subdirectories of the current drive. Furthermore, we want to display them without the directory header and summary format. Here's how we might define the macro:

```
DOSKEY DIRBAT=DIR *.BAT /p/s/on/b  Enter
```

After you define this macro, you can list all of the batch files in the subdirectories of the current drive by simply typing:

```
DIRBAT  Enter
```

DOSKEY lets you combine commands in a macro. To do this, separate the commands by the characters "$T". So, to change this example to list all BAT files in all subdirectories of the current drive, you would type:

```
DOSKEY DIRBAT=cd \$T dir *.bat /p/s/on/b  Enter
```

In this case, the DIRBAT macro first changes to the root directory before listing the BAT files.

Automatic DOSKEY macros

As you become familiar with macros, you'll find that they're indispensable for performing many of your computing tasks. So it's important to have an easy way to use predefined macros.

There are two basic ways to simplify macro definition:

1. Insert the DOSKEY macro definitions into your AUTOEXEC.BAT file.

2. Run a batch file, from your AUTOEXEC.BAT, which contains the DOSKEY macro definitions.

You'll first have to define each of your macros and then test them to ensure that they work properly. When you've defined them to DOSKEY, you can then list them by typing:

```
DOSKEY /MACROS  Enter
```

By redirecting the this command, you can write these definitions to a file on your hard drive. For example, to create a file called MACDEFS.BAT, you would type:

```
DOSKEY /MACROS >MACDEFS.BAT  Enter
```

All the definitions are then written to the designated file. To turn the file into a true batch file, use EDIT to add the DOSKEY command to each of the lines in the MACDEFS.BAT file. The MACDEFS.BAT file is now ready to run as a stand alone batch file to define each of the DOSKEY macros.

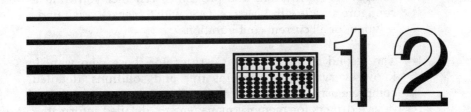

Memory Management

Just a short time ago, the amount of memory in a PC wasn't an important consideration. Most computers came with 640K or 1 Meg, adequate for most users. Nobody cared how much memory was really available, since users could run their computers without problems. The programs weren't as demanding as today's software.

Today, however, it's not unusual for a computer to have more memory. A PC containing from two to eight Megs of memory is not uncommon, and terms such as Upper Memory and High Memory are deciding factors in how well application programs run. That's why we're going to examine the various options for using memory in this chapter. We will use several steps:

- First, we'll explain special features, problems and terms using examples, analogies. Over and over again, we find that many users have great difficulty understanding the problems and distinguishing the various options and terms. This leads to misunderstandings or even errors when users work with their computers. This section introduces you to the special features of memory management. Those who understand the fundamentals so well that they don't need the examples and analogies can skip this first section and start at Chapter 12.2.

- The second section summarizes the fundamentals of memory management. The special features and problems explained through analogies in the first section are presented in computer terminology from MS-DOS' point of view. In addition, we clear up the problems that arise from varying terminology in different versions of DOS. Equating "Upper Memory" with "High Memory" is like calling apples oranges.

- Next, we introduce readers to practical problems and solutions. We'll show you how to choose the best setting for different computers, applications and programs. Whether you want to configure an AT with 1 Meg or a 486 with 8 Megs -- you'll find a solution for all current configurations.

- The second to last section is written for those who want to know everything. It contains tips and solutions, detailed, comprehensive information about all memory commands and device drivers for memory management, detailed information about the exact memory requirements of all important MS-DOS commands and many tips and solutions for optimizing your PC system. You will benefit from the experiences of many DOS installations when you read this section.

12.1 Overview

Here is a brief overview of memory management.

Importance and use of enough memory

The more memory available on a computer and the more memory programs use, the better and faster programs will run. We're talking about RAM memory, that is, the fast, fleeting memory that loses its contents when you switch off the computer, unlike hard drive memory.

Memory types

Not all memory can be used directly by DOS and application programs. Along with pure RAM (can be used by all programs), there are special kinds of memory that different programs use either completely, partially or not at all. The following explanation includes current abbreviations and typical MS-DOS terms.

Conventional Memory

This is the memory below the 640K limit that is available for MS-DOS applications without restrictions. This makes conventional memory the most important type of memory on a PC, with its size determining considerably the power and performance of a computer under MS-DOS.

Extended Memory (XMS)

Available for ATs and above starting at 1 Meg (1024K). Almost all ATs with 1 Meg have Extended Memory.

Expanded Memory (EMS)

This extra memory for all computers is "inserted" into the available memory in small portions, called memory pages. It can be "simulated" with other memory types.

High Memory (HMA)

High Memory refers to the first 64K of memory starting at 1 Meg, which can be used directly by some programs (DOS 6.0, Windows).

Upper Memory (UMB)

Upper Memory is memory in free areas between 640K and 1 Meg, that is, memory located in the same area where the hardware extensions, the video memory and the BIOS-ROM are located.

Video Ram

Video Ram is reserved for display of text and graphics on the screen. Unused parts of video Ram can be added to MS-DOS conventional memory.

Memory Management Programs

On ATs and 386/486 systems, extended memory is managed by the HIMEM.SYS driver, on 386 systems the EMM386.EXE driver provides expanded memory. The setting DOS=HIGH/UMB in the CONFIG.SYS causes MS DOS to swap out as many MS-DOS program and data fields from conventional memory as possible. On ATs and 386 computers, High Memory is available for this purpose, while 386/486 computers also provide Upper Memory.

Loading programs into High Memory

It's possible to relieve conventional memory by loading drivers into Upper Memory with DEVICEHIGH in the CONFIG.SYS. Adding LOADHIGH to the CONFIG.SYS lets you load memory resident programs (TSR programs) like KEYB into Upper Memory as well. You will notice the improvement by the additional conventional memory available on your PC. Use MEM /C to display the programs loaded into Upper memory.

Memory optimization

With MEMMAKER, you can have DOS automatically optimize your memory. MEMMAKER attempts to load the programs in a sequence and in those areas that will free up as much memory as possible.

Displaying memory

Use MEM to display the available memory. Special parameters allow precise display of individual memory areas and their uses.

12.2 Background

Memory is required for a computer to work. There are two types of computer memory:

Random Access Memory

> (RAM) - Your computer can write and then read data from this type of memory. When computer programs refer to memory, they are almost always talking about this type.

Read-Only Memory

> (ROM) - Your computer cannot write to ROM, hence the term read-only memory. This type of memory contains programs and data that are permanent and cannot be changed. ROMs are most often used to instruct hardware devices, such as video graphics adapters, how to operate in your PC.

Both types of memory are used to hold programs and data that the computer processes. The difference is that RAM is volatile - if you switch off your computer, the programs and data in memory are lost, whereas ROM is permanent - if you switch off your computer, the programs and data are retained.

Let's look at RAM more closely. Basically, this is how a program uses this type of memory:

```
Memory Type           Total  =  Used  +  Free
----------------------------------------------------
Conventional           640K      159K     481K
Upper                  187K      187K      0K
Adapter RAM/ROM        384K      384K      0K
Extended (XMS)        2885K     1861K    1024K
----------------------------------------------------
Total memory          4096K     2591K    1505K
Total under 1MB        827K      346K     481K
Largest executable program size            481K
Largest free upper mem blk                  0K
MS-DOS is resident in the high mem area
```

When a program such as a word processor is started, the file containing the program is loaded (i.e., copied) from the diskette or hard drive into the memory area of the computer. The DOS command interpreter tells the computer where in memory to load the program file.

As you type characters using the word processor, the data (characters) is also stored in another area of the computer's memory. The word processor tells the computer where in memory to store this data. The data remains in memory until you tell the word processor to save (i.e., write) the text to a storage device.

When you change the text, you're actually changing the data in the computer's memory. If you switch off your computer without saving the text to a storage device, the text is gone forever.

How much memory does my computer have?

By using the DOS 6.0 MEM command, you can easily determine how much memory your computer has. Type:

```
MEM
```

You'll see a display similar to the following:

DOS 6.0 MEM display

The first line tells us that DOS recognizes a total of 640K of conventional memory. There is 159K used which leaves 481K free.

If your computer has more than 640K of memory, the next three lines will contain capacity information for Upper, Adapter and Extended (XMS) memory. These terms will be discussed in more detail shortly.

The largest executable program size tells us that approximately 481K of memory remains to run programs.

12.3 Conventional and Extended Memory

Before discussing conventional and extended memory, let's take a few moments and talk about the early days of PCs.

Early IBM/PC computers were powered by the Intel 8088 and 8086 CPUs. They were capable of referencing or addressing up to 1 Meg of memory. This 1 Meg limit was determined by the number of *address lines* on the 8088 chip. Since the 8088 has 20 address lines, it was able to address 2^{20} = 1,048,576 memory (1 Meg) locations.

The 80286 CPU appeared a few years later in the AT model computers. The 80286 has 24 address lines so it is able to address 2^{24} = 16,777,266 memory (16 Meg) locations.

The 80386 and 80486 CPUs, which are found in the latest computers, both have 32 address lines. So they are able to address 2^{32} = 4,294,967,296 (4 gigabytes) locations.

From this historical perspective, we can see that all of the CPUs are able to address at least one megabyte of memory. The original DOS was designed around the 1 Meg limit and this range of memory has become known as *conventional memory*. To distinguish between this first megabyte of memory, additional memory beyond the 1 Meg limit is referred to as *extended memory*.

Since the 8088 and 8086 CPUs don't have enough address lines, computers with these processors cannot use memory beyond the 1 Meg limit. But PCs with 80286, 80386 and 80486 CPUs can use extended memory.

Why 1 Meg adds up to only 640K

If your computer has 1 Meg of memory, a program still may not be able to use this full amount of memory. In fact, most programs can only use up to 640K of memory.

To explain why this occurs, let's use an example. Suppose that you want to construct a small building and you need 1,024 square feet of property. You purchase 1,024 square feet, but later find out that it's actually divided by a six lane freeway that has the right of way.

The freeway divides your property into two sections: one 640 square feet in size and the other 384 square feet. Although you have 1,024 square feet of property, you won't be able to use the 384 square foot section to construct the building according to plan.

This is similar to how memory appears to DOS. When you load a program, DOS makes memory available to the program in a contiguous (undivided) section.

The maximum amount of memory that DOS can make available to a program is 640K. The other 384K is reserved by DOS. Although your computer may have 1024K of memory, you can use only 640K of it effectively.

More details about conventional memory

Before discussing extended memory further, let's look at conventional memory in more detail.

The figure below shows the layout of conventional memory.

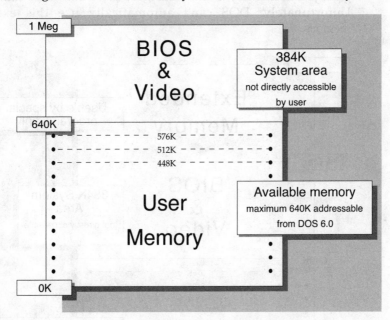

Conventional memory layout

You'll see that *low memory* ranges up to the 640K limit. This area of memory is sometimes referred to as user memory. Some portions of DOS are stored within low memory.

The remainder of low memory is for user programs and data. If your computer has less than 640K, the amount of user memory for the programs and data is reduced proportionally.

Above the 640K limit, conventional memory ranges up to the 1 Meg limit. The additional 384K of memory is reserved by DOS and is sometimes referred to as *upper memory*.

Within upper memory are the BIOS (basic input/output system) ROM, video memory and ROM and other hardware dependent programs (e.g., hard drive controllers, network cards, modem).

Usually only parts of upper memory are used by the computer. This leaves unused sections (or holes) of memory in this address range.

12.4 Extended Memory

An 80286, 80386 or 80486 computer can address much more memory than a 8086 or 8088 computer. As we mentioned, the memory above the 1 Meg conventional limit is called extended memory.

A maximum of 16 Meg of memory is addressable in an 80286. Up to 4 gigabytes of memory is addressable for 80386 and 80486 computers. Unfortunately, DOS can't automatically use this extended memory.

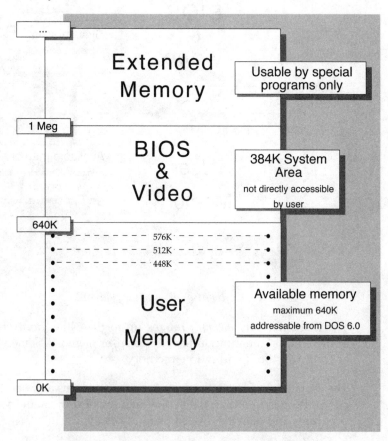

Extended memory layout

This is a layout of a typical AT-class computer (computers with 80286, 80386 and 80486 CPUs) with 1 Meg of memory. The layout of conventional memory is identical to that for 8086 and 8088 computers.

The AT has 640K of conventional memory and an area reserved for the BIOS, video and other hardware-dependent devices. The remaining 384K of memory is found in an area above the 1 Meg limit. So this 384K is part of extended memory.

In order to be compatible with the 8086 and 8088 computers, the AT-class computers operate in what is called *real mode*. In this mode, the computer operates as if it were an 8086 computer and therefore can address a maximum of 1 Meg of memory. So an AT-class computer in real mode cannot use memory beyond the 1 Meg limit.

Using extended memory

To use memory beyond the 1 Meg limit, the microprocessor must be switched to *protected mode*. Remember that only 80286, 80386 and 80486 CPUs are capable of running in protected mode. In this mode, the 1 Meg memory limitation is removed. So you can store and retrieve information beyond the 1 Meg line.

Problems in protected mode

Unfortunately switching to protected mode isn't easy. You must take precautions in order to avoid problems. For example, you can use the special instruction to switch from real mode to protected mode, but there isn't an instruction for switching back to real mode.

Problems in memory sharing

As long as programs use only conventional memory, DOS ensures that only one program uses that area of memory. DOS manages the memory by assigning or allocating parts of memory to the various programs (drivers, resident utility programs, applications).

However, DOS doesn't manage extended memory. Because of this, you may have problems if more than one program tries to use extended memory and conflicts with another program.

Different programs may not work together if they are both using extended memory. For example, a disk cache program to speed up hard drive access can be set up to store data in a portion of extended memory rather than taking away valuable conventional memory.

However, if your word processor is capable of using extended memory, it may try to store text into the same area. Both the word processor and disk cache program may overwrite each other's data and eventually cause the computer to crash.

There are a few ways to avoid these kinds of conflicts. For example, a disk cache program might use a portion of extended memory and then fool other programs into thinking that this memory area doesn't exist. Unfortunately, since extended memory isn't managed systematically the way DOS manages conventional memory, the problem may still occur.

Which DOS programs use extended memory

Two DOS 6.0 utilities can use extended memory:

RAM disk A RAM disk is a pseudo disk drive that uses a part of the memory for storing data. There are several advantages to using a RAM disk. The most important advantage is that data can be retrieved and written (stored) much faster than with a real (and relatively slow) disk drive.

The main disadvantage of a RAM disk is that the contents are lost when the computer is switched off. In many cases a RAM disk is useful for temporary data storage.

DOS 6.0 includes a utility program, called RAMDRIVE.SYS, for creating a RAM disk. Instead of calling this program by typing its name, you must install it by calling it from CONFIG.SYS. RAMDRIVE.SYS can use extended memory so you don't lose any conventional memory (the area from 0 to 640K).

Hard drive cache
Although a hard drive is considerably faster than a disk drive, it can still be relatively slow when working with large amounts of data. A cache program uses a part of memory to store data, from the hard drive, temporarily. The next time this data is needed, it doesn't have to be retrieved from the drive. Instead, it can be quickly accessed from this buffer.

When data is stored temporarily in conventional memory, less memory is available for programs. The special SMARTDRV.EXE cache can use extended memory for temporary storage. This speeds up your hard drive considerably.

There are programs that can use extended memory (e.g., Version 3.0 of Lotus 1-2-3 or Version 1.1 of dBASE IV). However, many other programs can only use only extended memory as expanded memory.

12.5 Expanded Memory

Extended memory has two disadvantages:

1. It can only be used on AT-class computers. Therefore millions of 8086 and 8088 computer users cannot take advantage of any memory beyond the 1 Meg limit.

2. Not all programs have been written to take advantage of extended memory. Therefore only a small universe of programs are able to address beyond the 1 Meg limit.

To try to solve these two extended memory limitations, several large companies joined forces to develop a uniform method for adding and using additional memory on the PC. This method is called the Expanded Memory Specification (EMS). The initials of the participating companies (Lotus, Intel and Microsoft) are sometimes added to the name, so you might see the standard referred to as LIM/EMS.

How does expanded memory work?

Expanded memory is a combination of hardware and software. The memory itself is contained on a printed circuit board with special electronics. One principle behind expanded memory is that it can be used by 8086 and 8088 computers. So memory that uses this scheme must be addressable below the 1 Meg limit.

An area in upper memory, between 640K and 1 Meg, is designated as a *page frame*. The page frame is a 64K area of memory that acts as a window to a much larger area of expanded memory. The electronic circuitry lets you select the part of expanded memory that appears in this window at any given time. Just as DOS manages memory up to the 640K limit, special software called an EMS driver manages the expanded memory. When a program references a section of expanded memory that isn't in the window, the EMS software/hardware combination replaces an unneeded section of memory out of the page frame with the section that is needed.

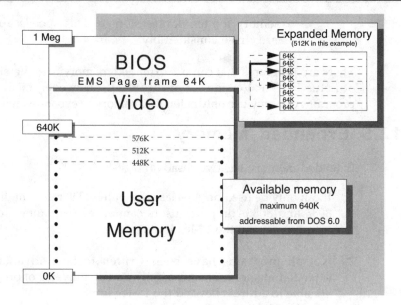

Expanded memory layout

The above figure shows the layout of expanded memory. The expanded memory on the EMS circuit board is completely independent of the computer's conventional memory (and extended memory, if present). The electronic circuitry on the board manages the data in the EMS memory.

Of course, a program must be especially written to be able to use expanded memory. But many programs are already set up to recognize and take advantage of a computer's expanded memory. Some of the major applications that can use expanded memory are: dBASE IV, Framework, Lotus 1-2-3, Microsoft Windows, Microsoft Word, Microsoft Works, Turbo Pascal and WordPerfect. There are many other applications that can use expanded memory.

Expanded memory - some variations

Earlier we said that you needed an EMS printed circuit board to use expanded memory. Computers that contain the NEAT chip set are already capable of using expanded memory without additional hardware. By adding a special EMS software driver, a computer's extended memory will behave as if it were expanded memory.

Also, computers that have 80386 and 80486 CPUs are also capable of converting extended memory into expanded memory without requiring additional hardware.

Utility programs for expanded memory

The DOS 6.0 driver called EMM386.EXE is used by 80386 and 80486 CPUs to convert extended memory into expanded memory. This driver makes the extended memory function according to the LIM/EMS standard.

In addition, EMM386.EXE has other capabilities. High memory between 640K and 1 Meg that isn't being used by DOS can be used to store driver programs and many Terminate and Stay Resident (TSR) programs using the LOADHIGH command. By moving drivers into high memory, additional conventional memory is freed up for applications.

12.6 High Memory

For AT-class computers, there is a small area of memory that has a unique characteristic. This area is located in the first 64K of extended memory (starting at 1 Meg) and is called the *high memory area*.

What makes this area so unique is that, due to a peculiarity in how the 80286, 80386 and 80486 CPUs handle addresses, it's possible to reference these 65,520 bytes of extended memory in real mode. So, you don't have to switch from real mode to protected mode in order to use this area of memory even though it is part of extended memory.

This unique property makes the high memory area a special variant of extended memory. But to take advantage of the high memory area, your computer must have extended memory. Using the high memory may not just free up enough conventional memory to get these applications to work.

The illustration on the following page shows that the high memory area is part of extended memory. Extended memory begins at address 1,048,576 (1 Meg). Again, the high memory area exists only if your computer has at least 64K of extended memory.

This diagram also shows that an 80286 computer can address up to 16 Meg of memory. But to do so, it must first be switched to protected mode.

By using the high memory area to store certain parts of DOS, you can free up parts of conventional memory for your applications. While 64K may not seem like much, some applications may not work unless there is a minimum amount of conventional memory available.

The DOS driver HIMEM.SYS is used to manage the high memory area. However, remember that only a few applications are capable of running from the high memory area.

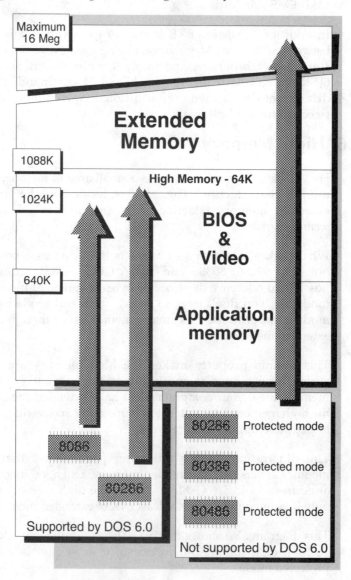

Special features of high memory

12.7 Upper Memory

The memory above the 640K line and below the 1 Meg is referred to as the upper memory blocks or *upper memory*. These areas are most often used for hardware-related memory requirements. For example, video graphics cards, network adapters and specialized hard drive controllers use memory addresses in upper memory to control their devices.

But upper memory is never completely filled. There are always "holes" in this range that are unused. On most computers, you can fill these "empty" areas by adding RAM chips. And since this range is below the 1 Meg line, 8086 and 8088 computers can address this area.

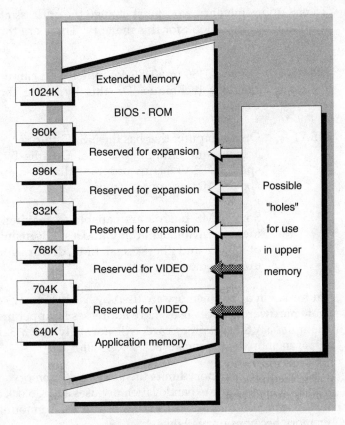

Special features of upper memory

The previous diagram shows the layout of memory between 640K and 1024K (1 Meg). On most computers, this area of memory is reserved for hardware add-ons. But if an area isn't being used, then the "hole" can be used.

With DOS 6.0 you can, under certain conditions, use many areas of upper memory just as you would use memory below the 640K limit. The LOADHIGH command is used to load a program into upper memory and the DEVICEHIGH command is used to load drivers into upper memory.

12.8 Requirements for Using Upper Memory

While high memory can be used on an AT computer that has extended memory, upper memory isn't as readily available. Remember that on an AT, memory above 640K begins at 1 Meg, not at 640K.

To use upper memory, you must change the address at which the computer begins to look for this memory. There are three ways to do this:

386/486   On an 80386 or 80486 computer, you can use a virtual memory technique. Do this by using the EMM386 driver.

NEAT   On a computer that has the NEAT chip set, you can use a technique similar to a 386. Do this by using the special NEAT setup program that re-maps memory above 1 Meg as upper memory.

EMS   Some EMS boards are capable of making additional memory available at any address. By using this type of board and the special EMS driver, you can add upper memory.

Addresses in upper memory are used by hardware devices. Adding more hardware devices uses more addresses in upper memory. For example, a VGA graphics card will normally use a 32K block of upper memory beginning at 786432 (C0000h).

Also, expanded memory limits the amount of memory available as upper memory. Since expanded memory uses a 64K block of memory in this range for its window, 64K of the total amount of upper memory becomes unavailable.

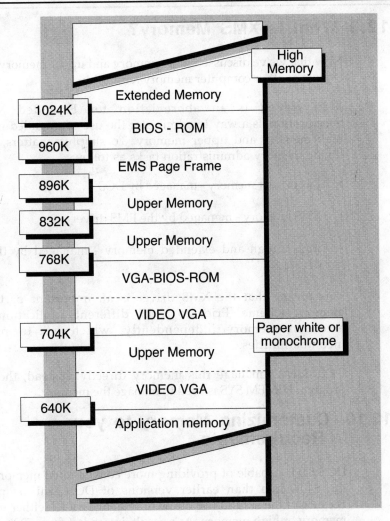

High
Memory

Extended Memory

1024K

BIOS - ROM

960K

EMS Page Frame

896K

Upper Memory

832K

Upper Memory

768K

VGA-BIOS-ROM

VIDEO VGA

704K   Paper white or
                                                        monochrome
Upper Memory

VIDEO VGA

640K

Application memory

Upper memory with VGA card and EMS page frame

The previous diagram shows a typical layout of upper memory.
One block of memory is occupied by the VGA graphics card.
Another block is occupied by an EMS board. The address range
occupied by the ROM BIOS at the end of upper memory is also
unavailable. This leaves a total of 128K of upper memory as
unused.

You'll also notice that upper memory isn't available as a
contiguous block of memory. To take advantage of the unused upper
memory, you have to be able to use the disjointed blocks.

12.9 What Is XMS Memory?

Now that we've discussed high memory and upper memory, we can explain another computer memory term: XMS.

XMS, which is an abbreviation for Extended Memory Specification, is a way to administer the use of extended memory, high memory and upper memory. To simplify matters, we can divide memory administration tasks as follows:

- low or user memory - managed by DOS

- EMS memory - managed by the EMS driver

- upper, high and extended memory - managed by the XMS driver

This means that the XMS driver is an important part of the memory scheme. Prior to XMS, different applications used extended memory independently, which led to program incompatibilities.

DOS doesn't manage this memory directly. Instead, the driver program HIMEM.SYS is used to manage the memory.

12.10 Customizing Memory to your Requirements

DOS 6.0 is capable of providing more conventional memory up to the 640K line than earlier versions of DOS. This is possible because of the skillful use of memory above 640K - either in upper memory or high memory. As a result, instead of from 520K to 540K of user memory available using DOS 4.01, DOS 6.0 users will find from 590K to 630K available for their applications.

Using high memory

If extended memory - beginning at 1 Meg - is available, DOS can use the first 64K as the high memory area and store part of itself there.

High memory requires extended memory. For example, if you use a memory manager on an 80386 or 80486 to convert all of extended memory to expanded memory, then extended memory no longer exists.

To use the high memory area, leave 64K of the extended memory unused by adjusting the EMM386.EXE driver.

The following conditions must be met for DOS to use high memory:

- The computer must have extended memory beginning at 1 Meg. This is only possible on ATs (80286 and upwards).

- A special driver program must make the first 64K of extended memory available as high memory. With DOS 6.0, use the XMS driver HIMEM.SYS for ATs. Some special memory management programs also have this capability.

  In any case, start this driver program as early as possible in the CONFIG.SYS file. HIMEM.SYS must even be started before EMM386.EXE is called. Then you can start the drivers that use EMS or XMS memory.

- A special command line in the CONFIG.SYS file must be used to instruct DOS to use the high memory for storing the DOS kernel:

  ```
  DOS=HIGH
  ```

  Entering the command line DOS=LOW in the CONFIG.SYS file tells DOS that high memory shouldn't be used directly for DOS. This allows Windows 3.1 to use the high memory area.

 The location of the line, DOS=HIGH/LOW, in the CONFIG.SYS file is not important.

Example

Suppose that you want DOS 6.0 to use high memory on an AT with a total of 1 Meg of available memory. To do this, type the following lines at the start of the CONFIG.SYS file:

```
DEVICE=HIMEM.SYS
DOS=HIGH
```

The remaining memory from 640K and above is available as XMS memory.

Use the MEM command to check the available memory. MEM also displays whether part of DOS is stored in high memory. The screen output of MEM might look like the following on an AT with extended memory and the DOS kernel in high memory:

```
C:\>mem

Memory Type        Total  =  Used  +  Free
Conventional        640K     146K     494K
Upper               187K      28K     160K
Adapter RAM/ROM     384K     384K       0K
Extended (XMS)     2885K    1241K    1644K

Total memory       4096K    1799K    2297K

Total under 1 MB    827K     174K     653K

Largest executable program size      493K  (505264 bytes)
Largest free upper memory block      159K  (163200 bytes)
MS-DOS is resident in the high memory area.

C:\>
```

Using upper memory

To use memory as upper memory, you must start the EMM386.EXE driver in the CONFIG.SYS file. The XMS driver must be loaded ahead of the EMM386 driver. The following is the correct order for using these drivers in the CONFIG.SYS file:

```
DEVICE=HIMEM.SYS
DEVICE=EMM386.EXE
```

  As a rule, EMM386 automatically converts all of the existing extended memory to expanded memory. Since this isn't always desirable, the parameter, NOEMS, tells the driver not to allocate any EMS memory but still allocate upper memory.

To use the extended memory as XMS memory and still use EMM386 to provide upper memory, call both driver programs as follows:

```
DEVICE=HIMEM.SYS
DEVICE=EMM386.EXE NOEMS
```

You must also tell DOS to reserve all of the existing upper memory and make it available as "ordinary" conventional memory (like the memory up to 640K).

```
DOS=HIGH,UMB
```

The abbreviation UMB represents the upper memory block. For example, to reserve upper memory and high memory for DOS on an 80386 or higher computer and use 512K for expanded memory, use the following command lines (provided that you have enough memory):

```
DEVICE=HIMEM.SYS
DEVICE=EMM386.EXE 512
DOS=HIGH,UMB
REM Other lines of the CONFIG.SYS follow
```

To use upper memory without storing the DOS kernel (the most important part of DOS, which must always be available in the memory) in high memory, use the line:

```
DOS=LOW,UMB
```

You can use NOUMB instead of UMB to prevent DOS from using the upper memory area as memory. Usually you won't have to specify NOUMB because:

```
DOS=LOW,NOUMB
```

is the default setting if there aren't any parameters specified in CONFIG.SYS.

We recommend using upper memory for applications as long as your programs are able to use it without any problems. If programs have problems using the memory area between 640K and 1 Meg, use NOUMB as your setting.

If necessary, use special memory management programs to "highload" drivers and TSR programs so you can use upper memory.

LOADFIXcan be used to load programs that aren't usually run in extra conventional memory.

This command can also be used to load programs that generate a "Packed file corrupt" error message when trying to load into low memory.

LOADFIX can also load some programs that won't load if a network is installed and running.

12.11 Partitioning Memory

As we've seen, DOS 6.0 is very flexible in managing your computer's memory. The following are some examples of the options that are available. Remember that a few of these options are mutually exclusive (can't be used together).

- On a computer with only 640K of memory, neither of these new options (upper memory or high memory) are available. Since DOS 6.0 uses more conventional memory on this kind of computer, less will be available for application programs.

- On an AT class computer or a 386 with 1 Meg of memory, you can either use this memory for shadowing or as extended memory (including high memory).

  If you use 64K of high memory, there is 64K less of extended memory for a RAM disk or a cache program. The computer must have either an 80386 microprocessor, 80486 microprocessor or a NEAT chip set to use upper memory.

- Computers with more than 1 Meg of memory can use both upper memory and extended memory (including high memory). You lose up to 384K of extended memory for upper memory (even if the ROM areas are accelerated by shadowing) and another 64K for high memory. The rest of the memory is available for programs.

The following table shows which options are applicable for different computer equipment:

Computer equipment	High Memory	Extended	Upper Memory
XT/AT up to 640K	- -	-	
AT with 1 Meg	yes	320K as XMS	-
386 with 1 Meg or	yes	320K as XMS	-
386 with more than 1 Meg	yes	yes as XMS	yes

12.12   Optimizing Memory with MEMMAKER

MS-DOS 6.0 comes supplied with MEMMAKER, a program for optimizing memory. MEMMAKER optimizes memory by moving the device drivers and resident programs in the CONFIG.SYS and the AUTOEXEC.BAT into upper memory.

With this type of memory optimization, the programs and drivers to be loaded into upper memory must already be present in the system files. Even MEMMAKER cannot automatically link a mouse driver that wasn't linked previously.

After linking all the desired programs and drivers to the system files, you can use MEMMAKER to optimize the distribution of the programs and drivers in memory. MEMMAKER inserts the programs in the most efficient order in the AUTOEXEC.BAT and CONFIG.SYS and uses the LOADHIGH /L and DEVICEHIGH /L commands to load the programs and drivers into specific memory areas that are free. To do this, MEMMAKER locates the free memory areas via MEM /F.

To start the program, enter the following command:

```
MEMMAKER
```

After startup, a welcome screen appears, displaying information about MEMMAKER and explaining the keys used to operate MEMMAKER.

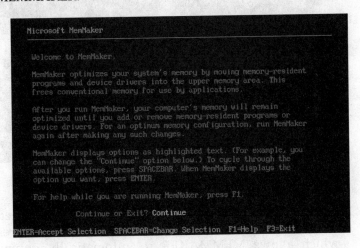

Welcome to MEMMAKER

12.12.1   Operating MEMMAKER

The following keys are available for operating the program:

[Enter]   Use this key to confirm the selection.

[↑][←][→][↓]   Use the cursor keys to select displayed options.

[Spacebar]   Use this key to change selection.

[F1]   Displays help on MEMMAKER.

[F3]   Changes MEMMAKER. After you press this key, a new
               screen appears, in which you can decide to accept the
               changes or undo them. You can also choose to continue
               optimization with MEMMAKER.

12.12.2   Optimizing with MEMMAKER

After the MEMMAKER welcome screen appears, you can continue
memory optimization by pressing [Enter].

Selecting the type of optimization

A new screen appears, in which you must choose between Express
Setup and Custom Setup. We recommend using Express Setup,
which allows MEMMAKER to automatically optimize your
computer's memory, since Custom Setup requires much technical
knowledge. Actually, the only time you should perform a Custom
Setup is when you have trouble with Express setup.

In the following section, we'll give a description of Custom Setup anyway, and explain the information for which MEMMAKER prompts you.

To perform an Express Setup, press ⌈Enter⌉. To perform a Custom Setup, press the ⌈Spacebar⌉ and then press ⌈Enter⌉.

In the next screen, MEMMAKER asks whether you use expanded memory (EMS) for your programs. If you aren't sure how to answer, choose "No". Using expanded memory always leaves you with less conventional memory. If you find later that your programs need expanded memory, you can run MEMMAKER again to change this setting.

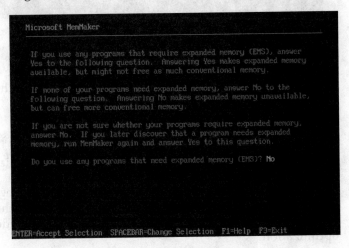

Use of EMS memory

What the program does now depends on which Setup you chose, Express or Custom.

12.12.3 Custom Setup

If you chose Custom Setup, the next screen displays a list of settings MEMMAKER wants to use for optimizing memory.

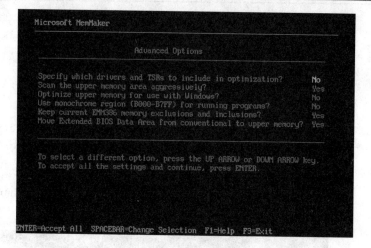

MEMMAKER settings

Press Enter to accept these settings. You could also choose to change each setting. To do this, use the cursor keys to highlight the desired setting and press the Spacebar to change it.

Now we'll give you a brief description of the individual settings.

Specify which drivers and TSRs to include during optimization?

If you choose "Yes", you will be prompted for each program and driver to include it in the optimization. If you choose the default setting, "No", all the programs and drivers will be included in the optimization.

This option is especially practical for users with old drivers that cannot be loaded into upper memory.

Scan upper memory aggressively?

This setting allows you to determine which memory areas MEMMAKER scans in upper memory. If you choose "No", MEMMAKER only scans memory with addresses between C600-EFFF. Choose "Yes" to have MEMMAKER include addresses F000-F7FF in the scan.

Choose "No" for this setting only if your computer doesn't run correctly when moving the UMBs into upper memory from F000-F7FF.

Optimize upper memory for use with Windows?

If you are running Windows, MEMMAKER optimizes memory so that as much conventional memory as possible is available for MS-

DOS programs in Windows. However, as a result, only a small amount of conventional memory is available when Windows isn't running.

Choose "Yes" if you work with MS-DOS applications frequently in Windows. If you only run Windows applications in Windows or seldom run Windows, choose "No".

Use monochrome region (B000-B7FF) for running programs?

If you have a monochrome monitor connected to your computer, you must choose "No" for this setting. If you have an EGA or VGA monitor, you can choose "Yes". This makes memory area B000-B7ff available for device drivers or programs.

Keep current EMM386 exclusions and inclusions?

If you linked the EMM386.EXE driver to the CONFIG.SYS, you may have excluded various memory areas from use or included other areas. It's also possible that some other program did this.

If you choose "Yes" for this setting, the inclusions and exclusions of memory areas will be ignored, if necessary, MEMMAKER will create new ones. By doing this, MEMMAKER frees up more memory. If you have trouble after choosing "No", choose "Yes" the next time you run MEMMAKER to keep the old EMM386 inclusions and exclusions.

Move Extended BIOS Data Area from conventional to upper memory?

Ordinarily, MEMMAKER loads the extended BIOS data area into upper memory. If you have trouble while MEMMAKER is attempting to load the extended BIOS data area into upper memory, choose "No" for this setting. However, you should try choosing "Yes" first, since this frees up one more K of memory.

After making the desired settings, press Enter to continue optimization.

12.12.4 The Actual Optimization

After that, MEMMAKER begins the actual optimization, regardless of whether you chose Express or Custom Setup. First MEMMAKER checks whether your computer has Windows.

If it does have Windows, by default, MEMMAKER attempts to make as much memory as possible available for MS-DOS programs under Windows when it optimizes the memory.

Then MEMMAKER tells you to restart the computer. Remember to remove all diskettes from the computer's disk drives when you do this.

☞   If a program starts up in your AUTOEXEC.BAT after you restart the computer, you must exit the program so you can continue with MEMMAKER.

After that, MEMMAKER checks different configurations and selects the best one for your computer. When it is finished, press (Enter) to have MEMMAKER restart the computer again with the new system files.

Pay careful attention to the messages that appear on the screen when you restart the computer. If you see error messages, either change the settings in Custom Setup or undo the changes made by MEMMAKER.

If you have trouble starting your computer, simply turn it off and on again. MEMMAKER automatically starts up again and you can press (F3) to exit, then choose "Exit and undo changes". Now, you can restart the computer with the old system files.

If you don't have any trouble restarting the computer, when MEMMAKER automatically restarts, accept the changes MEMMAKER made to the AUTOEXEC.BAT and CONFIG.SYS files by answering "Yes" to the prompt.

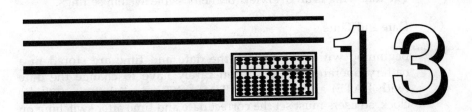

C h a p t e r

13

System Settings

MS-DOS is designed to be flexible. As you add new hardware, you can change DOS to accommodate these new devices. Also important is that you can "customize" or tailor DOS for your work habits or preferences.

For example, the system prompt can be changed, the number of buffers altered to speed up access to the hard drive and special function programs, such as the MS-DOS Shell or DOSKEY, can be installed.

DOS can be adapted to the computer and your special needs by modifying the two system files AUTOEXEC.BAT and CONFIG.SYS.

The best way to change these files is to use the DOS 5.0 editor, EDIT. Backup the original files before modifying them so you can use these copies in case a change you made creates problems.

You should also create a bootable diskette (use the FORMAT /S command). Then if one of the changes you make to the CONFIG.SYS file prevents your computer from booting properly from the hard drive, you can use the bootable floppy diskette.

You'll simply insert the bootable diskette into a disk drive and restart the computer; then recopy the original CONFIG.SYS file to the hard drive.

13.1 Overview

The following is an overview of the possible system settings.

Date and Time

Beginning with AT's (286's), the date and time are stored in a
battery operated clock, so you rarely have to change the date
(with DATE) and time (with TIME). XT's don't have a realtime
clock, so users must set the correct date and time after switching on
the computer. When users create or change files and then save
them, the date and time are included in the save.

Customizing the System Prompt

The PROMPT command is used to customize the system prompt.
You can add text to the system prompt, or use different codes that
are preceded by the special character "$".

Specifying the Command Interpreter

MS-DOS works with a command interpreter called
COMMAND.COM. In some cases, (especially when you exit
application programs), you must reload the command interpreter.
To ensure that MS-DOS can always find COMMAND.COM, an
environment variable named COMSPEC should always contain
the exact search path and name of the command interpreter when
it isn't located in the root directory. To do this, add the following
line to the AUTOEXEC.BAT file:

```
SET COMSPEC=C:\DOS\COMMAND.COM
```

In the CONFIG.SYS file, use the SHELL command to specify the
first command interpreter:

```
SHELL=C:\DOS\COMMAND.COM /P
```

Defining the size of the environment and the start directory

Use a parameter to set the size of the environment when starting
COMMAND.COM with /E:XXXX. For long search paths and
intensive use of environment variables, use a setting of /E:500 or
more. You can also define a start directory for the command
interpreter by searching the AUTOEXEC.BAT file afterward. To
do this, specify it right after the call. A complete line in the
CONFIG.SYS might look as follows:

```
SHELL=COMMAND.COM C:\ /P /E:500
```

Loading a new command interpreter

You can also load the COMMAND.COM command interpreter again after system startup by entering COMMAND. You can pass several switches to COMMAND.COM. However, do not specify the /P switch for the new command interpreter.

Environment Variables

Type SET without any switches to display existing variables. To create or make changes to variables, use SET Name=contents. Some environment variables have a special meaning to DOS. So, if you change their contents, DOS will change its behavior. These special variables include:

PATH   Search path for program files (C:\DOS).

APPEND   Search path for data files defined by the APPEND command.

PROMPT   System prompt displayed on the screen (PG).

TEMP   Directory for temporary files (C:\TEMP).

COMSPEC Path and name of the command interpreter in case it must be reloaded (C:\DOS\COMMAND.COM).

DIRCMD   Default parameters for the DOS DIR command. The DIR command handles these commands as if they were entered directly from the keyboard.

Special System Settings

Use the FILES command to define the maximum number of files that can be open at the same time (FILES=25). Use BREAK to specify whether MS-DOS checks attempts to interrupt commands during storage device accesses (BREAK=ON).

13.2 Setting the Time and Date

As part of its task of maintaining files and directories, DOS keeps track of the date and time at which a file or directory is created or changed.

It's important that the date and time be accurate. If your computer doesn't have a built-in clock, the correct time and date must be entered immediately after you start the computer.

Since these settings must be made each time you start your computer, you should include the DATE and TIME commands in your AUTOEXEC.BAT file, which automatically runs every time the computer is started. These two commands will prompt you to enter the date and time.

You may not have to use the DATE and TIME commands since most computers now have built-in clocks. In this case, the built-in clock automatically maintains the correct date and time.

The DATE and TIME commands are then used to alter the date and time for certain situations (e.g., set to daylight savings time).

 Some computer clocks lose or gain several minutes per day. So even if your computer has a battery operated clock, check the date and the time regularly.

Displaying and changing the date

Use the DATE command to display and make any necessary changes to the current date:

```
DATE
```

After pressing Enter, the current date that is set in your computer is displayed along with a prompt that asks you to enter a new date. Enter the new date in the MM-DD-YY format (or DD-MM-YY if you've specified a country other than the U.S. in your AUTOEXEC.BAT file):

MM   Month (1-12)

DD   Day (1-31)

YY   Year (80-99) or (1980-2099)

 Instead of a hyphen "-", you can also use a period "." or a slash "/" to separate the elements of the date. The year can be specified as either two or four digits (91 or 1991).

```
C:\>date
Current date is Wed 03-13-1991
Enter new date (mm-dd-yy):
```

The DOS DATE command

The new date can also be passed as a parameter to the DATE command. Use the same format as described when entering the date. For example, to set 6-20-1991 as the date, use the following:

```
DATE 6-20-91
```

Depending on the date format (e.g., UK), you may need to type:

```
DATE 20-6-91
```

```
C:\>date
Current date is Wed 13-3-1991
Enter new date (dd-mm-yy):
```

The DOS DATE command using UK format

In addition to the date, DOS displays the day of the week. So you can use this function to determine on which day of the week a certain date falls. To do this, simply enter the date as a parameter to the DATE command.

Remember to reset the current date before continuing your work on the computer. If you don't do this, all the new or changed files will have an incorrect date stamp in the directory.

Example

To determine on which day of the week New Year's Eve will fall in the year 2000, type the following date after calling DATE:

```
12-31-2000
```

```
C:\>date
Current date is Wed 03-13-1991
Enter new date (mm-dd-yy): 12-31-2000

C:\>date
Current date is Sun 12-31-2000
Enter new date (mm-dd-yy):
```

The DATE command shows December 31, 2000, will be
a Sunday

After you type the DATE command again, you'll see that the last
day of the year falls on a Sunday.

Depending on the format (e.g., UK), you may need to type:

```
31-12-2000
```

```
C:\>date
Current date is Wed 13-3-1991
Enter new date (dd-mm-yy): 31-12-2000

C:\>date
Current date is Sun 31-12-2000
Enter new date (dd-mm-yy):
```

The previous example using the UK format

Now you can reset the date to the current date. Otherwise, if you
press (Enter) instead of entering another date, the previous date
will be set.

If you try to enter an invalid date, DOS displays an error message
informing you of this and prompts you to enter a new date.

Viewing and changing the time

Use the TIME command to display and change the time stored by
your computer. If your computer doesn't have a battery operated
clock, include the TIME command as well as the DATE command in
your AUTOEXEC.BAT file.

If a built-in clock isn't installed, DOS sets the clock to 00:00:00.00
(0 hours, 0 minutes, 0 seconds, 0 hundredths of a second) each time
you switch on the computer.

```
TIME
```

After pressing ⌊Enter⌋, the time appears on the screen in the HH.MM.SS.XX format:

HH   Hours (0-23)

MM   Minutes (0-59)

SS   Seconds (0-59)

XX   Hundredths of a second (0-99)

If a new time isn't needed, simply press ⌊Enter⌋; the time remains unchanged. If you enter an invalid time, DOS indicates this with an error message and prompts you to enter a new time.

```
C:\>time
Current time is 12:04:30.94p
Enter new time:
```

The DOS TIME command

You can specify the complete time. For example, if only the hours and the minutes are entered, DOS sets the seconds and hundredths of a second to zero.

Example

Type 17:10; DOS interprets your entry as 5:10:00.00 PM.

DOS accepts the time entered in either the military format (24 hour) or in the standard 12 hour notation with an "A" or "P" (AM and PM) added to the time string. So the time in the preceding example could also be set by typing:

```
TIME 5:10P
```

Displaying the date and time on the command line

The date and time can be displayed as part of the system prompt. Use the DOS PROMPT command to include the following characters:

```
$d $t
```

The character sequence $d specifies the date, while $t specifies the time. The following command sets the system prompt to display both the date and time in addition to the current drive and path:

```
PROMPT $D $T $P$G
```

Here is the new prompt created by the previous command:

```
C:\>PROMPT $D $T $P$G

Mon 05-06-1991 11:47:40.37 C:\
```

Displaying the time in the MS-DOS Shell

 The MS-DOS Shell displays the time in the lower right corner of the screen. Use the TIME command to make sure the correct time is set.

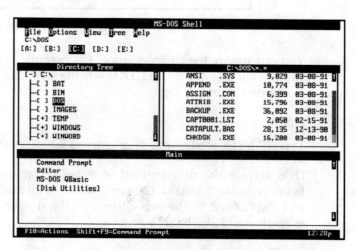

The time is displayed in the lower-right corner of the MS-DOS Shell

13.3 Customizing the System Prompt

The PROMPT command is used to customize the system prompt.

```
PROMPT Text
```

The Text string contains the parameters which specify how you want the system prompt to appear. We'll explain the parameters below.

Entering PROMPT without parameters resets the prompt to the default setting.

Some characters, which have special meanings, cannot be used with the DOS system prompt. Among these characters are "<" and ">", which are used to redirect input and output, and the pipe symbol "|", which is used for linking several commands.

There are some special codes for the system prompt that DOS doesn't treat like ordinary characters. These codes always start with the special character "$".

$B	Pipe symbol (	).
$D	Display of the current system date.
$E	The ESC character (ASCII 27) used to send commands to ANSI.SYS.
$G	Greater than character ">".
$H	Deletes character to left of cursor (backspace).
$L	Less than character "<".
$N	Displays the current drive.
$P	Displays the current drive and directory.
$Q	Equals sign "=".
$T	Displays the current system time.
$V	Displays DOS version.
$_	New line (CR/LF); permits defining system prompts of more than one line.

Since the dollar sign "$" identifies the special character sequences, it can't be entered by itself. So to use the dollar sign, type two dollar signs:

$$ Represents the "$" character.

Entering PROMPT without any parameters resets the system prompt to NG, which is the default system prompt that displays the drive letter and the greater than character. With this setting, you can use a disk drive as the current drive even if a diskette isn't in the drive, without receiving an error message.

This setting is useful for laptop computers without a hard drive because DOS won't have to access the drive after every command to determine the current directory. Using a simple system prompt without a directory is also useful because the hard drive doesn't have to be accessed unnecessarily, thereby saving valuable battery energy.

When you're working with subdirectories you should set the system prompt to PG from the AUTOEXEC.BAT file. This causes DOS to display the system prompt with the current drive and directory, followed by the greater than symbol.

Example

To display the current time (without hundredths of a second) and, in the next line, display the current directory as your system prompt, use the following command line:

```
PROMPT $_The current time is $t$h$h$h$_$p$g
```

The trick in this line is to use a backspace ($H) to remove the hundredths of a second.

```
C>prompt $_The current time is $t$h$h$h$_$p$g

The current time is 13:26:48
C:\>
```

Changing the system prompt

  The PROMPT command also allows you to enter spaces and displays them on the screen exactly as entered, as shown above.

If you load the ANSI.SYS device driver from within your CONFIG.SYS file (enter DEVICE=ANSI.SYS), you can create a more informative header:

```
prompt $e[7mTime: $t$h$h$h$h$h$h            $_Date:
$d$e[0m$e[K$_$e[0m$e[1m$p$g$e[0m
```

This special header always displays the date, time and the current directory.

To use this command line, ANSI.SYS must be installed from your CONFIG.SYS file. Use the following line to install ANSI.SYS:

```
DEVICE=ANSI.SYS
```

```
Time:  14:38
Date:  Wed 03-13-1991
C:>
```

Instead of being updated automatically, the date and the time are updated only after you press Enter.

You may have trouble typing the above PROMPT command because the proper ANSI codes must be used and the proper spacing must be maintained in the PROMPT string. So, on the companion diskette we've included a batch file, called HEADMSG.BAT, that can be used instead. This batch file can be edited as needed. You can also change the prompt by calling HEADMSG.BAT from your AUTOEXEC.BAT file. The CONFIG.SYS file must load the ANSI.SYS driver.

To make it easier for you to adapt this system prompt to your own requirements, the following is a brief summary of each code that is used:

$e[7m   This is an escape code for the ANSI.SYS driver. This code switches on the inverse mode for text.

Time: Displays the text string "Time:".

$t   Displays the current system time.

hhhhhh
               Backspaces and deletes six characters to remove the displayed seconds and hundredths of seconds from the screen.

Next it displays a string of 9 spaces in reverse video.

$_	Carriage return/line feed.
Date:	Displays the text string "Date:".
$d	Displays the current system date.
$e[0m	Switches off all text attributes. The "m" must be lowercase.
$e[K	Erases all characters from the cursor position to the end of the line. The "K" must be uppercase.
$_	Carriage return/line feed.
$e[0m	Switches off all text attributes. The "m" must be lowercase.
$e[1m	Switches on bold text. The "m" must be lowercase.
$p	Displays current path (drive and directory).
$g	Displays the greater than symbol ">".
$e[0m	Switches off all text attributes. The "m" must be lowercase.

 Sometimes when you try to execute the PROMPT command, MS-DOS displays the following message:

```
Out of environment space
```

If this happens, increase the space reserved for environment variables. To do this, specify a higher value for reserved space with the /E switch when opening COMMAND.COM with the SHELL command in the CONFIG.SYS file.

13.4 Specifying the Command Interpreter

The command interpreter accepts and responds to user commands that you type at the keyboard. The standard MS-DOS command interpreter is the file COMMAND.COM, which is usually found in the root directory of the hard drive.

Defining the command interpreter for booting

You can change the default command interpreter by using the SHELL command from within the CONFIG.SYS file (don't confuse this command with the DOSSHELL command).

You may want to use the SHELL command if COMMAND.COM isn't located in the root directory.

```
SHELL=Command_interpreter
```

The drive, path and name for the command interpreter are specified. For example, if the command interpreter is located in the DOS directory of the hard drive, the line in the CONFIG.SYS file would read as follows:

```
SHELL=C:\DOS\COMMAND.COM
```

If the command interpreter is run without any additional parameters, you can leave it at any time by using the EXIT command. However, the computer can no longer accept commands.

Also, a command interpreter started like this doesn't automatically run the AUTOEXEC.BAT file. So basic settings of the AUTOEXEC.BAT file (e.g., search path, keyboard, desired system prompt) aren't available.

You can prevent premature exits from the command interpreter by specifying the /P switch (permanent) after COMMAND.COM. This switch will prevent you from leaving this (the first) command interpreter using the command. The command interpreter also automatically runs the AUTOEXEC.BAT file.

Insert the SHELL command in your CONFIG.SYS file like this:

```
SHELL=C:\DOS\COMMAND.COM /P
```

Here, the CONFIG.SYS file is first run before the commands in your AUTOEXEC.BAT file. The SHELL command loads the command interpreter. Then COMMAND.COM runs the AUTOEXEC.BAT file.

 SHELL is only valid in the CONFIG.SYS file. Enter the same data that is specified in COMSPEC (name and path of the command interpreter) after SHELL.

Use the switches following the name of the command interpreter just as you would in a command line. For example, you could define the size of the environment memory for the first command interpreter. DOS stores important settings, such as the search path for programs or the current system prompt, in this environment memory.

Increasing the environment memory

To set the environment memory for COMMAND.COM, in the C:\DOS directory, to 512 bytes, use the following:

```
SHELL=C:\DOS\COMMAND.COM /P /E:512
```

By default, DOS provides only 256 bytes of environment memory.

You should only increase the size of the environment memory area if you get error messages when using SET to create new environment variables or if the changes made with PROMPT and PATH aren't functioning properly. Both of these switches (/P and /E) change the PATH and PROMPT environment variables.

Setting the command interpreter to reload

If an application program requires a lot of memory, DOS will temporarily remove part of the command interpreter from memory. When you exit the application, the command interpreter must be re-loaded.

If you haven't defined the command interpreter search path (with the SHELL command), DOS may ask you to insert the appropriate diskette into drive A:, even if the command interpreter is located on the hard drive. Usually DOS searches for the command interpreter in the root directory of the drive from which the computer is booted.

The command interpreter search path is kept as a system variable. To display the environment variables, type SET. You'll see a statement like this among the system variables:

```
COMSPEC=C:\COMMAND.COM
```

If your command interpreter isn't in the root directory, you'll want to add a line to your AUTOEXEC.BAT file that specifies the location of the command interpreter:

```
SET COMSPEC=C:\DOS\COMMAND.COM
```

The COMSPEC system variable tells DOS that the command interpreter COMMAND.COM is found on the C: drive in the DOS subdirectory. Remember that the name and search path of the

COMSPEC environment variable (set by AUTOEXEC.BAT) and SHELL (set by CONFIG.SYS) must match.

 If you see one of the following error messages after leaving an application program, an invalid path or filename for the command interpreter was specified. The following appears if the error was in drive A:

```
Invalid COMMAND.COM
Insert COMMAND.COM in drive A:
Press a key to continue...
```

The following appears if the error was in drive C:

```
Invalid COMMAND.COM

Cannot start COMMAND, exiting
```

Press Ctrl + Alt + Del to warm boot your computer and correct the specification for COMSPEC. If this error message appears again, you must boot from a DOS system diskette and correct the settings for SHELL in CONFIG.SYS.

In addition to the search path for reloading the command interpreter, a few other settings are specified in the environment variables. Type SET without any parameters to display the environment variables. The following variables are defined:

PROMPT   Specifies the system prompt.

PATH   Specifies the path specification for executable programs and batch files; DOS searches the directories specified in this path for the program to be executed.

COMSPEC Specifies the path and name of the command interpreter in case the command interpreter has to be reloaded.

These variables are called "environment variables" because they define the environment in which DOS operates.

If you change any of these variables, eventually you'll notice changes in DOS. The environment variables can be changed as follows:

```
SET Variable=contents
```

To set the system prompt, either use the PROMPT command or change the environment variable directly:

```
SET PROMPT=$P$G
```

Other system variables

The following are some additional system variables that can be set under certain conditions:

APPEND   This variable contains the DOS search path for data files (not programs). APPEND is used to define a search path.

                 The /E switch is used to store a copy of the appended directory list in an environment variable named APPEND. The /E switch can only be used the first time APPEND is called.

TEMP   This variable allows you to specify a directory that DOS can use to store temporary variables. If several commands are linked by a filter, the necessary temporary files are stored here.

                 The MS-DOS Shell also creates some temporary files which are stored in the specified directory. Example: SET TEMP=C:\TMP.

DIRCMD   This variable can be used to specify parameters that can be used as defaults for the DOS DIR command. The DIR command uses these parameters as if they were entered directly.

13.5 Using the Command Interpreter

The command interpreter is the heart of DOS. It's loaded automatically every time the computer is switched on and accepts and executes commands that you type at the keyboard. A second interpreter, sometimes called a secondary command interpreter, can also be started like other DOS commands.

Starting a secondary command interpreter

Use COMMAND to start a secondary command interpreter:

```
COMMAND
```

When you change the environment of a secondary command interpreter, the changes only affect the environment temporarily. When the secondary command interpreter terminates, the changed environment is lost and the environment of the first or primary command interpreter is restored. To terminate a secondary command interpreter type:

```
EXIT
```

The original command interpreter, with its unchanged environment, is then reactivated.

 Remember not to EXIT from the primary command interpreter. If you do this, you won't be able to send any commands to your computer. To avoid this problem, you can specify the /P switch of the SHELL command to set the command interpreter as permanent.

Example

Many compilers set up directories using special system variables, which are needed for the compiler to function properly. Usually a path to the program files of the compiler must also be defined. Working with these programs and other applications can create conflicts in system variables.

Example

The following sample batch file, STARTUP.BAT, defines the path and directories that are used with the Microsoft C Compiler 5.1:

```
PATH C:\MSC\RBIN;D:\MSC\DOS;D:\MSC;C:\DOS
SET LIB=C:\MSC\LIB
SET INCLUDE=C:\MSC\INCLUDE
SET TMP=C:\TEMP
SET INIT=C:\MSC\SOURCE\ME\INI
```

Suppose the following variables were defined before running the STARTUP.BAT file:

```
PATH=C:\DOS
COMSPEC=C:\COMMAND.COM
PROMPT=$p$g
```

After running STARTUP.BAT, the following environment variables became effective (previously defined variables and new variables). Any changes or deletions must then be made individually:

```
COMSPEC=C:\COMMAND.COM
PROMPT=$P$G
PATH=C:\MSC\RBIN;C:\MSC\DOS;C:\DOS
LIB=C:\MSC\LIB
INCLUDE=C:\MSC\INCLUDE
TMP=C:\TEMP
INIT=C:\MSC\SOURCE\ME\INI
```

It's easier to start a new command interpreter before calling STARTUP.BAT and leave it, after working with the compiler, by using EXIT. This method automatically restores the previous environment values:

```
COMMAND
STARTUP
```

Here, all of the new environment variables required by the compiler are defined. After working with the compiler, restore the original environment by typing:

```
EXIT
```

Many application programs let you execute one or more DOS commands from within the application program itself. To do this, a command interpreter is run by the application. Usually you can return to the application program by typing EXIT.

COMMAND.COM can be called from within an application in the same way that it is called from the system prompt. After entering EXIT, all the changed environment variables for the command interpreter are restored to their original values.

When a new command interpreter is started from within an application program, there is usually less memory available for programs. At least a part of the application program is occupying memory.

For example, if 550K of memory is available after booting your computer, after starting Microsoft Word 5.5 from DOS only 200K - 250K will be available. This means that only relatively small programs can be run. If a large program is called, an error message will appear.

Starting a command interpreter with a larger environment

If the environment memory isn't large enough, DOS displays an error message when you try to change or set up an environment variable.

```
Out of environment space
```

A new command interpreter can be started with a larger area reserved for environment memory:

```
COMMAND /E:xxxxx
```

For xxxxx, specify the size of the environment memory in bytes (256 default). Values between 160 and 32,768 bytes are acceptable.

 When this command interpreter is terminated by the EXIT command, the original setting for the environment will be effective again.

To permanently change the size of the memory area reserved for the environment variables, insert a line in the CONFIG.SYS file using the SHELL command:

```
SHELL=COMMAND.COM /E:xxxxx
```

Enter the correct path to the command interpreter and choose an appropriate environment size, in bytes, for xxxxx (512 bytes would be appropriate).

Using the command interpreter for a single command

The /C switch can be used to load a command interpreter and run a single command:

```
COMMAND /C Command_line
```

Enter the commands and parameters in place of command_line. DOS starts a new command interpreter, executes the command line and automatically stops and terminates the new, temporary COMMAND.COM command interpreter.

This method is useful for running batch files that change the environment. This is especially useful when the changes need to be cancelled immediately and the default environment restored.

 The /C and /P switches cannot be combined. /C loads the command interpreter for a single command and /P loads COMMAND.COM in memory permanently (can't exit).

13.6 Environment Variables

Each command interpreter contains an environment in a special area of memory. Important information about the working environment and system settings is stored there. Also, user defined variables can be defined in this area.

An environment variable is a basic setting of DOS that can be changed. There are many settings in DOS that either can't be changed or that can only be changed through very complicated procedures. However, the settings stored in environment variables can be adjusted easily by simply changing the variables.

Some variables change the way the system works (system variables). Other variables don't have any direct effect, but can be used by batch files (user defined variables). When using variables in batch files, enclose the variable name within percentage signs.

Displaying environment variables

Use SET to display the existing variables. The individual variables are displayed as:

```
Variable_name=value
```

Depending on the AUTOEXEC.BAT and CONFIG.SYS, most of the following variables are defined and displayed after entering SET:

```
COMSPEC=C:\COMMAND.COM
PATH=C:\DOS
PROMPT=$p$g
```

The first line specifies the path and filename of the command interpreter in case it must be reloaded after running an application. (For example, after exiting from Windows, COMMAND.COM must be reloaded into memory again.) The second line contains the search path for commands and batch files; use PATH to change this line. The third line contains the specification for the system prompt, which can also be changed as explained earlier in this chapter.

Defining and changing environment variables

New variables can be defined and existing variables can be changed by using the SET command.

```
SET Variable_name=value
```

If no values are specified after a variable in the SET command, the existing variable is deleted.

By default, DOS reserves only 256 bytes of memory for environment variables. So you may see the following error message if you're defining or changing several environment variables:

```
Out of environment space
```

One solution to this problem is to start a new command interpreter with a larger environment (/E switch) or change the SHELL statement in the CONFIG.SYS file by adding the /E switch.

SET is also used to change the environment variables for the search path and the system prompt. Using SET has the same effect as changing the variables with PATH and PROMPT.

Example

To set a new search path for commands and batch files that searches the C:\DOS and C:\WORD directories, use the following:

```
SET PATH=C:\DOS;C:\WORD
```

 Only changes in the system variables PATH, APPEND, COMSPEC and PROMPT and the TEMP and DIRCMD variables change the way DOS works. The user defined environment variables don't have any effect on DOS. However, batch files can read and use user defined environment variables.

For example, you can write a batch file that backs up a directory, specified in the environment variable BACKUP, onto diskettes. Use SET to define these environment variables before calling the batch file.

 The environment can't be changed from special user interfaces, such as the Norton Commander®. These types of programs use a copy of the environment. When you exit the program, the original environment is restored.

Special environment variables

The following is a list of several system variables:

PATH   Contains the search path for programs and batch files; DOS looks for programs in the current directory first, then in all the directories specified in the search path. The search path should contain at least the directory for DOS commands.

APPEND   Contains the current search path for data files defined by the APPEND command. If APPEND hasn't been used or the /E switch wasn't used with the APPEND command, the variable is not defined.

PROMPT   Contains the specifications for the system prompt for the command line.

COMSPEC Contains the path and name of the command interpreter in case it must be reloaded after running an application. Some programs also use the system variable COMSPEC to execute DOS commands.

TEMP   Specifies the directory DOS uses to store temporary files. If several commands are linked using filters, the necessary temporary files are stored in the directory specified here. The MS-DOS Shell also creates some temporary files that are stored in this directory.

DIRCMD   Contains the default parameters for the DOS DIR command. The DIR command handles these parameters as if they were entered directly from the keyboard. For example, you can use SET DIRCMD=/P to display the diskette directory one screen page at a time. You should define this environment variable from the AUTOEXEC.BAT file.

The environment variables mentioned above have a special meaning to DOS. Many applications also use environment variables. For example, Word 5.0 sets up temporary files in the WORD directory and in the current directory. If a directory is specified in an environment variable (TMP), WORD stores temporary files in this directory. The user manuals for application programs provide information about possible environment variables.

Unfortunately, some programs (Word 5.0, dBASE IV) use TMP as the variable for the temporary directory, while DOS 6.0 uses the TEMP variable. Both variables can be defined to use the same directory.

13.7 Special System Settings

This section describes three special commands that you can specify to DOS. One defines whether the [Break] key can be used to interrupt or stop commands and batch files during execution. Another specifies whether disk write operations should be verified. The third specifies whether commands should be displayed on the screen.

Switching the break on/off

You can use the [Break] key, or [Ctrl] + [C] (or also [Ctrl] + [Pause]), to interrupt commands when DOS is reading a character oriented device (keyboard) or displaying data (printer).

To use the [Break] key during read or write accesses to hard drives and diskettes (block oriented input/output), the BREAK command must be switched on with the following command:

```
BREAK ON
```

You can switch it off by typing:

```
BREAK OFF
```

Entering BREAK without any other parameters displays the current status. The default setting is OFF.

Usually the break option should be switched on. For example, if you accidentally copy an extensive file, you can abort this process by pressing [Ctrl] + [C] if BREAK is switched on. Many compilers require extensive file operations and can only be interrupted when BREAK is switched on.

However, [Ctrl] + [C] can't be used to interrupt all applications. For example, Microsoft Word 5.0 ignores the [Break] key.

Switching VERIFY on/off

Use the VERIFY command to specify whether or not DOS should check the data after writing it to your hard drive or diskette:

```
VERIFY ON
```

This command line switches on VERIFY. Unfortunately verifying each write access of a device slows down the system. Switch off this option by typing:

```
VERIFY OFF
```

To display the current status on the screen, enter VERIFY without any other parameters. The default setting is OFF.

Switching off ECHO

Use the ECHO command to specify whether or not DOS command lines are displayed from within batch files as they're executed:

```
ECHO ON
```

Enter ECHO ON to display command lines. This option can be switched off by typing:

```
ECHO OFF
```

If ECHO is switched off at the command line, remember that it must be switched on again. If ECHO isn't switched on, the system prompt will no longer be displayed. Entering ECHO without any other parameters displays the current status. The default is ON.

For example, you can easily change the status within the batch file by placing ECHO OFF at the beginning and ECHO ON at the end of a batch file. By doing this, only the messages of the commands that are being processed in the batch file will be displayed on the screen.

This is less complicated than displaying every command line before processing it. However, displaying all the command lines can be helpful when you're trying to find errors in a batch file.

If ECHO is switched off in the first line of the batch file, this line will still be displayed. If you don't want this line displayed, place a "@" symbol in front of the line. This symbol will prevent the line from being displayed.

Remember that ECHO is also used for displaying additional text messages in batch files. So this command has a double meaning.

If ECHO is switched off, you cannot use PROMPT to send any control sequences for the screen or the keyboard to ANSI.SYS. If you want to use this option in batch files, switch on ECHO before the PROMPT instruction and switch it off afterwards.

13.8 Setting the Number of Buffers and Files

The number of read/write buffers and the maximum number of files that can be open simultaneously can be set in the CONFIG.SYS file. By selecting the proper values for these settings, you can increase the performance of DOS. Remember that the changes made to any statement in the CONFIG.SYS file won't take effect until the computer is rebooted.

Setting the read/write buffer

Accessing the data on disk drives and hard drives is time-consuming. The more a drive needs to be accessed, the slower your computer operates. Rather than reading or writing individual bytes of data, the computer works with blocks of information. This information is collected in buffers.

To set the number of buffers, include the following line in the CONFIG.SYS system file:

```
BUFFERS=XX
```

For XX, specify the number of buffers needed. Each of these buffers uses 528 bytes of memory. Of this total, 512 bytes are used to store the data and 16 bytes are used to manage that data. You should specify between 15 and 20 buffers. However, if the directory structure on a hard drive is large, you can specify a larger number of buffers.

If you don't explicitly have a BUFFER statement in the CONFIG.SYS file, DOS reserves a number based on how much memory is available. DOS uses 10 buffers as the default setting for memory between 256K and 511K. If more than 512K of memory is available, DOS reserves 15 buffers.

If you use a cache program, such as SMARTDRV (which is part of MS-DOS 6.0), to speed up access to your hard drive, you must decrease the number of buffers set with BUFFERS. Otherwise, you will not only waste memory, but also reduce the speed of your computer.

Many installation programs for applications change the value of BUFFERS in CONFIG.SYS if the file doesn't contain the desired minimum value.

After installing a program, check whether such a change is really desirable. For example, if you use an acceleration program, such as SMARTDRV.EXE, usually it isn't necessary to increase the value for BUFFERS.

Number of files opened at the same time

For DOS to obtain information from a file or write to it, the file must be open. DOS requires a minimum of five open files and uses 7 as a default value.

Using the default, your applications would only be able to open two files. This usually isn't enough for most applications. Many applications require a series of files to be opened simultaneously.

For example, Microsoft Word 5.0 requires the text file, the style sheet, any glossaries and temporary files to be open at the same time.

To set the number of opened files, use the following line in the CONFIG.SYS:

```
FILES=XX
```

For XX, enter the number of files you want opened simultaneously. You should specify a value between 20 and 30. Each additional file that's specified requires an additional 48 bytes of memory.

  During installation, many application programs check the number specified after FILES and, if necessary, increase it to a larger value. Don't decrease this value; otherwise the application may not function properly.

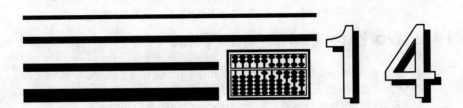

Chapter

Optimizing Data Storage

In this chapter we'll discuss how you can speed up access to storage devices.

14.1 Overview

The following is an overview of the guidelines presented in this chapter.

Speeding up work with files

Before you work with a file, you must open it. This can be a time consuming process, especially with extensive directory structures. By using FASTOPEN, you can speed up this process considerably.

Actively speeding up the hard drive

Use BUFFERS to define the number of buffers for storage device accesses (recommended setting: BUFFERS=20).

MS-DOS 6.0 includes a special cache program called SMARTDRV.EXE.

Passively speeding up the hard drive

You can also speed up access to data by improving the order of or shortening access paths. While this "passive" method doesn't require more memory, you must load an optimizing program at regular intervals.

Creating a RAM disk

Use a RAM disk to speed up your hard drive. To do this, define the RAM disk with: DEVICE=RAMDRIVE.SYS.

Doubling the hard drive capacity

Use DoubleSpace, Stacker or Double Density to increase the size of your hard drive to as much as twice its original size.

14.2 Working Faster with Files

Before working with a file, you must open it. This process can be very time-consuming, especially with large directory structures. FASTOPEN can speed up this process considerably.

Use the following command line to start FASTOPEN:

```
FASTOPEN Drive
```

After you start FASTOPEN, MS-DOS remembers up to 34 files and is able to open these files much faster. Since users ordinarily open more than 34 files, MS-DOS removes the files that haven't been used for the longest time and adds new files. FASTOPEN does this automatically.

The following command line starts FASTOPEN on the C: hard drive:

```
FASTOPEN C:
```

You can call FASTOPEN only once per work session on the PC. To change settings for FASTOPEN, restart the PC.

FASTOPEN works only on hard drives.

Specify the number of files that FASTOPEN remembers and opens when you call the command:

```
FASTOPEN Drive=Number
```

You can specify between 10 and 999 files. Since FASTOPEN requires approximately 48 bytes of memory for each file, don't use values that are too large.

Use the following command line to open up to 100 files quickly on hard drive C:

```
FASTOPEN C:=100
```

FASTOPEN memorizes the location of the files on the hard drive. Therefore, if you use a utility program to organize and optimize the hard drive, you may have problems. Don't run optimizing programs when FASTOPEN is active.

Add the /X switch to FASTOPEN to save all of FASTOPEN's information in expanded memory. This leaves more RAM available for programs.

14.3 Speeding up your Hard Drive Access

Although hard drives are faster than disk drives, extensive loading and memory processes still require a considerable amount of time. Faster hard drives are now available, but they are still expensive.

The basics of speeding up access to the hard drive

Decrease the amount of hard drive accesses...

However, there are also ways to speed up access on slower hard drives. One way is to use the hard drive as little as possible. This may sound strange, but it is actually a powerful method for accelerating the hard drive. To do this, you can use a cache.

...because RAM is faster than the hard drive

The basic concept behind a cache program consists of temporarily storing data, which the hard drive has already read once, in RAM. The next time you need this data, you can access it from RAM, which is much faster than accessing it from the hard drive. If there is no more room in memory and new data must be stored, the cache program makes room in RAM by removing older files, or files that are rarely used, from the cache.

Most cache programs only store information that is being read in RAM. Data is still written to the hard drive. This protects the written data, because the data isn't really safe until it's been saved on the hard drive. A power failure would wipe out everything stored in RAM.

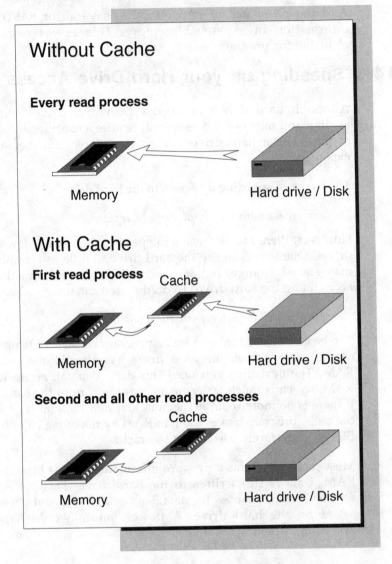

How a cache works

The previous illustration shows how a cache operates and demonstrates the importance of temporarily storing data on a cache.

Without the cache, the computer accesses the hard drive or diskette for every read operation (program or data), which is time-consuming.

With a cache, the first read operation also takes place on the storage device (hard drive or diskette). At the same time, however, the cache program stores the data in the part of RAM reserved for the cache.

The next time, it is no longer necessary to read the same data from the storage device. You can get the information directly from cache RAM, which is much faster.

There are also several other techniques for speeding up access that use the cache principle.

Speeding up access through BUFFERS

MS-DOS already has a built-in capacity for temporary storage. You can add a line (BUFFERS=XX) in the CONFIG.SYS that specifies the number of 512 byte buffers that MS-DOS uses for temporary data storage. If this statement is omitted, MS-DOS selects a value that depends on your PC system. Usually, however, the value MS-DOS selects is too small. For example, it's better to specify BUFFERS=30 for a computer with a 30 Meg hard drive. This change takes effect the next time you boot your PC. You'll notice the difference because your hard drive will be faster.

99 BUFFERS is only 50K

However, BUFFERS has some limitations. For one, the highest amount you can specify for BUFFERS is 99, which is about 50K. Also, the system for replacing older information with information currently being read is not very effective. Special cache programs can greatly improve the effect.

Speeding up access with SMARTDRV

One such cache program is SMARTDRV.SYS, which is included with MS-DOS 6.0. SMARTDRV uses only extended or expanded memory. Unlike BUFFERS, SMARTDRV can do the following:

- SMARTDRV can use extended memory or expanded memory for data storage. For example, an AT with 1 Meg of memory can have a cache of 384K with SMARTDRV, while the program itself only requires 14,064 bytes of RAM. Available RAM is only slightly reduced.

- SMARTDRV uses a clever system to replace older cache contents with new data. With SMARTDRV, the data you need is probably located in the cache.

Use SMARTDRV only if you have extended or expanded memory

The more memory that's available for temporary storage, the more effective the cache program will be. If the PC doesn't use extended or expanded memory, the memory the cache program uses would be taken from main memory. After a while, you wouldn't be able to load large programs. Even a smaller cache can lose some of its speed advantages because memory intensive application programs must move data from RAM to the hard drive. This wouldn't be necessary if all of RAM were available. That's why you can only use SMARTDRV if your computer has extended or expanded memory.

Using a cache in extended memory

Since SMARTDRV is a device driver, you must start the program from the CONFIG.SYS file. To use extended memory for temporarily storing data and programs, simply specify the size of the memory in kilobytes. Use the following line in the CONFIG.SYS file to specify the maximum 384K of extended memory:

```
DEVICE=SMARTDRV.SYS 384
```

If you are using the Extended Memory Manager HIMEM.SYS, you cannot define SMARTDRV until you define HIMEM.SYS. Also, HIMEM.SYS reserves the first 64K of extended memory as High Memory, leaving that much less memory available for extended memory.

Using a cache in expanded memory

To use expanded memory, use the /A switch. Enter the following command line in the CONFIG.SYS to use 256K of expanded memory for temporary data storage:

```
DEVICE=SMARTDRV.SYS 256 /A
```

The SMARTDRV statement in the CONFIG.SYS must follow the expanded memory driver statement. For example, in MS-DOS 6.0, it comes after EMM386.EXE.

 If you're using the EMM386.EXE device driver on an 80386 system to emulate expanded memory, (i.e., converting extended memory into expanded memory), don't assign this memory to SMARTDRV. This unnecessarily slows down access to this memory. Decrease the expanded memory by the value that you want to use for temporary storage, and allocate this amount as extended memory.

For example, suppose that you have 1 Meg of extended memory and want to convert it all to expanded memory. To do this, use the following line in the CONFIG.SYS file:

```
DEVICE=EMM386.EXE 1024
```

Now you want to use 512K for temporary storage with SMARTDRV. Reduce the expanded memory to 512K and use only 512 as a parameter when you use SMARTDRV in the CONFIG.SYS file:

```
DEVICE=EMM386.EXE 512
DEVICE=SMARTDRV.SYS 512
```

This uses 512K of extended memory for temporary storage, and you still have 512K of expanded memory for application programs.

Speeding up access with FASTOPEN

FASTOPEN speeds up access to files and directories significantly. Usually, MS-DOS must search the directory structure of the hard drive every time you access a file or a directory.

FASTOPEN notes the exact position

FASTOPEN remembers the exact location of a file or directory on the storage device, so that you can access it immediately next time. This is especially important for application programs that frequently open and close files. For example, FASTOPEN is valuable for database programs and also word processors. Instead of saving the entire text in RAM, these programs swap it to the hard drive.

To speed up access to files that you access regularly, specify the drive and desired number of files after FASTOPEN:

```
FASTOPEN X:=nnn
```

"X" represents an existing hard drive and "nnn" represents the number of files. For example, to have the program remember up to 50 file positions for the C: hard drive, use the following command line:

```
FASTOPEN C:=50
```

It's best to include the command line in your AUTOEXEC.BAT, so that FASTOPEN is immediately available when you start up your computer.

FASTOPEN requires about 48 bytes for each file it remembers, so that the command line in our example only takes away 2,400 bytes of RAM. If your computer has expanded memory, FASTOPEN can also store the file positions in expanded memory. To use expanded memory, add the /X option to the command line:

```
FASTOPEN C:=50 /X
```

Often files aren't stored contiguously on the hard drive, but consist of several contiguous areas. The FAT, or File Allocation Table contains the information about how the elements of the file go together. However, MS-DOS requires time to redetermine this allocation for each file access.

FASTOPEN can also note entries in the FAT

You can have FASTOPEN remember allocations in the FAT by using the following command line:

```
FASTOPEN X:=(nnn,mmm)
```

"mmm" represents the number of allocations. Possible values for "mmm" range from 1 to 999. Each entry takes up 16 bytes of memory.

For example, to have FASTOPEN remember 50 file positions and 25 allocations on drive C:, use the following command line:

```
FASTOPEN C:=(50,25)
```

Again, if your computer has expanded memory, you can specify the /X switch to relieve RAM.

Practical uses

We've found that FASTOPEN will speed up access only slightly, and you'll hardly notice the effect. However, memory requirements are also slight, since only 2 bytes are required per table entry (for each file to be noted). So the setting FASTOPEN=512 only subtracts 1K of memory.

Here are some guidelines for using FASTOPEN:

- FASTOPEN can only contribute to speeding up the PC system under MS-DOS if programs must frequently open the same files. For example, database programs and compilers work with the same files, so you will achieve a noticeable effect with FASTOPEN only if you make use of such programs intensively.

- FASTOPEN will have a greater effect if you don't use a cache program. Once you start using SMARTDRV for temporary storage of hard drive data, the cache will overshadow the effect of FASTOPEN.

 If necessary, test FASTOPEN on your PC yourself to see what kind of speed advantage FASTOPEN can give you. Measure the time the computer requires for typical activities (e.g., loading a word processor). Then compare the results of running your computer with FASTOPEN=0 in your CONFIG.SYS and with FASTOPEN=2048 in the CONFIG.SYS.

14.4 Hard Drive Management

The utility programs and DOS techniques used to increase the access speed of a hard drive can be divided into two categories:

14.4.1 Active techniques

These techniques change the way the hard drive is accessed. For example, you can use BUFFERS to install several memory buffers or allocate a large memory area as a cache buffer. Also, FASTOPEN can remember the location of files on the disk. So, MS-DOS doesn't have to search for these files the next time they are accessed.

These techniques are active because they need processor time or memory (or both) to increase access speed. So, when these techniques are used, they require system resources.

14.4.2   Passive techniques

Unlike active techniques, passive techniques are applied only once (or in regular intervals) and don't need any system resources (processor time, memory, etc.). Instead, these techniques must be used at regular intervals.

 Passive techniques are activated when the PC isn't being used. So, a convenient time to use them is when you've finished your work and will be leaving your computer for several hours. Instead of switching off your computer, you can activate another program. This is possible because these programs don't require regular user interaction (e.g., changing diskettes, answering prompts) in order to operate.

Improving data storage

The most important passive technique for increasing hard drive speed is improving data storage on your hard drive. The DEFRAG program moves data on the hard drive so that MS-DOS can access the hard drive more quickly. In the following section, we'll explain how DEFRAG does this.

Although the only passive technique we'll describe is DEFRAG, the following are some other ways to speed up hard drive access:

Order through directories

How files are stored on the hard drive can affect a computer's access speed.

- Store as few files as possible in your root directory. Instead, use subdirectories. When MS-DOS must access a file in a directory, it must search through all the preceding entries in that directory. So, if there are 120 entries before the desired file, this process could be very time-consuming.

- However, if a directory contains too many levels (especially five), MS-DOS must search through all the directories to reach the desired subdirectory. Since this is time-consuming, don't add too many levels to your directory.

- When using a new hard drive, it's important to install the directory structure before copying the actual files to the hard drive. This places the subdirectory entries at the beginning of the directories before the actual files. As a result, MS-DOS can find these files more quickly.

- Using properly constructed paths enables MS-DOS to find frequently used commands quickly.

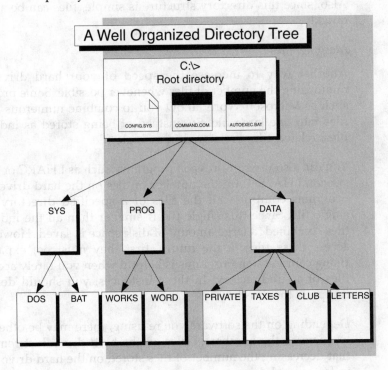

An ideal directory tree

The previous illustration is an example of a well-organized directory structure on a hard drive. The root directory is the base of the entire directory structure, which is available immediately after the hard drive is formatted. You should place only the most important files, such as AUTOEXEC.BAT, CONFIG.SYS, and COMMAND.COM, in the root directory.

This structure also contains three subdirectories. The SYS subdirectory includes subdirectories containing the external commands and programs of the operating system (MSDOS subdirectory) and batch files (BAT directory).

The PROG (programs) subdirectory contains subdirectories for the various application programs (in this example, MS-Word and Works). The next subdirectory is DATA, which contains the data files used by the application programs.

This organization is helpful because the files are arranged according to application. So, you can easily maintain a current copy of the data files by simply backing up the DATA directory. This saves both time and diskettes.

Also, since this directory structure is simple, files can be accessed quickly.

Merging files

Another way to increase the speed of your hard drive is by minimizing the number of files whenever possible. Some programs, such as Microsoft Word, allow you to combine numerous smaller files into one large file. So, instead of being stored as individual files, related files are stored in a single file.

You can also use compression programs, such as LHARC or its new version LHA, to limit the number of files on the hard drive. These programs compress all the files of a specified directory into a single file. Since this single file is smaller than all the individual files combined, a large amount of disk space is saved. However, to access these files in the future, first they must be "expanded". Using compression programs is helpful when you rarely access the files of a subdirectory. In these instances, you should definitely compress the directory.

Depending on the software you're using, there may be other ways to decrease the number of files on the hard drive. Just remember that decreasing the number of files stored on the hard drive results in faster hard drive access.

Setting an optimal interleave

A computer system isn't automatically able to read data from the hard drive at the speed with which the rotating disk passes data by the read/write head.

A typical hard drive (up to 80 Meg) with 17 sectors of 512K each, rotating at 3600 rpm (60 rotations per second), would require the computer to accept 510K of data for each rotation. Since the average PC (such as an AT) is able to process information at only half (or even less) this rate, at least two rotations will be required to read the information on one track. This also affects the sequence in which sectors must be arranged on a track.

If the sectors are arranged in numerical order, the sector following another would pass the read/write head before the hard drive is ready to read this sector. This happens because the information cannot be accepted as quickly as it travels by the head. The hard drive would then have to wait for the entire revolution to be completed before it could read this sector. Although this rotation would take only 0.02 seconds, this is a considerable amount of time for a fast hard drive. This will lead to a noticeable decrease in hard drive speed. So, a special technique, called interleave, is used to read and process data as fast as possible.

With this technique, the sectors are arranged so that the next sector is located at a specific distance from the preceding sector. With an optimal interleave setting, the distance between sectors would be set so that the controller would be ready to process the next data set exactly when the next sector approaches the read/write head.

The number of sectors skipped for every sector processed is determined by the interleave factor. A factor of 1 indicates that the sectors are arranged sequentially without additional sectors in between. So one sector is skipped and one sector is read. An interleave setting of 3 indicates that every third sector is accessed. An interleave factor of 3 will give the controller more time to transfer the data of the sector that was just processed before the next sector arrives at the read/write head.

An interleave setting of 5 or 6 is common for PC/XT's and a setting of 2 or 3 is common for AT's. An interleave setting of 1 can only be managed by 386's, 486's or fast AT's with very fast controllers.

It's very important that the interleave factor is adjusted to the speeds of the computer and the controller. Sometimes fast AT's claim to have a "1:1 controller", which means that the controller operates with an interleave setting of 1. So the sectors are arranged sequentially and can be read and processed immediately.

 Hard drive controllers are also capable of writing one or more sectors between sequential sectors. The more data the controller is capable of writing, the more effectively it will support the computer's data transfers.

A large interleave setting will result in only a slight decrease in speed. This occurs because the hard drive must wait only for an extra sector until the next sector in the sequence can be processed. However, a small interleave setting (e.g., 2 instead of 3) will result in a decrease in speed. This occurs because the next sector to be read will pass the read/write head when the controller is ready for the next operation. The disk will then have to complete an entire revolution before that sector can be accessed.

The interleave setting (the sequence of sectors on a track) is determined during the low level formatting of the disk. Unfortunately it's difficult to change this setting without destroying the data stored on the hard drive. However, some utility programs, such as CALIBRATE in Norton Utilities 5.0, can optimize the interleave without losing the information stored on the hard drive. This is done by reading a track into memory, formatting this track with the new interleave setting, and then rewriting the data to that track until all tracks on the hard drive have been reformatted.

14.4.3   Optimizing data storage

Hard drives become slower as more data is placed on them. The more often data is deleted and new data files are created, the more apparent the problem will become. To understand this completely, you must know more about how MS-DOS stores data on a drive.

If the hard drive is empty, MS-DOS stores data contiguously. This means that MS-DOS writes data on a track of the hard drive until it is full, then starts storing data on the next track.

Since a hard drive usually has at least two disks with two read/write heads each for the top and the bottom, MS-DOS can write on four tracks before the read/write head must be moved. These tracks, which can be processed without moving the heads, are called "cylinders".

On a typical hard drive with 17 sectors per track, you can fit 17 * 512 or 8,704 bytes on a track. So 34,816 bytes can be stored on the four tracks of a cylinder. Since the computer can read or write to a file with 34K without having to move the read/write heads, the process is very fast.

It's ideal if files are distributed consecutively on the disk sectors. When this occurs, the heads don't have to be moved several times, which causes waiting times while the heads "seek" a new position.

Files become "fragmented" during use

Files are constantly being deleted and saved on the hard drive. Even within the same file changes can be made to the text and saved. When a file is deleted, empty regions develop on the hard drive. Later these regions are used again to store data. If the newly saved files are bigger than the amount of free, contiguous space, the file is scattered over different places on the hard drive. When this happens, the file becomes fragmented.

When the computer reads or writes to these files, the head must be moved to new tracks continuously, so that it can read or write other parts of the file. As a result, the performance of the computer is diminished.

This process can be difficult if a hard drive is almost full. In this case, there are only several small areas in which MS-DOS can distribute files. Because of this you should never fill a hard drive to more than 90% of its capacity.

14.5 Using DEFRAG Effectively

MS-DOS 6.0 includes a special defragmenting program called DEFRAG. This program is based on the design of Speed Disk from the Norton Utilities.

DEFRAG has several advantages when compared with other defragmenting programs:

- DEFRAG is tailored to special programs and techniques in MS-DOS 6.0. This includes the cache program SMARTDRV, the hard drive doubler DoubleSpace and other special software. For the user, this means less errors, upward compatibility with future DOS versions and fewer problems.

- DEFRAG is included with MS-DOS 6.0. It's much more expensive to purchase a special defragmenting program from another manufacturer.

However, other defragmenting programs may have more options, execute faster or be more powerful.

Defragmenting requirements

Before using a defragmenting program, you should follow some important guidelines:

- During the execution of a defragmenting program, the data structure of the medium is seriously affected. During this procedure, data loss is possible. So, before defragmenting the hard drive, back up your data.

- The first time you use a defragmenting program, select a complete optimization even though this is time-consuming. Then you can perform a fast optimization regularly.

- The defragmentation can only be performed from the command level (DOS prompt). It cannot be executed from the MS-DOS Shell or from Windows. In Windows, a swap file should be stored before a complete optimization and installed again after the optimization. This is important because this swap file cannot be moved by DEFRAG to another position on the hard drive; this would prevent an effective optimization.

  Also, the swap file must occupy a contiguous area on the hard drive. Many Windows users can create only small swap files, because not enough contiguous hard drive space is available. After the complete optimization, the entire free contiguous area is available and a backup file can be optimally positioned.

Starting DEFRAG

After you start DEFRAG, a new display appears, allowing you to select the drive that must be compressed.

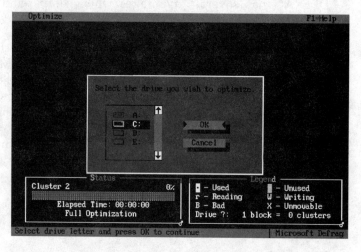

Selecting the drive to be defragmented

Select the desired drive and start the analysis of the drive with [OK]. For each file, DEFRAG determines how seriously it is fragmented. Depending on the computer, this may take a considerable amount of time. During this procedure, the program informs you which directory is currently being processed. When the testing is completed, the amount of fragmentation is represented in percentages. DEFRAG also recommends an optimization method.

If a hard drive hasn't been defragmented recently, DEFRAG recommends a complete defragmentation. Normally, this involves optimizing the storage device.

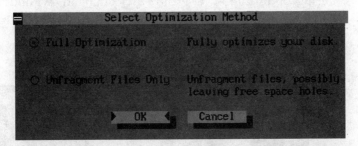

Full optimization or optimizing the storage device

DEFRAG graphically displays the fragmentation information. Do not assume that every cross on the screen represents a cluster, which is a unit of the hard drive. If this were true, the hard drive being displayed would have a capacity of less than 5 Meg. Since there is not enough space on the screen to represent each cluster of a hard drive, several of these units are combined for each cross on the display. What these symbols mean and how many clusters are included under one symbol, are displayed at the bottom of the screen.

Activating the optimization

After selecting the desired optimization method, start the process with **Optimize/Begin optimization** or Alt + B . DEFRAG begins the optimization, starting with the directories. You can easily follow the process on the screen. DEFRAG gathers the fragments of the files and writes them, sorted sequentially, to the beginning of the hard drive.

The progress of the optimization is represented in percentages and as a bar graph in the lower-left corner of the screen. To end the optimization process, press the Esc key. A window appears, allowing you to terminate the process by pressing Enter or continue with Esc .

At the end of the optimization, you'll hear a beep. In the dialog box, you can start the optimization of another drive, change the settings, or quit DEFRAG. You can quit DEFRAG at any time by selecting the **Optimize/Exit** command.

Sorting the files

DEFRAG can determine the sequence of the files in the directories during optimization. Use the DIR command, without a special parameter, to display the files in the indicated sort sequence.

Select the **Optimize/File sort...** command. A window, in which you can determine the sort sequence, appears.

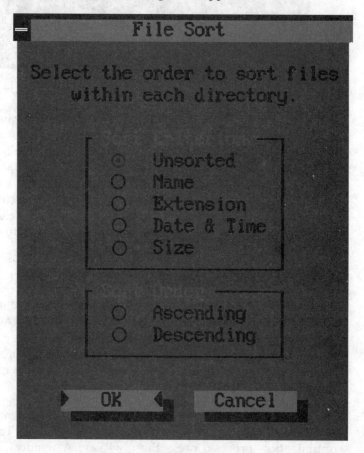

Determining the sort sequence

Determine the sequence of the file entries in the "Sort Order" group. MS-DOS 6.0 can change the position of the elements in a directory; these elements are called directory entries. This term refers to an entry or element in the directory, instead of a subdirectory.

The directory entries of the directories are listed first and the directory entries of the files are listed last. This enables DOS to find subdirectories more quickly. Also, the sequence of the file entries can be determined with the menu.

The sorting doesn't determine how the files are actually stored on the storage device. Instead, it determines the sequence in which they appear in the table of contents. The following possibilities exist:

Unsorted

The directory entries aren't sorted. They remain in the existing sequence. Usually the files are located in the sequence in which they were created.

Name

The directory entries are sorted alphabetically according to names. First to appear are the subdirectories followed by the alphabetically sorted files.

Extension

The directory entries are sorted according to file type (the file extension).

Date & time

The entries are sorted according to the date. The newest files are at the end.

Size

The files are sorted according to size. The smallest file is located at the beginning.

Ascending

The sequence is in ascending order, alphabetical order, numerical order or from the smallest to the largest files.

Descending

The sequence is in the opposite order from the above.

The sort order isn't related to the actual data optimization. The sequence of the file entries can be changed quickly on an optimized medium (for example, sorting according to filename to sorting according to date and time). To do this, MS-DOS 6.0 only must change the directory entries, but not the actual data. A sector with 512 bytes will fit 16 of these directory entries. Therefore, to sort 160 files, only 10 sectors must be read and the sorting of 160 files is changed. The data may be several megabytes for example, if every file is approximately 100K.

 The sorting can also be quickly changed for a non-optimized medium, by setting the desired sorting, starting the sort process and waiting until the first data actually moves on the screen. In the meantime, DEFRAG has already read the directories and sorted them in the desired sequence. Additional optimization can be terminated with (Esc). After the optimization ends, the directories and the desired sequence are restored.

14.6 Creating a RAM Disk

You can "borrow" part of the computer's memory (RAM) and use it as a fast RAM disk drive. To do this, you'll need a special device driver. In MS-DOS this device driver is called RAMDRIVE.SYS. If the driver isn't in the root directory, you must specify the complete path.

 Using PC-DOS, the driver is named VDISK.SYS.

Since a RAM disk is a lot faster than a disk drive or a hard drive, it speeds up many data intensive processes.

But every time you shut off the computer, the data stored in a RAM disk is lost. Remember to save any data stored in a RAM disk onto a diskette or hard drive before switching off the computer. Alternatively you might choose to store only non-changing data on the RAM disk so that data loss does not become a problem.

Special features of a RAM disk

A RAM disk has some advantages and some disadvantages when compared to disk drives and hard drives:

Advantages of a RAM disk

The most important advantage of a RAM disk is the speed with which the computer can access the data. The speed is greater than even the fastest hard drives.

• You can load programs from the RAM disk very quickly. If you use a program frequently, simply copy it to the RAM disk and load it from there.

It's best if you extend the search path by the drive specification of the RAM disk. First, include this in the search path so that you can load programs from the RAM disk.

For example, if D: is the drive letter of your RAM disk and MS-DOS is in the directory C:\DOS of the hard drive, the search path in the AUTOEXEC.BAT might look similar to the following:

```
PATH D:\;C:\DOS
```

• You can retrieve data from a RAM disk faster than from a diskette or hard drive. If you use the same files often, copy them to the RAM disk and always load them from there.

Since the contents of the RAM disk are lost after you switch off the computer or press reset, you shouldn't edit or make changes to data on the RAM disk without saving a copy of the data to a permanent storage device.

• Many programs use temporary files, in which information is stored for a short time. These programs often place the temporary files in a special directory if you define an environment variable (TMP or TEMP) which contains the desired directory.

Setting up a RAM disk and defining it as a directory for temporary files can increase the speed of your programs significantly.

For example, in order for Word 5.0 or 5.5 to place all of its temporary files on RAM disk D:, type the following command line before calling Word 5.0:

```
SET TMP=D:\
```

It's best to include this line, which sets the TMP environment variable, in the AUTOEXEC.BAT file.

• If your PC doesn't have a hard drive, you can copy the command interpreter and the most important external commands to a RAM disk. By doing this, you won't have to insert an MS-DOS diskette several times. You should set this up to run automatically in the AUTOEXEC.BAT file.

You should also include the special system variable COMSPEC for the new command interpreter in the RAM disk so that MS-DOS knows where it can load the command interpreter. For example, if drive D: is the RAM disk, define the environment variable COMSPEC with the following command line:

```
SET COMSPEC=D:\COMMAND.COM
```

Disadvantages of a RAM disk

The biggest disadvantage of a RAM disk is that the data is stored in the memory of the computer (RAM):

- Switching off the computer, using the reset button, performing a warm boot with Ctrl + Alt + Del , power failures and serious program errors all cause the data in the RAM disk to be lost forever. So it's very dangerous to edit and make changes to data in the RAM disk. It's safer to store data, which is also stored on a diskette or hard drive, to the RAM disk.

- Since the RAM disk is completely empty every time you reboot, first you must copy data or programs to the RAM disk. That's why you should place data, that you frequently use, on the RAM disk.

- If your computer doesn't have extended or expanded memory, the memory for the RAM disk is reduced to the available conventional memory. A RAM disk with 256K of memory (a lot less than the capacity of a 360K diskette) won't provide enough storage for extensive application programs.

  Reserve a maximum of 128K of memory for the RAM disk on PCs that don't have extended or expanded memory. Even with this amount of memory you can still have problems. If your computer has a hard drive, but not extended or expanded memory, use the hard drive instead of a RAM disk.

Alternatives to a RAM disk

Cache programs are an alternative to the RAM disk. They also use part of the main memory for storing data but don't function like a disk drive.

A cache program consists of taking information, that's already read, from the disk drive and temporarily storing it in the memory. Then if the information is needed again, it is taken from RAM, which is much faster than the hard drive. When the reserved amount of memory for the cache is filled and more information needs to be stored, available space must be made in the cache.

Using a cache has two distinct advantages over using a RAM disk:

- Unlike a RAM disk, you don't have to copy the data to memory before it's used. The cache program does this automatically the first time it retrieves the data from the hard drive.

- The cache program determines which data will be stored temporarily in the main memory. You must make this decision when using a RAM disk. For example, it isn't very useful to place the MS-DOS FORMAT command in the RAM disk when you use the DISKCOPY command more often. However, the cache program would notice this and automatically store the DISKCOPY command in RAM.

Creating a RAM disk with standard default

Remember to install the software for memory extension before the RAM disk. Since you ordinarily do this by calling the appropriate driver program in the CONFIG.SYS file, call the driver for the memory before defining the RAM disk.

Insert the following line in the CONFIG.SYS of your system diskette or hard drive:

```
DEVICE=C:\DOS\RAMDRIVE.SYS
```

  Remember to include the complete search path for your system.

The next time you start your PC you'll have a new drive, which has a capacity of 64K and can contain 64 files or directories. When you start your PC, the screen displays this information.

Creating a RAM disk with special defaults

When you define the RAM disk, you can set the capacity, the size of the sector and the number of possible entries. To do this, use additional parameters when defining the RAM disk in the CONFIG.SYS:

```
DEVICE=C:\DOS\RAMDRIVE.SYS disksize sectorsize entries
```

Disksize   Specifies the size of the RAM disk in K. The default size is 64K; 16K is the minimum size.

Sectorsize

> Here you specify the least amount of space a file occupies. Larger files always take up a multiple of this sector size. Possible values are 128, 256, 512 and 1024. The RAM disk has a default sector size of 512 bytes.

Entries

> Determines the number of files and/or directories that you can put on the RAM disk (4 to 1024). The default value is 64. RAMDRIVE.SYS automatically adapts this value to the sector size.

Placing a RAM disk in extended memory

A RAM disk can use extended memory. This enlarges the available main memory considerably.

RAM disk in extended memory

To use extended memory for storage, specify /E as your additional switch. The line in the CONFIG.SYS file is as follows:

```
DEVICE=C:\DOS\RAMDRIVE.SYS disksize sectorsize entries
/E
```

To use the 384K extended memory available on an AT with 1 Meg for the RAM disk and to have sector size and file entries work with default values, use the following line in the CONFIG.SYS file:

```
DEVICE=C:\DOS\RAMDRIVE.SYS 384 /E
```

Remember to install the software for memory extension before the RAM disk. Since you ordinarily do this by calling the appropriate driver program in the CONFIG.SYS file, call the driver for the memory before defining the RAM disk.

Define the RAM disk in the CONFIG.SYS file before other driver programs. The drivers EMM386.SYS and HIMEM.SYS are exceptions to this rule. EMM386.SYS allows you to use the extended memory in a 386 as expanded memory. HIMEM.SYS allows you to use extended memory in ATs as XMS memory and makes high memory (special memory area) available. Both of these drivers must be installed before the RAM disk.

☞ The new RAM disk driver RAMDRIVE.SYS, which is included with MS-DOS 6.0, follows the rules for extended memory (XMS specification) so that you can use it only if you install HIMEM.SYS beforehand.

As soon as you install HIMEM.SYS, the program automatically reserves 64K of memory for high memory. This area is no longer available to the RAM disk. On a computer with 1 Meg memory (384K extended memory), you would only have 324K available for the RAM disk.

RAM disk in expanded memory

You can also use expanded memory that conforms to the LIM 4.0 specification for the RAM disk. Use /A as your switch.

To use 1 Meg (1024K) of existing expanded memory for the RAM disk and work with default values for the sector size and the file entries, type the following line in the CONFIG.SYS:

```
DEVICE=C:\DOS\RAMDRIVE.SYS 1024 /A
```

 You cannot place a RAM disk in the expanded memory of the VDISK.SYS (PC-DOS).

Removing the RAM disk

To remove a RAM disk, delete the command line from CONFIG.SYS and reboot the computer. A RAM disk can't be removed without rebooting the computer.

14.7 MS-DOS Internals

Since this section is for the more advanced user, feel free to skip it and come back to it at a later time.

Basically, MS-DOS manages storage devices using block driver programs that can read or write a block of data at a time. This is why MS-DOS also arranges storage devices into blocks (sectors or clusters).

A storage device is set up in the following order:

```
Boot sector
FAT
Root directory
Actual data
```

Structure of storage devices

Diskettes are simply flexible plates (disks) that are coated with a magnetic material. When MS-DOS prepares (formats) a diskette, it divides the diskette into tracks and sectors.

Tracks and sectors

Let's use a 360K, 5.25 inch diskette as an example. Computers can't simply write on the diskette. If they did this, they would have trouble finding and recognizing information that belongs together. So, a diskette is divided into tracks. The computer numbers the tracks consecutively, which results in a specific arrangement.

This arrangement isn't flexible, since it allows you to write only 40 different groups of data in the 40 tracks.

The tracks are further divided into blocks (9 blocks on a 360K diskette) called sectors. Using this arrangement and a few additional pieces of information, MS-DOS can store 512 characters in one of these blocks. This would appear to be the minimum size for storing information as a unit. Since there are 40 tracks with 9 sectors on each side of the diskette, there are a total of 720 sectors numbered from 0 to 719.

But MS-DOS, instead uses two sectors. This unit of allocation is called a cluster. So, for a 360K diskette, one cluster refers to two sectors or 1024 characters. The reason for this is that when MS-DOS was introduced, diskettes were only single sided (180K) and contained 360 sectors. So, the management information on the diskette was only set up for 360 elements.

When the capacity was doubled to 360K, only the old space was reserved for the management information in order to remain compatible with older versions of DOS. Two sectors were integrated into one unit, called a cluster. A file always uses at least one cluster. Also, a file containing a single character uses 1024 bytes on a 360K diskette. This problem wasn't resolved until 1.2 Meg diskettes were developed. MS-DOS reserves more room for managing information on 1.2 Meg diskettes, which have clusters containing only one sector with 512 bytes.

Division into boot block, FAT and directory

Besides the data, a diskette contains a couple of special areas for managing this stored information.

Table of contents directory

MS-DOS always stores data on a diskette as a file. You can then refer to this data by its filename. To do this, MS-DOS must save information about each file. This is done in the disk directory, which is a collection of sectors reserved for managing files.

For each file in the directory, MS-DOS stores the name, creation date and time, the size of the file and the location of the first sector of data on the diskette.

The directory of a 360K diskette starts at the fifth sector. A small section of this directory would look like the following:

```
No      contents as hexadecimal numbers        character representation
-----------------------------------------------------------------------
0000   49 4F 20 20 20 20 20 20 53 59 53 27 00 00 00 00  IO           SYS
0016   00 00 00 00 00 00 00 18 81 15 02 00 BE 82 00 00
0032   4D 53 44 4F 53 20 20 20 53 59 53 27 00 00 00 00  MSDOS     SYS
0048   00 00 00 00 00 00 00 18 81 15 23 00 10 92 00 00
0064   43 4F 4D 4D 41 4E 44 20 43 4F 4D 20 00 00 00 00  COMMAND COM
0080   00 00 00 00 00 00 00 18 C7 15 48 00 4B A0 00 00
```

Notice that each entry for a file contains 32 bytes, which requires two printed lines. The first 11 bytes contain the filename (8 bytes) and the extension (3 bytes), without the period between the name and the extension. This results in the following structure for a file entry:

Byte	Length	Description
00-07	8	filename, padded with spaces
08-10	3	extension, padded with spaces
11	1	attribute, special features of a file
12-21	10	reserved
22-23	2	time of creation or last change
24-25	2	date of creation or last change
26-27	2	location of first cluster of file data
28-31	4	size of the file

When the computer stores numbers, the lower value digits are on the left, while the higher value digits are on the right (exactly the opposite of our decimal system). The last four bytes of the file size under IO.SYS "BE 82 00 00" correspond to "00 00 82 BE" in hexadecimal notation. Converted to our decimal system they read 33470. Attributes, date and time are even more complicated in their structure.

If you want to examine the directory of a 360K diskette, use a utility program such as PC Tools or Norton Utilities, or use the MS-DOS DEBUG command. Insert the 360K diskette into drive A: and make drive A: the current drive. After starting DEBUG, type the following command lines:

```
L 0100 0 5 1
D 0100
```

This instructs DEBUG to load the fifth sector into the memory and display it on the screen. Press Q and Enter to exit DEBUG.

FAT

In addition to a directory, two additional pieces of information are required to manage the data of a diskette: which sectors belong to a file and which sectors are still unused. This information is maintained in the File Allocation Table (FAT), which is where the storage units of a diskette are assigned to a file.

The FAT of a 360K diskette begins at sector 1, which is the second sector (start counting at 0), and is two sectors (1024 bytes) long. A section from the beginning of the FAT would look like the following:

```
0000   FD FF FF 03 40 00 05 60 00 07 80 00 09 A0 00 0B
0016   C0 00 0D E0 00 0F 00 01 11 20 01 13 40 01 15 60
0032   01 17 F0 FF 19 A0 01 1B C0 01 1D E0 01 1F 00 02
0048   21 20 02 23 40 02 25 60 02 27 80 02 29 A0 02 2B
0064   C0 02 2D E0 02 2F 00 03 31 20 03 33 40 03 35 F0
0080   FF 37 80 03 39 A0 03 3B C0 03 3D E0 03 3F 00 04
0096   41 20 04 43 40 04 45 60 04 47 80 04 49 A0 04 4B
0112   C0 04 4D E0 04 4F F0 FF 00 00 00 00 00 00 00 00
```

We didn't list the characters that would be displayed on the right side of the screen. These are nonsense characters that have no real significance. The filenames are not stored there.

To display the beginning of the FAT of a 360K diskette, use the MS-DOS DEBUG command with the following command lines:

```
L 0100 0 1 1
D 0100
```

It's difficult to interpret the FAT. On diskettes, not one or two bytes, but 1.5 bytes contain information (12 bits, 1 byte = 8 bits). The first line of our sample display consists of the following entries:

```
0000   FDF FFF 034 000 056 000 078 000 09A 000 0BC
```

The first entry (No. 0), with the hexadecimal value FDF, labels the diskette as a 5.25 inch diskette with two sides, 40 tracks per side and 9 sectors per track (360K). An AT diskette with 80 tracks per side and 15 sectors per track (1.2 Meg) would have the hexadecimal value of F9F. This information is also called the media descriptor. A value describes the medium being used. The second entry (No. 1) is reserved and always contains the value FFF.

The subsequent entries label the clusters where the data is filed. Let's return to the structure of a file entry in the table of contents directory. Bytes 26 to 27 specified the first cluster of the file. For the IO.SYS file entry, both bytes had "02 00" (the value 2). The file data begins with cluster number 2 (sector no. 12, the first sector after the table of contents directory).

Cluster 2 always contains the number of the cluster where the file continues. You cannot use this number as a 12 bit value (1.5 bytes) because MS-DOS files the values differently. In our example, the value seems to be 34 (hex) but it's actually 003 (the third cluster). The previous line should look as follows:

```
0000   FDF FFF 003 004 005 006 007 008 009 00A 00B
```

We're not really interested in where the data is located, since MS-DOS looks for the clusters that we use when we edit a file. You can use special utility programs, such as Norton Utilities, so that you don't have to convert the 12 bit values. Norton Utilities has a special FAT Editor. So whenever you try to display a sector of the FAT, the FAT Editor automatically shows the numbers correctly. The end of a file is marked as <EOF>.

```
   Object     Edit     Link     View     Info     Tools     Quit    F1=Help
Sector 1                                                                    ↑
      1         2       \3        4        5        6         7         8
      9        10       11       12       13       14        15        16
     17        18       19       20       21       22        23        24
     25        26       27       28       29       30        31        32
     33        34       35       36       37       38        39        40
     41        42       43       44       45       46        47        48
     49        50       51       52       53       54        55      <EOF>
     57        58       59       60       61       62        63        64
     65        66       67       68       69       70        71        72
     73        74       75       76       77       78        79        80
     81        82       83       84       85       86        87        88
     89        90       91       92       93       94        95        96
     97        98       99      100      101      102       103       104
    105       106      107      108      109      110       111       112
    113       114      115      116      117      118       119       120
    121       122      123      124      125      126       127       128
    129       130      131      132      133      134       135       136
    137       138      139     <EOF>     141      142       143       144
    145       146      147      148      149      150       151       152
    153       154      155      156     <EOF>      0         0         0    ↓
  FAT (1st Copy)                                                    Sector 1 -
  A:\BTPLUS2.DOC                                              Cluster 2, hex 2
  Press ALT or F10 to select menus                              | Disk Editor
```

FAT Editor of Norton Utilities

Instead of providing the next data portion of a file, some cluster values describe different special conditions:

000   Cluster is free

FF0 - FF6   Reserved cluster

FF7   Cluster is defective and cannot be used

FF8-FFF   Last cluster of a file <EOF>

The example we've been using is for a 360K diskette, which automatically has a FAT with 12 bit values (1.5 bytes or 12 bit FAT). On hard drives, the FAT usually contains 16 bit entries and a cluster may be composed of 4 or even 8 sectors.

The directory of a diskette has a file entry for each file with the number of the first cluster of the file. This allows MS-DOS to read the first two sectors (on a 360K diskette) directly. To find other data on the diskette, MS-DOS follows the "linkage" within the FAT until a cluster number between FF8 and FFF signifies the end of the file.

It's obvious that the directory and the FAT play a significant role in working with files. If there are problems, you can no longer work with the data of the diskette. Because of this, MS-DOS even places a copy of the FAT on the diskette. This copy follows the first FAT in sectors 3 and 4.

The boot block

The first sector of every diskette is important. This sector is called the boot block or boot sector. Booting refers to the processes that take place immediately after you switch on the computer. The boot block contains information for this booting process.

The boot block contains much more information than its name indicates. It has important details about the division of the diskette and the format of the diskette. This information enables MS-DOS to determine at which data capacity to prepare the diskette.

To display the boot sector of a diskette, use the MS-DOS DEBUG command with the following:

```
L 0100 0 0 1
D 0100
```

A section from the boot sector would look similar to the following:

```
0000   EB 3C 90 4D 53 44 4F 53 35 2E 30 00 02 02 01 00      MSDOS6.0
0016   02 70 00 D0 02 FD 02 00 09 00 02 00 00 00 00 00
0032   00 00 00 00 00 00 29 E0 11 20 31 41 52 42 45 49             WORK
0048   54 44 49 53 4B 20 46 41 54 31 32 20 20 20 FA 33   DISK FAT12   •
0064   C0 8E D0 BC 00 7C 16 07 BB 78 00 36 C5 37 1E 56
0080   16 53 BF 3E 7C B9 0B 00 FC F3 A4 06 1F C6 45 FE
0096   0F 8B 0E 18 7C 88 4D F9 89 47 02 C7 07 3E 7C FB
0112   CD 13 72 79 33 C0 39 06 13 7C 74 08 8B 0E 13 7C
0128   89 0E 20 7C A0 10 7C F7 26 16 7C 03 06 1C 7C 13
```

Beginning at position 3 (starting at 0), you can clearly recognize the name and version number of MS-DOS 6.0. The other areas of the boot sector usually contain the following text:

```
Non-System diskette or disk error
Replace and press any key when ready
IO      SYSMSDOS  SYS
```

It's interesting that there is a command at the beginning of the boot sector (in the first three bytes) to run a program that starts at a later position. In our example, this program begins at position 013E (hex). It loads both of the hidden system files (in our example IO.SYS and MSDOS.SYS) and in so doing, starts MS-DOS 6.0. The names of both files are in part of the boot sector.

There is important information about the storage device in the boot sector from position 0B to 1D (hex). For example, position 0B (decimal 11) provides the number of bytes per sector. In our example, it is "00 02" or 0200 (hex), which means 512 bytes per sector.

The boot block also contains the volume label of the storage device and the volume serial number. The volume serial number is located at 27-2A (hex, decimal 39 - 42) and is filed beginning with the lowest digits. So the number sequence "E0 11 20 31" must be turned around to get the volume number: 3120-11E0.

Position 15 (hex, decimal 21) contains the media descriptor, which describes the type of storage device. Our example has FD, which labels the storage device as a 5.25 inch diskette with 360K.

When you insert a 360K diskette into a 1.2 Meg disk drive on an AT, MS-DOS immediately recognizes, from the information in the boot sector, how the diskette was formatted and processes the data accordingly.

System information of different diskettes

In our examples we chose 5.25 inch diskettes with 360K capacity. If you want to look at the system information for diskettes with different capacities, you need to know the right sectors:

	360K	1.2 Meg	720K	1.44 Meg
Boot sector	0	0	0	0
FAT	1	1	1	1
Root directory	5	15	7	19

After calling DEBUG, load a sector into the memory with the following command line:

```
L address disk_drive start_sector number
```

For example, if you specify 0100 for the address, you can look at the data by typing:

```
D 0100
```

For disk drives, specify 0 for drive A: and 1 for drive B:. For your starting sector, specify the desired sector on the diskette, using the values from the table above. For number you can also enter a value larger than 1; then the program loads several sectors into the memory, one after the other.

☞   To exit DEBUG simply type Q Enter at the prompt.

What happens when you format a diskette

The division of the diskette into tracks and sectors and the management information (directory, FAT and boot block) are created during FORMAT. That's why you can't use a new diskette until it has been formatted.

During this formatting MS-DOS checks the diskette for defective areas and excludes them from data storage. (The clusters belonging to these defective areas are labeled FF7: Cluster is defective and excluded from use.)

This is why there is a difference between the amount of data that will fit on a diskette and the total capacity. The screen automatically displays this information after the formatting process or you can display this information by using the CHKDSK command. If the diskette contains defective regions, they will be documented.

When you use FORMAT to format a diskette, the command writes new, empty sectors to the diskette. That's why any information previously stored is lost when you format.

Differences in various disk drives

Since MS-DOS uses different kinds of management information, when formatting diskettes you must specify the various disk drive types and capacities.

360K disk drive (5.25 inch)

When you format a 360K diskette, it is divided into 40 tracks on each side. Each track is subdivided into 9 blocks (sectors). MS-DOS can file 512 bytes (characters) in one of these sectors. Multiplying 40 tracks * 9 sectors * 512 characters *2 sides results in 368,640 characters. Since one K contains 1,024 bytes, you have 360K storage capacity.

This diskette contains 720 sectors and 360 clusters. After subtracting the management information (boot sector, FAT and directory), you still have 354 clusters available for data storage. So a 360K diskette can store a maximum of 354 files.

The root directory is 7 sectors long and since each sector can contain 16 file entries with 32 bytes, there is a maximum of 112 files in the root directory. Because they are placed in the root directory as special file entries, the subdirectories and the name of the storage device are included.

1.2 Meg disk drive (5.25 inch)

1.2 Meg disk drives can store more than three times as much as a 360K diskette. Each side of the diskette is divided into 80 tracks and 15 sectors. You need special diskettes, called DSHD (double sided, high density).

A 1.2 Meg diskette contains a total of 2,400 sectors and 2,400 clusters. It has 2,400 clusters because each cluster has 512 bytes due to the expanded FAT (7 sectors instead of 2). After subtracting the management information (boot sector, FAT and directory), there are still 2,371 clusters available for data storage. A 1.2 Meg diskette has a root directory with 14 sectors (twice as many as a 360K diskette) and has room for 224 files in the root directory.

When reading and writing data, the disk drive can determine what kind of a diskette has been inserted by checking the media descriptor in the boot sector of the diskette. This media descriptor contains exact information about the capacity of the diskette. When formatting a diskette, a 1.2 Meg disk drive always formats diskettes with the highest possible capacity (1.2 Meg). However, you can use special parameters with the FORMAT command to change this.

720K disk drive (3.5 inch)

The 720K capacity of a 3.5 inch diskette with double density is a result of having twice as many tracks written as a 360K diskette (80 instead of 40). It has the same number of sectors (9) as a 360K diskette. A 720K diskette contains 3 sectors per FAT and 2 sectors per cluster. Out of 720 clusters, you can use 713 clusters for data storage. Since the root directory contains 7 sectors, you can have a maximum of 112 entries (files or subdirectories) in the root directory.

1.44 Meg disk drive (3.5 inch)

The higher storage capacity of a 1.44 Meg disk drive results from having 18 sectors per track. If we multiply 80 tracks * 18 sectors * 512 bytes * 2 sides, the result is 1,474,560 bytes = 1.44 Meg. Similar to 1.2 Meg diskettes, a cluster contains one sector with 512 bytes. There are a total of 2,880 clusters with 2,847 clusters available for data storage; MS-DOS requires the rest for management. The root directory consists of 14 sectors and can contain 14 * 16 =224 files.

These disk drives are similar to 1.2 Meg disk drives. You can operate them with high capacity and you can also edit 720K diskettes. By the media descriptor in the boot block, MS-DOS can tell which capacity the diskette was formatted for and treats it accordingly.

2.88 Meg disk drive (3.5 inch)

These new diskettes can store 2.88 Meg of data. Once again, the higher memory capacity is a result of doubling the number of sectors per track. The diskettes manage 36 sectors per track. Similar to 1.2 Meg or 1.44 Meg diskettes, a cluster contains one sector with 512 bytes.

Formatting diskettes as system diskettes

When you add the /S switch to the MS-DOS FORMAT command, MS-DOS automatically copies the operating system to the new diskette. The operating system consists of two hidden files and the command interpreter COMMAND.COM. In MS-DOS these hidden files are called IO.SYS and MSDOS.SYS and in PC-DOS by IBM they appear under different names.

You can start your PC using this system diskette. To boot your computer from a system diskette, place the diskette in drive A: and close the drive lever.

Remember that simply copying the hidden files to a diskette won't make it a system diskette. There are two crucial requirements:

- Both the IO.SYS and MSDOS.SYS files must be the first two files in the root directory of the diskette.

- Both files must be located in the first clusters of the storage device.

Leaving room for the system

If the /B switch is used when formatting a diskette, MS-DOS reserves room for the system. Then you can copy the system to the diskette with the MS-DOS SYS command. In this procedure, the FORMAT command creates two files with the correct names and sizes. This reserves, on the diskette, the amount of space necessary for the system. MS-DOS 6.0 creates an IO.SYS file with approximately 35,000 bytes and an MSDOS.SYS file with 37,000 bytes. Then the SYS command replaces these files with files of the same name containing the correct contents.

Diskette volume label and volume serial number

After formatting a diskette, you can specify a volume label for the storage device. You can also do this later with the LABEL command. The volume label of a storage device is stored in almost the same way as a filename. The root directory of a diskette looks like the following:

```
0000  49 4F 20 20 20 20 20 20 53 59 53 26 00 00 00 00  IO       SYS
0016  00 00 00 00 00 00 64 56 35 15 02 00 B8 88 00 00
0032  4D 53 44 4F 53 20 20 20 53 59 53 26 00 00 00 00  MSDOS    SYS
0048  00 00 00 00 00 00 65 56 35 15 47 00 88 90 00 00
0064  41 52 42 45 49 54 53 44 49 53 4B 28 00 00 00 00  WORKDISK
0080  00 00 00 00 00 00 81 58 35 15 00 00 00 00 00 00
```

You can see that the label of the diskette (in our example WORKDISK) is filed similar to the two system files, except that the filename and its extension aren't separated.

MS-DOS must be able to distinguish a filename from the diskette name. It can distinguish the two by using the attribute, beginning at position 11, in the file entry. For the first two file entries the value is 26 (hex). The diskette name has an attribute of 28. The attribute byte consists of 8 bits, 6 of which are used to identify different file entries:

Bit 0 = 1   File is write protected.

Bit 1 = 1   File is hidden, not usually displayed.

Bit 2 = 1   System file.

Bit 3 = 1   This entry is the name of the storage device.

Bit 4 = 1   This entry is not a file, but a subdirectory.

Bit 5 = 1   This file has been changed since the last backup.

If you break both attributes down according to this system, you get the following result:

Hex	Bit 5	Bit 4	Bit 3	Bit 2	Bit 1	Bit 0
26	1	0	0	1	1	0
28	1	0	1	0	0	0

The first two files have been changed since the last backup. They are hidden and labeled as system files. The third entry has also been changed and it's marked as a storage device name.

14.8 Increasing Hard Drive Capacity with DoubleSpace

Not long ago, AT systems were equipped with 20 Meg hard drives. Computers with 40 Meg hard drives were considered to be well-equipped for the future.

However, because of the success of the Windows user interface and other factors, these standards have changed. A fully equipped Windows system with some application programs requires about 20 Meg of hard drive storage capacity. If graphic data is also stored, the remaining 20 Meg are quickly filled.

In many cases, a second hard drive may be interfaced to the existing hard drive controller. This is not only expensive, but also the additional hard drive capacity is available only under a new drive letter (perhaps D:). Since MS-DOS Version 4.0, many DOS users no longer use partitioning.

Warning: Use DoubleSpace carefully

Be extremely careful when using compressed hard drives because data loss is possible. Do not select extreme settings during the creation of DoubleSpace. For example, don't try to compress a 100 Meg hard drive so that 95 Meg remain free.

 If you're working with a compressed hard drive, you should have a bootable system diskette available. This diskette should contain all the programs and drivers needed by the computer. You must store important data before compressing your hard drive.

An Overview of DoubleSpace

You've probably heard of the data compression programs LHARC, PKZIP or PKARC. Similar to DoubleSpace, these programs also pack files. However, these files must be unpacked before they can be used.

DoubleSpace is an on-line compression program. This means that the data on the hard drive are available in stored form. If they are needed in the working memory, they are unpacked directly. When the data is stored again on the hard drive, DoubleSpace packs them automatically again. DoubleSpace automatically packs and unpacks files by using the special device driver DBLSPACE.BIN.

DoubleSpace consists of several components. An installation program called DBLSPACE.EXE is used for the administration of the packed data. A driver called DBLSPACE.BIN packs/unpacks the data. This driver isn't started in the CONFIG.SYS file or in the AUTOEXEC.BAT file. DoubleSpace also contains a special device driver, DBLSPACE.SYS, which can be optionally started. This driver is used only for the special control of the storage administration; it doesn't have any other functions.

Before you can use the "expanded" hard drive, the hard drive must be converted from the unpacked to the packed condition. Use the DBLSPACE.BIN program to do this.

DoubleSpace and MS-DOS 6.0

DoubleSpace is important in MS-DOS 6.0 because data compression is now an integral part of MS-DOS. This offers the following advantages:

- Several problems, such as double system files on two drives or having to work with an unpacked boot partition and a packed partition, are prevented.

- DoubleSpace operates without problems because of special utilities, such as DEFRAG, SMARTDRV and DoubleSpace drives. Also, the security of the data stored in compressed form increases when the compression is standard.

- The compression standard set by Microsoft has also benefited other areas. For example, the new backup program uses this technology for compressing the backup data. This reduces the number of files needed. Soon incompatibility between various compression methods may no longer exist.

DoubleSpace Requirements

Before installing DoubleSpace on the hard drive, some requirements must be fulfilled.

Compressing a hard drive is a relatively fast and simple process. Although DoubleSpace drives can be removed, all data will be deleted. So, you must perform a complete backup. Later, this backup must be transferred to the decompressed hard drive.

- You must have a complete current backup of the data on the hard drive. This is important because if a problem occurs during the compression, you can remove the DoubleSpace drive and restore the data to the hard drive.

  Usually a compression that was interrupted by an error can be continued later without problems or data loss.

- If you use programs that can be installed only once on the hard drive and must be de-installed again, you should de-install these programs before the compression and install them again on the hard drive after the DoubleSpace drive is created.

- If you're working with Windows and have created a swap file, you must remove this file before the compression. If you're not sure whether a swap file exists, start the Windows Control Panel from the "Main" group of Windows, select **Settings/386 Enhanced...** and click the [Virtual Memory...] button.

  During the compression of the hard drive, you should also reserve an area large enough for a Windows swap file, if you want to install it permanently. This is important because this file must be located in an area that is decompressed.

- Before the compression, test the hard drive with the CHKDSK command. If this command reports errors, remove them with the /F Parameter and then test the hard drive again. The compression will be successful only on a hard drive that doesn't contain errors.

- The drive that will be compressed must have at least 1.5 Meg of free hard drive capacity. If this isn't possible, you must store data or programs on diskettes and then delete them from the hard drive in order to obtain sufficient free space for the compression. After the DoubleSpace drive is created, you should have enough space to copy the stored files back to the hard drive. The data that's copied later on the hard drive will also be compressed automatically.

- When the compression is activated, other programs, such as the MS-DOS Shell or Windows, cannot be active.

If you're using SMARTDRV as a cache program and the number of the DOS buffers BUFFERS in the CONFIG.SYS was set to a small value (3-5), you should set a higher value temporarily for the optimization. This is important because DBLSPACE performs a new start during the compression; during this time the AUTOEXEC.BAT file isn't executed. Then you would perform a compression without SMARTDRV and with a few buffers, which puts a strain on the hard drive. This lengthens the compression process and causes the hard drive to make noise.

After the hard drive is compressed, MS-DOS 6.0 can no longer be de-installed with UNINSTALL. This means that you can no longer use earlier DOS versions, which may still be available. For this reason, a compression should be performed only after MS-DOS 6.0 can remain securely on the hard drive without, for example, encountering compatibility problems with existing software.

After a compression, operating systems, such as DR DOS or PC-DOS, can no longer access the data on the hard drive. If, for some reason, you occasionally want to boot with another operating system's version from a diskette and use the hard drive data, you shouldn't use DoubleSpace.

On a hard drive compressed with DoubleSpace, all commands and tools of MS-DOS 6.0 can be used without limitations. The hard drive and its data can be checked with CHKDSK, or the arrangement of the data can be optimized with DEFRAG to accelerate the reading or writing of the data.

Performing the compression

Once these conditions have been met, you can start the hard drive compression by activating DoubleSpace. After the call, the program displays the following:

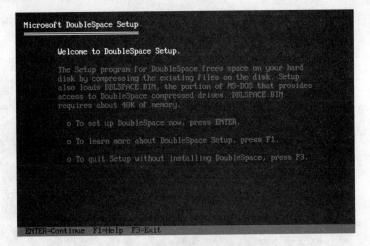

Starting DBLSPACE

The program informs you that you can access compressed drives with DoubleSpace and that it requires about 43K. You can continue the installation with (Enter), get help by pressing (F1) or exit by pressing (F3).

Under certain circumstances, DoubleSpace displays a warning message, indicating that your computer uses software that may not be compatible with DoubleSpace. You should end by clicking the (Exit) button or pressing the (E) key. First read the README.TXT file, which lists all systems that may be incompatible and suggests possible solutions. You can display this file with TYPE README.TXT, or load it into the MS-DOS Editor with EDIT README.TXT.

This message also appears if you're using an older version of SMARTDRIV, perhaps from Windows, instead of the SMARTDRV cache included with MS-DOS 6.0. The Windows 3.1 version isn't suitable for DoubleSpace. You can easily test the version of SMARTDRV by using the following command line:

```
SMARTDRV /S
```

SMARTDRV displays the currently valid parameter and the version number. Version 4.0 of SMARTDRV is included with Windows 3.1, but at least Version 4.1 is required. This is the version that's included in MS-DOS. If SMARTDRV isn't the cause of the error, it may be another driver from the system files. You should test whether all paths for the device drivers, which are concerned with storage or medium and are also included in MS-DOS 6.0, point to the DOS Directory.

After pressing [Enter], a screen, in which you can select the Express or Custom Setup, appears.

Express or Custom Setup

Custom Setup

In the following sections we'll describe the Custom Setup, since the Express Setup requires only a few selections. Normally you can use the recommended Express Setup, since your decompressed hard drive will be converted without problems. In this case, DoubleSpace operates with the following settings:

- Compress existing drive

- Use 2 Meg for the decompressed drive

- Drive letter H for the decompressed drive

Then the last screen, before the actual compression, appears.

If you made an error during an input or selection, you can return to the previous screen by pressing [Esc]. In an emergency, the installation program can be interrupted with [F3] and then terminated by continually pressing [F3].

When you select Custom Setup, a new screen, in which you can compress an available drive or make compressed capacity on this drive available as an additional drive, appears.

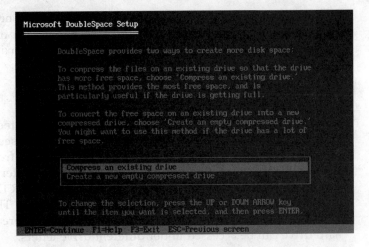

Compress Custom Setup

It may take a long time to compress an existing drive, depending on the capacity and speed, and whether the hard drive is full. However, it's faster to create an additional and compressed, but empty, drive.

After selecting "Compress an existing drive" and pressing ⎡Enter⎤, a screen, in which you must select the size of the portion that shouldn't be compressed and the drive letter for the decompressed drive, appears:

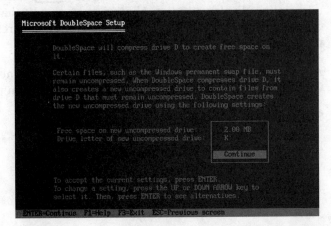

Decompressed capacity and determine new drive letter

Usually DoubleSpace provides 2 Meg of decompressed memory and the drive letter K as fallback. After the compression, a drive K: is available, besides the drive C:. On drive K:, the driver and the compression file areas are available as hidden files and about 2

Meg of decompressed memory, which Windows may need for a swap file, are available. However, remember that each megabyte of decompressed memory also means that there is approximately 2 Meg less capacity on the compressed drive.

Tips for the size of the decompressed area

Windows in enhanced mode for 386s can be accelerated with a swap file; this file can be created only on a decompressed area of the hard drive. If necessary, leave about 3-10 Meg of free space. Also, remember that all data that could be accessed after booting with a different DOS version (e.g., MS-DOS 5.0, DR DOS 6.0) must also be on a decompressed area of the hard drive. Therefore, with MS-DOS 6.0, the compressed and decompressed areas of the hard drive can be accessed under different drive letters.

With other DOS versions, you can access only the decompressed areas. If you try to access the packed drive, an error message appears.

Don't try to leave an area larger than half of the hard drive capacity free. If you're compressing a 100 Meg hard drive, you should not exempt more than 50 Meg from the compression, since this could cause problems.

To change a default value, move the highlight with the cursor keys to the displayed value and press (Enter). An extensive information display appears, allowing you to edit the value. You can accept the value with (Enter) and continue and return to the previous screen with (Esc).

After selecting both values according to your needs, select "Continue" and press (Enter) to continue the installation program.

Starting the compression

DoubleSpace is now ready to compress the drive:

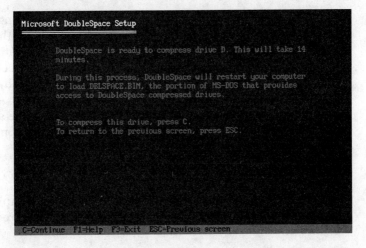

Starting the compression

DoubleSpace displays the estimated time requirement. Since this is only an estimate, it will be refined and updated during the compression. Also, the screen warns you that the computer will be restarted during this procedure to load the new device driver DBLSPACE.BIN. This occurs automatically. If a power failure occurs, an automatic start of DoubleSpace occurs and the optimization continues. To ensure that this occurs without problems, ensure that a diskette isn't in drive A:.

Later a line that loads the device driver doesn't appear in CONFIG.SYS. This occurs automatically, which is similar to the IO.SYS and MSDOS.SYS files during the start of the computer. DBLSPACE.BIN is a third systems file, newly added to DOS and is started when it is available in the root directory.

Finally, to start the compression, activate the C key; otherwise you can still terminate the program with Esc or F3 and make changes or remain with a decompressed hard drive.

Then the following steps occur:

- The hard drive is tested for errors with CHKDSK.

- A test is performed to determine whether diskettes are inserted in drive A: or other compressed drives.

- DBLSPACE.BIN is created in the root directory and a first DBLSPACE.INI.

- The computer is restarted; DBLSPACE.BIN is automatically loaded.

A message, indicating that compressed drive is still being created, appears at the end of the CONFIG.SYS. During the actual compression, a new screen appears, providing information about the duration of the compression and the file currently being used. During this process, DoubleSpace continuously adjusts the estimated finishing time and the remaining time. After the immediate compression, the DEFRAG program may be started to defragment the new drive and to reduce the size of the compression file to a minimum.

Ending the compression

At the end, a screen appears. DoubleSpace has completed the compression and provides information about the result. For example:

- Free space before compression: 67.4

- Free space after the compression: 142.5

- Compression ratio: 1.6:1

- Total time to compress: 17 minutes

DoubleSpace also reports, for example:

New drive K: with 2.0 Meg decompressed space, for files that cannot be compressed.

Then you're prompted to press (Enter) to exit DoubleSpace and to restart the computer again. A message, indicating that DoubleSpace has made changes in the AUTOEXEC.BAT and CONFIG.SYS files, appears. The system checks for a diskette in drive A: and then performs the reboot. The conversion and compression are finished and the hard drive has been exchanged for a larger one.

Using the packed hard drive

While using a hard drive that has been packed by DoubleSpace, you shouldn't encounter any problems, unlike with other compression programs. Besides the increased hard drive capacity, the changes made to the drive aren't very noticeable.

Compression and changes during operations

Usually when working with a compressed drive C:, it seems as if the hard drive has been replaced by a larger one and the data copied to the new drive. The amount of free space is almost doubled. The amount of increased storage capacity depends on whether the data is easy to compress.

Graphic data, for example, may be compressed to 10 percent, formatted text files to about 50 percent and EXE files only by a few percent. In the middle there is a packing rate of almost 50 percent and therefore not quite a doubling of the hard drive capacity. For us, the value was not quite 2:1 but 1.5:1, because of numerous EXE files.

To obtain more specific information about the compressed drive, you must activate the DBLSPACE command again. For example, the following display may appear:

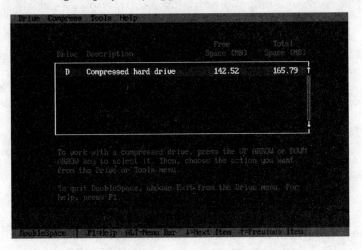

DoubleSpace displays compressed drives

The following two values are provided as basic information:

Free space:
> The available space of the compression.

Total space:
> The calculated total space of the compression.

Remember that both values are estimates based on the compression relationships up to now. In the future, you may store large amounts of data, which can be compressed more easily, resulting in more than the displayed free space. However, less than the displayed free space will be available to compress data. We'll discuss these problems in more detail later.

Decompressed drive K:

On drive K:, some hidden systems files, the large compression file and, if space was reserved during the compression, the decompressed parts of the hard drive are available. If you create a swap file for Windows, you must select drive K: for the drive in Windows.

You should be careful when working with drive K:, since the files marked as hidden are irreplaceable. If these files are accidentally destroyed, all data on drive C: is lost.

However, you can display the files on drive K: with ATTRIB K:*.*.

Speed of the compressed hard drive

The speed of the compressed hard drive is about the same as the decompressed hard drive. Sometimes the speed increases and other times the speed decreases. Apparently the loss of time through packing and unpacking is balanced by the smaller amount of data which must be read and written. The files are compressed in about half the space. You can optimize drives compressed with DoubleSpace with DEFRAG, if the hard drive has become "slow" because of fragmentation over time.

Peculiarities of the system files

If you inspect the system files on the compressed drive, you'll find references to a device driver DBLSPACE.BIN or DBLSPACE.SYS. This driver has become a new part of MS-DOS 6.0 and, along with IO.SYS and MSDOS.SYS, is in the root directory of the hard drive as DBLSPACE.BIN and is loaded automatically.

However, the driver is loaded in conventional memory and occupies about 43K of memory there, which of course could be missing somewhere else. If you want to load this driver into upper memory and have also created this memory area with EMM386.EXE, you can specify, with the device driver DBLSPACE.SYS in the CONFIG.SYS file, that DoubleSpace at the end of the boot procedure stores the driver in upper memory. Load DBLSPACE.SYS with the command LOADHIGH:

```
DEVICEHIGH=C:\DOS\DBLSPACE.SYS /MOVE
```

Perhaps you're wondering why a type of dummy device driver must be loaded, instead of adding another key word after DOS=. For example:

```
DOS=HIGH,UMB,DBL_HIGH
```

The dummy driver is necessary because of the MEMMAKER function, which searches for a corresponding memory block for every driver in the CONFIG.SYS. This determines the optimum distribution of programs in high memory. DEVICEHIGH=C:\DOS\DBLSPACE.SYS, MEMMAKER searches for a program, DBLSPACE.BIN, and includes it in the optimization.

Displaying information about the compressed drive

You cannot control DoubleSpace's compression of the hard drive. You must trust the compression program to handle the data. However, you cannot be sure if a certain amount of data will still fit on the hard drive, since this depends on the packing rate for the files.

All messages regarding the space needed and the free capacity aren't always accurate. Therefore, you should question any information CHKDSK provides about the available storage capacity.

Only **Drive/Info...** from the DoubleSpace program provides accurate information about the compressed hard drive. You can also move the highlight to the drive in the basic display and press Enter.

After the call, a window appears with important information about the packed and the unpacked drive.

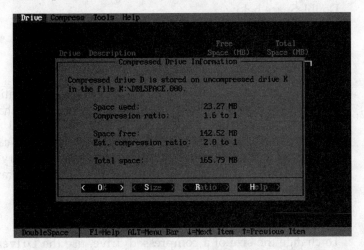

Compressed Drive Info

The information about the compressed drive D: have the following meanings:

The estimated compression ratio of 2:1 results in the total capacity for the compressed drive D:

Space used   This is the quantity of decompressed data, which is on the drive in compressed format.

Space free   Compared to the compression relationship of 2:1, this amount of data could still be stored on the compressed drive.

Since these values constantly change, a definitive statement cannot always be determined. Therefore, you should check these values regularly.

Other features of DoubleSpace

Of course DoubleSpace has many other features. You can access these features through various menus after starting DoubleSpace or they can be activated directly with parameters during the call of DoubleSpace.

To check a compressed drive for data integrity and errors, use DoubleSpace's **Tools/Chkdsk...** command, or run DBLSPACE from the system prompt using the following syntax:

```
DBLSPACE /CHKDSK
```

We'll briefly describe the various options of the main menu of DoubleSpace below.

Drive Menu

Obtaining information about the compressed drives

With the **Drive/Info...** command, you can obtain information about a compressed drive. This information is similar to that of the CHKDSK command. The data for the compressed and the decompressed drive pertaining to it, are displayed. You can obtain information about the available memory, the memory already used and the total memory available. The compression rate is also displayed.

Changing the size of the compressed drive

To change the size of a compressed drive, use the **Drive/Change Size...** command. You can either increase or decrease the size. For example, this command can be used if too much decompressed memory is available.

After selecting this command, the current data is determined and then displayed. Then the value for ":New free space:" can be changed at the uncompressed drive K:. It's helpful that the current free memory value is displayed at the "Current free space:" line.

Changing the compression ratio

With the **Drive/Change Ratio...** command, you can set the compression ratio for a drive. DoubleSpace uses this value to determine the storage space still available on the drive.

Increasing the compression ratio won't improve the data compression. Instead, doing this simply provides a more accurate calculation of the available storage space.

Formatting a compressed drive

To format a compressed drive, use the **Drive/Format...** command. You cannot do this by using the FORMAT command. During formatting, all the files on the medium are erased.

The boot drive C: cannot be formatted with the **Drive/Format...** command.

Deleting a compressed drive

To delete a DoubleSpace compressed drive, use the **Drive/Delete...** command. Remember that all data on this drive will be deleted. Unfortunately, it's impossible to reverse the creation process by unpacking the data to a decompressed drive.

The data can be stored before the deletion of the drive and then restored later. Before the deletion of the compressed hard drive, the data should be backed up and put in a safe place. Later, when needed, the data can be restored to the decompressed hard drive, if there is enough space available. During the backup, the data is automatically decompressed and made available in decompressed form for the restoration.

If you accidentally deleted a compressed drive, you can reverse this by restoring the DBLSPACE.XXX file with UNDELETE. Then you must use the DBLSPACE /MOUNT command.

Tools Menu

Defragmenting the compressed drive

With the **Tools/Defragment...** command, a program for defragmenting compressed drives starts immediately. The fragmented files are stored again in consecutive areas. Unlike the decompressed drive, the speed isn't improved. This process results in more available space on the compressed drive.

Testing compressed drive

With the **Tools/Chkdsk...** command, you can test a compressed medium for errors, as we previously mentioned. If you press the (Check) button, any errors that are found are only displayed; they aren't corrected. If you also want to correct errors, use the (Fix) button.

Load compression device driver high

During the start of the computer, the required parts of MS-DOS 6.0, with DBLSPACE.BIN, are loaded automatically. However, because of this, about 43K of conventional memory are lost. To ensure that the driver is loaded high, the following command line can be used in the CONFIG.SYS:

```
DEVICE=DBLSPACE.SYS /MOVE
```

/MOVE loads the DBLSPACE.BIN driver into high memory.

The driver isn't immediately loaded high because, during booting, the enhanced memory administration isn't available with HIMEM.SYS or EMM386.EXE. These are available only after the DBLSPACE.BIN driver is loaded and access to the compressed data is possible. For this reason, DBLSPACE.BIN is first loaded at the beginning of the conventional memory and, after the availability of high memory, can be moved by adding the previously mentioned command line to the CONFIG.SYS.

Start diskette for the compressed hard drive

If you're working with a compressed hard drive, keep a bootable system diskette available (e.g., the FAILSAFE diskette we had you create earlier in this book). This diskette should contain all the required programs and drivers for the computer (the IO.SYS, MSDOS.SYS and DBLSPACE.BIN files from MS-DOS 6.0).

If a problem occurs during the bootup, you can start your computer only from this diskette. You can access the data only on the hard drive and the CONFIG.SYS, if the device driver, DBLSPACE.BIN, is available on the start diskette.

14.9 Increasing Hard Drive Capacity with STACKER 3.0

Like DoubleSpace, STACKER is a compression program. We'll discuss the most important features and options of STACKER in this section.

 Use compressed hard drives carefully. Don't select extreme settings when you install STACKER. In other words, don't try to compress a 100 Meg hard drive to free up 95 Meg.

 If you work with a compressed hard drive, ensure that you have a bootable system diskette available. This diskette should contain all the necessary programs and drivers for the computer, including the STACKER.COM and SSWAP.COM files.

The basic principle of STACKER

Unlike the well-known compression programs LHARC, PKZIP or PKARC, which compress files that you must decompress before using, STACKER is an on-line compression program (i.e., your data is in compressed form on the hard drive). The data is decompressed immediately when needed in RAM for processing. If you save the data on the hard drive after processing, STACKER automatically compresses it again. The STACKER.COM. program automatically compresses and decompresses the data.

STACKER has several components, which include an install program (SETUP), a program for compressing/decompressing the data (STACKER.COM), and the SSWAP.COM utility program, which swaps the two drive labels, C: and D:.

Installing STACKER 3.0

Before benefiting from a "larger" hard drive, first you must install STACKER 3.0. The installation program performs several necessary tasks.

1. It enables the device drivers in CONFIG.SYS. This happens automatically when you install STACKER 3.0. The next time you start up your computer, it automatically loads the drivers.

2. The program also compresses the hard drive.

Compressing a hard drive is relatively quick and easy, but it's impossible to decompress it again. Although you can erase drives compressed with STACKER, this process deletes all the data. So, you must perform a complete backup of your compressed hard drive and then transfer the data back to your decompressed hard drive.

This compression technique refers only to one storage medium (e.g., the hard drive). When you copy, or backup, the data to a diskette, the data is in decompressed form on the diskette.

Compression requirements

- It's very important to backup your hard drive completely. If it's been a long time since your last backup, do another backup before installing STACKER. If you have trouble while STACKER is compressing your hard drive, simply delete the STACKER drive and transfer the backup data back onto the hard drive.

- If you're working with copy-protected programs that can only be installed on the hard drive once, de-install the programs before compression and reinstall them on the hard drive after installing STACKER.

- Use CHKDSK to check your hard drive before compressing it. If any errors occur, use the /F switch with CHKDSK to correct the errors and then check the hard drive again. The only guarantee you have for successful compression is a hard drive that is free of defects.

- You need at least 1.5 Meg of free disk space on the hard drive for the system files and the compression process. If necessary, back up data or programs on diskettes and delete them from the hard drive temporarily to get sufficient free disk space for compression. After installing the STACKER drive, you should have enough room to copy the files back to the hard drive. When you copy these files back to the hard drive, STACKER automatically compresses them for you.

- If you're working on a network, log out before installing STACKER; otherwise you could lose data.

- Also, be sure to quit any programs in RAM before installing STACKER. Otherwise, they will automatically abort during installation, which could also cause data loss.

- Installing STACKER requires 512K of free RAM. If you don't have that much available, you'll have to remove memory resident programs from RAM to free up the necessary amount of RAM.

You can use many MS-DOS 6.0 commands and tools on a hard drive compressed with STACKER. For example, you can still use CHKDSK to check the hard drive.

Starting the installation

After the above requirements are met, you can begin installing STACKER and compress your hard drive. To do this, insert the installation diskette of the STACKER 3.0 program into drive A: or B: and make it the current drive. Use the following line to call the installation program:

```
SETUP
```

First, the welcome screen of STACKER appears, providing some information about STACKER.

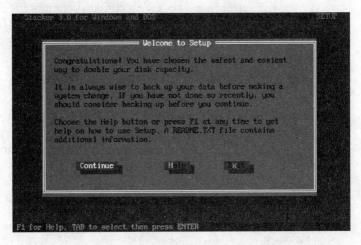

The Welcome screen of STACKER

To obtain information about the installation program, press F1 . Use the Tab key to select "Continue" and press Enter .

The next screen prompts you to type in your name and company. When you're finished, press Enter to move to the next screen.

You must select Express Setup or Custom Setup (the default is Express Setup). This will "stack" or compress all your hard drives and make the best choices for your system. You should select Custom Setup if you want to stack selected drives or make your own choices for configuration. Make your selection and press Enter.

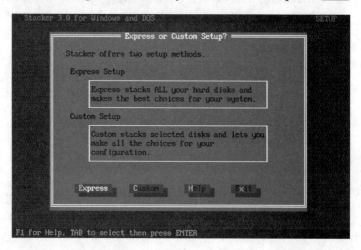

Express or Custom Setup

In this screen, you must specify the directory to which you want to copy the STACKER files. The default directory is STACKER. To accept the default, press Enter. You can also change the default to any other directory and confirm your selection by pressing Enter. Then the program copies the necessary files to the directory you specified.

Another screen appears and informs you that the installation program wants to change the AUTOEXEC.BAT file. The program only adds the directory with the STACKER files to the search path. Accept this change by pressing Enter. If you don't want to make this change, use the cursor keys to select "Do not modify AUTOEXEC.BAT" and then press Enter.

The following screen describes three choices for using the Tune Stacker. You can maximize the speed or the amount of compression by selecting one of these choices. Use the Tab key to move to the "Stacker Setting:" group, and use the cursor keys to highlight your selection and press Enter.

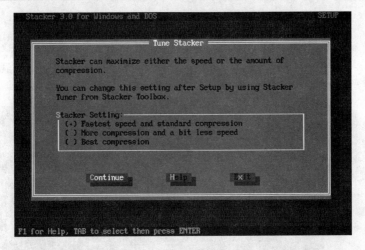

Choices for using the Tune Stacker

The next screen indicates the safest way to install STACKER. This involves closing all the resident programs (e.g., the ones in the AUTOEXEC.BAT). You are then prompted to restart your computer. To disable resident programs, select "Restart" and press [Enter].

The next screen asks whether you want to compress a hard drive or diskette. Use the cursor keys to select a drive or diskette and select [Enter].

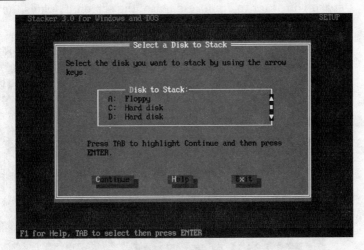

Select a drive or diskette to stack

The next screen displays the status of the drive you want to stack. To compress existing data, choose the "Entire Drive" option. To build an empty Stacker drive, choose the "Free Space" option. Select the "Entire Drive" option if the drive contains data you want to compress. This process takes longer than the "Free Space" option because you are compressing all the existing data on the drive. The "Free Space" option is faster because you are only preparing an empty space for receiving compressed data. Select the desired option and press Enter.

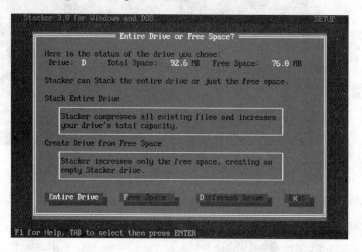

Entire Drive or Free Space options

The following screen appears if you select the "Free Space" option and if you choose to stack a disk that's already been stacked and has free space available. This screen asks the size of the free space you want to compress. Also, the screen displays the default, which is the highest possible free space.

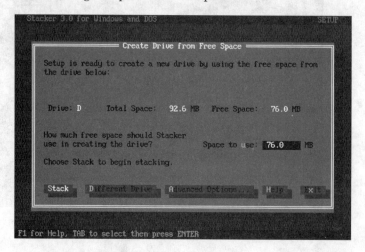

Create drive from Free Space

You can make other settings by choosing "Advanced Options...". For example, if you're compressing a storage device that already contains data, you can exclude an area of any size from compression. To do this, choose Amount to keep decompressed and enter the desired size in the next screen.

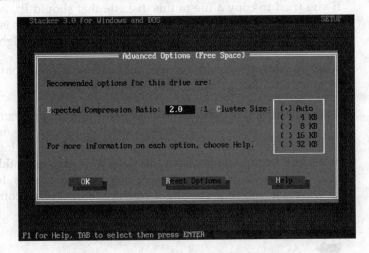

Advanced Options

You can also change the size of the clusters by selecting "Cluster Size:". The default cluster size is "Auto".

Choosing "Expected Compression Ratio:" lets you set the compression ratio. Choose a value between 1.1 and 8.0. Try to set the correct compression ratio. For example, if you are compressing a hard drive, accept the default value of 2, since this is the average compression ratio for a hard drive.

However, if you want to prepare a diskette for compression that you are going to use exclusively for copying illustrations, set a higher ratio, since illustrations can usually be compressed very well. We recommend using the highest ratio, which is 8.

Specifying the compression ratio is only important for displaying information about how much space is left on a storage device. STACKER calculates this information based on the specified value and then displays it. So if you specify a compression ratio of 2 on a 1.2 Meg diskette, you can store a maximum of 2.4 Meg of data on the diskette, regardless of which compression ratio STACKER uses to compress the data.

STACKER always tries to compress the data with the highest possible ratio. For example, if you compress illustrations and copy them to the diskette, you'll get only 2.4 Meg on the diskette, even if you specified a compression ratio of 7. However, if you specified a ratio that is too high for a hard drive or diskette, STACKER could display a large amount of free disk space.

If you tried to copy a file to this diskette that should fit, you could get an error message stating that the file cannot fit. This is because the file cannot be compressed with the specified (too high) ratio.

After making the desired selections, choose OK to continue the installation. Choose "Stack" to begin stacking.

After selecting this option, the actual work of the program begins. STACKER processes the storage device depending on which method you selected. If you chose a drive containing a lot of data, STACKER begins compressing this data. This process could take up to a half an hour on a 40 Meg hard drive that is half full. However, if you're preparing a free space to receive compressed data, the process takes only one or two minutes.

 You cannot cancel the compression process. Switching off the computer or resetting during conversion destroys the data on the drive.

After the program is complete, a screen, which informs you that the program has finished, appears. Now reboot the computer and begin working with the compressed data.

Drive C: is your new, compressed hard drive. Also, drive D: contains the most important device drivers for starting the computer in decompressed form:

```
D:\COMMAND.COM
D:\CONFIG.SYS
D:\STACKER\SSWAP.COM
D:\STACKER\STACKER.COM
D:\IO.SYS
D:\STACVOL.000
D:\MSDOS.SYS
D:\DOS\EMM386.EXE
D:\DOS\HIMEM.SYS
```

STACVOL.000 is a "System", "Hidden" and "Read-Only" file containing the compressed data for drive C:, which makes the data seem to be in two places.

Working with the compressed hard drive

When working with a hard drive compressed by STACKER, remember the following:

When you work with the compressed C: drive now, it's almost as though you added a new bigger hard drive and were copying data to this new hard drive. Suddenly you have about twice the space you had before the compression. It's difficult to determine exactly how much memory capacity you've gained. The reason is that different types of data are compressed at different ratios.

For example, graphic files can be compressed to about ten percent of their original size, formatted text files can be compressed to about 50 percent of their original size, and EXE files can only be compressed by a few percentage points. On the average, this results in a compression rate of about 50%, so you are doubling your hard drive capacity.

Each time you start your computer, you'll see a message indicating that drive C: is now compressed drive D:.

Next, SSWAP swaps the two drive letters, so you can work with C:.

```
Swapped drives C: and D:
```

Drive D: contains some system files, the big compression file and, if you excluded areas from compression, the decompressed parts of the hard drive.

Speed of the compressed hard drive

In our experiences, the compressed hard drive is about as fast as it was when it was decompressed. In some cases, you gain a little speed and in others you lose some speed. Apparently the time that's lost compressing and decompressing the files is compensated by the smaller amount of data read from and written to the hard drive. The files are compressed to about half their size. By the way, if your hard drive starts slowing down, you can optimize STACKER drives with a program called SDEFRAG, which is included with STACKER.

Fast computers with slow hard drives should gain speed after compression, while ATs with fast hard drives will probably slow down a little.

Features of system files

If you make changes to CONFIG.SYS and AUTOEXEC.BAT on a compressed hard drive, there are some features you should remember. When you start the computer, the CONFIG.SYS file of what will later be drive D: runs. However, right now it's still drive C:. The drivers for STACKER are loaded here and then drives C: and D: are swapped. The AUTOEXEC.BAT then starts from the drive that will later be drive C:.

After you install STACKER, the CONFIG.SYS and AUTOEXEC.BAT are on C: and D:. The files on these two drives should always be identical. If you make changes to one of these files on a particular drive, STACKER will notice after you restart the computer and prompts you to make an identical copy of the modified file.

In a sense, when you use STACKER to compress your hard drive, you're giving up part of your control over your data and relying on the compression program to handle the data. You can no longer be certain whether a specific amount of data will fit on your hard drive, because this depends on how high the compression rate is for the files.

Be especially wary of any information about required space and free capacity. The information provided by CHKDSK probably isn't accurate.

It's best to obtain information about the compressed hard drive from CHECK of STACKER. After you call CHECK, it displays information about the compressed hard drive/diskette.

How do you remove a STACKER drive?

To remove a STACKER drive from the hard drive, use SREMOVE. However, you'll lose all the data saved on the STACKER drive. Unfortunately, you cannot decompress the data back to the decompressed hard drive.

 It's possible to back up the data saved on the STACKER drive before removing it and then copy the data back to the decompressed hard drive, if there is enough room.

You'll encounter problems if you saved 60 Meg of data on a compressed drive that was 40 Meg prior to compression. Either you'll have to do without some of the data (on the hard drive) or purchase a bigger hard drive.

Special STACKER commands

In this section we'll introduce the special commands that are available after you install STACKER.

The SETUP command

Use this command to install additional STACKER drives after installing STACKER.

Syntax: SETUP option

Calling SETUP starts a program that enables you to set up new STACKER drives via menu selection. Installation is identical to the original installation of STACKER, except that you no longer have to copy STACKER files, etc. The first screen you see prompts you to restart the computer. For more information about installing new STACKER drives, refer to the section on installation.

Option:

/? Displays the SETUP help screen.

/AT Adapts SETUP for AT/16 coprocessor.

/MC Adapts SETUP for MC/16 coprocessor.

/XT Adapts SETUP for XT/8 coprocessor.

/M Displays SETUP in black and white.

/T=<dr:> Specifies a temporary drive.

The SATTRIB command

Choose this command to change file attributes.

Syntax: SATTRIB option file

Use SATTRIB to display or change file attributes. Don't specify any switches along with the command to display the set attributes of a file.

Option:

If you don't specify any of the following options, the command displays only the current valid file attributes.

+R Sets the Read-only attribute. This option write protects the file. You can no longer make changes to it or delete it.

-R   This option removes the Read-only attribute. Now you can delete the file or make changes to it.

+A   Sets the Archive attribute for the specified file. The file is archived and will be copied for the next BACKUP or XCOPY if you specify the correct option.

-A   Removes the Archive attribute from the specified file.

+H   Sets the Hidden attribute. The file is now hidden, and many commands can no longer access the file.

-H   Removes the Hidden attribute. Now you can access the file again.

+S   Sets the System attribute. Many commands can no longer access this file.

-S   Removes the System attribute. You now have access to this file again.

File

Specify a file here. You can't use wildcards. If you specify the filename without any path, the options affect the current directory. Specify the file without options to see a display of its current attributes.

The CHECK command

This command is similar in function to the MS-DOS CHKDSK command.

Syntax: CHECK options

Use this command to check a STACKER diskette in the specified drive or a STACKER hard drive for errors. Use this command before optimizing a STACKER drive with SDEFRAG.

Option

d: Specifies the STACKER drive you want to check. If no drive is specified, the current drive is the default.

/B   Specify this option to suppress breaks and system prompts during output of the command as long as CHECK doesn't find any errors. This option should be ideal for using CHECK in batch files. However, we didn't notice any difference in CHECK's performance when we used this option.

/F   Finds and fixes errors. If you don't specify this option, CHECK only displays errors.

/D   This option displays errors in detail when CHECK finds errors on the STACKER drive.

/V   During the check, the file currently being edited and any errors are displayed.

Here's more information about output from the CHECK /D command:

```
CHECK - 3.00, (c) Copyright 1990-92 Stac Electronics,
Carlsbad, CA

Volume in drive C is STACKER

No errors found

Stacker Drive Statistics:

                       Stacker Drive          STACVOL File
                       Drive C:               D:\STACVOL.000
                     ---------------        --------------------
     Total Bytes: 39,403,520                19,703,808
     Bytes Used:  24,317,952 ( 61.7%)       16,870,400 ( 85.6%)
     Bytes Free:  15,085,568 ( 38.3%)        2,833,408 ( 14.4%)

Stacker Drive Compression Ratio = 1.4:1
Projected Bytes Free            = 4,063,232
Fragmentation Level             = 0%
```

The data on the left side of the table show the same information that the MS-DOS CHKDSK command would have given about the STACKER drive. The data on the right side of the table provides information about the size of the STACVOL file, in which the information of the compressed drive is stored. You also see the name of the file and information about where the file is located.

The second to last line displays the average compression ratio used to compress the data on the STACKER drive. The last line contains an estimate of how many files will still fit on the STACKER drive.

The CREATE command

Use this command to install an empty STACKER drive from the DOS prompt.

Syntax: CREATE Drive File Options

This command gives you the opportunity to specify an empty STACKER drive with the necessary parameters directly from the DOS prompt.

Drive

Specify the drive on which you want to install an empty STACKER drive.

File

Specify the name of the file, to which the STACVOL file for the installed drive is backed up. If you don't specify a file, STACKER uses the default, STACVOL.DSK. It's important to define this filename for the root directory.

Option

/S=XXX.X   Specify the size to be used for the empty STACKER drive. Use megabytes in the specification. The minimum amount of megabytes for installing a STACKER is 0.1 Meg. To use the largest possible space for creating a STACKER drive, specify /S=0.

/R=X.X   Use this option to set the compression ratio for the STACKER drive. The compression ratio can be from 1.1 to 8.

/C=X   Specify the size of the clusters in kilobytes here. Use a value of 4 or 8. Use 4 only if you work with MS-DOS 3.3 or an earlier version. The default is 8, which is the optimum value for MS-DOS 6.0.

/M   Sets the output to black and white when you create an empty STACKER drive.

The SCREATE.SYS driver

This driver gives you the option of using a RAM disk when you create the empty STACKER drive.

Syntax: DEVICE=SCREATE.SYS Drive File Option

If you link this device driver to the CONFIG.SYS, an empty STACKER RAM disk is created when you restart the computer. There are two requirements for this: The RAM disk must be defined in the CONFIG.SYS and the command line for defining the RAM disk must come before the line that converts the RAM disk to a STACKER drive.

Drive

Specify the drive name for the RAM disk, on which you want to install an empty STACKER drive, here.

File

Specify the name of the file, to which the STACVOL file for the installed drive is backed up. If you don't specify a file, STACKER uses the default, STACVOL.DSK. It's important to define this filename for the root directory.

Option

/S=XXX.X   Specify the size to be used for the empty STACKER drive. Use megabytes in the specification. The minimum amount of megabytes for installing a STACKER is 0.1 Meg. To use the largest possible space for creating a STACKER drive, specify /S=0.

/C=X   Specify the size of the clusters in kilobytes. Use a value of 4 or 8. Use 4 only if you work with MS-DOS 3.3 or an earlier version. The default is 8.

The SDEFRAG command

This command calls a program for optimizing a STACKER drive.

Syntax: SDEFRAG Drive Option

Use this command to "clean up" a STACKER drive. That is, this command takes files that are fragmented, stores them contiguously and moves free memory to the end of the storage device. This speeds up access to the files on the storage device.

☞   Before optimizing, use CHKDSK and CHECK to remove any errors from the drive you are going to optimize.

Drive

Specify the drive you want optimized here.

Option

/R   Compresses the data to minimum size. Use this option
        when you update to STACKER from an earlier version and
        when you install a coprocessor.

/G   When you specify this option, after optimizing you can
        press (Enter) to increase or reduce the size of the STACKER
        drive from a menu.

/D   This option only optimizes the structure of the directory, it
        does not store fragmented files contiguously. If you add the
        /Sorter option to specify a sorting sequence, the files are
        stored in that sequence. When you use SDEFRAG with this
        option, optimization takes only a short time.

/SX   Use this option to specify a sorting sequence for the files on
        the storage device. Use the following values for X:

        N   Sorts files by name. This is the default.
        E   Sorts files by extension.
        T   Sorts files by time of creation.
        S   Sorts files by size.

/FDriveFile
        This option guarantees that you will be able to restore the
        STACKER drive in case the optimizing program is
        interrupted while it is running, whether the interruption
        is due to a power failure or a computer reset.

The SDIR command

Use this command to display the contents of a STACKER drive.

Syntax: SDIR File Option

If you don't specify a file, SDIR displays all the files in the
current directory. In addition to the file display, you also get
information about the size of the files, the date and time they
were last saved. System files and hidden files usually aren't
included in the display. At the end of the display, SDIR gives you
the compression ratio of all the displayed files.

File

Specify the files you want displayed here. To check whether a file is in the current directory, enter the filename here. You can also add a drive letter and a path to the filename to display the contents of any directory. Use the wildcards "*" and "?" to define the files you want displayed, just as you do with the MS-DOS DIR command.

Option

☞ The following options function in the manner described here only when you call them from the STAC program. If you use SDIR from the DOS prompt, strange things can happen on the screen. For example, when we called SDIR from the DOS prompt without any options, the screen changed to the large display format.

/H   Includes HIDDEN files in the display.

/P   Displays the contents of a directory one page at a time. Includes information about memory size, date and time of creation for each file; this is similar to using SDIR without any options.

/W   Displays contents of a directory in two columns, the wide display format.

The ED command

Use this command to activate the full screen editor that's included with STACKER.

Syntax: ED File

Use this simple editor to create or make changes to ASCII files.

Use the normal editing keys to move around in the text. The following are other keys you can use in the editor:

[Ins]   Switches between overtype and insert modes.

[Del]   Deletes the character under the cursor.

[Esc]   Exits the editor. If you made changes to the text, you are prompted to save the changes.

Ctrl + Z

        Saves the text under its current name and exits the editor.

F2   Loads a new text into the editor.

F3   Saves the text under a new name.

File

Specify the name of the file to be edited here. If the file doesn't exist yet, ED creates it.

The REMOVDRV command

Use this command to remove a STACKER drive.

Syntax: REMOVDRV Drive

Use REMOVDRV to remove a compressed drive. Remember that you'll lose all the data on the drive when you do this. If you still need the data, back them up before using REMOVDRV. You can use COPY, XCOPY or BACKUP (can be found on the Supplemental Disk from Microsoft) to do this.

Drive

Specify the STACKER drive you want removed here (e.g., REMOVDRV I:).

The SSWAP.COM driver

This driver switches two drive letters.

Syntax: DEVICE=SSWAP.COM Drive1 Drive2 Option

When you use SETUP to install STACKER on a drive that has data on it, the program automatically adds this driver to the CONFIG.SYS file. You can also call SSWAP from the DOS prompt; however, you must omit DEVICE= from the command.

Drive1 or Swapfile

Up to Version 1.X:, Drive1 is the unstacked drive; use "Drive2:" if you specify a second drive.

Starting with Version 2.0:, specify the STACKER swap file instead of Drive1 (for example, C:\STACKVOL.DSK). You no longer need to specify an additional Drive2.

Drive2

This is the stacked drive. Specifying two drives is only practical for downward compatibility with Version 1 of STACKER.

Option

/SYNC   Specify this option to have SSWAP compare the AUTOEXEC.BAT, CONFIG.SYS and COMMAND.COM files of the DOS drive and the STACKER drive when you start the computer. If the files don't match, you're prompted to modify the files so that they do match. STACKER also does this automatically for you.

Example

Here's a typical line for using SSWAP:

```
DEVICE=C:\STACKER\SSWAP.COM C:\STACKVOL.DSK /SYNC
```

The STAC command

The STAC command calls the Stacker Toolbox program to load the STACKER commands. When you type STAC at the DOS prompt, a screen, displaying all the commands you can call, appears. When you select a command, Stacker Toolbox displays help text for that command. Press Enter to start the command. After the command is finished, press any key to return to Stacker Toolbox. Press F10 to exit.

The STACKER command

Syntax: STACKER Drive

Use STACKER to switch a removable STACKER drive (a STACKER drive whose data are stored on a removable storage device) from DOS use to STACKER operation. When you install STACKER, the STACKER.COM drive is automatically installed in the CONFIG.SYS for storage media that will be used continuously as STACKER drives. Above all, the STACKER command is practical for disk drives.

Drive

Specify the drive you want to switch from DOS operation to STACKER operation here. You can switch a STACKER drive back to DOS operation by placing a minus sign in front of the drive.

Instead of a drive, you can also specify the complete path of the STACKER file (C:\STACVOL.DSK). For example, this is especially useful when you have several files and you want to create several STACKER drives. Additionally, by using an equal sign you can specify which drive letters your newly created STACKER drive gets.

Example

```
STACKER A:
STACKER C:\STACVOL.DSK
STACKER D:=C:\STACVOL.DSK
```

The STACKER.COM driver

Add this device driver to the CONFIG.SYS to make STACKER drives possible.

Syntax: DEVICE=STACKER.COM Option

Option

/B=1   Specifies that an MC/16 coprocessor for Stacker is in the system. This is a special coprocessor similar to the math coprocessor. This special "Stacker processor" is only for compressing and decompressing files.

/B=xxx   Specifies the base address for the AT/16 Stacker coprocessor. Valid addresses are 200, 220, 240, 260, 280, 2A0 and 2E0 (all hexadecimal addresses).

/B=xxxx   Specifies the base address for the XT/8 Stacker coprocessor. Valid addresses are C400, C800, CC00, D000, D400, D800 and DC00, which are all hexadecimal addresses.

/M=nn   Specifies the amount of system memory, in kilobytes, that STACKER uses for temporarily storing data to speed up data transfer (cache). Possible values range from 0 to 64. This specification is ignored when you use the /EMS option.

/EMS   Instructs STACKER to use 64K of EMS memory.

*   Tells STACKER to use the next available drive letter as a compressed drive.

@   Sets STACKER drive as replaceable drive that can be addressed only as a STACKER drive. The original drive isn't available as a DOS drive again until you log off the STACKER drive, as shown in the following command line:

```
STACKER -Drive:
```

File   Sets the name and path of the STACKER file. STACKER uses C:\STACVOL.DSK as the default file for the C: hard drive.

Drive   Replaceable "Drive" is available with the STACKER file as a compressed drive, but is no longer available as a decompressed drive.

Encountering problems with compressed data

Earlier we mentioned some of the errors that may occur when using STACKER. The following are some tips on what to do if you encounter these problems:

Read or write errors

When the following error message appears

```
Input/Output Error Reading Drive C
Abort, Retry, Ignore, Fail ?
```

try to narrow down the error. If the error occurs when you are copying several files, try to determine the name of the file and restore it from the backup. If you receive this message for a diskette, it indicates a defective area. If this message appears for a hard drive that is otherwise free of defects, it indicates problems with the STACKER device driver. If the error frequently occurs, remove the STACKER hard drive and transfer the data from the backup onto the decompressed hard drive.

          You can easily create a data backup of a compressed drive and then copy it to a decompressed hard drive, if there is enough room. When the data for the backup are being read, the files are automatically decompressed and saved in decompressed form on the backup diskettes.

Boot diskettes and deleting a STACKER drive

If you're working with a compressed hard drive, you must have a bootable system diskette available. Along with all the necessary programs and drivers for the computer, this diskette should also include the STACKER.COM and SSWAP.COM files.

If you have trouble starting the computer (e.g., the computer crashes while running the CONFIG.SYS), you can start the computer only from this diskette. The only way you will be able to access the data on the hard drive and the CONFIG.SYS file (which you will probably have to modify) is to add the STACKER device driver to the CONFIG.SYS file on the start diskette.

To remove a STACKER drive from the hard drive, start up the computer and choose the REMOVDRV command. Remember to back up the drive before removing it; otherwise all your data will be lost.

14.10 Increasing Hard Drive Capacity with DoubleDensity

DoubleDensity, like STACKER, is a "hard drive doubler" for DOS and Windows. In this section we'll describe the most important features and options of DoubleDensity.

Installing DoubleDensity

It's very easy to install DoubleDensity. However, you should be extremely careful when doing this because data loss may occur.

 When working with a compressed hard drive, be sure that a bootable system diskette is available. This system diskette should contain all the necessary programs and drivers, including the D_D.SYS file for DoubleDensity. The diskette should also contain an editor.

After backing up, check the storage device for files with a set system attribute. Most MS-DOS commands cannot back up these files and it's also not possible to change the position of these files on the storage device.

To check the storage device, use the ATTRIB command. This command finds all files with a set system attribute, except IO.SYS and MSDOS.SYS.

Note the displayed files and remove their system attributes by using the following line:

```
ATTRIB Filename -S
```

 Do not remove the system attribute from the IO.SYS and MSDOS.SYS files under any circumstances.

Then install DoubleDensity and assign the system attribute to the system files again with the following command line:

```
ATTRIB Filename +S
```

This procedure is important for getting the greatest possible capacity for your DoubleDensity drive. If there are system files anywhere on the DoubleDensity drive, the capacity may shrink to a minimum, because DoubleDensity will create only a compressed contiguous drive.

Use the INSTALL program to install DoubleDensity. The diskette from which you install DoubleDensity must be writeable, so you must remove any write protection from the diskette before installation so that the program can save your name and the registration number. To be on the safe side, be sure to make a backup copy of the diskette before removing its write protection.

After copying the DoubleDensity files to the hard drive, you can set the size of the compressed drive. In normal cases, use the recommended maximum value to get the most out of DOS. However, to work with Windows, leave 5-20 Meg free. The installation program automatically installs the CONFIG.SYS. After that, the actual process of conversion and creation takes quite a while. When the installation is complete, the system resets. Access your new drive under the next available drive letter.

Working with DoubleDensity

Your new drive with the increased capacity is available as a logical drive. In addition, drive C: now has a new file containing the compressed data.

If for some reason you don't start the D_D.SYS device driver (perhaps because you booted from a DOS diskette), you won't be able to access the DoubleDensity drive or the data on the drive.

You can use the new drive almost without restrictions. However, do not create any Windows swap files there. Also, you can use the SMARTDRV.EXE cache program on the DoubleDensity drive for read operations, but not for write operations. For example, to prevent SMARTDRV.EXE from caching write accesses for drive D:, specify the drive letter directly. If you add a minus sign, data for this drive won't be cached at all. Use the following command line to display status information that will protect you from possible misunderstandings:

```
SMARTDRV /S
```

The following is an example of what the status information should look like:

```
            Hard drive-Cache-Status
Drive   Read-Cache   Write-Cache   Caching
-------------------------------------------------
  A:         yes          no          no
  B:         yes          no          no
  C:         yes          yes         no
  D:         yes          no          no

Enter "smartdrv /?" to display a help screen about the
SMARTDRV program.
```

The driver for the compressed drive also takes up space in memory. However, this is hardly a problem on 386 computers and above with MS-DOS 6.0. If you installed Upper Memory and place the driver there with DEVICEHIGH, you should ordinarily get all the conventional memory back.

Other DoubleDensity Options

Along with the DoubleDensity's low price and easy installation, we also liked the option for assigning a password for a DoubleDensity drive. While other efforts to protect sensitive data fail because you are able to start the computer from your own DOS diskette or use a special utility program to view hidden files, it's impossible to do these things with data on a DoubleDensity drive unless you know the password.

However, we urge you to store this password in a safe place for reference, in case you forget it.

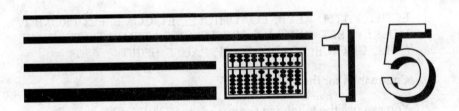

C h a p t e r

Optimizing AUTOEXEC.BAT And CONFIG.SYS

In the following sections we'll discuss two files that are especially important for your PC. These files are responsible for starting your computer so you can immediately begin working with it. If you didn't have these two files and tried starting your computer, you could experience problems and be forced to do without a number of conveniences that these files contain.

You can give your PC instructions that it notes in these two special files. We'll introduce these files and explain their effects in detail. We'll also explain how to change these files to adapt them to your own preferences.

15.1 Overview

The following is a brief overview of the system files.

Installation programs

Most installation programs make changes to the AUTOEXEC.BAT and CONFIG.SYS files. Because of this, always back up these two files before installing a program. Later you can decide whether to keep the changes or use the backup versions of these files.

Changing AUTOEXEC.BAT and CONFIG.SYS

Before making changes to the system files, create a boot diskette by formatting a diskette with FORMAT A: /S. Then copy the AUTOEXEC.BAT and CONFIG.SYS files to this diskette, making any necessary changes.

Commands for the AUTOEXEC.BAT

You can use the following commands in AUTOEXEC.BAT:

ECHO, PATH, KEYB, LOADHIGH, SET COMSPEC, PROMPT, DOSKEY, SET DIRCMD, SET TEMP=C:\TEMP, DATE, TIME, CALL, CHOICE, FOR, GOTO, IF, PAUSE, SHIFT

Commands for the CONFIG.SYS

You can use the following commands in CONFIG.SYS:

BREAK, BUFFERS, COUNTRY, DEVICE, DEVICEHIGH, DOS, DRIVPARM, FCBS, FILES, INSTALL, LASTDRIVE, REM, SHELL, STACKS, SWITCHES

Device drivers for CONFIG.SYS

MS-DOS contains the following device drivers, which you can add to CONFIG.SYS:

ANSI.SYS, DISPLAY.SYS, DRIVER.SYS, EGA.SYS, EMM386.EXE, HIMEM.SYS, KEYBOARD.SYS, PRINTER.SYS, RAMDRIVE.SYS, SETVER.EXE, SMARTDRV.EXE

15.2 Installation Programs

You may be familiar with the following situation. While running SETUP for Windows, a message states that some of the device drivers in the CONFIG.SYS file are incompatible. SETUP offers you the option of updating some old device drivers (usually MOUSE.SYS and HIMEM.SYS). You confirm this action.

Later, you install Word, whose SETUP program also gives you the option of updating the existing mouse driver. You confirm this action also.

However, when you use MS-DOS 6.0, the SETUP program informs you that it has automatically updated some device drivers.

Although user-friendly installation packages are very helpful, they can also disrupt system files.

A 386 with MS-DOS 6.0 installed for optimum memory management has a CONFIG.SYS that can provide up to 50K more conventional memory, with the drivers arranged in the proper order. However, if another installation program adds its own drivers and replaces existing ones, problems can occur.

If you're not sure whether you have control over your PC or if it's taken on a life of its own at your expense, look at the CONFIG.SYS file. This section explains the important device drivers. Once you understand how CONFIG.SYS works, you can eliminate anything that's unnecessary and perhaps even increase your system's speed.

15.3 Changing AUTOEXEC.BAT and CONFIG.SYS

Very important: The DOS failsafe diskette

When you make changes to the CONFIG.SYS file, error messages may appear or your computer may crash. In extreme cases, you may not even be able to start your PC from the hard drive.

To avoid these problems, create a DOS failsafe diskette before editing CONFIG.SYS. Format a diskette using FORMAT A: /S. Copy any other files you may think necessary to the DOS failsafe diskette, and copy the CONFIG.SYS and AUTOEXEC.BAT files as well.

One last step: Copy your AUTOEXEC.BAT and CONFIG.SYS file to the hard drive under different names (e.g., AUTOEXEC.OK and CONFIG.OK) before editing either file.

15.4 AUTOEXEC.BAT

The first file we'll discuss is called AUTOEXEC.BAT. This file is located in the root directory of your hard drive or on the start diskette. To display the contents of this file, type the following command:

```
TYPE AUTOEXEC.BAT
```

The screen displays the contents of the AUTOEXEC.BAT file. We'll use a sample file to explain the most important elements of this file.

Here's an example of what the AUTOEXEC.BAT file could look like:

```
@ECHO OFF
PATH C:\DOS;C:\BATCHES
LOADHIGH C:\DOS\KEYB UK,,C:\DOS\KEYBOARD.SYS
SET COMSPEC=C:\DOS\COMMAND.COM
PROMPT $P$G
LOADHIGH C:\SYS\DOS\DOSKEY
SET DIRCMD=/P
SET TEMP=C:\TEMP
```

```
REM WORD needs the following setting
SET TMP=C:\TEMP
LOADHIGH C:\DOS\SMARTDRV.EXE 1024 256
CHOICE /C:NY /T:Y,15 Should the MS-DOS Shell be started
IF ERRORLEVEL 2 GOTO NOSHELL
IF ERRORLEVEL 1 GOTO RUNSHELL

:RUNSHELL
  DOSSHELL
  GOTOEND

:NOSHELL
  ECHO MS-DOS SHELL NOT STARTED
  GOTO END

:END
```

The lines of the file are made up of MS-DOS commands. The computer runs these commands in the sequence in which they appear in the file. In other words, you could also enter these commands manually after starting your PC. However, having the commands executed in this file saves you the trouble of entering them by hand. Now we'll explain the meaning of each MS-DOS command in the file.

The ECHO command

As you can see, we used ECHO twice in our sample file, each time in a different way. By using this command, you determine whether the command lines will be displayed on the screen as AUTOEXEC.BAT is running. The first time we added OFF to the command, the second time we added ON.

By adding OFF to ECHO, we specified that the rest of the commands processed in this file would not appear on the screen prior to execution. By placing the "@" character at the beginning of this line, you can prevent this line from appearing on the screen as well.

Adding ON to the ECHO command specifies that any other commands will be displayed on the screen before execution.

The PATH command

If you have a hard drive with all MS-DOS commands in a specific directory, PATH can be of great importance. This command specifies that all MS-DOS commands will be found, regardless of which directory you are working in.

This command lets you specify the path for other directories as well as for the MS-DOS commands. For example, this is helpful if you frequently work with a certain word processor or other program. If you define a path to the directory in which the program is located, you can call the program any time from any directory or drive.

To create paths to different directories, specify the directory names separated by semicolons. For example, to define paths to a directory containing all your batch files, to your word processing program (C:\WORD), and to the directory containing your MS-DOS commands, add the following line to your AUTOEXEC.BAT:

```
PATH C:\DOS;C:\BAT;C:\WORD
```

By doing this, you can create a path to all your application programs. Specify the directories in the sequence in which you use them most. This is important because MS-DOS searches the directories in the order listed with the PATH command each time you start one of the programs.

The LOADHIGH command

Use this command to load programs in upper memory instead of conventional memory. If you have upper memory that is available and active, programs are swapped to this memory if possible. This can greatly increase the amount of available RAM. If there isn't enough upper memory available, the specified program is loaded into conventional memory instead.

To be able to load programs into upper memory, you must allocate the appropriate memory. The driver EMM386.EXE, which is included with MS-DOS 6.0, is used to do this. Also, upper memory must be enabled in the CONFIG.SYS with the entry DOS=UMB.

You should use upper memory only with memory resident programs. For example, you can load KEYB into upper memory, but not QBASIC. Another program that is well suited for upper memory is called DOSKEY.

After LOADHIGH, specify the name of the program you want to load in upper memory. If necessary, specify the name of the program with its complete path specification.

The /L switch is also available so you can directly specify the memory block where you want to load the program. Use the MEM /F command to view the free memory blocks that are available.

If you specify a memory block, the program can be loaded in this block only. Some programs require several blocks, however. You can specify several blocks by separating them with semicolons.

You can also specify a minimum size for each block. This means the program will load only in a block that's big enough for the program and also bigger than the specified minimum size.

The following is an example of a command line that loads a program in a certain block:

```
LOADHIGH /L:1,6400 C:\DOS\DOSKEY
```

The ability to load programs in a specific block is used by the MEMMAKER program to achieve optimal memory utilization.

The KEYB command

The following command line in your AUTOEXEC.BAT file can be used to create the keyboard definition for the United Kingdom keyboard:

```
LOADHIGH C:\KEYB UK,,C:\DOS\KEYBOARD.SYS
```

If you don't specify a keyboard definition when you start your system, the default setting (American keyboard) is used. In this example, the United Kingdom keyboard definition is loaded into upper memory to save conventional memory.

The SET COMSPEC

The next command line in the AUTOEXEC.BAT file

```
SET COMSPEC=C:\DOS\COMMAND.COM
```

finds the command interpreter on the hard drive and loads it after you exit a large program. This speeds up your work with MS-DOS.

The PROMPT command

This command line is used to set your system prompt from within the AUTOEXEC.BAT file.

The PROMPT command line used in our example defines a prompt that includes the current drive letter and directory name, followed by the ">" character.

The DOSKEY command

The command line

```
LOADHIGH C:\SYS\DOS\DOSKEY
```

automatically loads the DOSKEY program into upper memory from your AUTOEXEC.BAT file. Use this program to edit command lines and create macros. By adding this line to your AUTOEXEC.BAT, the program is available immediately after you start your system. Loading this program in upper memory leaves more conventional memory free for other applications.

The SET command

Use the SET command to set environment variables. Some environment variables are important for working with MS-DOS. The operating system uses these variables to store information about the environment and the system settings. The following are some of the most important environment variables:

```
SET DIRCMD=/P
SET TEMP=C:\TEMP
SET TMP=C:\TEMP
```

The DIRCMD environment variable defines the default format for the DIR command. In our example, we specified the /P switch, which ensures that the contents of a directory are always displayed page by page.

Use the TEMP environment variable to specify the directory in which MS-DOS stores temporary files.

The next set variable in our example is for the word processing program, Word. It defines the directory in which this program will store its temporary files.

The REM command

We've also used the REM command in our example AUTOEXEC.BAT file. This command is used to add comments to this file. MS-DOS doesn't consider the comments you enter after this command as commands, so you can add them for your own personal information.

The cache program SMARTDRV.EXE

This command sets the size of the cache memory that's used. You can use this command only if your computer has extended memory or expansion memory. Part of the contents of a data storage device is stored in the cache memory. This reduces the number of times the system has to read or write to the data storage device and accelerates access to the information. In our example, the cache program is loaded into upper memory with a hard drive cache of 1024K. The minimum size of the cache is set to 256K.

The CHOICE command - Queries in AUTOEXEC.BAT

The CHOICE command can be used to insert queries in your AUTOEXEC.BAT file and then branch to different commands or programs depending on the response. The result of the query is returned as an Errorlevel. The Errorlevel is queried by the batch file to determine how to proceed.

Our example includes a query asking the user whether the MS-DOS Shell should be started when the computer is booted. If a response to the query isn't entered within 15 seconds, then the MS-DOS Shell automatically starts. The command lines used in our example are:

```
CHOICE /C:NY /T:Y,15 Should the MS-DOS Shell be started
IF ERRORLEVEL 2 GOTO NOSHELL
IF ERRORLEVEL 1 GOTO RUNSHELL

:RUNSHELL
   DOSSHELL
   GOTOEND

:NOSHELL
   ECHO MS-DOS SHELL NOT STARTED
   GOTO END

:END
```

With these lines in your AUTOEXEC.BAT file, the following query will appear on your screen:

```
Should the MS-DOS Shell be started [N,Y]?
```

If you press Ⓝ, the message "MS-DOS Shell not started" appears. If you press Ⓨ or if 15 seconds pass without a response, the MS-DOS Shell starts automatically.

This occurs because the Ⓝ and Ⓨ keys have been defined as answers to the query. The Ⓝ key is assigned as Errorlevel 2. The Ⓨ key is assigned as Errorlevel 1. Using /T:Y,15 indicates that the Ⓨ key is the default response and that this will be returned automatically if a response isn't given within 15 seconds. The Errorlevel returned by the query then determines which of the next two lines in the file is processed.

Other commands in the AUTOEXEC.BAT - DATE and TIME

If your computer doesn't have a real time clock, you must enter the current date and time each time you start your computer. You can also add these commands to your AUTOEXEC.BAT so you don't have to enter them manually each time your start up your PC. Use the DATE and TIME commands. Add the two commands in separate lines at the end of the AUTOEXEC.BAT to have your computer prompt you for the current date and time every time you start it up.

A PC can accomplish a great deal of work with a well-designed AUTOEXEC.BAT file. Therefore, you should take advantage of this option.

15.5 Getting the Most from CONFIG.SYS

Not all too long ago, computers were able to "get along well" without a CONFIG.SYS. In emergencies, users inserted a bootable diskette and started the computer without the CONFIG.SYS and AUTOEXEC.BAT files. These times are over.

 Starting the computer without the CONFIG.SYS: The first time you start the word processor Word 5.5, the program fails to run because the standard setting for the FILES command is too low. Or, you can't move the mouse because the mouse driver was not loaded. Also, it's impossible to run programs such as Windows without a CONFIG.SYS file.

The following diagram shows the different steps executed when you start up (boot) a PC system. You can clearly see which steps the user can control and customize.

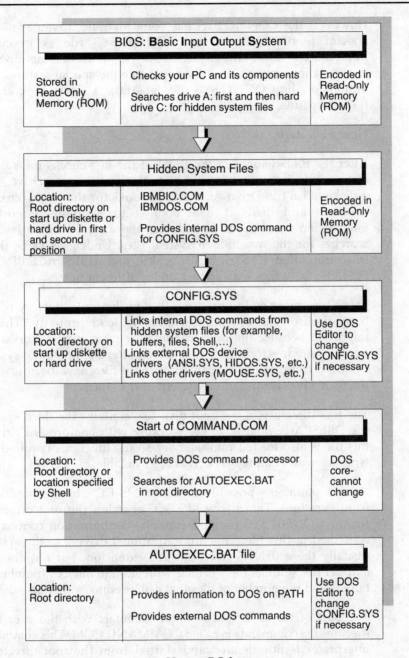

BIOS: Basic Input Output System

| Stored in Read-Only Memory (ROM) | Checks your PC and its components

Searches drive A: first and then hard drive C: for hidden system files | Encoded in Read-Only Memory (ROM) |

Hidden System Files

| Location:
Root directory on start up diskette or hard drive in first and second position | IBMBIO.COM
IBMDOS.COM

Provides internal DOS command for CONFIG.SYS | Encoded in Read-Only Memory (ROM) |

CONFIG.SYS

| Location:
Root directory on start up diskette or hard drive | Links internal DOS commands from hidden system files (for example, buffers, files, Shell,...)
Links external DOS device drivers (ANSI.SYS, HIDOS.SYS, etc.)
Links other drivers (MOUSE.SYS, etc.) | Use DOS Editor to change CONFIG.SYS if necessary |

Start of COMMAND.COM

| Location:
Root directory or location specified by Shell | Provides DOS command processor

Searches for AUTOEXEC.BAT in root directory | DOS core-cannot change |

AUTOEXEC.BAT file

| Location:
Root directory | Provdes information to DOS on PATH

Provides external DOS commands | Use DOS Editor to change CONFIG.SYS if necessary |

How a PC boots

First there is the BIOS, which is stored in the ROM of every PC. The BIOS checks the components (including the memory) and searches for hidden system files.

These hidden system files are part of the operating system. They contain the internal commands needed to execute the setup commands found in the CONFIG.SYS file.

Next, the CONFIG.SYS file runs. This is also the first step where the user can influence the boot procedure.

After this, the PC searches the root directory of the boot drive for the COMMAND.COM file, which is the unmodifiable kernel of every operating system.

In the next step, the AUTOEXEC.BAT file runs. This file gives the user another chance to influence the boot procedure.

Finally, the operating system appears in a form in which you can begin working. You can enter DOS commands after the prompt, or use the options of the graphical user interface, the DOS Shell.

Installation programs for application software provide a convenient way to modify your system files. However, this doesn't mean that the computer will be optimally configured.

MS-DOS 6.0 contains a program called MEMMAKER that automatically optimizes your system files. Before using MEMMAKER, however, you should add all the necessary driver commands. MEMMAKER optimizes the location of programs in memory, but it can't know which drivers (such as mouse drivers or keyboard drivers) to load.

It's best if you find out about the commands and device drivers in the CONFIG.SYS for yourself, and then decide which commands are needed and how you can change parameter values to improve system performance.

15.5.1   What does CONFIG.SYS do?

Basically, the CONFIG.SYS and AUTOEXEC.BAT work together to set up your PC with the optimum configuration to suit your particular needs. However, most PC users are more familiar with the AUTOEXEC.BAT file and its commands than with the CONFIG.SYS file. This is because AUTOEXEC.BAT uses normal DOS commands that can be run directly from the MS-DOS prompt. However, the commands and device drivers found in CONFIG.SYS are used only in this file. So most users aren't familiar with the commands in this file.

However, the CONFIG.SYS has some definite advantages and special features. Since the CONFIG.SYS file is executed immediately after the system starts, it has some special configuration options. To fully appreciate the special features and options of the CONFIG.SYS file, let's take a closer look at the boot procedure.

How a PC starts

After the BIOS (stored in the ROM of the PC) checks the system components, it searches for and loads the boot sector in Drive A:. If a diskette isn't in Drive A:, the BIOS looks for the boot sector on drive C: and loads it. The boot sector contains important information about the storage device and a start program, which searches for the two hidden system files. Under MS-DOS, these files are called IO.SYS, MSDOS.SYS, and DBLSPACE.BIN. In PC-DOS, these files may appear under different names.

These files must be the first two files in the root directory of the boot disk for the operating system to load properly. This is important because the BIOS cannot recognize subdirectories yet (reading subdirectories is possible only after the operating system has been completely loaded). After these files have been loaded, the BIOS gives control of the system over to them.

The root directory of the boot disk also contains the third system file DBLSPACE.BIN. If you're working with compressed drives, this file is also loaded into memory so the functions required for working with compressed drives are available.

At this point, it's possible to adapt MS-DOS to the hardware (configuration). That's why MS-DOS searches the root directory for the CONFIG.SYS file and runs the configuration commands contained in this file. This links additional drivers to the system (usually these drivers have the SYS extension, but not always) and defines settings for working with storage devices (number of buffers and the number of files that can be edited simultaneously).

The part of MS-DOS that maintains contact with the user and executes the commands is called COMMAND.COM. This command interpreter is now loaded and started from the root directory. However, you could also specify a different command interpreter through a special configuration command called SHELL. For example, you could start the new command processor with the enhanced options from Norton Utilities. The CONFIG.SYS file then starts this command interpreter, which can be in a subdirectory, in place of the COMMAND.COM.

The COMMAND.COM file searches for a batch file called AUTOEXEC.BAT and executes the commands in this file. This file must also be located in the root directory. After AUTOEXEC.BAT is processed, MS-DOS (or more specifically COMMAND.COM) displays the system prompt, which indicates that it's ready to process commands input by the user.

As you can see, CONFIG.SYS is processed very early in the boot procedure. For example, this makes it possible to load a driver for extended memory early. Later, the driver makes this additional memory available to all the other programs. It is possible to bypass both the AUTOEXEC.BAT and CONFIG.SYS files in an emergency by pressing the [F5] key while your computer is displaying the "Starting MS-DOS..." message.

Pressing [F8] will cause a prompt to be displayed for confirming each step in the CONFIG.SYS. You will also be asked if AUTOEXEC.BAT should be run.

15.5.2   Configuration commands

The following commands are internal DOS commands, in other words, they are not device drivers on the DOS diskettes or the hard drive. Unlike other DOS commands, such as COPY or DIR, these internal commands aren't stored in the COMMAND.COM file. Remember that COMMAND.COM isn't even loaded into memory when the CONFIG.SYS is being processed. These special commands are located in a hidden file called IO.SYS.

Each command is followed by a brief description and tips for using the command. If possible and practical, we also provide a basic setting that is suitable for most systems:

BREAK   Determines when MS-DOS prompts for the [Ctrl]+[C] key combination, which makes it possible to abort. Doesn't require memory or system resources. It can usually be omitted, since MS-DOS uses the default setting, ON.

             Suggestion: Omit

BUFFERS Specifies how much memory MS-DOS uses for transferring data between RAM and storage devices. It's an important command; each buffer takes up 532 bytes in memory and can store 512 bytes of data. This leaves about 20 bytes for management information.

Suggestion: Without a cache program (e.g., SMARTDRV.EXE), 20-30; with a cache program, use BUFFERS=3.

COUNTRY

Determines which country specific features MS-DOS will use. These are stored in the COUNTRY.SYS file. For example, COUNTRY=044,,COUNTRY.SYS instructs MS-DOS to use the United Kingdom date and time formats. Extra memory isn't needed. The two commas serve as a placeholder for an omitted parameter. If you want to use something other than the standard character set, enter the number of the desired code page between the two commas (for example, 850=international). Usually the code page can be omitted.

Suggestion: COUNTRY=044,,COUNTRY.SYS for UK; otherwise omit the entire command to use the standard American configuration.

DEVICE   Loads an external device driver (usually with SYS extension). DEVICE itself is merely the command for loading a driver; the actual amount of memory required depends on the device driver being loaded.

Suggestions and examples appear given below, under loadable device drivers. If you have extended memory, use DEVICEHIGH if possible.

DEVICEHIGH

Loads an external device driver in upper memory on computers that have this memory. If upper memory isn't available, conventional memory is used (an error message doesn't inform you of this).

Suggestion: If you have a 386 computer and have used the DEVICE=EMM386.EXE command to make reserved memory available, replace all DEVICE commands in the CONFIG.SYS with DEVICEHIGH.

DOS — Determines whether DOS should load as many programs and data in the first 64K of upper memory as possible and whether DOS should fill up all of upper memory. This command helps you save valuable conventional memory. It doesn't require any memory itself.

Suggestion: Use HIMEM.SYS on ATs along with DOS=HIGH. On 386 computers, load the EMM386.EXE driver with DEVICE=EMM386.EXE and use the setting DOS=HIGH,UMB. This tells DOS to use upper memory for memory management functions as well.

DRIVPARM
Sets the drive parameters for the available floppy and hard drives. This command is rarely used and doesn't require any memory.

Suggestion: Omit

FCBS — Sets the maximum number of files that can be open at one time under the old File Control Block method. This command can be omitted if there are no error messages specifically requesting the creation of File Control Blocks.

Suggestion: Omit or FCBS=0,0

FILES — Determines the maximum number of files that can be open at once.

Suggestion: Use 20 as the default setting. If you use database programs, program switching in the DOS-Shell or Windows 3.0, use the setting FILES=30.

INSTALL Loads a program while CONFIG.SYS is being processed. For example, you could add a password program here.

LASTDRIVE
Defines the maximum number of valid drive letters. The default setting is LASTDRIVE=E. Change this only in special circumstances.

	Suggestion:	Omit

REM   Indicates non-executable program lines (REM = remark).

Suggestion: Use this command to write notes about the function and use of the settings in the CONFIG.SYS file. For example, after the line

```
SHELL=COMMAND.COM /E:500 /P
```

```
REM /E:500
REM /P
```
for 500 bytes of environment memory and because otherwise the AUTOEXEC.BAT won't be executed.

SHELL   Enables changes in setup of the command interpreter, which is loaded after the CONFIG.SYS file is processed. Important when the command interpreter is in a subdirectory, needs a larger environment (/E:XXXX), or an alternative command interpreter is used (e.g., the new powerful command interpreter of Norton Utilities 6.0).

Suggestion: SHELL=C:\COMMAND.COM /E:1024 /P

STACKS   Specifies the number and size of memory areas allocated for hardware interrupts. This command is necessary only if the program's manual refers to it. By default, DOS uses the setting STACKS=0,0 and the currently running program provides the memory for the stack.

Suggestion: Omit

SWITCHES

Allows you to set switches that will influence the way certain devices work. Up to now, it's possible to set SWITCHES=/K to disable extended keyboard functions and SWITCHES=/W to place the special WINA20.386 file in a subdirectory.

Suggestion: Omit

15.5.3 DOS device drivers in CONFIG.SYS

Besides the internal configuration commands previously listed, MS-DOS also has several other commands called device drivers. A device driver is a special program that is responsible for the proper configuration and operation of a certain device. Devices can be a piece of peripheral hardware (printer, screen, mouse, etc.), part of the PC system (device drivers for extended memory or the version of DOS), or a virtual device, such as a RAM disk.

The following is a brief description of each device driver:

ANSI.SYS Device driver for screen and keyboard. Necessary for changing the number of screen lines and columns displayed on the screen with the MODE command and for enhanced screen control and changing the keyboard layout with PROMPT. ANSI.SYS uses about 4K of memory.

Suggestion: Omit

CHKSTATE.SYS

This device driver is used only by the MEMMAKER program for optimizing the use of your system memory. If you use MEMMAKER, this driver is temporarily added to your CONFIG.SYS file.

DBLSPACE.SYS

This driver is used only for data compression. It's automatically installed in CONFIG.SYS when you call DBLSPACE. You can also install this driver yourself, which lets you load it into high memory. DBLSPACE.SYS is not the actual driver for working with compressed data storage devices (the actual driver program is DBLSPACE.BIN, which is loaded with IO.SYS and MSDOS.SYS). DBLSPACE.SYS's only purpose is to allow you to load DBLSPACE.BIN in UMB.

DISPLAY.SYS

Help file for using code pages. Many versions of DOS automatically execute the command line DEVICE=DISPLAY.SYS CON= ... during installation to set up the screen for using code pages.

Suggestion: Omit, then also remove MODE CON CODEPAGE PREPARE, NLSFUNC, and CHCP from the AUTOEXEC.BAT.

DRIVER.SYS

Can manage external disk drives (rarely) or allocate logical drives (more frequently). A logical drive is created when an existing drive is configured with new parameters and assigned a new drive letter (/D:Drive letter).

Suggestion: Omit

EGA.SYS

Special driver for eliminating disadvantages of an EGA graphics card when switching programs or using Windows 3.0. This driver is necessary only in special cases.

Suggestion: Omit

EMM386.EXE

Important device driver for memory management on 80386 systems. Allows the use of expanded memory (EMS) and upper memory (UMB).

Suggestion: On 386 systems without Windows, use DEVICE=EMM386.EXE RAM and DOS=HIGH,UMB. On 386s with Windows in 386 Enhanced mode, use DEVICE=EMM386.EXE NOEMS instead. Do not use EMM386.EXE if you have to run Windows 3.0 in Standard mode.

HIMEM.SYS

Very important device driver for extended memory on all AT or higher computers. HIMEM.SYS is a requirement for using high memory, upper memory, and XMS memory. It must be loaded by the CONFIG.SYS file before EMM386.EXE.

Suggestion: DEVICE=HIMEM.SYS

KEYBOARD.SYS

Only necessary in the KEYB command line if KEYBOARD.SYS isn't located in the current directory.

Suggestion: Omit, or add the following line to the AUTOEXEC.BAT file (for example, when using the UK keyboard):

```
KEYB UK,,C:\DOS\KEYBOARD.SYS
```

POWER.EXE

Loading this driver in CONFIG.SYS activates a program that reduces the amount of electricity used. This driver should be used only with notebook and laptop computers.

PRINTER.SYS

Only necessary for code pages (character set tables) on a printer. For more information, refer to DISPLAY.SYS.

Suggestion: Omit

RAMDRIVE.SYS

Reserves part of the system memory for a RAM disk. This command is useful only if you have a lot of extended memory.

Suggestion: Omit and use SMARTDRV.EXE instead to speed up hard drive accesses.

SETVER.EXE

Must be loaded in the CONFIG.SYS file as a device driver if you want to run a program that is dependent on the DOS version.

Suggestion: Omit

SMARTDRV.EXE

This driver is required to use double-buffering of the hard drive cache. This is needed when running Windows in extended mode. Often required with SCSI hard drives.

Suggestion: Include the command line DEVICE=C:\DOS\SMARTDRV.EXE/ DOUBLE_BUFFER when running Windows in extended mode.

15.5.4 Device drivers from other programs

There are other device drivers besides DOS device drivers. A number of hardware and software companies offer special programs with their products. The most well known program is MOUSE.SYS, the mouse driver for Microsoft and compatible mice.

Your CONFIG.SYS file may also have a special driver for your hard drive, or perhaps you have a memory expansion card that provides expanded memory via a special driver.

Some drivers even replace DOS drivers, offering enhanced, improved options. For example, your CONFIG.SYS may contain Quarterdeck's QEMM386.SYS driver. This driver is important for using the multitasking interface, DesqView.

Be very careful when changing or removing such drivers, since this can significantly alter the way your PC works.

15.6 Using System Configurations

There are several ways to use AUTOEXEC.BAT and CONFIG.SYS system files in MS-DOS 6.0. We'll discuss these possibilities in this section.

Booting without the system files

As we've already discussed, MS-DOS lets you start your system without processing the AUTOEXEC.BAT and CONFIG.SYS files.

To boot without executing these files, press the F5 key when your computer displays the message "Starting MS-DOS" while booting. This will prevent the two system files from being processed, giving you direct access to your computer. This is useful when you've made some changes to these system files and your computer won't boot.

 Unlike other compression programs, such as STACKER, DBLSPACE doesn't require a driver in the system files. This means that you can still access your hard disk even if the system files aren't executed.

Skipping portions of the system files

MS-DOS also provides an option that lets you partially execute the system files when you boot. If you press F8, the CONFIG.SYS file is displayed one line at a time. So you can decide whether each line should be processed as it's displayed. Press Y to execute the displayed line or Ⓝ to skip the line and move to the next one. This is a good way to determine exactly which line in the system file is causing your system to crash.

Once you've gone through every line in the CONFIG.SYS file, you're asked whether AUTOEXEC.BAT should be executed. Press Ⓨ to execute the file or Ⓝ to skip it.

Queries in AUTOEXEC.BAT

The CHOICE command can be used to insert queries into your AUTOEXEC.BAT file and to branch to different commands or programs, depending on the response. The result of the query is returned as an Errorlevel. The Errorlevel is queried by the batch file to determine how to proceed. The following is an example of how this command works:

Defining response keys for the query

The /C: switch lets you define the keys that will be valid as a response to the query. If you don't enter anything here, CHOICE uses the Ⓨ and Ⓝ keys as the default. You can define your own response keys by entering the appropriate characters immediately after the colon. Do not insert spaces between each response character. A distinction isn't made between upper and lowercase letters unless you use the /S switch.

For example, the following command line is used to create a query with the Ⓐ, Ⓑ, Ⓒ keys as the valid responses:

```
CHOICE /C:ABC
```

The order in which you specify each response character determines the corresponding Errorlevel. Therefore, the first character will be Errorlevel 1, the second will be Errorlevel 2, etc. In our example, the Ⓒ key is Errorlevel 3. When one of the defined response keys is pressed, the corresponding Errorlevel is returned to the batch file.

The response keys that you define are displayed on screen in square brackets separated by commas and followed by a question mark.

Suppressing the display of response keys

Use the /N switch to switch off the display of valid response keys. CHOICE will display the keys by default.

Distinguishing between upper and lowercase characters

The /S switch makes the query case sensitive.

Default response and timeout

You can use /T:Key,Time to define the default response to the query and the timeout period. If the timeout period expires and a key hasn't been pressed, the batch file receives the Errorlevel for the default response and continues processing. Values from 0 to 99 seconds are valid for Time.

Text for the query

At the end of the CHOICE command, you can also enter some text that will be displayed on screen to define the query. This text appears before the list of valid query response keys. If you want to use the "\" character in the text, then the entire text must be enclosed in quotes.

The following example shows a query that can be added to the AUTOEXEC.BAT file to ask the user whether the DOS Shell should be loaded. The user has 15 seconds to respond; otherwise the Shell is automatically started. These lines are added to the end of AUTOEXEC.BAT to create the query:

```
CHOICE /C:NY /T:Y,15 Should the MS-DOS Shell be started
IF ERRORLEVEL 2 GOTO NOSHELL
IF ERRORLEVEL 1 GOTO RUNSHELL

:RUNSHELL
  DOSSHELL
  GOTOEND

:NOSHELL
  ECHO MS-DOS SHELL NOT STARTED
  GOTO END

:END
```

If you've added these lines to your AUTOEXEC.BAT file, the following query appears on screen after this file has been processed:

```
Should the MS-DOS Shell be started [Y;N]?
```

If you press N, then the message "DOS Shell not started" appears. If you press Y or if 15 seconds pass without a response, then the MS-DOS Shell starts automatically. This happens because the N and Y keys have been defined as answers to the query.

The N key is assigned as Errorlevel 2 and the Y key is assigned as Errorlevel 1. Using /T:Y,15 indicates that the Y key is the default response and that this will be returned automatically if a response isn't given within 15 seconds. The Errorlevel returned by the query then determines which of the next two lines in the file is processed.

Different configurations within CONFIG.SYS

MS-DOS 6.0 has the capability to create a CONFIG.SYS file that gives the user a choice between various configurations while booting. We'll demonstrate this with an example and an explanation of all the commands found in such a CONFIG.SYS file.

```
[MENU]
MENUITEM= SIMPLE, Standard Configuration
MENUITEM= WINDOWS, Additional Configuration for Windows
SUBMENU= SUB_NETWORK,Novell

MENUDEFAULT= WINDOWS, 30
MENUCOLOR 7,4

[SUB_NETWORK]
MENUITEM= NOVELL, Novell 3.11 Network Configuration
MENUITEM= NETLITE, Novell Netware Lite Configuration

[SIMPLE]
DOS=HIGH
DEVICE=C:\DOS\HIMEM.SYS /A20CONTROL:ON /SHADOWRAM:ON
BUFFERS=10,0
FILES=75
lastdrive=M
FCBS=4,0
DEVICEHIGH /L:1,12048 =C:\DOS\SETVER.EXE
SHELL=C:\DOS\COMMAND.COM C:\DOS\ /E:160 /p
BREAK ON

[WINDOWS]
INCLUDE=SIMPLE
DEVICE=C:\DOS\EMM386.EXE RAM I=E000-EFFF X=C600-C6FF
DOS=UMB

[NOVELL]
INCLUDE=WINDOWS
REM Any special drivers required by Novell 3.11 go here

[NETLITE]
INCLUDE=WINDOWS
REM Any special drivers for Novell Netware Lite go here
```

If your CONFIG.SYS file is set up like this, you'll be asked which configuration you want to use each time you boot. Since each configuration is assigned a number, simply type the number for the desired configuration and press [Enter].

The commands used in this special file are explained with the following:

The MENUITEM command

This command defines the entries in the boot menu. A maximum of 9 entries is allowed.

This command must be followed by a block name that contains the name of the menu. The corresponding block will contain all the CONFIG.SYS command lines that will then be executed if this menu item is selected.

It's also possible to include text for each menu item, separated from the block name by a comma. If you do not enter additional text, then the block name will be displayed on screen as the menu name.

The SUBMENU command

This command defines a submenu within the CONFIG.SYS start menu. If the submenu item is selected, then other menu items are displayed, each of which must be defined in CONFIG.SYS with the MENUITEM command.

The SUBMENU command is followed by the block name that contains the definition of the items for the submenu. The main menu will always have the name MENU, but you can assign any name to a submenu.

As before, you can also add additional text separated from the block name by a comma. If no additional text is given, then only the block name will appear on screen.

The MENUDEFAULT command

This command determines which menu will be the default. The name of this menu item will be highlighted and its number will appear as the default response. If you don't use this command, then the first menu item in the list will become the default.

You can also set a timeout period with this command. If the timeout period expires, the default menu is automatically selected and the boot procedure continues.

If you want to use this command, you must give the block name of the menu item that you want to be the default.

The timeout period is entered after the name, separated by a comma. Valid values are 0 to 90 seconds. If you define a timeout period of 0, then the default menu is automatically selected.

The MENUCOLOR command

This command can be used to set the text and background colors for the boot menu.

The first entry sets the text color. Valid values are 0 to 15. The table below indicates which color corresponds to each value. The second value sets the background color. The entries are separated by commas. The valid values for the background color are also listed below.

Table of Color Values:

0	Black	1	Blue	2	Green
3	Cyan	4	Red	5	Magenta
6	Brown	7	White	8	Gray
9	Bright Blue	10	Bright Green	11	Bright Cyan
12	Bright Red	13	Bright Magenta	14	Yellow
15	Bright White				

The INCLUDE command

The INCLUDE command is used to call another block and process it as part of the current block. Enter the command followed by the name of the block that you want to call.

The menu blocks

Each menu block within the CONFIG.SYS file is identified by its name enclosed in square brackets. Below the name of the block, you can then enter the commands that should be executed when the corresponding menu item is selected. You can use the INCLUDE command within any menu block to call and process another set of commands.

This provides an easy way to configure your PC several different ways without having to change your CONFIG.SYS file each time.

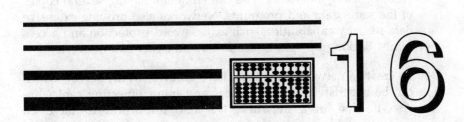

Chapter 16

MS-DOS In The Network

In this chapter, we'll explain the advantages and options of using MS-DOS as the basic operating system in a network.

Since networks are a complex subject, we won't discuss the advantages and disadvantages of networks or provide detailed technical information about networks. Instead, we'll discuss using MS-DOS on an existing network.

We'll begin by discussing some basic information about networks. So if you don't have any experience with networks, you can quickly learn the basics. This chapter should be helpful if you've never used a network and are trying to determine whether you need a network.

Most likely you're familiar with the Novell network system because this operating system has been very successful and is currently the standard for networks. For these reasons, the explanations in this chapter are based on using a Novell network.

16.1 Overview

A network is a group of computers that are connected so they can exchange data and share hardware. Networks can be arranged in various ways (e.g., star, ring, or bus). There are local and worldwide networks.

Network basics

Using a network has many advantages. One of the biggest advantages is the ability to share data among several computers.

Another advantage is the ability to divide hardware so there is one powerful server and several less powerful workstation computers.

Also, by using a network, you can eliminate having several copies of the same data and programs. Networks also provide extensive data security capabilities, such as password protection and access rights. Backing up data is also faster and easier in a network.

To create a network, you must have a powerful file server, which can be expensive. Network cards and interconnecting cables are also needed in a network. It's also important to have an uninterruptable power supply.

Installing a Novell Network

Installing a Novell network involves preparing the file server, installing the network drivers system on the file server, and preparing network drivers and a network shell for the workstations.

The person installing the system can declare him/herself system supervisor and enter a password, establish additional user code words and assign their access rights. It's also important to create efficient directory structures on the file server for programs and data.

To install programs that are able to use the network, normally you must use a special option to install them on the file server and then configure them individually for each user. Program files should be marked "read-only" and "shareable".

Also, users should be assigned only the access rights they need. However, several users can be assigned common rights by using a group defintion.

Installing DOS on the network

To install DOS on the network, first you must install DOS on the file server and then create the appropriate startup files (DOS: AUTOEXEC.BAT and CONFIG.SYS, Novell: Login Script). Access to the network can take place via IPX, NET5 and LOGIN, once the workstation is running. You should add these commands to the AUTOEXEC.BAT file.

DOS environment variables usually control the programs that can operate in a network. These and various search paths for different user identifiers should be established in a user's Login Script.

Working in the network

From the standpoint of DOS, the network makes one or more new drive letters available. Some DOS commands (FORMAT, SYS, etc.) cannot be used on network drives. You can use a special SHELL.CFG configuration file to solve problems with changing directories (..).

Printing in the network

A network printer is usually connected to a file server and can be used from all workstations. To print from a workstation, a print outlet is "seized" on the workstation with the CAPTURE command and redirected to the server.

The file server supervises a print queue that you can view and change by using PCONSOLE.

Exchanging data and messages

Use the Novell commands SEND and SESSION to exchange data in the network. However, these commands can be used to send only brief mesages to users currently at their workstations.

16.2 Types of Networks

The best feature of networks is their ability to swap data quickly and easily between computers. Worldwide networks provide information on weather, stock market quotations, etc. to computer users around the world. Also, with Local Area Networks (LANs), it's possible to use existing hardware components (printers, hard drives) from different computers joined together into a network.

Depending on their capabilities, networks place special demands on the programs used in the network. You must ensure that different users don't change the same data at the same time. So, the programs must be "networkable". Basically, this means that the programs must be able to lock (i.e., block access to) a file that's currently being used by a user. This capability is called file locking.

Local networks differ in three ways:

- Arrangement of the individual components

- Transmission media and techniques

- Access procedures

The simplest type of network consists of two computers connected by a cable. For example, you could swap data between a desktop system and a laptop system using INTERLNK in DOS 6.0. The cable required for this is available from Abacus; see the offer in the back of the book. Since it's very easy to exchange data between computers in this way we won't discuss this option in detail (see Section 16.4).

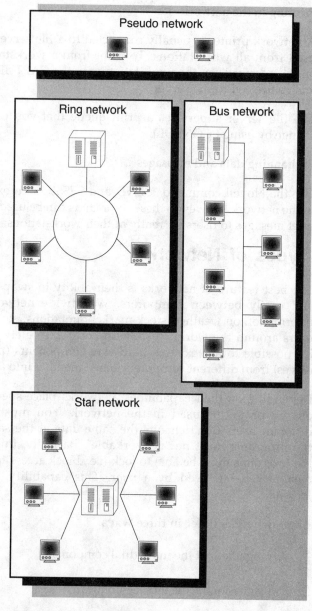

Various network types

Network arrangements

At the next level, you can join several computers together in the form of a star, ring or bus. In the star arrangement, all PCs (workstations) are connected to a powerful main computer (the server) in the shape of a star. In the ring arrangement, all computers are attached in series to a cable whose ends are connected to form a ring. Lastly, in a bus arrangement, the ends of the "ring" are simply left open.

The advantages and disadvantages of the different network arrangements depend on your data exchange needs. In the star network, for example, each workstation can exchange data directly with the server, but workstation-to-workstation data exchange requires a detour through the server. Also, the star network is rarely used because of the amounts of cable required.

In a ring network, on the other hand, data must be passed on from one computer to the next. The data "circulates" in the ring network. The disadvantage here is that if a single computer crashes, or becomes disconnected, the entire network becomes inoperative (goes down).

The bus network offers the most advantages over the other two configurations, with two disadvantages. First, the ends of the bus cable must be ended with terminators (resistors that indicate the end of the bus). Second, you are limited in the number of workstation cables you can add to the bus.

The advantage of a network

The particular advantage of a network is that only the server needs to have the data and programs stored on it. The workstations can then access data and programs from the server. That makes it relatively easy to keep data continually updated. There is no need to fear that an obsolete copy of the data on one computer is being edited.

Another advantage lies in cost containment. The workstations can function efficiently with the server, without being as powerful as the server. In fact, if all data and programs can be loaded from the server, these workstations can even operate without disk drives. The workstations can often be instructed to boot from the server through boot ROM chips.

A network usually also offers the option of presenting extended services available to workstations that wouldn't normally be available. One example is the print server, which accepts print jobs (documents for printing) from the workstations, then sends the print job to a printer connected to the network. Another example would be a workstation with FAX board capability, which would allow any other network station to send FAXes through the FAX station.

16.3 Network Basics

Much has been written lately about networks. Why are increasing numbers of PC users becoming interested in this technology? What advantages and disadvantages do networks offer?

16.3.1 Working with more than one computer

Increasing numbers of users have more than one computer. We would like to clarify this statement with a few examples.

First, businesses use networks world-wide. Several employees in a company can access the same software and the same data. This makes sense, especially when one address must be kept in a central location for access by all.

Let's take two examples. First, in a non-networked medical practice, changing a patient's address on his/her file card doesn't ensure that the billing department will receive that change of address. The result may be mismailed (and unpaid) bills, and strained relations between patient and practice. A network could solve this problem, provided it was properly set up.

Second, let's say a non-networked car dealership generates a repair order on one computer, and someone must carry a diskette containing the repair order to a different computer in the billing department.

Multiple customers, increases and decreases in estimates, and other factors can change between the time the repair order is created and the time that file is taken to billing. Most dealerships, especially conglomerate groups that handle multiple car makes under one roof, now have networks to alleviate some of this problem.

Networking could eventually make its way into the private sector, and perhaps your own home. Here are some reasons there might be a network in your future:

- You upgrade computers every year or two because of technological advances. You may not want to sell the old system(s), because of sentimental value, or because you know you won't get much money for it. Also, the older system is still quite useful for games or educational software.

- You buy a laptop to supplement your desktop computer. The problem now is keeping data on both machines current.

- One computer suffers from a chronic problem, and spends a lot of time in the repair shop. You buy a second machine to continue working. Later, the old computer comes back fixed, and the old unit sits unused.

- Perhaps you would also like to have a second PC system, because you just simply cannot afford to have your only computer die suddenly in a critical phase of your work, and repairs take too long.

Data transfer creates problems

Once you have more than one computer, you will soon see that shuffling data back and forth can cause big problems.

- If you update one copy of a file, you must be really conscientious about updating the others. If you do happen to forget, you may end up editing an older (and possibly obsolete) version of the file.

- One postulate of Murphy's Law decrees that the file or program you need won't be on the computer you're using. Few things are as frustrating as trying to run a word processor that isn't on your system, to edit a file on your system that is compatible only with that word processor.

- Anyone frequently swapping data or programs between computers will quickly find out how slow and inconvenient it is to work with diskettes. Data transfer by diskette is particularly inefficient, when the data no longer fits on one diskette (that is quickly the case with graphics files and texts) and have to be distributed over several diskettes using BACKUP, or compressed with a special compression program, transferred to diskettes and again uncompressed.

- Even using a null modem cable with appropriate software (e.g., LapLink) can be rather slow with larger amounts of data. If you need 10-15 minutes to transfer 2 Meg, the thrill of data transfer fades quickly.

Network technology can solve these problems.

16.3.2 Network components

A network in the sense used by us has the following components:

- At least two computers connected by means of a cable, of which at least one acts as the server (performs services) and acts as a supervisor.

- Special network software, the network operating system, which handles data management and access rights.

In addition to those components mentioned, a network includes still more:

- An operating system which permits network access. In our case, MS-DOS 6.0.

- Special programs which will run on a network. That means that the word processing program must accept tasks beyond writing, saving and printing texts. In other words, this same program must be able to keep different users separate, and control access rights as needed (more on this later in this chapter).

- A system manager, also called the supervisor. This is the user who handles the network's basic operations and setup. The better this person sets up the network, the more efficiently the network will run, and the more all the other users will profit from it.

Of course, the "conditions" just mentioned are not absolutely necessary for a network.

The buzzword "network" has been applied to such inexpensive solutions as multiple drives cabled together, and assigning other computers logical drive letters rather than actual ones. These don't really fit into the network description that we've laid out so far.

16.3.3 Network advantages

You may be wondering about the advantages of a network as a whole. We've seen a long list of requirements, and simple data transfer can't be the only benefit. A well installed, well configured network offers a series of important benefits. We'll list these benefits here to help you make some decisions:

Working on a project

- A network greatly simplifies the task of several people working on a single project. Networking allows access to a common body of data.

- Networks minimize data redundancy (multiple copies of the same file on different computers). Data redundancy wastes resources, and presents the danger that an old version may overwritten a current version of a file, or worse, that multiple users will be working on duplicate versions of the same file.

Data security

- Networks allow easy and relatively inexpensive data backup. Single computers would require each user to back up his or her data to diskettes, which is time-consuming, or add a tape streamer to each computer for backups, which is expensive. On a network, a single tape streamer can do the job of backing up the server's hard drive.

Communication options

- Networks allow communication between users. A user can send messages to single users, or an entire group of users. Also, network mail software is available, so users not on the system at the time of the message can receive messages, then refer to them at their leisure. All the options just named represent optimal conditions for teamwork and can significantly increase the productivity of a department.

Better use of peripheral devices

- A network permits better use of peripheral devices. Network users can access network printers, modems or FAX boards, with proper planning.

Money saved

- If you start with a powerful server, the workstations can "lean on" the server's capabilities. For example, if your server has a 300 Meg hard drive and you install the programs you need on that drive, then your workstations don't need 80 Meg hard drives, and may even survive without hard drives.

Protecting data from destruction

- Computer programs and data can be easily protected not only against destruction, but also against unauthorized access. In a well organized net you set an inexperienced person down at a workstation computer and let him try out something, because this person does not have the access rights to delete or destroy data.

Protecting sensitive data

- Any data can be protected from inspection by users. A properly configured network server can even be made available to others, or brought to a workplace with all data and programs, without the need to fear that anyone will take a peek into your protected files.

Greater control

- Supervisor (system manager) control can be a blessing to some, and a curse to others. Supervisors can easily determine what programs and data a person is working with, and how long their computer was connected to the network.

16.3.4   Network disadvantages

Naturally a network does not have only advantages. Rather, there is an entire list of more or less important disadvantages:

Hardware costs

- The hardware necessary within the network can involve significant expense. A file server, for example, is expensive, because it should have a 386 processor at minimum, with a large hard drive (more than 100 Meg) and a lot of memory (more than 4 Meg).

  Besides, since the file server will be dedicated (used only for network operations), you will need another computer to act as a workstation for access. If a program on the server crashes the server, this will take the network down and cause loss of data currently in the workstations not recently saved, but still in the server's cache.

Expensive add-ons

- The more you want the network to accomplish, the more the costs for the hardware. Because all data are only available in one place (on the file server), it's a good idea not to rely exclusively on the built-in hard drive.

  So, you should install an especially reliable (i.e., expensive) hard drive, and use "disk mirroring". For that you have to install a second, identical hard drive into the computer and always have all data from the network operating system (for example, Novell NetWare) written onto both hard drives.

During a read operation the two identical stores of data are read and compared. If there is a difference, or one hard drive drops out due to a hardware defect, you can always read the data from the second disk and use this to continue working for the time being.

Uninterruptable power supplies

- Although in MS-DOS there are usually no consequences in normal operation (solo) if the computer is abruptly shut down due to power loss, that can mean considerable data losses in a file server. Since the network won't tolerate an uncontrolled shutoff, and the server must be properly shut down to store data, you'll need an "uninterruptable power supply" (UPS).

This UPS is basically a large battery able to maintain the power for yet another 15-30 minutes, if the house current from the outlet is interrupted. The longer the period during which the computer can be operated on this battery power, the more expensive the UPS.

Costs for the network operating system

- Even the costs for the network operating system are rather high. The more speed and performance desired, the more expensive the operating system. The price strongly depends upon the maximum number of users. If only up to five workstations are managed, the operating system will be much cheaper than if 100 workstations are provided.

Network software more expensive

- That usually means that more expensive software is used, or must be used. Software frequently exists in a relatively inexpensive single-station version and a more expensive network version. You will also save money, of course, if a network version for five users costs "only" double the price of the single-station version, because five users will then be able to use the program at the same time.

- Anyone wanting to take optimal advantage of the benefits of a network will also require special software for the network. This must be capable of network operation. That means essentially that the programs must have a protective mechanism available, permitting a file currently being worked on by another user to be locked (file locking). Specially structured files being worked on at the moment can also be locked (record locking).

Getting into it

- Acquiring the necessary know how for operating a network means an additional outlay of time and money. Although there is an extensive amount of literature covering all available application programs and problems which may arise, the information on networks is frequently still highly theoretical and of little help in solving practical problems.

  Unfortunately, most of us are not personally acquainted with a "network expert" whom we can call upon for advice. As a result, expensive schooling or very expensive service contracts are frequently the only solution.

Extra system managers

- But it is also often possible to assume responsibility for data care and maintenance on your PC yourself. Within a network, a supervisor (system manager) should take charge of the basic tasks and installations. It makes no difference whether someone devotes himself exclusively to this job, or takes it on only as a sideline, it will in any case take up a lot of time. And as the saying goes, time is money.

16.3.5   The prerequisites

Anyone deciding, after having weighed the pros and cons, that the implementation of a network makes sense, should read the prerequisites below. You are undoubtedly already aware of some of the aspects and concepts.

Server: The server must be at least an AT with 2 Meg of memory. But of course a server like that might be completely inadequate for the job. Therefore, we advise you to get a machine with at least a 386SX processor running at 25 MHz, a hard drive with a capacity of at least 100 Meg and at least 4 Meg of working memory.

A server can get along without VGA and a mouse, however, because you should run it only as a "dedicated" unit (i.e., only as a server, no DOS operation). A low-priced Hercules card is good enough for the video display.

In the case of a server, you may even be able to get along without a keyboard and a monitor. If you later have need of a monitor, or of a means of input, you will need a correspondingly equipped workstation available from which you can temporarily borrow the monitor and keyboard.

The lack of a keyboard and monitor also prevents anyone from using the server to log onto the network and enter dangerous commands (MONITOR, SHUTDOWN etc.).

Workstations:

Workstations have fewer hardware demands than a server. In our experience, for example, relatively inexpensive 386SX units with 2 Meg of RAM will yield nearly the performance of 25 MHz 386DX models, if the server itself is adequately configured for rapid data transfer.

A further advantage of 386 machines (whether SX or DX) over 286/AT units is the required network program requires about 60K of memory. This amount of memory would severely reduce the amount of working memory available on a 286.

On the other hand, on 386 machines, the network driver can be swapped along with MS-DOS into the reserved memory region (Upper Memory, High Memory), enabling you to still make use of 600K and more of working memory despite the network.

Network cards:

The actual transfer of data in a network is taken care of by network boards installed in the server and workstations.

These boards, and the hard drive of the server, are significant factors in determining the overall performance of the network. Anyone choosing the cheapest (and usually the slowest) network cards won't be very happy when confronted with the high data transfer-rates of programs like Windows.

In any case, we recommend a 16-bit board for the server, while fast 8-bit boards can also be used for workstations.

Cabling: Although the cabling for the computer is not really all that expensive, you'll also need special tools for the special cables and connectors. It's best to buy the cables ready-made and estimate their length on the long side.

It's really irritating, when a cable can no longer be used, because a workstation has been moved to another part of the room. The ends of the lines must be equipped with terminators.

   In addition, network cables are doubly sensitive, which should be considered in your planning. They should not be subjected to mechanical stress (e.g., avoid laying the cables so chair wheels connect with them). Breaking a single connection can lead to disturbances in the entire network's operation.

For correct data transfer, the network needs closed circuits, which an accidentally broken connection will not provide.

Network operating system:
As mentioned, you'll need a special network operating system for the server (and corresponding programs on the workstations). Here, of course, various suppliers will promote different products. Many manufacturers accept Novell NetWare as a standard capable of high performance.

For example, we've run Version 2.15 for the 286 without problems on a 386 machine, and have had no performance difficulties under Windows, with 3 to 5 workstations attached.

Additional speed and performance is offered, for example, by the special 386-targeted Version 3.11. There is, naturally, a series of further possibilities (like the OS/2-based LAN Manager).

Operating system:
If you thought you could simply equip all computers with a network operating system, think again. Both

the server and the workstations still require the installation of a DOS operating system. Which DOS version you choose will depend upon the hardware and your personal preferences.

We generally advise you use the most recent version of MS-DOS because this DOS version makes use of special memory management techniques to put an end to the continually arising problems with memory space on network computers. In MS-DOS Versions 5.0 and 6.0 you can swap the network drivers into special regions of the computer (High Memory, Upper Memory).

Security: We urge every network operator to turn attention to the network's data security at an early stage. We've already suggested uninterruptable power supplies and tape streamers.

Additional security measures, like mirrored disks and the like, should be considered according to need. These security measures make up a significant portion of network costs.

Besides, server failure due to a defect leads in most cases to a crash of the entire system.

☞ To prevent disaster, you can ensure yourself rapid help from your dealer by signing a service contract or using a removable hard drive, and keeping a second PC on hand as a "spare server".

In case of emergency you pull the removable hard drive out of the defective server and insert it in the spare. You will then have one workstation less. Provided that you reconfigure the hardware properly, the substitute server will fill the bill temporarily.

Quality: These hints show that saving money in hardware purchases (for example, of the server) with cheap components would be better off to leave networks alone.

Hardware provided by Novell includes "Novell Approved" notations. This may not always refer to the top seller in the market, but great value must be placed on quality.

16.3.6 Novell at the outset

Essentially there are many choices of operating systems for network use. There is also a whole series of reasons for the use of Novell Netware.

Novell is standard

- Novell has set a standard for powerful PC nets; and the effect of this experience and maturity in practice is very positive.

- Novell is being continually further developed. You thus have no need to worry that it will someday no longer be possible to accommodate your network operating system to new hardware and software.

- Novell is well supported by many programs. This is true not only for the very popular user interface, Windows, but also for application programs like the database program Superbase.

- When problems and questions do turn up relating to the use of Novell, you will have at least a chance of finding competent advisors among your friends for the solution of problems.

Tested by a magazine

And finally: six network operating systems were tested and compared in a recent magazine (among them Novell versions 2.2 and 3.11), and both Novell versions received unequivocal recommendations from the editors.

This not only made us as Novell users very happy, but also confirmed our very positive experiences with the performance and compatibility of this software.

The competition: LAN Manager

Now for a word on the great competitor—the LAN Manager. This software is based on OS/2 rather than MS-DOS. For DOS users Novell NetWare is surely the better choice.

16.3.7 Examples and tips

Our discussion in this chapter is based on a bus network.

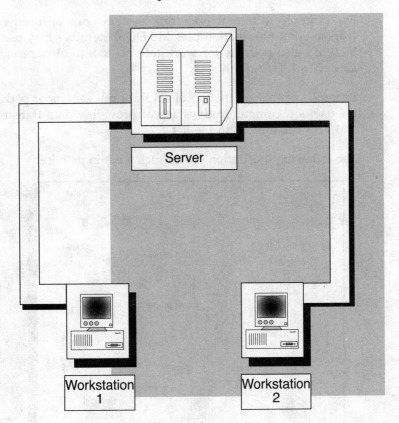

A simple net

The drawing shows the basic principle and the simplest meaningful variant of a network. This network comprises a server and one or more workstations, attached to the server by means of special cables.

This makes it possible for all workstations to access programs and data on the server, and for these programs and data to exist in one location (the server). The result is, among other things, data integrity:

All workstations work with the same store of data.

The examples and procedures in this chapter are based on a Novell network with the ELS Level II version, Version 2.15. The small of the procedures may differ slightly in the case of other networks.

However, the essential steps, results and problems can be easily adapted. On the whole, a network has more to offer than our simplified example.

For example, different operating systems can be used on the workstations: One station uses MS-DOS, the other may use OS/2 V2.0. It's also possible for workstations, too, to offer services for all network participants.

Examples of this are the use of several print servers or perhaps of the use of a communications server providing data transmission and FAX capabilities in the net.

The following illustration shows such a net in practice:

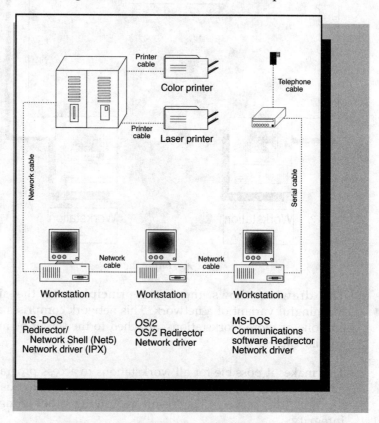

Network with workstations, server, printer and modem

The drawing shows a network with three workstations, each with a specific job. The central element is the file server to the upper left, acting as a print server and connected to the available printers (here a color printer and a laser printer).

The three workstations on the lower level are attached to the file server through network cables. One workstation runs under MS-DOS, the other under OS/2, and the one at the far right also runs under MS-DOS.

This particular workstation contains all the communication software. Also found here are the connections to the mail network (serial cable to the modem, from there the telephone cable to the public mail net).

16.4 Connecting Computers with INTERLNK

The INTERLNK program provides a simple means of data transfer between two computers connected by a cable. This eliminates the time-consuming transfer method of diskettes. Of greatest interest here is the possibility for data exchange between a laptop/notebook computer and a desktop PC.

16.4.1 What INTERLNK does

A distinction is made during data exchange between server and client, at which point the typical network concepts come into play:

Commands are entered on the client, the server delivers the data. Let's take an example: If you want to use your laptop to load data from your desktop PC, the laptop is then the client, and the desktop PC is the server.

The INTERSVR is locked and cannot be used for other tasks, when it is running on the server.

In practice it looks as if the drives on the server are available as supplementary drives on the client. For the purpose of this example, you have perhaps the following drives on your laptop and are able to address them entirely in the normal manner under DOS:

Laptop/client in practice:

A: Laptop A: (its own installed drive)

B: Not available or installed (the laptop has only one drive)

C: Laptop C: (the client's own hard drive)

D: Server A: (the server's drive A)

E: Server B: (the server's drive B)

F: Server C: (the server's hard drive)

Take an example: When you want to transfer data from your desktop PC, as the server, to your laptop, you can switch with F: on the laptop to hard drive C of the desktop PC/server.

If you then want to load the text of a letter in the \TEXTS\LETTERS directory from there onto your laptop, you need only change to the corresponding directory, and the data on the hard disk of your desktop PC will be available to you. F:\TEXTS\LETTERS is then displayed as the directory. On the server you would find the same data under C:\TEXTS\LETTERS.

You will in any case quickly get used to the fact that F is the letter for the hard drive of the server supplying the data. And normally you will limit your accesses almost exclusively to the server hard drive.

In the case of disk drives, you could as a rule insert the diskette directly into the client—but if it has the wrong diskette format, you will still have to use INTERLNK.

Let's assume that you have only a 3.5 inch drive on the laptop and want to copy data from a 5.25 inch diskette onto its hard drive. In that case you can simply insert the "incorrect" diskette into the disk driver of the server and type

```
COPY D:\*.* C:
```

to copy the data onto the hard drive of your laptop. These are only brief reflections to get you used to network concepts and procedures.

Prerequisites

Aside from the INTERLNK program, the corresponding hardware must also be available.

• A free serial or parallel port on both computers.

• A 3-line or 7-line null modem cable or a two-way parallel cable (refer to the offer in the back of this book).

• MS-DOS 3.0 or higher (We're assuming you have MS-DOS 6.0).

• 16K of free memory on the client, and 130K of memory free on the server, in other words, no significant amount of memory.

16.4.2 Installing the Link

Let's get connected:

1. Connect the two computers using the cable.

2. Copy INTERLNK.EXE onto the client, making the new drive letters available in DOS.

3. Copy INTERSVR.EXE onto the server, thus making data and services available on the server.

4. If the computers are able to do so, copy the two programs onto both computers.

5. Install INTERLNK in the CONFIG.SYS file of the client, for example, with the following command line (see the Appendix for complete parameter explanations):

```
DEVICE=C:\DOS\INTERLNK.EXE /drives:5
```

6. Start INTERSVR from the DOS prompt on the server. When INTERSVR is active, task swapping in the DOS shell and Windows is deactivated. Thus you can't switch to a different application.

16.4.3 Using the Link

After rebooting with INTERLNK added to CONFIG.SYS, and after running INTERSVR on the server, simply activate a new drive on the client (for example, F:) and switch to it.

Printer ports can likewise be used from both computers; LPT1 on the client accesses LPT2 on the server and LPT2 on the client LPT3 of the server. In practice, that means you will be able to print something from your laptop on the printer of the server without difficulty, once the link is established.

To break the link between server and client, you have to press Alt + F4 on the server. You can restore the link again later by starting the INTERSVR.EXE program.

16.5 Windows for Workgroups

MS-DOS 6.0 isn't limited to operation in a Novell network. We've found that MS-DOS 6.0 also works extremely well with networks based on Windows for Workgroups, Windows NT or the LAN Manager.

In this way, different computers running under Microsoft operating systems like DOS, Windows or Windows NT can exchange data simply and easily.

Prerequisites for using Workgroups in DOS 6.0

To install a DOS 6.0 computer in a network, you will naturally require suitable network hardware. For a simple network you will need:

- a network card

- a network cable

- a terminator (terminal resistor)

We'll discuss hardware installation below in more detail.

Summary of installation

Installation consists of the following steps:

- Install the hardware

- Configure the hardware and network card

- Start the SETUP program from the Windows for Workgroups Setup diskette

- Set the configuration

- Copy the Windows for Workgroups files

- Adjust AUTOEXEC.BAT and CONFIG.SYS

- Restart the computer with the changed values

- Log onto the system for the first time with your logon name and password

16.5.1 Installing the network hardware

When installing the network card in the computer, you have to be particularly careful to see that it is correctly configured. A network card requires an unused interrupt (IRQ) and an input/output base (I/O base). Many network cards also require an additional memory range of a few kilobytes in the upper memory area (upper memory).

Configuring the network card

Many users find configuring the network card very confusing, because the settings are unfamiliar. Because of this, we want to give you the following information:

IRQ number

The following table shows the typical assignment of the IRQ numbers in a PC:

IRQ Number	PC/XT	PC/AT
2	EGA/VGA	EGA/VGA
3	COM2	COM2
4	COM1	COM1
5	Hard disk	LPT2
7	LPT1	LPT1

If all the devices listed are installed in your machine, the search for a free interrupt will be a little more difficult. Fortunately, there are still a few numbers free, which are listed below.

I/O base address

Even selecting the I/O base address can lead to conflicts which will impair the network card's operation, or even of the entire system.

I/O address	Possible device conflicts
200	Game port/joystick/expansion card
220	Novell Netware master card
240	
260	LPT2
280	Special LCD displays (Wyse 2108)
2A0	
2C0	
2E0	COM4
	COM2
300	Prototype card

I/O address	Possible device conflicts
	3COM Etherlink setting
320	XT hard drive
340	
360	LPT1
380	SLDC/Bi-Sync interface 2
3A0	Bi-Sync interface 1
	Monochrome monitor
3C0	EGA controller
	CGA controller
3E0	COM3
	Floppy disk controller
	COM1

If several entries are made at one address, the named devices will use this address range. However, these devices cannot be present all at the same time, or use this range simultaneously.

Base address for RAM

The use of certain RAM regions for data transfer can also lead to problems and memory conflicts. For that reason you should have accurate knowledge of the memory regions claimed by certain devices. This essentially concerns the special adapter region between 640K and 1 Meg. The following table shows the allocation of this memory:

Device	A000	B000	C000	D000	E000	F000	10000
MONO		B000-B100					
CGA		B800-BFFF					
EGA	A000-AFFF	B000-BFFF					
VGA mono	A000-AFFF	B000-B7FF	C000-C800				
VGA color	A000-AFFF	B800-BFFF	C000-C800				
Expanxsx memory					E000-EFFF		
XT BIOS						F400-FFFF	
AT BIOS (IBM)					E000-EFFF	F000-FFFF	
AT BIOS (compatible computer)						F000-FFFF	

The presentation of the numbers and ranges is not completely accurate, because the VGA card range begins at A0000 rather than A000. However, the last zero is usually omitted.

Furthermore, on many computers with an 80386 processor or higher, portions of this memory range are used as upper memory for swapping device drivers and TSR programs.

The following table shows information on the designation of the various memory areas in different operating systems.

Address in K	MS-DOS	DR DOS
0 - 640	Conventional Memory	Conventional Memory
> 1024	Extended Memory	Extended Memory
?	Expanded Memory	Expanded Memory
1024-1088	High Memory	High Memory
640 - 1024	Upper Memory Block	Upper Memory
0 - 64	Lower Memory	Lower Memory

The EMM386.EXE device driver should be appropriately configured to prevent memory conflicts from occurring with the use of upper memory.

16.5.2 Avoiding memory conflicts with EMM386.EXE

The EMM386 device driver can recognize whether certain memory regions are occupied by devices or able to be used as upper memory. But if a network card sets aside memory for data transfer, conflicts nearly always result. For that reason, you have to use a special parameter to exclude the address area from use as high memory:

X=AAAA-BBBB

        Excludes the address area from A000 to B000 in the adapter segment from use as high memory.

For example, if a network card uses 8K, starting with base address E000, it will then be necessary to exclude the region from E000 to E1FF:

```
DEVICE=EMM386.EXE NOEMS X=E000-E1FF
```

Some network cards, however, use a memory area with a sized of 16K, making it then necessary to exclude E000-E3FF from use as upper memory.

16.5.3 Network card features

Some network cards have very few setting options; others can be very flexibly configured. We would like at this point to explain the advantages and disadvantages of each operating with Windows for Workgroups.

Various factory settings

Often, it's possible to set network cards to different IRQ values and
I/O addresses, making it possible to select a different setting in
the case of conflicts with other devices. The factory defaults
follow the most frequently used settings. The values of these
settings can generally be found in the documentation supplied with
the network cards. For example, an EtherCard Plus Elite 16
(WD/8013EP) has an IRQ setting of 3 and the I/O base set at 280.

If your network card does have such a factory setting, and this is
not automatically recognized during installation, it is best that
you make the entry manually, if the information asks for it.

Configuring network cards by changing hardware

Many network cards are configured with jumpers on the adapter
board. That's good if the values never change, but very bad if you
need to make changes, say, if a new device causes a conflict with
the network card. The network card can only be changed by
changing the network card configuration. If that happens, you
must:

- shut down the network computer

- remove the network cables

- open the computer

- pull out the card

- reset the jumpers

- put everything back

- test it

- if everything works, restore the network; otherwise, reset the
  jumpers again

- restart the network

Software configuration

Adapters that can be set through software are much more easily controlled. In this case, you run the network card's setup program, enter the new values, test them on the spot and save them, if everything has worked properly. In this case there is no need to fiddle with screws and no need to take the network card off-line, because it is not necessary to disconnect the cable. However, you will need to log off, because the network link is interrupted.

With an EtherCard Plus Elite 16 (WD/8013EP), you use, for, example the EZSETUP program to change the values and get the following display:

```
Board Type:  8013EPC
Node Address: 0000C0716B61

           Current Setup

I/O Base Address  240
IRQ          10
RAM Size       16 K
RAM Base Address  0C8000
Add Wait States   Yes
Network Connection BNC

ROM Size       Disabled
ROM Base Address   Disabled

Do you want to change the setup ? (y) ->
```

The values can then be directly changed. The correct and current values are automatically recognized in the installation program. These settings can later continue to be used without problems, unlike those set using jumpers on the card. DOS automatically recognizes and accepts the new values when you next start the computer.

We suggest you avoid making the adjustments while accessing network functions in an MS-DOS Shell task. For that it is best to leave the data store and switch to a local drive.

But if you do change the jumpers of a hardware-configurable card, it would then be necessary to change the settings in Windows for Workgroups. Under certain circumstances a reinstallation may be necessary.

Tips for correct selection of the settings

At this point we would like to give you a few tips on correct choices for the settings:

Retain the factory settings if possible

You should, if possible, use the preset values from the factory. These are also for the most part the values used by the Windows for Workgroups drivers as settings for the recognized network cards. The odds are best that the defaults will cause the fewest problems.

Write down the network settings

If you do must change the network card settings, write down the factory default settings on a piece of paper and tape the paper in your computer's case. You could even use a diskette label.

If the preset values don't work, you should use the following guidelines when making the changes:

If possible use an IRQ address which is completely free

If possible use an IRQ number which is completely free (perhaps number 10). This will minimize conflicts with existing devices. If this doesn't work, use the IRQ number of a port not in use. If you have only one serial port, you can use IRQ 3 of the second serial port. In 80286 computers and up, equipped with only one parallel port, you can use IRQ 5 pretty much without difficulty.

For the I/O base address you can use the values 300, 240, or 280, which are good alternatives if your computer is not equipped with an LCD display.

The RAM area you choose would be free, and you should also take care that it lies as close as possible to the beginning or to the end of a block.

Get as much upper memory as possible

In many computers the region between C800 and EFFF is free, ahead of it is the VGA BIOS (in case you have VGA) and after it the computer BIOS. Try to avoid using D000 as the starting address if you are working with an upper memory area, because the total memory block will then be split into two parts:

• C800-CFFF

• D400-EFFF

This could make it impossible to load the larger drivers completely, the available working memory being reduced. If possible, use the C800 or EC00 region, that is, the beginning or end of the free area. Don't forget to lock out this area in the EMM386.EXE device driver with X=....

The following table shows once more the most important devices and their possible conflicts with the network card. Enter the exact dates of further devices installed by you directly into the table in the book. A few terminal programs for modems permit the use of different COM ports with different settings. In the case of the ProComm Plus terminal program, this can look like the following:

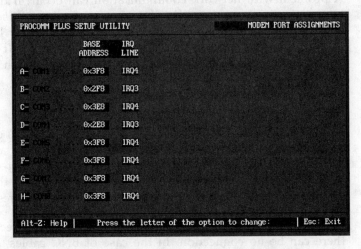

COM definition in terminal programs

Different settings can be likewise entered. Write the settings down in the printed table along with the settings for the network card. You can even use a pencil, if the settings are to be changed later; or make a copy of the page.

This information should make it possible for you to correctly configure the network card without great difficulty and to install Windows for Workgroups. If problems do turn up, the following section will provide help with the most frequently occurring breakdowns and problems.

Avoiding crashes

The following list of breakdowns and problems comes directly from exprience:

Crash: IRQ 2 used

A network card ran DOS applications without difficulty in a network. But as soon as Windows was started, the screen remained dark and the computer suspended activity.

Solution: The card was set to IRQ 2 (EGA/VGA), disabling Windows' screen driver. As soon as IRQ had been reset to 5, the card ran without problems. In the case of Novell networks, the setting is also saved in the NET$OS.EXE file, so be careful when restoring from backup diskettes or streamers, because the corrected values will then reset back to the old values which don't work.

Crash: Cable connection severed

A problem with network communication can occur, if the cable connection is temporarily broken. In many cases, the synchronization between the network cards is thereby lost and does not reappear when the connection is restored. It is then necessary to restart the software and the driver, which usually means rebooting the computer.

Crash: No terminal resistor attached

Not only a parted cable leads to errors and crashes, this can also result from an absent or incorrect terminal resistor.. Attached to each network card is a T-connector, one end of it connected to the cable to the next computer, the other either to a cable in the other direction (to form a chain) or to a terminator or terminal resistor.

If this resistor is not present, or does not have the correct value, there can be no connection. In the case of BNC cables, 50 ohm resistors must be used. Whether not the value is correct can usually be determined from the label.

Crash: SCSI controller occupies memory space

Problems with the selection of a memory area for the network card can also occur, if a SCSI controller (perhaps for a SCSI hard drive) is used. The associated BIOS will then take up space in memory and come into conflict with the network card memory. In these cases, it is best to select a different area. For example, if you are working with color VGA, the B000-B7FF area can be used.

Other drivers or hardware expansions can also lead to memory conflicts with the network card. Look through your computer documentation or use the MSD program supplied by Microsoft for diagnosis.

Crash: Errors in configuration files

Many errors come about from failures and conflicts in the configuration files. For example, it can happen that memory management errors, which have already been around for a while, will abruptly appear if the doubly allocated memory is suddenly used. In cases of doubt, it is best to set up special minimal configuration files to prevent such problems.

Successful installations with minimal system files

Anyone with problems during installation (for example, of network cards) should give it a try with minimally configured AUTOEXEC.BAT and CONFIG.SYS files. It's often some driver, specially used memory area or doubly allocated I/O-addresses, which make the installation impossible. In an emergency use the following configurations:

```
REM CONFIG.SYS
Device=C:\HIMEM.SYS
DEVICE=SETVER.EXE
FILES=30
BUFFERS=20

REM AUTOEXEC.BAT
PROMPT $P$G
PATH C:\DOS
```

It may be necessary merely to adjust the path if HIMEM.SYS is not in the main directory or DOS is not in the C:\DOS. Once when everything is working, make a backup of your AUTOEXEC.BAT and CONFIG.SYS files, then run MEMMAKER to maximize your free memory.

16.5.4   Installing Windows for Workgroups

Most network cards are correctly recognized automatically during installations. The basic requirements during an installation are a user name and the name of a work group. The work group is important and must also be that with which you will want to work in the Windows for Workgroups network.

Otherwise, you will not have access to the resources of the group (drives, printer). You can enter any user name you like and are then asked for a password that must be entered a second time for security purposes.

Windows for Workgroups is installed from a special diskette and is actually very simple. Insert the SETUP diskette in drive A: and run the SETUP.EXE. Type:

```
A:SETUP
```

and press ⌷Enter⌷. The first to appear, of course, is the opening screen:

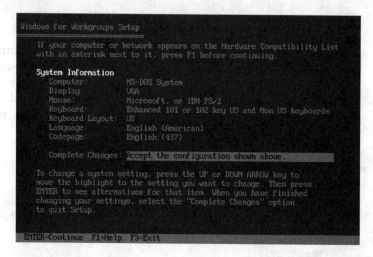

The Windows for Workgroups opening screen

After the opening screen appears, you can select the method of setup, similar to normal Microsoft Windows.

Next, you can specify the path in which you want Windows for Workgroups installed.

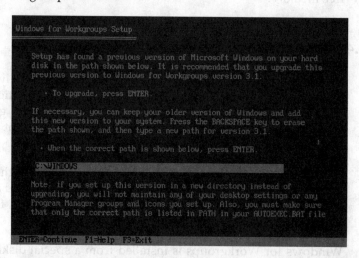

Installing the Windows for Workgroups directory

The installation program looks through the computer for setup information. Once SETUP finds the configuration satisfactory, it begins copying files to your hard drive.

Copying files

The system periodically asks you to change diskettes.

Prompting for diskette changes

Halfway through the installation process, SETUP changes from DOS mode into Windows mode and requests your name, your company's name, the name of your system and the name of the workgroup which you want to set up.

Once setup is complete in Windows for Workgroups, you'll be asked to return to DOS or restart your computer. We recommend you restart altogether.

When the system reboots, you'll see some activity taking place in your AUTOEXEC.BAT file that wasn't there before. Windows for

Workgroups adds a number of files to the system, which go under Microsoft's general title of Workgroup Connection:

PROTMAN.EXE or Protocol Manager supervises the cooperation of the network hardware with various network protocols. WORKGRP.SYS is the device driver for managing workgroups.

The SETUP program added the following line to AUTOEXEC.BAT:

```
C:\DOS\net start
```

This command line creates the link to a Windows for Workgroups network. You are then asked by NET for the user name and password.

Changes in the network configuration

The Workgroup Connection settings can be easily updated, if you must make changes in the configuration of either the computer or the network. This requires running the Setup application from within Windows.

To manually connect yourself to the network and log into the Workgroup from DOS, you enter the line command line:

```
NET LOGON
```

NET prompts you to enter your user name and password. Windows for Workgroups also prompts for this information when you start it.You are then prompted to enter your user name or merely to confirm it with (Enter), if it is the user name entered during installation.

The password can have a length of up to 14 characters and should be at least 5 characters long.

Accessing Workgroup Connection resources from the POPUP interface

Microsoft Windows for Workgroups boots the system prepared for connection access. You make your connections through the File Manager's **Disk/Connect Network Drive...** item.

In DOS, the NET POPUP program is a TSR (Terminate and Stay Resident) program that can be accessed by pressing (Alt) + (N). You cannot make changes to NET during operation, but you can connect to and disconnect from resources.

To access the interface directly from the DOS system prompt, enter the command line:

    NET

To load the interface permanently into memory and have it available for use at any time, the following command line is used:

    NET START POPUP

Appearing at this point is a message telling you that the program has been started and can be activated with [Alt] + [N].

You can now activate the indicated key combination in any application you desire to call the network interface. In your word processor, for example, you can connect with another computer in the network to load a text. Or connect to a printer available in the network to print something on it.

```
Disk Connections                          [Show Printers]

  Drive: G:                               [ Connect  ]
  Path:
  [ ] Reconnect at startup                [  Browse  ]

           Current connections            [Disconnect]

                                          [   Exit   ]

                                          [   Help   ]

```

POPUP

If you select the [Exit] check box, the window will disappear and you will be able to continue working in the application program.

To remove the POPUP program again from memory, type the following entry at the DOS system prompt:

    NET STOP POPUP

A message then tells you that the program for forming the link to the Workgroup Connection was removed from memory. The links aren't actually removed—you just cannot assign new network paths from within running programs.

If you have removed the POPUP program from memory and want to make changes in the network allocations, you can immediately enter the NET command from the DOS system prompt and make the changes.

Connecting to a directory on another computer

When a connection is made to a directory released for use by the various network users, a network path is assigned to a drive letter. If the computer with the Workgroup Connection uses only the drive letters A:, B:, C:, then letter D: could be assigned to a network path.

Since you won't have a listing right at hand of available computers in the network, click on the [Browse] button or press [Alt] + [B]. The "Browse" window lists directories currently shared, and directories on which you would like sharing to occur.

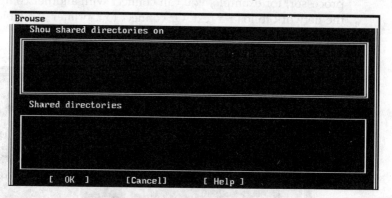

Searching the network connections

For example, to establish the network path to the C: directory on the 386_40 computer and assign it drive letter D:, you choose 386_40 in the upper window and select line C in the lower area. Clicking on [OK] makes the connection.

The [Connect] button makes the connection to the path. You can manually type in this path, but we recommend using the [Browse] button.

If you would like to have the connection established permanently and automatically restored the next time you boot the computer, enable the "Reconnect at startup" check box. You can click in this check box with the mouse, or press [Alt] + [R]. A permanent connection to a released directory makes sense, if you frequently have to access the same data or programs in released directories. Many programs store paths and expect them to be available again the next time the program starts.

If you later want to remove a connection to a directory, run the POPUP program and select the desired connection. Select the [Disconnect] button (press Alt + D).

Select the [Exit] button to exit, or press Alt + X or Esc .

Using a network printer

The Workgroup Connection lets you print on a network printer in the network, as if it were attached to your PC. For this purpose, a printer, available in the network and released, is assigned to a port.

After you start the POPUP program, select Alt + S to display a list of all printers in the network. Like the directories, you can [Connect], [Disconnect], [Browse] for printers. In addition you can display the print queue by selecting [Show Queue].

The "Print Queue" window lists printer, user, ID, file size of the print job and status of the print job.

16.5.5 Using the Workgroup Connection with NET

Using the Workgroup Connection from the POPUP program is very reliable and quite convenient. Connections once established through MS-DOS 6.0 can be restored automatically. If released drives and commonly utilized printers have been in operation for relatively long periods of time without changes, you will have very little more to do with the POPUP program.

But if you want to set up the options within the network to run more automatically and control them from batch files, the POPUP program will be of little use to you. It is however possible to reach all the network options with a new and very comprehensive command: NET. This command has an entire series of key words at its disposal.

You already became acquainted with the command in its simplest form, without additional parameters, when you used NET to start the POPUP surface directly, or with

```
NET START POPUP
```

to install the interface permanently in memory.

Summary of the NET commands

NET   Loads the Workgroup Connection interface.

NET CONFIG
> Displays the current network and Workgroup Connection settings.

NET HELP
> Displays Help information on the individual NET commands.

NET LOGOFF
> Terminates access to the network and severs all connections to the commonly used resources.

NET LOGON
> Creates the link to the network and restores access to the commonly used resources, if permanent was selected when making the connection.

NET PASSWORD
> Changes the code word for the user's code word file. It is here that all the code words employed by the user are saved, to permit the Workgroup Connection to restore connections previously made. The old code word must be entered once more to establish the new one.

NET PRINT
> Displays a list of the files waiting to be printed in the print queue. When making this entry, NET PRINT must be followed by the name of the computer containing the print queue, or to which the printer is attached. Printing can also be stopped, continued; or a file can be removed from the print queue.

NET START
> Starts the Workgroup Connection or loads the POPUP program into memory. You can use BASIC or FULL to specify whether the basic interface or the extended one is to be loaded. Following the entry of POPUP, the interface becomes resident in memory and can be activated with the $\boxed{\text{Alt}}$ + $\boxed{\text{N}}$ key combination.
>
> Entering WORKSTATION loads the standard interface specified during installation (BASIC or FULL).
>
> NETBIND binds the protocols and drivers of the network card. This is a prerequisite for any work with the Workgroup Connection and normally takes place

automatically when you boot the computer, if the NET command is included in AUTOEXEC.BAT. NETBEUI loads the interface to the NETBIOS network operating system.

/LIST displays a list of the elements/services in the Workgroup Connection, which are started or active (for example, FULL and NETBEUI).

NET STOP   Ends the Workgroup Connection or removes the POPUP program from the memory of the computer. To do this, follow the NET STOP entry with the service you want to stop, or with POPUP to remove the Workgroup Connection from memory. The possible services or elements are listed with NET START.

NET TIME   Sets the system time of the PC to that of the server/LAN Manager. For this you will need a time signal in the network.

NET USE   Restores the connection to a shared resource (printer interface or directory).

NET VER   Displays the Workgroup Connection version number.

NET VIEW

Displays a list of the computers and shared resources available in the Workgroup.

16.6 Mail and Mailboxes for Workgroups

Windows for Workgroups includes an application called Mail (MSMAIL.EXE). You and your groupmates can send messages to one another online or offline. This is similar to the EMAIL (Electronic MAIL) you might exchange with others on online services such as Compuserve Information Service (CIS), only limited to the network.

Mail is automatically associated with the appointment calendar, Schedule+. Invitations to group meetings, which can be sent to users from Schedule+, can also be received and read in Mail. From both programs it is possible to edit a personal address book and inspect the list of post office users. This avoids a continual swapping of the two programs to control mail access or look for user addresses.

Mail lets you do the following:

- Send messages to Workgroup members.

- Receive messages from Workgroup members.

- Respond to messages received.

- Print messages.

- Save and delete messages.

- Attach files to messages.

Overview of Mail

The first time you run Mail in Windows for Workgroups, you must either connect to an existing postoffice or create a new postoffice.

Like its real-time namesake, a postoffice contains the mail for all registered users, placed in individual mailboxes. A postoffice manager or administrator (as opposed to "postmaster") is the person responsible for maintaining the postoffice.

This postoffice can be on a hard drive of one of the networked PCs or, if available, on a server. For each Workgroup there must be one postoffice—no more and no less. Users of different postoffices are not able to exchange mail with one another.

The administrator separates the users into their proper groups and gives each one an account: a mailbox with a name or a password. All the information on each postoffice user is kept in these accounts.

Only the administrator can inspect this information, change or delete accounts. Any new postoffice participants can register on their own, without the administrator's help. However, the administrator can view information such as passwords, user names and postoffice names.

The first time you run Mail, you'll need to set up a mailbox in the existing postoffice.

16.6.1 Connecting through the post office

If you want to send and receive messages in Windows, you must connect to a post office.

Run Mail from Windows for Workgroups.

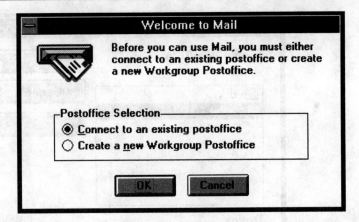

The opening screen of Mail

Select whether you want a new postoffice created, or if you want to connect with an existing postoffice. If you're running Mail on a server for the first time, you should create a new postoffice. Select the "Create a new Workgroup Postoffice" option button and click OK.

The following dialog box appears, confirming that you want to create a postoffice, and reminding you that you must take care of this postoffice. Click OK.

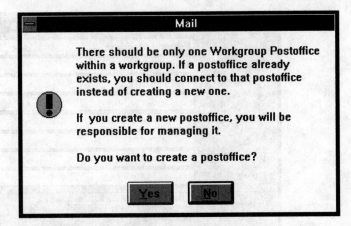

Confirmation

The next dialog box prompts you to select a directory into which you want the WGPO directory placed. Select a directory and click OK.

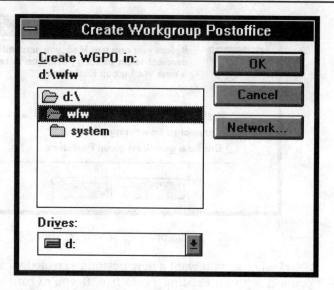

Specifying the postoffice directory

A dialog box prompts you for administrator account details. Enter
your name, the mailbox name, the password and other important
information (we entered "Edmund Klaassen" for the name, "MAIL"
for the mailbox name, and "PASSWORD" for the password). Click
OK.

Naming the mailbox

Once you've selected this information, the "Mail" postoffice
window appears. In its barest form, this window looks like this:

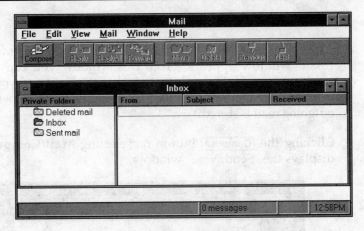

Mail window

From this window, you can create new folders that can be shared by other users, or for your private use; you can send or receive mail; add or remove other users from this postoffice; and more.

You can now take a quick first look into your "Inbox" folder, or select **File/Exit** to exit Mail.

The next time you start Mail, you will be prompted for the postoffice name (the default is displayed, which in this case is "MAIL") and a password.

Entering the mailbox name a second time

Type the password and click [OK].

16.6.2 Sending and receiving mail

EMAIL can be broken down into two basic elements—sending mail and receiving mail. Mail is designed to make sending and receiving messages easy. You can even send messages using an address book included in Mail, or using the postoffice user list.

Sending a message

After you start Mail and enter the necessary information, the "Mail" window appears. From this window you can send and receive messages. Move this window to the right and you'll see an icon named "Outbox". As its name suggests, this is where your outgoing mail is stored.

Clicking the [Compose] button or selecting **Mail/Compose Note** displays the "Send Note" window.

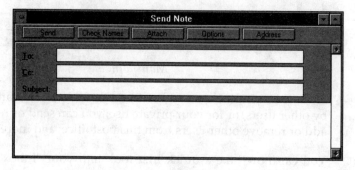

Send Note window

Clicking on the [Address] button in this window displays the users connected to this postoffice.

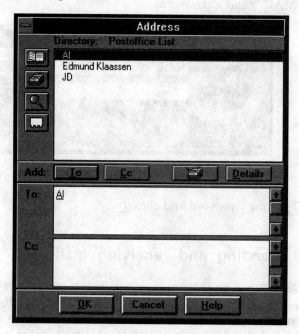

Address book

From the address book you can click on a name, then click on the [To] button to place that name in the "To:" text box (to send a message to that name), or click on the [Cc] button to place that name in the "Cc:" text box (to send a copy of that message to that name). Select the "To:" and "Cc:" names and click [OK].

When Mail returns to the "Send Note" window, click on the [Options] button. This displays a series of options for keeping messages or records of messages sent, as well as message priority.

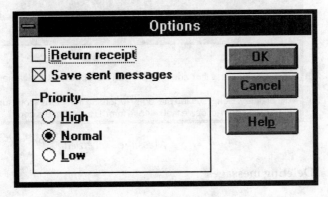

Message options

The "Subject:" text box lists the subject of the message. This information also appears in the title bar of the window displaying the message. If no subject was listed, the title bar lists "Send Note" when being sent, and "Read Note" when being read.

The lower half of the window is your message space. You can type the message, or paste in the contents of the Clipboard (more on this later). When you've completed the message, click [Send].

Message ready to send

When you exit Mail, a dialog box informing you that an unsent message is in your Outbox appears. Click [Yes] to send the message.

Receiving messages

Select **View/New Messages** to see a list of new messages. If a
message exists, just double-click it. A window appears containing
the note's contents.

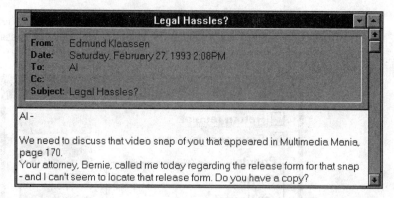

Message received

Deleting messages

You'll find that sent messages pile up in the "Sent mail" folder.
Use the **File/Delete** item to delete these messages.

16.6.3   Further options in mail

In addition to these basic capabilities, there are other options in
Mail:

Setting priority

You can adjust message priority by clicking on the (Options) button in
the "Send Note" window. The priority can be sent to low, medium
or high.

Editing messages

In addition to the direct entry of text in the message window, you
also have the following editing options at your disposal:

* **View/Change Font** toggles text between fixed pitch and
  normal (proportional) font.

- You can paste existing data from the Clipboard using **Edit/Paste**, provided you previously copied data to the Clipboard from another application by marking the data and selecting **Edit/Copy**.

Replying to messages

After you have read a message, you are frequently forced to write a reply immediately. Select **Mail/Reply**. Enter your reply and click on (Send).

To forward a message, select **Mail/Forward** and specify the user to whom you want the forwarded message sent. Click on (Send).

Reading several messages

To read several messages one after the other, press (Shift). Click on each message, then double-click on the last message selected. This displays all the messages you want to read.

Attaching files

Here's a truly remarkable feature of Mail—the ability to attach files to a message. These files can be text, graphics, WAV files or MIDI files. If the recipient has the application for playing the file, the recipient can view the file by double-clicking it.

When in the "Send Note" window with the "To:" text specified, click down in the work area of the window. Click the (Attach) button. The "Attach" dialog box appears. Select a file and click (Attach). When the hourglass icon changes back to a mouse pointer, click (Close). When you click (Send), the user receives this note and its contents.

Saving messages

You can save messages as ASCII text by selecting **File/Save As...** while viewing them. You can also print a message while viewing it by selecting **File/Print...**.

16.7 Working in the Novell Network

In addition to the option of working with the Workgroup Connection in a Windows for Workgroups network, MS-DOS 6.0 also permits you to work in a Novell network. This section examines how this is done and what you must watch for.

16.7.1 Installing a Novell Network

The installation of a network imposes significant demands upon the user—greater ones than those needed for setting up a single PC under MS-DOS. Even if you are already working in a network which is already set up, a brief description of the individual steps can be very helpful in understanding how networks interrelate.

Summary of the individual steps

The installation of a network consists of a whole series of necessary or at least important steps, which in part are very time-consuming.

All hardware and software requirements must be met.

Hardware Requirements:

- A 286, preferably a 386 machine with at least 2 or 4 Meg of memory as the server (we recommend a 386DX with 33 MHz and 4 Meg of memory).

- A hard drive with a capacity of at least 80 Meg for the server (we recommend 200 Meg with a < 17 ms access time).

- A network card for the server (we recommend a fast 16-bit card).

- A PC with a 386 processor and at least 1 Meg of memory and a network card for each workstation.

Software Requirements:

- A network driver system (e.g., Novell 2.2 or 3.11, or the Microsoft LAN Manager).

- An operating system for the server (either MS-DOS or DR DOS or, if you are using the Microsoft LAN Manager, OS/2).

- An operating system for each workstation. If DOS is on the server, a basic system should be enough.

The following illustration shows the prerequisites for the installation of a Novell network, a distinction being made between workstation hardware and server hardware. The demands imposed on the server hard drive and memory are always greater than on the workstation components.

There is also a listing of the individual steps in the installation, the type and scope of the latter also being different for servers and workstations.

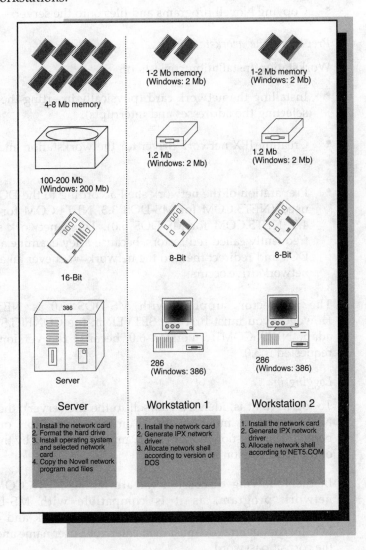

The steps in the installation

Preparing servers

Server installation consists of:

- Installing the network card in the server (physically inserting the card and selecting the addresses and interrupts).

- Formatting the hard drive.

- Installing the operating system for the server and the network card chosen.

- Copying Novell programs and files onto the server.

Preparing the workstations

Workstation installation consists of:

- Installing the network card (physically inserting the card and selecting the addresses and interrupts).

- Creating IPX network driver for the workstation and network card.

- Preparation of the network shell according to the DOS version used (NET3.COM for MS-DOS 3.3, NET4.COM for MS-DOS 4.0, NET5.COM for MS-DOS 5.0). These network shells are frequently called redirectors, because they examine accesses to DOS and redirect them to the network whenever an access to a network drive occurs.

The redirector supplied with MS-DOS 6.0 is NETX.COM. However, you must first use SETVER in the CONFIG.SYS file to adapt NETX.COM to Version 6.0, because the version actually requested is 5.0.

Logging in

To log in (that is, identify yourself to the file server), the IPX and NET? programs must be started on the workstation, once it has booted. The question mark in NET? must be replaced by the number of the DOS version in your call.

In the following discussion we are taking NETX.COM as our network program, as it is compatible with MS-DOS 6.0. Furthermore, you have to change to the network and enter the LOGIN command. You must then enter your user name and, if used, the correct password.

A workstation must thus have a bootable diskette or hard drive at its disposal. It is best to include the necessary commands in the AUTOEXEC.BAT file:

```
IPX
NETX.COM
F:
LOGIN
```

The first login is always done as supervisor (system manager) and without a password. In this state the network is uninstalled and still unprotected. Therefore, the supervisor's password should be specified immediately using the SYSCON program. It is also necessary (as on a local hard drive) that the necessary directories be created and the programs and data installed.

We suggest that you back up the hard drive as soon as possible. With NARCHIVE or LARCHIVE you can back up the entire network hard drive, assuming your supply of diskettes is sufficient. Backing up 80 Meg of data requires about seventy 1.2 Meg diskettes.

Installing directory structures

It is absolutely necessary to create order on a hard drive with directories. That is especially true for network hard drives, because a whole group of users will have to be able to find their way there.

Besides, a well thought out directory structure greatly simplifies and speeds up access to the data. Even the basic structure of the data on the hard drive can already have a positive influence on access to the data, if the latter are simpler and more easily found.

The directory tree and later access rights

When planning directory tree structure, it's especially important to configure branches of the tree structure depending on users' access rights. On the other hand, it's much easier to deny a user access to an entire directory tree than to lock out 20 individual subdirectories.

- Store as few files as possible in the root directory. It should contain only directories. You will find your way around the root directory much more easily, if a DIR command displays only 10 directories instead of hundreds of files.

- Very deep directory structures with five or more levels do of course have a good logical structure, but they force the system to search through all the overlying directories on the way downward. For this reason, we suggest you keep the directory tree relatively "shallow," or "flat."

- Whenever you install a new hard drive, the very first thing you should do is set up the directory structure and only then copy the files onto the hard drive.

This will position subdirectories themselves at the very beginning of each directory, ahead of the data, permitting them to be found more quickly.

Arranging the directory tree

Novell automatically creates a series of directories on the hard drive during installation:

SYSTEM   Contains those programs and data important to the system manager.

LOGIN   Contains the programs and files needed for logging in on the file server.

MAIL   Contains additional subdirectories for each user and for defined groups. A name for this purpose consists of a "random" number and letter combination. Only the system manager receives a 1 as his directory name. The MAIL directory could, for example, look like the following:

```
F:\
Ã---MAIL
≥    Ã---1
≥    Ã---20007
≥    Ã---10004D
≥    Ã---11005D
≥    Ã---120065
≥    Ã---13006F
≥    Ã---170079
≥    Ã---180085
≥    Ã---1A0091
≥    Ã---A0031
≥    Ã---B0051
≥    Ã---C0041
≥    À---D003B
Ã---SYSTEM
 . . .
```

PUBLIC   Contains all the commands needed by the user. This roughly corresponds to the DOS directory of a "local" hard drive on a PC that has not been networked.

The directories you add should have some logic in tune with the network. You could install the following directory tree:

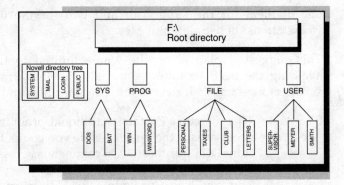

An optimal directory tree

The above illustration shows a directory tree with a structure particularly suitable for work in the network.

The first to branch out from the root directory (here F:\) are the directories installed by Novell itself (SYSTEM, LOGIN, MAIL and PUBLIC), which (except for MAIL) have no additional subdirectories.

The user should then create four subdirectories, from which all other directories branch off, resulting in a relatively flat structure. This prevents unnecessary searching through the directory tree.

The SYS subdirectory contains all the directories and data important to system operation. The DOS directory of course branches off here. This is also a good place to put the directory for the batch files you create yourself.

The PROG subdirectory contains, first of all, the Windows directory, and then the many directories for the different programs used (WINWORD is the only one shown in this case, as an example).

The DATA subdirectory is provided for routine data backup. Branching out from here is everything having to do with the results of users' work and is usually changed frequently. In our example there are only four directories on the third level (PRIVATE, CONTROL, GROUP and LETTERS). This subdivision is of course more dependent upon individual needs and preferences than those cited above.

Located to the far right is the USER directory containing the data and settings important for work with the netwok. In the case under consideration there are three additional directories branching off, one of them for the supervisor and two for the users of the workstations (here Smith and Meyer).

This suggested plan is on the whole limited to three levels, avoiding the need to follow unnecessarily long trails through subdirectories and their data in the search for files and programs.

SYS   This directory contains additional programs and files necessary for the system. Here you could, for example, store DOS (for those DOS commands accessible by all).

You could also provide a BAT directory for storing batch files and small tools. We advise that you do not merely copy these into the Novell directory, PUBLIC, because Novell and DOS files should be kept apart, like DOS files and self-created programs or batch files.

As we'll explain later, read-only protection makes a lot of sense for the Novell directories and at least the DOS directory and is much more easily implemented with the procedure described.

PROG   In this directory you create the program directories as subdirectories. In our example, that would be perhaps WIN for Windows and WINWORD for Microsoft Word for Windows. In any case you should also keep the different programs in different directories and separate from the data of the programs to simplify backing up the data.

DATA   You should also install several directories for data. There are in this case two options relative to organization: Directories can either be organized according to their contents (LETTERS, CONTROL, PRIVATE) or according to the programs they belong to (TEXTS, ICONS, PICTURES). A general answer to this question is not possible. The apportionment depends entirely upon the programs used.

USER   When there are several users working within the network, a separate directory should be created for each. These are best organized as subdirectories of a USER directory. The advantage of this is that it eases the later work with programs which generate user-specific files, for example, Windows and the user-specific Windows files. Moreover, you can easily back up all user-specific settings by backing up the USER directory tree.

 At first only the supervisor has access to the directory structure. If (later) a newly defined user is to obtain access to a directory, this must be expressly determined in advance. It therefore makes sense to organize the component directory trees in advance so a user can receive read or read/write access to an entire series of related directories.

Installing data and programs on the server

After installation of the directory tree you will have the basic structure of the programs and data installed on the disk and will still have to fill them up with the actual data.

The installation of the data is relatively simple. You merely use an attached workstation to copy the data into the desired subdirectory on the server from a diskette. If the data were previously stored on an individual PC, now connected as a network workstation, you can simply log into the network from this computer and copy the data onto the server with XCOPY:

```
XCOPY C:\DATA F:\DATA /S
```

Installing networkable programs

The installation of programs capable of network operation is relatively simple. Once a suitable program directory has been set up as a subdirectory of F:\PROG, you start the installation program.

For most programs you must select network installation in advance or when selecting the installation options. With Windows, for example, calling SETUP /A permits a complete installation of all files and programs on the server. SETUP /N can then be used for installing Windows on each workstation.

Even with the word processing program, WORD 5.5, it is first necessary to install all files on the server with the installation program, before a network installation useful to each user can be implemented with the /USER parameter. There are, of course, a few tricks:

- You can implement a normal single-workstation installation in the F:\PROG\WORD directory of the server.

- It is then possible to copy the user-specific data MW.INI, SCREEN.VID, STANDARD.TBS and STANDARD.DFV and the like into a user directory manually, for example, F:\USER\SMITH.

- You can use SET to set the MSWNET55 environment variable to the respective subdirectory for each user.

For user SMITH with WORD files in the F:\USER\SMITH directory, it would thus be necessary to execute the following command line:

```
SET MSWNET55=F:\USER\SMITH
```

Such lines are of course best included in AUTOEXEC.BAT (referenced to the workstation) or in the LOGIN script (referenced to the user). Both procedures are further explained below.

☞ You must use WORD /N the first time you run Word in the network. This setting will then be saved by Word in the MW.INI file, permitting subsequent calls to be made as usual without parameters or with a file name.

☞ You should if possible provide the program directory of a networkable program with write-protection. This prevents the program from being accidentally deleted or changed. Moreover, you should declare the files in the program as "shareable", usable in common by several persons. Both can be done with the Novell command FLAG, for example. To characterize the WORD files in the manner described, you would use the following command line:

```
FLAG F:\PROG\WORD\*.* S RO
```

This line states: Set all files in the WORD directory to "Shareable" and "Read Only".

Installing programs not capable of network operation

Programs not capable of network operation can be set up on a server in principle just like on the local hard drive of an individual PC. Because the programs are not networkable, they can, strictly speaking, be used only by a single user.

The problems for the most part begin when each change in the screen settings for the program made by user SMITH also immediately produces a change in the settings of user MEYER, because the program is unable to keep track of the different settings of different users.

A program incapable of network operation is likewise unable to provide limited access rights to a directory or a file. Whereas the networkable program, Word 5.5, when access is attempted by another user to a file currently in use, displays this or a similar message:

```
Another user is currently processing the file:
F:\DATA\TEXTS\LETTERS.DOC
```

and automatically opens some files in such a case in the read-only mode; another program may display: " File cannot be opened" or perhaps also "Hard disk/Diskette full".

You will be quite safe in most cases, if you do not install the files and programs of non-networkable applications on the server at all, or at least declare them "non-shareable" with FLAG.

If you have set the program up optimally for network operation, and have then declared all program files including the INI files of the program as "Read-Only", the various users will then not be able to change the program settings or remove them from memory.

Why should you install Novell for users?

At the latest, after having installed most and the most important program data on the server, you should think about data backup. To be sure, you will later be able to improve and optimize the backup mechanism still further, but the work done thus far should already be backed up. Backup is particularly simple and easy, if you work with a streamer (tape drive).

Why shouldn't all users be supervisors?

You may think it best at this point to let each network participant log in as a supervisor. At first glance, this would be a big advantage: You would save yourself the chore of allocating access rights for all necessary directories to each individual user. Whenever you define a new user (see below), that individual has initially only an absolutely minimal access right to the server, scarcely permitting him or her to work.

You can of course also solve the problem by setting up directory trees containing all directories with shared access rights. Or you simply define a group, establish the general access rights for it and then shove all the individual users into the group.

Nevertheless, eliminating different user categories has some serious disadvantages:

Security

Security loss is first. If you assign supervisor rights to all, you as system manager will have no privacy. One wrong file deletion made by a user (e.g., LOGIN) and the network can be rendered useless. Limiting access rights prevents (or at least alleviates) this problem.

Differentiating users

If all users log into the net as supervisors, the network and networkable programs will be unable to differentiate users.

Login script

A starting script can be established for each user, similar to the AUTOEXEC.BAT file. For example, each user can install a series of automatic operations to make his or her work simpler. You can, as system manager, start a "safety shell" for a still really inexperienced network participant, either an MS-DOS Shell with limited options or a Novell shell. You can only do this once users have been defined.

Setting up Novell for users

Once the system manager installs the basic options in the network, preparations should be made for users.

Immediately after installation, the supervisor is without a password. Assign this password as soon after installation as possible, before you begin installing additional users.

Defining a supervisor password

Let's assume you have the network "up and running" and have logged into the file server as supervisor. Start the SYSCON installation program. If no search path has yet been established, change to the \PUBLIC directory.

After calling SYSCON, use the cursor keys to select the "User Information" menu option and the "SUPERVISOR" entry in the list of user names. Then select "Change Password" in the "User Information" window.

After the initial entry of the password, you will have to re-enter the password to avoid typing errors because the characters are not displayed when passwords are entered, for security reasons.

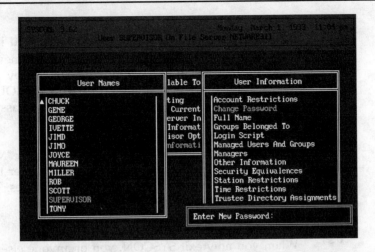

A password for the supervisor

If the two passwords agree, you can exit SYSCON by pressing [Esc] several times (or the [Alt]+[F10] key combination) several times. Confirm that you wish to exit to return to the operating system.

 You must not forget this password under any circumstances. Either write it down in a really safe place, or deposit it in your safe or bank's safe deposit box. Without this password any further installation of the network is virtually impossible.

Installing the network for a new user

To install the file server for a new user, you use SYSCON. Before setting up passwords for several users, however, you should first have a clear idea of the individual steps and then inform yourself about the groups involved and how you install them. For the definition of several users is a rather laborious procedure, which should be as simple and as coherent as possible to prevent crashes.

 We will now work through the installation procedure for a user named MILLER, this name now acting as a general user name for our example.

The definition of a new user consists of the following steps: Begin by starting SYSCON and selecting "User Information" from the menu. A list of all the existing user names then appears. Press [Ins] to insert a new name.

If the Ins key doesn't work, you are not logged in as the supervisor. Only the supervisor can install new users, meaning that you will have to exit SYSCON by pressing Esc several times and logging out with LOGOUT. You must then log in again with the appropriate password as the supervisor.

You are then prompted to enter the "User Name:". Enter "MILLER" here and confirm the entry with Enter. An instant later the new user will appear in the alphabetical list of user names. You are now done.

 When you now exit SYSCON, you or anyone else can log into this file server with the user name MILLER. No password has been specified; and the access rights are absolutely minimal. We advise in any case that you at least assign a password and extend the minimal access rights somewhat. For now, user MILLER has only the option of opening files from the \LOGIN and \PUBLIC directories and to use and change files in that user's special MAIL subdirectory.

To assign a password to the new user, MILLER, mark this name in the list of user names and press Enter. You then use Enter to select the "Change Password" option in the "User Information" window.

After entering the password, you must enter it a second time to avoid typing errors, because characters are not displayed when passwords are entered for security reasons. If the two password entries coincide, you can either leave SYSCON or assign further access rights.

 There is an entire series of rules governing the assignment of passwords. The most important thing is to know what you should not do. Without going into the details at this point, would like briefly to give you the most important rules of thumb:

Rules for passwords

- A password should be at least five characters in length, and different from the user name.

- All those words readily coming to mind as passwords are also quickly guessed, for example, the first names of your family members, your birthday, etc.

We don't know how important your data are and, consequently, how important the protection against access by unauthorized persons or destruction. Choose your passwords with care. Write them down and kep them in a safe place.

Displaying the existing access rights of user MILLER

If anyone is to do any real work with the user name MILLER, you will at least have to assign it some more extensive access rights in the net.

We'll go into the problems involved and the various options somewhat further down, for now we will limit ourselves to explaining what the initial situation is and how you can define new access rights for user MILLER: In the "User Information" window, select "Trustee Directory Assignments".

A new window will then appear containing directories to the left and, to the right, access rights:

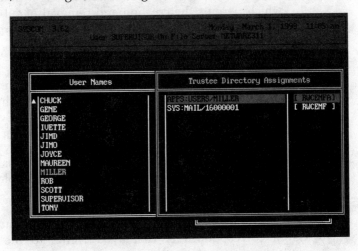

User MILLER's access rights

At the present time, in addition to rights in the \PUBLIC and \LOGIN standard directories, user MILLER merely has access to a SYS:MAIL/16000001 directory, and even there only to the one abbreviated between the two parentheses by letters:

Access rights and their meaning

R   Read permits reading from an already opened file.

W   Write permits writing to an already opened file.

C   Create allows the creation of new files.

E   Erase permits the deletion of files.

F   File Scan allows the display of the names of files (not of
           the contents) in a directory. If this right has not been
           granted, a DIR command in a directory returns the message
           "File not found" without any hint of the reason.

M   Modify enables the renaming of files, the modification
           and deletion of the file attributes and the changing of
           directory names.

A further access right is in any case still absent, and for that
reason there is a location between the parentheses left blank:

P   Parental Rights is the most extensive right in a directory,
           which permits the creation and removal of subdirectories
           and the assignment of access rights to other users.

Changing access rights for programs and data

If MILLER is to use the \ETC directory and the programs contained
in its subdirectories, he must at least be granted the rights R and F.
Use (Ins) in the "Trustee Directory Assignments" window to enter a
new directory in the list of access rights.

This displays a new window, "Directory In Which Trustee Should
Be Added", in which you can directly enter the complete path of
the directory.

However, it's simpler to press (Ins) a second time and then to use it
to assign correspondingly displayed rights to the directory
interactively, one step at a time.

A "File Servers" window appears in which you confirm the server
with (Enter), and then a "Volumes" window in which you in this
case confirm the SYS: entry with (Enter). This opens a new
"NetWork Directories" window with the available directories.

☞   The "File Servers" option makes it possible, moreover, to
           install more than one server in a net. The "Volumes"

correspond to the partitions in DOS, that is to say, the option dividing up a hard drive into several regions.

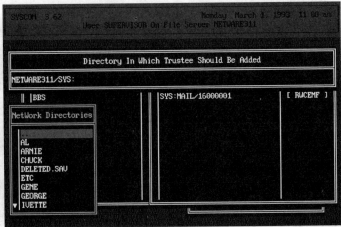

Selecting a new directory

Standard rights - RF

To select the \ETC directory as the first, move the cursor to this directory and press (Enter). The directory name will then also appear above in the window "Directory In Which Trustee Should Be Added".

Now you're now able to conclude the further definition of the directory with (Esc). The "Network Directories" window than disappears. The "Directory In Which Trustee Should Be Added" window now contains the correct path (in our example, NETWARE311/SYS:ETC) and can be concluded with (Enter).

However, we also still want to include the \DATA directory in the list, likewise expanding the rights. Use the same procedure you used to insert \ETC to insert the \DATA directory with the standard right.

You use (Ins) to initiate the insertion process, (Enter) to move one level down in the directory structure or confirm a selection, (Esc) or .. to move one directory level higher or end the selection procedure.

If the directory has been inserted in the "Trustee Directory Assignments" window and highlighted by the marker, you can initiate the change in access rights with (Enter). This displays all available rights. To remove a right, you would press (Del) and respond to the confirmation.

However, you want to insert new rights and therefore press the [Ins] key. An additional window appears with a list of the rights not yet allocated for this directory:

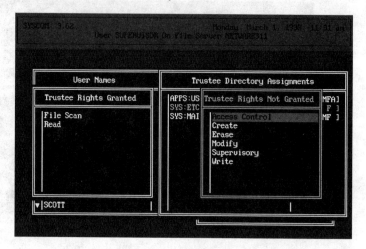

Assigning further rights for a directory

You should concede at least Create, Erase and Write, the rights required for processing data. Thus, select "Create" and press [Enter], causing the window to disappear, and the new right will be included in the list of available rights, "Trustee Rights Granted". Repeat this procedure for the two remaining rights, Erase and Write.

Amazingly, the procedure for granting rights is ended with [Esc], and the changes nevertheless remain in place. If you are then satisfied with the existing settings, you can use [Esc] to return to the main menu or even leave SYSCON immediately by pressing [Alt]+[F10] and confirming the exit.

Defining characteristics for several users by grouping

You can easily see that a precise installation for many users can mean more than an evening's work for the supervisor. For that reason Novell gives you the option of assembling identical characteristics for several users into a group.

You could thus specify access to the \ETC and \DATA directories once for a group with the name TEXTS and would then need to define several users further only as members of this TEXTS group. You could of course define a CAD group in the same way and grant it access to the engineering program and the current drawings.

This procedure has in particular, in addition to a considerable saving of work in the configuration of the system for several users, two advantages:

- When making changes (for example, the insertion of new directories), it will not be necessary to assign access rights individually for each user.

- The danger will not so likely arise that a user will be overlooked when changes are made, with the result that users with essentially identical job assignments will have different access rights, always a source of failures and problems. Whatever works for Smith, as a member of the TEXTS group, will surely then also work for Meyer.

In our example, you would withdraw the access rights to the two directories, \ETC and \DATA, for user SMITH and define them for a new group TEXTS.

Let's define the new group, TEXTS, in the main menu of SYSCON. Press Enter to select "Group Information" in the menu; and a "Group Names" window appears with all the existing groups.

During installation Novell automatically defined a group called EVERYONE, which automatically includes all users. But you want to insert a more specific group TEXTS and press Ins. At the "New Group Name:" window type TEXTS; and the new group will be added to the "Group Names" list.

Selecting this group and pressing Enter displays a "Group Information" window which permits you to define access rights with the "Trustee Directory Assignments" option in the menu just as you did for an individual user.

After completing the definition for the two directories (as described above for user SMITH), you will still have to define SMITH as the first member of this group. This is very simple: With the TEXTs group active, select the "Member List" entry in the "Group Information" window.

Appearing then is a new window, "Group Members", which still contains no entries. Pressing Ins displays a new window, "Not Group Members", in which you can merely select SMITH. Pressing Enter makes him a member of the group, and you can use Esc to exit the group definition process.

Finally, you can remove the rights specially defined for the user, SMITH, because he will get these rights as a member of the TEXTS group. In the main menu of SYSCON, select the "User Information" entry and, in the window then appearing, SMITH.

The "User Information" window then appears. There you select "Trustee Directory Assignments".

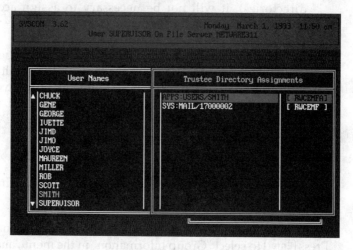

SMITH gets added

The window with the defined directories appears, and you are able to mark the two inserted lines with the cursor keys and trigger the deletions with Del:

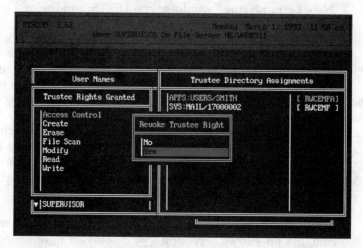

Deleting an access right with Del

Following a confirmation prompt, the access rights definition in question is deleted.

The change becomes effective immediately, though Novell checks access rights for a directory only if a change is made in the directory. Someone can thus select a directory, \DATA, containing files to which he has no access right.

If he's now granted such a right by the system manager, he will still be unable to access the files in the \DATA directory. Only if he again makes use of CD.. and CD DATA to switch back into the directory does Novell check the (now changed) access right and then permit access.

What are the minimal access rights you need to work?

Novell generally grants only minimal access rights to a new user. These are:

- The right to file scan and read files in the \PUBLIC und \LOGIN directories.

- Each user also receives a special subdirectory in the MAIL directory for the storage of user-specific data. This is in particular a login script to be created by the user, in other words, a batch-like sequence of commands comparable to AUTOEXEC.BAT.

These access rights enable a user to fiddle around a bit on the server, but not to change or delete anything.

To start programs, he needs at least the same rights (File Scan and Read) for the program directories. He will also need a directory in which he can save the data of the programs. For this data directory, it will be necessary in practice to have the rights, "Create", "Modify" and "Write".

The drawing distinguishes between minimally necessary access rights and those rights needed in daily practice. A distinction is also made between File Scan/Read rights and Write/Modify rights.

With minimal access rights a user can, of course, log into a system (LOGIN), but that's about all, apart from running SYSCON or HELP.

Therefore, the second group of lines shows the rights necessary in practice.

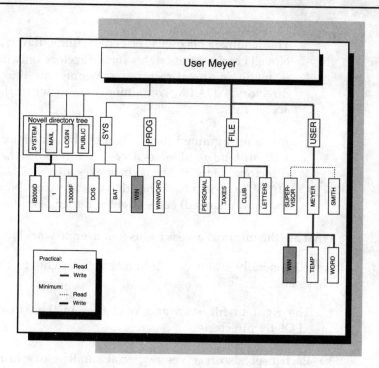

Minimal and practically needed access rights

16.7.2 Installing DOS in the Network

The correct organization of DOS is an important prerequisite for working in a network. Moreover, the installation options within DOS (such as CONFIG.SYS or AUTOEXEC.BAT) interact well with the options in Novell (for example, the login script).

The diagram shows the interaction of the single-station operating system normally used, MS-DOS, and Novell NetWare system.

When the user calls an application program, this application program will access devices such as disk drives and the printer. MS-DOS starts the network shell on the workstation computer. The shell checks all accesses and either relays them unchanged to DOS (right-hand bundle) or sends them over IPX and the network card to the server, where the network operating system (not shown here) takes charge of them from then on.

Because of this ability to screen and "redirect" accesses to the disk drives of the network, the network shell is frequently also called the "redirector".

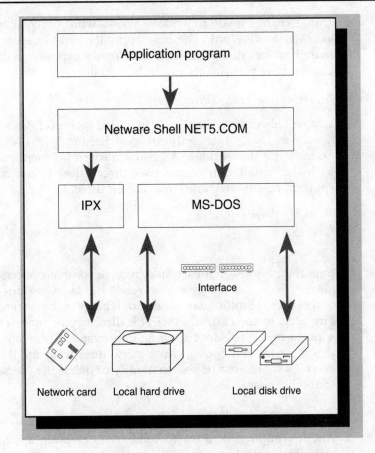

How DOS and Novell work together

What directories should be installed for users?

The correct choice of directories and directory structures is an prerequisite for optimal work and the most effective backing up of data possible. Whenever several users are working on a project, it must be possible to effectively delimit those files on which each user is working. On the other hand, there must be provision for the most rapid file exchange possible.

Directories for project work

This problem is easy to solve in the case of a networkable database like Superbase, because the smallest "unit" in a database is a data field. The directory intended for user access is the top priority. If the project-participant group has been defined as a group in Novell (see our example above for the TEXTS group), an access right to this directory can be defined for the group and the project participants enrolled as group members.

Things change if you're working with a word processing program like Microsoft Word. The best approach is to use one or more shared project directories and use Word's capacity to distinguish among those participants currently working on the text.

Accessing the USER directories

You will also create directories in which each user can store his or her "personal" data without restriction. INI files can, for example, be stored there. A good approach (as mentioned earlier with the installation of the user directories) is the creation of appropriate subdirectories in a \USER directory:

```
F:\USER\SMITH
F:\USER\MEYER
. . .
```

Important here is that each user receive complete access rights to his directory, and, if possible, "read" rights to the directories of other users. Smith may thus do whatever he wants in "his" directory. In the F:\USER\MEYER directory he may at least take a look around. To adopt a setting improvement from another user, you must for this copy at least a few lines from the INI file. But one user should not be able to modify or delete the "personal" files of another user.

A temporary directory for data exchange

Another important factor to consider is creating a directory for temporarily storing data, and for data exchange. We suggest that you create a \USER\TMP directory to which all users have read/write access.

If it happens that user SMITH wants to send an interesting text to MEYER, he would copy it into \USER\TMP and then notify MEYER that the text is available there. It is important that all network participants clearly understand that files may only be stored briefly in the TMP directory. Each can make room there prior to a copy operation.

 The TMP directory just described is not the same as the directory defined in the DOS environment with SET TEMP=.

Installing DOS on the server

Naturally, you can also install MS-DOS directly on the server. For this you merely create an appropriate directory (for example, F:\SYS\DOS) and copy the DOS files into it.

Installing the workstations

You cannot boot the workstations from this DOS directory, because these units aren't connected to the network during bootup (unless a workstation includes a boot ROM on the network card).

You can boot each workstation from a DOS system diskette, and load the remaining DOS commands from the file server after loading the network driver. Instead of a diskette, you can also use the workstation's hard drive if one is available.

 For a workstation operating under Novell 2.15, the CONFIG.SYS and AUTOEXEC.BAT files on the boot diskette could perhaps look like the following:

```
REM CONFIG.SYS
SHELL=COMMAND.COM /E:1000 /P
DEVICE=HIMEM.SYS
DEVICE=EMM386.EXE NOEMS
DOS=HIGH
DEVICE=SETVER.EXE
FILES=30
BUFFERS=30
BREAK=ON
```

 The programs and files used, HIMEM.SYS, EMM386.EXE, SETVER.EXE and COUNTRY.SYS, must of course also be present on the boot diskette.

These command lines install MS-DOS in high memory with a command interpreter having 1000 bytes of environment memory. Moreover, EMM386.EXE installs upper memory without EMS. In this way you get more upper memory for loading network drivers high.

```
@REM AUTOEXEC.BAT
@ECHO OFF
IPX
NETX
F:
LOGIN
PATH F:\SYS\DOS;F:\SYS\BAT;F:\USER\SMITH;F:\PROG\WIN
SET COMSPEC=F:\SYS\DOS\COMMAND.COM
```

```
SET TEMP=F:\USER\SMITH
SET TMP=F:\USER\SMITH
PROMPT $P$G
```

The IPX network driver and the NETX shell start, and the file server becomes available after LOGIN. The appropriate search path can then be set up with PATH. The search path for the command interpreter can then be redirected to the network DOS directory (a valid COMMAND.COM must also be there), the temporary directories being defined as environment variables.

    If a hard drive is installed in the computer, you can of course store the temporary files on this local hard drive and thereby unburden the net.

Securing the DOS files with write-protection

You should protect the server's operating system from accidental overwriting by users. For this you can either deny users write rights in the directory in question, or set the corresponding read-only attributes for the files.

We suggest the latter approach, which permits special files (for example, INI files) to be purposely excluded from write-protection, which is often absolutely necessary (see below).

Careful with INI files

You have to be careful with programs which back up changes in special files (for example, the MS-DOS Shell's DOSSHELL.INI). Such programs have serious problems, if they cannot write into the files. The least damage may be from an error message, while the most damaging result may be a crash.

For these (mostly non-networkable) programs, you should remove all directories from write-access, and deny a write and delete right to the users (e.g., per the definition of their group), a read-only attribute then being set for all files, with the exception of the INI files.

For the DOS directory and the TEXTS group, that could look like the following:

1.   You activate the TEXTS group via SYSCON and insert the following access rights for the F:\SYS\DOS directory:

```
SYS:SYS\DOS              [RWOCD F ]
```

This permits all members of the TEXTS group to read, write, open, close, delete and scan for files in the DOS directory.

2. Use the Novell command, FLAG, to set the file attributes to "Shareable by several users" and "ReadOnly".

```
FLAG F:\SYS\DOS\*.* S RO
```

3. Then set the attributes for all INI files to read and write (ReadWrite) and usable by one user only (NonShareable).

```
FLAG F:\SYS\DOS\*.INI NS RW
```

 You can change the file attributes, if you are the system manager (supervisor), or change (Modify) the right of others in this directory. Because the TEXTS group was not given this right, only the supervisor can undertake a change of attributes, which cannot be done accidentally by a user.

You can use this trick in principle even for the entire \PROG directory tree, but should then also take care of other file extensions for INI files, for example, SYS for CDCONFIG.SYS in Corel Draw. To set all the files in the directories from \PROG onward, including the subdirectories, to Shareable and ReadOnly, use the command line:

```
FLAG F:\PROG\*.* NS RW SUB
```

SUB in this case stands for subdirectories.

Defining special settings for users

The description of the options for various users and groups, with their respective access rights, has surely provided you with an idea of the many and varied installation options within a network.

However, these are not all the options. With Novell it is possible, for example, to make highly customized settings for different users. This can be done by the system manager (as a point of departure), but also modified and refined by each user. The setting options concern, for example, the following points:

• The installation of special search paths for the user.

• The automatic starting of programs.

- The definition of special environment variables, which in turn control the work of the different networkable programs.

We would like at this point to explain only the general mechanism and present a few practical examples.

The function of AUTOEXEC.BAT and CONFIG.SYS

The system files, AUTOEXEC.BAT and CONFIG.SYS, play an important role in the installation of the workstations. CONFIG.SYS contains the necessary device drivers and system settings, AUTOEXEC.BAT for the most part, the definition of the system prompt. It also starts the IPX network driver and the NETX network shell.

These functions and procedures are, however, independent of the user: It makes no difference who logs into a workstation, the same CONFIG.SYS and the same AUTOEXEC.BAT run in each case.

This procedure imposes no restriction, if Smith is permitted or able only to log into workstation 1, and Meyer only into workstation 3. However, a net is essentially much more flexible.

Smith, at his workstation 1, is perhaps able to use data from 3.5 inch diskettes in a drive of the corresponding type, but has only 4 Meg of total memory available and a 386 CPU without a math coprocessor.

However, if he wants to work on a very extensive drawing with Corel Draw, he can simply change places with Meyer, log onto the more powerful 486 machine with 8 Meg of memory, as Smith, and continue his work there without restrictions. There is a special technique for this: the Login Scripts.

The function of the login script

A login script is a special starting file in Novell NetWare, permitting each user to create a special working environment. Unlike AUTOEXEC.BAT, this login script executes as soon as the user logs into the network.

The login script can define an entire series of activities. The most important activities are:

- Defining a special name for the user/workstation.

- Defining search paths for programs and commands.

- The automatic starting of programs.

- The setting of special environment variables, which in turn control the work of the different networkable programs.

We would like at this point merely to explain the general mechanism and give you a few practical examples.

Creating a login script

To create a Login Script for a user, you use the SYSCON program. This program contains a built-in editor for creating and editing the login script:

 Please don't change the supervisor login script, without having sufficient knowledge and without having created a "security user" for the system manager. If you make an error while producing the login script of the supervisor, it may become impossible to make a valid connection to the net. Because only the supervisor is able to change his or her login script, the error leads into a blind alley.

Solution:

It is best to define a user with the same access rights as the user and the same password. We'll call this user SM.

To install such a second supervisor, you of course have to define the user in the manner described. You then select "User Information" in the SYSCON main menu and, from the list of "User Names", the user who is to be assigned the right, in our case, the newly created user SM.

In the "User Information" menu, then select the "Security Equivalences" entry and confirm this with [Ins] to create a new "equivalence". Displayed in the list then appearing, "Other Users And Groups", are all defined groups and users, and you are able to select the SUPERVISOR entry and confirm the selection with [Enter]. Finally, you can exit SYSCON with [Alt]+[F10].

Following these security operations, you are then also essentially able to modify the login script of the supervisor. It is nevertheless perhaps not a bad idea to practice first on a different user, or even better on a test user.

The background for this bit of advice comes from our practical experience that Novell uses a default script as long as no login script has been created for the user. Once this has been done, the default script is no longer used.

To create a login script for user MILLER, you proceed as follows:

Start SYSCON and select "User Information" in the main menu. After selecting MILLER from the list of "User Names", select "Login Script" under "User Information".

If there is still no login script for this user (as assumed), you can then decide whether the login script of a different user is to be employed: "Read Login Script From User". Suggested in this case is the name of the current user, SMITH. If this is confirmed with Enter, an empty editor screen will appear: "Login Script For User MILLER".

☞   But here you could also specify an already existing user to appropriate his login script.

Only one corresponding script can be entered in the editing window.

An example might look like the following:

```
REMARK Login Script for user MILLER
MAP F:=SYS:
COMSPEC=F:\SYS\DOS
DOS SET MSWNET55="F:\USER\MILLER"
DOS SET WINDIR="F:\USER\MILLER"
DOS SET TEMP="C:\TEMP"
DRIVE F:
MACHINE="MILLER"
EXIT "\PUBLIC\MILLER"
```

The login script works as follows:

REMARK   Introduces a comment line and prevents Novell from processing the rest of the line. REMARK corresponds to the REM command in batch files.

MAP   Models a drive letter on a path to the server. In this case, the first volume on the server (corresponding to a partition under DOS) can then be used as F:.

COMSPEC Defines the path and filename of the command interpreter.

DOS SET Permits the setting of system variables in a manner comparable to the MS-DOS command SET. Specified in the Login Script are a TEMP directory for DOS ad Windows and the directory F:\USER\MILLER for the user-specific WORD and Windows files.

DRIVE   Switches to the indicated drive.

MACHINE
         Defines a name for the computer.

After entering the lines, you can press [Esc]. Then appearing is a query (Save Changes) on whether the entries or changes are to be saved. After confirmation, you can exit SYSCON with [Alt]+[F10] and then try out the login script by logging on again as user MILLER A batch file, F:\PUBLIC\MILLER.BAT, should be available.

Changing a login script

To change an existing login script, select the same steps used in creating a new login script. However, the existing script appears automatically, without the option of selecting a user name.

[Del] and [Backspace] are used to delete a character. [F5] and the cursor keys are used to mark a block. With [Del] you can delete a block and, if desired, reinsert it in a new position with [Ins].

The changes are saved, when you press [Esc] and confirm that you want the file saved.

 You cannot, unfortunately, insert several lines directly from an existing script into another user's existing script, because you cannot load more than one script at a time.

What should be in a login script

We've found that a user-defined login script should at minimum access the MAP entry, because otherwise no access to the server will be possible. The reason appears to be that that Novell uses a sort of default login script for a user, as long as no special script file has been created. This default script images a network drive letter. If your own login script exist, it overrides the automatic reference.

 You can in any case also modify your login script without being logged in as the supervisor. Only for changing the scripts of another user do you have to log in as supervisor.

16.7.3 Working in the Net

Much of the work on a network is practically no different from that at an individual workstation. The additional drive letters of the network appear in the drive line of the DOS shell and are also represented differently than diskette drives or hard drives, but they can be used in exactly the same way.

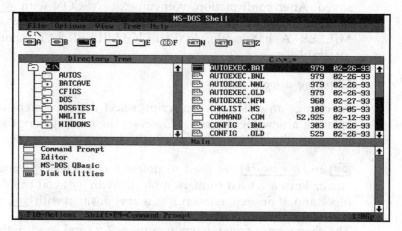

Diskette, hard drive and network icons

If a network drive on the server is selected, the available files and directories appear just as they would in the case of a local hard drive or diskette drive. However, some operations are not available, such as naming and formatting disks. These functions are also not available from DOS.

The following commands either cannot be used on network drives, or can be used only to a limited extent on network drives:

CHKDSK	Test and correct storage media
DISKCOPY	Copy diskettes
DISKCOMP	Compare diskettes
FASTOPEN	Accelerated opening of files
FORMAT	Prepare and delete storage media
RECOVER	Restore files
SYS	Create data storage medium for system
UNFORMAT	Cancel formatting operation

Quirks arising from access rights

Access rights also produce some quirks within a network. As long as you are not logged into a Novell network, the only directory you will be able to access is the LOGIN directory on the file server. The LOGIN directory usually contains only those commands needed for logging in.

Any attempt to exit or view the contents of other directories displays an error message. The basic law: If you don't have access rights to a directory, you won't be able to view the files in that directory. From the outside it looks as though no files are stored there.

This peculiarity can generate a whole series of crashes and problems. For example, if a new program has been installed on the file server, but no access rights were granted to the user, the program is not usable, quasi unavailable.

Problems when changing to a directory one level higher

Many programs have problems selecting directories on the next level up when loading or storing files, if a network is in operation. That comes from the fact that two special entries are automatically present in all subdirectories on a local DOS drive: "." and "..".

With these two entries you can specify the current and the next-higher directory. But directory management on a network drive is completely different, these two entries being thus not available there.

But how do you get to the next higher level without ".."? Meanwhile, the system of representation used by many new programs during directory selection is now different, all intervening directories, up to the current one, being individually displayed and available for selection. An example of this is provided by Works for Windows.

If ".." is omitted

You can reach the next directory level up by double-clicking. But if the program does not have this new technology, your only alternative is to look for the file name in the main directory by entering the drive letter followed by wildcard characters:

```
F:\*.*
```

You will then have to tediously "sift through" the root directory to find the correct subdirectory.

The solution to the problem is already provided by Novell and consists of writing the command

```
SHOW DOTS = ON
```

into a configuration file named SHELL.CFG. This file is automatically processed by the NETX.COM network shell each time the computer boots, if it is present in the current directory. If the IPX and NETX files are processed in the AUTOEXEC.BAT file in the root directory of the C: hard drive, and this is indeed the current directory, the SHELL.CFG file will also have to be in the current directory.

As soon as the network shell starts in this configuration, it will insert the two points for the next higher directory ".." with the corresponding search commands ("Search First" and "Search Next") automatically.

16.7.4   Printing in the Network

The MS-DOS PRINT command offers many options for document printing in the background. PRINT slows the foreground application program, however. This makes it virtually impossible to continue working productively. The network print queue offers a fix for this problem, as well as a host of other advantages.

The advantages of a network printer

A network printer is available to all workstations, as though connected to a local computer. This can be a real money saver for small businesses.

A network printer can manage print jobs in a print queue. MS-DOS's PRINT command and the Microsoft Windows Print Manager also perform this task, though the working speed suffers greatly. When the file server takes control of a print job, you have the feeling that your workstation is connected to a fairly fast printer. But the printing speed is determined more by the printing software than by the network, as printing barely affects the network's speed.

Let's look at an example. We'll examine the network printing process using an HP DeskJet 500, connected to an LPT1 parallel port.

Installing a shared printer

A network printer must be installed to make this operation work, using the following steps:

- Connect the printer to the file server using a printer cable.

- Install printer configuration as needed using PRINTCON.

- Redirect print jobs to workstations using CAPTURE.

- Install printer drivers for application programs as needed.

We'll skip the first step. PRINTCON lets you edit an existing print job configuration, select a default print job configuration, or copy a configuration from a user's system.

The CAPTURE command redirects print jobs to the network printer in a Novell network. You can access this command from the workstation's AUTOEXEC.BAT file, or place in each user's login script.

   The command is named CAPTURE because it captures all data sent to the port, and sends the data over the network cable to the file server for printing.

The CAPTURE command offers a wide variety of switches; we'll discuss some important ones here. Let's say we want to print to LPT2:, sending the data to the first PRINTQ_0 queue, omitting printed banners (title pages) for each print job, and omitting automatic formfeeds for each print job. To perform these tasks, CAPTURE requires the /NB (No Banner), /No FormFeed, /L=2 (LPT=LPT2), and /Queue=PRINTQ_0 switches. The command would look like this:

```
CAPTURE /NB /No FormFeed /L=2 /Queue=PRINTQ_0
```

   We purposely selected the LPT2 (/L=2) printer port on the workstations, to leave LPT1 free local printers. The file server's printer is still connected to LPT1.

Any data you send to the parallel port under MS-DOS is rerouted to the network printer for printing.

   You can also display the current print jobs in the print queue. Simply use the Novell PRINTCON command.

16.7.5   Exchanging messages and data

One of the greatest advantages of a network over individual and independent computers is the option of joint work on projects. It can be necessary and useful in a school for the classroom teacher and the front office to have access to student data. If the classroom teacher changes a pupil's address in the network, the "report card" from the office will go to the correct address, to the joy or dismay of the pupil. In this case all participants will need access to the same pupil data.

Mutual access to data is also important in business. This type of data exchange will prevent sales manager Smith from promising 20 machines to a good customer, when sales rep Miller has just sold these machines to another client a few minutes before Smith closed the deal. Again, all network participants must have access to the same data.

The aspects discussed in the examples are usually provided automatically by good, networkable software. The database, the warehouse management or the business office can really only consider themselves "networked" if provision is automatically made for such problems, or if solutions are easily implemented.

There are a few additional problems which turn up relating to optimal network teamwork on projects, and neither Windows 3.1 nor Novell provide convenient solutions. In this section we want to show you concrete practical examples for data exchange among several users. Although the examples and solutions come directly from our own fields and experience, they can be very easily adapted to different problem situations.

Windows for Workgroups offers a multitude of solutions, including optimal data and information exchange, and works together splendidly with MS-DOS 6.0. If you have connected your DOS computer to a Windows for Workgroups network, you can skim over or even skip the following sections. The following section is aimed at those MS-DOS 6.0 users who are running a Novell network without Windows for Workgroups.

Organizing data exchange between users

What do you do, if user SMITH has changed the CONFIG.SYS file on her workstation hard drive for maximum RAM use, and now user Smith wants to do the same for his system. Or someone has created some new icon files, and now all the other users want to decorate "their windows." In each of these cases, files must be exchanged between users.

Prerequisites for data exchange

Important:

- All participants must have unlimited access to a shared directory, enabling the one to deposit data there and everything else who is interested to fetch it.

- The files present in the directory for exchange must be removed as quickly as possible to prevent data "garbage" from taking up too much valuable file server space and backup capacity.

- A user should be able to inform the others that the files are now available, and other users should be able to receive messages.

We have already discussed sensible directory structures and access rights. Both play an important role in smoothly running data exchange. Unfortunately there are no available network buffers which are automatically supervised. You'll have to install something of the kind yourself.

If you want to follow our recommendations on directory structures, you should install a F:\USER\TMP directory for data exchange and a F:\USER\UMAIL directory for the exchange of messages, granting appropriate group rights to all users:

```
F:\USER/TMP        [RWOCDPSM]
F:\USER/UMAIL      [RWOCDPSM]
```

The F:\USER\TMP directory can then of course be used for data exchange, while the \USER\UMAIL directory allows the exchange of user messages. You should think about these matters in any case, and discuss them with all network participants:

- Files in the F:\USER\TMP directory can be deleted at any time. This directory is used for unimportant files, or duplicates, nothing more.

 Never use the F:\USER\TMP directory as a temporary directory for DOS or Windows. Do not set the TMP (SET TMP=) or TEMP (SET TEMP=) environment variables to this directory, otherwise important TMP files (e.g., those used by Microsoft Word) could be deleted accidentally, resulting in data loss. For TEMP, use a directory on your local hard drive (SET TEMP=C:\TEMP) or in your user directory (SET TEMP= F:\USER\MILLER\TEMP).

- If User A wants to send data to User B, then User A copies the data into the F:\USER\TMP directory and sends User B a message using the SEND command. User B must then copy the data into a "safe" directory as quickly as possible to prevent data loss during the next deletion. We recommend the MOVE command from MS-DOS 6.0—this command copies the data from the TMP directory to User B's system, then deletes the file from the TMP directory.

Organizing the data exchange between users

In a smaller company, User A would poke her head over the partition and tell User B that the data he wanted is in the TMP directory. This isn't a simple task in a larger firm, especially if the data needs to be passed to many users.

A network offers the most basic electronic means for exchanging information and establishing contacts in such situations. Novell NetWare Versions 2.15 and 3.11 provide two methods of communication (SEND and SESSION).

We would therefore like in this section to introduce to you not only a solution for Windows far more elegant than "direct message exchange", but also to recommend a simple message system that reports to the user the next time he is logged into the network.

Direct messages with SEND and SESSION

Novell gives you two options for sending messages to a single user or to all members of a group. These messages appear in the bottom line of the DOS screen (and in Windows if everything is properly configured), and can have a maximum length of 45 characters.

Sending messages with SEND

To send a message to a user with SEND, you should first try to determine whether the recipient is logged into the network through the USERLIST command.

```
USERLIST
```

This displays a list of all the users currently active in the network. The information after your own user name is marked with an asterisk:

```
User Information for Server NETWARE311
Connection  User Name        Login Time
----------  ---------------  --------------------
    1         MILLER          3-12-1993  10:23 am
    2       * SUPERVISOR      3-12-1993  10:02 am
```

To send a message to user MILLER, enter the following command line:

```
SEND "Is the text ready?" TO MILLER
```

A message then appears telling you to which file server and to which user the message was sent. If MILLER wasn't logged in at the time, an error message appears on your screen. MILLER's system beeps and the following message appears in the bottom line of the screen:

```
>> From SUPERVISOR[2]: Is the text ready?      (CTRL-ENTER to clear)
```

As soon as MILLER presses Ctrl+Enter, the message disappears, and he or she will be able to respond to it.

Receiving messages in Windows

If you wanted to receive a message in Windows 3.0, you had to make a few small preparations. For example, you had to start a special program, NWPOPUP.EXE, with the following line in the WIN.INI file:

```
RUN=NWPOPUP.EXE
```

In Windows 3.1 this is no longer necessary, because Novell NetWare drivers handle the message passing. Some Windows systems reserve the message until the user exits to DOS. As long as you have a DOS task in text mode running in Windows, you will receive the message in the lowermost line just as if Windows wasn't even there.

How you receive the message depends on which task is active and how the screen output of the active task looks.

 If you have installed a screen saver, the receipt of a message on this computer will lead to the end of the screen output. If a password is also still active, the dialog window for entry of the password will still appear first. If you weren't logged in while the message was being sent, you of course will not receive a report, the sender getting simply an error message.

Sending messages with SESSION

SEND has a disadvantage in the entry of parameters. These parameters are hard to remember, and you can always mistype the user name.

It is much safer to use the Novell SESSION command, which offers the "User List" menu option after you start it. There you can make a selection from the list , press (Enter), then select "Send Message" from the "Available Options" window.

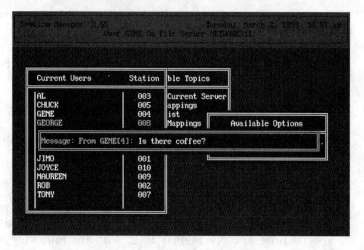

Sending messages with SESSION

Unlike SEND, SESSION lets you select the name of a user conveniently and reliably from a list. You can also use the same procedure for a group of users. That makes message exchange within a project group very simple.

To leave SESSION again, press (Esc) several times or press (Alt)+(F10).

16.8 Network Glossary

The following glossary reviews the concepts most important for working in a network.

Access rights
>Rights of a user to the use of programs or data can be assigned and changed with the SYSCON utility by the supervisor. In Novell it is possible to define the access rights for each user and each directory individually. In addition to DOS attributes like "read-only" or "hidden", there are also special rights for the opening or closing of files and for the creation of subdirectories.

Dedicated Opposite of non-dedicated. A file server is dedicated if it can no longer be used as a workstation. The total performance of the computer is thus available for network management.

File server Often called the server, this is the most powerful computer in the network. Stored on it are the data which each user wants to access. These computers usually have high computing power for the management of the central tasks. 386 or even 486 computers with large hard drives and at least 4 Meg of main memory are for that reason used for this purpose. The actual work of computing is done on the workstations.

Group One or several users with (at least partially) equal rights. In practical terms, the organizational principle of a group corresponds to a work group. Within a network, it is frequently possible to use a group designation instead of individual user names to identify several users—like a wildcard symbol. This is particularly important for sending messages.

LAN (Local Area Network). Unlike "global networks", a local area network allows you to share available hardware resources.

Local Net A network available only in a local area. In a local network there is the option of using hardware components, like printers and modems and fax machines, from different networked computers; this type of networking is also termed a LAN and stands in contrast to "global networks".

Login User "sign-on" to a network (mostly on a workstation). It's usually also necessary to enter a password. Login permits the user to receive a valid drive letter for the file server. A drive letter is thereby assigned to a directory on the server.

LOGIN Command for identifying yourself to a file server.

Login script
A command file which can be created for each user. If a login script is available for a user, it is automatically processed as soon as the user logs into the network.

Log off Disconnection of a workstation from the network.

Log on   Login of a user on a workstation.

Logout   Opposite of login. Following this entry no further access to data and programs on the file server is possible.

LOGOUT   Command to exit from a network.

Microsoft LAN Manager
              A network operating system from Microsoft. The competing product is the Novell network, Novell NetWare.

Network   The connection of several computers (file servers and workstations) into a system permitting the exchange of data and the sharing of hardware.

Network card
              Network cards control sending data in the network over the connecting cables. They represent, in addition to the computing power of the file server (main memory, processor and data storage) significant factor in determining the overall performance of the network.

              Typical network cards yield up to 10 Meg per second, more than 1 Meg of data transmission per second. The maximum transmission rate normally possible over a serial cable is 115,200 baud (or 14K per second).

              The computer would be so intensively involved with data transmission in such a case that it would scarcely have time for other jobs. Data transfer through a network card, on the other hand, imposes a much smaller burden upon the processor.

Network drive
              A drive letter assigned with MAP or by the use of the Connect drive to network option in the file manager. This drive letter is only available if the file server is available in the net and the user is logged into net with a valid user name.

              The file manager is in a position to save the connections made to the file server and to restore them automatically the next time the computer is booted from Windows.

Network driver

> A special device driver for the network card which defines the transmission protocol (language for communication). The Novell network driver is called IPX.

Network path

> A directory path on the file server, to which a drive letter was assigned. If a user is given access via the drive letter D:, for example, to the SERVER_1/SYS:PROG network path, he/she can move only within the \PROG directory path.

Network printer

> A printer essentially available to all users in the net. This printer is normally connected to the server.

Network shell

> After the network driver for the special network card has started, the network or redirector is able to establish the link to the file server.
>
> Providing the user has not used LOGIN to connect to the file server, he will have access only to the \LOGIN directory containing data and programs for logging into the network.
>
> In the case of Novell NetWare, the names of the redirectors, depending on the DOS version, are NET3.COM through NETX.COM for MS-DOS 3.X through MS-DOS 6.0.

Non-dedicated

> Opposite of dedicated. A file server is non-dedicated if it can also be used as a workstation. It can then likewise be operated in the operating system mode in addition to console mode (network operation). In any case, a program crash in the operating system mode can have serious consequences for network operation, so only dedicated file servers can be used starting with Novell NetWare 3.0.

Novell network

> A local network installed with Novell NetWare. Novell represents virtually the standard for local PC networks and is supported by all networkable programs.

Password   A code word which, together with a user name, controls access to a file server.

Print server

A computer on which the print jobs from the individual workstations are processed. A file server in the network is usually also given the job of a print server. Print jobs on the workstations are intercepted with the CAPTURE command and fed to the wait queue of the print server.

Redirector Another name for network shell.

Server   The abbreviation for file server.

Shareable   File attribute in a network; characterizes data and programs as "simultaneously usable by more than one user".

Streamer   A streamer is a tape drive, similar to a cassette recorder, which "records" data. A streamer is a good alternative to diskettes for data backup, for example, because the hard drive backup is on a cassette instead of 20 diskettes.

Data exchange, too, is relatively simple, because it is necessary merely to play the cassette, while handling files larger than 2 Meg is rather awkward on diskettes due to the need to distribute the backup over several diskettes.

The streamer has the advantage that files of up to 50 or more Meg can simply be copied by means of cassettes.

Supervisor System manager.

SYSCON   Novell program for managing users, groups and access rights. SYSCON enables you to do this quite conveniently via the program menu.

System managers

Those users with the user name supervisor, having unlimited rights in the network and responsible for administrative tasks. Only the supervisor can install and remove new user names and grant or withdraw user rights.

User A person having direct access to the data on the file server and with a user name (and usually also a code word) and able to log onto a workstation. A special user is the supervisor who has unlimited rights in the network and supervises the users and their rights.

User name A name under which the user is known to the network. Such a name is usually paired with a password; and a user is able to work on several file servers under different user names. User names can be installed by the system manager with SYSCON.

Workstation

A PC in a network on which the actual work takes place. By way of contrast, the file server is used only for managing the users and storing the data. To enable a workstation to access the data on the file server, it needs a cable connection, network card and special software (network driver and network shell).

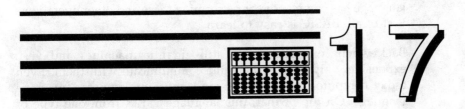

Using QBasic

Some PC users are content to use only commercial applications. Others, however, are more open to the possibilities that programming languages offer for writing their own applications. QBasic is one of these programming languages and is part of MS-DOS 6.0. This new language replaces the GW-BASIC language that was part of the earlier versions of DOS.

QBasic includes an extensive set of online documentation. You'll be able to learn about using the various commands and functions by using these help screens. Whenever you need information, simply access the **Help** menu from the QBasic Editor. However, further documentation is always desirable.

This chapter isn't intended to cover all aspects of QBasic. That would be impossible in one small chapter of a book. We recommend obtaining other reference sources such as *QuickBASIC for Beginners*, also published by Abacus. *QuickBASIC for Beginners* includes additional useful information about programming with QBasic.

We'll introduce a few of the fundamentals of BASIC programming and create some small sample programs. Mostly, we'll confine ourselves to explaining how to use QBasic and the QBasic Editor.

17.1 Working with QBasic

A computer language is a system of command words, that a compiler or interpreter changes into instructions that your computer understands. To be more precise: It tells the computer what to do.

Your computer also understands MS-DOS commands like DISKCOPY or TYPE, but MS-DOS commands can't be used to perform calculations or create graphics. The BASIC programming language has commands for performing these and other operations. Best of all, BASIC is easy to learn.

Back when computers were still gigantic machines and very expensive, only specialists could communicate with them. Even today computers really understand only one language, machine language. On top of that, this language varies from one type of computer to another.

As computers became smaller and more reasonably priced, it wasn't practical for every user to learn how to write complicated machine language programs to communicate with their computers. Languages were developed that were easy to learn. One such language was BASIC.

How does BASIC communicate with a computer?

BASIC uses a set of defined commands, much like the ones used in MS-DOS. These commands are linked together in such a way that the computer solves problems for us, step by step. Each problem presented to the computer must be divided into small steps, which are combined into programs. A program is a series of steps for solving a problem.

17.1.1 Special features of QBasic

Computers are all different inside. They have different amounts of RAM (random access memory) and even use different microprocessors. A microprocessor is the central control unit of your computer. MS-DOS computers today use microprocessors such as the 8086, 8088, 80286, 80386 and 80486.

Computers such as the Apple Macintosh use microprocessors from the 68000 family. These microprocessors are quite different and understand different instructions.

Machine language, the lowest level for communicating with your computer, is very different for each family of microprocessors.

There are even great differences in languages like BASIC. Different versions of BASIC exist for each type of computer. QBasic was developed by Microsoft especially for MS-DOS computers.

Since the different PCs usually conform to a standard, called the industrial standard, QBasic can be used on any MS-DOS computer. That means that you can write programs, then share them with your friends, and - more importantly - you can also use programs written by other people.

QBasic is a further development of the programming language, GW-BASIC, which was part of earlier versions of MS-DOS for a long time. QBasic is a lot easier to use and more efficient. Beginners will find helpful menus making it much easier to use.

QBasic also uses an intelligent editor, checking each line for proper syntax and providing hints on correcting the error.

The QBasic Editor offers an easy and convenient way to enter a program since it is a full-screen editor similar to a word processor. This makes QBasic a lot handier for creating large programs.

Although you can still use line numbers (for reasons of compatibility with other BASIC language programs), they are no longer necessary in QBasic. QBasic can use programs created with GW-BASIC language. This makes it easier to switch over to using QBasic.

If you want to convert your QBasic programs to stand alone programs which don't require the QBasic interpreter to run, you can buy Microsoft's QuickBASIC. Then you can transform the completed programs into an EXE program which runs independently. QuickBASIC is more powerful than QBasic and is compatible with QBasic.

17.1.2 Starting QBasic

To work with QBasic, you must first install the program. If you installed all files provided with MS-DOS 6.0 on the hard drive and the DOS directory is in the search path, you can start the QBasic program easily.

If QBasic is not in a directory defined by your search path (as explained previously) you must make the directory containing QBasic the current directory. It's a good idea to put QBasic and the programs created with it in a separate directory, such as \QBASIC.

To start QBasic from the system prompt in the command interpreter, type the program name:

```
QBASIC
```

The startup screen of QBasic will appear:

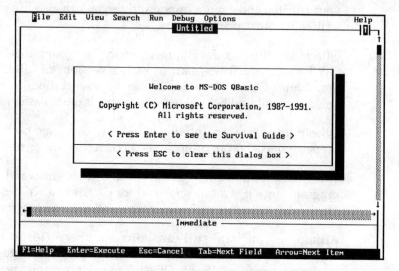

The QBasic startup screen

A dialog box appears in the middle of the screen with a note about online help information. Press [Esc] to clear this dialog box from the screen.

The QBasic startup screen

The first line of the screen is the menu bar. You can use the menus to choose the QBasic operations and processes.

The next line is the area title and displays the name of the program currently in the memory. If a program has not been loaded yet, the line displays "Untitled". This is the default screen you always see when starting QBasic without entering any optional parameters.

The actual work area takes up the greatest amount of space on the screen.

Beneath the work area, is an area titled "Immediate". You can use this area to enter one line commands directly. The computer executes these commands as soon as [Enter] is pressed. Press [F6] to make this area current. Pressing [F6] again will return to the work area.

The last line on the screen is the status bar. It displays information about the selected menu. If no menu has been selected, the commands displayed in the status bar can be selected by pressing the appropriate function key, or with your mouse.

The lower right corner displays the line and column number of where your cursor is located. This is practical, especially when working on lengthy programs.

17.1.3 Running QBasic

QBasic allows you to:

- Enter a program just as you would text in a word processor. As you enter a program, QBasic operates much like EDIT, the MS-DOS Editor.

- Select operations from the menus at the top of the screen. You can load and save finished programs as files, start the current program, etc.

- Use QBasic commands to write and modify a program.

The QBasic Editor

The QBasic Editor is a full screen editor that lets you create, view and modify program files quickly and easily. It is similar in many ways to the MS-DOS Editor. You can view a file on the entire screen and use the cursor keys to easily change the contents of the file.

Moving the cursor in the program editor

When QBasic is first started, the cursor is located in the upper left corner of the work area. You are ready to begin making entries in QBasic. The following list summarizes the keys you can use to move the cursor:

QBasic Cursor Control Keys

Key	Function
↑	Move one line up
←	Move one character to the left
→	Move one character to the right
↓	Move one line down
PgUp	Move one page up

Key	Function
PgDn	Move one page down
Home	Jump to beginning of line
End	Jump to end of line
Ctrl + ←	Move one word to the left
Ctrl + →	Move one word to the right
Ctrl + PgUp	Move the cursor left 78 characters
Ctrl + Home	Jump to beginning of program
Ctrl + End	Jump to end of program
Ctrl + PgDn	Move the cursor right 78 characters

Editing programs

Simple corrections to programs are made by deleting the mistake and inserting the correction (in Insert mode) or by typing the change over the error (in Overtype mode). To switch between Insert and Overtype modes, press the Ins key.

You can tell which mode you are in by observing the cursor. If the cursor is a line beneath the characters, QBasic is in Insert mode. If the cursor appears as a small rectangle, then QBasic is in Overtype mode.

Using menus

You can select the QBasic menus by pressing the Alt key to activate the menu bar, then pressing the highlighted letter's key to open the menu. Select a command with the cursor keys and press Enter.

It's even easier to select menus with the mouse. Point to the desired command and click with the left mouse button.

If a command has three periods after the name "...", the command is not executed when you press Enter. Instead, a dialog box appears where you enter additional information. Pressing Esc will cancel a menu selection or input to a dialog box.

The pull-down menus

The pull-down menus are lists of commands. For each command, one letter is highlighted. To select a command, press the desired highlighted letter. You can also use the ↑ and ↓ cursor keys to select a command. When the selection cursor covers the desired command, press Enter to select it.

The QBasic scroll bar

On the right margin of the screen is a vertical strip with arrows pointing up and down. This is the scroll bar. Within this strip is a rectangle. This is the scroll slider. Its position within the scroll bar indicates which section of the file is being displayed.

If the slider is at the top of the scroll bar, the start of the file is being displayed. If it is in the middle of the scroll bar, you are seeing the middle portion and if it's at the bottom, the area contains the last part of the file.

Use the ↑ or ↓ cursor keys to move through the file one line at a time. Press PgUp and PgDn to scroll the entire screen contents up or down by one screen.

You can also click the mouse pointer on either of the two direction arrows at the top and bottom of the scroll bar to scroll the data in the area up or down. You can even move the slider with the mouse.

Place the mouse pointer on the slider, press the left mouse button and, while holding down the mouse button, move the mouse pointer in the desired direction. The scroll slider will move along in the direction of the mouse arrow and display the corresponding contents of the file in the area.

The horizontal scroll bar on the bottom of the screen works exactly like the vertical bar, except that it moves horizontally. Use the key combinations Ctrl + PgDn to move right and Ctrl + PgUp to move left.

17.2 The QBasic Menus

Using the letter keys

Press Alt to activate the menu bar. Then press the highlighted letter key to pull down the individual menus. Pressing the highlighted letter opens the menu.

The menu bar displays the titles for each of the menus. These titles are **File**, **Edit**, **View**, **Search**, **Run**, **Debug**, **Options** and **Help**. Various commands are available only at specific times and some commands open dialog boxes for further input.

Using the cursor keys

The ↓ and ↑ cursor keys can also be used to open the pull-down menus, while the → and ← cursor keys can be used to select a pull-down menu. Press one of the cursor keys to highlight the desired command and press Enter to execute the command.

Using the mouse

If you are using the mouse, point and click to the desired menu and
the pull-down menu will open. You can also activate individual
commands by clicking on them with the mouse.

Here's how the menus are organized and what the commands do.

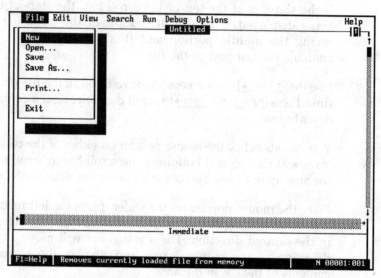

The QBasic File menu

The File menu

New   Clears the screen and deletes the file contents.

Open...   Loads an existing file from a diskette or hard drive to
             command memory.

Save   Saves a file which has been previously saved. If you
             haven't saved a file yet, this command prompts you to
             enter a filename.

Save As...   Saves a new file, or saves an existing file with a new
             name.

Print...   Prints the entire file or a marked block of text on the
             printer.

Exit   Leaves QBasic and returns to the MS-DOS Shell or
             command line.

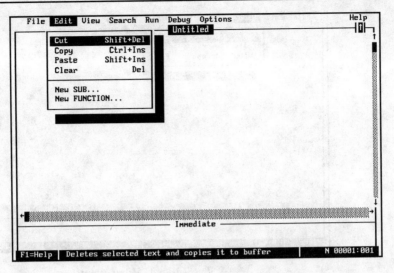

The QBasic Edit menu

The Edit menu

Cut   Deletes a marked block of text from the file and copies the block to the buffer.

Copy   Copies a marked block from the file to the buffer.

Paste   Inserts the contents of the buffer (block of text) at the position of the cursor in the file.

Clear   Deletes a marked block of text. The deleted text is not copied to the buffer.

New SUB...

Creates a new SUB procedure.

New FUNCTION...

Creates a new FUNCTION procedure.

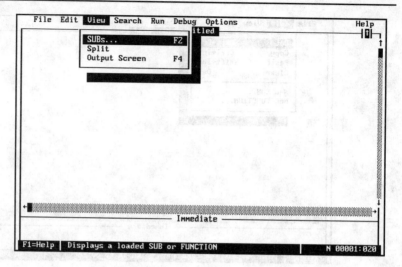

The QBasic View menu

The View menu

SUBs...   Displays a loaded SUB or FUNCTION.

Split   Divides the screen into two View windows.

Output Screen

Displays the output screen.

Selecting SUBS with the cursor or the mouse, or pressing F2 displays a dialog box containing the names of SUB and FUNCTION procedures which may be edited or deleted.

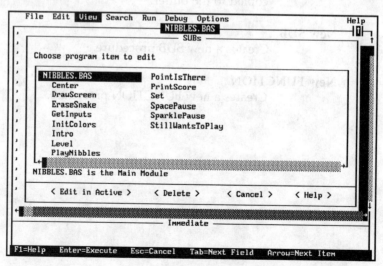

The SUBS dialog box

The Search menu

Find... Use this command to search for any character string in the file. You can specify whether to search for upper or lowercase letters, search for the target string as a separate word (and not as a part of another word) as well as the target string itself.

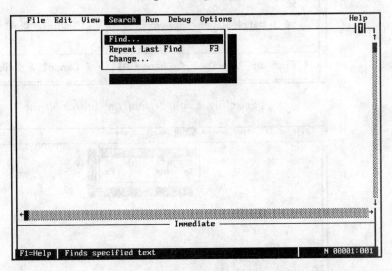

The QBasic Search menu

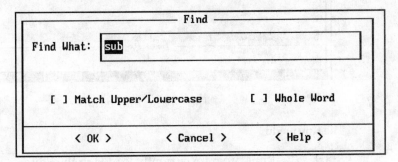

The Find dialog box

Repeat Last Find

Use this command - or press F3 - to repeat the last search.

Change... Use this command to replace any character string in the document with any other string of characters.

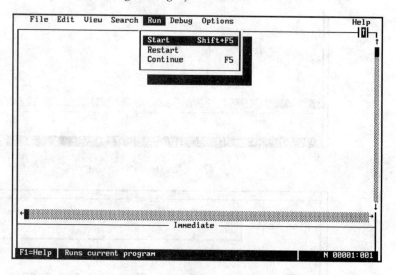

Selecting Change from the Search menu

The QBasic Run menu

The Run menu

Start   Runs program currently loaded in the Editor.

Restart   Clears all variables in preparation for single-stepping
               through a program while debugging. The first
               executable statement in the program is highlighted.

Continue   Continue execution of a program after it has stopped.
               Continue is often used after a breakpoint. Variables
               are not cleared. The program continues running with
               the line immediately following the breakpoint.

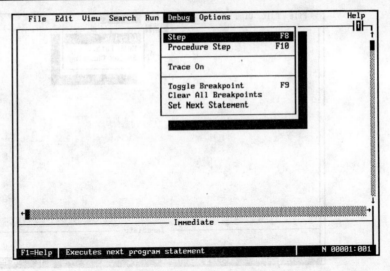

The QBasic Debug menu

The Debug menu

Step
: Executes next program statement. This command permits moving through a program one statement at a time while checking for program logic errors.

Procedure Step
: Single steps through a program, but executes procedure calls as a single statement.

Trace On
: Highlights each statement in a program as it is executed. This permits viewing the flow of a program.

Toggle Breakpoint
: Use this command to turn breakpoints on and off. Breakpoints are markers in your program. To turn on a breakpoint, move the cursor to highlight the line where you want the breakpoint, then press F9 or choose this command. Your program will run until it reaches this line, then it will stop, permitting printing variables in the Immediate area or single stepping from this point forward.

Clear All Breakpoints
: Removes all previously defined breakpoints.

Set Next Statement
: Changes the program execution sequence so that the next line executed is the one the cursor is on.

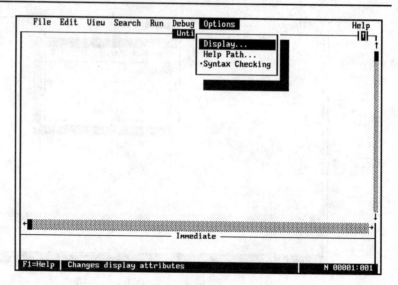

The QBasic Options menu

The Options menu

Display... Use this command to select the color of the screen background and the color of the font (the foreground), to switch the scroll bar on and off and to set the distance between the tabs.

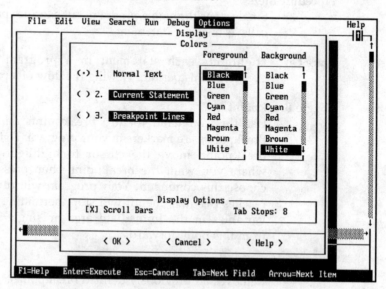

The Display dialog box

Help Path...

Use this command to specify the path for the directory containing the QBASIC.HLP file.

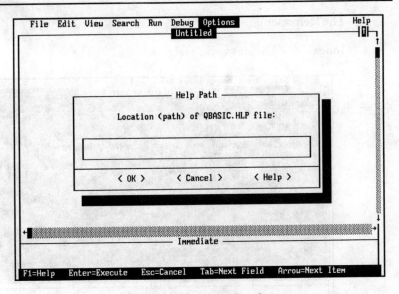

The Help Path dialog box

Syntax Checking

This command is a toggle for turning syntax checking on and off. When activated, QBasic checks each line entered for syntax errors, formats the line and translates the line to executable form if the syntax is correct.

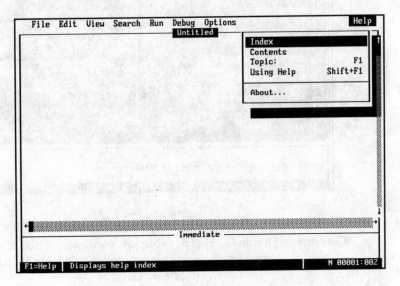

The QBasic Help menu

The Help menu

Index   Displays the Help index.

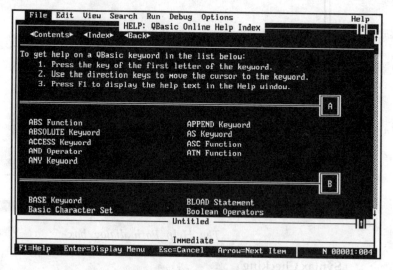

The QBasic Help index

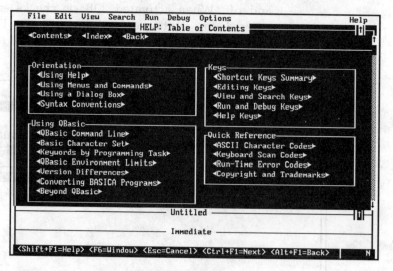

Contents of QBasic Help

Contents   Displays **Help** table of contents. This command
             provides a guide organized according to topics to
             information in QBasic Help.

Topic   Displays information about the QBasic keyword the
             cursor is on.

Using Help

This displays information on getting general help (see "QBasic Help").

About...   This displays information about the copyright and version number of QBasic.

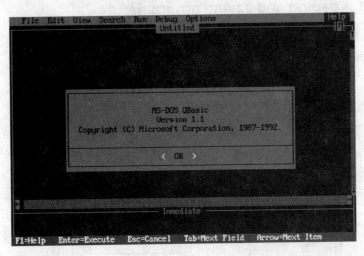

The About... window

QBasic Help

Using Help may be the most important command of QBasic to understand. The information provided in the help screens covers virtually every subject about QBasic you're likely to encounter.

Information about keywords includes the proper syntax, variable types and small example programs.

To get help with the available QBasic commands, simply press Shift + F1. A help screen appears. Select the keyword "Index" by pressing Tab and then press Enter. You can also double-click the icon with the mouse.

An alphabetical list of all commands and keywords appears. Use either the cursor keys or the mouse (and the scroll bar) to view all of the commands.

Move the cursor to a command you would like to know more about. After pressing Enter or double-clicking with the mouse, detailed information about the function and meaning of the command is displayed. Press Esc to leave the Help screen and return to the QBasic Editor.

You can also display a Help screen for each command in the current program by moving the cursor into the command and pressing F1. Most help screens for commands even have short sample programs that demonstrate the use of a command.

17.2.1 Loading and saving programs

After entering a program, you'll want to save it. The first time a program is saved, select an appropriate filename. After the first save, you can use the same filename whenever you save.

Saving programs

Use the command **Save** from the **File** menu to save an untitled program and assign it a new filename. After you select **Save**, the following dialog box appears:

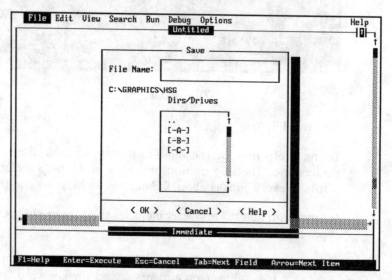

The dialog box for Save

Enter the name under which you want to save the program in the dialog box. After pressing Enter, the program is saved in the current directory of the hard drive or diskette. QBasic automatically attaches .BAS as the filename extension.

You can also specify the path of the directory where the program is to be saved. Enter the complete path including the filename in the File Name text box. As an alternative, you can also select the correct path under "Dir/Drives" and then enter just the filename.

When selecting filenames for your programs, remember that filenames can only use eight characters. If a name with more than eight characters is entered, the first three excess characters will be used as the filename extension and all other characters are simply omitted.

If you make changes to the program after saving it the first time, make sure you save it again. Select **Save** from the **File** menu. The dialog box for defining the filename and directory won't be displayed again. The program will be saved with the previously selected name.

Loading a saved program

To run a previously saved program, you must first load it into the work area. You can do this in the **File** menu also, using the **Open...** command.

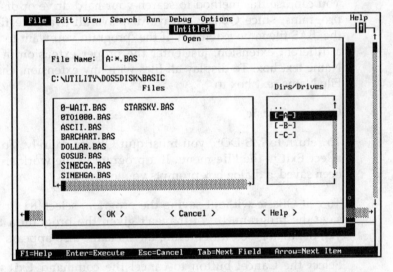

Selecting Open... from the File menu displays this dialog box

Enter the filename (and path, if necessary) of the program in the top line of the dialog box.

There is another way to select a program to be loaded. Enter a wildcard in the File Name text box. This will display all QBasic files in the current directory which satisfy the conditions of the wildcard in the list box.

Press ⌈Tab⌉ (or use the mouse) to move to the list box. Use the cursor keys (or the mouse) to select the desired file. The filename is automatically placed in the File Name list box.

The drive and path can be changed by using ⌈Tab⌉ (or the mouse) to select the Dirs/Drives list box and select the desired drive and directory.

You can move to the next highest directory by moving the cursor to the two periods ".." and pressing ⌈Enter⌉. To go to the next lowest directory, move the cursor to the directory name (which is always in capitals) and press ⌈Enter⌉.

These directories also display the QBasic files. Select the desired file from the list box. After pressing ⌈Enter⌉ or clicking with the left mouse button, the file is loaded and displayed on the work area.

You can use this method to search your hard drive or diskette for programs, since QBasic always displays all available files with the .BAS filename extension. If the program you want to load has a different extension, just enter the proper extension in the File Name text box. To display all files with any extension, change the File Name text box to *.*.

Quitting QBasic

To return to MS-DOS, you must quit QBasic entirely. To do this, select **Exit** in the **File** menu. If a program in the work area hasn't been saved, a dialog box prompts you to save it.

To exit QBasic without saving the program, select ⌈N⌉. Press ⌈Y⌉ to save the program. If you haven't given the program a filename yet, the dialog box for entering the filename also appears.

Select the Cancel button to cancel the command **Exit without saving** and return to QBasic.

After quitting QBasic you return to the command area of MS-DOS and can enter MS-DOS commands. If you started QBasic from the MS-DOS Shell, you will return to the MS-DOS Shell screen.

17.3 Commands and Functions

Even though QBasic is powerful and easy to use, some programming knowledge is required. A thorough explanation of all of the facets of BASIC programming is beyond the scope of this book. In fact, to adequately cover a subject like QBasic with programming examples and detailed keyword explanations would require a book at least as large as this one.

At first glance it appears complex to learn to program in BASIC, but BASIC programming is certainly within the grasp of the average user. Programming isn't dark and mysterious. If you haven't tried programming before, we recommend working through the following example programs. You'll be pleasantly surprised at what you can do on your own.

To learn more about programming, we recommend *BASIC Programming Inside & Out* or *QuickBASIC for Beginners*.

The purpose of this section is to provide a general overview of the most important commands and functions in QBasic. This section does not provide an introduction to the fundamentals of BASIC programming.

 Refer to Appendix F for a full listing of the QBasic keywords.

17.3.1 Using variables for simple calculations

The basis of ordinary programming consists of finding a solution to a problem and describing the solution with the "command" words of the programming language. You can't just think up any solution, but must use the available commands and options of the programming language. This means, a solution in the programming language BASIC is necessarily different than the solution in Pascal or Assembler.

If you have created a program using QBasic commands, use either **Start** from the **Run** menu or press (Shift) + (F5) to start it. QBasic then switches to another screen where all of the program's messages appear. After the program ends, press any key to return to the QBasic Editor.

One of the advantages of every programming language is the fact that it uses variables. Imagine the problems you would encounter if you had to write a separate program for each number whose square root you wanted to calculate. This would be so tedious as to cancel the advantages of programming. Instead of writing a new program for every instance, you can use a general calculation equation with placeholders (the variables) and assign these variables different values for different calculations.

It's not necessary to write a new program every time you calculate a square root. Instead, create a program for calculating the square root of the variable X and then run this program for X=3, X= 4537, and so forth.

Essentially, there are two different types of variables: Numeric variables and alphanumeric variables. Alphanumeric variables are better known as string variables.

Simply put, numeric variables can only contain numeric values, and you can perform any kind of calculation with them.

Strings can consist of almost any character, but you can't perform calculations with them.

Choosing a plain, clear variable name makes a program more understandable. The variables in QBasic can have names up to 40 characters long. This makes it possible for users to give their variables very meaningful, expressive names. However, there are a few restrictions when choosing variable names:

- Names must be at least one character long and can be up to 40 characters long.

- Names can only contain letters (a-z) and numerals (0-9). Spaces are forbidden just as in filenames, since they serve as separators.

- Names cannot start with a numeral and shouldn't contain any QBasic keywords (such as PRINT).

Alphanumeric variables (character strings) have the character "$" at the end of the variable name. Character strings themselves must be defined in quotation marks, to distinguish them from numbers. 147 is a number, while "147" is a character sequence of three alphanumeric characters. In this case the numbers "1", "4" and "7".

Numeric variables can also contain different kinds of numbers. The exact type of variable is indicated by a special character at the end of the variable name. The integer variables are especially important and can contain only whole numbers from -32768 to 32267 and have a percentage sign following the variable name.

The practical thing about numeric variables is that you can use them just like numbers in all arithmetic equations. The four fundamental arithmetic operations (addition, subtraction, multiplication and division) are easy to use in QBasic:

Program line	Output to screen
PRINT 4 + 9	13
PRINT 5 - 3	2
PRINT 3 * 5	15
PRINT 7 / 3	2.333333

Examples of variables

Here are a few examples that should explain how to use variables and variable names correctly:

Strings/Character strings

`Name$ = "Miller"`   Character string with 6 characters

`Character$ = "a"`   Character string with 1 character

`Street$ = "25 Star Street"`
     Character string with 14 characters, spaces and numbers

`Number$ = "119"`   Character string with 3 characters/numbers

Numeric variables

`Number = 119`   Single precision number

`New_number = 9.5`   Simple precision number

`Number% = 9.5`   Integral number (whole number) with the content of 9, the remainder is cut off during the allocation

17.3.2 Input and output of data

Commands provide a way to enter data into a program and control the way a program runs. In most cases, you'll want to display the results of your program on the screen. QBasic also has methods for displaying data as well.

Using PRINT to output data

The PRINT command sends data to the screen. Numbers, character strings or variable names may be specified after PRINT. When a variable name is used, the screen displays the contents of the variable.

```
PRINT 3
PRINT "Three"
Number = 3
PRINT Number
```

QBasic moves the cursor to a new line after each PRINT statement. To prevent this, end the line with either a comma or a semicolon. After a comma, the next information printed to the screen is displayed at the next tab position. When a semicolon is used, the next data printed to the screen follows immediately. In this way, you can output several items with a single PRINT statement:

```
PRINT 3,4,5
PRINT "One";"Two"
```

```
3      4        5

OneTwo
```

Screen display from the program lines shown above

Notice that in the figure above that the commas in the first line positioned the cursor at the next tab position. Also, the semicolon in the second line printed the two strings without a space between them.

Using INPUT to put data in a variable

The INPUT command can be used to pause a program to get input from the keyboard. The computer displays a question mark to indicate that it is expecting input:

```
INPUT Number
```

The variable type used in the INPUT line determines the type of input that is permitted. In the example above, only numbers can be input. Entering "Miller" would result in an error message and you would have to enter something else. On the other hand, if you specified a character string variable after INPUT, almost any kind of input would be accepted.

Since a question mark prompt doesn't provide information about the kind of input the program expects, you can insert comments, in quotation marks. The variable name is separated from the comments by a semicolon:

```
INPUT "What is your name"; Name$
```

This causes the comment to appear in front of the question mark. If you separate the variable name from the comment by a comma instead of a semicolon, the question mark is not displayed.

```
INPUT "Please enter your name: ", Name$
```

Checking the keyboard

In some cases, INPUT is not flexible enough. For example, you must press (Enter) after the input. Also, there is no way of checking the input for length or special characters.

You can use the special INKEY$ command as an alternative. Actually, INKEY$ is not a command, but rather a string variable updated by QBasic: It always contains the next character read by the keyboard. If there is no character available, INKEY$ contains an empty string "".

For example, to have a program wait for a key to be pressed before continuing, use the following:

```
PRINT "Please press any key..."
Delay:
KBENTRY$ = INKEY$
IF KBENTRY$ = "" THEN GOTO Delay
```

INKEY$ enables limiting input to a specific length. You can count characters and automatically stop when the maximum limit is reached.

17.3.3 Commands and functions

We've discussed some simple rules for arithmetic. Up until now we have learned arithmetic rules as commands. By using the instruction:

```
Number = 3 + 4
```

QBasic calculates the result and assigns it to the variable "Number". A variable name can also appear on the right side of the equation:

```
Number = Number + 1
```

By now it should be clear that the equals sign isn't really an "equals" sign as expressed in mathematics, but represents an assignment. You are assigning the value on the right of the equals sign to the variable on the left.

QBasic consists of commands and functions. Functions play an important role in programming. You should know the fundamental differences between commands and functions.

Commands are used to have QBasic perform actions, while functions require QBasic to supply a value or result.

For example, to determine the character with an ASCII code of 33, you can use the CHR$() function.

```
PRINT CHR$(33)
```

The exclamation point is displayed as a result of this function. More often, functions are used in an assignment and then the result is assigned to another variable:

```
Character$=CHR$(33)
```

Many functions (like CHR$() in our example) require at least one piece of information to be able to work at all. The function CHR$(), for example, requires the ASCII code of the character. These values are specified within parentheses.

When a function like CHR$() is used, there are two things to keep in mind: Usually you must specify a value within the parentheses and you must use the result (function value).

For example, you could display the result on the screen, assign it to a variable and so forth.

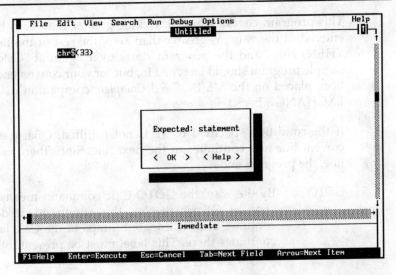

A function entered in a command line without an assignment results in an error message

17.3.4 Program control

If it weren't for program loops, a program would always run from the first line to the last line. QBasic uses commands that control a program so that some commands can be executed several times.

Conditions: IF ... THEN

You can use the IF command to check for a condition. Commands which are executed if the specified condition is satisfied are written after the THEN portion of the statement.

The following example program converts U.S. dollar amounts into DM (German marks) after the current exchange rate for the dollar has been entered at the beginning of the program. The program continues to execute until a zero is entered as a value for dollar:

```
CLS
INPUT "Please enter rate of exchange: 1 U.S. dollar = ??
DM: ", Rate

Calc:
INPUT "Please enter desired amount in dollars (Enter 0
to end): "; Dollar
DM = Dollar * Rate
PRINT "$";Dollar; " equals "; DM; " DM"
IF Dollar > 0 THEN GOTO Calc
```

This program checks whether a value greater than zero has been entered. If the value is greater than zero, the rest of the line (after THEN) runs, and the program starts over again at "Calc". (This sample program should be typed in, but for your convenience, it has been placed on the *MS-DOS 6.0 Complete* companion diskette as EXCHANGE.BAS.)

If the condition specified by IF is not fulfilled, QBasic ends the current line and continues in the next line. Since there is no next line, the program ends.

GOTO   By the way, the GOTO Calc command means that as soon as QBasic reaches this command, it does not continue line for line, but jumps to the Calc label and continues there. This label must be present, otherwise the program gives you an error message.

Define the label by entering it at the desired place in the program. Labels are a name followed by a colon. More information about GOTO can be found in the section about subroutines.

Conditional options for IF

There are a number of conditional operations used to make comparisons. These operators are called logical operators, because they cause something to happen that demands logical "thinking":

QBasic Logical Operators	
=	equals
<	less than
>	greater than
>=	greater than or equal to
<=	less than or equal to
<>	not equal to

Setting limits: FOR ... NEXT

Many times users want to run a part of a program several times with different numerical values each time. Sometimes it's necessary to run a portion of a program a specified number of times. FOR...NEXT loops are ideal for both of these purposes.

What would be an easy way to display all characters with ASCII codes between 32 and 255 on the screen? Here's a simple solution:

```
CLS
FOR AsciiNumber = 32 TO 255
PRINT CHR$(AsciiNumber);
NEXT AsciiNumber
```

In QBasic, the line "FOR AsciiNumber = 32 TO 255" means that the initial value for AsciiNumber is 32. All of the lines which follow the FOR statement are executed until the line NEXT AsciiNumber is encountered.

The value of AsciiNumber is then increased by "1". If the value of AsciiNumber is not greater than 255, the program "jumps" back to the line containing FOR. (The lines between FOR and NEXT are called a "loop").

 This loop begins with 32 because some ASCII characters below this value are not printable characters. This would spoil the results. For example, CHR$(7) emits a warning beep, not a printable character.

Other options

Besides these two options, QBasic has a number of other commands for special uses, such as those in the following list. Look them up as you need them in the appropriate QBasic Help screen.

To get help for a specific command, just type the command word and press F1 .

DO... LOOP
> Execute as long as or until a condition is fulfilled.

WHILE...WEND
> Execute as long as a condition is fulfilled.

SELECT CASE
> Run one of several different parts of a program based on the selection of a value.

17.3.5 Using subroutines

Users once complained that BASIC couldn't be used to create structured, easy to read programs. With QBasic, this is no longer the case, partly because of its very efficient, powerful subroutines.

Jumping with GOTO and GOSUB

QBasic ordinarily runs the lines of a program one after the other from beginning to end. You can use the GOTO command to have QBasic continue in a different place in the program. Just mark the target area with a label and GOTO the label.

It should be noted that using GOTO is frowned upon by many programmers. Using GOTO often leads to very inelegant program structures. Overuse of GOTO can lead to programs which are extremely difficult to follow. Using subroutines is the preferred method of program flow control.

One problem with GOTO is that when QBasic jumps to another program line, it no longer knows where it came from.

Quite often it would be convenient to return to the line where you made the jump from. One reason could be that you want to use one part of a program several times. For example, you might want to use the lines for user input or for displaying information on the screen.

The following short program shows you why you can't do that with the GOTO command. The program assigns different values to a variable at the beginning, and then jumps to a small output program, which represents the program section to be repeated:

```
VARIABLE = 10
GOTO Type
Back:
VARIABLE = 20
GOTO Type
VARIABLE = 30
GOTO Type
END
Type:
 PRINT "The variable is "; VARIABLE
 GOTO Back
```

 By the way, instead of letting the program run to the last line, the END command in the fourth line from the bottom immediately ends the program.

The program functions correctly the first time. It outputs 10 and sets VARIABLE to 20. After displaying 20, the program jumps back again and outputs 20 a second time. The problem is that VARIABLE can't be set to all of the values, because the program always jumps back to the same line.

What's needed is a way to jump from anywhere in the program to a section that you need often and then return to the original line. You can solve this problem using subroutines together with GOSUB and RETURN.

A subroutine is a part of a program that may be executed numerous times, may be called from anywhere in the program and always returns to the line immediately following the calling line.

Instead of using GOTO, you use GOSUB to jump to the first line of this program section. QBasic remembers it's present position in the file, continues execution at the label, reaches RETURN and goes back to the line immediately following the GOSUB statement. Here's an example:

```
CLS
MARK = 100
GOSUB Calculate
MARK = 500
GOSUB Calculate
MARK = 10
GOSUB Calculate
END
Calculate:
 CLS
 PRINT "                  Conversion: DM - Dollars "
 PRINT
 DOLLARS = MARK / 1.5
 PRINT MARK ; " DM are "; DOLLARS ; " Dollars"
 PRINT
 INPUT "Continue (ENTER) "; KBENTRY$
RETURN
```

The subroutine starts in the line with the label CALCULATE and ends in the line with RETURN. It's executed three times. The first time it is called in the third line. MARK was set to 100. The subroutine calculates the appropriate number of DOLLARS and displays it on the screen. After RETURN, QBasic continues in the fourth line. The same thing happens with 500 and 10 in the following lines.

The END at the bottom of the main program, before the subroutine, is important. If the program didn't end here, it would run the subroutine again beginning at the label and would encounter RETURN at the end. Since there is no GOSUB calling the subroutine, QBasic would return an error message.

Subroutines and their practical uses

Although in many cases larger programs can be structured in such a way that they run continuously from "top" to "bottom" (i.e., from the first to the last line), there are several reasons why you wouldn't want to do this. For example:

- readability

- simple variability and expandability

- it's difficult to search for errors

Instead, build programs from program parts and give them a hierarchical structure. It's best if you use small, closed task areas to separate program parts.

Programs that aren't too large begin with a main program and execute different tasks and activities in subroutines. Programs that are very large often have subroutines that use subroutines of their own.

```
REM Start the main program
..
GOSUB SR1
GOSUB SR2
IF Result < 100 THEN GOSUB SR3
GOSUB SR1
END

REM Subroutine 1
SR1:
..
RETURN

REM Subroutine 2
SR2:
..
RETURN

REM Subroutine 3
SR3:
..
RETURN
```

 The lines with the periods represent any command lines within the program.

This outline of the program structure clearly shows that the actual work is delegated to the various subroutines, which are called from the main program in the correct sequence.

The outline should also demonstrate that you can very easily make certain tasks dependent on conditions (indicated in the example by "IF Result < 100 THEN GOSUB SR3") and that you can also call a subroutine more than once (SR1 in the example).

The following example illustrates the use of subroutines. In the main program, a counter is increased in the loop and calls the subroutine Delay after displaying to the screen.

This subroutine uses delay loops to delay the program (QBasic counts from 0 to 1000). At the same time, you can terminate the delay loop prematurely by pressing a key.

```
REM Main program
CLS
FOR WaitLoop = 1 TO 10
PRINT WaitLoop
GOSUB Delay
NEXT WaitLoop
END

REM Subroutine Delay
Delay:
Counter = 0
WHILE INKEY$ = "" AND Counter < 1000
Counter = Counter + 1
WEND
RETURN
```

More options using SUB and FUNCTION

QBasic has other structures that are even more powerful. These structures start with SUB, end with END SUB and are called "procedures". You can start procedures like commands, by entering the name of the procedure. This allows you to expand QBasic by adding your own commands. Here's what our sample program from above would look like with the Delay procedure:

```
DECLARE SUB Delay ()
CLS
FOR Y = 1 TO 10
PRINT Y
Delay
NEXT Y
END

SUB Delay
Delay:
Counter = 0
WHILE INKEY$ = "" AND Counter < 1000
Counter = Counter + 1
WEND
END SUB
```

At the beginning of the program you have to tell QBasic that the program contains a Delay procedure. After that you can call it in the main program. The procedure follows at the end of the main program.

QBasic usually divides the program into the main program and its procedures, displaying only one coherent part of the program.

To enter the program above, you ordinarily use the **New SUB...** command from the **Edit** menu in the (empty) BASIC editor. QBasic will prompt you for the name of the procedure. Enter Delay. The beginning and end lines of a procedure appear on the screen:

```
SUB Delay
END SUB
```

In between these two lines, enter the lines for the procedure from the example above. To enter the actual main program, select **View SUBs....** This displays the existing elements of the program. The first line in the display is the name of the main program, Untitled. Select this command and press (Enter) to display it on the screen. Then enter the name of the main program.

Just as you can use **New SUB...** to create new subprograms, you can use **New FUNCTION...** from the **Edit** menu to create new functions in QBasic. A typical example of such a new function could be a subroutine that waits for the press of a key and then delivers this keypress to the main program.

17.4 QBasic and Graphics

QBasic has some powerful options for creating graphics. The sample programs that are supplied with MS-DOS 6.0 demonstrate that you can even use these options to create computer games.

Graphics made of ASCII characters

To be able to take advantage of the QBasic graphics commands, you need a graphics card which is a special expansion to your PC that corresponds to the IBM standard. However, different graphics cards vary considerably in the number of dots that can be displayed (resolution).

If you want to program QBasic programs with special graphics commands, the programs frequently have to do complicated calculations so that the results on different computers are identical.

There is another option for creating graphics that is a lot easier because it doesn't use either a graphics card or the special QBasic graphics commands. This option uses ASCII characters. ASCII is the acronym for American Standard Code for Information Interchange.

A PC can only "think" in numbers and has to translate each character transmitted from the keyboard into one of these numbers. ASCII codes translate into characters. The numbers begin at 49 (Alt + 4 9 =1) and the letters begin at 65 (Alt + 6 5 = A).

The following sample program creates a random bar chart out of the "*" character:

```
CLS
RANDOMIZE TIMER
FOR I = 5 TO 60 STEP 5
 HEIGHT% = 24 - ((22 * RND) + 1 )
  FOR Y = 24 TO HEIGHT% STEP -1
  LOCATE Y,I
  PRINT "***";
 NEXT Y
NEXT I
```

The program looks somewhat complicated because the chart is created randomly and starts at the bottom, working its way to the top. Since you can easily get help and information about unknown commands by placing the cursor on the command and pressing F1, you can find out everything you need to know about the program by using the QBasic online help screens.

It's especially easy to display a trigonometric function with ASCII graphics. The following example displays the sine function on the screen:

```
CLS
FOR I = 1 TO 80
Y = I * 3.14 * 2 / 80
Y = INT(SIN(Y) * 12) + 13
LOCATE Y, I
PRINT CHR$(249);
NEXT I
WHILE INKEY$ = "": WEND
```

The most difficult thing about this program is the "scaling" (i.e., the conversion to the screen coordinates). Since the sine repeats itself after 2 PI, this range of numbers is divided into the 80 columns of the screen.

17.4.1 Different graphics modes

In our last example we confined ourselves to ASCII graphics, since anyone can use this form of graphics regardless of the graphics capacities of their PC. On the other hand, if you do have a PC with a graphics card, QBasic provides some powerful commands for high resolution graphics. For example, one interesting option involves changing the screen display from 640 pixels in width and 200 pixels vertically.

Since lines and circles are made up of many pixels and are a lot of trouble to make from individual pixels, QBasic provides special commands for making them. For example, with graphics commands it's easy to display mathematical functions on the screen in graphics.

There are two things to keep in mind when using these graphics options:

1. Depending on the kind of graphics card, there can be a considerable difference in the commands for turning on graphics and the maximum number of pixels (resolution) in the screen display.

2. If your PC has a Hercules Graphics card, start the MSHERC.COM program before starting QBasic. Displaying graphics is impossible otherwise.

17.4.2 Basic graphics commands

The easiest way to learn the basic graphics commands and the correct sequence is through examples. In the previous section we showed you a sine in text mode (ASCII graphics).

For comparison, here is the same sine function using the graphics options of QBasic. We added a "V" in front of the variable names since WIDTH is a QBasic keyword:

Example of the sine in Hercules Graphics

```
VMode = 3
VHeight = 348
VWidth = 720

SCREEN VMode
CLS
FOR I = 1 TO VWidth
Y = I * 3.14 * 2 / VWidth
Y = INT(SIN(Y) * VHeight / 2 + VHeight / 2)
PSET (I, Y), 15
NEXT I
WHILE INKEY$ = "": WEND
```

Example of the sine function with EGA/VGA Graphics

For EGA/VGA cards with 640 * 350 pixels, change the following lines:

```
VMode = 9
VHeight = 350
VWidth = 640
```

You must use the SCREEN command to switch the screen to graphics mode. The kind of mode that is possible depends a great deal on the kind of graphics card and results in very different pixel display widths and heights.

The PSET command actually draws the pixels.

QBasic can do a lot more than just draw pixels. You can use LINE to create lines and rectangles and you can draw circles with the CIRCLE command.

17.4.3 Preserving your screen

In conclusion, here's a screen saver program. You should not allow the screen to display a motionless image over a long period of time. This can leave "traces" in the phosphorus layer of the screen. This is called "burning in" an image.

Although you can create a screen saver in two simple BASIC lines:

```
CLS
WHILE INKEY$="":WEND
```

a screen that is completely empty can be rather boring.

The following program (on the companion diskette under the name STARSKY.BAS) draws a "colorful starry sky" until you press a key.

```
REM Starry sky as a screen saver
DEFINT A-Z
RANDOMIZE TIMER
VidMode = 9
VHeight = 350
VWidth = 640

SCREEN VidMode
WHILE INKEY$ = ""
   VColor = RND * 15
   y = VHeight * RND
   x = VWidth * RND
   PSET (x, y), VColor
WEND
SCREEN 0
```

If you have a Hercules Graphics card and want to use this program, change the following lines:

```
VidMode = 3
VHeight = 348
VWidth = 720
```

Remember that you have to start the MSHERC.COM program before starting QBasic if you have a Hercules Graphics card.

To use the screen saver, start QBasic, load and start the program. Create a small batch file called PRESERVE.BAT, containing the following line:

```
QBasic /RUN C:\BASIC\STARSKY.BAS
```

The BASIC program must be in the specified directory, otherwise you will need to change the line.

If you want to exit QBasic automatically at the end of the program so that you can continue working in the command interpreter, just add the following line after SCREEN 0:

```
SYSTEM
```

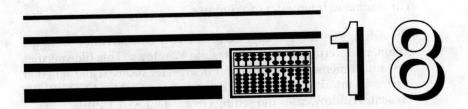

C h a p t e r

MS-DOS 6.0 And Windows 3.1

The following chapter describes the best way to organize MS-DOS 6.0 for working together with Windows and tells you how to set up the programs supplied with MS-DOS 6.0 for operation in Windows.

18.1 Overview

Here is an overview about running DOS and Windows together.

Basic cooperation

MS-DOS 6.0 and Windows 3.1 work very well together and complement each other in various areas.

Special features with storage media

Speeding up access to diskettes and hard drives with SMARTDRV harmonizes well with DOS and Windows. SMARTDRV is able to loan memory to Windows.

The DEFRAG program can speed up Windows' access to storage media and should be used before creating a permanent swap file in Windows. Before using DEFRAG, remove any permanent swap file in Windows and reinstall it after the program is finished.

Windows requires a great deal of hard drive capacity. With MS-DOS 6.0, you can use DBLSPACE to compress storage media so they will be able to hold about twice the amount of data.

Special features using memory

If you run MS-DOS 6.0 together with Windows, avoid using expanded memory. By using MEMMAKER, not only can you optimize memory, you can also adapt it for use in DOS and Windows.

The command interpreter in Windows

The settings in the PIF file, COMMAND.PIF, determine how the command interpreter runs as a task in Windows. This file specifies how much memory the command interpreter receives and whether it runs in multitasking or not. If there is no COMMAND.PIF file present, Windows uses the settings from _DEFAULT.PIF.

You can specify the prompt of a DOS task in Windows with the WINPMT environment variable. In many cases, the deciding factor in whether TSR programs will run in all DOS tasks under Windows or only in one depends on whether you referenced the TSR program before starting Windows, from a DOS task.

Windows Tools from MS-DOS 6.0

MS-DOS 6.0 comes with three utility programs for Windows:

Backup   A program for backing up and recovering data.

Virus protection
              A program for scanning files for viruses.

Undelete   A program for recovering deleted files.

18.2 Running MS-DOS and Windows

Windows 3.1 and MS-DOS 6.0 work well together. Since both are Microsoft products, they contain the XMS memory manager HIMEM.SYS and the 386 memory manager EMM386.EXE.

However, it's possible to refine and optimize this cooperation between Windows and MS-DOS. When installing either product, you may need to decide whether your PC should be Windows-oriented or MS-DOS-oriented. For example, if you plan on using Windows often, you'll want the Windows mouse driver running when you start the computer. If you prefer MS-DOS, you may want to run the mouse driver as needed, instead of including it as a device driver.

Calling MS-DOS based applications from Windows can be difficult and sometimes impossible. For example, some tape drive backup programs won't work from Windows and hard drive optimizers shouldn't be used from within Windows.

One option consists of either selecting the best possible compromise between Windows and MS-DOS during installation or working with different system files and simply switching between the two files when necessary. The special setup options of MS-DOS 6.0 are especially advantageous.

18.2.1 Reasons for running DOS and Windows

In this chapter, you'll learn how to maximize your productivity with MS-DOS and Windows. Here's an overview:

- MS-DOS 6.0 and Windows are both Microsoft products, so they (almost) always work well together, updating each other with the latest drivers.

- Windows started as an attachment to MS-DOS, but now offers a number of operating system functions: Printer, networks, memory management, OLE, DDE etc.

- With MS-DOS 6.0, DOS is developing in Windows niches, for example with the supplied Windows Utilities, DoubleSpace and Defrag (Windows doesn't have this program, but needs it to free up large contiguous free areas on the hard drive for a permanent swap file).

- Windows complements DOS in those areas in which DOS is at a disadvantage, and DOS complements Windows in those areas in which Windows cannot perform, or performs poorly. Examples:

- FDISK, DEFRAG and DBLSPACE are not present in Windows.

- Multitasking, data exchange, OLE and the like, although desirable, are not present in DOS.

18.3 Storage Media

The better Windows is able to work with the existing storage media, the faster Windows will work. The hard drive plays the major role. The following section shows you ways of improving how Windows works with storage media.

18.3.1 Active methods of speeding up access

The methods described in this book for speeding up access also apply to Windows, in fact, these methods are especially important because in Windows, temporary files are created on the hard drive much more often than in DOS and portions of programs are swapped out of memory.

Of the active methods, the cache program SMARTDRV is the best because it works especially well with Windows, can loan memory reserved for the cache to Windows and works very well in compressing the hard drive with DBLSPACE.

18.3.2 Passive methods of speeding up access

Of the passive methods, optimizing the hard drive with DEFRAG is especially important. In connection with Windows, there are two important considerations:

- Do not run the optimization program from a DOS task in Windows. You must exit Windows and start DEFRAG from the system prompt.

- Hard drive optimization is of central importance if you want to set up a permanent swap file. However, before optimization, remove any existing permanent swap file (Control Panel in Windows) and then reinstall it afterwards. Also, when using DEFRAG, you must perform a complete defragmentation to free up the largest possible contiguous area.

When using SMARTDRV, check whether double buffering is necessary to use Windows 386 Enhanced mode on a 386 computer. A detailed description of the exact procedure for this is in Chapter 19.

If you run Windows in 386 Enhanced mode, use a second value as needed to specify the amount of memory to which Windows can reduce the cache. We recommend using the following values depending on the amount of total memory capacity available on your computer:

Memory	DOS	Windows
<= 1 MEG	320K	0K
<= 2 MEG	512K	256K
<= 4 MEG	1024K	512K
<= 6 MEG	2048K	1024K
<= 8 MEG	4096K	2048K

To specify the correct values, call SMARTDRV as shown in the following example:

```
SMARTDRV DOS WINDOWS
```

Specify the two values from the preceding example. For a computer with 4 Meg of memory, use the following command line:

```
SMARTDRV 1024 512
```

18.3.3 Compression

One very interesting option for using DOS with Windows is related to MS-DOS 6.0's ability to compress storage media, resulting in double the space on a storage medium.

We recommend this technique to anyone who works with Windows and runs out of disk space. The technique used in MS-DOS 6.0 works very well with Windows.

Make sure you leave a part of the hard drive uncompressed so you can create a permanent swap file for Windows on the uncompressed drive.

If you forget to do this and you have a compressed drive but not enough room on the uncompressed drive to create a permanent swap file, use DBLSPACE to change the size of the compressed drive. By reducing the size of the compressed drive you will create enough room for the permanent swap file on the uncompressed drive. As a rule, 6 to 10 Meg is enough.

18.4 Memory Management

When planning memory management for a system with DOS and Windows, it's important to find the right compromise.

18.4.1 Expanded memory in DOS and Windows

For example, if at all possible, avoid using expanded memory in DOS programs, because this memory would no longer be available for Windows and Windows applications. Also, the page frame necessary for expanded memory means losing 64K of upper memory, so your available memory could be reduced.

If DOS applications require expanded memory, you no longer have to specify the exact amount of extended memory to be converted by EMM386.

In MS-DOS 6.0, EMM386.EXE alternatively provides available memory as extended memory and as expanded memory and can change the distribution at any time.

We described options for managing memory in MS-DOS 6.0 in Chapter 12. We also included a special section on memory management in Windows there, which covers all the aspects.

18.4.2 Using MEMMAKER

You can optimize your computer memory with the help of the MS-DOS MEMMAKER command. MEMMAKER checks for Windows on the hard drive, and if it finds Windows, optimizes memory so DOS and Windows work as well as possible together. You can also specify that part of the memory is to be reserved for Windows and have MEMMAKER carry out optimization in such a way that DOS applications running in Windows get as much memory as possible.

18.5 The Command Interpreter in Windows

It's possible to work with a command interpreter in Windows at least as well as you can at the system prompt. However, by making a few settings, you can usually improve the performance of the command interpreter.

18.5.1 Multitasking for DOS

In this section, we'd like to show you the solution to a problem that you may not even have noticed. If you work with DOS applications often in Windows, you normally don't benefit from Windows' Multitasking capability.

DOS applications are always started from a PIF file. The easiest method is to have Windows create the PIF files for the DOS applications itself. This is what happens when you link a DOS application to a group with the Windows Setup program.

If you link a DOS application to a group and use the COM or EXE file as your start file in the command line, or if there is no PIF file of the same name available, Windows uses the _DEFAULT.PIF file to start this file.

Multitasking is not possible with the PIF files created by Windows or with the _DEFAULT.PIF file, since in all these files the Background check box is not active.

To make multitasking possible in your DOS applications, you must modify the PIF files with which these programs are started. To find out which file is used to start a DOS application, highlight the application and press Alt + Enter. The Program Item Properties dialog box appears on the screen. Check the entry for Command Line to see whether the program is started with the help of a PIF file.

If the entry is a PIF file, note the name of the file and load it in the PIF Editor. Start the PIF Editor, which is usually in the Main group, and open the file by selecting the Open command from the File menu. Check whether the Background check box is enabled for Execution. If the check box is not active, enable it now and save the file.

To run DOS applications that do not have their own PIF file in multitasking mode, you also need to change the _DEFAULT.PIF file which is used for those DOS applications. Enable the Background check box for this file also.

☞ If you have trouble running a DOS application in multitasking mode, you can always disable the Background check box. We haven't ever had any problems with this setting.

18.5.2 TSR programs

If you start a TSR program from the DOS system prompt, this program is resident in memory, or permanently available. Many of these programs can be started by pressing a special hot key combination. However, a TSR program takes memory away from other programs.

If you want to make a TSR program available in all running DOS applications in Windows, you must start the program before starting Windows. For example, to install Desktop from PC Tools in resident memory and be able to use it in all DOS applications, add the following command line to the AUTOEXEC.BAT before starting Windows:

```
DESKTOP /R
```

All TSR programs started before Windows are available in all DOS tasks running in Windows, which means that much less memory is available for DOS applications. All TSR programs started after Windows in a DOS task are only available in this one DOS task. So if you want to start the DOS application Word in Windows and shoot screen dumps with Hotshot, you must start Windows, open a DOS task, install the TSR Grab program from Hotshot, start Word in the same DOS task and then make the TSR program active with the hot key combination to shoot the screen dumps.

When you are finished, you can quit Word and close the DOS task to remove the TSR program, Grab, from memory. This option is practical when you only need a TSR program for a certain amount of time and want to free up the memory afterwards.

18.5.3 Environment variables in DOS tasks

All environment variables are usually available from the original command interpreter, from which you started Windows. That means that all the command interpreters started from Windows are actually copies of the original.

However, if you change an environment variable in a DOS task started from Windows, this change is only valid in this particular DOS task and is lost as soon as you leave this task with EXIT.

Time and time again, we would see a system prompt on the screen and want to switch off the computer. At the last moment, we would realize that this might not be the only command interpreter, but instead, could be a DOS task running in Windows.

Shutting down while Windows and other DOS applications are still running is dangerous; any data that hasn't been saved in the Windows and DOS applications is lost. We'll show you an easy, but effective solution: Simply make sure that you are able to recognize a DOS task in Windows and can distinguish it from the normal system prompt:

The following command line in the AUTOEXEC.BAT before Windows assigns a different system prompt to a command interpreter running in Windows:

```
SET WINPMT=$p$G-Win-$G
```

This prevents you from switching off the computer from a DOS task running in Windows. This command line changes the prompt for all DOS tasks, including command interpreters called from DOS applications started in Windows, such as Word. You can specify your own contents for WINPMT.

18.6 The Backup Program in Windows

When you purchase MS-DOS 6.0, along with the comfortable, menu-driven MSBACKUP program, the virus scan program and the UNDELETE program, all intended for use at the DOS command prompt, you also get Windows versions of the same programs.

The Backup program for Windows is a program package that you can use to perform a backup (back up the hard drive data), then compare the backup (to ensure that the data you backed up matches the data on the original file from the hard drive) and restore (transfer the backup data back to the hard drive) the backup. Like the DOS version of Backup, the Windows version first determines the configuration and, if necessary, runs a compatibility test.

In Windows you have the advantage of being able to perform a backup without interrupting your work on the computer. You can run Backup in the background and continue working on the computer after making all the necessary settings and starting Backup.

☞　　When you run Backup in background mode, you may require more diskettes, since the data can't be compressed as much.

Configuration menu

If you installed the Backup program correctly in Windows, the first time you start the program, a dialog box prompts you to automatically determine the computer configuration. If you click on the OK button, make sure there are no diskettes in your disk drives, since a compatibility test will be run afterwards. If you have more than one disk drive, select the desired drive for the compatibility test.

Since you have the option of multitasking in Windows (running different applications simultaneously), you are informed that during a backup, compare or restore operation, you cannot and should not access your disk drives from any other application.

You will need two diskettes to run the test. If there are files on the diskettes, a dialog box displays the contents of the diskettes and gives you the option of overwriting the files. If you would rather use a different diskette, you still have the chance to remove the first diskette, insert another one and repeat the process.

If the test is successful, you are guaranteed of safe backups. Run this test before every backup.

When you are finished with configuration and the compatibility test, you automatically go to the Configure dialog box. You can tell by the highlighted Configure button. You can always call Configure again later to change the configuration or run the compatibility test.

Main menu

After that, you go to a Windows program window. You see a menu bar with the commands of the main menu and an icon bar underneath it. From this menu you can choose among the various programs (such as Backup, Compare, Restore, or Configure). Depending on which button is active in the icon bar, the bottom of the screen displays the appropriate commands and options in Windows dialog boxes.

The menu bar contains the **File**, **Catalog** and **Help** menus. You can also call Help by pressing F1. The **File** menu contains commands for opening, saving and deleting a Setup file, for printing, printer installation and quitting the program. By saving a Setup file you save yourself the trouble of repeatedly setting the Backup configuration. Selected parent directories and options as well as selection criteria are stored in a Setup file.

With the **Catalog** menu you can load, retrieve, rebuild and delete a catalog file. A catalog file contains the backup data and directories and the setup file used. Depending on which routine is active (Backup, Compare, Restore, or Configure), not all menu commands are always selectable.

Starting Backup

After clicking on the Backup button in the icon bar, a screen appears, in which the same options and commands are available as in MSBACKUP. You can choose the setup file, set the drives, backup type and the options.

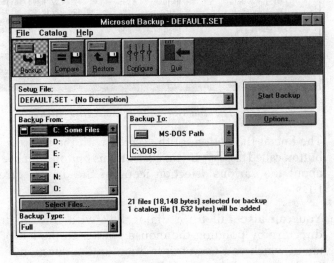

The Backup Menu

To back up all the files on a drive, you can also click on the drive in the Backup From list with the right mouse button to select all the files. When you select all the files on a drive for backup, "All Files" appears next to the drive letter. Detailed information about the selected files appears in the lower area of the screen.

Click on Select Files to display a screen similar to the screen of the DOS version. In addition, there is a menu bar with the **File...** and **Tree...** commands. With the **File** menu you can either select everything (**File/Select All**) or cancel (**File/Deselect All**) the selection. The **Tree** menu gives you the option of expanding or collapsing directories, like the Windows File Manager.

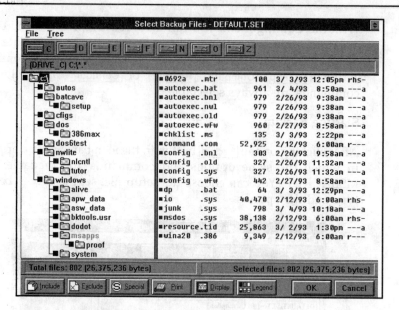

The Backup Menu: Selecting files

The line at the bottom of the screen with the buttons has an extra button called [Legend]. If you click on this button, you see information about the various selection icons of the drives, directories and files.

You can also call up a dialog box with information for each directory by pointing the mouse pointer to the left of a directory about which you want information until a question mark appears. Click on the left mouse button to display a dialog box with information about the directory, date of creation, total files, selected files and the backup files. The last two values are different, because you could exclude files from the backup but still select them.

See Chapter 10 for information on the options for selecting files and setting the display.

After clicking [OK], you return to the **Backup** menu and can begin the backup. A dialog box informs you of the progress and status of the backup.

Compare and Restore

To compare or restore files, click on the [Compare] or [Restore] button in the icon bar. [Compare] and [Restore] are identical in appearance and operation. The only difference is that the **Options** button in the **Restore** menu has some extra options.

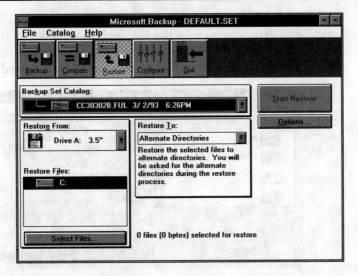

The Restore menu

The **Catalog** menu lets you load, retrieve and rebuild Catalog files.

Other operations, such as specifying a default catalog file, setting the drive and selecting files are identical to the ones described in Chapter 10.

When you quit the Backup program, a dialog box appears, prompting you to save your configuration and (or) your settings by clicking the appropriate buttons.

18.7 The Anti-Virus Program

The Anti-Virus program for Windows operates similar to the DOS version of the program. The working screen is a typical Windows Program window, easy to operate. All the functions and options are identical in both the DOS and the Windows version of the program.

Again, users have the advantage of running the virus scan in Windows in the background. While the program is running, you can continue working on the computer.

18.7.1 Starting a virus scan

After starting the Anti-Virus program, you see the Microsoft Anti-Virus for Windows work screen. You can call Help at any time by choosing the **Help** menu or pressing F1 .

In the Drives box on the left, you can set the desired drive. All the available drives appear in the list, including network drives. The Status box on the right contains information about the contents of the current directory as well as viruses found and cleaned.

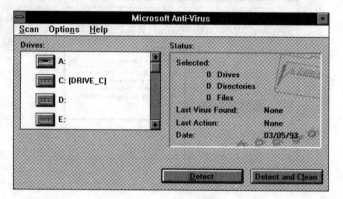

The Anti-Virus menu

You can set one or more drives by clicking the desired drives. To "deselect" a selected drive, simply click it a second time to cancel the selection.

After selecting the desired drives, you can enable or disable different options in the **Options** menu.

The different options are defined in Section 10.11.

To begin the virus scan, click on either the [Detect] or [Detect] and [Clean] button. You will also find these commands in the [Scan] menu. If you click the [Detect] button, you can still choose to clean any viruses that are found.

A dialog box informs you of the progress and status of the virus scan. When the scan is complete, a Statistics screen appears with the results of the scan. A listing of the scanned drives and files is displayed, along with found and cleaned viruses.

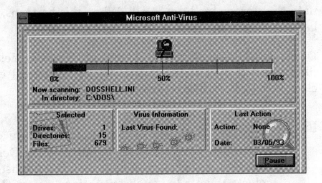

The information dialog box during a virus scan

For a detailed list of all known viruses, choose Virus List from the **Scan** menu. You can keep this list current by updating it. Microsoft will offer different options for updates, for example, via data transfer from a BBS.

To delete your checklist file (CHKLIST.CPS), choose the Delete Checklist Files command from the **Scan** menu. The checklist file contains important information about the file size, file attributes, date and the checksums (see also Section 10.11).

When this file is deleted, it disables the Verify Integrity check box. To enable this check box, a checklist file must be created.

To save the settings when you exit the program for later work sessions, choose the **Options/Save Settings on Exit** command.

18.8 Windows Undelete

The Windows Undelete program gives you an option for recovering deleted files and directories in Windows. If you accidentally delete one or more files, they could still be present on the storage medium.

If no substantial changes have been made since the deletion, it's almost always possible to undo the deletion. Only in cases where deleted files have been overwritten are they irretrievably lost, and not even Undelete can bring them back.

To make certain that it is possible to recover deleted files, you can prevent deleted files from being overwritten by choosing either Delete Sentry or Delete Tracker.

If the Delete Sentry is active, deleted files are stored in a hidden directory. Files protected by Delete Sentry won't be overwritten until the storage medium is full. When this happens, UNDELETE begins overwriting files, starting with the oldest.

Delete Tracker registers the cluster addresses of deleted files. A file protected by Delete Tracker can be recovered even if some clusters have been overwritten.

 Windows Undelete is not able to restore damaged or incomplete files that aren't protected by Delete Tracker. Although such files can appear in the file list, you cannot select them. In such situations, use the MS-DOS UNDELETE command from the command prompt.

18.8.1 Protecting files

To be on the safe side, you should install delete protection first, so you can restore your files and directories in an emergency. To do this, start the Undelete program from the Windows program group.

The program screen is easy to operate. Under the Windows style menu bar, there is an icon bar, in which you can also directly select the most frequently used commands.

Below the icon bar is a window in which the deleted files of a directory are listed after you enable a search (see the following). More information about the files is at the bottom of the screen.

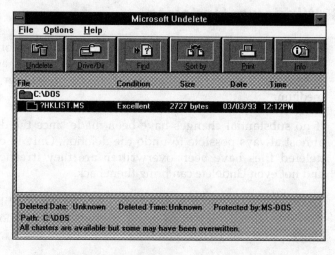

The Undelete screen with a list of deleted files
that can be restored

Choose **Options/Configure Delete Protection** to install the desired level of protection. You can choose between Delete Sentry or Delete Tracker. The Standard option disables delete protection. The right side of the window provides brief definitions of the protection options.

Installing Delete Sentry

Delete Sentry stores all deleted files in a hidden directory named /SENTRY. Files protected by this method are in perfect condition and can be restored quickly.

However, Delete Sentry also requires a certain amount of disk space on the storage medium to be used when your hard drive is full. At this point, files are overwritten until there is enough room, starting with the oldest files.

If you choose the more memory intensive Delete Sentry, you can limit the number of files you wish to protect.

In the dialog box that appears after you select Delete Sentry, you can choose to protect either All Files or Only Specified Files and add filenames, extensions to either Include or Exclude.

You can also exclude archived files from delete protection. There are also settings for the number of days before the deleted files are removed from Delete Sentry and the maximum amount of disk space to be used for protected files.

The (Drives) button allows you to select which drive you want to provide with delete protection. You can use the settings we just described to reduce the memory requirements of Delete Sentry to a minimum.

After you select (OK), the program automatically changes your AUTOEXEC.BAT system file. You could also choose to save the change under a different filename specified by the program. This change is necessary for the successful installation of the delete protection.

To make this change manually, add the following entry to your AUTOEXEC.BAT:

```
UNDELETE /LOAD
```

Delete protection doesn't go into effect until you reboot your computer and the additional entry in your AUTOEXEC.BAT has been processed.

If you no longer require the Delete Sentry files (e.g., after a backup), you can delete them from the directory to make more disk space available.

To do this, select the desired files in your window and then choose the **File/Purge Delete Sentry File** (see "Searching for files").

     It's possible that you won't be able to select the **File/Purge Delete Sentry File**. For example, if you accidentally select one or more files that aren't delete protected, you won't be able to select the command. Files with delete protection are in "Perfect" condition.

Enabling Delete Tracker

The Delete Tracker protects deleted files by registering their position on the storage medium. The files can be completely restored, provided none of the clusters have been overwritten. That's why you should restore files protected by Delete Tracker as quickly as possible when something happens and you need the files.

When you install Delete Tracker, you can specify which drives you want Delete Tracker to protect and are prompted to make the entry cited above in your AUTOEXEC.BAT. When you install Delete Tracker, you cannot limit the number of files that are protected.

18.8.2 Restoring files

After configuring the kind of delete protection you want, you can be sure of restoring files that are under such protection. However, it's always wise to restore the files as quickly as possible after deletion.

To restore deleted files, start the UNDELETE program as soon as possible.

Specifying a directory

Use the **File/Change Drive/Directory** command or click the appropriate button in the icon bar to set the directory in which the files were located before the deletion. A dialog box appears, in which you can specify the complete path yourself, or you can choose the directory from the list box.

If this is the directory from which you deleted the files, they are automatically listed with corresponding file information and a note about their condition in the window. To view information about a file or directory, use the **File/File Info...** command (or the Info button in the icon bar) to call an information window with file information.

Sorting files

If there are quite a few deleted files in the directory and you don't want to restore all of them, you can sort them. To do this, either choose **Options/Sort** by or click on the **Sort by** button in the icon list.

In the dialog box that appears you can sort by name, extension, size, Deleted Date and Time, Modified Date and Time and Condition. You can also enable the Sort files first by directories check box.

Finding files

If you no longer know which directory contained the deleted files, you can use a command to find them. You don't even have to specify the complete filename.

Just click on the Find icon in the icon bar or choose the **File/Find Deleted Files** command. In the Find Deleted Files dialog box, you can specify the name of the file(s) in the File Specification text box. Wild cards are allowed, so you could limit your specification to the file extension, for example:

```
*.TXT
```

To search for all deleted files, specify the following:

```
*.*
```

In the next box, Containing, you can specify text from the contents of the file. You can ignore case or enable the Whole Word check box. The set directory, starting with the root directory, will be searched for files corresponding to your specifications.

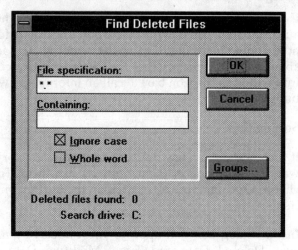

Finding deleted files with Undelete

Defining search groups

To speed up a search, you can install search groups for later searches that limit the search to specific file groups. Click on the (Groups) button, and then click on the (Edit) button in the Search Groups dialog box.

In the Group Name text box you can give your group a name, for example, if you work a lot with text files, you could name the group "Texts". Then specify the files in the File Specification text box, for example:

```
*.TXT
```

After you choose the (Save) button, the name of the group is transferred to the Search Groups list box at the top and your group specification is saved for later use. After clicking (OK), you have finished configuring a personal file group that you can use for a quick search.

To search for files that match this group specification, select the desired group in the Search Groups dialog box and click on (OK). The entry is then transferred to the Find Deleted Files dialog box. After clicking on (OK), the search begins.

Undeleting files

If deleted files or directories appear in the list, you can select one or more of them and restore them with the **File/Undelete** command or by clicking on the Undelete icon.

As we mentioned, a delete protected file is in "Perfect" condition and is 100% undeletable. A file that is not delete protected, but is still complete is described as "Excellent" and can also be undeleted. A file in "Good" condition can probably be restored. A "Destroyed" file cannot be undeleted. A "Poor" file has overwritten clusters and you may be able to undelete it with the DOS version of the UNDELETE program.

If you have a large list of deleted files, you can use either **Options/Select by Name** or **Unselect by Name** to mark specific files easily, without having to view the entire list. In the File Specification text box you can use wild cards in your specification.

You can select any file with the mouse by clicking it. You can also use the cursor keys to choose files and then highlight them with the [Spacebar]. To cancel the selection, click the mouse or press the [Spacebar] a second time.

If you chose the **Undelete** command, you are prompted to specify the first character of the filename or name of the directory. You can choose any character you wish. If you selected more than one file or directory, all the files will be restored after you specify the first character of each file or directory name.

If you deleted a directory and the files contained in the directory, you must first undelete the directory before you can copy the files into the directory.

Unlike the DOS version of Undelete, Windows Undelete also lets you undelete deleted files to a different drive and even save them under a new name. This is a protective measure for cases where there aren't enough data available for Undelete in Windows (clusters are overwritten, Poor condition). Then you can try using the advanced DOS methods of UNDELETE to undelete these files to their original directories.

In such cases, choose the **Undelete** command from the **File** menu and click on the [Directory] button. In the directory list box you can then choose the desired drive. Specify the new name and another directory if necessary. In the New Drive and file name: text box the path changes accordingly. You can also change the filename in the same text box.

After you click [OK], the undelete process begins. You won't be able to select the [OK] button again unless you also set another drive.

If you used the **File/Undelete** command to copy a file protected by Delete Tracker to another drive, all the clusters that the file originally had will also be copied to the other drive. In other words, those clusters overwritten by other files are also transferred to the new drive.

18.9 Future Developments for DOS and Windows

Now that you've read this chapter, we're certain that you are aware of how MS-DOS 6.0 and Windows are coordinated with each other and that they work very well together. You have also learned about how the two complement each other and that together, MS-DOS 6.0 and Windows can increase the benefits of the user.

It's our opinion that this division of labor will be improved and refined even more in the future. Windows offers you several new options that will make your work much easier.

For example, there is the option for exchanging data between different applications, or the simplified memory management. If you want to learn all there is to know about Windows, including all the tips and tricks for running Windows, we recommend "Windows 3.1 Complete" from Abacus. It discusses all the topics about Windows in detail.

Perhaps in the not too distant future, Windows will no longer be an operating system attachment for MS-DOS, but rather MS-DOS will be a special way of running the Windows operating system. The first Beta versions of Windows NT have already made it clear that Microsoft will probably take this route in the long run.

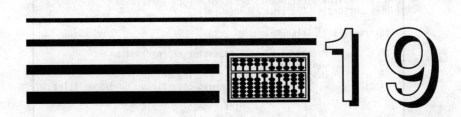

Chapter 19

The MS-DOS 6.0 Commands

When working with MS-DOS, you often need to know the name, syntax and parameters for a specific command.

One added feature to MS-DOS 6.0 is the online help for every command. To display a list of all MS-DOS commands, type the following at the system prompt:

```
HELP
```

This command displays a list of all commands, with a brief description of the function of each command.

If more information about a specific command is needed, type the command followed by the switch "/?". This displays all of the parameters and switches for the command. The following figure shows the results of typing DIR /? at the MS-DOS command line.

```
C:>DIR /?
Displays a list of files and subdirectories in a directory.

DIR [drive:][path][filename] [/P] [/W] [/A[[:]attribs]]
[/O[[:]sortord]] [/S] [/B] [/L] [/C[H]]

  [drive:][path][filename]
              Specifies drive, directory, and/or files to list.
  /P          Pauses after each screenful of information.
  /W          Uses wide list format.
  /A          Displays files with specified attributes.
  attribs        D Directories  R Read-only files  H Hidden files
                 S System files  A Files ready to archive
                          - Prefix meaning "not"
  /O        List by files in sorted order.
  sortorder   N  By name (alphabetic)      S By size (smallest first)
          E  By extension (alphabetic)  D By date & time (earliest first)
                 G Group directories first   - Prefix to reverse order
  /S        Displays files in specified directory and all subdirectories.
  /B        Uses bare format (no heading information or summary).
  /L        Uses lowercase.
  /C[H]     Displays file compression ratio; /CH uses host
            allocation unit size.

Switches may be preset in the DIRCMD environment variable.  Override
preset switches by prefixing any switch with - (hyphen)--for example,
 /-W.

C:\>
```

*Entering DIR /? displays information about using the DIR
command*

However, sometimes you may need additional information. This
chapter provides information about all the MS-DOS commands.

19.1 Types Of MS-DOS Commands

MS-DOS commands can be divided into two groups:

- resident commands

- external commands

A resident command can be used at any time, because it is copied
into a protected area of memory every time you start your
computer. You can execute a resident command simply by typing its
name.

An external command is stored on the DOS diskette or hard drive
and has the file extension .COM or .EXE. If you want to execute one
of these external commands, it must be stored on the current
diskette or hard drive.

In the following section, we indicate whether a command is
resident or external. Either term will appear in parentheses
following the DOS command name (e.g., FIND (external)).

All MS-DOS commands for Version 6.0 can be found in this chapter.

19.2 Command Reference

In this section we'll present the MS-DOS commands listed alphabetically.

The commands are described in Syntax, Switches and Description sections. The Syntax section for each command provides all of the possible forms of that command, the Switches section lists the switches that can be used with the command and the Description section explains each of the commands in more detail.

The following is an explanation of the notation used in these sections:

[ ]   Parameters enclosed in square brackets are optional.

| Alternative parameters are separated by a vertical bar. Only one of the parameters separated by a vertical bar can be entered in the command.

path   Specifies the hierarchical order of the directories separated by a backslash.

filename
      Specifies the name of the file and may include an extension.

pathname
      Specifies the path followed by the filename.

*   Any character or combination of characters may be replaced by an asterisk (*). This wildcard character can be located in any position of the filename or extension, but wildcards are permitted only when explicitly noted.

?   Any single character may be replaced by a question mark (?). This wildcard character can be located in any position of the filename or extension, but wildcards are permitted only when explicitly noted.

So that you can easily find them, switches are listed after each command's syntax description.

APPEND   (external)

Permits data files to be opened in specified directories as if they are in the current directory.

Syntax: APPEND [[drive:]path[;...]]
             /x[:on | :off] [/path :on | path:off] [/e]

path   The path in which you want to search for files. Multiple paths can be defined, separated by semicolons.

;   The semicolon, when used by itself, cancels the list of appended directories.

Switches:

/x [:on | :off]
             Determines whether MS-DOS is to search the appended directories when executing programs. /x:on searches appended directories. /x:off does not search appended directories. x:on must be specified the first time APPEND is used.

/path:on | path:off
             Determines whether a program is to search the appended directories for a data file when the path is included with the program name. The default setting is path:on.

/e   The search path set in APPEND is assigned to an environment variable named APPEND. The list of appended directories can be displayed with SET. This switch can only be used the first time APPEND is used after starting your system.

Description:

Sets the search pattern for data files. APPEND works like PATH, but APPEND uses the specified path when opening a data file, not a command or program file.

Normally when a file is opened, the current directory is searched for the file. When you use APPEND, then all paths listed in the APPEND search path are searched for this file. An error message is displayed if the file is not found.

This is useful, for example, when you use programs such as WordStar 3.3, which doesn't support paths. The example below checks for the file DEMO.TXT first in the DOS subdirectory then in the LIB subdirectory.

```
APPEND C:\DOS;\LIB
TYPE demo.txt
```

If all parameters are omitted, the current APPEND path is displayed. If the parameter is a semicolon, the APPEND search path is canceled. To define multiple paths, separate each path with a semicolon. Blank spaces within the specification are not allowed.

APPEND is an external program. The first use of APPEND can include the /e switch, which stores the search path in an environment variable. You can then display the APPEND search path with SET. Applications can access a file through this search path. If you omit the /e switch on the first use of APPEND, then the search path is not stored in the environment area.

You can also specify /x on the first use of APPEND. This specifies that the defined paths should be searched for executable program files (extensions .BAT, .EXE and .COM). For example:

```
APPEND /e /x
APPEND c:\dos;d:\utility
```

has the same meaning as:

```
APPEND /e
APPEND c:\dos;d:\utility
PATH  c:\dos;d:\utility
```

Prior to DOS 4.0, the /x switch was used to extend the search path. First the current directory is searched and then the appended paths are searched. You should be aware of the differences between versions.

When a file is to be opened, it is searched for first in the current directory and then in the directories defined by APPEND. In some cases, you may not want the search to include all of the directories. Use the APPEND search path when the corresponding filename is defined without a drive statement and without a directory name. So if the following filename is specified:

```
DEMO.TXT
```

the entire APPEND search path is used. If a filename is specified as:

```
D:\DOS\KEYBOARD.SYS
```

then the search path from APPEND is not used because an explicit filename was specified. APPEND searches for a file in the appended directories with the /path:on switch. If the APPEND search directory should not be used for files that have a drive statement and/or a directory name, then use the /path:off switch:

```
APPEND /path:off
```

 When a file within the defined search path is found and is opened for reading, some applications may open a NEW file in the current directory; the original file remains unchanged.

Type:

APPEND ; to clear the appended directory list

APPEND   to display the appended directory list

See also: PATH, SET

ASSIGN   (resident)

 This command isn't included with DOS 6.0. However, if you need this command, you can order a supplemental disk from Microsoft that contains this command.

Redirects disk operations from one drive to a different drive.

Syntax: ASSIGN [drive1:[=]drive2: [...]]
            ASSIGN /status

drive1:   The drive letter to reassign.

drive2:   The new drive to which input and output will be redirected.

/status   Displays current drive assignments.

Description:

ASSIGN redirects all disk operations from drive1: to drive2:. The equal sign (=) can be replaced by a space. For example, you can use the ASSIGN command if a program does not permit the active drive to be changed.

Multiple assignments can be combined in a single ASSIGN command:

```
ASSIGN a=c b=a
```

If drive2: is omitted, redirection from an earlier ASSIGN command is terminated. If no parameters are specified, all redirection is terminated.

 ASSIGN should be used carefully, since it "hides" the drive characteristics that a program might need for correct execution. The ASSIGN:FORMAT, ASSIGN:DISKCOPY and ASSIGN:DISKCOMP commands ignore the ASSIGN command.

 A complete path must be specified if a file is to be opened for writing.

See also: JOIN, SUBST

ATTRIB (external)

Displays or changes file attributes.

Syntax: ATTRIB [+r | -r] [+a | -a] [+s | -s] [+h | -h] [[drive:] [path] filename] [/s]

drive: path filename
The complete path and name of the file whose attributes are displayed or changed. Wildcards are allowed, but if a file has system or hidden attributes set, they must be cleared before any other attributes can be changed.

Switches:

+r   Set read-only flag
-r   Clear read-only flag
+a   Set the archive flag

-a	Clear the archive flag
+s	Set the system flag
-s	Clear the system flag
+h	Set file as hidden
-h	Clear hidden file attribute
/s	Includes all the entries in the current directory and any subdirectories

Description:

ATTRIB displays or changes the file attribute of a specified file or files.

The read-only flag is bit 0 of the FCB at address 00Bh. The read-only flag determines whether a file may be changed or deleted:

```
+R sets the read-only flag (file cannot be changed or
deleted).
-R clears the read-only flag (file can be changed or
deleted).
```

For example, to protect all of the commands in the \DOS subdirectory from being overwritten or deleted, use the following command:

```
ATTRIB +R C:\DOS\*.COM
DEL COMMAND.COM
Access denied
```

The archive flag is used by the MSBACKUP and XCOPY commands:

```
+A sets the archive flag
-A clears the archive flag
```

To display the status of the files, omit all of the ATTRIB command's parameters. Filenames preceded by an "R" are read-only files. Filenames preceded by an "A" have been modified or created since the last XCOPY:

```
ATTRIB D:\DOS\*.COM
R A    C:\DOS\DISKCOPY.COM
A      C:\DOS\LABEL.COM
R      C:\DOS\COMMAND.COM
```

DOS has an option for displaying all pertinent entries as well as the subdirectories. The following example displays all the BAK files on the hard drive C:

```
ATTRIB C:\*.BAK /s
```

See also: XCOPY

BACKUP	(external)

 This command isn't included with DOS 6.0. However, if you need this command, you can order a supplemental disk from Microsoft that contains this command.

Makes a backup copy of one or more files from one storage device to another.

Syntax: BACKUP ;source_drive:[pathname] target_drive: [/s][/m][/a][/f[:size]][/d:date][/t:time][/l[:[drive]][path]logfile]]

source_drive:pathname
The name of the drive and the path to be backed up. If pathname is omitted, all files on source_drive are copied. Wildcards are allowed.

target_drive:
The target diskette to which the files are copied. A path may not be specified. If target_drive is a hard drive, the files are copied into a subdirectory named \BACKUP.

Switches:

/s   Backup all files from every subdirectory of the source drive.

/m   Copies only the files which were modified since the last backup and clears the archive bit for each.

/a   Add backup files to an existing backup diskette. (Normally the target diskette is erased before BACKUP begins.)

/f[:size]   Specifies the size of the target disk for formatting. This switch causes BACKUP to format floppy diskettes that do not match the default size of the drive. size specifies the size, in kilobytes, of the diskette to be formatted. If size is not specified, the /f switch uses the default size of the drive.

/d:date   Backup only files which were modified after the specified date. The date is specified in the format as set by the country command. (In the United States, the format is MM-DD-YY.)

/t:time   Backup only the files which were modified after a specified time. The time is specified in the format set by the country command. (In the United States the format is HH:MM:SS.)

/l[:[drive][path]logfile]
Creates a log file called BACKUP.LOG on the target diskette. This file contains information about the number of disks required, date and time of backup, etc. A filename can also be specified.

Description:

BACKUP makes archive copies of files from the hard drive. If for some reason the original files are damaged or completely destroyed, the backup files can be recovered with the RESTORE command.

BACKUP's advantage over COPY is that it preserves the structure of the original directory hierarchy. The subdirectories are automatically recreated by RESTORE as needed. Also, RESTORE prompts the user to insert the correct disks if necessary. Copies created with BACKUP can be restored only with RESTORE.

DOS informs you if more than one diskette is required for the backup copy. RESTORE requires the diskettes to be in the same order that BACKUP created them. RESTORE will reject incorrect diskettes. Number the diskettes so that you know their correct order.

The /f switch permits specifying the size for formatting diskettes. Sizes may be specified according to the following table:

Value	Kbytes	Type
160	160K	Single-sided, double density, 5.25-inch diskette
180	180K	Single-sided, double density, 5.25-inch diskette
320	320K	Double-sided, double density, 5.25-inch diskette

Value	Kbytes	Type
360	360K	Double-sided, double density, 5.25-inch diskette
720	720K	Double-sided, double density, 3.5-inch diskette
1200	1200K	Double-sided, double density, 5.25-inch diskette
1440	1440K	Double-sided, double density, 3.5-inch diskette
2880	2880K	Double-sided, double density, 3.5-inch diskette

The following BACKUP command creates a specific type of backup on drive B:. This backup consists of all the files in the CPROGS directory of the current drive, which have .C filename extensions. The /m switch instructs BACKUP to include files that have been modified since the last time the user ran BACKUP.

```
BACKUP \CPROGS\*.C B: /m
```

When the copy is completed, BACKUP returns the following values to a batch file that may be tested with IF ERRORLEVEL:

Code	Meaning
0	No error during BACKUP
1	No files were found to backup
2	Some files could not be copied due to time-sharing conflicts
3	User terminated procedure by pressing Ctrl + C
4	Process terminated due to an error

See also: COPY, REPLACE, RESTORE, XCOPY

BREAK   (resident)

Sets or clears extended Ctrl + C checking.

Syntax: BREAK [on | off]

Description:

MS-DOS normally tests to see if Ctrl + C was pressed during input or output to one of the standard I/O devices. Extended checking tests for Ctrl + C during disk operations.

If the BREAK command is specified without parameters, the current status is displayed. The default status is OFF, unless previously changed by CONFIG.SYS or AUTOEXEC.BAT.

When using compilers, it's often useful to enable BREAK so that you can halt the compiler if an error is encountered:

```
A>BREAK ON

BREAK is on
```

CALL   (resident)

Calls one batch program from within another batch program.

Syntax: CALL [drive:][path]batchfile [parameter]

batchfile   The name of the batch file to be called. drive: and path must be specified if batchfile is not in a defined search path.

parameter   A list of parameters used by the batch file. This list of parameters can be any length.

Description:

The CALL command lets you call a batch file from within another batch file as you would call a subroutine. After executing the batch file, the CALL command returns to the point immediately after the CALL command in the original batch file and executes the remaining commands.

You can pass parameters to the new batch file by listing them after batchfile.

The following example calls the batch procedure DEMO2.BAT and uses parameters of 11, 22 and 33. After DEMO2.BAT is completed, control returns to the main batch routine.

```
echo off
echo first batch
call demo2 11 22 33
echo back to first batch
```

CD (resident)

Displays the name of or changes the current directory.

Syntax: CD [drive:][path]

drive: The drive where the new current directory is located.
            If drive: is omitted, the current drive is assumed.

path   The name of the new current directory. The directory
            must exist.

Description:

CHDIR or CD displays or changes the current directory.

To display the current directory, omit the parameters.

By changing the current directory, all subsequent references to files
are assumed to be found in that directory.

The directory that is hierarchically above the current directory
can be abbreviated to two periods (..):

        `C:\CPROG\UTILITY>CD ..`

is the same as typing:

        `C:\CPROG\UTILITY>CD \CPROG`

If the current directory is \CPROG, you can select the subordinate
directory, UTILITY, with the following command:

        `CD UTILITY`

From any other directory you must specify the entire pathname:

        `CD\CPROG\UTILITY`

See also: MD, RD

CHCP (resident)

Displays or sets the active code page number.

Syntax: CHCP [code_page_number]

code_page_number

> Specifies the system code pages defined by the COUNTRY command in the CONFIG.SYS file.

Description:

CHCP defines the active code page to be used for all devices that support code page switching. This code page is defined by the country command of the CONFIG.SYS file.

Before you can use CHCP, both the location of the COUNTRY.SYS file must be specified and the NLSFUNC program must be loaded into memory.

The code_page_number codes are:

437	U.S.
850	Multilingual
852	Slavic
860	Portuguese
863	Canadian-French
865	Nordic

See also: KEYB, MODE, NLSFUNC

CHDIR   (resident)

Displays the name of or changes the current directory.

Syntax: CHDIR [drive:][path]

or

> CD [drive:][path]

drive: The drive where the new current directory is located. If drive: is omitted, the current drive is assumed.

path   The name of the new current directory. The directory must exist.

Description:

CHDIR or CD displays or changes the current directory.

To display the current directory, omit the parameters.

By changing the current directory, all subsequent references to files are assumed to be found in that directory.

The directory that is hierarchically above the current directory can be abbreviated to two periods (..):

```
C:\CPROG\UTILITY>CD ..
```

is the same as typing:

```
C:\CPROG\UTILITY>CD \CPROG
```

If the current directory is \CPROG, you can select the subordinate directory, UTILITY, with the following command:

```
CD UTILITY
```

From any other directory you must specify the entire pathname:

```
CD\CPROG\UTILITY
```

See also: MD, RD

CHKDSK   (external)

Checks storage media for errors and displays a status report.

Syntax: CHKDSK [drive:]pathname[/f][/v]

drive: The drive to be checked. If drive is omitted, the current drive is assumed.

pathname   The name of the file or files to be checked for fragmentation. Wildcards are allowed.

Switches:

/f   Correct any errors found (if possible). If this switch is omitted, errors are displayed and MS-DOS asks you if the error is corrected.

/v   Display the names of all files that were checked. This switch helps localize the errors.

Description:

CHKDSK checks the directories, files and memory allocation of a disk and displays a status report.

To check the entire disk, omit the drive and pathname parameters.

The status report contains information about the disk's total storage, remaining capacity, number of hidden files, number of directories, etc. For example:

```
Volume PROGRAMS     created 03-04-1993 10:35a
Volume Serial Number is 1A62-6E61

42366976 bytes total disk space
   79872 bytes in 3 hidden files
    4096 bytes in 16 directories
 4401152 bytes in 985 user files
37881856 bytes available on disk

    2048 bytes in each allocation unit
   20687 total allocation units on disk
   18497 available allocation units on disk

  655360 bytes total memory
  636352 bytes free
```

If CHKDSK encounters an error, an error message is displayed. For example, a file may not be linked properly, or a sector may be damaged. If /f is specified, errors are corrected when possible.

☞ You should not use CHKDSK to check drives that were referenced by the SUBST command. The combination of drive information can lead to false error messages. Correcting these errors may destroy important data on the disk.

If CHKDSK is run on a DoubleSpace compressed drive, DoubleSpace will also check the drive for errors using DBLSPACE /CHKDSK.

See also: DISKCOMP

CHOICE   **(resident)**

Syntax: CHOICE [/c[:]choices] [/n] [/ s]
            [/t[:]choice,time] [text]
            CHOICE /c:yn

This command allows you to prompt within batch files. The result of the prompt is returned via an errorlevel. By evaluating this errorlevel, you have the option of branching somewhere in the batch file, depending on the results.

For more information on CHOICE, see Chapter 11.

/c:choices Gives you the option of defining which keys are available as possible answers to the prompt. If you don't specify any keys, CHOICE uses Ⓨ and Ⓝ as the default keys. You can define any keys you want, and as many as you want. Specify the keys right after the colon. Make sure there are no spaces between keys. Choice ignores case unless you use the /S switch.

For example, to define the keys Ⓐ, Ⓑ and Ⓒ as possible answers to the prompt, use the following command line:

```
CHOICE /C:ABC
```

The returned errorlevels are also affected by the keys defined after this switch. The first key is errorlevel 1, the second key is errorlevel 2, and so on. In our example, Ⓒ would be errorlevel 3. The batch file will return this errorlevel when a user presses this key.

When the command is being processed, the keys you define appear on the screen in brackets separated by commas and ending in a question mark.

/n Suppresses display of the possible keys after CHOICE.

/s Use this switch to differentiate between uppercase and lowercase letters in the prompt.

/t:choice,time
   Use this switch to define a default key for processing the batch after a specified time. For choice, specify the default key for the batch file. For time, specify the number of seconds (between 0 and 99) before the command uses the default choice.

If you use this switch within the CHOICE·command, the command waits the time specified. If a key is pressed during this time, the command continues running with the error level that the key returns, if no key is pressed during the specified time, the command continues with the default key.

text   Use Text to explain the prompt. The text will always appear at the beginning of the prompt. Remember, if you use the "\" character in the text, you must place the entire text in quotation marks.

CLS   (resident)

Clears the screen.

Syntax: CLS

Description:

CLS clears the screen, except for the system prompt and cursor.

The cursor is repositioned to the upper-left corner of the screen. The screen's attributes are not changed.

COMMAND   (external)

Starts a new command interpreter.

Syntax: COMMAND [[drive:]path][device] [/e:nnnnn][/p] [/[c│k] command][/msg]

drive: path
           The drive and directory from which COMMAND.COM is loaded. This value is stored in the COMSPEC environment variable.

device   Specifies a different device to be used for command input and output (see CTTY).

Switches:

/e:nnnnn   Specifies the size of the environment, where nnnnn is the size in bytes. This number is rounded up to a multiple of 16 bytes and must be in the range of 160 through 32768 bytes. The default value is 256 bytes.

/p   Installs the new command interpreter as permanent. In other words, you can't enter EXIT to end it.

/c command

> This is a DOS command that is executed after loading the command processor, which then stops.

/k command

> Use this switch to call a program or batch file before starting the command interpreter you are loading. For example, you might use this switch to change settings in the AUTOEXEC.BAT file for the new command interpreter.

/msg

> This switch causes all error messages to be stored in memory. /P must also be specified with this switch.

Description:

The command processor COMMAND.COM is automatically loaded when DOS is started. It is responsible for interpreting user commands and batch files, displaying screen prompts, executing application programs, etc. COMMAND copies the command processor and allows you to change the environment.

It is possible to load a second command processor. However, you may not want to change the environment memory during a program's execution. In this case, run the program in a copy of the command processor. This has the advantage that the environment memory of the original command processor is undisturbed. Each copy of the command processor needs about 3K.

The environment is a group of values that can be changed with the SET command. If a new command processor is started, the environment of the parent command processor is copied. Changes in the environment of the new command processor have no effect on the parent command processor.

If a new command processor is loaded, the environment of the current command processor is copied into the environment memory of the new command processor. Changes in the environment of the new command processor have no effect on that of the first command processor. The new command processor is terminated by the EXIT command and the original environment is restored. The EXIT command has no effect if the command processor was entered as permanent.

/p makes the new command processor permanent. The values specifying the drive and path of the new COMMAND.COM are stored in the environment in a variable called COMSPEC. If the command processor ever becomes defective—for example, if an application overwrites part of the command processor—MS-DOS will try to reload the command processor from the location specified at COMSPEC.

/c causes the new command processor to be temporary. It executes only the command specified by command and terminates. Control is returned to the parent command processor. The /c switch must be the first switch specified.

Example

In the following example, the CHKDSK command is executed in a copy of the command processor.

```
C>COMMAND /c CHKDSK A:
```

The following line specifies that the permanent command processor should be replaced with the COMMAND.COM file stored in the \DOS directory. The environment memory is defined as 512 bytes:

```
C>COMMAND C:\DOS\ /p /e:512
```

The following line specifies that DOS system messages should be stored in memory and the new command processor is made permanent:

```
C>COMMAND /p/msg
```

The following example calls a second batch file, DEMO2, inside a batch file. Give this batch the first three parameters of the main batch:

```
@echo off
cls
command /c demo2 %1 %2 %3
```

See also: SHELL (CONFIG.SYS)

COMP   **(external)**

 This command isn't included with DOS 6.0. However, if you need this command, you can order a supplemental disk from Microsoft that contains this command.

Compares the contents of two files or sets of files.

Syntax: COMP [drive:][pathname1][drive:][pathname2] [/d][/a][/l][/n=number][/c]

drive: pathname1
> The complete path and name of the first file to be compared. Wildcards are allowed.

drive: pathname2
> The name of the second file to be compared. The two files must be the same length. Wildcards are allowed.

Switches:

/d Displays difference in decimal format. The default setting is to display in hexadecimal format.

/a Displays differences as ASCII characters.

/l Displays line numbers of differences.

/n=number Compares only the specified number of lines of both files. This is useful when files are different sizes.

/c Ignore case when comparing ASCII characters in files.

Description:

COMP compares the contents of two files. The files may contain ASCII, binary or program data.

Any differences between the two files are displayed showing the position and contents of the mismatched bytes in hexadecimal format:

```
Compare error at OFFSET xxxx
File 1 = yy
File 2 = zz
```

If one of the files is shorter than the other, a message indicating this is displayed.

See also: DISKCOMP

COPY (resident)

Copies one or more files from one location (directory or disk) to another. The COPY command has several different forms. This form of COPY copies individual files.

Syntax: COPY [drive1:][pathname1] [drive2:][pathname2]
               [/a][/b][/v]

drive1: pathname1
               The source file to be copied; it is mandatory.
               Wildcards are allowed. If drive1: is omitted, the
               current drive is assumed.

drive2: pathname2
               The target file. Wildcards are allowed. If drive2: is
               omitted, the current drive is assumed. If the filename
               is omitted from pathname2, the copy is given the same
               name as the source file.

Switches:

/a   Source file is in ASCII format and is terminated by
               Ctrl + Z.

/b   Source file is in binary format.

/v   Verify target file after the copy operation.

Description:

The following example copies the file ORDERS.DAT to
ORDERS.BAK in the current directory:

```
A> COPY ORDERS.DAT ORDERS.BAK
```

To copy all of the files from the current directory with a file
extension of .TXT to the \DATA subdirectory and rename them
with "T" as the first character and the file extension .TEX, type:

```
C>COPY *.TXT \DATA\T*.TEX
```

COPY   (resident)

This form of COPY combines multiple source files into a single
target file.

Syntax: COPY [drive:][path]filename1 [+[[drive:]
               [path]filename2]...] [drive2:][path][target][/a][/b][/v]

drive: path filename1
               The source file to be combined; it is mandatory.
               Wildcards are allowed. Multiple filenames are

specified by separating their names with a plus sign (+).

drive2: path target
The target file resulting from combining the source files. If you omit target, the source files are combined into filename1.

Switches:

/a   Source file(s) is in ASCII format and is terminated with Ctrl + Z.

/b   Source file(s) is in binary format.

/v   Verify target file after the copy operation.

The /b switch copies the entire source file(s) (including all Ctrl + Z characters). Ctrl + Z is not appended to the target file. If several source files are specified, all of the files following the /b switch are treated as binary files until explicitly disabled with the /a switch. This procedure can be used to create ASCII files from binary files or binary files from ASCII files.

The /v switch checks the target file to verify that it's the same as the original file.

If all switches are omitted or the /a switch is used, COPY copies ASCII text files. These files are terminated with a Ctrl + Z (ASCII value 26). COPY terminates the copy process after a Ctrl + Z in the source file is encountered. COPY also appends a Ctrl + Z to the end of the target file. This is not very helpful if you want to copy binary files.

COPY	(resident)

This form of COPY copies files from "from_device" to "to_device".

Syntax: COPY from_device to_device

from_device
The device or file whose data is to be copied.

to_device   The device or file to accept the data to be copied.

The following device names are allowed:

AUX
COM1
COM2
CON
LPT1
LPT2
LPT3
NUL
PRN

Description:

You can also use COPY to send data from one device to the other. For example, you can print a file with COPY:

```
COPY READ.ME PRN:
COPY CON AUTOEXEC.BAT
```

One way COPY can be used is to create small files, such as a batch file, from the keyboard. By doing this you don't have to use a word processor to enter a few lines of text. To create an AUTOEXEC.BAT file, type:

```
COPY CON AUTOEXEC.BAT
```

Now you can enter text from the keyboard on separate lines. To end the file, press either Ctrl + Z or F6. Each line entered is ended by pressing Enter. These lines are stored in the file AUTOEXEC.BAT. Once you have completed a line by pressing Enter, you cannot revise or correct it.

You can also send characters to a printer directly from the keyboard. Type the following (terminate with F6 or Ctrl + Z):

```
COPY CON PRN
```

See also: DISKCOPY, REPLACE, RESTORE, XCOPY

CTTY   (external)

Changes the terminal device used to control your system.

Syntax: CTTY device

device   The device that becomes the new standard input/output device.

Description:

CTTY specifies the input and output devices used. The default input and output devices are the keyboard and screen, which collectively are called the console or CON.

The following I/O devices are allowed:

Name	Device
CON	Screen and keyboard (normal)
AUX	Auxiliary port; RS-232
COM1	Communications port 1; RS-232
COM2	Communications port 2; RS-232
COM3	Communications port 3; RS-232
COM4	Communications port 4; RS-232
LPT1	Printer port 1; Parallel
LPT2	Printer port 2; Parallel
LPT3	Printer port 3; Parallel
PRN	Default printer port

For example, you can convert your PC into a "dumb terminal". Assuming you have the proper hardware and have made the necessary connections, you could use the following configuration with a modem to communicate with a mainframe computer:

```
CTTY AUX
```

If you change the standard I/O device, a device capable of input and output must be connected to the AUX interface. For example, a printer would not be suitable for this because it is only capable of output, not input. To restore input and output to the standard keyboard and screen (console), type the following (from the new standard input device):

```
CTTY CON
```

To use a device other than AUX, COM1, COM2 or CON, the device must have a device driver specified by the DEVICE command in the CONFIG.SYS file.

☞ Only applications that use the DOS interrupts can reference the input and output devices defined with CTTY.

See also: MODE

DATE   (resident)

Displays or sets the system date.

Syntax: DATE [date]

date   This is the new system date.

Description:

If date is omitted, the current system date is displayed and you are asked to enter a new date. The current system date is unchanged if you press (Enter) without entering a new date.

date has one of the following formats, depending on the country code you enter in COUNTRY of CONFIG.SYS:

```
MM-DD-YY              or
MM-DD-YYYY            or
DD-MM-YY             or
YY-MM-DD
```

MM represents the month, DD represents the day and YY or YYYY represents the year. The year can be entered as either two or four digits. The period (.), dash (-) or slash (/) can be used as the separator between the elements of the date. Which separator is used when the date is displayed depends on the setting of COUNTRY in the CONFIG.SYS file. Dashes are used in the U.S.

See also: TIME

DBLSPACE   (external)

Syntax: DBLSPACE
            DBLSPACE

This program lets you compress a drive, so you can store more data on it than ordinarily possible. This program increases the capacity of your drive by storing the data in packed, or compressed form.

The first time you call this program, you automatically go to the DBLSPACE SETUP program. SETUP is menu-driven, and gives you the option of compressing a drive that already contains data, or creating a new compressed drive. You can also choose how much of the drive is excluded from compression, for example, to leave enough room for a swap file for Windows. Depending on your choices, the program compresses the selected drive and automatically defragments it. While the process takes time, afterwards you will have more memory capacity available on the drive.

After installing DBLSPACE, the next time you call the program a menu-driven interface appears on the screen, providing you with menus and commands for working with compressed drives. While we won't go into the menus and commands here, we will explain those commands that you can call directly from the command line.

DBLSPACE /CHKDSK	(external)

Syntax: DBLSPACE /CHKDSK [/f] [drive:]
DBLSPACE /CHKDSK

Use this command to check a compressed drive for errors. Errors found are displayed, but not corrected.

Drive   Specify the drive letter here. If you don't specify anything here, the command checks the current drive.

Switches:

/F   Specify this switch to correct errors found by DBLSPACE. Answer the prompt that appears with Y.

DBLSPACE /COMPRESS	(external)

Syntax: DBLSPACE /COMPRESS drive:
[/NEWDRIVE=drive2:] [/RESERVE=size]
DBLSPACE /COMPRESS A:

Use this command to compress other drives after installing DBLSPACE. The compression process is identical to the first one. However, the program no longer gives you a menu-driven guide through compression; instead, you can begin entering the necessary information.

Drive   Specify the drive or part of a drive here that you want compressed. If you specify only the drive without any other switches, DBLSPACE compresses the entire drive with all of the data.

Switches:

/NEWDRIVE=Drive

To exclude part of a drive from compression, specify this switch, to define which name can be used to address the uncompressed area. If you don't use this switch, the command uses the next free letter.

/RESERVE=size

Use this switch to determine how much of the drive should not be compressed. Specify the size in megabytes.

DBLSPACE /CREATE   (external)

Syntax: DBLSPACE /CREATE Drive Switch
            DBLSPACE /CREATE E:

Use this command to create a compressed drive from free space on an uncompressed drive.

Drive   Specify the name of the drive in which you want to create a new compressed drive.

Switches:

/NEWDRIVE=drive

Specify the name of the new compressed drive here. If you don't specify a name here, DBLSPACE uses the next free drive letter.

/SIZE=size

Specify the size of the new compressed drive here in megabytes.

/RESERVE=size

Specify the amount of the drive, that remains uncompressed, here.

DBLSPACE /DEFRAGMENT   (external)

Syntax: DBLSPACE /DEFRAGMENT Drive
             DBLSPACE /DEF A:

Use this command to start a program for optimizing (defragmenting) compressed drives. Non-contiguous files are stored together again.

Drive   Specify the drive to be optimized here. If you don't specify a drive, the command optimizes the current drive.

DBLSPACE /DELETE   (external)

Syntax: DBLSPACE /DELETE Drive
             DBLSPACE /DEL A:

Use this command to delete a compressed drive. When you delete a compressed drive, keep in mind that all the data on the drive will be lost.

Drive   Specify the compressed drive to be deleted here.

  If you accidentally delete a compressed drive, use UNDELETE to restore the DBLSPACE.XXX file. After undeleting the drive, you still must use the DBLSPACE /MOUNT command.

DBLSPACE /FORMAT   (external)

Syntax: DBLSPACE /FORMAT Drive
             DBLSPACE /FORMAT A:

Use this command to format a compressed drive. You cannot use the FORMAT command to format a compressed drive. When you format a compressed drive, all the files on the drive are destroyed.

  You cannot unformat a drive formatted with the DBLSPACE /FORMAT command.

Drive   Specify the compressed drive to be formatted here.

DBLSPACE /INFO   (external)

Syntax: DBLSPACE /INFO Drive
           DBLSPACE /INFO A:

Outputs information about a compressed drive. The information is
similar to that of the CHKDSK command. Data for the
compressed drive and its uncompressed drive are displayed. You
get information about the total available disk space, the amount
of disk space being used and the free disk space. The command also
displays the compression ratio and which factor DBLSPACE tried
to use for compression.

Drive   Specify the drive for which you want DBLSPACE to
           display information.

DBLSPACE /LIST   (external)

Syntax: DBLSPACE /LIST
           DBLSPACE /L

Use this command to get information about all the drives on your
computer. The command displays whether the drive is compressed
or uncompressed, how much memory the drive has as well as the
free memory. With compressed drives, you also get the name of the
CVF file.

DBLSPACE /MOUNT   (external)

Syntax: DBLSPACE /MOUNT=XXX drive switch
           DBLSPACE /MOUNT A:

Use this command to restore the connection between the compressed
drive and CVF file. DBLSPACE /MOUNT is necessary for working
with compressed diskettes or if the DBLSPACE /UNMOUNT
command has already been used. For example, if you used an
uncompressed diskette in a disk drive and then switched to a
compressed diskette, DBLSPACE will not automatically recognize
the diskette. You must first establish a connection with the CVF
file. To do this, use DBLSPACE /MOUNT.

    /MOUNT=XXX

Specify the CVF file you want to mount here. CVF files are
always named DBLSPACE.XXX. XXX stands for a number between

000 and 254. Specify the number here. Do this only if the name of the file is not DBLSPACE.000.

Drive   Specify the drive, in which the compressed volume is located, here.

Switches:

/newdrive=drive
> Specify the name of the new compressed drive here. If you don't specify a name, DBLSPACE /MOUNT uses the next free drive letter for the compressed drive.

DBLSPACE /RATIO   (external)

Syntax: DBLSPACE /RATIO=X.X drive switch
             DBLSPACE /RATIO=4.0 /ALL

Use this command to set the compression rate for one or all drives. DBLSPACE will then attempt to pack the data at the greatest possible compression. You can also use the compression ratio to determine how much free disk space the drive contains.

```
/RATIO=X.X
```

Specify the compression ratio here. You can choose a ratio of between 1.0 and 16.0.

Drive   Specify the drive whose compression ratio you want to change. If you don't specify a drive here, DBLSPACE changes the compression ratio for the current drive.

Switches:

/ALL   Sets the compression ratio for all drives.

DBLSPACE /SIZE   (external)

Syntax: DBLSPACE /SIZE=size1 /RESERVE=size2 Drive
             DBLSPACE /SIZE=50 C:

Use this command to change the size of a compressed drive. You can enlarge or reduce the compressed drive. For example, you could use this command if you needed uncompressed disk space, or, in the reverse situation, if you had too much uncompressed memory.

/SIZE=size1

Specify the amount of memory in megabytes to be used for the compressed drive.

/RESERVE=size2

Specify the amount of memory in megabytes to be left uncompressed.

Drive   Specify the drive whose size you want to change.

DBLSPACE /UNMOUNT   (external)

Syntax: DBLSPACE /UNMOUNT Drive
             DBLSPACE /UNMOUNT A:

Use this command to break the connection between a compressed drive and the CVF file. You won't be able to access the compressed data on this drive anymore. Instead, you will only have access to the uncompressed portion of the drive.

Drive   Specify the drive you want unmounted from the CVF file. If you don't specify a drive, DBLSPACE /UNMOUNT unmounts the current drive.

DEBUG   (external)

Starts DEBUG, a program testing and editing tool.

Syntax: DEBUG [drive:][path]filename [switches | parameters]

drive: path filename

The program or file to be analyzed with DEBUG. The file is loaded at its defined starting address. If omitted, the current contents of memory are used.

Switches:

These are additional parameters. You may specify these switches after DEBUG is started.

parameters

Any command line information required by the executable file to be tested.

Description:

The DEBUG program analyzes machine language programs during execution. Memory locations can be displayed, printed, changed, stored, etc. The prompt symbol for DEBUG is the minus sign (-).

If you omit a filename when you start DEBUG, the current memory area is assumed. You can load a file with the DEBUG commands N or L.

Once DEBUG is started, the segment registers are all set to the lowest memory boundary. The flags are cleared. The instruction pointer IP is set to 0100h, which is where most programs start (at least the COM programs). All registers except for SP are set to zero. Register pair BX/CX contains the length of the program.

Addresses can be specified with or without segment specification. When the segment address is omitted, DS is the default (except for the commands G, L, T, U and W, where the code segment is assumed).

The segment registers themselves can be used as the segment address. The following address specifications are allowed:

```
400
CS:1022
SS:900
```

To specify a range of memory, use either two hexadecimal values separated by a space or a starting value followed by a length (also separated by a space). The length (in hexadecimal) is prefixed with an L. In this case, the segment is specified only once. If CS contains the value 196a, then the following six commands all specify the memory area 196A:0100 to 196A:019F:

```
100 19f
100 L1a0
CS:100 19F
CS:100 L1A0
196a:100 19F
196a:100 L1A0
```

To define a list of data, separate the hexadecimal values from one another with spaces:

```
E DS:3000 20 30 31 32 33 34 35 36 37
```

ASCII strings are enclosed by quotation marks. If a quotation mark is present in the string itself, enter it as a double quotation mark ("").

```
31 32 "345""6789"   yields      12345"6789
```

In addition to executable programs, you can also load and edit text files with DEBUG.

   Be careful with EXE files. These files are not saved by DEBUG because they are relocatable.

The following information provides only a brief overview of the DEBUG commands.

?   Displays a list of the Debug commands.

a [address]

Assembles 8086/8087/8088 mnemonics. DEBUG supports the 8087 instruction set. The length of each operation, byte or word must be specified. All numeric values must be entered in hexadecimal.

```
A 1000
1af0:1000 inc byte [1fff]
1af0:1004 dec word [1ffd]
1af0:1008 db "Here is a string"
1af0:1018 db fd, 3, 09
1af0:1018 dw 2000, 9dfe
1af0:101F movsb
```

c [range] [address]

Compare two areas of memory. The first parameter, range, specifies the starting and ending addresses and the second parameter, address, is the starting address of the second memory area to compare. The length of range determines the length of the comparison.

If the range and address memory areas are identical, Debug displays nothing and returns to the Debug prompt. If there are differences, they are displayed in the following format:

```
address1 byte1 byte2 address2
```

address1 is in range. address2 is in the second area. The two bytes are displayed side by side.

d range

Display (dump) the specified memory range in hexadecimal format. Both the hexadecimal and ASCII values are displayed. ASCII values which cannot be displayed are represented as periods. Sixteen bytes are displayed per line.

If only a starting address is specified, 128 bytes are displayed. If the starting address is omitted, the area at CS:0100 or the last address dumped is displayed:

```
d 3000:9222 L200
```

e address list

Enter data in memory. If list is omitted, the memory contents beginning at address are displayed and you can enter values to replace the current contents. To leave memory unchanged, press the (Spacebar). To move back by one memory location, press the (-) key. To terminate this command, press the (Enter) key.

The following displays the contents of memory one byte at a time from 2000 thru 3331 and allows you to change the contents:

```
e 2000:3331 43 90 "Grand total:"
e 2000:3331
2000:3331 20. 01  ff. 02  31. ff
```

f range list

Fill a range with the values in list. For example, to fill the screen with the letters DOS, type the following command:

```
fb000:000 Lfa0 "D" 09 "O" 09 "S" 09 20 07
```

 Replace B000 with B800 if you have a color monitor.

g (go) [=address] [breakpoints]

Start a program at the address CS:=address. This address must be the first byte of an instruction.

You can define up to 10 breakpoints. When one of these addresses is encountered, the program is halted and control is passed back to DEBUG. The breakpoints call interrupt CCh.

If =address is omitted, the program is started at the address CS:IP. You can use this form of the command after a breakpoint has been encountered:

```
g=0100 0110 0212 9fd
```

h value1[,] value2
>   Adds the first two parameters value1 and value2, then
>   subtracts the second parameter from the first. value1 and
>   value2 can be any hexadecimal number between 0 and
>   FFFFh.

```
-h 2c78 421
3099 2857
```

>   If value2 is larger than value1, the result is represented as
>   a two's complement number.

```
-h 3d00 3e00
7B00 FF00
```

i port   Reads and displays one byte of data from the specified
>   port. The value is displayed in hexadecimal format.

l address drive sector num_sectors
>   Load a file or specified disk sectors into memory.

Parameters

>   address   Specifies the memory location where the file
>   or disk sector should be loaded.

>   drive   Specifies the drive which contains the disk
>   from which sectors are to be read. This is a
>   numeric value: 0=A, 1=B, 2=C, etc.

>   sector   Hexadecimal number of the first sector to load.

>   num_sectors
>   Hexadecimal value of the number of
>   consecutive sectors to load.

>   Using L without parameters loads the file
>   specified when DEBUG was started or the file was
>   last defined by the N command. The filename
>   cannot be specified from the L command. The file is
>   loaded starting at CS:0100, or at address, if
>   specified.

>   The other form of L loads a specified number of
>   sectors from drive, starting at memory location
>   address, beginning at the relative sector, sector.

drive is not a letter but a digit from 0 to 255, where 0=A, 1=B, etc.

```
l              load   the last file
l 4000         load   the last file at 04000h
l 200 2 0 D    load   13 sectors from drive c,
                      starting with sector 0,
                      to address SC:200
```

m range address

Copies the contents of memory at range to address.

range   The starting and ending address, or the starting address and length, of the memory to be copied to address.

address

The starting address of the location to which the contents of range will be copied.

n filename

Sets the filename for subsequent load (l) and write (w) commands.

```
ntextomat.exe
```

o address byte

Output the data value byte to port address:

```
o 02f8 2e
```

p [=address][number]

Proceed; executes a loop, a repeated string instruction, a software interrupt or a subroutine. May also be used to trace through any other instructions.

=address

The location of the first instruction to execute. If no address is specified, the default address in the CS:IP is used.

number

Specifies the number of instructions to execute before returning control to Debug.

q   Quit DEBUG without confirmation and without saving the current file. If you have made changes that you want to save, you must save them before quitting DEBUG.

r register

Display and/or change the register contents.

R without parameters displays the contents of all registers.

R register displays the contents of the corresponding registers.

You can change the contents of these registers. The following register names are recognized by DEBUG:

```
AX BX CX DX CS DS ES SS DI SI BP SP F IP (or PC)
```

You can change more than one flag register by separating the register names with spaces.

The following codes can be used to change the corresponding flag:

Flag	Flag set	Flag cleared
Overflow	OV	NV
Direction	DN (Down)	UP (Up)
Interrupt	EI (Enabled)	DI (Disabled)
Sign	NG (Negative)	PL (Plus)
Zero	ZR (Zero)	NZ (Nonzero)
Aux Carry	AC (Aux Carry)	NA (No Auxiliary)
Parity	PE (Parity even)	PO (Parity odd)
Carry	CY (Carry)	NC (No Carry)

For example, the following command clears the interrupt and carry flags in the flag register:

```
-r f
OV DN EI ZR NA PO CY  -  di nc
```

s range list

Search for the characters list within memory range. The address at which the characters are found is displayed in the form segment:offset. For example, if you're searching for all occurrences of the string "error", use the following command:

```
s0100 ffff "error"
6abd:3a94
```

The search is case sensitive. For example, the above example will find "error", but not "ERROR".

t=start_number

Trace the program in memory beginning at address start for number executions. If start is omitted, execution begins at the current value of CS:IP. If number is not specified, a single instruction is executed. When the specified number of instructions have been executed, the following is displayed:

```
t            start at CS:IP    (1 instruction)
t=0400       start at CS:0400  (1 instruction)
t=0400 8     start at CS:IP    (8 instructions)
```

u range

Unassemble (disassemble) memory at range. The hexadecimal opcodes are displayed in their equivalent mnemonic form as follows:

```
u2000
20FE:2000   BAFFFE      MOV     DX,FEFF
20FE:2003   2E          CS:
20FE:2004   8A0E2020    MOV CH,[2020]
```

If you enter only a starting address, 32 bytes of memory are disassembled. If you omit range, the 32 bytes of memory at CS:IP are disassembled.

w[address] [drive] [first_sector sectors]

Write the data to disk.

w without parameters or with address writes the file specified when DEBUG was started or last defined by the N command.

Using parameters writes the specified number of sectors to drive, starting at memory location address, beginning at relative sector first_sector.

drive is a hexadecimal value with 0=A, 1=B, 2=C, etc. Files with .EXE or .HEX extensions cannot be rewritten—DEBUG will display an error message if you try to do this.

Be careful when you write directly to sectors. Under certain conditions, writing directly to sectors can overwrite important data, the FAT or the directory.

xa count   Allocates a specified number of pages of expanded memory.

       count   The number of 16K pages of expanded memory to allocate.

             If this command executes successfully, a message, similar to the following, is displayed:

```
Handle created=0004
```

xd handle
        De-allocates a handle to expanded memory.

        Example

```
XD 0004
```

        This example de-allocates handle 0004. If successful, DEBUG displays the following message:

```
Handle 0004 deallocated.
```

xm [lpage] [ppage] [handle]
        Maps a logical page of expanded memory, associated with a specific handle, to a physical page of expanded memory.

       lpage   The number of the logical page of expanded memory to map.

       ppage   The number of the physical page to which lpage is mapped.

       handle
           The handle associated with a logical page of expanded memory.

   xs   Displays information about expanded memory in the following format:

Handle x has x pages allocated
Physical page x - Frame segment x
x of a total x EMS pages have been allocated
x of a total x EMS handles have been allocated

| **DEFRAG** | **(external)** |

Syntax: DEFRAG drive: switch

Use this command to start a program that defragments files on the specified storage device. The program stores the files on the storage device in such a way that they can be accessed faster. For example, incontiguous files are stored contiguously.

After you call DEFRAG, the program begins. You can make the desired settings from the menus. As an alternative, you could also specify the desired settings when calling the command by adding switches. Optimization would then start right after you called DEFRAG.

drive   Specify the drive whose files you want defragmented here.

Switches:

/f   Defragments all files and arranges them in sequential order, so there are no empty spaces in between the files.

/u   Files are defragmented, but there can be empty spaces in between the files.

/s:x   Specify a sorting sequence here that determines the order in which files are placed on the storage device. The following values for x are available:

n   Files stored on the hard drive in alphabetical order by name.

n-   Files stored on the hard drive in reverse alphabetical order by name.

e   Files placed on storage device in alphabetical order by file extension.

e-   Files stored in reverse alphabetical order by file extension.

d   Files stored on the drive in order by date, beginning with the earliest.

	d-	Files stored on the drive in reverse order by date, beginning with the latest.
	s	Files placed on storage device in order by size, beginning with the smallest.
	s-	Files placed on drive in reverse order by size, beginning with the largest.

/b   Computer automatically restarts after optimization.

/skiphigh   Loads program into conventional memory. Ordinarily, DEFRAG is loaded into upper memory.

/lcd   Starts the program in LCD graphics mode.

/bw   Starts the program in monochrome mode.

/g0   Starts the program in text mode. Disables the mouse and graphical elements.

/h   Moves hidden files.

DEL   (resident)

Deletes specified files.

Syntax: DEL [drive:][path]filename [/p]

[drive:][path] filename
            Specifies the drive, path and filename of the file or files to delete. Wildcards are permitted as filenames.

Switches:

/p   Prompts for confirmation before erasing a file.

If the /p switch is used, a prompt appears asking for confirmation before each file is deleted.

To erase all files in the DOC directory of drive C:, type:

```
DEL C:\DOC\*.*
```

    or

```
ERASE C:\DOC\*.*
```

See also: ERASE, UNDELETE

DELOLDOS (external)

Removes previous version of DOS (saved in the OLD_DOS.1 directory when MS-DOS 6.0 is installed).

Syntax: DELOLDOS [/b]

DELOLDOS removes all files saved in the OLD_DOS.1 directory from your disk drive. This command also removes itself from the DOS directory after running because there is no further use for it.

Switches:

/b   When you specify this switch, DELOLDOS displays data in black and white (monochrome) instead of color.

When you install MS-DOS 6.0, the previous version of DOS is saved in case you want to reinstall this version for any reason.

If MS-DOS 6.0 is installed more than one time without running DELOLDOS, multiple copies of your DOS directory will be created named OLD_DOS.1, OLD_DOS.2, etc.

DELTREE (external)

Syntax: DELTREE [/y] directory

Use this command to delete whole directories or directory trees. DELTREE automatically deletes all the files in a directory, as well as any subdirectories and files in the subdirectories. Be careful when you use this command, since it also deletes all hidden and write-protected files in the selected directory.

Switches:

/y   When you specify this switch, specified directories are deleted without a security prompt.

Directory   Specify the directory to be deleted here. Any subdirectories of the specified directory will also be deleted. If the directory you are deleting is a subdirectory of the current directory, it's enough to specify the name of the directory. Otherwise, you must specify the entire path of the directory you want deleted.

DEVICEHIGH   (resident)

Loads device driver into upper memory.

Syntax: DEVICEHIGH region1 file region2

Use this command to install device drivers in the CONFIG.SYS file. If upper memory is available (reserved memory in the area between 640K and 1024K), the drivers are relocated to this memory. If there is not enough upper memory available, the drivers are loaded into conventional memory.

Region1

/l:region,minsize

This switch allows you to determine a specific area in memory for loading the device drivers. To display the memory areas, call MEM /F. When you define the memory area, it is only possible to load the device drivers into this particular memory area, no other areas may be used. However, some device drivers require several areas. To select more than one memory area, use semicolons in between each memory area you specify.

You can also define a minimum size for each area.

/s   The UMBs (Upper Memory Blocks) are reduced to minimum size when the drivers are loaded. This switch makes the best use of memory. Ordinarily, you only use this switch with MEMMAKER.

file   Specify the filename of the device driver here, if necessary, with the complete path. MS-DOS comes with the following files: ANSI.SYS, DISPLAY.SYS, DRIVER.SYS, EMM386.EXE, HIMEM.SYS, POWER.EXE, RAMDRIVE.SYS and SETVER.EXE.

You will find a brief description of the device drivers in the appendix. If you allocate upper memory with EMM386.EXE, you cannot load this driver into upper memory. However, EMM386.EXE only takes up a few kilobytes in conventional memory.

Region2

Specify the switches accepted by the individual device drivers here. For more information, read the appendix for a description of the device drivers.

To load device drivers into upper memory, it is necessary to reserve enough memory. MS-DOS comes supplied with a device driver that handles this task, called EMM386.EXE. Also, the CONFIG.SYS must have the entry, DOS=UMB to make upper memory active.

DIR	**(resident)**

Displays a list of files and subdirectories in the current directory.

Syntax: DIR [drive:][path][filename][/p][/w][/a[[:]attributes]][/o[[:]sortorder]][/s][/b][/l][/c]

drive: The drive containing the directory. If you omit drive:, the current drive is assumed.

path   The subdirectory to be displayed. If you omit path, the current path is assumed.

filename   The name of a specific file to be displayed. If you omit filename, the entire directory is displayed. Wildcards are allowed.

Switches:

/p   Page switch: Displays the filenames one screen page at a time. You can view the next page by pressing any key.

/w   Wide format switch: Displays the filenames across each line with as many as five filenames per line. No other information about each file is displayed.

/a[:]   Displays only the names of files and directories with specified attributes. (See the table below.)

/o[:]   Display files by specified sort order (see following table).

/s   All files and subdirectories in specified directory.

/b   Bare format (no heading information or summary).

/l   Display in lowercase.

/c   Includes the compression ratio in the directory
            display. You have the option of adding the H switch
            to display the compression ratio in relation to the
            cluster size of the uncompressed drive.

Description:

DIR displays the directory of the files on a disk, the number of
files in the directory and the number of available bytes on the
disk.

To display the external COM commands for DOS (assuming you're
in the correct subdirectory), use the following command:

```
DIR *.COM
```

If these external COM commands are in a different subdirectory
named DOS, the following command could be used:

```
DIR \DOS\*.COM
```

The following commands display the files in the current directory
of a specified drive:

```
DIR
DIR A:
```

The following commands display all of the files in the \DOS
directory:

```
DIR \DOS
DIR \DOS\*.*
```

The wildcard parameter *.* (representing all of the files) can be
omitted because it is the default.

To print a hardcopy of the directory, redirect output to the printer.
Do this with the > symbol:

```
DIR *.COM > PRN
```

It's also possible to display only files with specific file attributes.
The following table lists the attribute codes to use with the /a:
switch:

Attribute Code	Meaning
h	Hidden files
-h	Files that are not hidden
s	System files
-s	Files other than system files
d	Directories
-d	Files only (no directories)
a	Files with archive bit set
-a	Files with archive bit cleared
r	Read only files
-r	No read only files

For example, to display a directory of only those files in the current directory which have their archive bits set, you could use the following command line:

```
DIR /a:a
```

To display the filenames in a different order, use the /s:order switch to specify the order as shown below:

Sort order Code	Meaning
n	Alphabetical order by name
-n	Reverse alphabetical order
e	Alphabetical order by filename extension
-e	Reverse alphabetical order by filename extension
d	By date and time, earliest first
-d	By date and time, last first
s	By size, smallest to largest
-s	By size, largest to smallest
g	Directories grouped before files
c	The files are displayed by compression ratio, lowest first
-c	The files are displayed by compression ratio, highest first
-g	Directories grouped after files

To display the filenames in the current directory sorted alphabetically by name, type:

```
DIR /o:n
```

Using the /s switch displays all files in the current directory, as well as files in any subdirectories.

/b displays the files with no heading and summary information.

/l displays an unsorted list of file and directory names in lowercase letters. This switch does not convert external characters to lowercase.

You can also preset these switches by setting the DIRCMD environment variable.

You can insert the default setting with DIRCMD in the AUTOEXEC.BAT so that your custom display of DIR is always available when you start up your computer.

DISKCOMP   (external)

Compares the contents of two floppy diskettes.

Syntax: DISKCOMP [drive1:[drive2:]][/1][/8]

drive1:   The drive containing the first diskette.

drive2:   The drive containing the second diskette. If drive2: is omitted, the current drive is assumed.

Switches:

/1   Compare only the first sides of double-sided diskettes.

/8   Compare only the first eight sectors of each track, regardless of the number of sectors per track.

Description:

DISKCOMP compares the contents of two diskettes. These diskettes are compared track by track. Any differences are displayed; the location of the mismatched data is indicated.

Remember that two disks which contain the same files are not necessarily identical.

DISKCOMP works only with floppy diskettes. An error message is displayed if a hard drive is specified.

If the current drive is A: and both drive1: and drive2: are omitted, DOS assumes you want to use a single drive (A:) and asks you to insert one diskette at a time into drive A:.

 Don't use DISKCOMP with drives that have been processed with the SUBST command.

DISKCOPY	(external)

Copies the contents of one floppy diskette to another.

Syntax: DISKCOPY [drive1:][drive2:][/1][/v]

drive1:   The drive containing the source diskette to be copied. If omitted, the current drive is assumed.

drive2:   The drive containing the target diskette. If omitted, the current drive is assumed.

Switches:

[/1] one   Copies only the first side of the source diskette, even if both sides are formatted. The target diskette is also formatted as single-sided.

[/v]   Verifies that the information is copied correctly.

Description:

DISKCOPY makes a copy of the source diskette, track by track. If you have only one drive, DOS assumes that you are copying to the same drive and prompts you to insert the correct diskette as necessary.

If the target diskette is not formatted before the copy operation, DOS recognizes this and reformats the diskette with the same number of sides and sectors per track as the source diskette. If errors occur during copying, they are displayed; the side, track and sector are indicated.

If the source diskette has a volume serial number, DISKCOPY creates a new volume serial number for the destination diskette and displays this number when the copy operation is complete.

Specify the /1 switch to copy only the first side of the source diskette. If the target diskette is unformatted, it's then formatted as single-sided.

When the /v switch is used, DISKCOPY checks that all information is copied correctly. Verifying the copy operation requires additional processing time.

Since DISKCOPY makes an exact copy of the source disk, it does not eliminate any file and disk fragmentation. To de-fragment the files, use the COPY or XCOPY commands.

The ERRORLEVEL parameter of the IF command line may be used in a batch file to process exit error codes returned by DISKCOPY.

DISKCOPY Exit Error Codes

0   The copy operation was successful.
1   A nonfatal read/write error occurred.
2   The Ctrl+C key combination was pressed by the user.
3   A fatal error occurred.
4   An initialization error occurred.

 Don't use DISKCOPY with drives that have been processed with the SUBST command.

See also: COPY, DISKCOMP, REPLACE, RESTORE, XCOPY

DOSKEY	**(external)**

Allows command line editing. Recalls and edits commands and defines macros.

Syntax: DOSKEY [/reinstall][/bufsize=size]
             [/macros][/history][/insert | /overstrike]
             [macroname=[text]]

/reinstall   Installs a new copy of the DOSKEY program, even if one is already installed.

/bufsize=size
             Specifies the size of the command history buffer for storing commands and macros.

/macros   Displays a list of all DOSKEY macros.

/history   Displays the contents of the command history buffer.

/insert | /overstrike

> Determines how new characters entered in a command line will be handled. INSERT specifies that new text will be inserted into old text; OVERSTRIKE specifies that new text is to write over previous text.

macroname

> Specifies a name for a created macro.

text   Specifies commands to be recorded.

Description:

DOSKEY is a Terminate and Stay Resident (TSR) program that lets you automate and customize MS-DOS command lines. DOSKEY requires about 3K of memory.

The following keys have special uses from the command line when DOSKEY is installed:

[↑]   Recalls the MS-DOS command issued prior to the command line being displayed. Subsequent key presses move further back through the command history.

[↓]   Recalls the MS-DOS command issued after the command line being displayed. Subsequent key presses move further ahead through the command history.

[PgUp]   Recalls the oldest MS-DOS command in the history buffer.

[PgDn]   Recalls the most recent MS-DOS command issued.

The DOSKEY command lets you edit a displayed command line. If /insert has been set, all keystrokes are inserted into the command line at the cursor location, while /overstrike replaces the character at the cursor position with the newly typed character.

Other editing keys and their functions are used as follows:

[←]   Moves the cursor back one character.

[→]   Moves the cursor forward one character.

[Ctrl]+[←]   Moves the cursor back one word.

[Ctrl]+[→]   Moves the cursor ahead one word.

[Home]   Moves the cursor to the beginning of the line.

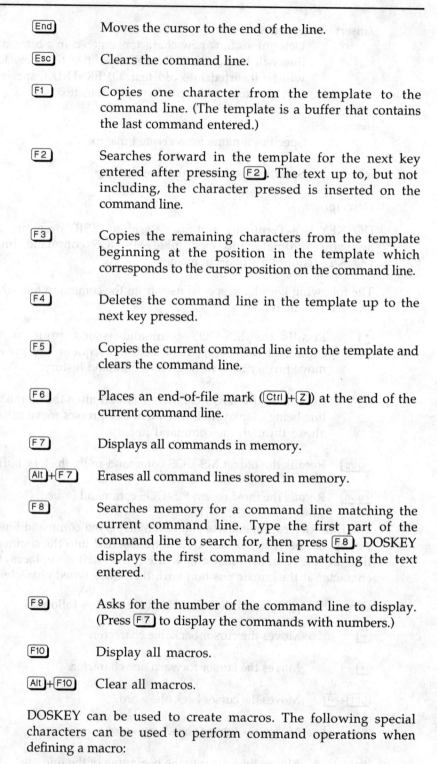

End   Moves the cursor to the end of the line.

Esc   Clears the command line.

F1   Copies one character from the template to the command line. (The template is a buffer that contains the last command entered.)

F2   Searches forward in the template for the next key entered after pressing F2. The text up to, but not including, the character pressed is inserted on the command line.

F3   Copies the remaining characters from the template beginning at the position in the template which corresponds to the cursor position on the command line.

F4   Deletes the command line in the template up to the next key pressed.

F5   Copies the current command line into the template and clears the command line.

F6   Places an end-of-file mark (Ctrl+Z) at the end of the current command line.

F7   Displays all commands in memory.

Alt+F7   Erases all command lines stored in memory.

F8   Searches memory for a command line matching the current command line. Type the first part of the command line to search for, then press F8. DOSKEY displays the first command line matching the text entered.

F9   Asks for the number of the command line to display. (Press F7 to display the commands with numbers.)

F10   Display all macros.

Alt+F10   Clear all macros.

DOSKEY can be used to create macros. The following special characters can be used to perform command operations when defining a macro:

$G or $g	Redirects output. Sends output to a device or file instead of the default display device.
$L or $l	Redirects input. Takes input from a device or a file instead of the keyboard.
$B or $b	Pipes commands. Sends the output of the macro to another command.
$T or $t	Command separator. Separates commands when creating a macro or entering commands directly.
$$	The dollar sign filename character. This is equivalent to $.

$1 through $9

Replaceable parameters. Use $1 through $9 to specify parameters that may be entered from the command line when the macro name is entered. The $1 character is equivalent to %1 in batch files.

$*   Replaceable parameter in macros.

DOSSHELL   (external)

Starts the MS-DOS Shell.

Syntax: DOSSHELL [/t | /g[:res[n]]][/b]

Switches:

/t   Starts the MS-DOS Shell in text mode.

/g   Starts MS-DOS Shell in graphics mode.

:res[n]   A letter representing the screen resolution (l=low, m=medium, h=high).

/b   Starts MS-DOS Shell using black-and-white color scheme.

The /t and /g switches are mutually exclusive. You can reset the resolution in the MS-DOS Shell. All the settings are stored in the DOSSHELL.INI.

Description:

The MS-DOS Shell user interface is started by typing the DOSSHELL command. If your computer does not use a hard drive, the appropriate diskette must be in the drive. You do not need to define any parameters to configure the MS-DOS Shell because these are given in the DOSSHELL.BAT batch file.

If you leave the Shell by pressing [Shift] + [F9] or with a corresponding menu command, you can restart the Shell again by typing the EXIT command; you don't need to run the DOSSHELL command again.

The DOSSHELL command may be added to your AUTOEXEC.BAT file to start the Shell whenever your computer is started.

ECHO   **(resident)**

Turns on or off the command message display.

Syntax: ECHO [on | off]
            ECHO [message]

on | off   Specifies whether the command-echoing feature is on or off. To display current ECHO setting, enter ECHO with no parameters.

message   Displays specified text on the screen.

ECHO is especially useful with batch files. When ECHO is set to off, ECHO *message* can be used to display a message without displaying all other command lines.

EDIT   **(external)**

Starts the MS-DOS Editor for creating and changing ASCII files.

Syntax: EDIT [[drive:][path]filename][/b][/g][/h][/nohi]

drive: path filename
            The name of the file to be edited. If it does not exist, it is created.

Switches:

/b   Permits a monochrome monitor to be used with a color graphics card.

/g   Provides fastest screen updating for a CGA monitor.

/h   Displays the maximum number of lines possible for the monitor you are using.

/nohi   Enables using 8-color monitors with the MS-DOS Editor. Usually MS-DOS uses 16 colors.

The MS-DOS Editor is used for editing ASCII files quickly and easily. If the QBASIC.EXE file is not in the current directory or search path or not in the same directory as EDIT.COM, you cannot use the MS-DOS Editor.

The MS-DOS Editor uses predefined keys and menus to edit an ASCII file with a full screen editor. This is a vast improvement over EDLIN which was supplied with previous versions of MS-DOS.

For more information about the MS-DOS Editor, refer to Chapter 8.

EDLIN	external)

☞   This command isn't included with DOS 6.0. However, if you need this command, you can order a supplemental disk from Microsoft that contains this command.

Starts the line editor.

Syntax: EDLIN [drive:][path] filename [/b]

drive: path filename
            The name of the file to be edited. If it does not exist, it is created. You cannot edit a file with a .BAK extension.

Switches:

/b   File to be loaded is a binary file. The end-of-file marker Ctrl+Z is ignored.

Description:

EDLIN is a text line editor with very simple commands. EDLIN can be used to create or edit small batch files. EDLIN loads a file until it encounters a Ctrl+Z (ASCII 26 or 01Ah). To ignore this

end-of-file marker, use the /b switch. EDLIN has the following
commands:

Command	Syntax
Append	line_number a
Copy	first_line,last_line,target num c
Delete	first_line,last_line d
Edit	line
End (Save file)	e
Help	?
Insert	line i
List	start_line,end_line l
Move	first_line,last_line m
Page display	first_line,last_line p
Quit (disregard changes)	q
Replace	first_line,last_line ?r oldtext ^Z newtext
Search	first_line,last_line ?s string
Transfer	targett[drive:][path]filename
Write	lines w

A text file is composed of one or more lines. Each line may contain
up to 253 characters and is preceded by a line number when
displayed.

The line numbers are not part of the text file, but are
automatically maintained by EDLIN. After each EDLIN command
that inserts or deletes a line of text, the lines are renumbered to
readjust.

All EDLIN commands consist of a single letter preceded by
parameters. You can use either uppercase or lowercase characters.
If the line number is not specified, the last line processed is
assumed. The last line processed is designated by an asterisk. Press
Enter without a command to edit this line.

You can enter multiple commands on a line, separated by
semicolons (;).

In addition to specifying an absolute line number, you can use the
following characters to represent a position relative to the current
line number or a symbol for certain line numbers:

Symbol	Meaning
#	The last line number in the EDLIN buffer
.	The current line
+ I -	A line number relative to the current line

The I command is used to enter new lines. Here is an example of creating an AUTOEXEC file:

```
EDLIN AUTOEXEC.BAT
New file
*i

    1:*echo off
    2:*cls
    3:*echo Please enter the date and time:
    4:*echo -
    5:*date
    6:*time
    7:*^z
*q
Abort edit (Y/N)? N
*e
```

To save the edited text, you must exit EDLIN with the E command. A backup copy of the file with a .BAK extension is made before the file is edited.

If you exit EDLIN with the Q command, DOS asks you to confirm this without saving the changes.

EMM386   (external)

Turns EMM386 expanded memory on or off.

Syntax: EMM386 [on I off][w=on I w=off]

on I off   Activates or suspends EMM386.EXE device driver or places it in auto mode. (Auto mode enables expanded memory support only when a program calls for it.) Default value is ON.

w=on I w=off
             Enables or disables Weitek co-processor support. The default value is w=off.

The EMM386 device driver must have been installed using the DEVICE command from your CONFIG.SYS file before using this command. Your computer must have an 80386 (or higher) microprocessor.

ERASE	(resident)

Erases files from disk.

Syntax: ERASE [drive:][path]filename [/p]

drive: path filename
          The path and name of the file to be deleted. Wildcards are allowed.

Switches:

/p   Prompts for confirmation before erasing a file.

Description:

This command is identical to DELETE and uses the same syntax.

ERASE removes a file from disk. The files are not immediately physically erased, but the filename in the directory is marked as erased and the sectors occupied by the file are marked as free (and thus subject to overwriting).

If you attempt to erase all of the files on a drive or a directory, DOS asks for confirmation. If you don't confirm the operation, the command is terminated:

```
ERASE FILE.DAT
ERASE *.HLP
ERASE O??O.*
ERASE *.*
All files in directory will be deleted!
Are you sure (Y/N)?n
```

If the /p switch is used, a prompt appears asking for confirmation before each file is deleted.

To erase all files in the DOC directory of drive C:, type:

```
ERASE C:\DOC\*.*
```

See also: DEL, UNDELETE

EXE2BIN   (external)

   This command isn't included with DOS 6.0. However, if
you need this command, you can order a supplemental disk
from Microsoft that contains this command.

Converts an EXE file to a BIN file.

Syntax: EXE2BIN [drive1:]path1 input_file[drive2:]
             [pathname2 output_file]

drive: pathname1
             The complete path for the input file.

drive: pathname2
             The complete path for the output file.

input_file   The name of the input file.

output_file
             The name of the output file. If omitted, a BIN file
             with the same filename as the input is assumed.

Description:

EXE2BIN converts an executable file (EXE) into a binary file. It is
used by programmers, not general PC users.

EXE files are created by an assembler or compiler. EXE files can be
executed by simply entering the name of the file. In contrast to EXE
files, COM files are neither relocatable nor segment-oriented.
They always start at address 0100h.

There are some restrictions to remember when using EXE2BIN.

The input file must be a valid EXE file produced by the linker and
must not be packed. The EXE file may not contain a stack segment.
The program and data segments may not exceed 64K.

If the EXE file does not start at address 0100h and the entry point
is not defined with the END pseudo-op of the assembler or if a
segment-oriented command occurs, EXE2BIN will simply create a
binary file. This binary file cannot be correctly loaded and
executed by the COMMAND.COM command processor. In this
case, EXE2BIN requests a starting address for this binary file. This
binary file can be loaded and started only from an application.

EXIT	**(resident)**

Quits the COMMAND.COM program and returns to the program which started it, if one exists.

Syntax: EXIT

Description:

When a second command processor is loaded in addition to the permanent command processor COMMAND.COM, the alternate command processor is terminated with EXIT (see also COMMAND). If you load multiple command processors, each copy takes up about 3K of memory.

If you leave COMMAND.COM with EXIT, the original environment is restored.

The EXIT command has no effect on the last command processor, which you cannot leave any more.

If you have left the MS-DOS shell with [Shift] + [F9] or with a corresponding menu command, use the EXIT command to return to the Shell.

In many applications you have the possibility of jumping to the operating system. A second command processor is loaded and started. All commands that are entered have no influence on the original environment of the application program. You leave this copy with the EXIT command:

```
EXIT
```

See also: COMMAND

EXPAND	**(external)**

Unpacks compressed files.

Syntax: EXPAND filename destination

Almost all MS-DOS commands on the installation diskettes are in the form of compressed files that cannot be used until they are unpacked. When you install MS-DOS, SETUP automatically expands (unpacks) these files.

Use EXPAND to unpack one or more of these compressed files. For example, this is practical when you accidentally delete a file from the DOS directory.

filename   Specifies the drive, directory and filename of the compressed file to be expanded here. On the installation diskettes, the compressed files all have "_" as the last character in the extension. You can also specify more than one file in sequence. Wildcards are not allowed.

destination

Specifies the drive, directory and filename of the destination (expanded) file. If only one file is being expanded, you can also specify a new name for the file here. If you are expanding more than one file, you can only specify one directory. The files are then stored there under their original filenames.

FASTHELP	(external)

Displays brief help descriptions of MS-DOS commands.

Syntax: FASTHELP [command]

command   The command for which you need help.

Description:

Typing FASTHELP without parameters displays the MS-DOS commands with single-line descriptions of each command. Entering a command name after FASTHELP displays the same command information that you would get by typing the command name with the /? switch. For example, FASTHELP VSAFE displays the same information as VSAFE /?.

Command:

An MS-DOS command listed in the special help file, DOSHELP.HLP. When you call FASTHELP without any switches, the DOSHELP.HLP file is displayed on the screen, page by page.

FASTOPEN   (external)

Decreases the amount of time required to open frequently used files and directories.

Syntax: FASTOPEN drive: [[=]number][drive:
            [[=]number][....]][/x]

drive: The hard drive whose filenames are to be cached.

number   The maximum number of filenames to be cached. Values may range from 10 to 999. The default value is 48.

Switches:

/x   Creates the filename cache in expanded memory.

Description:

When opening a file, DOS searches multiple directories to locate the file. This can be time consuming if you are using a hard drive with many subdirectories. FASTOPEN caches the filenames and their locations. If one of these files is accessed again, it can be located very quickly from the cache.

FASTOPEN works only with hard drives and does not work on networks.

A FASTOPEN command can be defined for any disk drive with up to 24 partitions. FASTOPEN requires 48 bytes for each entry. If the number of files opened exceeds the amount specified by number, un-referenced filenames are deleted from the list and the new filenames are inserted in the list accordingly.

Use the INSTALL command with your CONFIG.SYS file to automatically run FASTOPEN when booting your computer. You can also run FASTOPEN from your AUTOEXEC.BAT file.

The following starts FASTOPEN from the CONFIG.SYS file. It caches a maximum of 100 filenames on the C: drive:

```
INSTALL=C:\DOS\FASTOPEN.EXE c:=100
```

If FASTOPEN is to work with multiple hard drives, a corresponding assignment must be made for each drive. Only one FASTOPEN command is allowed. You cannot cache two drives by using two FASTOPEN commands. A single command is necessary. In the following example the access to filenames on drives C: and D: are cached:

```
FASTOPEN c:=100 d:100
```

 Do not use disk optimization programs such as Norton's Speed Disk or DEFRAG when FASTOPEN is installed. Running a disk optimization program with FASTOPEN installed may cause loss of data.

FC	(external)

Compares two files or sets of files and displays the differences between them.

Syntax: FC [/a][/c][/l][/lbn][/n][/t][/w][/nnnn]
            [drive1:][path1]filename1 [drive2:][path2]filename2
            FC /b [drive1:][path1]filename1 [drive2:][path2]
            filename2

Switches:

/a   Displays only the first and last lines for each set of differences.

/b   Performs a binary comparison.

/c   Ignore upper and lowercase letter differences.

/l   Compares files as ASCII text.

/lbn   Sets the number of lines for the internal line buffer. The default length of the line buffer is 100 lines. If the files being compared have more than this number of consecutive differing lines, only the first 100 lines are compared.

/n   Displays line numbers during ASCII comparison.

/t   Do not expand tabs to spaces.

/w   Compress white spaces (tabs and spaces) during comparison.

/nnnn   Specifies the number of consecutive lines that must
             match before FC considers the files synchronized again
             after a mismatch.

Description:

FC compares two files and reports differences between the files.
When used for an ASCII comparison, the differences between the
two files are reported in the following order: the name of the first
file, the lines that differ between the files and the first line to
match in both files. Then the name of the second file is displayed
followed by the lines from that file that differ and the first line
to match.

The following format is used to report mismatches during a binary
comparison:

    xxxxx: yy zz

The value represented by xxxxx specifies the hexadecimal address
for the pair of bytes, offset from the start of the file. yy and zz
represent the mismatched bytes from the two files being compared.

Wildcards are permitted in filenames.

FDISK   (external)

Configures a hard drive for use with MS-DOS.

Syntax: FDISK [/status]

Switch:

/status   Specify this switch to display the partition
             information without starting FDISK.

Description:

Hard drives can be divided into several different areas called
partitions. A hard drive is often pre-partitioned and preformatted when you buy your computer. If not, you must prepare
the hard drive using the FDISK command.

FDISK may be used to:

• Create a primary MS-DOS partition.

• Create an extended MS-DOS partition.

- Create logical MS-DOS drives.

- Change the active partition.

- Delete a partition.

- Display partition information.

- Select the next hard drive for partitioning on a system with multiple hard drives.

The hard drive can be divided into different partitions of varying sizes. A different operating system can then be assigned to each of these partitions.

Two different types of partitions may be placed on a hard drive: The primary DOS partition and the extended DOS partition. The primary partition contains the information necessary for booting from DOS.

The maximum partition size with MS-DOS 5.0 is 2 gigabytes, which is 2×10^9 or 2 billion bytes of storage area.

FDISK is menu-oriented. You select the options through menus instead of by parameters.

FDISK menus allow you to create a partition, change the size of a partition, delete a partition, display all of the information about a partition or select a different hard drive. This option is available only if your PC has access to several hard drives.

 It is not possible to create or delete a partition for another operating system. To do this, you must consult the documentation for each different operating system. Also, you cannot change or delete an active partition.

The information about a DOS partition looks like this:

```
                    Display Partition Information
Partition Status Type Volume Label Mbytes  System  Usage
  C: 1     A   PRI DOS DOS600        119    FAT16   100%




Total disk space is 119 Mbytes (1 Mbyte = 1048576 bytes)

Press Esc to return to FDISK Options
```

In this example, the entire drive is available as a DOS partition. If bad sectors (or tracks) are found on the hard drive, they are marked as unusable when the partition is installed. If you define the entire drive as a DOS partition, then you do not have to switch the DOS partition to active. FDISK asks you to insert the system diskette into drive A: to format the hard drive.

It's important that you format the hard drive with the /s (System transfer) switch of the FORMAT command. This copies the operating system files IBMBIO.COM, IBMDOS.COM and COMMAND.COM to the DOS partition after formatting.

The active partition is always the partition that is booted. If the entire hard drive is a DOS partition, it is always active. Otherwise FDISK displays the status of the defined partitions from which you can choose the partition you want to activate.

Setting up an unformatted hard drive

Insert the system diskette in drive A: and boot it. (For an IBM AT, you must use the diagnostics program to indicate that the drive is attached so that you can access it.)

Next use FDISK. To define the entire hard drive as a DOS partition, select menu option 1. FDISK asks if you want to use the entire hard drive as a DOS partition. Answer yes. Next you are asked to insert the system diskette in drive A:. Type the following command to format the hard drive as a system diskette:

```
FORMAT C: /s/v
```

FIND   (external)

Syntax: FIND [/v][/c][/n][/i]"str"[[drive:][path]filename[...]]

str   The character string to be searched for in a file. string must be enclosed in quotation marks. Upper and lowercase letters are searched for exactly as entered. (See switch /i below.)

drive: path
            The path to the file to be searched. Wildcards are allowed. Multiple filenames may be specified.

filename   The name of the file to be searched.

Switches:

/v   Inverts the search process — the lines which do not contain the specified string are displayed or counted.

/c   The number of lines which contain the search string are simply counted and not displayed. The /c switch disables the /n switch and has higher priority. The number of lines which contain the string are displayed adjacent to the filename.

/n   Numbers the displayed lines. The line number is displayed in square brackets without leading zeros.

/i   Specifies that the search is not case sensitive.

Description:

FIND searches a specified file or group of files for a character string and displays the line containing the string.

To search for a string containing quotation marks, enter each quotation mark as a double quote (""). For example:

```
FIND /c ".said ""You know how to format diskettes.""
demo.txt
```

To search an entire file for two specific strings, chain together two FIND commands. For example, to find all of the lines of a Pascal program that contain a BEGIN statement and a comment, type the following:

```
FIND "BEGIN" DEMO.PAS | FIND "(*"
```

See also: MORE, SORT

FOR   **(resident)**

Performs a specified command for each file in a file list.

Syntax: FOR %variable IN list DO command [parameters]
               FOR %%variable IN (list) DO command [parameters]

%%variable or %variable
            Represents a replaceable variable.

list   Specifies a list of one or more files. Wildcards are allowed.

command   Specifies the command to be performed for each file.

parameters

>   The parameters or switches for the specified command.

Description:

FOR performs a specified command for each file in a list of files. IN and DO are not parameters, but are required keywords for the FOR command.

To avoid confusion with batch file parameters, use any character other than the numerals 0 through 9 for variable.

list may be a single group of files or several groups of files. Wildcards may be used to specify a file list. Some valid file lists are:

```
(*.DOC)
(*.DOC *.TXT)
CHAPT??.DOC)
```

Example

```
FOR %a IN (*.TXT) DO TYPE %a
```

This command line displays all files, in the current directory, on the screen using the TYPE command.

This line could be used in a batch file by replacing %a with %%a.

FORMAT	(external)

Prepares a diskette or hard drive for use with MS-DOS.

Syntax: FORMAT drive: [/v[:label]][/q][/u][/f:size][/b | /s]
FORMAT drive: [/v[:label]][/q][/u]
>   [/t:tracks /n:sectors][/b | /s]
FORMAT drive: [/v[:label]][/q][/u][/1][/4][/8][/b | /s]
FORMAT drive: [/q][/u][/1][/4][/8][/b | /s]

drive: Specifies the drive containing the diskette or hard drive to be formatted. The drive must be specified.

Switches:

/v[:label]   Assigns a volume label to a diskette or hard drive.

/q	Perform a "safe" (quick) format.
/u	Perform a complete (unconditional) format.
/f:size	Specifies the size of the floppy diskette. Valid sizes are 160, 180, 320, 360, 720, 1.2, 1.44 and 2.88.
/t:yy	Format a disk with yy tracks. When possible, use the /f switch instead of this switch.
/n:xx	Format a disk with xx sectors per track. When possible, use the /f switch instead of this switch.
/1	Format the diskette as single-sided. This switch is necessary if you are using single-sided diskettes.
/4	Format a 5.25 inch diskette with a capacity of 360K in a high density drive. This switch is only relevant when formatting with 1.2 Meg drives.
/8	Format the diskette with eight sectors per track.
/b	Reserves space on a diskette for system files. (This switch is no longer necessary, but is maintained for compatibility with early versions of DOS.)
/s	Format the diskette as a system diskette. The two hidden files IO.SYS and MSDOS.SYS are copied to the formatted diskette.

Description:

A diskette or hard drive must be formatted before data can be stored on it. Formatting divides the disk into sides, tracks (cylinders) and sectors. In addition, formatting creates a File Allocation Table on the new disk. A FAT contains information about a disk's used sectors.

Since formatting erases essentially all data on a diskette or hard drive, a confirmation is required after the program is started. (Actually, MS-DOS 6.0 saves information for recovering an accidentally formatted diskette. See UNFORMAT.) FORMAT automatically assigns a volume serial number to the formatted diskette. This serial number is displayed after the format operation.

The FORMAT command defaults to formatting at the highest density possible. This density depends on the drive's capabilities.

For example, a 5.25 inch drive capable of writing to 1.2 Meg diskettes will format diskettes at 1.2 Meg, unless you instruct the drive to do otherwise. You can control the format density by using the /4 or /f:*size* switches.

To format your hard drive, make sure that the hard drive is correctly installed and partitioned. (See the FDISK command.) Format the hard drive with:

```
FORMAT c: /s /v
```

When formatting a hard drive, you'll be asked the following as a precaution:

```
WARNING! ALL DATA ON NON-REMOVABLE DISK
DRIVE C: WILL BE LOST!
Proceed with Format (Y/N)?
```

To continue to format the hard drive, press Ⓨ. Pressing Ⓝ cancels the command.

If the /u switch is not specified, or the disk is not formatted to a different size, MS-DOS performs a "safe" format. This means that the FAT (File Allocation Table) and the root directory are cleared but data is not erased. The UNFORMAT command can be used to recover this information.

Formatting checks to ensure that each sector can store data properly. If a sector is found that cannot store data, it is marked to prevent MS-DOS from using it.

If the /u switch is specified or the size of the diskette is changed, an unconditional format is performed and all data on the disk is erased.

The /n switch specifies the number of sectors per track. The /t switch specifies the number of tracks per side. These switches are alternatives to using other switches - /1, /8, etc.

The /f switch specifies the capacity of the formatted diskette in bytes, kilobytes or megabytes. This simplifies using the FORMAT command. All of the allowable formats and the corresponding switches are shown in the following table:

Format	Possible Switches
160K	/f:160 /f:160K
180K	/f:180 /f:180K
320K	/f:320 /f:320K
360K	/f:360 /f:360K
720K	/f:720 /f:720K
1.2 Meg	/f:1200 /f:1200K
	/f:1.2 /f:1.2 M
1.44 Meg	/f:1440 /f:1440K
	/f:1.44 /f:1.44M
2.88 Meg	/f:2880 /f:2880K
	/f:2.88 /f:2.88M

Not all switches are allowed with each drive. The following table provides an overview of the switches.

Drive	Allowable Switches
160/180K	/1 /4 /8 /b /n /t /v /s /f
320/360K	/1 /4 /8 /b /n /t /v /s /f
720K	/b /n /t /v /s /f
1.2 Meg	/b /n /t /v /s /f
1.44 Meg	/b /n /t /v /s /f
2.88 Meg	/b /n /t /v /s /f
hard drive	/b /v /s

Diskette Type	Drive	Tracks	Sectors	tpi	in DOS
5.25" 1s/dd	60K	40	8	48	1.0
5.25" 1s/dd	180K	40	9	48	2.0
5.25" 2s/dd	320K	40	8	48	1.1
5.25" 2s/dd	360K	40	9	48	2.0
5.25" 2s/dd	1.2 Meg	80	15	96	3.0
3.5" 2s/dd	720K	80	9	135	3.3
3.5" 2s/hd	1.44 Meg	80	18	270	3.3
3.5" 2s/hd	2.88 Meg	80	36	540	6.0

Return Values for Batch File Processing (error level):

Code	Meaning
0	FORMAT was successful, no errors
3	stopped with Ctrl + C
4	error during formatting
5	negative response to message: "Proceed with Format (Y/N?)"

GOTO   (resident)

Jump to a labeled line during execution of a batch file.

Syntax: GOTO label

label   Specifies the line in a batch program to which MS-DOS should jump.

GOTO jumps to a line, identified with a label, during a batch program. The batch file continues executing commands at the line following the label.

Labels in batch files begin with a colon and can contain spaces, but cannot include other separators, such as colons or equal signs. Only the first eight characters of a label are used.

GOTO is often used to perform conditional operations in conjunction with IF.

For more detailed information on the use of GOTO in batch files, refer to Chapter 11.

GRAFTABL   (external)

 This command isn't included with DOS 6.0. However, if you need this command, you can order a supplemental disk from Microsoft that contains this command.

Sets up MS-DOS to display an extended character set in graphics mode.

Syntax: GRAFTABL [nnn]
           GRAFTABL [/status]

Switches:

nnn   Specifies the code page number which defines the
                appearance of the characters.

/status   Identifies the active code page.

Description:

GRAFTABL affects only the appearance of external characters
(ASCII characters 128-255) in the specified code page, but does not
change the code page. To modify the code page, use MODE or
CHCP.

The following shows each valid code page ID number and its
country or language.

Code	Meaning
437	USA (standard)
850	Multilingual (Latin I)
852	Slavic (Latin II)
860	Portuguese
863	Canadian-French
865	Nordic

The /status switch displays the active code page.

If GRAFTABL is entered without switches the following
information is displayed:

```
C:>GRAFTABL
Previous Code Page: None
Active Code Page: 437
```

GRAFTABL resides in memory after being run and requires about
1K of conventional memory.

Returns Values for Batch File Processing (error level):

Code	Meaning
0	GRAFTABL was installed as resident
1	An existing table was overwritten
2	A file error occurred
3	An incorrect switch was specified, GRAFTABL terminated

Code	Meaning
4	Incorrect DOS version, DOS 5.0 is required

See also: CHCP, GRAPHICS, MODE, NLSFUNC

GRAPHICS   (external)

Loads a program to print graphics on a printer when using a color or graphics adapter.

Syntax: GRAPHICS [type]
            [[drive:][path]filename][/r][/b][/lcd]
            [/printbox:std | printbox:lcd]

drive:path filename
            Specifies the path and filename containing printer information.

Switches:

type   Specifies the type of printer. See the table below for a list of valid printer types.

[/r]   Prints the image with white characters on a black background, as it appears on your screen.

[/b]   This switch is valid for COLOR4 and COLOR8 printers. The background is printed in color.

[/lcd]   Uses the liquid crystal (LCD) aspect ratio instead of CGA aspect ratio.

/printbox:std | printbox:lcd
            Selects the size of the print-box, either std or lcd.

Description:

GRAPHICS loads a program to print graphics. The GRAPHICS command supports CGA, EGA and VGA display modes.

type is one of the following printers:

Mode	Printer
color1	IBM personal computer color printer with black ribbon
color4	IBM personal computer color printer with red, green, blue and black color ribbon
color8	IBM personal computer color printer with cyan, magenta, yellow, black ribbon
hpdefault	Any Hewlett-Packard PCL printer
deskjet	Hewlett-Packard DeskJet printer
graphics	IBM personal computer compact printer or a compatible
graphicswide	Graphic printer with wide paper (11 in.)
laserjet	Hewlett-Packard LaserJet printer
laserjetii	Hewlett-Packard LaserJet II printer
paintjet	Hewlett-Packard PaintJet printer
quietjet	Hewlett-Packard QuietJet printer
ruggedwriter	Hewlett-Packard RuggedWriter printer
ruggedwriterwide	Hewlett-Packard RuggedWriter wide printer
thermal	IBM PC convertible Thermal Printer
thinkjet	Hewlett-Packard ThinkJet printer

There is extensive information about the supported graphic printer in a file named GRAPHICS.PRO.

See also: CHCP, MODE, NLSFUNC

HELP (external)

Displays on screen help for MS-DOS commands.

Syntax: HELP [command] [/b][/g][/h][/nohi][topic]

command Specifies the name of the command about which information is required. If no command is specified, HELP displays every command and a brief summary of its function.

Switches:

/b Starts the program in monochrome mode on a color monitor.

/g Starts the program in CGA mode.

/h   Displays the maximum possible number of lines.

/nohi   Allows use of a low-resolution monitor.

The HELP command displays on screen help for every MS-DOS command. All parameters and switches are listed. A brief description of the command's function and a description of the effect of the various switches are displayed.

IF	(external)

Performs conditional processing in batch files.

Syntax: IF [NOT] ERRORLEVEL number command
            IF [NOT] string1==string2 command
            IF [NOT] EXIST filename command

[NOT]   Specifies that the command should be executed only if the condition is false.

ERRORLEVEL number
            Specifies a true condition only if the previous program run by COMMAND.COM returned an exit code equal to or greater than the value specified by number.

command   The command to execute if the preceding condition is met.

string1==string2
            The condition is true if string1 and string2 are the same. These values can be literal strings or batch variables.

EXIST filename
            If filename exists, the condition is true.

In a batch file, IF tests for specified conditions and performs or skips commands based on the outcome of the test. If the text condition is met, the command is performed; otherwise it skips to the next line of the batch file.

The double equal sign (==) tests for equality.

IF can also be combined with other conditions:

IF NOT condition

Here, if the condition is met, then the batch file execution continues with the next line. If it's not met, then the rest of the line is executed.

IF EXIST filename

Checks to see if the specified file exists. If it does, then the rest of the command line is executed. Otherwise, processing continues with the next line. A variation of this command is IF NOT EXIST. In this case, the rest of the line is processed only if the specified file does not exist.

IF ERRORLEVEL number

Checks for an error number. When certain MS-DOS commands encounter problems or errors, they return an error number to a batch file. The batch file can determine the error number by using the ERRORLEVEL parameter. If there is no error, ERRORLEVEL is 0. Otherwise the various MS-DOS commands return different values of ERRORLEVEL depending on the specific problem or error.

The commands in the IF ERRORLEVEL line are executed if the ERRORLEVEL returned is greater than or equal to the specified number. Otherwise, it skips to the next line.

INCLUDE   (resident)

Allows selection of different configurations.

Syntax: INCLUDE=blockname

This command can only be used in the CONFIG.SYS file. With INCLUDE, you can include the contents of one configuration block within another configuration block.

blockname Specify the name of the block here to be included within the current block of defined commands.

```
.....
[Normal_CONFIG]
DOS=HIGH
DEVICE=C:\DOS\HIMEM.SYS

[NETWORK_CONFIG]
INCLUDE=Normal_CONFIG
DEVICEHIGH=C:\DOS\NETWORK.SYS
.....
```

INTERLNK   (external)

Syntax: INTERLNK [client[:]=[server][:]]

Use this command to redirect requests for operations on a client drive or even on printer ports. For example, this allows you to access files from a laptop that is connected to another computer via the computer.

client   Specify the drive letter of the client drive to be redirected to a drive on the server here.

server   Define the letter of the drive here that is to be redirected.

To use this command, you must first install the INTERLNK.EXE device driver in the CONFIG.SYS file.

Type the command without any parameters to see a display of the current status of the program.

INTERSVR   (external)

Syntax: INTERSVR [drive:[...]][/x=drive:[...]]
            [/lpt:[n|address]][/com:[n|address]][/baud:rate]
            [/b][/v][/rcopy]

Use this command to start the INTERLNK server. This enables data transfer from serial or parallel ports as well as redirection of print jobs.

drive   Specify the letter of the drive being redirected here. By default, all drives are redirected.

Switches:

/x=drive   Specify drives that you don't want redirected here. By default, all drives are redirected.

/lpt:n   Specify the parallel port here to be used for data transfer. For n specify the number of the port. You can also specify the address of the parallel port for n. If you don't specify anything for n, all the ports are scanned, and the first one found will be used. By default, INTERSVR searches for both serial and parallel ports. If you specify the /lpt switch without /com, the command only searches for parallel ports.

/com:n   Specify the serial port here to be used for data transfer. For n specify the number of the port. You can also specify the address of the serial port for n. If you don't specify anything for n, all the ports are scanned, and the first one found will be used. By default, INTERSVR searches for both serial and parallel ports. If you specify the switch /COM without /LPT, the command only searches for serial ports.

/baud:rate Sets the maximum baud rate for serial connection. Possible values are: 9600, 19200, 38400, 57600 and 115200. The default value is 115200.

/b   Displays the screen of the server in black and white. Use this switch only if you have trouble reading a monochrome screen.

/v   Specify this switch to avoid problems with the computer timer. Use this switch when there is a serial connection with another computer and one computer stops running.

/rcopy   Allows copying of files from one computer to another. The computers must be connected via a 7 wire null-modem cable to each other from serial ports.

JOIN   (external)

 This command isn't included with DOS 6.0. However, if you need this command, you can order a supplemental disk from Microsoft that contains this command.

Redirects a disk drive to a directory on another disk drive.

Syntax: JOIN [drive1:][drive2:][path][/d]
          JOIN drive1: /d

drive1:   Specifies the disk drive or hard drive to be joined to a different drive and directory.

drive2:   Specifies the drive to receive the combined capacity.

path   A subdirectory of drive2; it must be empty. It must also
            be a directory other than the root directory. If the
            directory does not exist, MS-DOS tries to create it.

Switches:

/d   Cancels any previous JOIN commands for the specified
            drive.

JOIN lets you access drive1: as though it were the subdirectory
drive2:path. When you join drive1:, it becomes accessible only
through drive2:path. Trying to access drive1: produces the error
message: "Invalid drive specification".

JOIN lets you run certain software applications that don't support
a hard drive. You can set up a directory (called \HD in this
example) that points to the hard drive C:

```
JOIN A: C:\HD
```

Directory \HD is created on drive C: if it does not already exist.
Type the following line to display this directory of drive A:,
which can only be accessed as C:\HD:

```
DIR \HD
```

See also: ASSIGN, SUBST

KEYB	(external)

Sets up the keyboard for a specific language.

Syntax: KEYB [keyboard_code[,[code_page][,[drive:]
            [path]filename]]][/e][/id:idn]

keyboard_code
            The two-character codes used to define the country-
            specific keyboard.

code_page   The code page. The default is the standard character
            table.

filename   The keyboard definition file, usually the file
            KEYBOARD.SYS. This parameter is required if it is
            not in the root directory.

Switches:

/e   Specifies that an enhanced keyboard is installed.

/id:idn   Defines the keyboard used in countries that have different models. This switch is only necessary in countries that have more than one keyboard layout for the same language (France, Italy and the United Kingdom).

Description:

The following table shows valid values for keyboard_code, the code_page and idn (when necessary):

Country	Keyboard code	Code Page	ID
Australia	US	850,437	
Belgium	BE	850,437	
Brazil	BR	850,437	
Canada (Fr.)	CF	850,863	
Canada, Engl.	US	850,437	
Czech	CZ	852,850	
Slovak	SL	852,850	
Denmark	DK	850,865	
Finland	SU	850,437	
France	FR	850,437	120,189
Germany	GR	850,437	
Hungary	HU	852,850	
Italy	IT	850,437	141,142
Latin America	LA	850,437	
Netherlands	NL	850,437	
Norway	NO	850,865	
Poland	PL	852,850	
Portugal	PO	850,860	
Spain	SP	850,437	
Sweden	SV	850,437	
Switzerland (French)	SF	850,437	
Switzerland (German)	SG	850,437	
United Kingdom	UK	850,437	166,168
United States	US	850,437	
Yugoslavia	YU	852,850	

There are different keyboard arrangements available for Great Britain, France and Italy. The value of idn specifies the keyboard model required.

The code page specifies the character set table that should be used to display the character on the screen when a given key is pressed. The supported character set tables are:

Character table
437   USA (standard IBM character set)
850   multi-language
852   Slavic
860   Portugal
863   French Canadian and French
865   Nordic countries (Denmark, Norway)

Not every character set table can be used with each keyboard arrangement. The following table lists which keyboard driver may be combined with the respective character set tables:

Set	Country
437	BE, BR, SU, FR, GR, IT, LA, NL, SP, SV, SF, SG, UK, US
850	BE, BR, CF, CZ, SL, DK, SU, FR, GR, HU, IT, LA, NL, NO, PL, PO, SP, SV, SF, SG, UK, US, YU
852	CZ, SL, HU, PL, YU
860	PO
863	CF
865	DK, NO

To use a Portuguese keyboard arrangement, type the following command:

```
KEYB po, 860
```

If the file KEYBOARD.SYS is not in the main directory, specify the path:

```
KEYB po, 860, c:\dos
```

If you don't want to define a character set table, you can omit the second parameter:

```
KEYB po, ,c:\dos\keyboard.sys
```

If KEYB is entered without parameters, the current settings are displayed:

```
KEYB
Actual keyboard code: UK Character set table:   437
Active character set table not usable from    unit CON
```

See also: CHCP, MODE, NLSFUNC, SELECT

LABEL	(external)

Creates, changes or deletes the volume label of a disk.

Syntax: LABEL [drive:][name]

drive: The drive that contains the disk to be named. If omitted, the current drive is assumed.

name   The volume label.

Description:

LABEL assigns a volume label to a disk. The volume label may contain up to 11 characters.

If name is omitted, the following DOS message prompts you for a new volume label:

```
Volume label (11 characters, ENTER for none)?
```

To change the volume label, type the new volume label and press Enter.

To delete the previous volume label, press Enter:

```
LABEL C:harddisk
LABEL A:
Volume label (11 characters, ENTER for none)?
```

If a volume label exists, pressing Enter without entering text at the "Volume label" prompt displays:

```
Delete current volume label (Y/N)?
```

LH   (resident)

Loads a program into the upper memory area of the computer.

Syntax: LH [drive:][path]filename [parameters]
            LH [/l:region1[,minsize1]
            [;region2[,minsize2]...][/s]]
            [drive:][path]filename [parameters]

parameters
            Any command line information required by the
            program to be loaded.

Switches

/l:region1,minsize1;region2,minsize2
            This switch allows you to determine a specific area in
            memory for loading the device drivers. To display the
            memory areas, call MEM /f. When you define the
            memory area, it is only possible to load the device
            drivers into this particular memory area; no other
            areas may be used. However, some device drivers
            require several areas. To select more than one memory
            area, use semicolons in between each memory area you
            specify.

            You can also define a minimum size for each area.

/s   The UMBs (Upper Memory Blocks) are reduced to
            minimum size when the drivers are loaded. This
            switch makes the best use of memory. Ordinarily, you
            only use this switch with MEMMAKER.

Description:

LH loads a program into the upper memory area leaving more room
in conventional memory for other programs.

Before you can use LH, you must install the HIMEM.SYS driver
and include the DOS=UMB command in your CONFIG.SYS file.

If there is insufficient space to load a program into the upper
memory area, MS-DOS loads the program into conventional
memory. There is no indication from MS-DOS as to which memory
area was used.

For convenience, you can use the LH command from your
AUTOEXEC.BAT file.

See also: LOADHIGH

LOADFIX   (external)

Loads a program into the memory area above 64K and runs the program.

Syntax: LOADFIX [drive:][path]filename

[drive:][path]filename
            Complete path and name of file to load and execute.

MS-DOS 6.0 is able to "free" certain areas of conventional memory. Some programs won't run properly, especially ones which expect to be loaded at a specific memory location. LOADFIX loads and runs programs that produce the "Packed file corrupt" error message.

LOADFIX can also load some programs which fail to load in a network environment.

LOADHIGH   (resident)

Loads a program into the upper memory area of the computer.

Syntax: LOADHIGH [drive:][path]filename [parameters]
            LOADHIGH [/l:region1[,minsize1]
            [;region2[,minsize2]...][/s]]
            [drive:][path]filename [parameters]

parameters
            Any command line information required by the program to be loaded.

Switches

/l:region1,minsize1;region2,minsize2
            This switch allows you to determine a specific area in memory for loading the device drivers. To display the memory areas, call MEM /F. When you define the memory area, it is only possible to load the device drivers into this particular memory area; no other areas may be used. However, some device drivers require several areas. To select more than one memory area, use semicolons in between each memory area you specify.

            You can also define a minimum size for each area.

/s   The UMBs (Upper Memory Blocks) are reduced to
            minimum size when the drivers are loaded. This
            switch makes the best use of memory. Ordinarily, you
            only use this switch with MEMMAKER.

Description:

LOADHIGH loads a program into the upper memory area leaving
more room in conventional memory for other programs.

Before you can use LOADHIGH, you must install the HIMEM.SYS
driver and include the DOS=UMB command in your CONFIG.SYS
file.

```
DEVICE=HIMEM.SYS
DEVICE=EMM386.EXE RAM
REM or DEVICE=EMM386.EXE NOEMS
DOS=UMB
REM or DOS=HIGH,UMB
```

If there is insufficient space to load a program into the upper
memory area, MS-DOS loads the program into conventional
memory. There is no indication from MS-DOS as to which memory
area was used.

For convenience, you can use the LOADHIGH command from your
AUTOEXEC.BAT file.

MD   (resident)

Creates a new directory.

Syntax: MD [drive:]path

drive: The drive on which the new directory is to be created.

path   Name and location of the new directory.

Description:

MD creates a new subdirectory on drive:.

If the new subdirectory is to appear in the root directory, path
must be preceded by a backslash symbol (\). If this symbol is
omitted, the subdirectory is created as a subdirectory of the current
directory.

     Don't use MD when the SUBST command is active.

See also: MKDIR

MEM	(external)

Displays information about memory usage in your system.

Syntax: MEM [/classify | /debug | /free |
           /module modulename] [/page]

Switches:

/classify or /c
:   Displays summarized information about the memory usage of programs and unused space.

/debug or /d
:   Displays information about the memory usage of programs, drivers, internal buffers, etc.

/free or /f   Displays the free memory areas in conventional and upper memory. Also includes the total memory allocation.

/module or /m
:   Displays information about the about how the specified program is being used in memory. The display includes the memory areas being allocated by the program with the address and size of each area.

/page or /p
:   Page by page display. When the screen fills up, the display stops, and doesn't start again until you press a key.

Description:

The MEM command displays information about the memory of your computer. Information about the extended and expanded memory as well as the main memory is given.

Typing MEM with no switches displays a screen similar to the following:

```
Memory Type         Total =   Used +  Free
----------------    ------    ------  ------
Conventional         640K      25K     615K
Upper                155K      82K      73K
Adapter RAM/ROM      256K      256K     0K
Extended (XMS)       1635K     1265K   15092K
                    ------    ------  ------
Total memory        17400K    1629K   15779K

Total under 1 MB     795K      108K    687K

Largest executable program size      615K (629472 bytes)
Largest free upper memory block       72K (74144 bytes)
MS-DOS is resident in the high memory area.
```

Entering MEM /c will display information similar to the following:

```
Modules using memory below 1 MB:

  Name        Total        = Conventional  + Upper Memory
  --------    ----------     ------------     ------------
  MSDOS       17293  (17K)   17293  (17K)        0    (0K)
  HIMEM        1152   (1K)    1152   (1K)        0    (0K)
  EMM386       4144   (4K)    4144   (4K)        0    (0K)
  COMMAND      2960   (3K)    2960   (3K)        0    (0K)
  SBPCD       10048  (10K)       0   (0K)    10048   (10K)
  SMARTDRV    26784  (26K)       0   (0K)    26784   (26K)
  MSCDEX      46576  (45K)       0   (0K)    46576   (45K)
  FIXDSK        560   (1K)       0   (0K)      560    (1K)
  MODE          480   (0K)       0   (0K)      480    (0K)
  Free       703952 (687K)  629568 (615K)    74384   (73K)

Memory Summary:

Type of Memory        Total      =      Used       +      Free
----------------    -----------     -----------         -----------
Conventional         655360 (640K)     25792  (25K)     629568  (615K)
Upper                158832 (155K)     84448  (82K)      74384   (73K)
Adapter RAM/ROM      262144 (256K)    262144 (256K)          0    (0K)
Extended (XMS)     16749456 (16357K) 1295248 (1265K) 15454208 (15092K)
                   ---------          ---------        ---------
Total memory       17825792 (17408K) 1667632 (1629K) 16158160 (15779K)

Total under 1 MB    814192   (795K)   110240  (108K)   703952  (687K)

Largest executable program size      629472   (615K)
Largest free upper memory block       74144   (72K)
MS-DOS is resident in the high memory area.
```

Entering MEM /d will display information similar to the following:

```
Conventional Memory Detail:

Segment          Total            Name        Type
-------          ----------------  -----------  --------
00000            1039    (1K)                  Interrupt Vector
00040             271    (0K)                  ROM Communication Area
00050             527    (1K)                  DOS Communication Area
00070            2864    (3K)     IO           System Data
                                  CON          System Device Driver
                                  AUX          System Device Driver
                                  PRN          System Device Driver
                                  CLOCK$       System Device Driver
                                  A: - E:      System Device Driver
                                  COM1         System Device Driver
                                  LPT1         System Device Driver
                                  LPT2         System Device Driver
                                  LPT3         System Device Driver
                                  COM2         System Device Driver
                                  COM3         System Device Driver
                                  COM4         System Device Driver
00123            5136    (5K)     MSDOS        System Data
00264           12688   (12K)     IO           System Data
                 1136    (1K)     XMSXXXX0     Installed Device=HIMEM
                 4128    (4K)     EMMQXXX0     Installed Device=EMM386
                 2368    (2K)                  FILES=45
                  256    (0K)                  FCBS=4
                  512    (1K)                  BUFFERS=40
                 1152    (1K)                  LASTDRIVE=M
                 3008    (3K)                  STACKS=9,256
0057D              80    (0K)     MSDOS        System Program
00582            2640    (3K)     COMMAND      Program
00627              80    (0K)     MSDOS        -- Free --
0062C             320    (0K)     COMMAND      Environment
00640             256    (0K)     MEM          Environment
00650           88608   (87K)     MEM          Program
01BF2          540880  (528K)     MSDOS        -- Free --

Upper Memory Detail:

Segment  Region    Total           Name        Type
-------  ------   ----------------  -----------  --------
0C93A      1      10032   (10K)    IO           System Data
                  10000   (10K)    MSCD001      Installed Device=SBPCD
0CBAD      1         48    (0K)    MSDOS        -- Free --
0CBB0      1      26784   (26K)    SMARTDRV     Program
0D23A      1        192    (0K)    MSDOS        -- Free --
0D246      1      46576   (45K)    MSCDEX       Program
0DDA5      1        208    (0K)    FIXDSK       Environment
0DDB2      1        480    (0K)    MODE         Program
0DDD0      1        352    (0K)    FIXDSK       Program
0DDE6      1      74144   (72K)    MSDOS        -- Free --

Memory Summary:

Type of Memory      Total         =      Used    +     Free
----------------  ----------------     ---------------  ----------------
Conventional       655360   (640K)      25792    (25K)   629568   (615K)
Upper              158832   (155K)      84448    (82K)    74384    (73K)
Adapter RAM/ROM    262144   (256K)     262144   (256K)        0     (0K)
Extended (XMS)   16749456 (16357K)    1295248  (1265K) 15454208 (15092K)
----------------  ----------------     ---------------  ----------------
Total memory     17825792 (17408K)    1667632  (1629K) 16158160 (15779K)

Total under 1 MB   814192   (795K)     110240   (108K)   703952   (687K)

Memory accessible using Int 15h              0     (0K)
Largest executable program size         629472   (615K)
Largest free upper memory block          74144    (72K)
MS-DOS is resident in the high memory area.

XMS version 3.00; driver version 3.09
```

Entering MEM /f displays information similar to the following:

```
Free Conventional Memory:

  Segment          Total
  -------    ----------------
  00627           80    (0K)
  00640          256    (0K)
  00650        88608   (87K)
  01BF2       540880  (528K)

  Total Free: 629824  (615K)

Free Upper Memory:

  Region   Largest Free      Total Free       Total Size
  ------   ------------      ----------       ----------
     1      74144  (72K)     74384  (73K)    158832  (155K)
```

Entering MEM /m:COMMAND displays information about COMMAND.COM similar to the following:

```
COMMAND is using the following memory:

  Segment  Region     Total         Type
  -------  ------   ----------     -------
  00582             2640    (3K)   Program
  0062C              320    (0K)   Environment
                   ----------
  Total Size:       2960    (3K)
```

See also: CHKDSK

MEMMAKER   (external)

Optimizes memory.

Syntax: MEMMAKER [/b][/batch][/session][/swap:drive][/t]
            [/undo][/w:size1,size2]

Use this command to start a program for optimizing the memory of
your computer. It loads a menu-driven program that installs device
drivers and linked programs in CONFIG.SYS in such a way that
optimum memory division is achieved.

You can only use this program with a 386 or 486 computer.

Switches:

/b   Runs MEMMAKER in black and white (monochrome)
            mode.

/batch   Program automatically runs without user
            specifications. If the program encounters an error, your
            old configuration files are automatically used again
            and the changes made by MEMMAKER are discarded.

/session   Used by MEMMAKER during optimization.

/swap:drive

Specifies the drive that was originally your startup drive. This is only necessary if the startup drive has changed since the last start.

/t   Disables IBM Token-Ring network detection.

/undo   Undoes the last changes MEMMAKER made to the configuration files.

/w:size1,size2

If you are running Windows, you can specify how much upper memory to reserve for the Windows translation buffers. This requires two memory areas. By default, MEMMAKER reserves two 12K memory areas for these buffers. However, you can specify your own sizes here. If you don't use Windows, specify /w:0,0 here so that MEMMAKER doesn't reserve any memory for Windows.

MENUCOLOR   (resident)

Specifies menu colors in the startup menu as called by CONFIG.SYS.

Syntax: MENUCOLOR x[,y]

You can only use this command in the CONFIG.SYS file. Use it to specify the color of the text and the background color of the startup menu.

x   Specifies the text color of the startup menu. Possible values range from 0 to 15. The table below lists the colors associated with the values.

y   Specifies the background color of the startup menu. Possible values range from 0 to 15. The following table lists the colors associated with the values.

Table of color values:

0	Black
1	Blue
2	Green

3	Cyan
4	Red
5	Magenta
6	Brown
7	White
8	Gray
9	Bright blue
10	Bright green
11	Bright cyan
12	Bright red
13	Bright magenta
14	Yellow
15	Bright white

See also: MENUDEFAULT, MENUITEM

MENUDEFAULT   (resident

Specifies the default menu item that appears in the startup menu.

Syntax: MENUDEFAULT blockname[,timeout]

You can only use this command in the CONFIG.SYS. Use it to specify which menu is used as the default menu when you start the computer. This menu is highlighted and its number appears as the default selection after the "Enter a choice:" prompt. If you don't use this command, the first choice appears after the prompt by default.

You can also set a timeout for this command, after which the default menu will automatically be used to configure the computer.

blockname Specify the name of the menu to be used as the default here.

timeout   Specify a timeout here, after which the specified default menu will automatically be used. Set a value between 0 and 90 seconds for Timeout. If you define a timeout of 0, the default menu is automatically used.

See also: MENUCOLOR, MENUITEM, SUBMENU

| MENUITEM | (resident) |

Defines a menu item on the startup menu as called from CONFIG.SYS.

Syntax: MENUITEM blockname[,menu_text]

This command can only be used in the CONFIG.SYS file. Use it to define an item in the startup menu. You can define up to 9 items for the startup menu.

blockname Define the name of the menu item to be entered in the startup menu. This menu item must defined somewhere in the CONFIG.SYS file. When this item is selected from the menu, MS-DOS runs all the configuration commands that go with it.

menu_text Specify text for the menu item. If you don't specify any text, MS-DOS displays the block name as the menu text.

See also: MENUCOLOR, MENUDEFAULT, SUBMENU

| MIRROR | (external) |

☞   This command isn't included with DOS 6.0. However, if you need this command, you can order a supplemental disk from Microsoft that contains this command.

Saves information about disks for use by the UNFORMAT and UNDELETE commands.

Syntax: MIRROR [drive: [...]] [/1][/tdrive:[-entries][...]]
           MIRROR [/u]
           MIRROR [/partn]

drive: Specifies the drive about which information will be saved.

Switches:

/1   Save only the most recent information about the disk. If this switch is omitted, MIRROR makes a backup copy of the existing disk information file before saving the current information.

/tdrive[- entries]

Loads a program for recording information (deletion tracking file) to be used by the UNDELETE command. The required parameter, drive, specifies the disk to be mirrored. The entries parameter specifies the maximum number of entries to be contained in the deletion tracking file (PCTRACKR.DEL). The value must be in the range of 1 - 999.

/u   Removes the program for recording UNDELETE information (deletion tracking file) from memory.

/partn   Saves hard drive partitioning information.

MIRROR saves a copy of the File Allocation Table (FAT) and the root directory of the disk of the specified drive. This information is used by the UNFORMAT command to rebuild a disk which has accidentally been formatted.

This information should be saved frequently. You can add a MIRROR command to your AUTOEXEC.BAT file.

You can also save information about the partitioning of your hard drive. Every hard drive has at least one partition and the information about the partition is stored in a special disk partition table. If this table becomes corrupted, MS-DOS can't access the hard drive.

The partition information can be saved by using MIRROR with the /PARTN switch. This switch creates a file called PARTNSAV.FIL. This file is used by the UNFORMAT command to reconstruct the partition table. This file (PARTNSAV.FIL) should not be saved on your hard drive.

See also: UNDELETE, UNFORMAT

MKDIR   (resident)

Creates a new directory.

Syntax: MKDIR [drive:]path
          MD [drive:]path

drive: The drive on which the new directory will be created. If omitted, the current drive is assumed.

path   The name and location of the new directory.

Description:

MKDIR or MD creates a new subdirectory on drive:.

If the new subdirectory is to appear in the root directory, path must be preceded by a backslash symbol (\). If this symbol is omitted, the subdirectory is created as a subdirectory of the current directory.

    Don't use MKDIR or MD when the SUBST command is active.

See also: CD, RD

MODE (Set Display Mode)   **(external)**

This form of MODE selects the display mode or reconfigures the active display adapter.

Syntax: MODE [display_adapter][,shift[,t]]
            MODE [display_adapter][,n]
            MODE con[:][cols=c][lines=n]

display_adapter
            This is one of the following:

Code	Meaning
mono	Sets the display for the monochrome adapter (80-character text)
40	Sets the screen width to 40 characters per line for the CGA
80	Sets the screen width to 80 characters per line for the CGA
co40	Sets display for CGA using 40 columns
co80	Sets display for CGA using 80 columns
bw40	Sets the display for the CGA using 40 columns in monochrome
bw80	Sets the display for the CGA using 80 columns in monochrome

shift	Shift the display to the right or left. An 80-column display is shifted by two columns and a 40-column display is shifted by one column. Valid values for shift are L (for left) and R (for right).
t	Enables aligning screen by using a test pattern.
con:	Refers to monitor.
cols=	Specifies the number of characters per column.
lines=	Specifies number of lines that can be displayed on the screen.

Description:

MODE sets the CGA for 40- or 80-column display in either monochrome or color.

The optional parameters allow for the adjustment of the display.

MODE (Configure Printer)   (external)

This form of MODE configures a printer connected to the parallel printer port (generally, LPT1).

Syntax: MODE lptn[:][cols=c][,[lines=l][,retry=r]]

lptn	The printer port device. It can be LPT1, LPT2 or LPT3.
cols	The number of print characters per line. It can be either 80 or 132. The default value is 80.
lines	The number of lines per inch for vertical spacing. It can be either 6 or 8. The default value is 6.
retry	Specifies the retry action to take if a time-out occurs. This parameter causes a part of MODE to remain resident in memory. See below for a list of valid values for r.

Description:

MODE sets the printer device for 80 or 132 column line widths and/or 6 or 8 lines per inch of vertical spacing.

Valid values for retry

b	Return "busy" from a status check of a busy port
e	Return an error from a status check of a busy port
p	Continue retrying until printer accepts output
r	Return "Ready" from a status check of a busy port
n	Take no retry action (default value)

You can interrupt a time-out loop by pressing ⌐Ctrl⌐+⌐C⌐.

MODE (Configure Serial Port)   (external)

This form of MODE sets the operating characteristics of the serial port.

Syntax: MODE comn[:][b[,p[,d[,s[,r]]]]]
            MODE comn[:][baud=b] [parity=p]
            [data=d][stop=s][retry=r]

comn   Specifies the number of the asynchronous communications port. This can be COM1 through COM4.

b or baud   The baud rate. baud can be 110, 150, 300, 600, 1200, 2400, 4800, 9600 or 19,200. You may abbreviate baud to its first two digits.

p or parity The type of parity checking. Parity can be E (even), O (odd) or N (none), M (mark) or S (space). If omitted, E is assumed. Not all computers support the M and S switches.

d or data   The number of data bits. bits can be in the range of 5 through 8. If this parameter is omitted, 7 is assumed.

s or stop   The number of stop bits. stop can be 1, 1.5 or 2. If omitted and baud is 110, than 2 is assumed. Otherwise 1 is assumed.

r or retry Specifies the retry action if a time-out occurs when port is busy.

Description:

MODE sets the asynchronous communications port parameters.

Valid retry actions

e	Return an error from a status check of a busy port
b	Return "busy" from a status check of a busy port
p	Continue retrying until printer accepts output
r	Return "Ready" from a status check of a busy port
n	Take no retry action (default value)

MODE (Redirect Printing)   (external)

This form of MODE redirects all output from the parallel port to the serial port.

Syntax: MODE lptn[:]= comn[:]

lptn   The printer port device. This device can be LPT1, LPT2 or LPT3.

comn   The serial communication port. Valid ranges for comn port are 1 through 4. The serial port must be initialized with MODE comn before redirecting the output to the parallel port.

Description:

MODE redirects the data from the printer port to the asynchronous communications port (the serial port).

MODE (Set Device Code Pages)   (external)

This form of MODE prepares, selects, refreshes or displays the numbers of the code pages for parallel printers or the console.

Syntax: MODE device codepage prepare= ((yyy [...])
             [drive:][path][filename])
             MODE device codepage select=yyy
             MODE device codepage [/status]
             MODE device codepage refresh

device   One of the devices CON, LPT1, LPT2, LPT3 or PRN.

yyy   Number of the code page to prepare.

437	United States
850	Multilingual (Latin I)
852	Slavic (Latin II)
860	Portuguese
863	Canadian-French
865	Nordic

drive:path filename
> The complete path parameters of the file containing the code page information. The system diskettes contain these parameters with the file extension .CPI.

/status
> Returns status of the current code pages selected or prepared for the specified device.

refresh
> Reinstates the prepared code pages if they are lost as a result of a hardware problem or other error.

Description:

The MODE command handles code page activity for device. The keyword codepage (abbreviated cp) is required.

You prepare a device driver for a character set table with the prepare parameter.

```
MODE lpt1 codepage prep=((437,860) 4201.cpi)
MODE lpt1 codepage prep=(437 4201.cpi)
```

Following the prepare keyword (abbreviation prep) you can specify a character set table as a file. The following files are on the system diskette:

```
4201.CPI   IBM PC graphic printer II
4208.CPI   IBM Proprinter, IBM Proprinter XL
5202.CPI   IBM PC Quietwriter III Model 5202
EGA.CPI    Enhanced graphics adapter (EGA) or IBM PS/2
LCD.CPI    IBM PC Liquid Crystal display
```

A character set table can be selected after this definition at any time. Select the next set with the select keyword. The following example selects the character set table 860 for the LPT1 device driver:

```
MODE lpt1 codepage select=860
```

When you want to know the current status of a device driver, use the /status switch to display the current character set table and a driver list:

```
MODE lpt1 codepage /status
```

The refresh command reactivates the last defined character set table of a device driver. For example, if the printer has been switched off, reactivate it as follows:

```
MODE lpt1 codepage refresh
```

Programming the keyboard

```
MODE con[:] rate=repetition delay=delay
```

When you hold down a key on the keyboard of your computer, the corresponding character is repeated after .5 seconds with a repeat frequency of 10 characters per second. This operation is called typematic. With old AT keyboards the delay and the repeat frequency can be programmed. The repeat frequency should be set to 32 characters per second and the delay to .25 seconds:

```
MODE con rate=32 delay=1
```

If the keyboard on your computer cannot be programmed, you'll receive the following error message:

```
Function is not supported by this system
```

Output of device status

```
MODE [device] [/sta[tus]]
```

The MODE command can influence components of the input/output devices. MODE can display a device status list. To do this, give the MODE command without parameters.

See also: CHCP, GRAPHICS, KEYB, NLSFUNC

MORE   **(external)**

Displays one screen of output at a time.

Syntax: MORE < [drive:][path]filename
            command | MORE

[drive:][path]filename

Displays the name and path of the file to be used for storing the temporary file used by MORE.

command   Any MS-DOS command.

Description:

MORE is used to prevent the screen from scrolling. It temporarily halts screen output of lengthy files before information scrolls off the screen.

MORE is a filter command that is used in conjunction with other DOS commands such as TYPE or DIR.

For example, to display the contents of a large subdirectory, the following command line could be used:

```
DIR | MORE
```

When one full screen is displayed, DOS waits for you to press any key, except Ctrl + Break, to display the next screen. This key combination terminates the command.

You can redirect input to MORE with the < symbol:

```
MORE < file.txt
```

Note that a space separates MORE from the < symbol. When all but the last line of the screen is filled, the following message appears:

```
--More--
```

Press any key to display the next full screen of data.

See also: DIR, FIND, SORT, TYPE

MOVE   (external)

Moves files (copies files to new location then deletes original files).

Syntax: MOVE filename destination

Use this command to move files. When you move files, they are deleted from their original location and copied to the destination.

You can also use this command to rename directories. Specify a directory name for both the filename and the destination.

filename   Enter the name of the file you want moved here. You can also use wildcards in the filename. You can include the entire path in the filename. Instead of a file, you can also specify a directory and/or a drive here.

destination
            Specify a directory or drive here as the destination for the file, file group or directory being moved.

The following command line moves all files with the BAT file extension from the TEST directory to the BAT directory.

```
MOVE C:\TEST\*.BAT C:\BAT
```

MSAV	(external)

Runs Microsoft Anti-Virus program.

Syntax: MSAV [drive:][/s|/c][/r][/a|/l][/n][/p][/f][/video]

Use this command to start the MS-DOS virus protection program. Call the command without any switches to start MSAV; you can then begin working with the menu-driven program.

drive   Specify the drive you want to check for viruses here. In addition to specifying the drive, you can also specify a path so that only the files in the specified path are checked for viruses.

Switches:

/s   Checks the files specified under drive for viruses. If any viruses are found, they won't be corrected. This is the default setting.

/c   The files specified under drive are checked for viruses, and MSAV corrects any viruses it finds.

/r   Creates an information file called MSAV.TXT, which displays the number of files checked for viruses. The file also displays the number of viruses found and corrected.

/a	All drives are checked for viruses except for drives A and B.
/l	All drives are checked for viruses except network drives.
/n	Disables the display of MSAV. After the program is finished running, the MSAV.TXT file is displayed, containing information about the number of files searched, the number of viruses found and corrected.
/p	MSAV is displayed in command line mode.
/f	Disables display of the filenames checked for viruses. Use this switch only with /p or /n.
/video	Sets display in specified screen mode. The following settings are permitted:

25	Display in 25 lines. This is the default setting.
28	Display in 28 lines, only possible with VGA monitors.
43	Display in 43 lines, possible for EGA and VGA monitors.
50	Display in 50 lines, only possible with VGA monitors.
60	Display in 60 lines, only possible with Video 7 monitors.
in	Runs MSAV in color mode, even if no color graphic is found.
bw	Runs MSAV in black and white mode.
mono	Runs MSAV in monochrome mode.
lcd	Runs MSAV in LCD mode.
ff	Only for CGA monitors. Uses the fastest screen updating, which may decrease the quality of the display.

bf   Video output using information from the
              computer's BIOS.

nf   No alternate fonts may be selected.

bt   Enables use of a graphics mouse under
              Windows.

ngm   Runs MSAV with default mouse character
              instead of graphics character.

le   Switches left and right mouse buttons.

ps2   Resets mouse when it locks up or disappears.

MSBACKUP   (external)

Syntax: MSBACKUP [setup_file][/bw I /lcd I /mda]

Use this command to make backup copies of one or more files,
directories, the hard drive or a diskette. You can also use this
command to restore data.

setup_file Loads the specified SETUP file with the program.

Switches:

/bw   Runs the program in black & white mode.

/lcd   Runs the program in LCD mode.

/mda   Starts the program in monochrome mode.

MSD   (external)

Displays technical information about your computer system.

Syntax: MSD [/i][/f[drive:][path]filename]
            [/p[drive:][path][filename][/b]

Use this program to display information about your computer. If
you call MSD without any switches, the menu-driven program
appears, and you can display information about your computer.

Switches:

/i   Use this switch to bypass the hardware check at the start of the program. Instead, you must enable the various highlighted letters to check the hardware. This is practical when you have problems starting MSD.

/ffilename

When you specify this switch, MSD prompts you to enter your name, company, address, country, telephone number and other comments. After that, the program writes a complete report to a file, whose name and path you enter after the switch.

/pfilename

Specify this switch to have MSD write a complete report to a file, whose name and path you specify after the switch.

/sfilename

Specify this switch to have MSD write a short report to a file, whose name and path you specify after the switch.

/b   Runs the program in black and white mode.

NLSFUNC   (external)

Loads information to support extended country-specific code-page switching.

Syntax: NLSFUNC [drive:][path] filename

[drive:][path] filename

The name of a file containing country-specific information. By default this is the file COUNTRY.SYS in the root directory.

Description:

NLSFUNC loads country-specific information used by CHCP, MODE CP, KEYB and other device drivers.

If filename is omitted, the file specified by the country command in the CONFIG.SYS file is used. If the country command is not in the CONFIG.SYS file, the file COUNTRY.SYS is used.

See also: CHCP, MODE

NUMLOCK   (resident)

Syntax: NUMLOCK=[on | off]

Use this command in the CONFIG.SYS to specify whether the
Num Lock key is enabled or disabled after the computer boots up.

Switches:

on   Num Lock key is enabled.

off   Num Lock key is disabled.

PATH   (resident)

Sets the search path for executable files.

Syntax: PATH [[drive:][path][;[drive:]path]...]

drive: path
             The drive and path of the directories to be searched.
             Multiple drives and directories are searched in the
             order they appear. If drive: path is omitted, the
             current search path is displayed.

Description:

PATH specifies the directory or directories that are to be searched
for commands or batch files not found in the current directory. The
search path is defined as the directories specified by the
parameters drive:path. Multiple parameters are separated by a
semicolon (;).

Each use of the PATH command replaces any previous search
path.

The PATH command with only a semicolon (;) clears the search
path.

The maximum length of the PATH command is 127 characters.

See also: APPEND, SET

PAUSE   (resident)

Suspends processing of a batch program.

Syntax: PAUSE

PAUSE temporarily suspends the processing of a batch file and displays the message: "Press any key to continue...".

It is often used to allow the user to respond to a prompt or condition, such as to insert a diskette into the disk drive. Processing of the batch file continues when a key is pressed.

POWER   (external)

Syntax: POWER [adv[:max | reg | min] | std | off]

Use this command to reduce your computer's power consumption when it is idle. If you call the command without any switches, it also displays the current status of the program. To enable the program, link the POWER.EXE device driver to the CONFIG.SYS.

Switches:

adv[:max | reg | min]
> This switch determines how much power is saved. Since the power consumption of the computer can change when an application is not idling, you should experiment with different values. The following values are available:

> max   Maximum power conservation.

> reg   The default value. Balances power conservation with the performance of applications and devices.

> min   Minimum power conservation. Use this value only if you have trouble with the other two values.

adv:std   Use this switch only if the computer supports the APM specification (Advances Power Management). If this switch is specified, only the power management features of your computer are used. If your computer does not support this specification, specifying this switch disables power management.

adv:off   Disables power management.

PRINT   (external)

Prints a text file in background mode while processing of other commands continues.

Syntax: PRINT[/d:device][/b:buffersize][/u:ticks1]
               [/m:ticks2][/s:ticks3][/q:qsize][/t][[drive:][path]
               filename[...][/c][/p]

/d:device   Specifies the printer device. Valid devices are PRN:, LPT1:, LPT2:, LPT3:, COM1: and COM2:. If device is omitted, PRN is assumed.

/b:buffersize

               Specifies the size of the memory area reserved for storing data before it is sent to the printer. The default buffer size is 512 bytes. The maximum size is 16384 bytes.

/u:ticks1   Specifies the maximum number of timer ticks that PRINT will wait while the printer is busy. Ticks occur about 18 times per second. The valid range is 1 - 255. If this parameter is omitted, 1 is assumed.

/m:tick2   Specifies the number of timer units that PRINT can take to send a character to the printer. If this parameter is omitted, 2 is assumed.

/s:tick3   Specifies the number of clock ticks that the MS-DOS scheduler allocates for background printing. The valid range is 1 to 255. If this parameter is omitted, 8 is assumed.

/q:qsize   Specifies the maximum number of files in the print queue (4 to 32). If this parameter is omitted, 10 is assumed.

Switches:

/t   Removes all files from the print queue.

/c   Removes a specified file from the print queue.

drive: pathname

The filename to be added or deleted from the print queue. Wildcards are allowed.

/p   Adds preceding and subsequent filenames to the print queue.

The previous parameters can be specified only the first time PRINT is used.

Description:

PRINT prints a series of files to the printer while you are performing other tasks. This is known as print spooling.

You cannot send any other output to the printer while PRINT is running.

PRINT automatically sends a form feed after a file has been printed.

The advantage of using the PRINT command is that you can define multiple files to be printed and they are all printed in sequence.

The following defines a print queue for LPT1, a queue size of 32 files and a buffer of 2048 bytes:

```
PRINT /d:LPT1 /q:32 /b:2048 /s:10 /m:4 /u:3
```

The following command prints all of the files with an extension of .TXT, as well as the file READ.ME. The file OLD.TXT is removed from the print queue:

```
PRINT *.TXT /p OLD.TXT /c READ.ME /p
```

PROMPT   (resident)

Defines the appearance of the MS-DOS system prompt.

Syntax: PROMPT [string]

string   The new system prompt. If string is omitted, the standard system prompt is assumed.

Description:

Normally the system prompt appears as the current drive identifier followed by the greater than symbol (e.g., A:>). The PROMPT command changes the appearance of the system prompt.

To define the appearance of the prompt, you can include the PROMPT command in an AUTOEXEC.BAT file. The string parameter is composed of printable characters and/or the following codes. These codes can be used anywhere in the string and as often as necessary:

Code	Meaning
$b	Pipe symbol (│)
$d	System date
$e	Escape character (01bh)
$g	Greater than symbol (>)
$h	Backspace deletes the previous character
$l	Less than symbol (<)
$n	Current drive
$p	Current drive and path
$q	Equal symbol (=)
$t	System time
$v	DOS version number
$_	CR/LF (new line)
$$	Dollar sign symbol

If the dollar sign is followed by a character not found in the above table, the character pair in the prompt string is ignored.

For example, use the following PROMPT command to display the date and time in the prompt (omitting the year) and the current drive and directory:

```
PROMPT $d$h$h$h$h$h, $t$h$h$h$_$p$g
```

DOS may respond with a message similar to:

```
Not enough environment memory!
```

If this error message is displayed, you must shorten the PROMPT command parameter, increase the size of the MS-DOS environment or remove unnecessary variables from the environment.

Since escape characters can also be contained in the system prompt, it is possible to send escape sequences. This is useful only if the ANSI.SYS device driver is loaded through the CONFIG.SYS file. ANSI.SYS lets you use the standard control sequences. For example, the following PROMPT command displays the current directory in reverse video if ANSI.SYS is active:

```
PROMPT $e[7m$p$e[0m$g
```

The <, >, = and | symbols are also used in normal DOS commands for operations like loading and saving files. This is the reason why they must be replaced by the escape sequences $g, $l and $b.

See also: PATH, SET

QBASIC	(external)

Starts the MS-DOS QBasic program.

Syntax: QBASIC [/b][/editor][/g][/h][/mbf][/nohi][/run]
                [drive:][path]filename

[drive:][path]filename
    Specifies the name of an optional file for QBasic to load when the program begins.

Switches:

/b   Displays QBasic in black and white on a color monitor.

/editor   Calls the MS-DOS full screen text editor.

/g   Provides the fastest update for a CGA monitor.

/h   Displays the maximum number of lines possible for your screen.

/mbf   Converts the built-in function MKS$, MKD$, CVS and CVD to MKSMBF$, MKDMBF$, CVSMBF and CVDMBF.

/nohi   Permits using a monitor that doesn't support high-intensity video. This switch does not work with COMPAQ laptop computers.

/run   Loads and runs a specified BASIC program. (A filename must be specified.)

QBasic provides a complete programming environment for the BASIC language. It also includes extensive online help screens.

RD   (resident)

Removes a directory.

Syntax: RD [drive:]path

[drive:][path]
            Specifies the location and name of the directory to be
            removed.

Description:

RD removes a subdirectory from its parent directory. The specified
subdirectory cannot contain any files or subdirectories.

You cannot remove the current directory or the root directory.

For example, to delete subdirectory SAM from the directory
C:\NAMES, type:

    A>RD C:\NAMES\SAM

Or, if the current directory is NAMES, type:

    C:\NAMES>RD SAM

 RD should not be used if the SUBST command is active.

See also: RMDIR

RECOVER   (external)

 This command isn't included with DOS 6.0. However, if
you need this command, you can order a supplemental disk
from Microsoft that contains this command.

Recovers readable information from a defective diskette.

Syntax: RECOVER [drive:][path]filename

To recover the files on a diskette when the directory is unusable,
type:

    RECOVER drive

Do not attempt to recover all files in a directory unless it's absolutely necessary.

drive: pathname

The path and name of the file to be recovered. Wildcards are allowed, but only the first matching filename is rebuilt.

drive:

The drive (in the second optional syntax) containing a damaged directory that will be recovered in its entirety.

Description:

RECOVER rebuilds files from a disk that contains bad sectors or rebuilds all files on a disk whose directory has been damaged. The data in the bad sectors are not recovered.

When a single file is RECOVERed, a copy of the file is made without the data in the bad sectors. You'll probably have to edit and delete erroneous parts of the file using a text editor or another method.

When a complete disk is RECOVERed, the directory structure is rebuilt using the File Allocation Table (FAT). The recovered files are renamed to FILEnnnn.REC where nnnn starts at 0001. You'll have to examine each of these files to determine their previous contents.

 Use the second form of RECOVER only as a last resort. Also, don't use RECOVER with a SHAREd drive, or with drives which have been redirected with JOIN, SUBST or ASSIGN.

REM (resident)

Inserts a comment into a batch file or in CONFIG.SYS.

Syntax: REM comment

comment   Any string of characters to be included as a comment.

MS-DOS ignores any line in a batch file or CONFIG.SYS which begins with REM. If ECHO is ON, the line is displayed on the screen but any executable commands in the line are ignored.

IF ECHO is set to OFF, the comments are not displayed on the screen. Redirection or pipe symbols are not permitted with a batch file comment.

RENAME   (resident)

Changes the name of a file or group of files.

Syntax: RENAME [drive:][path]oldname newname
             REN [drive:][path]oldname newname

drive: pathname oldname
             The name of the file to be renamed. Wildcards are allowed.

newname   The new filename for drive: pathname.

Description:

RENAME or REN renames one or more files. The contents of the file remain unchanged.

If the two names are identical, if the file to be renamed does not exist or if filename *newname* already exists, the following error message is displayed:

```
Duplicate file name or file not found
```

RENAME displays the previous message and does not change the filename. Either delete one file or enter a different newname.

To change the name of the file READ.ME in the directory \COMPLEX\SCOMPLEX\ECOMPLEX to IGNORE.ME, use the following command:

```
REN \COMPLEX\SCOMPLEX\ECOMPLEX\READ.ME IGNORE.ME
```

To rename all files with the extension .TXT as files which start with the letter "T" and have an extension of .BAK, use the following command. Only the first letter of the renamed file and the filename extension will be replaced with "T":

```
REN *.TXT T*.BAK
```

See also: ATTRIB, COPY, DEL

| **REPLACE** | (external) |

Replaces files in the specified destination directory with files with the same name from the source directory.

Syntax: REPLACE [drive1:][path1]filename [drive2:][path2] [/a][/p][/r][/w][/s][/u]

drive1:path1 filename
: Specifies the drive, path and name of the source file. Wildcards are allowed.

drive2: path2
: Specifies the destination for the new files.

Switches:

/a
: Add files to the destination. Only files that do not already exist are copied from the source. This switch cannot be used with /s or /u.

/p
: Prompt before replacing a destination file or adding a source file.

/r
: Replace read-only files as well as unprotected files in the destination.

/w
: Waits for a disk to be inserted before beginning to search for files.

/s
: Search all subdirectories of the destination for matching source files. Switches /s and /a cannot be used together.

/u
: Updates only files in the destination directory that are older than those in the source directory. This switch cannot be used with /s or /a.

Description:

REPLACE selectively copies files from drive1:path1filename to the destination disk. This operation replaces the files on the destination disk with more recent versions of the files (updates files) or adds new files to the destination disk if they are not already there.

For example, the following command replaces all of the Pascal programs in directory \PASCAL on drive C: with Pascal programs of the same name on drive A:. DOS prompts you for confirmation before overwriting each file:

```
REPLACE A:\PASCOPY\*.PAS C:\PASCAL /s /p
```

When completed, REPLACE returns the following values to a batch file that can be tested with IF ERRORLEVEL:

Code	Meaning
0	Files added or replaced successfully
2	Source files not found
3	Source/destination path not found
5	User does not have access to the files to be replaced
8	Not enough memory
11	Syntax error in command line

See also: COPY, RESTORE, XCOPY

RESTORE   (external)

Restores files that were backed up using the BACKUP command from MS-DOS Versions 2.0 through 5.0.

Syntax: RESTORE drive1: [drive2:][path filename]
            [/s][/p][/b:date][/a:date][/e:time][/l:time][/m][/n][/d]

drive1:   Specifies the drive containing the backup files.

drive2:   Specifies the drive to which the files are to be restored. If omitted, the current drive is assumed.

path filename
            Specifies the path and name of the file to be restored. Wildcards are allowed. If omitted, all files in the current directory of drive2 are restored.

Switches:

/s   Restore all subdirectories.

/p   Prompt before restoring read-only files or files that have changed since the last backup.

/a:date   Restore only files that were modified on or after the specified date. The format for entering the date can vary according to the country setting in your CONFIG.SYS file.

/b:date   Restore only files that were modified on or before the specified date. The format for entering the date can vary according to the country setting in your CONFIG.SYS file.

/e:time   Restore only files that were modified before the specified time. The format for entering the time can vary according to the country setting in your CONFIG.SYS file.

/l:time   Restore only files that were modified at or after the specified time. The format for entering the time can vary according to the country setting in your CONFIG.SYS file.

/m   Restore only files modified since the last BACKUP.

/n   Restore only files no longer on the destination. Existing files on the destination are not restored.

/d   Display files on drive1 that match specifications.

Description:

RESTORE copies files that were backed up by the BACKUP command. Only files backed up by BACKUP can be restored. The files are copied into the same directory from which they were backed up. You cannot RESTORE a file to a different directory.

For example, to restore all of the files on the diskette in drive B: that have been changed since the last backup (the diskette with the backup files is in drive A:), use the following:

```
RESTORE A: B: /m
```

The following command replaces all files with a .C extension, in the directory \CPROGS on drive A:, that have been changed since 11-5-1986. Read-only files are confirmed:

```
RESTORE A: C:\CPROGS\*.C /b:11-5-86 /a /p
```

When completed with its tasks, RESTORE returns the following values to a batch file that may be tested with IF ERRORLEVEL:

Code	Meaning
0	RESTORE successful
1	No files were found to restore
2	Some files could not be restored
3	RESTORE was terminated by the user with <kbd>Ctrl</kbd>+<kbd>Break</kbd>
4	Hardware error (critical error) terminated program

    Do not use RESTORE if a drive has been redirected with
SUBST.

See also: COPY, DISKCOPY, REPLACE, XCOPY

RMDIR   (resident)

Deletes a directory.

Syntax: RMDIR [drive:]path
            RD [drive:]path

drive: The drive that contains the directory to be removed.

path   The path and/or name of the directory to be removed.

Description:

RMDIR or RD removes a subdirectory from its parent directory.
The specified subdirectory cannot contain any files or subdirectories.

You cannot remove the current directory or the root directory.

For example, to delete subdirectory SAM from the directory
C:\NAMES, type:

    A>RD C:\NAMES\SAM

Or, if the current directory is NAMES, type:

    C:\NAMES>RD SAM

Neither RMDIR nor RD should be used if the SUBST command is active.

See also: CD, CHDIR, MD, MKDIR

SET (resident)

Displays, sets or removes environment variables.

Syntax: SET [variable=[value]]

variable   A variable name. All characters in variable are internally converted to uppercase characters.

value   The string of characters that specifies the current value of variable.

Description:

SET is used to define, display or remove an environment variable name and value.

If both variable and value are omitted, all of the current environment variable names and values are displayed.

IF value is omitted, variable and its value are deleted from the environment.

For example, one of the environment variables is called COMSPEC. It contains the path used to reload COMMAND.COM. Other programs can then reference COMSPEC as necessary.

Two other standard environment names are PATH and PROMPT (not to be confused with the DOS commands of the same name). These names can be displayed and modified with the SET command or the PATH and PROMPT commands.

The following command informs a program that the user is named Smith (provided the program reads the environment variable USER):

```
SET USER=Smith
```

The next command deletes the variable USER:

```
SET USER=
```

The following command tells DOS that COMMAND.COM is located in a different location:

```
SET comspec=C:\DOS\COMMAND.COM
```

Entering SET without parameters displays the current environment:

```
SET
COMSPEC=:\DOS\COMMAND.COM
PATH=C:\DOS
LIB=C:\LIB
TMP=C:\
USER=Smith
```

☞   If you load a new command processor and then modify the environment, the changes made will not be preserved following the EXIT command. The environment of the calling (original) command processor will be restored.

See also: APPEND, COMMAND, PATH, PROMPT

SETVER   (external)

Sets the version number that MS-DOS reports to a program.

Syntax: SETVER [drive:path][filename n.nn]
            SETVER [drive:][path][filename [/delete][/quiet]]

To display the current version table, type:

            SETVER [drive:path]

drive:path
            Specifies the location of the SETVER.EXE file.

filename   The filename of the program (.EXE or .COM) to be added to the version table. Wildcards are not permitted.

n.nn   Specifies the MS-DOS version number (e.g., 3.3 or 4.01) for MS-DOS 6.0 to report to the specified program.

Switches:

/delete   Deletes the version table for the specified program file.

/quiet   Does not display messages as entries are deleted from the version table.

Description:

SETVER is a device driver and must be installed from your CONFIG.SYS file with the following line:

```
DEVICE=SETVER.EXE
```

Many applications run only on a specific version of the MS-DOS operating system. The SETVER command is used to "trick" the application into thinking that MS-DOS 6.0 is really a different version.

As developers upgrade products to work with MS-DOS 6.0, SETVER will be used less frequently.

To move SETVER.EXE to upper memory:

```
DEVICEHIGH=C: \DOS\SETVER.EXE
```

SETVER Exit Error Codes

0	SETVER completed successfully
1	Invalid command switch specified
2	Invalid filename specified
3	Insufficient memory
4	Invalid DOS version number specified
5	SETVER could not find the specified entry in the version table
6	SETVER.EXE not installed
7	Invalid drive specified
8	Too many command line parameters specified
9	Missing command line parameters
10	Error while reading SETVER.EXE file
11	SETVER.EXE has been corrupted
12	SETVER.EXE does not support version table
13	Insufficient space in the version table for new entry
14	Error while writing to SETVER.EXE

SHARE   (external)

Installs file sharing and locking capabilities on your hard drive.

Syntax: SHARE [/f:file_buffer][/l:max_locks]

You may also install SHARE.EXE from your CONFIG.SYS file by using the following command line:

INSTALL=[drive:][path] SHARE.EXE [/f:file_buffer] [/l:max_locks]

file_buffer
Specifies the number of bytes of memory to be reserved for storing file sharing information. The default size is 2048 bytes.

max_locks   The maximum number of files that may be locked at one time. The default value is 20 files.

Switches:

/l:max_locks
Specifies the number of files that can be locked.

/f:file_buffer
Sets memory space available for file sharing.

Description:

SHARE loads a program that allows files to be shared. If several PCs are used in a network, a method for sharing files must be implemented to prevent more than one user from accessing the same file at the same time.

Preventing other users from accessing a file on a network is known as locking. The /l switch specifies how many files can be locked. The system normally reserves space for 20 locked files.

The /f switch sets the memory space available for file sharing. Normally 2048 bytes are set up for this data. The system needs 11 bytes plus the length of the filename for each file.

The following command increases the size of both default values:

```
SHARE /f:4096 /l:40
```

SHIFT   (resident)

Changes the position of replaceable variables in a batch file.

Syntax: SHIFT

The SHIFT command changes the values of the replaceable parameters (%0 through %9) by copying each parameter into the previous parameter. For example, parameter %1 is copied into %0, %2 is copied into %1, %3 is copied into %2, etc.

Batch files can perform the same operation on any number of parameters.

SMARTDRV   (external)

Starts or configures SMARTDrive, which creates a disk cache in extended memory.

Syntax: [drive:][path]SMARTDRV[[drive[+ | -]]...]
            [/E:ElementSize]
            [InitCacheSize][WinCacheSize]][/B:<BufferSize>]
            [/C][/R][/L][/Q][/V][/S]

            Or, if SMARTDrive is running:

            SMARTDRV [[drive[+ | -]]...]] [/C] [/R]

[drive:] [path]
            Specifies the location of the SMARTDRV.EXE file.

[[drive+ | -] Specifies the letter of the disk drive for which you want to control caching. Include the plus (+) sign to enable caching for the specified drive; include the minus (-) sign to disable caching for that drive. You can specify multiple disk drives.

InitCacheSize
            Specifies the size in kilobytes of the cache when SMARTDrive starts (when Windows is not running). The size of the disk cache affects how efficiently SMARTDrive runs.

WinCacheSize
            Specifies, in kilobytes, how much SMARTDrive will reduce the cache size for Windows.

Switches:

/E:ElementSize

> Specifies in bytes the amount of the cache that SMARTDRIVE moves at a time.

/B:Buffersize

> Specifies the size of the read-ahead buffer.

/C   Writes all cached information from memory to cached disks.

/R   Clears the contents of the existing cache and restarts SMARTDRIVE.

/L   Prevents SMARTDrive from automatically loading into upper memory blocks (UMBs), even if there are UMBs available.

/Q   Instructs SMARTDrive not to display status messages when its starts.

/V   Instructs SMARTDrive to display status and error messages when it starts.

/S   Displays additional information about the status of SMARTDrive.

SORT	**(external)**

Sorts data into ascending and descending order.

Syntax: SORT [/r][/+n][<][drive1:][path1]filename1
           [>[drive2:][path2]filename2]
           [command |] SORT [/r][/+n][>
           [drive2:][path2]filename2]

drive1:   Drive containing data to be sorted.

path1   Path to data to be sorted.

filename1 Input file with data to be sorted.

drive2:   Drive for output file for sorted data.

path2   Path to file for sorted data.

filename2 File for storing sorted data.

Switches:

/r   Sort the input data in descending (reverse) order: Z, Y, X, ... A.

/+n   Sort beginning at column n. For example, you can sort a disk directory according to size by beginning the sort at column 12.

Description:

SORT reorders the lines of the standard input file into ascending or descending sequence and rewrites them to the standard output file.

SORT is normally used by redirecting the standard input and output files using the < and > symbols. For example, the following sorts a file named INPUT and rewrites the sorted data to a file named OUTPUT:

```
SORT < INPUT > OUTPUT
```

You should use a different name for both files; otherwise the contents of the input file might be overwritten.

SORT does not distinguish between upper and lowercase characters. SORT can sort files up to 63K in size.

To enter a list of words from the keyboard and sort them, use the SORT command with no switches. Press Ctrl+Z following the last entry. SORT then displays the sorted word list on the screen.

The following command lets you enter data from the keyboard and outputs the sorted list to the printer:

```
SORT > PRN
```

You can chain SORT to another DOS command (using the pipe symbol) to send the output of the first command to the second command. The following chained commands sort the directory and send it to the printer:

```
DIR | SORT > PRN
```

See also: FIND, MORE

STACKS   (external)

Supports the dynamic use of data stacks to handle hardware interrupts. This command can be used only in your CONFIG.SYS file.

Syntax: STACKS=n,s

n   Specifies the number of stacks. Valid values for n are 0 and numbers between 8 and 64.

s   Specifies the size, in bytes, of each stack. Valid values for s are 0 and numbers between 32 and 512.

SUBMENU   (external)

Specifies a submenu as called from CONFIG.SYS.

Syntax: SUBMENU=blockname,menu_text

You can only use this command in the CONFIG.SYS file. It allows you to choose from different computer configurations within this file.

Use this command to define a submenu within the startup menu of the CONFIG.SYS. When you select the submenu, you get another set of choices.

blockname Specifies the blockname in which the submenu is defined. Unlike the main menu, which is always named MENU, you can use any name for the submenu. The name can be up to 70 characters long and cannot contain the following characters: Spaces, commas, semicolons, equal signs, square brackets, forward slashes and backslashes.

menu_text Specify a text for display here. If you don't enter any text, the blockname will be displayed. This text can also have up to 70 characters.

See also: MENUCOLOR, MENUDEFAULT, MENUITEM

| **SUBST** | **(external)** |

Associates a path with a drive identifier.

Syntax: SUBST [drive1: [drive2:]path]
            SUBST drive1: /d

drive1:   The drive identifier to be substituted for a subdirectory.

drive2:path
            The drive and path to be accessed. drive1: and drive2: must be different.

Switches:

/d   Disables the redirection of the specified drive. The data on this drive can be accessed again or the drive can be redirected to a new directory.

Description:

SUBST redirects all references from a drive to a directory.

Some applications, such as Wordstar, do not support directory structures. You can use the SUBST command to overcome this limitation and access files in a directory as if the directory were a disk drive. For example, the following allows Wordstar to access text files in the \WSFILES subdirectory of drive C: as if they were located on drive B:

```
SUBST B: C:\WSFILES
```

SUBST can also be used to shorten long pathnames. For example, you can define drive D: as the drive on which all DOS commands are located. Then you can execute all of the DOS commands by typing D: before the command:

```
A> SUBST D: C:\DOS
A>D:ATTRIB *.EXE
```

Omit all parameters to display the current list of substitutions.

You can use the TRUENAME command to display the real name (the original directory name) of the pseudo drive.

To do this, simply type the command along with the drive whose true name you want to display:

```
TRUENAME drive
```

The screen then displays the correct name of the directory.

SWITCHES	**(resident)**

Syntax: SWITCHES=/w /k /n /f

Use the SWITCHES command to disable the functions of enhanced keyboards to avoid compatibility problems. You can also use this command to specify that the WINA20.386 file has been moved from the root directory to another directory. This command also allows you to disable the option for partially or totally bypassing the startup commands in CONFIG.SYS (by pressing F5 and F8).

Switches:

/w   Allows you to move the WINA20.386 file to a different directory than the root directory when you are running Windows. Add this command to the CONFIG.SYS and add the following command to the Windows SYSTEM.INI file:

```
DEVICE=Drive Directory WINA20.386
```

in the passage for 386 Enhanced mode.

/k   Turns an enhanced keyboard into a conventional keyboard.

/n   The F5 and F8 functions keys can no longer be used when you start up the computer. It's no longer possible to bypass the CONFIG.SYS file.

/f   Skips the two-second delay that occurs after the "Starting MS-DOS..." text.

SYS	**(external)**

Copies MS-DOS system files and command interpreter to a specified disk.

Syntax: SYS [drive1:][path] drive2:

drive1: path

> Location of the system files. If not specified, MS-DOS searches the root directory.

drive2: The destination disk to which the system files are to be copied.

Description:

SYS transfers the two system files to the disk in the specified drive. SYS also transfers the COMMAND.COM file to the disk.

The disk in drive: must be empty or must have been previously formatted with the /s switch of the FORMAT command. This ensures that the first two entries in the disk's directory are reserved for the two system files.

TIME	**(resident)**

Displays or sets system time.

Syntax: TIME [hh:[mm[:ss[.cc]]][a | p]]]

Switches:

h h   Hours (0-23).

mm   Minutes (0-59).

ss   Seconds (0-59); optional.

cc   Tenths of seconds (0-99); optional.

a | p   A.M. or P.M.

Description:

TIME sets the system clock.

If time is omitted, the current system time is displayed and you are prompted to enter a new time.

See also: DATE

TREE   (external)

Graphically displays the directory structure of a drive or path.

Syntax: TREE [drive:][path][/f][/a]

drive:path
>   The drive and path containing the directories to be
>   displayed. If omitted, the current drive is assumed.

Switches:

/f   Display filenames within each directory.

/a   Specifies that the tree structure should display text
>   characters instead of graphics characters.

Description:

TREE displays the structure of the directories of the disk in the
specified drive.

Type the following command to output the directory structure to
your printer:

```
TREE C: /f/a >PRN
```

In order to display all subdirectories on the current disk and drive,
type:

```
TREE \
```

TYPE   (resident)

Displays the contents of a text file.

Syntax: TYPE [drive:][pathname]filename

drive: pathname
>   The path and drive of the file to be displayed.

filename   The name of the file to be displayed. Wildcards are
>   not allowed.

Description:

TYPE displays the contents of a file to the standard output device.

If the file contains a tab (code 09h), it is replaced by spaces until the next tab position (every 8 columns).

You can use TYPE with MORE to prevent the displayed output from scrolling off the screen. So, the command:

```
TYPE read.me | MORE
```

is the same as:

```
MORE < read.me
```

You can also redirect the output to your printer:

```
TYPE read.me > prn
```

UNDELETE   (external)

Recovers file previously deleted with the DEL command.

Syntax: UNDELETE [[drive:][path]filename][/dt | /ds | /dos]
            UNDELETE
            [/list | /all | /purge[drive] | /status | /load | /unload |
            /s[drive] | /t[drive]-entries]]

drive:path filename
            The location of the file or files to be recovered.

Switches:

/dt   Recovers only files listed in the MIRROR command's
            deletion tracking file. Before recovering each file, a
            confirmation prompt is required.

/ds   Recovers only those files listed in the SENTRY
            directory. For each file, UNDELETE prompts you to
            confirm the undelete operation.

/dos   Recovers only those files that are internally listed as
            deleted by MS-DOS.

/list   Lists all deleted files which may be recovered, but
            does not recover any files.

/all   Recovers all deleted files without prompting for
            confirmation.

/load   Loads the resident UNDELETE program into RAM,
             creating an UNDELETE.INI file as well as the
             SENTRY directory and the deletion tracking program.

/unload   Removes the resident UNDELETE program from
             memory.

/purge[drive]
             Use this switch to clear the SENTRY directory. If no
             drive is specified, MS-DOS searches the current drive
             for the directory, deleting it if necessary.

/status[drive]
             UNDELETE is loaded into memory with the
             information of the UNDELETE.INI file, enabling the
             SENTRY. If you don't specify a drive, the DELETE
             SENTRY is installed on the current drive.

/t[drive][-entries]
             Enables a resident program for securing information
             required by UNDELETE for recovering deleted files.
             You must specify the drive whose information you
             want to secure. You can also specify -entries to
             determine the maximum number of entries in the
             deletion tracking file. The number of possible entries
             ranges from 1 to 999.

UNDELETE recovers accidentally deleted files whenever
possible.

UNDELETE cannot recover a directory that has been removed and
cannot recover a file if the directory which contained the file has
been removed. The UNFORMAT command may be able to assist
you with recovering such files.

UNFORMAT   (external)

Restores a disk erased by the FORMAT command or restructured by
the RECOVER command.

Syntax: UNFORMAT drive: [/j]
             UNFORMAT drive: [/u][/l][/test][/p]
             UNFORMAT /partn [/l]

drive: Specifies the drive that contains the disk to be
             recovered.

Switches:

/j   Verifies mirror files with system information.

/u   Unformats without using MIRROR files.

/l   Lists every file and subdirectory when used without the /partn switch. When used with /partn, UNFORMAT displays the partition table of the current drive.

/test   Simulates how UNFORMAT would restore the information on the disk without actually performing UNFORMAT.

/p   Sends output to the printer on LPT1:.

/partn   Restores disk partition tables.

Although UNFORMAT is a powerful command, it has some limitations. If a disk was formatted with the /u (unconditional format) switch of the FORMAT command, it cannot be recovered.

UNFORMAT can usually restore an accidentally formatted disk.

It is also possible to recover data from diskettes with UNFORMAT. To do this, information for recovering the diskette must be saved during formatting. In addition to the restrictions that apply for unformatting hard drives, there can be no change to the capacity of the diskette.

VER   **(resident)**

Displays the version of MS-DOS being run.

Syntax: VER

Description:

VER displays the version number of DOS. Many applications test the DOS version number to ensure that the application is compatible with the operating system.

For example:

```
C>VER
MS-DOS Version 6.00
C>
```

See also: SETVER

VERIFY   (resident)

Tells MS-DOS whether to verify that files are written correctly to disk.

Syntax: VERIFY [on | off]

on   Enables write verification.

off   Disables write verification.

Description:

VERIFY ensures that data written to a disk is verified.

If on or off is omitted, the current status of write verification is displayed:

```
C>VERIFY
VERIFY is off
```

VOL   (resident)

Displays the volume label (if any) and volume serial number of a disk.

Syntax: VOL [drive:]

drive: The drive containing the disk whose volume label is displayed. If omitted, the current drive is assumed.

Description:

VOL displays the volume label of a disk. For example:

```
A>VOL C:
Volume in drive C is PROGRAMS
Volume Serial Number is 1699-5914
```

If a disk was not labeled during formatting or with the LABEL command, the following message is displayed:

```
Volume in drive A has no label
Volume Serial Number is 1699-5914
```

VSAFE   (external)

Syntax: VSAFE option1 option2
               VSAFE

Use this command to load a memory-resident program that continuously checks your computer for viruses. To ensure that the program always runs, start it in the AUTOEXEC.BAT.

option1

Use the following options to specify the type of virus check. To disable an option, place a minus sign after it. To enable an option, place a plus sign after the option.

/1   Gives a warning about formatting the hard drive. The default setting is "on".

/2   Gives a warning when a program tries to load itself into resident memory. The default setting is "off".

/3   This option prevents programs from writing to a hard drive or diskette. The default setting is "off".

/4   Checks executable files for viruses before starting them. The default setting is "on".

/5   Checks all boot sectors on drives. The default setting is "on".

/6   Warns when a program attempts to write to the boot sector or the partition table of a hard drive. The default setting is "on".

/7   Warns when a program attempts to write to the boot sector or partition of a diskette. The default setting is "off".

/8   Warns when programs try to modify executable files. The default setting is "on".

option2

/ne   Prohibits VSAFE from loading into expanded memory.

/nx   Prohibits VSAFE from loading into extended memory.

/ax   Specifies the hotkey for calling VSAFE. The key
               combination consists of [Alt] and the key you choose for
               x.

/cx   Specifies the hot key for calling VSAFE. The key
               combination consists of [Ctrl] and the key you choose for
               x.

/n   Instructs VSAFE to check network drives.

/d   Disables checksum generation.

/u   Unloads VSAFE from memory.

XCOPY   (external)

Copies files (except hidden and system files) and directories,
including subdirectories.

Syntax: XCOPY [sourcedrive:][sourcepath]filename1
               [dest_drive:][dest_path]filename2][/a | /m][/d:date]
               [/p][/s[/e]][/v][/w]

sourcedrive: sourcepath
               The drive and path from which the source file will be
               copied.

filename1   The name of the file to be copied. Wildcards are
               allowed. If drive: is omitted, the current drive is
               assumed. If only drive: is specified, all of the files in
               the current directory are copied. If you specify only a
               path without a filename, all files in the specified
               directory are copied.

dest_drive:dest_path
               The destination drive and path.

filename2   Specifies the name of the destination file. Wildcards
               are allowed. If omitted, the current drive and
               directory are assumed.

Switches:

/a   Copy files with set archive flags. The flag isn't
               changed.

/m	Copy only files with set archive flags. This switch resets (turns off) the archive flags.
/d:date	Copy only files created or modified on or after the specified date.
/p	Prompts before copying each file to the destination.
/s	Copy directories and subdirectories.
/e	Copy subdirectories in the destination path, even if they are empty. Used in conjunction with /s.
/v	Verify the copied files.
/w	Display a message and wait for a keypress before starting to copy files. This switch allows switching diskettes.

Description:

XCOPY makes a copy of a file. XCOPY can also copy existing directories and subdirectories if specified by the /e and /s switches. For example, the following use of XCOPY copies all files, directories and subdirectories from drive A: to drive B:, then verifies the copied files:

```
XCOPY A:*.* B: /e /s /v
```

☞   Do not use XCOPY when the SUBST command is active.

See also: COPY, DISKCOPY, REPLACE, RESTORE

Appendix A: Glossary

This chapter covers important terms used in working with MS-DOS. If you are already familiar with terms such as "current directory", "batch file" or "device driver", then skip those terms and read only the terms whose meanings you aren't sure about.

Access rights

Rights of a user to use programs or data. Access rights can be set up and changed by the *supervisor* with the *SYSCON* utility program. In Novell, you can specify access rights individually for each user and each directory. Along with DOS attributes such as "Read-Only" or "Hidden", there are also special rights for opening or closing files and creating subdirectories.

ASCII

Acronym for American Standard Code for Information Interchange. ASCII is the standard for keyboard character codes, which applies to some extent to keyboards and printers. The ASCII standard covers key codes 0 to 127; individual computer manufacturers assign their own characters to code 128 to 255.

ASCII file

ASCII files are readable text files. Many word processing programs save a great deal of additional information along with the text. When you try to view such files with the TYPE command, you will only see strange special characters on the screen. The same applies to program files.

ASCII files consist of only letters, numbers and the normal sentence characters. For example, if you write and save a text with the MS-DOS Editor, it is automatically saved as an ASCII file.

Attribute

File attributes are the possible "characteristics" of a file. These attributes determine how DOS handles a file or a directory. For example, when a file has a set "Hidden" attribute, it won't display when you use DIR to view the contents of a directory. Use the ATTRIB command to set the attributes:

A   Archive attribute (indicates that the file is "unsaved").

R   Read-only attribute (file cannot be changed or deleted).

H   Hidden (by default, hidden files are not included in the display).

S   System attribute (indicates that the file is a system file, cannot be moved on the storage medium).

AUTOEXEC.BAT

Abbreviation for AUTOEXECute BATch file. This text file contains a series of commands stored in a group. Immediately after you switch on the PC, the computer searches for an AUTOEXEC.BAT file. If one exists, the commands in this file execute automatically.

AUTOEXEC.BAT commands often include the display of the version of DOS in use (VER), the DATE and TIME commands.

The AUTOEXEC.BAT file is a special form of batch file. Like all other batch files, AUTOEXEC.BAT can also be called and executed directly from the system prompt.

Batch file A file containing a collection of commands (see *AUTOEXEC.BAT*). MS-DOS executes these commands in sequence when you type the name of the file.

Batch files are created using the COPY CON command (e.g., COPY CON FILE.BAT), the MS-DOS Editor, a word processing program, or the EDLIN (can be found on the Supplemental Disk from Microsoft) line editor. The .BAT extension must be included with any batch filename.

Buffer   Every access to disk drives and hard drives for read or write operations costs time. The more frequently such accesses are necessary, the slower your PC becomes. That's why individual units of information are not read or written, but instead, information blocks are used. To do this, the information is gathered beforehand in a buffer. You can determine the number of buffers used by MS-DOS with the BUFFERS command in the CONFIG.SYS file. Each buffer provides 512 bytes for temporary storage of data.

Cache   A cache can help speed up read operations on hard drives and diskettes considerably. During a read access (e.g., when a user loads a file), the data are placed in temporary storage in a special memory area. During the second read access, this buffer area is checked first for the desired data. If the data are located in this buffer area, then it's not necessary to load them from the diskette or hard drive. The device driver, SMARTDRV.EXE is available as a cache in MS-DOS.

Cluster   A cluster (allocation unit) is the smallest possible memory allocation unit on a storage medium.

On hard drives, clusters contain 2,048 bytes or a multiple of this number. On diskettes with 360K and 720K, an allocation unit contains 1,024 bytes, while clusters on diskettes with 1.2 Meg or 1.44 Meg contain only 512 bytes.

Code page   Code pages (character set tables) are tables used by MS-DOS to convert characters so that it can process special characters from various countries. Beginning with MS-DOS 3.3, users can use these special characters on keyboards, screens and printers, although the special characters do take up valuable memory. That's why you should only install code pages if you really need them.

Command interpreter

This is the COMMAND.COM program, which acts as the mediator between user and PC. The command interpreter can be accessed through the system prompt or the MS-DOS Shell.

Conventional memory

Conventional memory is memory below the 640K limit. Because this memory area has been reserved for DOS programs and data since the development of the first PCs, it can be used by programs without restrictions or compatibility problems. All other forms of memory have special requirements for programs that use these memory types or else result in incompatibilities.

Due to internal management and procedures, it's not the entire amount of conventional memory, but the largest available memory block that provides the most important limitation for programs. Most programs use only the largest available block; other memory blocks are ignored.

Current directory

To access a file or a directory, DOS uses the current directory. You make a directory current by showing the position relative to the current directory using the CD.. command.

A second method is to use the CD NAME command. You must indicate the drive (letter and colon) and then the path through the subdirectories separated by the backslash.

Current drive

The standard drive or current drive is the drive to which all disk commands of the computer apply. Usually, and especially for systems with only one drive, this is drive A:. If two drives are available, the second drive can be selected with B:. This command can be reversed with A:. The hard drive can be selected with C:. The standard drive is displayed in the system prompt.

Defragmenting

Since data are constantly being deleted and resaved on computers, the space on the hard drive is not filled up in sequence with files. As a result, areas with and without data of varying size break up or "fragment" the contiguous free space on the hard drive.

To create an optimum area of contiguous free memory on the hard drive, you can use special defragmentation programs like DEFRAG, which comes supplied with MS-DOS 6.0. Defragmentation programs reorganize the allocated memory areas to create a contiguous area of allocated and free memory on the hard drive.

Data exchange

Any method of transferring data between at least two computers is called data exchange. For example, users who are connected to a *network* can exchange data via the special network connection. Modem users can exchange data over the telephone line. MS-DOS 6.0 includes two programs, INTERLNK and INTERSVR, which allow a user to exchange data between two computers using a cable connecting the two computers through parallel or serial ports.

Device driver

Device drivers are special programs in charge of the hardware. MS-DOS doesn't have to address the hardware directly, but instead deals with the device driver. By using various drivers for devices with hardware specific differences, it is possible to adapt MS-DOS to different kinds of hardware. Some device drivers are built into MS-DOS (for example, the programs for working with diskettes or hard drives), while others are loaded from a storage medium. For instance, there's the KEYB program which is in charge of the keyboard, making it possible to adapt MS-DOS to a different country's keyboard. Device drivers ensure that MS-DOS is adapted to each peripheral device.

What is more, by improving a driver, it is possible to make an adjustment or improvement without changing MS-DOS. For example, if you switch to a new keyboard, it's not necessary to change MS-DOS itself, but only the keyboard driver. Most device drivers have the SYS extension and can be called in the CONFIG.SYS.

Whenever you connect a new device to the computer, you must tell MS-DOS about it. For example, you cannot use a connected mouse until you have started a special utility program for requesting the mouse.

Device name

Devices connected to the PC get special names to differentiate them from files and directories. Along with drives, which are marked with a letter and a colon, there are CON, AUX, COM1-4, PRN, LPT1-4 and NUL. These abbreviations refer to the following devices:

CON	Console; both keyboard and screen
AUX	First serial port (COM1)
COM1-4	Four serial ports
PRN	First parallel port (LPT1)
LPT1-4	Four parallel ports
NUL	A special dummy device that can receive data, but simply lets the data disappear.

The driver doesn't place or store the data anywhere. NUL, in other words, constitutes the "trash can" in MS-DOS.

Directory   Part of a storage medium. Before the hard drive was commonly used, all files were stored in one directory. Because of the large capacity of the hard drive, separate directories became necessary.

They're arranged in a tree structure where the root directory can contain files and subdirectories. Every subdirectory in turn can contain files andsubdirectories.

Diskettes   Removable data storage media. PC systems use two sizes: 5.25 inch diskettes and 3.5 inch diskettes. Each diskette size has two types-double density (capable of holding 1.2 Meg and 1.44 Meg of data respectively).

Drive letter

The drive letter consists of a letter followed by a colon. To indicate the standard drive, enter the drive letter that pertains to it.

Error messages

When users make mistakes working on computers, it's important that they be informed about the mistake and its possible causes.

If an MS-DOS command is used incorrectly or errors occur in using the hardware (e.g., problems working with a diskette), MS-DOS outputs an error message on the screen. Usually an error code, or errorlevel is returned to the program.

If the program was started by the command interpreter, in other words, was started by a command line after the system prompt, you won't be able to use this error number. However, when a command or program is running within a batch file, you can prompt for the errorlevel using a special batch command called ERRORLEVEL. If the return value of the command is zero, it means there was no error.

Expanded memory

Expanded memory is a method of breaking through the basic 640K limit of conventional memory. This limit results from the fact that a PC/XT can only process addresses of up to 1 Meg. The area up to 640K is reserved for conventional memory; the rest contains special expansions (e.g., memory for a special graphics expansion, EGA or VGA card) or is free.

Expanded memory is additional available memory that is below the 1 Meg memory address limit. Such memory could be present on special memory expansion cards, for example. Special electronic circuitry makes this kind of memory available to the computer in "small amounts". MS-DOS or application programs are then able to use this memory. Such programs must support working with expanded memory.

MS-DOS is not able to use expanded memory directly, but some auxiliary programs can store data in this kind of memory. For example, SMARTDRV, the program for speeding up hard drives and RAMDRIVE are able to use expanded memory. The BUFFERS and FASTOPEN commands also use expanded memory. Many application programs can also work with expanded memory.

Extended memory

Extended memory is memory present beyond the 1 Meg limit of memory that can be used by MS-DOS. Only ATs (286, 386 etc.) are able to use this type of memory. Expanded memory is not "inserted in a window" via special hardware and software the way expanded memory is, but can be used by different programs without additional hardware or software.

Extended memory can by used by MS-DOS for the RAMDRIVE RAM disk and SMARTDRV.

Extension Any filename can have a three-character extension separated from the filename by a period. The extensions .COM, .EXE and .BAT have special meanings in MS-DOS, but any other combination of letters can be selected for various files. There are some conventions which are observed, such as TXT for ASCII text.

The following extensions are commonly used in MS-DOS:

.BAK   Backup copy of file (e.g., generated by programs)
.BAS   Program written in the computer language BASIC
.BAT   Batch file
.COM   Executable program file
.DOC   Word processing document file
.EXE   Executable program file
.TXT   ASCII text file

External   Commands which must be read from the DOS disk before they can be executed. The best known and most often used of these commands are FORMAT and DISKCOPY.

FAT   Basically, a diskette contains three management units, the boot sector (with a mini-startup program and data about the type and capacity of the diskette), the directory (a listing of the files and directories in the root directory including information about size, type, start position, etc.) and a file allocation table containing the allocation of *clusters* to the individual files. Specifically, the FAT only contains information about whether a cluster is free, damaged, or part of a file. If it is part of a file, each cluster contains the name of the next cluster belonging to the file.

File   Data stored under a name assigned by the user or manufacturer. Data files (for example, programs, text, graphics, etc.) appear in the directory of a diskette or hard drive as an entry containing the name, extension, size and date it was saved.

File Allocation Table
See *FAT*

Filename   A unique group of letters and numbers assigned to a file. You assign the filename when you create it.

The length of the filename cannot exceed eight characters. The optional extension can have no more than three characters. The name and extension must be separated by a period.

Note that spaces are not allowed in either the name or extension.

File server This is the master computer in the network, the data which all users want or need to access is stored on this computer. Usually file servers are 386s or 486s with large hard drives. File servers are also referred to as servers.

Group In Windows you can combine individual programs into groups (program groups) in the Program Manager. The groups can be displayed in their own windows, making it easier to keep track of programs.

High memory

High Memory is the first 64K of extended memory. Unlike the rest of extended memory, high memory can also be used in real mode on an AT without difficulty. High memory is part of XMS memory and is managed by HIMEM.SYS. MS-DOS can relocate a large portion of the DOS kernel to high memory, freeing up more conventional memory.

Installation

Installation refers to the adaptation of MS-DOS to hardware and country specific features. This happens by creating AUTOEXEC.BAT and CONFIG.SYS files. In addition, during installation, SETUP creates a copy of MS-DOS, either on diskettes or on the hard drive.

LAN LAN is the abbreviation for Local Area Networks. See also *Local Network*.

LIM/EMS 4.0

Lotus, Intel, Microsoft Expanded Memory Specification. Unlike the older specification for expanded memory, Version 3.2, the newer version of 4.0 is the standard for using expanded memory and is supported by MS-DOS.

Local network

A local network is a network that is only available in one place (locally). It's possible to use hardware components such as hard drives or software from different network computers. This kind of *network* is also referred to as a *LAN (Local Area Network)*. The opposite of a local network is a global network.

Logging in   Entering a *workstation* in the network. Usually when you log in, you must specify a *password* and user ID.

Logging out

Logging out a workstation from the network. After you log out, it is no longer possible to access the data and programs of the *file server* from that workstation. To regain access to the data you must first *log in* again.

Logical drives

Logical drives are parts of the hard drive that can be addressed by a separate drive letter. They are defined in an extended DOS partition. In this way, it is possible to divide a hard drive into several drives when formatting with FDISK. The need for these "logical drives" comes from a time prior to MS-DOS 4.0, when MS-DOS was only able to process hard drives with up to 32 Meg capacity. The solution was to divide larger hard drives into several logical drives. For compatibility reasons, there are also logical drives in newer versions of MS-DOS, although hard drives of up to 2,048 Meg can easily be managed as a single drive.

Login script

A login script or start script can be defined for each user of a network. This login script is similar to the AUTOEXEC.BAT used by a PC with MS-DOS. For example, the login script enables users to install a number of automatic processes to simplify work on the computer. These processes are executed as soon as users log in.

Logout   The command for logging out of (exiting) a workstation in a network.

Mail   Refers to a message, usually used for message programs, with which users of a network can exchange data (mail) with each other.

Microsoft LAN Manager

A network operating system that protects programs from simultaneous access by more than one person and organizes the interplay of the individual components. The competitor's product is the Novell network.

Multitasking

Technical term for simultaneously running more than one program. For example, Windows 3.1 and the OS/2 operating system both allow multitasking. With multitasking, both a word processor and a database program can be in memory at the same time, provided there is enough memory. Users can switch back and forth between the two programs by pressing a hot key combination. MS-DOS doesn't permit genuine multitasking.

MS-DOS 6.0 comes supplied with the DOS-Shell user interface, with which you can start up more than one program and switch back and forth. Only the active program is located in conventional memory; the other programs are frozen and swapped to the hard drive. While this is not genuine multitasking, it does make working on a PC a lot easier, since you don't have to completely exit the program you are currently running when you start a new program.

NEAT chip set

Electronic chips that can significantly increase the performance of 286 computers. These chips enable a multitude of changes to the internal settings of a computer. For example, with NEAT chips you can specify the use of the available memory within wide limits. With NEAT chips you can also speed up a computer significantly by increasing the speed of accesses (see also *Shadow RAM*, *Paging*).

Network When several computers are connected to each other, we call this a network. In most cases a network is made up of a central computer (file server), which is equipped with a large hard drive, and which can be accessed by the individual computers (*workstations*). The essential advantage of networks is that the entire database only needs to be present once, but is accessible to all stations. Also, the entire periphery of the central computer (e.g., an expensive laser printer) can be used by the individual stations.

Network card

> The necessary hardware for a network, plugged into the appropriate port of the system as a network card. The network card transfers data in the network via the connection cable.

Network connection

> A network connection refers to the connection of a computer to a *network* via a special network cable and hardware.

Network drive

> A network drive is a drive on a network that can be accessed by all workstations. This drive is also referred to as a *file server* or server.

Network driver

> A special program in charge of direct use of the network hardware. MS-DOS doesn't have to address the hardware directly, but only the network driver (see also *device driver*).

Network path

> A directory path on the file server that is assigned a drive letter. For example, if a user gets access to the SERVER_1/SYS:PROG network path via the drive letter D:, he/she can move only within the \PROG directory path.

Network printer

> A printer that is available to all *users* of a network. Usually this printer is connected to the server.

Network print jobs

> When a printer is connected to a network so that the users of the workstations can print with it, a print job is termed a network print job. The print job doesn't go directly to the printer from the workstation, but is instead directed from the network.

Network shell

> The user interface of the network software for issuing network commands.

Novell network
> A local network set up with Novell NetWare. Novell is practically a standard for local PC networks and is supported by all current network capable programs.

Packed file corrupt
> Error message from programs when using the first 64K of conventional memory (in conjunction with intensive swapping of DOS and device drivers). Can be prevented by LOADFIX.

Paging
> When the processor inquires the contents of a specific memory location, it tells the memory chip the line and then the column of this address and then receives the results. With paging, the processor can read several memory addresses in half the time by sending the line specification only once and then specifying the different column addresses.

Parameter Command elements of a DOS command separated from the command name by a space. For example, the command COPY CON FILENAME uses the command name COPY and the two parameters CON and FILENAME.

Partition DOS can work with a hard drive only if it has a DOS partition (a DOS area). By dividing the hard drive into several partitions (areas) with FDISK, you can use another operating system on the hard drive as well as DOS (e.g., OS/2 with the HPS = High Performance System or Unix).

> MS-DOS can boot from the hard drive only if the DOS area is startable (primary partition). A second area can be set up as an extended partition with one or more logical drives.

Password To protect your data from unauthorized access, you can provide password protection for logging into the network or opening certain files. You can specify that a password (text string of up to 8 characters) must be entered before access is allowed. The password does not appear on the screen when it is typed.

Print server
> A computer that processes the print jobs of the *workstations*.

Program   Products which instruct a computer to perform a specific task or group of tasks (for example, a word processor). Sometimes called applications.

RAM   Abbreviation for Random Access Memory. This is your PCs most important area of memory. Data and other instructions are stored in RAM so that the CPU can write to and read from them quickly.

            The contents of RAM are deleted when you switch off your PC.

RAM disk   An area created in RAM by a program to act as a disk drive temporarily on the DOS disk.

            Since it is not a mechanical device, the RAM disk allows very fast file access, but loses all data when you switch off your PC.

            PC users with only one disk drive will find the RAM disk extremely helpful. Anything can be kept in a RAM disk, provided the files do not exceed the memory limits.

Redirector Another term for network shell.

Resident commands

            Commands loaded into the memory of the PC as MS-DOS boots. Resident commands are always available. Resident commands which we described include: CD, CLS, COPY, DATE, DEL, DIR, ECHO, MD, PATH, PROMPT, RENAME, RD, TIME, TYPE, VER, and VOL.

SETUP   SETUP is a special program that can be started right after booting up. You can use SETUP to make adjustments to the computer (memory, drives, etc.). Frequently you can start SETUP with a special key combination that displays on the computer screen after startup. Usually, a hard drive must be registered in the SETUP program so that MS-DOS can work with the drive.

            The adjustment is stored in a small memory area that continues to be supplied with power even after the computer is switched off (battery). Beginning with 286 computers, this memory area also ensures that users don't have to reset the date and time every time they boot up the computer. Make notes about the values entered in SETUP, because if the battery fails, these values are lost. This could result in serious problems. The ID number for the internal hard drive is especially important.

Shadow RAM

Shadow RAM is a copy of ROM memory in RAM. Since accessing RAM is much faster than accessing ROM, this can speed up the operation of the computer.

Shareable File attribute in a network. Identifies data and programs as "usable by several users at the same time".

Storage media

The various devices used to store the contents of the PC's memory outside the computer. Generally these include disk drives, hard drives and tape drives.

Streamer A streamer is a tape drive, similar to that of a cassette recorder, that can be used to record data instead of music. A streamer is a good alternative to diskettes for data backups, since you can back up a hard drive to a single cassette instead of 20 diskettes. Data exchange is also relatively easy, since you only have to play back the data from the cassette. Otherwise, a file of more than 2 Meg would have to be backed up to several diskettes. With streamers, you can copy files of 50 or more megabytes easily from cassettes.

Supervisor The supervisor is the user with unlimited rights in the network; he/she is responsible for administrative tasks. Only the supervisor can set up and remove user ID's and assign rights to or revoke rights from users.

Swap file A swap file is a file in Windows that simulates a larger memory by temporarily swapping data to the hard drive. You can adjust the size of a swap file in Windows to the computer configuration.

SYSCON Novell program for managing users, groups and access rights. SYSCON is a menu-driven program that lets you accomplish these tasks easily.

System diskette

>This is a special diskette containing information for starting MS-DOS (hidden system files and COMMAND.COM). If MS-DOS isn't installed yet, the diskette is called "Installation 1" (OEM-Version) and is the first of the supplied diskettes. When you install MS-DOS on a diskette system, the program automatically creates a system diskette. You can also use the FORMAT or SYS command to create system diskettes.

>If a system diskette is in drive A: when you start the computer, the PC loads the basic components of MS-DOS and prepares to receive commands. If a diskette isn't in drive A:, but the PC has a hard drive, the computer attempts to load the operating system from the hard drive.

System prompt

>The character or set of characters that MS-DOS uses to show that the PC is ready to accept a command or other input.

>The default (normal) prompt in MS-DOS consists of the current disk drive and a greater than character (for example, C>). The PROMPT command lets you change the appearance of the prompt.

TSR program

>Usually programs are loaded into memory, where they stay until they are ended. Some programs remain in memory after being started. Such programs are referred to as TSR programs (Terminate and Stay Resident).

>If you load a TSR program before the DOS Shell or before Windows, it is available to all processes started in the DOS Shell or in Windows, but it also allocates the memory for all processes. If you start a TSR program in a DOS Shell task, it is available only in this one task, but also allocates memory only there.

Upper memory

>Upper memory is the memory between 640K and 1 Meg; this is also called "reserved memory" in other operating systems. Both names describe aspects of this memory type. Upper memory is above 640K, or

conventional memory. Upper memory is also "reserved" for video display, the BIOS and expansions.

However, usually this memory area is not allocated by expansion cards, so that you can install an EMS window (page frame) for expanded memory there. MS-DOS attempts to fill free areas on computers with 386 processors with extended memory and then use it as upper memory for swapping TSR programs and device drivers. To do this, you need a 386 or above and a special device driver (EMM386.EXE).

User   A user is a person who has direct access to the data of the *file server* and works at a *workstation*. A user usually has a *user* name and a *password* to be used for logging in to the system.

User ID   The name (ID) of a user who is able to work in a *network* and has been assigned the appropriate *access rights*. When logging in, the user must specify his user ID.

Virtual drive
        An installed RAM disk is called a virtual drive, since it has the properties of a drive, but is not really present as a drive (see *RAM disk*).

Virus   A virus is a program that is able to multiply itself in a computer system and cause damage. Viruses are transmitted by copying diskettes to a computer system. They can remain undetected for a long time, until the damage they can cause becomes noticeable.

There are special anti-virus software programs for protection against viruses.

Workstation
        A PC in a network, on which the actual work takes place. A workstation requires a cable connection, a network card and special software to access the data of the file server.

A computer connected to the network, on which a *user* is working. Workstations are connected by cable to the *server* in a star network, and don't need a great deal of computer performance, since the server does most of the work. On a ring network, each computer is linked to the next one with a cable. In the third type of network, the bus network, the workstations are connected both to each other and to the server via a cable, which is open to the sides.

XMS   EXtended Memory Specification (XMS) defines a protocol for controlling access to the memory area between 640K and 1 Meg (upper memory), high memory and extended memory. The MS-DOS driver, HIMEM.SYS, manages the memory in accordance with the XMS specification.

Appendix B: Device Drivers

A device driver is a program used to control a peripheral device.

Normally each device (such as a disk drive, system clock or keyboard) needs a device driver. The standard device drivers are automatically loaded by DOS. You can also install device drivers that replace the standard input and output devices, or create a virtual disk (also known as a RAM disk).

The syntax for installing a device driver from your CONFIG.SYS file is:

```
DEVICE=[drive:]path driver
```

The following commands install a device driver:

```
DEVICE=ANSI.SYS
DEVICE=CHKSTATE.SYS
DEVICE=DBLSPACE.SYS
DEVICE=DISPLAY.SYS
DEVICE=DRIVER.SYS
DEVICE=EGA.SYS
DEVICE=EMM386.EXE
DEVICE=HIMEM.SYS
DEVICE=INTERLNK.EXE
DEVICE=POWER.EXE
DEVICE=RAMDRIVE.SYS
DEVICE=SETVER.EXE
DEVICE=SMARTDRV.EXE
```

ANSI.SYS

Driver which supports use of ANSI escape sequences.

Syntax: DEVICE= [drive:][path]ANSI.SYS [/x][/k][/r]

drive: path
    Drive and path for ANSI.SYS file.

Switches:

/x   Remap extended keys independently on 101-key keyboards.

/k   Ignore extended keys on 101-key keyboards.

/r   Improves line scrolling for screen reader programs. This makes it easier for users with physical disabilities to access a PC.

The ANSI.SYS driver enables the ANSI escape sequences for screen control. These escape sequences perform operations such as clearing the screen and defining the cursor position.

Escape sequences begin with the hexadecimal codes 01Ah and 05Bh (^Z[). These characters may be entered by pressing Alt+2 6, Alt+9 1.

The following is the list of recognized escape sequences.

ESC[2J   Erase screen and move the cursor to the Home position (line 0, column 0).

ESC[K   Erase all characters from the cursor position (including the character under the cursor) to end of line.

ESC[x;yH   Define the cursor position. If no position is specified, cursor is moved to home position.

ESC[x;yf   Positions the cursor in column x, line y. If one or both of the parameters are omitted, the default is 1.

ESC[xA   Move cursor up. Moves the cursor up x lines without changing the column. If the x parameter is omitted, the cursor is moved one line. The cursor cannot be moved past the top of the screen.

ESC[xB   Move cursor down. Moves the cursor down x lines without changing the column. If the x parameter is omitted, the cursor is moved one line. The cursor cannot be moved past the bottom of the screen.

ESC[xC   Move cursor right. Moves the cursor x characters to the right. If the x parameter is omitted, the cursor is moved one character. The line remains unchanged. The cursor cannot be moved past the rightmost column.

ESC[xD   Move cursor left. Moves the cursor x characters to the left. If the x parameter is omitted, the cursor is moved one character. The line remains unchanged. The cursor cannot be moved past the leftmost column.

ESC[s   Save current cursor position.

ESC[u   Restore cursor to saved position.

ESC[=xh   Set screen mode.

0	40x25 monochrome (text)
1	40x25 color (text)
2	80x25 monochrome (text)
3	80x25 color (text)
4	320x200 4-color (graphics)
5	320x200 monochrome (graphics)
6	640x200 monochrome (graphics)
7	Enable word wrap
13	320x200 color (graphics)
14	640x200 color (16 color graphics)
15	640x350 monochrome (2 color graphics)
16	640x350 color (16 color graphics)
17	640x480 monochrome (2 color graphics)
18	640x480 color (16 color graphics)
19	320x200 color (256 color graphics)

ESC[x;y;...;zm

Set screen attribute. The following control sequences can be accessed in normal text mode, from most video controller cards:

Text Attributes

0	None
1	Bold
2	Normal
3	Italic
5	Blinking
6	Fast blinking
7	Reverse video
8	Invisible

Foreground Colors

30	Black foreground
31	Red foreground
32	Green foreground
33	Yellow foreground
34	Blue foreground
35	Magenta foreground
36	Cyan foreground
37	White foreground

Background Colors

40	Black background
41	Red background
42	Green background
43	Yellow background
44	Blue background
45	Magenta background
46	Cyan background
47	White background

Parameters 30 through 47 satisfy the requirements for the ISO 6429 standard.

ESC[x;y;...p

Assign string y+...+z to key x.

Allows you to assign string variables to a specific key. For example, you could assign the DOS commands to their starting letters plus the (Alt) key. The string must be enclosed in quotes, or you can define the ASCII code or a single character in decimal. The parameters are separated by semicolons.

You can define more than one key in a single escape sequence by repeating Esc-[. A semicolon (;) cannot precede the terminating p.

All of the codes listed in the Key Code table (on the next page) are preceded by a zero (0). For example, the following causes (Alt)+(D) to clear the screen and display the current directory:

```
PROMPT $e[0;32;"cls";13;"dir";13p
```

```
PROMPT
```

A null PROMPT command restores the standard system prompt, and reassign the default key definitions. To restore (Alt)+(D) to its normal state, type the following:

```
PROMPT $e[0;32;0;13p
```

Key code 13 represents the (Enter) key, and is needed to end a line. Key code 0;32 represents the key combination (Alt)+(D) (see the Key Code Table below).

☞ Some applications may not operate correctly with a redefined keyboard.

Key Code Table

Code	Key	Code	Key	Code	Key
3	Null	63	F5	101	Ctrl + F8
13	Enter	64	F6	102	Ctrl + F9
15	Shift + Tab	65	F7	103	Ctrl + F10
16	Alt + Q	66	F8	104	Alt + F1
17	Alt + W	68	F9	105	Alt + F2
18	Alt + E	69	F10	106	Alt + F3
19	Alt + R	71	Home	107	Alt + F4
20	Alt + T	72	↑	108	Alt + F5
21	Alt + Y	73	PgUp	109	Alt + F6
22	Alt + U	75	←	110	Alt + F7
23	Alt + I	77	→	111	Alt + F8
24	Alt + O	79	End	112	Alt + F9
25	Alt + P	80	↓	113	Alt + F10
30	Alt + A	81	PgDn	114	Ctrl + Prt Sc
31	Alt + S	82	Ins	115	Ctrl + ←
32	Alt + D	83	Del	116	Ctrl + →
33	Alt + F	84	Shift + F1	117	Ctrl + End
34	Alt + G	85	Shift + F2	118	Ctrl + PgDn
35	Alt + H	86	Shift + F3	119	Ctrl + Home
36	Alt + J	87	Shift + F4	120	Alt + 1
37	Alt + K	88	Shift + F5	121	Alt + 2
38	Alt + L	89	Shift + F6	122	Alt + 3
44	Alt + Z	90	Shift + F7	123	Alt + 4
45	Alt + X	91	Shift + F8	124	Alt + 5
46	Alt + C	92	Shift + F9	125	Alt + 6
47	Alt + V	93	Shift + F10	126	Alt + 7
48	Alt + B	94	Ctrl + F1	127	Alt + 8
49	Alt + N	95	Ctrl + F2	128	Alt + 9
50	Alt + M	96	Ctrl + F3	129	Alt + 0
59	F1	97	Ctrl + F4	130	Alt + −
60	F2	98	Ctrl + F5	131	Alt + =
61	F3	99	Ctrl + F6	132	Ctrl + PgUp
62	F4	100	Ctrl + F7		

CHKSTATE.SYS

Syntax: DEVICE=CHKSTATE.SYS

This device driver is used exclusively by the MEMMAKER program, which optimizes the memory of your computer. When you use MEMMAKER, the device driver is automatically entered in the CONFIG.SYS.

DBLSPACE.SYS

Syntax: DEVICE=DBLSPACE.SYS /move

This driver is used exclusively by DBLSPACE for data compression. When you call DBLSPACE, the driver is automatically installed in the CONFIG.SYS file. You can also install this driver in advance, and have the option of specifying a switch.

/move   Causes the driver to be loaded into upper memory.

DISPLAY.SYS

Driver to support code page switching. Prepares screen for character set tables.

Syntax: DEVICE=[drive:][path]DISPLAY.SYS CON[:]=(type
            [,[hwcp][,n]])
            DEVICE=[drive:][path]DISPLAY.SYS CON[:]=(type
            ,[hwcp][,(n,m)]])

[drive:][path]
            Defines the location of the DISPLAY.SYS file.

type   Specifies the display adapter type being used. Valid
            values are EGA and LCD. EGA supports both EGA and
            VGA video adapters. If type is omitted,
            DISPLAY.SYS checks the hardware to determine
            which display adapter is in use. CGA and MONO may
            also be specified, but these values have no effect.

hwcp   Defines the number of the code page supported. Valid
            values are 437, 850, 852, 860, 863 and 865.

n   Number of code pages that can be supported.

m   Number of subfonts for each code page.

DISPLAY.SYS configures the screen device driver for use with the specified character set table.

Using DISPLAY.SYS with monochrome or CGA graphics cards has no effect as code page switching is not supported.

DRIVER.SYS

Installs a logical disk drive with different default characteristics from the physical disk drive.

Syntax: DEVICE=[drive:][path]DRIVER.SYS
             /d:n[/c][/f:factor][/h:heads][/s:sectors][/t:tracks]

[drive:][path]
             Defines the location of the DRIVER.SYS file.

/d:n   Specifies the number of the physical disk drive. Valid numbers are 0 through 127.

/c   Specifies that the physical disk drive can detect whether the drive door is open or closed.

/f:factor   Specifies the type of disk drive.

             0   160K/180K or 320K/360K
             1   1.2 Meg
             2   720K (3.5 inch disk)
             7   1.44 Meg (3.5 inch disk)
             9   2.88 Meg (3.5 inch disk)

The default value is 2. If the /f switch is used, the /h, /s and /t switches may be omitted.

/h:heads   Defines the number of heads in the disk drive. Valid values range from 1 through 99. The default value is 2. Refer to your drive manufacturer's documentation to determine the correct value for your drive.

/s:sectors   Specifies the number of sectors per track. Valid values are 1 through 99. The default value is dependant on the value of /F:factor as shown in this table:

             /f:0   /s:9
             /f:1   /s:15

                                    /f:2   /s:9
                                    /f:7   /s:18
                                    /f:9   /s:36

/t:tracks   Specifies the number of tracks per side. Valid values
               range from 1 through 999. The default value is 80,
               unless the /f switch is set to 0. In this case, the default
               value is 40.

DRIVER.SYS cannot be used with hard drives.

EGA.SYS

Syntax: DEVICE=[drive:][path]EGA.SYS

To use an EGA monitor when task switching in the DOS Shell, you
must install the EGA.SYS device driver in the CONFIG.SYS. To
save disk space, install EGA.SYS before the mouse driver if you
are using a mouse.

EMM386.EXE

Syntax: DEVICE=[drive:][path]EMM386.EXE [on l off l auto]
             [memory][w=on l w=off][mx l frame=address l /pmmmm]
             [pn=address][x=mmmm-nnnn][i=mmmm-nnnn]
             [b=address][L=minXMS][a=altregs][h=handles]
             [d=nnn][ram][noems][novcpi][highscan][verbose]
             [win=mmmm-nnnn][nohi][rom=mmmm-nnnn]
             [nomovexbda][altboot]

Driver which simulates expanded memory using extended memory.
Provides access to the upper memory area on computers using an
80386 (or higher) microprocessor.

[drive:][path]
             Defines the location of the EMM386.EXE file.

[on l off l auto]
               Set to on the device driver is activated. Set to off
               suspends device driver. Auto enables expanded
               memory support only when a program calls for it.

memory   Specifies the amount of memory (in K) to allocate to
             EMM386.EXE. Valid values range from 16 to 32768.
             The default value is 256.

Switches:

w=on | off   Enables or disables support for the Weitek coprocessor. The default setting is off.

mx   Specifies the address of the page frame; valid values are 1 through 14, as shown in the following table of base addresses:

1	C000h
2	C400h
3	C800h
4	CC00h
5	D000h
6	D400h
7	D800h
8	DC00h
9	E000h
10	8000h
11	8400h
12	8800h
13	8C00h
14	9000h

Values of 10 through 14 should only be used on computers with 512K of memory.

frame=address
              Specifies the page frame segment base. Valid values for address are 8000h through 9000h and C000h through E000h, in increments of 400h.

/pmmmm   The address of the page frame. Valid values are 8000h through 9000h and C000h through E000h, in increments of 400h.

pn=address
              Segment address of a specific page. n is the number of the page, address is the segment address. Valid values for n are 0 through 255. Valid values for address are 8000h through 9000h and C000h through E000h, in increments of 400h.

x=mmmm-nnnn
              Prevents EMM386.EXE from using a specified range of addresses.

i=mmmm-nnnn

> Specifies a range of address to be used for an EMS page.

b=address Lowest segment address available for EMS page swapping.

L=minXMS

> Ensures that a specified amount of extended memory is still available after loading EMM386.EXE. The default value is 0.

a=altregs This switch is used for multitasking and specifies how many fast alternate register sets are to be allocated to EMM386.EXE.

h=handles

> Specifies how many handles EMM386.EXE can use. Valid values are 2 through 255. The default value is 64.

d=nnn Reserves memory for direct buffer access.

ram Provides access to both the expanded memory area and the upper memory area.

noems Provides access to the upper memory area but prevents accessing expanded memory.

novcpi Disables support for VCPI applications (Virtual Control Program Interface). This switch must be used together with NOEMS.

highscan

> No scanning of high memory. Use this option if you have trouble using EMM386.EXE,SYS.

verbose Displays status and error information while loading EMM386.EXE.

win=mmmm-nnnn

> Use this switch to indicate that the specified memory can only be used by Windows. The memory would then no longer be available for EMM386. The areas for this switch are between A000h and FFFFh. If this area overlaps with an area defined by X, the area defined by X has priority. If the area overlaps with areas

defined by I, RAM or ROM, the WIN area takes precedence.

nohi   Prevents part of EMM386.EXE from being loaded in high memory.

rom=mmmm-nnnn
   Use this switch to define a memory area that EMM386 can use for Shadow-RAM with possible access to ROM memory. Valid values for this area range between A000h and FFFFh. Specify this switch to speed up a computer that doesn't have Shadow RAM.

nomovexbda
   Prohibits EMM386 from loading extended BIOS information into upper memory from conventional memory.

altboot Specifies use of an alternate handler to EMM386 when the user reboots the computer. Use this parameter only if your system locks up when EMM386 is loaded and you press `Ctrl`+`Alt`+`Del`.

The EMM386.EXE device driver uses extended memory to simulate expanded memory for programs that can use expanded memory. This device drive also enables loading programs and device drivers into the upper memory area.

HIMEM.SYS must be installed before using the DEVICE=EMM386.EXE command.

HIMEM.SYS

Driver which manages the use of extended memory.

Syntax: DEVICE=[drive:][path]HIMEM.SYS [/hmamin=m]
     [/numhandles=n][/int15=xxxx][/machine:xxx]
     [/a20control:on | off][/eisa][/verbose]
     [/shadowram:on | off][/cpuclock:on | off]

[drive:][path]
   Defines the location of the HIMEM.SYS file.

Switches:

/a20control:on | off

> Determines if HIMEM.SYS is to take control of the a20 line.

/cpuclock:on | off

> HIMEM.SYS attempts to control the clock speed of the computer via software. If the speed changes during installation of HIMEM.SYS, this setting will probably eliminate the problem. Set OFF to turn off control of the clock speed.

/eisa

> Only necessary for EISA computers with more than 16 Meg of memory. This switch specifies that HIMEM.SYS allocates all available extended memory.

/hmamin=m

> Defines the amount of memory (in kilobytes) a program must use before using the high memory area. Valid values are 0 through 63. The default value is 0.

/int15=xxxx

> Allocates a specified amount of memory for the Interrupt 15h interface.

/numhandles=n

> Maximum number of extended memory block handles that can be used at the same time. Valid values are 1 through 128. The default setting is 32.

/machine:xxxx

> Specifies the a20 handler to be used. The default value is at or 1.

Code	Number	a20 handler
at	1	IBM PC/AT
ps2	2	IBM PS/2
pt1cascade	3	Phoenix Cascade BIOS
hpvectra	4	HP Vectra (A and A+)
att6300plus	5	AT&T 6300 Plus
acer1100	6	Acer 1100
toshiba	7	Toshiba 1600 and 1200XE

Code	Number	a20 handler
wyse	8	Wyse 12.5 MHz 286
tulip	9	Tulip SX
zenith	10	Zenith ZBIOS
at1	11	IBM PC/AT
at2	12	IBM PC/AT (alternative delay)
css	12	CSS Labs
at3	13	IBM PC/AT (alternative delay)
philips	13	Philips
fasthp	14	HP Vectra
ibm7552	15	IBM 7552 industrial computer
bullmicral	16	Bull Micral 60
dell	17	Dell XBIOS

/shadowram ON | OFF

      Determines whether HIMEM.SYS should switch off shadow RAM and add that RAM to its memory.

/verbose   Specifies that HIMEM.SYS displays status and error information while loading.

HIMEM.SYS manages the way a program uses extended memory and the high memory area.

INTERLNK.EXE

Syntax: DEVICE=[drive:][path]INTERLNK.EXE
                [/drives:n][/noprinter]
                [/com[:][n | address]][/lpt[:][n | address]][/auto][/noscan]
                [/low][/baud:rate][/v]

Install this device driver in the CONFIG.SYS to redirect requests from one computer to another.

[drive:][path]

      Defines the location of the INTERLNK.EXE file.

Switches:

/drives:n   Use n to define the number of drives for redirection. The default value is 3. Set the value to 0 to use redirection only with the printer.

/noprinter   Choose this switch to disable redirection of printers. By default, INTERLNK.EXE redirects all printer ports.

/com:n   Specify the serial port to be used for data transfer. For n, set the number of the port. You can also specify the address of the serial port for n. If you don't specify n, INTERLNK.EXE checks all serial ports and uses the first one it finds. By default, INTERLNK.EXE looks for serial and parallel ports. Specify /COM without /LPT to have INTERLNK.EXE look only for serial ports.

/lpt:n   Specify the parallel port to be used for data transfer. For n, set the number of the port. You can also specify the address of the parallel port for n. If you don't specify n, INTERLNK.EXE checks all parallel ports and uses the first one it finds. By default, INTERLNK.EXE looks for serial and parallel ports. Specify /LPT without /COM to have INTERLNK.EXE look only for parallel ports.

/auto   Driver is only installed if the client is able to make a connection to the server when the computer is started. Ordinarily, INTERLNK is installed by default.

/noscan   The device driver is installed, but there is no connection established during startup.

/low   The device driver is loaded into conventional memory. By default, INTERLNK.EXE is loaded into upper memory.

/baud:rate   Sets the maximum baud rate for the serial connection. Possible values are: 9600, 19200, 38400, 57600 and 115200. The default value is 115200.

/v   Specify this switch to avoid problems with the computer timer. Use this option when there is a serial connection to another computer and one of them stops running while you access the other computer.

POWER.EXE

Syntax: DEVICE=[drive:][path]POWER.EXE
[adv[:max | reg | min] | std | off][/low]

Link this driver to the CONFIG.SYS to load the program for reducing power consumption active.

[drive:][path]
          Defines the location of the POWER.EXE file.

Switches:

adv[:max | reg | min] | std | off
          This switch determines how much power is saved. Since the power consumption of the computer can change when an application is not idling, you should experiment with different values. The following values are available:

      max   Maximum power conservation.

      reg   The default value. Balances power conservation with the performance of applications and devices.

      min   Minimum power conservation. Use this value only if you have trouble with the other two values.

adv:std   Use this switch only if the computer supports the APM specification (Advances Power Management). If this switch is specified, only the power management features of your computer are used. If your computer does not support this specification, specifying this switch disables power management.

adv:off   Disables power management.

/low   Loads the program in conventional memory. By default, the program attempts to load into upper memory.

RAMDRIVE.SYS

Driver to create a virtual disk.

Syntax: DEVICE=[drive:][path]RAMDRIVE.SYS
            [size][sectors][/e | /a]
            DEVICE=[drive:][path]RAMDRIVE.SYS
            [size sectors[entries]}[/e | /a]

[drive:][path]
            Defines the location of the RAMDRIVE.SYS file.

size   Number of kilobytes to be reserved for the RAM disk.
            This value can range from 1 to the upper limit of
            memory. At least 64K of memory must be left
            available for applications.

sectors   Size of the virtual sector. *sectors* can be 128, 256 or 512
            bytes.

entries   Number of virtual directory entries (from 2 to 512). The
            default is 64.

Switches:

/e   Specifies that the virtual disk is located in extended
            memory above the 1 Meg boundary.

/a   Creates the RAM disk in expanded memory instead of
            extended or conventional memory.

A virtual disk (or RAM disk) is a device that simulates a disk
drive. The virtual disk is actually located in the PC's memory.

The following example defines a RAM disk with a capacity of
150K. Each sector is 256 bytes long and 100 directory entries are
allowed:

```
DEVICE=C:\DOS\RAMDRIVE.SYS 150 256 100
```

SETVER

Sets the version number that MS-DOS reports to a program.

Syntax: SETVER [drive:][path][filename n.nn]
            SETVER [drive:][path][filename [/delete][/quiet]]

To display the current version table, type:

SETVER [drive:path]

drive:path
Specifies the location of the SETVER.EXE file.

filename   The filename of the program (.EXE or .COM) to be added to the version table. Wildcards are not permitted.

n.nn   Specifies the MS-DOS version number (e.g., 3.3 or 4.01) for MS-DOS 6.0 to report to the specified program.

Switches:

/delete   Deletes the version table for the specified program file.

/quiet   Does not display messages as entries are deleted from the version table.

Description:

SETVER is a device driver and must be installed from your CONFIG.SYS file with the following line:

```
DEVICE=SETVER.EXE
```

Many applications run only on a specific version of the MS-DOS operating system. The SETVER command is used to "trick" the application into thinking that MS-DOS 6.0 is really a different version.

As developers upgrade products to work with MS-DOS 6.0, SETVER will be used less frequently.

To move SETVER.EXE to upper memory:

```
DEVICEHIGH=C: \DOS\SETVER.EXE
```

SETVER Exit Error Codes

0	SETVER completed successfully
1	Invalid command switch specified
2	Invalid filename specified
3	Insufficient memory
4	Invalid DOS version number specified

5	SETVER could not find the specified entry in the version table
6	SETVER.EXE not installed
7	Invalid drive specified
8	Too many command line parameters specified
9	Missing command line parameters
10	Error while reading SETVER.EXE file
11	SETVER.EXE has been corrupted
12	SETVER.EXE does not support version table
13	Insufficient space in the version table for new entry
14	Error while writing to SETVER.EXE

SMARTDRV.EXE

Driver to create a disk cache in extended memory. You can start the cache program in the AUTOEXEC.BAT.

Syntax: DEVICE=[drive:][path]SMARTDRV.EXE
                    /double_buffer

[drive:][path]
            Specifies the location of the SMARTDRV.EXE file.

Switches:

/double_buffer
            Enables double buffering in SMARTDRV.EXE.

Do not run disk compression (defragmentation) programs while using SMARTDRV.EXE, unless the disk compression program is compatible with SMARTDRV.EXE. The BeckerTools Compress disk optimization program from Abacus is compatible with SMARTDRV.EXE.

Appendix C: A Short History Of MS-DOS

MS-DOS's life began in the fall of 1981 with the invention of the first IBM PC. This PC had from 16 to 64K of main memory and used single sided diskettes with 160K storage capacity. MS-DOS 1.0, supplied with these PCs, supported equipment that would be spartan by today's standards and had fewer commands and options than the latest versions of MS-DOS.

Shortly thereafter, MS-DOS Version 1.1 appeared. It was able to support 320K of memory and also increased the storage capacity of diskettes by using both sides - up to 320K.

In 1983 the IBM PC/XT (XT is an abbreviation for eXTended), with a 10 Meg hard drive, appeared on the market. This hard drive could store 10 million characters. To manage the larger number of files, developers built into MS-DOS the option of setting up subdirectories. That is, there wasn't just one directory, but subdirectories where users could keep information that belonged together, just like the drawers of a desk. This new version of MS-DOS was Version 2.0. MS-DOS 2.0 made it possible for users to specify a search path for MS-DOS commands and programs with the PATH command.

In addition, Version 2.0 was better able to support new devices and peripherals. The new version had new commands for configuring the computer (DEVICE for adding additional utility programs, BUFFERS and FILES for adapting to different storage media) and a special driver called ANSI.SYS for extending the screen and keyboard control system.

In 1984 developers added the option of customizing for different countries. To do this, Version 2.1 got a program called COUNTRY.SYS. In the same year MS-DOS was translated into many different languages and licensed to many personal computer manufacturers. Thanks to this, Version 2.11 became widely distributed.

Next came the development of the successor to the PC/XT, the new PC/AT (referred to as AT nowadays). This new computer was not only faster, but could also manage more than 640K of memory and was outfitted with a hard drive and a disk drive with 1.2 Meg capacity. In 1984, MS-DOS 3.0 came out as a temporary solution for use with the AT, with support for the new disk drives and hard drives. In the same year, Version 3.1 came out. It offered network capabilities, simulated drives and keyboard adaptation to special characters such as accents in foreign countries.

With MS-DOS 3.1, it was possible for the first time to use extended memory for the AT. MS-DOS 3.1 included the driver VDISK.SYS, which could use a part of the main memory or extended memory for file storage (RAM disk).

In 1986 Version 3.2 brought support for the new 3.5 inch disk drives with 720K storage capacity. The configuration command, DRIVPARM, allowed users to change the parameters of drives. The new APPEND command not only made it possible to find commands in any directory (see *PATH*), but also allowed users to define a search path for files. MS-DOS finally had a command for copying files that included subdirectories and had special options for data backup: XCOPY.

In 1987 Version 3.3 appeared, still the most widespread version of MS-DOS. It allowed users to adapt to country specific characters that could be displayed on the screen and printed on IBM printers. You could also use CALL to call other batch files from a batch file as subroutines. What is more, the new configuration command, FASTOPEN, enabled users to find subdirectories and files quickly, speeding up their work with storage media.

Many believed that MS-DOS's successor, the multitasking operating system OS/2, meant the end of MS-DOS. Soon, however, it turned out that OS/2 required a lot of memory (from 2 Meg and upwards) and a speedy computer. Since memory was rather expensive at the time (1 Meg was about 500 dollars - today it's under 200 dollars), in 1988 another version appeared: MS-DOS 4.0. The most important innovations were:

- For the first time, a graphical user interface was available with the DOS Shell, which could be operated using pull-down menus, a mouse or a keyboard.

- The 32 Meg limit for hard drives was lifted. Hard drives could now be up to 2 gigabytes (2048 Meg) in size.

- EMM386.SYS and XMA2EMS.SYS enable users to manage expanded memory; some MS-DOS commands could also make use of it.

- Installation went smoothly, was menu-driven, the system files AUTOEXEC.BAT and CONFIG.SYS were automatically created during installation.

Then MS-DOS 5.0 was introduced with several new functions.

Finally: MS-DOS 6.0

For the first time there is a new version of MS-DOS that can not only do more on most computers, but still makes more memory available to applications. We'll tell you how this is possible and about all of the other innovations in the next section.

Hassle-free installation

Installation is not only menu driven and extremely simple, MS-DOS 6.0 also automatically backs up all of the important data of the hard drive onto a backup diskette and can restore the status prior to installation if problems develop (UNINSTALL). Also, existing versions of DOS are not overwritten, but backed up to a special directory. This guarantees a maximum amount of security. By the way, you don't even have to boot MS-DOS 6.0 for the installation. On the contrary, you can start the installation program, SETUP, from other versions of DOS, too.

A DOS Shell for everyone

If you set up the MS-DOS Shell during installation, the next time you start the system you will automatically go to its user interface. The elements of the MS-DOS Shell borrow heavily from the elements in Windows 3.1.

The new MS-DOS Shell operates according to SAA (System Application Architecture) standards. You can press F10 to activate the menu, or use Alt key combinations.

The new MS-DOS Shell has a lot of other improvements: Along with colors, users can set different graphics modes. It is also possible to divide up different tasks practically, since you can finally create new groups in program groups. This allows you to create specific user shells.

"Multitasking" in the DOS Shell

Although MS-DOS 6.0 remains a single-user, single-program operating system, the Task Swapper in the MS-DOS Shell can easily overcome this limitation of running one program at a time. If you activate the appropriate menu item in the MS-DOS Shell, the Program List opens one area for active programs. When you then start a program from the MS-DOS Shell, you can press Alt + Tab to switch to the next program, and press Ctrl + Esc to return to the MS-DOS Shell. The current program is "frozen" and saved on the hard drive.

In the MS-DOS Shell, the program appears in the list of active programs. In this way you can start several programs and switch between them. Although you cannot run several programs parallel to each other the way you can in real multitasking, switching between several programs is enough in most cases.

QBasic

The QBasic interpreter comes with MS-DOS 6.0, while earlier versions up to MS-DOS 4.01 had GW-BASIC. With QBasic you can develop programs comfortably, as the editor also supports a mouse. Anyone who is used to BASIC, a powerful, user friendly programming language, and would like to create EXE files, can just use QuickBASIC 4.5 to compile QBasic programs.

Full Screen Editor

Users who had a hard time getting used to EDLIN (can be found on the Supplemental Disk from Microsoft), the line oriented editor that came with older versions of MS-DOS, can breathe a sigh of relief with MS-DOS 6.0: The MS-DOS Editor (EDIT.COM) which comes with MS-DOS 6.0 is very similar to the editor of QBasic. You might look at the file length of EDIT.COM (less than 1K) and wonder how Microsoft was able to pack such a versatile editor in such a small program. Call QBasic with /Editor:. That should reveal the secret, because the small program, EDIT.COM does all of that.

Help included

The MS-DOS commands come with an integrated help screen, which you can activate with the /? switch. This help screen is not only available for the external commands (as is the case with the competition, DR DOS 6.0), but also for the resident commands stored in the command interpreter. That means that you don't have to go through reference manuals looking up the exact syntax of a command. The HELP command displays a list of the commands for which MS-DOS 6.0 provides a help screen.

New commands and extensions

MS-DOS 6.0 contains a number of extensions and improvements. For example, the DIR command can sort files according to various criteria (name, date, file size) and can also work over subdirectories. Aside from that, users can limit the display to files with certain file attributes. The ATTRIB command also allows users to change the attributes "System" and "Hidden".

A series of new commands expands MS-DOS 6.0's performance. The UNFORMAT command allows you to restore a hard drive or diskette that was accidentally formatted to its original state. You can use UNDELETE to recover deleted files. With SETVER you can run individual programs under different versions of MS-DOS. SETVER manages a list which is stored in the MSDOS.SYS file, making changes the next time you boot the computer. A number of programs are already included in this version list and can be displayed by entering SETVER without any parameters.

The DOSKEY command lets users reactivate command lines entered previously and edit them comfortably with the cursor keys. One error in a long command line no longer leads to frustration. What's more, DOSKEY has a type of "built in batch language" with which users can assign extensive command sequences to a single command. Microsoft refers to these command sequences as macros. These macros are very similar to batch files— you can even pass parameters.

The big advantage compared to other utility programs that are designed for the same purpose: If you assign the name of an internal MS-DOS command such as DIR to one of these macros, the macro is called first, superseding the original command for the user's own command. It allows you to create your own "personal" MS-DOS.

MS-DOS 6.0 and memory requirements

Users who are excited about the many new options and improvements but are afraid that the new DOS could require more memory, leaving even less memory available for applications, can breathe a sigh of relief if they own an AT with at least 1 Meg of main memory. MS-DOS, with the help of the extended memory manager HIMEM.SYS, uses the first 64K of extended memory (high memory), placing 50K more of main memory at your disposal for applications. If you start MS-DOS without any driver program (in a sense, naked), this leaves about 623K of memory available for applications.

To make use of this option, you need at least an AT with extended memory and the appropriate commands inserted in your CONFIG.SYS file. When you install MS-DOS 6.0, these lines are automatically added to CONFIG.SYS.

All the important MS-DOS commands prompt you for the MS-DOS version you are using (i.e., you couldn't boot from MS-DOS 3.3 and then use MS-DOS 4.0 commands). Other than that, though, MS-DOS is upwardly compatible. You can install a new version of MS-DOS and continue working with all of the programs and data.

Appendix D: ASCII Table

Dec	Hex	Char	Dec	Hex	Char	Dec	Hex	Char	Dec	Hex	Char
0	00		32	20		64	40	@	96	60	`
1	01	☺	33	21	!	65	41	A	97	61	a
2	02	☻	34	22	"	66	42	B	98	62	b
3	03	♥	35	23	#	67	43	C	99	63	c
4	04	♦	36	24	$	68	44	D	100	64	d
5	05	♣	37	25	%	69	45	E	101	65	e
6	06	♠	38	26	&	70	46	F	102	66	f
7	07	•	39	27	'	71	47	G	103	67	g
8	08	▫	40	28	(	72	48	H	104	68	h
9	09	○	41	29	)	73	49	I	105	69	i
10	0A	■	42	2A	*	74	4A	J	106	6A	j
11	0B	♂	43	2B	+	75	4B	K	107	6B	k
12	0C	♀	44	2C	,	76	4C	L	108	6C	l
13	0D	♪	45	2D	–	77	4D	M	109	6D	m
14	0E	♫	46	2E	.	78	4E	N	110	6E	n
15	0F	☼	47	2F	/	79	4F	O	111	6F	o
16	10	►	48	30	0	80	50	P	112	70	p
17	11	◄	49	31	1	81	51	Q	113	71	q
18	12	↕	50	32	2	82	52	R	114	72	r
19	13	‼	51	33	3	83	53	S	115	73	s
20	14	¶	52	34	4	84	54	T	116	74	t
21	15	§	53	35	5	85	55	U	117	75	u
22	16	▬	54	36	6	86	56	V	118	76	v
23	17	↨	55	37	7	87	57	W	119	77	w
24	18	↑	56	38	8	88	58	X	120	78	x
25	19	↓	57	39	9	89	59	Y	121	79	y
26	1A	→	58	3A	:	90	5A	Z	122	7A	z
27	1B	←	59	3B	;	91	5B	[	123	7B	{
28	1C	∟	60	3C	<	92	5C	\	124	7C		
29	1D	↔	61	3D	=	93	5D	]	125	7D	}
30	1E	▲	62	3E	>	94	5E	^	126	7E	~
31	1F	▼	63	3F	?	95	5F	_	127	7F	⌂

Dec	Hex	Char	Dec	Hex	Char	Dec	Hex	Char	Dec	Hex	Char
128	80	Ç	160	A0	á	192	C0	└	224	E0	α
129	81	ü	161	A1	í	193	C1	┴	225	E1	β
130	82	é	162	A2	ó	194	C2	┬	226	E2	Γ
131	83	â	163	A3	ú	195	C3	├	227	E3	π
132	84	ä	164	A4	ñ	196	C4	─	228	E4	Σ
133	85	à	165	A5	Ñ	197	C5	┼	229	E5	σ
134	86	å	166	A6	ª	198	C6	╞	230	E6	µ
135	87	ç	167	A7	º	199	C7	╟	231	E7	τ
136	88	ê	168	A8	¿	200	C8	╚	232	E8	Φ
137	89	ë	169	A9	⌐	201	C9	╔	233	E9	Θ
138	8A	è	170	AA	¬	202	CA	╩	234	EA	Ω
139	8B	ï	171	AB	½	203	CB	╦	235	EB	δ
140	8C	î	172	AC	¼	204	CC	╠	236	EC	∞
141	8D	ì	173	AD	¡	205	CD	═	237	ED	Ø
142	8E	Ä	174	AE	«	206	CE	╬	238	EE	∈
143	8F	Å	175	AF	»	207	CF	╧	239	EF	∩
144	90	É	176	B0	░	208	D0	╨	240	F0	≡
145	91	æ	177	B1	▒	209	D1	╤	241	F1	±
146	92	Æ	178	B2	▓	210	D2	╥	242	F2	≥
147	93	ô	179	B3	│	211	D3	╙	243	F3	≤
148	94	ö	180	B4	┤	212	D4	╘	244	F4	⌠
149	95	ò	181	B5	╡	213	D5	╒	245	F5	⌡
150	96	û	182	B6	╢	214	D6	╓	246	F6	÷
151	97	ù	183	B7	╖	215	D7	╫	247	F7	≈
152	98	ÿ	184	B8	╕	216	D8	╪	248	F8	°
153	99	Ö	185	B9	╣	217	D9	┘	249	F9	•
154	9A	Ü	186	BA	║	218	DA	┌	250	FA	·
155	9B	¢	187	BB	╗	219	DB	█	251	FB	√
156	9C	£	188	BC	╝	220	DC	▄	252	FC	ⁿ
157	9D	¥	189	BD	╜	221	DD	▌	253	FD	²
158	9E	₧	190	BE	╛	222	DE	▐	254	FE	■
159	9F	ƒ	191	BF	┐	223	DF	▀	255	FF	

Appendix E: The Companion Diskette

The companion diskette has two subdirectories, TEMPEST and DOS6CPLT. The Tempest files are located in the TEMPEST directory and the DOS6CPLT directory contains files for batch, COM and EXE files discussed in this book. See the last section in this book for information on Tempest.

Both the TEMPEST and DOS6CPLT directories include self-extracting archive files. The root directory of the companion diskette contains two installation programs:

- INSTALL.EXE installs the batch and executable files in the DOS6CPLT directory to your hard drive.

- SETUP.BAT installs the Tempest graphical shell files in the TEMPEST directory to your hard drive.

If you're a newcomer to DOS, or to PCs, you may want to wait on installing the *DOS 6.0 Complete* batch and executable files using INSTALL, because these files require some modifications to the AUTOEXEC.BAT and CONFIG.SYS files. Instead, you may feel more comfortable working with Tempest. Run SETUP on the companion diskette, and see the last section of this book for information on Tempest.

The *DOS 6.0 Complete* batch and executable files are installed using the INSTALL program. Simply insert the companion diskette in your drive, make that drive the current drive, type

INSTALL

and press Enter. Follow the instructions displayed on your screen. More information is contained in the README.TXT file located on the companion diskette.

After running INSTALL, you'll find two directories on your hard drive:

- The BASIC directory contains the QBasic program listings from Chapter 17 (Using QBasic).

- The TOOLS directory contains a group of ready-to-run programs to streamline your sessions with DOS.

The TOOLS directory contains many of the batch files described throughout this book. We've included a set of utilities in this directory that we'll describe now.

Listing of TOOLS programs:

Filename	EXT	Purpose
CLEAR	.BAT	Clears all environment variables
COLOR	.BAT	Configures screen colors
FINDFILE	.BAT	Find files on a storage medium
FONT	.BAT	Sets DOS font attributes
GETFUNC	.BAT	Displays function key assignments
HEADMSG	.BAT	Displays parameter as text in inverse video header
HELPME	.BAT	Invokes help screens for companion diskette files
HELPME1	.TXT	Text file read by HELPME.BAT
HELPME2	.TXT	Text file read by HELPME.BAT
HELPME3	.TXT	Text file read by HELPME.BAT
HELPME4	.TXT	Text file read by HELPME.BAT
KEYBOARD	.BAT	Sets keyboard speed
RUNDIR	.BAT	Runs applications from anywhere
SETFUNC	.BAT	Assigns keys to function keys
SFORMAT	.BAT	Formats without danger to hard drive C:
SIZE	.EXE	Determines space free on storage medium
SPRINT	.BAT	Configures printer
TCD	.EXE	Tornsdorf-CD changes to any directory (incl. wildcards)
WAIT	.EXE	Pauses the system or screen display

The TOOLS directory also contains a group of data files, batch files and programs not directly accessible from DOS, but important to the TOOLS files.

Listing of TOOLS utility files:

Filename	EXT	Purpose
CAPITAL	.EXE	Converts characters to uppercase
DIRDAT	.COM	Directory data
DOSVERS	.COM	Gets DOS version
FINDPRG	.EXE	Program finder
INPUT	.EXE	Input reader
NEXT	.EXE	Next call
PATH_ADD	.DAT	Path addition data
SETINP	.BAT	Input data generated by some files

AUTOEXEC.BAT and CONFIG.SYS

These files can be found in the root directories of almost every PC in existence. AUTOEXEC.BAT and CONFIG.SYS perform some general DOS housekeeping chores (e.g., loading special driver software for mouse or keyboard input). To use the contents of the TOOLS directory, you'll need to alter the contents of your AUTOEXEC.BAT and CONFIG.SYS files. Before doing this, remember to make backup copies of these files. If you must revert to the original files, you can copy the old files to their original names and reboot your system.

INSTALL defaults

INSTALL defaults to the C: hard drive when installing the tools. INSTALL also assumes that you are installing the data from drive A: and that your DOS commands are in a directory named \DOS.

You must have COMMAND.COM and ANSI.SYS located in the root directory of your hard drive. If this is not the case, copy these files from your DOS directory. Otherwise, edit the CONFIG.SYS and AUTOEXEC.BAT files after installation to indicate the locations of COMMAND.COM and ANSI.SYS.

Final preparations

Before you can reboot and test out your new tools, you must make some modifications to your CONFIG.SYS and AUTOEXEC.BAT files. Start by creating backup copies of CONFIG.SYS and AUTOEXEC.BAT. Make your hard drive the current drive (e.g., C:), and change to the root directory (CD \). Type the following, pressing Enter at the end of each line:

```
COPY CONFIG.SYS CONFIG.BAK
COPY AUTOEXEC.BAT AUTOEXEC.BAT
```

IMPORTANT

Create a DOS FAILSAFE diskette for rebooting from diskette in case you make an error editing your CONFIG.SYS and AUTOEXEC.BAT files. Insert a diskette in drive A: and type:

```
FORMAT A: /S
```

This creates a system diskette. Copy your CONFIG.SYS and AUTOEXEC.BAT files to this diskette. Now remove this DOS FAILSAFE diskette, label it, and keep it close at hand.

Modifying CONFIG.SYS and AUTOEXEC.BAT

First, run the MS-DOS Editor (EDIT.COM) and select File/Open.... When the dialog box appears, type "\CONFIG.SYS" and press Enter. This loads the CONFIG.SYS file into memory.

Look for a group of lines starting with the word "DEVICE=". After the DEVICE listings, move the insertion point to the first column and type the following lines:

```
DEVICE=C:\ANSI.SYS
SHELL=C:\COMMAND.COM /P /E:1000
```

Save the file by selecting File/Save. Select File/Open... again. This time, type "\AUTOEXEC.BAT" and press Enter. Look for the PATH statement, which looks something like this (yours will probably look different):

```
PATH C:\DOS;\C:\WORD;D:\WORKS
```

Add ;\TOOLS to the PATH statement so that it has the following at the end of the line:

```
PATH C:\DOS;\C:\WORD;D:\WORKS;C:\TOOLS
```

While you're editing the PATH statement, add the following data to AUTOEXEC.BAT:

SET COMSPEC=C:\COMMAND.COM
SET BatDir=C:\TOOLS

Once installation is complete you will need to reboot the computer. This puts the information included in the new AUTOEXEC.BAT and CONFIG.SYS files into effect. After installation press (Ctrl) + (Alt) + (Del) to reboot.

Using these utilities

We'll go into detail about each file soon. For now, here are some ground rules about running the files.

How they work

Most of the files on the companion diskette are batch files - a set of MS-DOS commands, which access MS-DOS commands (e.g., DISKCOPY). These batch files are identified by their file extensions of .BAT. The other files are executable programs compiled with Turbo Pascal, distinguished by .EXE and .COM file extensions. These executable files act as support for the batch files - few of them will run on their own, without access through batch files.

There are two methods of running batch files: Direct input from the system prompt, including all batch file parameters; and dialog mode, when provided in the batch file.

What are parameters?

We mentioned batch file parameters earlier. These parameters provide important information to a command or file. Parameters entered in direct access mode must be separated from one another by single spaces. For example, if you wanted to view the directory listing in drive A: of all files, and have this listing displayed in wide (columnar) mode, you would type the following with the /W (wide) switch:

```
DIR A:*.* /W
```

In either the direct access method or dialog mode method, the end result is the same: The batch file acts upon the parameters provided by the user.

Let's take a closer look at both methods, using the COLOR.BAT file, which controls screen colors.

Direct input

Many of the batch files on the companion diskette can be called right from the system prompt without further communication between the user and the system. The syntax of the COLOR.BAT reads:

```
COLOR FOREGROUND BACKGROUND
```

The following changes the screen colors to a red foreground and white background:

```
COLOR RED WHITE
```

Dialog mode

Many of the batch files on the companion diskette also provide a dialog mode, in case users forget a parameter or two. If you enter the COLOR command without any parameters, COLOR displays a dialog box. You can then respond to the prompts displayed by the batch file.

Headers and user information

A batch file named HEADMSG.BAT displays additional information at the top of the screen in a header. Here you may find the name of the file currently running, or text intended to help you execute the batch file. If it does not display properly, make sure your ANSI.SYS file is accessible.

Canceling and clearing

You can easily exit the dialog mode of a batch file by pressing the Esc key.

However, if you started a batch file from the system prompt in direct mode, you can exit the batch file by pressing either Ctrl+C or Ctrl+Pause (also referred to as the <Break> key). After doing so, run the CLEAR command to ensure that all important system variables are reset to their earlier status. This is especially important if your system prompt has become invisible (it will if @ECHO OFF has been called in a batch file).

Getting general help

Change to the TOOLS directory and run the HELPME.BAT file. HELPME displays five separate screens listing the batch files available from the companion diskette files. You may prefer to call HELPME from a function key. For more information on assigning data to function keys, see the description of SETFUNC which appears later in this Appendix.

Batch file descriptions

The following paragraphs describe each TOOLS file in detail. The syntax of each batch file is as follows:

COMMAND

Short description

Syntax: COMMAND parameters

Detailed descriptions with examples where applicable.

Here a few rules you should remember about the characters:

- If you plan to enter a path as a File-group parameter, remember to begin the path with a backslash. If you do not do this, the batch file will begin searching at the current directory. Here's an example:

    \DOCS\PRIVATE

- If a path and file identifier is to be entered as a File-group parameter, you must end the directory path with a backslash, immediately followed by the file identifier. The following specifies all DOC files in the \DOCS\PRIVATE directory:

    \DOCS\PRIVATE*.DOC

- Parameters enclosed in [brackets] are optional, but must be entered if you want to take advantage of this parameter.

- Parameters not enclosed in [brackets] must be entered as part of the batch file. Unbracketed parameters indicate data needed by the batch file.

If you call a batch file using incorrect or missing parameters, the computer beeps and the batch file shifts into dialog mode.

CLEAR

Clears environment variables

Syntax: CLEAR

Pressing Ctrl+C or Ctrl+Pause (also referred to as the <Break> key) during batch file execution stops the batch file, but environment variables may still contain data.

Calling CLEAR resets existing system variables to their original values, or removes variables that may have been added since booting the computer. CLEAR also restores the default prompt if the prompt has been changed since booting the computer.

COLOR

Selecting screen colors

Syntax: COLOR Foreground [Background]

The COLOR program changes foreground and background screen colors. If you enter only the Foreground parameter, the foreground color is affected. If you enter the Background parameter as well, the foreground and background colors will change.

If no parameters are specified when calling the COLOR.BAT file the following help screen is displayed:

```
╓──────────────────────────────────────────────────────────╖
║  COLOR.BAT lets you change the colors of the screen      ║
║                                                          ║
║    Syntax: COLOR Foreground [Background]                 ║
║                                                          ║
║  If you enter only one parameter it will be applied to   ║
║     the foreground.  If entered the second will apply to ║
║     the background.                                      ║
║                                                          ║
║         Possible foreground and background colors:       ║
║            Black              Blue                        ║
║            Red                Magenta (Violet)           ║
║            Green              Cyan                       ║
║            Yellow             White                      ║
║                                                          ║
╙──────────────────────────────────────────────────────────╜
```

Available colors:

```
Black
Blue
Red
Magenta (Violet)
Green
Cyan (Light blue)
Yellow
White
```

FINDFILE

Find file on hard drive

Syntax: FINDFILE Filename

As directory structures become more and more complicated, the problems with keeping track of files increase proportionally. It gets harder to know where a file is on a disk drive, or if duplicates of the same file exist. FINDFILE is the answer.

FINDFILE.BAT searches the current storage medium for a file, informing you of the location of that file in the directory tree.

The Filename parameter specifies the file you want to find. Wildcards are not allowed here - if you do use a wildcard, FINDFILE assumes that all the other characters entered are wild as well.

The following searches for CONFIG.SYS:

```
FINDFILE CONFIG.SYS
```

The following searches for all files using the name/extension/path CON:

```
FINDFILE CON
```

It is also possible to search for files with more than one extension if you enter a period followed by one or more characters. The following searches for every file with an extension beginning with C:

```
FINDFILE .C
```

The following searches for all files with .TXT extensions:

```
FINDFILE .TXT
```

FINDFILE can also be instructed to find filenames immediately to the left of the "dot" and extensions immediately to the right of the "dot". The following searches for files ending with BOOK, and with extensions starting with TX:

```
FINDFILE BOOK.TX
```

A backslash at the beginning of the Filename parameter searches for files beginning with the characters immediately following the backslash. The following searches for files and directories starting with BOOK:

```
FINDFILE \BOOK
```

   Do not use wildcards (* or ?) with FINDFILE. FINDFILE
will then search for files containing these characters.

The first time you run FINDFILE it will generate a file named
FINDFILE.TMP. This contains all the available files. Each time
you call FINDFILE, the batch file refers to FINDFILE.TMP on
subsequent calls, thus speeding up access time. Entering FINDFILE
/INIT starts the TMP file from scratch.

If no parameters are specified when calling the FINDFILE.BAT
file the following help screen is displayed:

```
╔══════════════════════════════════════════════════════════╗
║      FINDFILE.BAT searches the current drive for a given  ║
║         file and gives the directory name if found.       ║
║                                                            ║
║ Syntax:    FINDFILE filename                               ║
║ Example:   FINDFILE CONFIG.SYS                             ║
║            Finds the CONFIG.SYS file.                      ║
║ Example:   FINDFILE CON                                    ║
║            Searches for all file names which include CON   ║
║ Example:   FINDFILE .SYS                                   ║
║            Finds all files with a .SYS extension           ║
║ Note:      FINDFILE /INIT                                  ║
║            This will update the contents of FINDFILE.TMP   ║
╚══════════════════════════════════════════════════════════╝
```

FONT

Change text display on the screen

Syntax: FONT Parameter

This program changes the text attributes as they appear on the
screen.

Available options

N	Normal
K	Blinking
B	Bold
I	Inverse
U	Underline
X	Hidden

   The underline attribute changes the foreground color.

These attribute changes apply only to DOS - most applications (e.g., word processors) may use their own special screen drivers, thus overriding attributes set by FONT.

GETFUNC

Display function key assignments

Syntax: GETFUNC

This command displays the function key assignments dictated by SETFUNC. Default DOS assignments (e.g., [F3] for retyping commands) will not be displayed.

HELPME

Display help text

Syntax: HELPME

This command displays a brief help text about the new commands contained on the companion diskette. Change to the TOOLS directory and run HELPME. The following screens are displayed when this batch file is called:

```
┌─────────────────────────────────────────────────────────────┐
│            TOOLS - Information about these files              │
├─────────────────────────────────────────────────────────────┤
│ _CD       BAT Data for CD_GET & CD_SET                        │
│ &ADDPATH  BAT Adds path data                                  │
│ &FORMAT   BAT Safe format command for drive A:                │
│ &GCOPY    BAT General copy command to A:                      │
│ &GOTO     BAT Goto command                                    │
│ ACD       BAT Modified CD                                     │
│ CAPITAL   EXE Capitalize text                                 │
│ CD        DAT Data for CD_GET & CD_SET                        │
│ CD_GET    BAT Get current directory                           │
│ CD_SET    BAT Set current directory                           │
│ CLEAR     BAT Clear environment vars                          │
│ COLOR     BAT Set screen colors                               │
│ DELBAK    BAT Delete backup files                             │
│ DIRALL    EXE Create ALLDIR.TMP file                          │
│ DIRD      BAT Subdirectory display                            │
│ DIRDAT    COM Sort files by date                              │
│ DIRSORT   BAT Displays sorted directory                       │
│ DOSVERS   COM DOS version as ERRORLEVEL                        │
├──────────┬───────────────────────────────────┬───────────────┤
│  Page 1  │ Change pages with PgUp ↑ and PgDn ↓│ END the HELP with ESC │
└──────────┴───────────────────────────────────┴───────────────┘
```

```
┌─────────────────────────────────────────────────────────────────┐
│              TOOLS - Information about these files                │
├─────────────────────────────────────────────────────────────────┤
│ ENDWRK    BAT Documents end time of work                         │
│ ENTER         [Enter] key data                                   │
│ ENTER     DAT [Enter] key data                                   │
│ ERROR     BAT Errorlevel control                                 │
│ FINDFILE  BAT Locate file                                        │
│ FINDPRG   EXE Find path to executables                           │
│ FONT      BAT Set screen font attribute                          │
│ FONT09    BAT Changes font attributes                            │
│ FORMAT1   BAT Safe formatter                                     │
│ FORMATA   BAT Formats drive A: only                              │
│ GETFUNC   BAT Get function key settings                          │
│ HEADMSG   BAT Display screen header                              │
│ HELPME    BAT Help file                                          │
│ INPUT     EXE Send input to SETINP.BAT                           │
│ KEYBOARD  BAT Speed configuration                                │
│ NEXT      EXE CD to next logical dir                             │
│ NOTE      BAT Generate _CD.BAT data                              │
│ PATH_ADD  DAT PATH DATA (don't modify)                           │
├──────────┬──────────────────────────────────┬───────────────────┤
│ Page 2   │ Change pages with PgUp ↑ and PgDn ↓ │ END the HELP with ESC │
└──────────┴──────────────────────────────────┴───────────────────┘
```

```
┌─────────────────────────────────────────────────────────────────┐
│              TOOLS - Information about these files                │
├─────────────────────────────────────────────────────────────────┤
│ PCX-DOC   BAT Back up PCX and DOC files                          │
│ PCX-DOC2  BAT Back up PCX and DOC filenames                      │
│ PRDIR     BAT Print directory to dot matrix printer              │
│ READTHIS  TXT Important information about this diskette data      │
│ RUNDIR    BAT Run apps from any dir                              │
│ SETFUNC   BAT Set function key commands                          │
│ SETINP    DAT INPUT DATA (don't modify)                          │
│ SFORMAT   BAT Safe format (floppies)                             │
│ SHOWPRG   BAT Show file extensions of executable programs        │
│ SHOWPRG2  BAT Show file extensions of executable programs        │
│ SIZE      EXE Sizes of selected files                            │
│ SPRINT    BAT Set printer within DOS                             │
│ STARTWRK  BAT Documents starting work time                       │
│ STRADD    EXE Add string                                         │
│ STRFIND   EXE Find string                                        │
│ TCD       EXE CD from anywhere                                   │
│ TEXTDIR   BAT Switch to DOC directory and display files          │
│ TEXTDIR2  BAT Switch to DOC directory and display files          │
├──────────┬──────────────────────────────────┬───────────────────┤
│ Page 3   │ Change pages with PgUp ↑ and PgDn ↓ │ END the HELP with ESC │
└──────────┴──────────────────────────────────┴───────────────────┘
```

```
┌─────────────────────────────────────────────────────────────────┐
│              TOOLS - Information about these files                │
├─────────────────────────────────────────────────────────────────┤
│ TEXTDIR   BAT Switch to DOC directory and display files          │
│ TEXTDIR2  BAT Switch to DOC directory and display files          │
│ TIME      DAT Time data                                          │
│ TYPEM     BAT Type command with MORE parameter                   │
│ TYPEM2    BAT Type command with MORE parameter                   │
│ WHERE     BAT Find file                                          │
│ WAIT      EXE Wait for time/keypress                             │
│                                                                  │
│                                                                  │
│                                                                  │
│                                                                  │
│                                                                  │
│                                                                  │
├──────────┬──────────────────────────────────┬───────────────────┤
│ Page 4   │ Change pages with PgUp ↑ and PgDn ↓ │ END the HELP with ESC │
└──────────┴──────────────────────────────────┴───────────────────┘
```

```
┌─────────────────────────────────────────────────────────────────────┐
│             BASIC - Information about these QBASIC programs            │
├─────────────────────────────────────────────────────────────────────┤
│ O-WAIT    Wait loop                                                   │
│ OTO1000   Wait loop - Counts 0 to 1000                                │
│ ASCII     Generates simple ASCII table with numbers                   │
│ BARCHART  Simple bar chart using asterisks                            │
│ DOLLAR    Monetary exchange (Dollars to Deutschmarks)                 │
│ GOSUB     Subroutine demo                                             │
│ SINECGA   Sine wave demo (CGA)                                        │
│ SINEHGA   Sine wave demo (Hercules, w/ optional VGA parameters)       │
│ STARSKY   Screen saver - stars in the sky                             │
│ WHERFILE BAT Simple file search                                       │
│                                                                       │
│                                                                       │
│                                                                       │
│                                                                       │
├──────────┬──────────────────────────────────┬───────────────────────┤
│ Page 5   │ Change pages with PgUp ↑ and PgDn ↓ │ END the HELP with ESC │
└──────────┴──────────────────────────────────┴───────────────────────┘
```

KEYBOARD

Configures keyboard speed

Syntax: KEYBOARD Speed

Sometimes adjusting the speed of your keyboard is a practical move. Many high-speed PCs actually require slowing keyboard response, because the user's hands cannot keep pace with the PC. This utility lets you adjust the speed of the keyboard repeat on your system.

The Speed parameter has two options:

Fast   Keyboard speed increases to maximum.

Normal   Keyboard speed reverts to normal.

RUNDIR

Start program from any directory

Syntax: RUNDIR Programname [Parameter]

Most applications are placed in their own directories. Before you can start an application, you may have to change to that directory. Frequent use of this application may force you to write a batch file to run the program, or you can use RUNDIR (RUN in own DIRectory).

RUNDIR searches on the current storage medium for an application with a .COM, .EXE or .BAT extension and the specified program name, changes to the directory containing that application and runs the application.

You can also include parameters in RUNDIR which control the way a program runs.

The following runs PCSHELL:

```
RUNDIR PCSHELL
```

The Parameter parameter lets you add switches or filenames to the command call. The following runs Microsoft Word and instructs Word to load the last file edited:

```
RUNDIR WORD /L
```

The following runs Microsoft Word and loads a file named BENZER.DOC from the PRIVATE directory:

```
RUNDIR WORD \PRIVATE\BENZER
```

   The PATH command in AUTOEXEC.BAT must be configured to direct RUNDIR to the application.

SETFUNC

Function key setup made easy (F1 - F10)

Syntax: SETFUNC Function-key [Assignment] [/RETURN]

The MS-DOS function key allocations don't allow for much flexibility. SETFUNC (SET FUNCtion keys) lets you give new assignments to function keys, whether these assignments access DOS commands or call applications.

Entering SETFUNC Function-key without any other parameters clears that function key of its current setting.

The following clears any settings from F3:

```
SETFUNC F3
```

SETFUNC with an Assignment parameter designates the specified function key as having that assignment. Pressing the function key and the Enter key executes that command.

The following assigns the DIR command to the F3 key:

```
SETFUNC F3 DIR
```

The /RETURN switch adds the ability to execute commands immediately, as if you entered the command by hand and pressed the (Enter) key.

The following assigns the DIR command to the (F3) key and adds the (Enter) key for immediate command execution:

```
SETFUNC F3 DIR /RETURN
```

SETFUNC concludes with a listing of current function key assignments.

 These function key assignments are lost when you reboot the computer. If you would like to have permanent function key re-assignments, you can add the definitions in your AUTOEXEC.BAT file (see your DOS documentation for more information on MS-DOS, or read *MS-DOS for Beginners*, published by Abacus). AUTOEXEC.BAT requires a CALL command to access SETFUNC. Inserting the following line in AUTOEXEC.BAT calls SETFUNC and makes the (F4) key the "official" DIR key:

```
CALL SETFUNC F4 DIR /RETURN
```

If no parameters are specified when calling the SETFUNC.BAT file the following help screen is displayed:

```
Syntax: SETFUNC F-KEY [Assignment] [/RETURN]

When you assign function to F1 to F10, the previous
       function key assignment will be erased.

Function key assignment can be almost anything.

If you want the function to simulate the user pressing
the Enter key, include the /RETURN switch as the last
or the third parameter.
Examples:
SETFUNC F3 : Deletes the current assignment of F3
SETFUNC F3 DIR : Assigns the DIR command to F3
SETFUNC F3 DIR /RETURN : Assigns the DIR command to F3
                and executes it by simulating a RETURN.
```

SIZE

Returns memory used by selected files

Syntax: SIZE [Path][File-group]

It is often necessary to know how much space a selected group of files takes on a disk. This can be useful when you plan to copy the contents of a subdirectory to a diskette, but you want to be sure that enough space exists on the diskette to complete the copy operation. The SIZE command is useful for this.

If you enter SIZE without a File-group parameter, SIZE checks the file allocation for the entire storage medium on the current drive and directory. It displays how many bytes would be needed for transfer to a 360K (or 720K) diskette, and for transfer to a 1.2 Meg (or 1.44 Meg) diskette.

The differences between normal and high-density diskettes appear because of the way MS-DOS reserves memory on varying diskette types.

SIZE provides the option of entering a path and File-group to limit the file check.

The following checks the amount of memory occupied by the DOC files in the TEXTS directory of the current drive:

```
SIZE \TEXTS\*.DOC
```

SFORMAT

Format floppy diskettes

Syntax: SFORMAT Drive: [Options]

The FORMAT command is an important but dangerous command. As it will format any storage medium, there is the possible danger of accidentally formatting a hard drive or diskette, thus destroying valuable data.

The SFORMAT (Safe FORMAT) command will not allow access to drive C: for formatting. If you enter C: as the Drive: parameter, the computer beeps and SFORMAT informs you that you cannot format the hard drive from within SFORMAT.

The Drive: parameter specifies the drive you want used for the format. Type the drive identifier followed by a colon.

The following invokes SFORMAT for formatting drive A:

```
SFORMAT A:
```

The Options designate the type of formatting you want performed. The following switches are available:

/Q　　Performs a quick format.

/V　　Allows the entry of a volume label. The /V switch must be immediately followed by a colon and the volume label name (e.g., /V:RALPH).

/U　　Unconditional format (no UNFORMAT possible).

/4　　Formats a diskette as 360K (XT format). Available only to AT users.

/B　　Allocates space on the storage medium for system files.

/S　　Copies system files to the diskette, making it a bootable (system) diskette.

The following formats the diskette in drive A:, assigns a volume label of BOOTDISK and makes the disk a system diskette:

```
SFORMAT A: /V:BOOTDISK /S
```

If no parameters are specified when calling the SFORMAT.BAT file, the following help screen is displayed:

```
┌─────────────────────────────────────────────────────┐
│         SFORMAT.BAT formats floppy disks only.        │
│                                                       │
│         Syntax: SFORMAT Drive: [Options]              │
│   Options:                                            │
│     /v    : Volume label (disk name).                 │
│     /q    : Quick format.                             │
│     /u    : Unconditional format.                     │
│     /f    : Disk size.                                │
│     /b    : Reserve space for system files.           │
│     /s    : Copy system files to disk.                │
│     /t:yy : Number of tracks/side.                    │
│     /n:xx : Number of sectors/track.                  │
│     /1    : Format one side only.                     │
│     /4    : Double-sided 360K format.                 │
│     /8    : Format 8 sectors per track.               │
└─────────────────────────────────────────────────────┘
```

SPRINT

Configure printer parameters

Syntax:　　SPRINT Parameter

This program configures a few printer parameters (e.g., character height or line height) for printing under MS-DOS.

Remember the following when using this program:

- If you call SPRINT in direct mode, you have the option of entering a parameter for line height as well as character height.

- In dialog mode you can only enter one parameter per execution of the program. The following parameters are available in SPRINT:

Character size

Wide: Printing at 80 characters per line

Compressed:
             Printing at 132 characters per line

Line height

Tall: Printing at 6 lines per inch

Short: Printing at 8 lines per inch

Default parameter

Normal: 80 characters per line, 6 lines per inch

 This program will only work under MS-DOS (e.g., printing directories). Applications such as word processors usually contain their own special printer configuration commands.

TCD

Fast directory change with wildcards

Syntax: TCD Directoryname

Complicated directory structures are important for maintaining order on your hard drive. It becomes tiresome after a while, however, to enter complete pathnames every time you wish to change directories with the CD command. The TCD (Tornsdorf CD) command offers an alternative.

TCD lets you switch to any directory on the current disk without your having to enter the full pathname. It works similarly to the Norton Utilities NCD command, except that TCD doesn't require a companion file. This saves you the trouble of updating the companion file every time the directory structure changes.

You can even use wildcards with TCD. For example, TCD DB* will change to the DBASE directory from any other directory on the storage medium.

TCD searches the hard drive for a directory with the specified name and changes to it. This works even if the directory name you enter is a subdirectory of another directory.

Use TCD as you would the CD command. Unlike the CD command, however, TCD can only be used on the current drive. You may want to place a copy of TCD on each hard drive available on your system.

The following changes to the next highest directory in the directory tree:

    TCD

The following changes to the root directory:

    TCD \

The following changes to a directory name starting with PRIV (e.g., C:\DOCS\LETTERS\PRIVATE):

    TCD PRIV*

 Avoid using duplicate directory names in different subdirectories of a disk. TCD will find only the first available occurrence, ignoring any subsequent occurrences.

TEMPEST

Graphic DOS Shells

Syntax: Tempest

As an added BONUS to this book, we've included the complete Graphic User Interface for DOS 6.0, Tempest. Tempest is a complete, independent software package included with this book. The complete Tempest manual is the last section of this book.

Tempest is an intuitive shell for DOS 6.0 that allows you to graphically display all of the program and files on your hard drive. Using Tempest anyone can easily master complex DOS computer commands with a simple point and click of the mouse. See the Tempest section for more information on Tempest.

Appendix F: QBasic Keywords

QBasic is a rich and powerful language, as is demonstrated by the
following list of keywords. To view all QBasic keywords from the
QBasic Editor, select **Help**, then choose the **Index** command. To
obtain information about a specific keyword, place the cursor in
the word, then press F1.

An alternate method of obtaining information is to type the
keyword in the Editor, move the cursor into the keyword and press
F1. The Help screen for the keyword will be displayed.

$DYNAMIC	CVD	EXP
$STATIC	CVDMBF	FIELD
ABS	CVI	FILEATTR
ABSOLUTE	CVL	FILES
ACCESS	CVS	FIX
AND	CVSMBF	FOR...NEXT
APPEND	DATA	FRE
AS	DATE$ Function	FREEFILE
ASC	DATE$ Statement	FUNCTION
ATN	DECLARE	GET(FileI/O)
BASE	DEFDBL	GET(Graphics)
BEEP	DEF FN	GOSUB
BINARY	DEFINT	GOTO
BLOAD	DEFLNG	HEX$
BSAVE	DEF SEG	IF..THEN...ELSE
CALL	DEFSNG	IMP
CALL ABSOLUTE	DEFSTR	INKEY$
CASE	DIM	INP
CDBL	DO...LOOP	INPUT
CHAIN	DOUBLE	INPUT$
CHDIR	DRAW	INSTR
CHR$	ELSE	INT
CINT	ELSEIF	INTEGER
CIRCLE	END	IOCTL
CLEAR	ENVIRON	IOCTL$
CLNG	ENVIRON$	IS
CLOSE	EOF	KEY(Assignment)
CLS	EQV	KEY(EventTrapping)
COLOR	ERASE	KILL
COM	ERDEV	LBOUND
COMMON	ERDEV$	LCASE$
CONST	ERL	LEFT$
COS	ERR	LEN
CSNG	ERROR	LET
CSRLIN	EXIT	LINE(Graphics)

LINEINPUT	PCOPY	SQR
LIST	PEEK	STATIC
LOC	PEN	STEP
LOCATE	PEN	STICK
LOCK...UNLOCK	PLAY	STOP
LOF	PLAY(Event	STR$
LOG	Trapping)	STRIG Function
LONG	PLAY(Music)	STRIG Statement
LOOP	PMAP	STRING
LPOS	POINT	STRING$
LPRINT	POKE	SUB
LPRINT USING	POS	SWAP
LSET	PRESET	SYSTEM
LTRIM$	PRINT	TAB
MID$ Function	PRINT USING	TAN
MID$ Statement	PSET	THEN
MKD$	PUT(FileI/O)	TIME$ Function
MKDIR	PUT(Graphics)	TIME$ Statement
MKDMBF$	RANDOM	TIMER Function
MKI$	RANDOMIZE	TIMER Statements
MKL$	READ	TO
MKS$	REDIM	TROFF
MKSMBF$	REM	TRON
MOD	RESET	TYPE
NAME	RESTORE	UBOUND
NEXT	RESUME	UCASE$
NOT	RETURN	UNLOCK
OCT$	RIGHT$	UNTIL
OFF	RMDIR	USING
ON	RND	VAL
ON...GOSUB	RSET	VARPTR
ON...GOTO	RTRIM$	VARPTR$
ON COM	RUN	VARSEG
ON ERROR	SCREEN Function	VIEW
ON KEY	SCREEN Statement	VIEWPRINT
ON PEN	SEEK Function	WAIT
ON PLAY	SEEK Statement	WEND
ON STRIG	SELECTCASE	WHILE...WEND
ON TIMER	SGN	WIDTH
OPEN	SHARED	WINDOW
OPENCOM	SHELL	WRITE
OPTION BASE	SIN	XOR
OR	SINGLE	
OUT	SLEEP	
OUTPUT	SOUND	
PAINT	SPACE$	
PALETTE	SPC	

Appendix G: Quick Index

MS-DOS 6.0 Commands

Index

Tempest
The Graphics Shell
for
MS-DOS 6.0

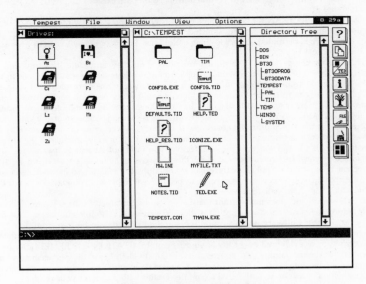

Tempest

by Martin Grümpel

Abacus
A Data Becker Product

Contents

1. Tempest The Graphic Program Manager

Tempest is a graphics program manager for DOS that makes using your computer easier. If you have been using your computer for a while, you know that a good deal of your time is spent with various file management chores. Your hard drive can contain thousands of files, all of which need to be backed up and kept in order.

Your computer's operating system already has a number of commands and utility programs for copying, deleting, viewing and editing files. For the most part, however, these commands are inconvenient and complex to enter.

This is where Tempest steps in. Tempest combines all of the files on your hard drive and diskettes into a single system. Files are displayed as symbols called "icons". You know immediately if a file is a text file or a database file. If you want to do something with a particular file, you don't have to type in any commands. With Tempest, a few clicks of the mouse will do it all.

1.1 Hardware and Software Requirements

Tempest runs on all IBM XT/AT computers and 100% compatibles equipped with an EGA or VGA graphics card. You will need a hard drive and DOS 5.0 or higher. We also recommend using a mouse.

1.2 Installation

Make a backup copy of your original diskette before installing Tempest. For this special edition of DOS 6.0 Complete, two directories have been placed on the companion diskette, DOS6CPLT and TEMPEST. The files needed for installing Tempest are located in the TEMPEST directory.

If you are connected to a network, reboot your computer and do not enter the commands necessary to establish a connection to the network. Tempest will recognize and run properly with network drives. However, the installation program may not run correctly if network drives are detected.

Tempest may be installed by either of two methods. First, make the drive containing your companion diskette the current drive and type "SETUP". Press Enter and follow the instructions which appear on your screen to install Tempest.

The other installation process is to change to the TEMPEST directory on the companion diskette, type "INSTALL" and press Enter. Follow the instructions on your screen to complete the installation process.

You may also choose to have Tempest run automatically every time you boot your computer by allowing the installation program to insert a line in your AUTOEXEC.BAT file.

If you decide not to install Tempest automatically when running the installation program, then decide at some future time to autoload Tempest, add the following sequence (using the correct pathname for your system) to your AUTOEXEC.BAT file:

```
PATH C:\TEMPEST
TEMPEST
```

Make sure you edit your PATH statement and add the path for Tempest to the end of it, preserving previously defined paths necessary for other applications.

1.3   Starting Tempest

Start Tempest by changing to the directory containing the Tempest files and type "TEMPEST Enter" on the DOS command line.

Most Tempest commands are executed with the mouse. This manual will use the following terms when describing mouse operations:

Click   Move the mouse pointer to an object and press the left mouse button.

Drag   Move the mouse pointer to an object, press and hold the left mouse button, and move the object to its destination.

Double-click
               Click the mouse button twice in rapid succession.

In many cases, it will not matter whether you click the left or right mouse button. However, some special functions (e.g., marking multiple files) do require the use of the right mouse button.

The mouse pointer normally appears as an arrow. This arrow will change its appearance under certain circumstances. For example, it turns into a thinking bubble when the computer is busy doing something, or a hand when the mouse pointer is located over a button.

2. First Steps

This chapter includes some practical examples to provide a brief introduction to Tempest. This is only intended as a first glance - no attempt is made to cover all of Tempest's features here. Following these examples will allow you to become familiar with the basics of Tempest, making it easier for you to use the more advanced features presented later.

2.1 The Main Screen

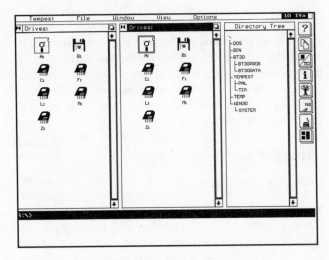

Figure 1: Tempest's main screen

Start Tempest. The screen will go blank, and then the mouse pointer and Tempest's main screen will appear.

Across the top of the screen is a menu bar that contains most of Tempest's commands. Along the right edge of the screen is the Toolbar with eight buttons, each of which also represents a Tempest command. The rest of the screen consists of three windows.

The left and center directory windows represent the contents of your drives. The directory tree of your hard drive is in the right directory tree window.

The center window is currently active in the previous figure, as indicated by the highlighted title bar. You will also notice a frame around one of the icons in the selected window. This is the selection cursor. You can move it using the cursor keys. When you click on an icon with the mouse, it is surrounded with the frame to indicate that it is the currently selected object.

2.2   The Directory Windows

Selecting Drives

Move the cursor to the drive where you installed Tempest (usually C:). Double-click on the icon for this drive or select it and press Enter. This puts you in the root directory of your hard drive. The files in this directory are represented as different kinds of icons: AUTOEXEC.BAT is a stack of paper, subdirectories are file folders, etc.

Viewing Directories

If you can't see all of the files in a given directory at once, you can scroll the window contents using the vertical scroll bar. You can also move the slider in the scroll bar to any position to move quickly to the end, or any other part, of the window. If you want to use the cursor keys to browse through the icons in the window, the contents will automatically scroll when you reach the top or bottom of the window. You can also use PgUp, PgDn, Home, and End to move quickly through the contents of the window.

Changing Directories

You can take a look around your hard drive by selecting one of the subdirectories. Double-click on the desired icon, or select it and press Enter. You can quickly move back to the directory just above this one (known as the parent directory) by clicking the Parent Directory icon located in the upper left corner of the window.

Starting Programs From a Directory

Starting a program is the same as selecting a directory. Try it with the DOS command processor program COMMAND.COM. The COMMAND.COM file will either be in the root directory of your hard drive or in the DOS directory. Like all other files, it is represented by an icon.

Tempest does not know the function of a program, so it simply represents all program files as an abstract cube or a rounded square. Start COMMAND.COM with a double-click or by selecting it and pressing Enter. The Tempest screen will disappear and be replaced with the DOS command line prompt. When you exit the program again (by typing "EXIT" in the case of COMMAND.COM), you will be returned to the Tempest screen.

Using Several Windows

If you now want to use the middle window, simply click anywhere within it with the mouse or press the [Tab] key. The middle window will be activated and the selection cursor will appear. [Tab] can be used to move to the next window again, or you can use [Shift] + [Tab] to move back to the previous window.

2.3 Working With Files

Creating a Text File

For the following exercise, we will need a test file that we can experiment with. In the left window, change to the root directory of your hard drive and press [Shift] + [F4]. A dialog box with the title "Create file" will appear. You can use the cursor keys to switch between the elements in a dialog box just as you can to switch between icons in a window.

This particular dialog box contains four elements: two input fields, the [OK] button, and the [Cancel] button. Activate the small input field by clicking on it with the mouse or by using [Tab]. The input cursor will appear in the field.

Type "MYTEXT.TXT" (if you make a typing error, you can correct it with [Backspace] and press [Enter]. The editor screen will appear for you to enter the contents of the file. You can type anything you like. When you have finished entering the contents of your text file, press [Esc] + [Enter] to save the file. A file called MYTEXT.TXT will appear in your root directory.

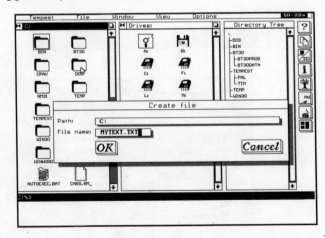

Figure 2: A dialog box

Assigning Icons

Tempest will assign the default icon to the file - a piece of paper with one corner folded over. If you want to assign another icon to your file, select the current icon for the file and press F9. A dialog box called "File info" will open. Click the Change button in this dialog box. Another dialog window will open containing the list of icons from which you may choose.

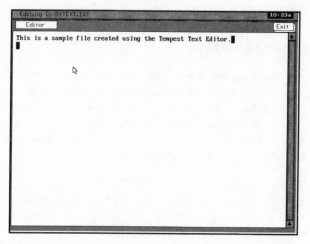

Figure 3: The text editor

The selection bar, which indicates the currently selected icon, can be moved the same way as in the directory windows. Select the icon you want and click OK. This dialog box will close and you will be back in the "File info" dialog box. Click OK in this dialog box as well. Your file will now be displayed in the directory window with the new icon.

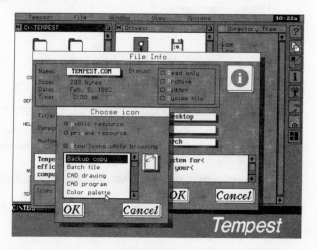

Figure 4: Assigning icons

Copying Files

Change to the center window and select the Tempest directory. Now move the mouse pointer to your test file in the left window and click and hold the left mouse button. Move the mouse so that the icon is dragged over to an empty space in the Tempest directory. When you let go of the mouse button, a dialog box will open to tell you that you are about to copy the file to the new directory. Click [OK] to confirm this action. In a moment, your test file will appear in the Tempest directory.

If another dialog box is displayed, which would happen if you accidentally moved the test file icon on top of another icon, you can always get out of any dialog box by clicking [Cancel] or pressing [Esc].

You can copy any file in this way, simply by dragging its icon from the source directory to a free space in the destination directory. You can also copy complete directories, with all their files and subdirectories in this way. In each case, Tempest will inform you how many files will be copied. During the copy operation, Tempest will show you how much is left to be copied.

2.4   Help

If you ever get stuck and don't know what to do next, you can press the [F1] key at any time to call up Tempest's on-line help files. If you are at the Tempest main screen, you can also call up help by clicking the question mark button in the Toolbar. A window will open containing general information or specific information on the function you are currently trying to use.

The words highlighted in red are cross-reference help topics. If you click on a cross-reference word (or use the cursor keys to move the selection cursor to a cross-reference word and press [Enter]), a help text on that topic will appear.

The [Return] button will take you back to the previously selected help text. The desktop will save up to 20 help texts and notify you with a beep when there is no more help information available.

The [Index] button will give you a listing of the most important help topics.

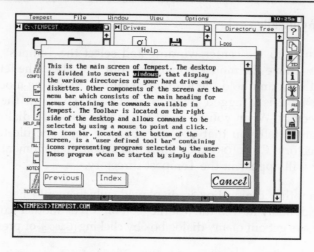

Figure 5: The help utility

2.5 What Next?

The next chapters describe Tempest in detail. Chapters 4 - 9 describe the desktop functions and other Tempest features. We won't describe every mouse or keyboard action as we did in this introductory chapter. Now that you've been introduced to the basic concepts of working with Tempest, you'll find it easy to work with the more complex functions.

3. The Control Elements

This chapter gives a detailed description of all the dialog elements of the Tempest interface.

3.1 Dialog Boxes

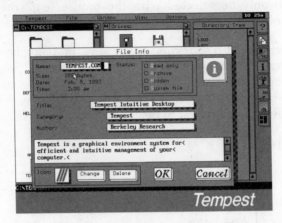

Figure 6: A typical dialog box

Most actions take place in dialog boxes. Dialog boxes are windows in the Tempest working screen in which you perform actions such as entering names or viewing information. Press Enter to confirm the contents of a dialog box or execute the action, press Esc to cancel. Mouse users click OK or Cancel. Press Tab to move to the next dialog element (item box, input box etc.), or press Shift + Tab to go back to the previous dialog element. Mouse users can simply click the desired element. You can also press the highlighted letter of an element, called the hot key, to get to the dialog element.

Tempest also uses dialog boxes to warn you of errors or have you confirm critical actions. Some warning dialog boxes have special icons. Urgent warnings are highlighted in a yellow or red window background.

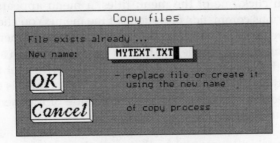

Figure 7: A Warning Message

3.2   Buttons

Buttons are used to give commands or answer questions in a dialog box. Select the button by clicking the mouse button while pointing to the desired button. The (Tab) key may be pressed to select the desired mouse button in dialog boxes. There are also buttons that can only be selected with the mouse (e.g., the buttons in the Toolbar or the scroll arrows).

There are also shortcuts, or hot keys, in dialog boxes. For instance, always press (Esc) to select the (Cancel) button, press the first letter of any other button to select it (e.g., "y" for Yes or "c" for Change). If you cannot find an (OK) button in a dialog box, press (Enter), which is always equivalent to the (OK) button.

3.3   Menus

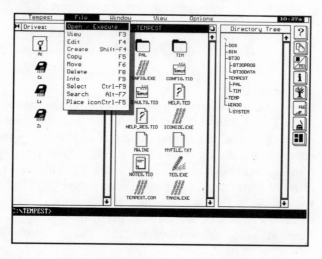

Figure 8: A typical Tempest Menu

Most of the commands are grouped in menus. At the top screen border you can see the menu bar, with the various menu titles. If you click one of the menu titles, a menu appears containing the various commands or options of the menu. You click a command to execute it (for example, **Info** from the **Tempest** menu). You can also point at a menu title, hold down the mouse button and move around in the menu bar and in its menus. When you let go of the mouse button, the command which the mouse pointer is currently over is executed. To exit a menu, click outside of the menu or release the mouse button.

Along with commands, there are also options for actions such as sorting in the **View** menu. The currently active option has a checkmark beside it. Commands and options that are not available are displayed in a "ghosted font". The selection bar also doesn't appear in these menu items.

Keyboard users can press [F10] to access the menu bar and can exit it by pressing [Esc]. Use the cursor keys to move the selection bar; press [Enter] or [↓] to open a menu. You can also use the cursor keys to move in the menu and select menu items by pressing [Enter]. You can also call a menu directly by pressing [Alt] + <Hot key> and use the <Hot key> to select a menu item (hot keys are the highlighted letters). You can also call a command with the function keys listed after the menu item.

Windows can also contain menu bars (the **Icon Editor**, for example). They function the same way the main screen does.

3.4 Input Boxes

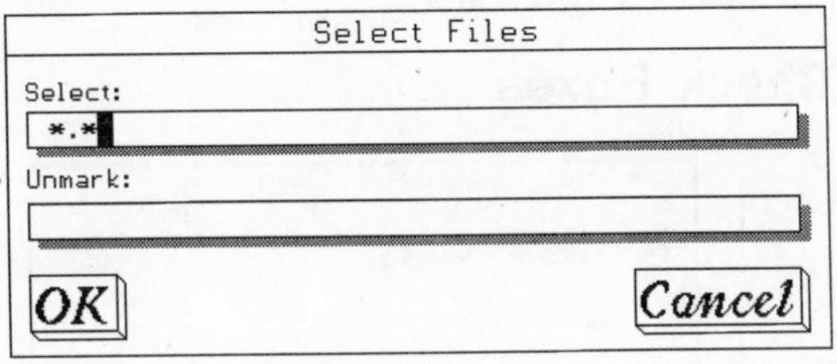

Figure 9: Input box

Input boxes are similar to the DOS command line. The characters entered appear at the current cursor position. The cursor keys as well as [Home] and [End] can be used to reposition the cursor. You can also click your mouse to move the cursor. Pressing [Backspace] deletes characters to the left of the cursor, while pressing [Del] deletes characters to the right of the cursor. Press [Ctrl] + [Backspace] to delete the entire input text.

3.5 Options Boxes

File Search
OK
Cancel
Tempest

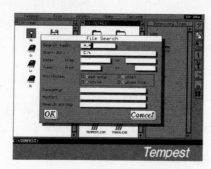

Figure 10: Options Box

Options boxes give you several options, from which you can choose one. Use the cursor keys or appropriate hot key to move to the desired option. You can also click the option. The selected item appears in a dotted border.

3.6 Check Boxes

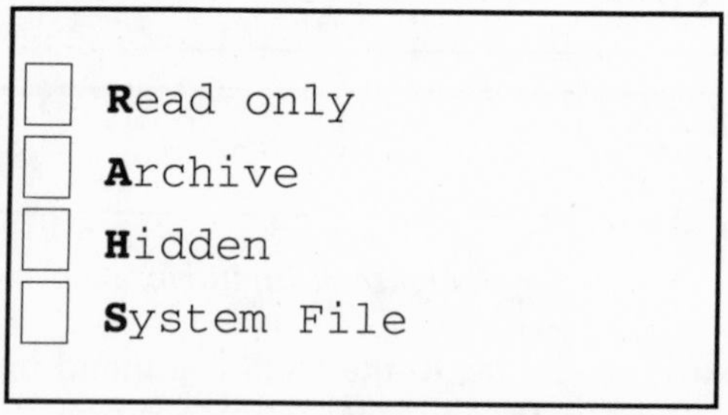

Read only
Archive
Hidden
System File

Figure 11: Check Box

Like options boxes, check boxes usually have several items (or sometimes, only one) that can be selected independently of one another. Press the Spacebar to select/unselect an item in a dotted border.

3.7 List Boxes

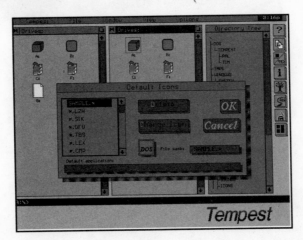

Figure 12: List Box

List boxes allow you to select an item from a list (e.g., a file or an icon name). You can move the selection bar with the cursor keys (or use `PgUp` and `PgDn` for quick browsing). Pressing `Home` and `End` moves the selection bar to the top or the bottom of the list. In lists that are in alphabetical order, you can enter a letter to jump to the first name beginning with that letter.

Mouse users can move the selection bar by clicking, you can scroll through the contents of the list with the scroll arrows. The position bar of the scroll box to the right of the item box shows the size of the list section in proportion to the entire length of the list (the position bar is a fixed length for extremely long lists, since it would otherwise be too small). By dragging this bar, you can quickly change to a different location in the list.

If an item box is currently active, its border is highlighted. The selection bar is always visible, even when it is inactive.

4. The Functions Of The Desktop

In this chapter you will learn the functions for managing your hard drive.

4.1 Directory Window

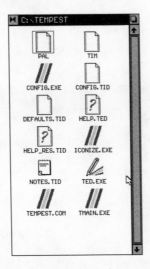

Figure 13: Directory Window

The directory windows let you view directories and edit the contents. The directory windows form the core of file management.

Selecting directories

To change to a directory, double-click its icon or press ⟨Enter⟩. You can also open a highlighted directory by selecting the **Open/Execute** command from the **File** menu. You can move to the root directory or the parent directory by clicking the button in the upper left corner of the window, by pressing ⟨Alt⟩ + ⟨F4⟩ or using the **Windows/Parent Directory** menu command. If you are already in the root directory of a drive, you are in a position to select another drive.

Zooming windows

To display a window in its full size, click the Maximize/Minimize button in the upper right corner of the window. The button is highlighted and the window overlaps all other directory windows. To return the window to normal size, click the button again. You can also use the key code ⟨Alt⟩ + ⟨F4⟩ or the **Windows/Zoom** menu command.

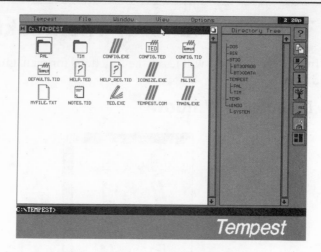

Figure 14: Zoomed Window

Switching to Text mode

Select **View/Text** or click the third button from the Toolbar to switch the active directory window to text mode. This mode displays several files at a time, and you also see additional information such as the file size or the date of the last change. This mode functions exactly like the other mode, except you cannot use the mouse to drag the files to other windows.

Select **View/Icons** or click the same button to return to graphics mode.

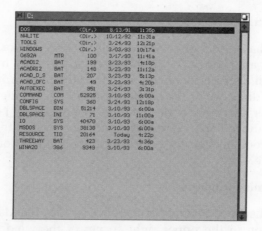

Figure 15: Window in Text mode

Sorting

By default, files are listed in alphabetical order. However, in the **View** menu you can also choose to have files displayed by file extension (e.g., ".DOC"), file size or date of creation, or simply leave the directory unsorted, just as it is saved on the disk. This setting only applies to the active directory window, you must change the settings for other windows separately.

Filtered file display

For a better overview, you can have only certain files displayed. Select **View/Filter** to display a dialog box in which you can determine whether all files, only programs or only those files specified by a file mask are displayed.

A file mask has the following format:

```
XXXXXXXX.XXX
Name      Extension
```

You can use the DOS wildcard characters '*' and '?' to replace one or more characters in the name or extension:

* represents any sequence of characters:

"*.TXT" displays "ABC.TXT", "LALL.TXT", "94704.TXT", ...

"A*.*": displays "ABC.TXT", "A.BAT", "ALL.OK", ...

"TE*.D*" displays "TEMPEST.DOC", "TEILE.DAS", "TEXT.D", ...

? replaces a single character:

"TEIL?.B?T" displays "TEILE.BAT", "TEIL1.BIT", ...

"AB????.TXT" displays "ABLASS.TXT", "ABFALL.TXT", ...

(but not "ABGAS.TXT", since each question mark must stand for a character).

Subdirectories are always displayed.

When you no longer need the filter, change the setting back to "All Files"; otherwise you'll wonder why your directories are always empty.

Updating the contents of a window

Use the **Windows/Read again** menu command to reread the directory of the active directory window. For example, you would use this command if you were displaying a diskette's directory and you just changed diskettes.

Changing the window arrangement

If you need to change the screen arrangement, select **Windows/Arrange** (or press Ctrl + F10 or click the last button of the Toolbar). A dialog box appears, displaying the current window arrangement. Click the column between the two windows to merge them into one, click the center of a window to split it. This allows you to display up to four windows simultaneously, or makes other arrangements possible, such as one large window and two smaller ones. Keyboard users can use the cursor keys to split or merge windows. For example, to make four windows, press ← and then →. With a little practice, you will be able to get the layout you want quickly.

To accept the new screen layout, press OK; pressing Cancel leaves the layout as it was.

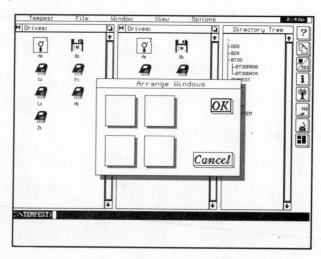

Figure 16: Changing the screen layout

4.2   Starting Programs

You can start programs from the desktop by double-clicking their icons (the filename in text mode) or by moving the selection bar to the program file and pressing Enter. You can also select **Open/Execute** from the **File** menu after moving the selection bar to the program. However, if you use the menu command you will be prompted to type in parameters for the program (for example, if you chose a formatting program, you could enter the drive letter). Keyboard users can also force the program to prompt for parameters by pressing Ctrl + Enter instead of Enter. You also have the option of starting "data" files, such as text files. In this case, a standard application will be loaded, for example a word processor. We go into more detail about this process later in this book.

Mouse users have a clever option: If you drag the icon of a file (or directory, drive or some other program, in Tempest, the term "file" is variable) to a program icon, this program loads with the file as its parameter. For instance, if you move the icon of drive A to the FORMAT program of MS-DOS, this drive will be formatted (be careful when doing this). Before the program starts you will also be prompted for additional parameters.

4.3 Working With Files, Directories and Drives

Selecting Files

The functions described here, which you can use on files ("file" also stands for directories and drives), always apply to the file that is currently highlighted. Some functions let you process a group of files. You can select or unselect the desired files with the right mouse button (or hold down Shift and press the left mouse button) or the Spacebar. Then the names will appear in red, instead of black, to show that they are selected. Any copying, delete or move function that follows will always refer to these selected files, regardless of the position of the selection bar. Files that have already been processed are then automatically unselected.

To select only certain files (for example, all .DOC files), use the **File/Select** menu command (or press Ctrl + F9 or the sixth button of the Toolbar). A dialog box appears, in which you can enter the files to be selected as well as the ones to be unselected. You can enter several file masks in the input boxes, separated by commas. For example, to mark all files except .TXT files and files beginning with "A", type "*.*" in the top input box and type "*.TXT, A*.*" in the bottom box. See "Filtered file display" in Section 4.1 for information on using wildcard characters.

Direct selection with initial letters

In windows that are in alphabetical order, you can jump to the first file beginning with a certain letter by typing that letter. If you have your windows in a different order, you will go to the next file.

Copying Files

To copy files, directories or even whole drives, select the desired icons or names as previously described and, in another window, change to the target directory. Use the **File/Copy** command (or the F5 key). In the dialog box that follows, Tempest outputs the number of files and directories to be copied as well as the total number of bytes and lists the path names for all the directories currently being displayed. Select your target directory from here and confirm the selection by pressing OK.

Tempest uses counters and a bar display to give you a continuous display of how the copying process has progressed. The top bar shows the current file being copied, the bottom bar displays the entire copying process. To cancel the copying process, just press Esc or click the Cancel button.

If there is not enough free memory on the target drive, Tempest displays an error message before copying. With disk drives, it also tells you how many extra diskettes will be needed and prompts you to change diskettes during the copying process. The information Tempest calculates is only approximate, since the disk space cannot be completely used due to DOS management data, defective sectors and unfavorable file lengths. Keep a couple of extra diskettes on hand, just in case.

Copying with the mouse

It's much easier to copy with the mouse. Just drag the desired icon to a free area in the target window. If you drag the icon to a directory or drive icon, the selected file will be copied to this directory or drive. If you drag an unselected file, only that file will be copied. If you drag a selected file, all of the selected files will be copied.

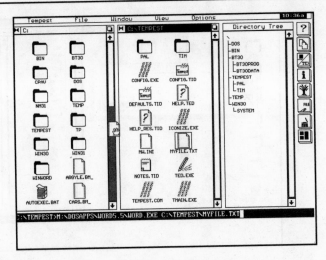

Figure 17: Preparing to copy a file with the mouse

Moving

You can move files from one directory to another, or, in contrast to
the REN (rename) command of DOS, also between different drives.

The process is identical to copying (select **File/Move** or press F6).

Mouse users can toggle between copying and moving with the
second button of the Toolbar. If the button shows two pages, **Copy** is
active. If the back page is empty and surrounded by dotted lines,
Move is active. You can also tell the current mode by either moving
a copy of the selected icon or the icon itself. When **Copy** is active,
the original icon is left in the directory window and a copy of the
icon is moved with the mouse pointer. When **Move** is active, the
original icon is moved with the mouse pointer.

After moving, set the Toolbar button back to copying mode as soon
as possible.

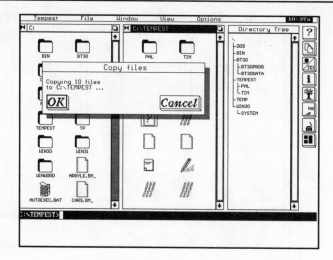

Figure 18: Copying multiple files with the mouse

Deleting Files

You can delete files with the **Delete** command from the **File** menu, by pressing F8 or by clicking the trashcan icon in the Toolbar.

Use this command carefully, because you can also delete entire directories and their contents or even your entire hard drive. If this seems too risky for you, you can also configure Tempest so that it only allows deletion of files (see Chapter 8).

Getting information about files

You can display a dialog box with information about a file by using the **File/Info** menu command, pressing F9 or by clicking the button with the i icon. This dialog box displays information about the file size as well as the date of creation. You can also change the name, file attribute or icon (see the following). Press OK to accept the changes, or press Cancel if you do not want to accept the changes.

The info window for drives shows the drive type, total and free storage capacity as well as the files and directories contained there. You cannot make any changes here. We'll tell you how to change drive icons later.

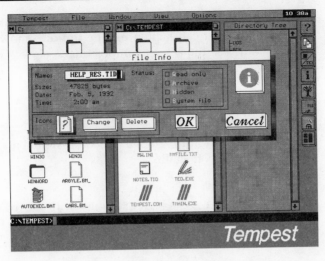

Figure 19: The File Info dialog box

Renaming Files

Call **File/Info**, edit the name in the input box and confirm by pressing OK. Tempest warns you if a file of the same name already exists and asks you whether you want to overwrite it.

Changing File Attributes

You can set and delete the following file attributes in the File Info dialog box:

Read only: The file cannot be deleted or overwritten. Although you can still perform these actions in Tempest, you are prompted explicitly each time the situation arises.

Hidden: The file does not appear in the listing when the MS-DOS DIR command is used (no significance for Tempest).

Archive: This attributes indicates that the file has been changed since the last backup.

System: The file belongs to the operating system.

Assigning and removing icons

The name of the icon displayed for a file is output in the File Info window. If an icon has not been defined for the file, then a default icon is used. Use the Change button to assign a different icon to the file. In the Icon dialog box you can choose an icon from the list. The option buttons "public/private resource" can be left at public (we'll explain later), you can switch off the option "Show icons while browsing" in case the screen composition is slowed down due to continuous drive accesses.

Now close both dialog boxes with (OK). The icon has been assigned to the file and will be "passed on" to copies.

Use the (Delete) button to remove an icon assignment. The file then carries a default icon again.

    To assign a given icon to all files with the .DOC extension, you can use a default icon. You can read about the procedure in the section on "Default Icons".

Extended Information

The File Info window has another feature. You can add more information for a file than what DOS makes available. For example, you can specify the name of the author and a short comment.

To toggle the normal Info window to extended mode, click the Icon button in the window or press (F10). The window increases its size and makes several additional input boxes available. If a file already has extended information, the Info window automatically appears in its increased size.

Now you can type in a title for the file (for example, "Tempest Intuitive Desktop" or "Competing with MacroSoft"), the author and the subject of file (for example, "Graphics", "Tools", "Programming", "Private", etc.). The multiple line input box is intended for a short comment about the file.

If you close the Info window with (OK), the information you typed will be saved. To remove it later, press (F10) or click the icon button to reduce the window and exit after pressing (OK). The extended information will be deleted after you confirm the prompt.

Please keep in mind that you can only use the extended information on diskettes or hard drives that contain a Resource file (see the **Options** menu).

Displaying, creating and editing files

See Chapter 5 "Editor & Viewer" for more information on this subject.

File Search

Tempest also provides you with a powerful File Search command. Along with a file mask, you can also specify a time period for the files specified in the search. You can also search for files with a given attribute or a specified search text. If you begin the search on a drive with a Resource file, you can also search for files that contain extended information for author or subject.

Use the **File/Search** command or press F7 to call the **Search** command. Type in all of the search parameters in the dialog box that appears. In the first input box you specify a mask large enough to hold all of the desired files. For example, "A*.TXT" searches for all .TXT files whose name begins with "A". In "Start Dir." you specify the directory for the search. Any subdirectories of this directory are included in the search. The default setting is the root directory of the current active drive (i.e., this entire drive will be searched from top to bottom).

In the following fields, specify the time period in which the files of the search should fall. The following formats are valid for the time and the date:

6.24.91, 06-24-91, 6-24-91 for "June 24, 1991"

8:05, 8.5, 08:05, 08.5   for "5 minutes after 8"

If the "from" field is left blank, the beginning of the search goes back to the time when MS-DOS was introduced, if the "to" field is left blank, the search continues until doomsday.

In the Attribute check box, you can set an attribute that the files in the search should have, for example, specifying Archive and Hidden, causes Tempest to find all hidden files that have been changed since the last time they were saved.

The next two boxes are for specifying the author and the subject used to search the entries with extended info. This is only possible on diskettes or hard drives equipped with a Resource file.

In the last input box, you can define a search text, which Tempest then searches all the files in the search path.

Pressing OK starts the search in the background (i.e., the files that have been found are displayed in a list). The selection cursor can be moved thru the list while the search is in progress. If you press Enter or double-click the mouse, the search is terminated and you change to the corresponding directory of the file under the selection cursor.

You can also end the search with ⌈Stop⌋, pressing ⌈New Search⌋ starts another search. Pressing ⌈Cancel⌋ stops the search and closes the dialog box.

If you call the search function again, the list of the previous search reappears. Press ⌈New Search⌋ to go back to the Search dialog box.

4.4   Defaults Icons for Files

To avoid having to manually assign an icon to each file, you can select **Options/Default Icons** to display files with an icon of your choice (for instance, all .TXT files with the Text file icon). You can also specify which application program is to be automatically loaded when the icon for the file is double-clicked.

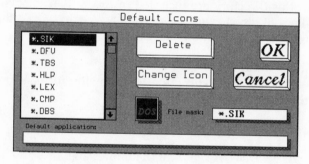

Figure 20: Default Icons

Creating a New Default

To add a new default, select "New entry" from the list. Now type in the file mask in the appropriate input box. As soon as you select another entry in the list, the new file mask is added. Once the file mask has been added, you can set the default icon that is to be used for the file mask.

Default Icons

Select a list entry and click the ⌈Change Icon⌋ button. The Select Icon dialog box appears, which you read about in the section titled "Assigning and removing icons". All the files that fit the file mask and don't already have an icon will be displayed with this icon.

Default Application

You can also set an application program for a file mask that starts when such a file is double-clicked. Type in the name of the program, (including the .COM, .EXE or .BAT extension) along with its complete path and any parameters in the input box. In the place where the filename is supposed to be used, type a percentage sign (%). To insert the file with its complete path as a parameter, type "%\%".

For example, let's suppose we had a word processing program called "WP" in a directory name WP51, that is supposed to start when you double-click on a file with the .DOC extension. Add the "*.DOC" file mask to the default list. Type the following line in the Default Application field:

```
C:\WP51\WP.EXE /m %\% /r /d
```

In this case, "/m", "/r" and "/d" are sample parameters. Now, when you press (Enter) or double-click "DOCUMENT.DOC" from the "D:\DOC" directory, WP.EXE is called with the parameters:

```
C:\WP51\WP.EXE /m D:\DOC\DOCUMENT.DOC /r /d
```

WP would then automatically start and load DOCUMENT.DOC.

Deleting a default

Use the (Delete) button to remove the selected Default Icon file mask from the list.

Press (OK) to save your defaults, or press (Cancel) to discard them.

   The new defaults don't take effect until you restart Tempest (you could also start any program, since Tempest will be initialized after this).

If more than one default exists for the same file mask or if they overlap (e.g., "*.DAT" and "A*.DAT"), the first default in the list is used. If necessary, delete the first one or define the one that forms the "generic term" ("*.DAT" in the previous example), as last in the list.

4.5   Resource Files

Tempest stores all icons and their associations to files as well as other information in what are called resource files. To provide files on a diskette or hard drive with icons, the files must be equipped with resources. The hard drive, where Tempest is located, was equipped with resource files during installation. These are called public resources. That means that files on other drives can access the icons of these resources. Resources created on other disks are private (i.e., they are only intended for use on that particular disk). While this may sound complicated, it is only important in special cases. It's best if you save your icons in the public resource and only use private resources when you assign icons to files on other disks.

Creating Resources

Change to any directory of the drive on which you want to create resources and select **Options/Create Resource**. Tempest creates the "RESOURCE.TID" file in the root directory of the drive and creates its directory tree.

4.6   The Directory Tree

You can use the directory tree to change directories easily. The directory tree is displayed in a separate window on the right side of the screen and displays the directory structure of your hard drive as a tree diagram. Select **Windows/Tree**, press (Shift) + (F10) or click the "Tree" Toolbar button to turn it on or off. When you select the Tree window, the last directory window used continues to be active. You can display another directory in this window by selecting a directory name in the tree and pressing (Enter) or double-clicking the name.

Displaying Directory Trees of other drives

Ordinarily, the drive from which you started Tempest is displayed in the Tree window. To display the directory tree of another drive, it must be equipped with a resource file. All you need to do then is select a window displaying any directory of this drive and turn the tree on and off again. You can also set a configuration option (see Chapter 8) to have the "correct" tree automatically displayed.

Creating a new directory

To create a new directory, use **Windows/Make Directory** menu command or press (F7).

Updating the directory tree

To properly display directories created outside of the Tempest interface, select **Windows/Update Tree**. After you answer a confirmation prompt, the directory structure is completely read and the tree is reconstructed.

Keep in mind that all file operations affect the active directory window, not the tree itself.

4.7   The Icon Bar

The bottom screen border serves as a "User defined tool bar", called the Icon bar, where you can place up to 14 programs that you use often. Select the program to place in the Icon bar and then call **File/Place Icon** (Ctrl + F5) or simply drag its icon to the bottom of the screen. Select **File/Delete** to remove an icon from the Icon bar (the program itself will not be deleted) or move it from the Icon bar anywhere on the screen.

You start programs in the usual way by double-clicking on the icon in the Icon bar. Keyboard users can use the Tab key to switch to the Icon bar and then use the cursor key to select the icon; the Enter key will start the program. You can also call **File/Info** for the icon displayed in the Icon bar. However, you cannot make changes to names, icons or attributes within the Icon bar.

Keep in mind though, that the program icons in the Icon bar are in virtual display, that is, they will also be displayed if the program that goes with the icon no longer exists.

4.8   Other Functions

Help function

Select **Tempest/Help**, click the "?" Toolbar button or press F1 to call the Online Help system, described in detail in Chapter 2 "First Steps".

Requesting the Tempest Version Number

Tempest/Info displays both the version number of Tempest as well as the copyright statement.

Entering DOS commands

You can type in DOS commands in the input line above the Icon bar, called "DOS Command Line". Like all desktop components, you can select the DOS Command Line with the Tab key or Esc. It functions like an input box, but will scroll if the cursor reaches the right margin.

If you select an executable file in a directory window or in the Icon bar, the command is displayed in the DOS Command Line. Press Enter or double-click the command to execute it.

Temporary exit to DOS

Select the **Options/DOS Shell** command to go to the DOS Shell without having to exit Tempest. Type "EXIT" to go back to the Tempest desktop.

Configuring Tempest

Select **Options/Configure** to call the Setup Utility configuration program for customizing Tempest (see Chapter 8).

Icon Editor

You can also call the **Icon Editor** from the **Options** menu. Chapter 5 is devoted to the Icon Editor.

Notepad

Select **Options/Notepad** (or press F2) to write down your ideas or thoughts (see Chapter 7, "Other features").

Returning to DOS

Select **Tempest/Exit** to exit the Tempest desktop.

5. Editor & Viewer

Tempest also has a built-in Viewer for displaying files and a Text editor for editing text files. This chapter describes how to operate these features.

5.1 Displaying Files

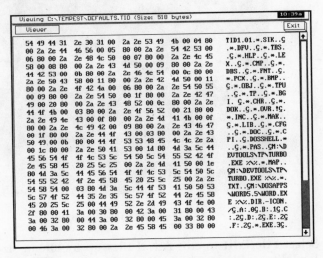

Figure 21: The Viewer in hexadecimal mode

Select **File/View** to activate the Viewer. You can display any file in formatted or unformatted text mode or in hexadecimal mode. Use ⬆/⬇ and (PgUp)/(PgDn) or the scroll bar to scroll through the file, use (Ctrl) + (PgUp)/(PgDn) to jump to the beginning or the end of the file.

Changing the display form

By default, files are displayed as formatted text (i.e., with paragraphs and indents). Files of approximately 100K and more are displayed in unformatted ASCII mode. Press (F2) to switch to formatted text display, press (F3) to switch to unformatted ASCII display and press (F4) to switch to hexadecimal mode. You can also select the corresponding menu option. However, a formatted display is only possible up to approximately 4000 lines and requires a few seconds for file analysis.

Text search

Press (F7) to have Tempest search for a character string in the file. The search begins at the current file position and can be continued by pressing (Shift) + (F7).

Exiting the Viewer

Press Esc or click the Exit button to exit the display mode.

5.2   Editing Text Files

Figure 22: The Editor

Select **File/Edit** to edit ASCII files up to 40K in size. Operating the Editor is like running an input box. Press Ctrl + PgUp/PgDn to jump to the beginning or the end of the text, press Ctrl + Y to delete the lines. When you reach the right margin in typing, you can continue typing at the beginning of the next line; the text will be written to the file without a paragraph break. You must press Enter to create a paragraph, which is then displayed as a colored checkmark.

Saving text

Select **Save** from the **Editor** menu (F2) to save your text without having to exit the Editor. Select **Save as ...** (Shift + F2) to save the file under a different name or save it in another directory.

Text search

Searching for text is identical to the search function in the Viewer, and also starts at the cursor position.

Exiting the Editor

Like the Viewer, you can also exit the Editor by pressing Esc or clicking the Exit button. Tempest prompts you to save any changes before exiting.

5.3 Creating Text Files

Use the **File/Create** command ([Shift] + [F4]) to create a new text file. A dialog box appears, prompting you for the path and name of the new file you are creating.

6.   The Icon Editor

This chapter discusses creating custom icons with the integrated
Icon Editor.

6.1   Calling and Exiting the Icon Editor

Select the **Icon Editor** command from the **Options** menu to call the
Editor; press (Esc) or click the (Cancel) button to exit the Editor.

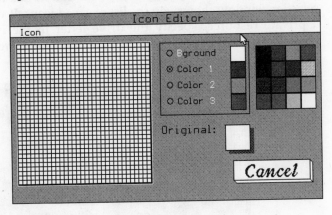

Figure 23: The window of the Icon Editor

6.2   The Editor Window

The left half of the window is covered with the drawing grid,
upon which you paint the icons. To the right of the grid are the
palettes; the icon is reproduced in its original size in the small
display box underneath. The window has its own menu bar.

6.3   Painting Icons

Changing colors

Icons are displayed in three colors, which you select from a palette
of 16 colors. To change colors, select one of the four color selection
fields (you can also define the background color, which appears
transparent in the original icon) and click the desired color in the
palette. The icon will not be displayed in this new color until you
set or delete a pixel (see the following).

Setting and deleting dots

When you move the mouse pointer to the drawing grid, it turns into
a pencil icon. You paint with the active color by holding down the

left mouse button and moving the mouse, pressing the right mouse button deletes pixels (they appear transparent in the original).

Deleting the drawing area

Use the **New** menu command to delete the drawing area.

6.4   Loading Icons

Use the **Load** command (F3) to load an icon from a resource. The selection window shows you the list of saved icons. If you are using a private resource, specify the drive letter in the input box. If there was still an icon in the drawing grid, Tempest prompts you to save it.

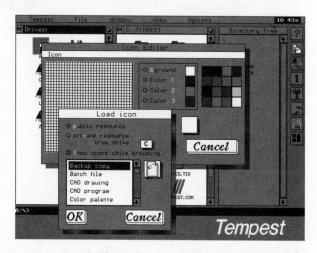

Figure 24: The Load Icons dialog box

6.5   Loading an ILBM Brush

If you have a paint program that produces ILBM image files (DeluxePaint, for example), you can use icons created with the paint program in Tempest. Save your icon as a brush in the format of 32 by 32 dots. Use the **Load ILBM Icon** command (Shift + F3) to load the brush in the Icon Editor.

6.6   Saving Icons

Use the **Save** command or press F2 to save your work. Select **Save as...** (Shift + F2) to save it under a new name or in a different resource. Icon names can have up to 16 characters.

6.7 Deleting Icons

Use the **Delete** menu command to remove icons from a resource. If you select a name and click ⌐OK⌐, the window stays open so that you can delete more than one icon. Select ⌐Cancel⌐ to close the dialog box.

 When you change icons that are already being displayed on the desktop, it's possible that the changes won't be displayed immediately after you exit the Editor, since Tempest still has the old icons in its buffer memory. Tempest will access the resources and display the new icons when you run another program and return to the desktop or restart Tempest.

7. Other Features Of Tempest

Along with the Viewer, Text Editor and Icon Editor, Tempest also has some other useful utilities, which are described in this chapter.

7.1 Clock

Tempest displays the current system time in the upper right corner, next to the menus. If you would rather not think about the time while working in Tempest, you can switch off the clock in the Setup Utility configuration program (described in Chapter 8).

7.2 Notepad

Use the integrated Notepad to write down your ideas or thoughts (select the **Notepad** command from the **Options** menu or press F2). It functions like the regular Text Editor (see Chapter 5). Your notes will automatically be saved in the NOTES.TID file in the Tempest directory if you exit the Notepad by clicking OK. Tempest also notes the position of the cursor, so if you call the Notepad again, the cursor will be in the same place it was when you last exited Notepad.

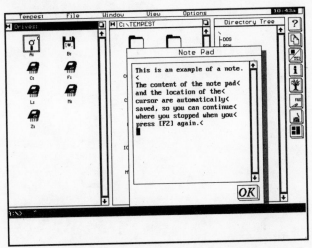

Figure 25: The Tempest Notepad

7.3 Screen Saver

Normal computer monitors have the unpleasant characteristic of burning the screen contents into the picture tube if the same picture is displayed on the monitor over a long period of time.

Tempest saves the screen by creating a moving picture on the screen after a given time period without user activity (mouse movements, key presses). When you move the mouse or press a key, the old screen contents return to the screen, unchanged.

You can also switch on the Screen saver yourself by moving the mouse pointer to the upper right corner of the screen.

8.   Configuring Tempest

Tempest has an additional program for customizing the interface. This chapter describes how you can set screen colors and operating options in accordance with your personal wishes.

8.1   Calling the Setup Utility Configuration Program

Call **Options/Configure** or start the CONFIG.EXE program. A main menu appears, containing various topics.

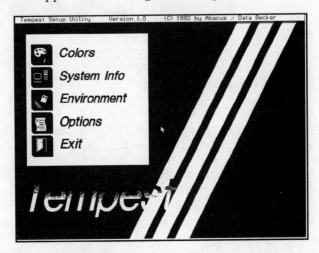

Figure 26: The Main Menu of the configuration program

8.2   Setting Colors

If you select Colors, you go to the Color Selection dialog box. On the left is the RGB sliders for setting palette colors, while you can color in the individual elements of the interface in the item boxes on the right.

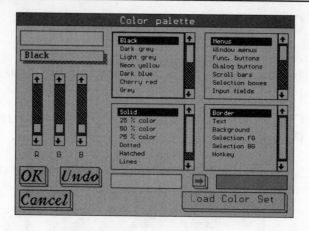

Figure 27: Setting colors

Loading predefined color sets

Tempest has a number of predefined color sets that you can use or modify. Click the [Load Color Set] button to display a list of the color settings. The following color sets are supplied with Tempest:

- Lemon Flavor, a flashy, exotic color set, the default for VGA cards (not available for EGA).

- Classic Frisco, blue like the Pacific, the default for EGA.

- Creative Berkeley, California Desktop Flair (VGA only).

- Vanilla Flavor, an alternative for EGA cards.

- Sweet dreams, a wistful harmony of color (VGA only).

- Intuitive Art, another artistic VGA color set.

Palette

The 16 colors of the current window are listed in the upper left list box of the palette window.

To change a color, select it and use the sliders to adjust the values for Red, Green and Blue. Keyboard users can also use [Tab] to select the sliders and move them with the cursor keys. By additive color mixing (red and green yields yellow, red and blue yields violet, etc.), you can set all 256,144 color shades of the VGA card, or 64 different colors of the EGA card.

Type in a new name for your color in the input box above the RGB sliders. Your setting is transferred to the list as soon as you select another list entry. Click (Undo) to retrieve the old color.

"Coloring in" the interface

After customizing the color palette with the method previously described, you can set the colors of the individual elements of the interface in the two list boxes on the right.

If you click one of the elements in the top right list box, the individual components of the element, such as foreground color or border, appear in the bottom right list box. The color field displayed underneath contains the color of the selected item. To change the color, select the desired color in the palette box and the pattern in the bottom left list box, if an area is to be filled in. Then click the arrow button between the two color boxes. Follow this procedure for all the items of the dialog elements that you want to change.

8.3   System Info

Pressing the (System Info) button displays a dialog box, in which you can enter the name of your computer system and your own name.

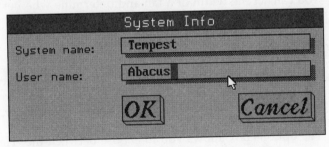

Figure 28: System Info

8.4   Environment Settings

The (Environment) button allows you to set the parameters of the environment. The following settings are possible:

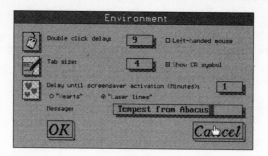

Figure 29: Environment parameters

Mouse settings

In the "Double-click delay" field you can enter the time period (in 1/18 seconds) that's allowed between two mouse clicks in order to be recognized as a double-click. The default setting is 9, or 1/2 second.

The "Left-handed mouse" option allows you to switch the functions of the left and right mouse buttons.

Editor/Viewer options

You can set the width of a tab and determine whether to display a paragraph in the Editor as a colored checkmark.

Screen saver

In the Screen saver input box you can specify the number of minutes that must pass without user activity before the Screen saver is switched on. Type in a zero to disable the Screen saver.

The options box allows you to choose between the "Hearts" screen saver and the "Laser lines" screen saver.

With the "Hearts" screen saver you can specify a message that displays on the screen from time to time.

8.5   Other Options

Selecting Options opens a dialog box in which you can enable and disable various Tempest features:

Sound: Allows warning beeps.

Clock: On slow computers, the clock can cause the mouse pointer to flicker, so you can switch off this feature here.

Quick info:
> A small information window will appear when you change directory windows. It displays the number of files and directories of the window as well as the kind of sorting and the filter mode.

Tree adjusting:
> When you change directories or windows, the current Directory Tree display is updated and the directory is displayed in color. If you have a slow computer, disable this feature.

Disable directory deletion:
> Since inexperienced users can sometimes cause a great deal of damage by deleting a single directory, you can prevent this by enabling this option. Files in these directories can only be deleted by group selection (more work).

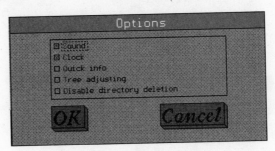

Figure 30: Options

8.6 Quitting the Configuration Program

Select the [Exit] button to exit the configuration program. If you answer the prompt in the dialog box that appears with [Yes], your settings are saved; otherwise they will be discarded.

9.   The Iconize Utility

The Tempest Iconize utility enables the user to integrate other software packages into the Tempest system. It allows software developers to create "TIM" files (Tempest Icon Maps) for their products. A TIM file is used to install icons and default settings for the product.

This chapter will show you how to use Iconize to create your own TIM files.

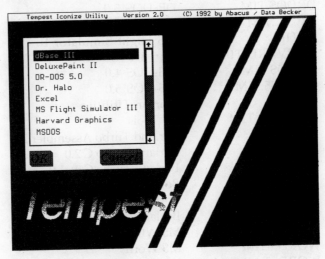

Figure 31: The Iconize utility

9.1   "Iconizing" a Software Package

Start ICONIZE.EXE from the Tempest directory. The selection box in the Iconize screen will list the TIM files stored in the **Tempest** directory. Select the program for which you want to install icons and click (OK). You can also do this by moving the icon of a **TIM** file to the ICONIZE.EXE icon. Tempest will then bring up a dialog box to ask you the name of the directory where the selected software package is stored. You have to enter the complete path, but you may leave off the filename (for example "C:\WP51" instead of "C:\WP51\WP.EXE"). Tempest will then look for the program files.

The icons are then installed automatically for the selected application program. Some questions may pop up in dialog boxes during this procedure (e.g., to ask if you want to change the existing defaults). You may also get an error message if the TIM file is defective. You will then be able to configure another application or exit from Iconize with (Cancel).

TIM Files Included

Tempest is delivered with TIM files for popular software packages including:

DBASE.TIM	dBase III
DPAINT.TIM	DeluxePaint II
DRHALO.TIM	Dr. Halo
DRDOS.TIM	DR-DOS 5.0
EXCEL.TIM	MS Excel
FS.TIM	MS Flight Simulator III
HARVARD.TIM	Harvard Graphics
MSDOS.TIM	MS-DOS 4.0
MSDOS5.TIM	MS-DOS 5.0
NU.TIM	Norton Utilities
PCTOOLS.TIM	PC Tools
TASM.TIM	Borland Turbo Assembler 2.0
TC.TIM	Borland Turbo C 2.0
TCPP.TIM	Borland Turbo C++ 1.0
TD.TIM	Borland Turbo Debugger 2.0
TPROF.TIM	Borland Turbo Profiler 1.0
TURBO.TIM	Borland Turbo Pascal 5.0
WINDOWS3.TIM	MS WIndows 3.+
WORD5.TIM	MS Word
WORDSTAR.TIM	Wordstar 5.0

The following TIM files are not for specific programs. They were created for use with certain application types. You may specify any pathname when loading one of these TIM files.

SOFTWORK.TIM	Symbols for programming languages (compilers, source code, libraries).
SYMBOLS.TIM	Various abstract symbols.
STANDARD.TIM	Standard symbols for drives and Tempest files. This is used when you install Tempest, and can be replaced with ALTERNAT.TIM.
TEXT.TIM	Icons for word processing.

9.2 Creating Your Own TIM Files

Structure of a TIM File

As mentioned in the introduction to this chapter, you can create TIM files for your own application software so that users can easily add these programs to the Tempest system.

Tempest Icon Maps are pure ASCII files that can be created with the integrated text editor. A typical TIM file for a word processing program could look like this:

```
Tempest Text
USE        icon_lib.tid, palette.ttx
LOOKFOR    ttext.exe
CARRY      "letter"
           "book"
           "report"

DEFAULT    *.txt         "Text file"        ttext.exe %\%
           *.drv         "printer driver"

SET        ttext.exe     "Tempest Text"
           fontcvrt.exe  "Converter"
           read.me       "ReadMe file"
```

The first line in every TIM file gives the complete name of the software package, up to 20 characters.

The lines that follow contain the actual TIM statements. Each statement begins with a command word in capital letters. The command words are followed by filenames. If there is more than one filename for a command, they must be separated with white spaces (comma, tab, space, or paragraph characters).

The USE Command

USE indicates the resource files that store the icons and the source color palette. Resource files should always be stored in the same directory as the corresponding TIM file. Iconize will convert the colors if the colors in your resource file do not match those in the palette of your Tempest system.

If the icon resource file is named ICON_LIB.TID, you may omit the USE command.

The LOOKFOR Command

The LOOKFOR command specifies the filename that Iconize will use to locate your software package. It is best to specify a name that is unique to this particular package. If the package uses subdirectories (as many compilers do), then choose a filename from the main directory. If you do not include a LOOKFOR command, Iconize cannot automatically look for your program.

The CARRY Command

CARRY copies icons from the resource associated with the TIM file to the main Tempest resource. You can enter as many icon names as you like after this command, separated by white space characters. If the name contains a white space itself, you must enclose the entire name in quotes. If an icon name contains quotes, they must be preceded by a backslash. A backslash in an icon name must be preceded by an additional backslash.

The DEFAULT Command

Like the CARRY command, DEFAULT transfers icons to the main resource. In addition, DEFAULT links the icon to a set of defaults. The syntax for this command is:

```
DEFAULT FileMask IconName <Default Application>
```

The FileMask and Default Application parameters have the same formats described in Chapter 4. The Default Application parameter is optional and does not require a pathname, since Tempest automatically determines the program directory. You can specify a number of defaults after the command word, but each must be on its own line.

The SET Command

The SET command assigns an icon to a specified file. The syntax is:

```
SET FileName IconName
```

The SET command may also be followed by as many definitions as you like, as long as each is on a separate line.

The INFO Command

INFO can be used to associate various information with a file. This information will be displayed in an additional window. Each piece of information must be entered on its own line, preceded by an identifying keyword. The syntax looks like this:

```
INFO FileName <Name : Author : Icon : Class : Infotext>
= text
```

The keywords have the following meanings:

Name: The actual name of the program (such as "Borland
            Turbo C++ 1.0).

Author: The author of the software (for example "Abacus").

Icon: The icon for the file (this saves you an additional SET
            command).

Class: The program class (such as "Graphics", "Tools",
            "Programming", etc.).

Infotext: Comment text that may be several lines long. If you use
            this keyword, it must be placed last in the command.

An example:

```
INFO fdisk.com
        Name=       "Fix Disk"
        Class=      "System"
        Author=     "Digital Research"
        Icon=       "Disk-Utility"

        Infotext=   "Hard drive maintenance program -
                    formats"
                    "hard drives, creates and deletes
                    partitions"
```

The USE and LOOKFOR commands may only be used once each in
any given TIM file. The other commands may appear after these
two commands as many times as you need. If an icon is used many
times, it is only copied once. If an icon of the same name already
exists in the main resource, you will be asked if you want to replace
it.

Procedure for Developing a TIM File

Before you write your TIM file, you should create a new resource
file on a diskette and use the icon editor to copy all of the icons you
will need.

Then copy the file ICON_RES.TID from the resource directory of
the diskette to the program file directory. Name this resource
ICON_LIB.TID (or use your own name).

Now you can write a TIM file using the commands previously
described. If you did not name your resource file ICON_LIB.TID, be
sure to include a USE command along with whatever name you
assigned to the resource file.

When you install your software package, make sure that this resource file is available to the user.

9.3   The Iconize Command Line Parameters

Iconize can also be started with the following parameters:

```
ICONIZE TIM_File
    </A:application program path>
    </T:Tempest directory>
```

The /A and /T parameters are optional. If you do not use /T, Iconize will assume that all the other Tempest files are located in the same directory as Iconize.

Potential Errors

You will encounter errors if filenames or icon names are too long, if the command syntax is not correct, or if a resource file could not be found. Please note also that the maximum size of a TIM file is 40K.

10. The External Text Editor TED

TED, the external text editor of the Tempest desktop, complements the integrated editor with functions such as window techniques and block functions. Once you have started it, you will notice that it is somewhat different from the other Tempest utilities, because TED is the latest offspring of the Tempest evolution.

Starting TED

Start the Tempest Editor by calling "TED". You can also specify the name of the file you wish to edit along with "TED". If you enter the switch "/c" after the name, the text window zooms to full size and closes at the end of the program, in other words, TED behaves like the integrated editor.

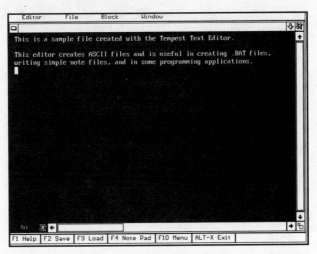

Figure 32: The Editor

TED is also called when you start a TXT file from the Tempest desktop.

Quitting TED

Select **TED/End** or Alt+X to exit TED. A security prompt follows if you neglected to save a text file that has been changed.

Window technique

With TED, you can edit more than one text at the same time, the number of windows is only limited by the amount of free memory available. The **Window** menu offers you various functions for working with windows:

Close Alt + F3

The current window closes, followed by a security prompt if the text hasn't yet been saved. Mouse users can also click the Exit button in the upper left corner of the window.

Zoom F5

Enlarges the current window to full size or returns it to its previous size. You can also do this by clicking the "arrow to top" buttons in the upper right corner of the window.

Size/Move Ctrl + F5

Moves the window or changes its size. A frame appears, which you can move with the cursor keys. You can size the window with the cursor keys and the Shift key: Shift+→ and Shift+↑ enlarge the window while Shift+← and Shift+↓ reduce the window. Press Enter to redraw the window; pressing Esc leaves the window in its original state. Mouse users can move the window by holding down the mouse button and dragging the title bar. To change the size of the window, drag the size icon in the lower right window corner.

Next F6

Activates the next window. Mouse users can activate a window by simply clicking.

<---> Icon Shift + F5

Reduces the window to an icon or restores it to a window if it was an icon. The "down arrow" button next to the zoom button reduces the window to an icon, you can also press Enter or double-click to restore an icon back to a window.

The dialog boxes from the Tempest desktop are also a feature of TED; they remain in the foreground until an action has been performed or the dialog box is canceled.

Loading and saving files

To load files, press F3 or use the appropriate menu command. You can select a file from the displayed directory or enter a filename or file mask. Confirm your selection or entry by pressing Enter or clicking the OK button; press Esc to cancel.

Press F2 to save the text file. Choosing **Save as...** lets you chose a new name for the file.

Block operations

Press [Shift] and the cursor keys or drag the mouse to mark a text block. When you type a character or press [Del], the block is replaced or deleted. Press [Ctrl] + [Ins] to copy a block to the clipboard, press [Shift] + [Del] to clip it from the text at the same time. The previous contents of the clipboard are then replaced. Press [Shift] + [Ins] to paste the contents of the clipboard to your text.

The **Editor** menu has some useful functions:

Notepad [F4]

Inserts a notepad whose contents are saved in the "NOTES.TIS" file when the window is closed.

"Clock" [Shift] + [F4]

Displays a digital clock.

11. Tempest Studio

Tempest Studio is an advanced, multi-window icon editor. It is useful for creating your own icon resources because of its resource management functions. It also contains a screen snapshot function to easily capture icons created with other graphics programs.

11.1 Starting Studio

Start Tempest Studio by clicking on "STUDIO.COM" in the Tempest directory. "STUDIO.EXE" is the main program that is loaded by "STUDIO.COM" and can be started directly. When STUDIO.EXE is started directly, it does not allow calling other programs (see 11.8) or the snapshot function (see 11.7).

11.2 Quitting Studio

Select "Studio/Exit" to exit Tempest Studio. A security prompt appears for all unsaved changes.

11.3 Window Techniques

The window functions are exactly the same as for TED (see previous chapter).

11.4 The Icon Editor

The icon editor window called with "Icon/New" works like the internal icon editor (see Chapter 6). Notice that this editor allows using the keyboard (cursor keys move the drawing cursor; Spacebar sets pixels). You can select the drawing color by clicking on it in the color selector or pressing Alt in combination with the numbers 0 - 3. To change the palette, click on the "Palette" button (Alt P) and select the desired color in the dialog window.

Load icons

To load an icon, select "Load" from the "Icon" menu, select the desired one from the dialog window and press return (or double click on it). To switch to another resource file, select a drive letter (the icon is loaded from the "RESOURCE.TID" file in the root directory of the specified drive then), or select the asterisk and enter the file name (like "C:\TEMPEST\TIM\ICON_LIB.TID" for the main icon library). Notice that there is a history list available, from which you can choose a prior file name; just click on the "arrow down" symbol or press ↓ and pick one of the given choices.

As soon as the icon choice box becomes active again, it's updated to display the desired resource file.

Save icons

To save an icon, use the "Save" or "Save as..." command from the "Icon" menu. In the dialog box, the resource selection works like described in the previous section. In the input field below you can enter an icon name which can be up to 16 characters long.

11.5 The Resource Viewer

The resource viewer displays all icons saved in a resource. You display this window with the "View" command from the "Resource" menu. It is similar to the icon load dialog window, yet it has some additional functions.

Load icons from the resource window

To load an icon directly from the resource viewer, select it and press Enter or perform a double click.

Delete icons

You can delete icons with "Icon/Delete". Select the icon you wish to delete or mark a group of icons using Spacebar or holding Shift and clicking on the icons. To delete a marked group of icons, the selection cursor has to be placed on one of the marked icons; otherwise just the icon with the cursor on it will be deleted.

Copy icons

To copy icons from one resource to another, use "Icon/Copy" and enter the name of the target resource in the dialog window. If you use the mouse, you can simply drag the desired icon holding the right mouse button and drop it on any other resource window. You can copy either single icons or whole groups; like for deleting, the selection cursor has to be on a marked icon to copy a whole group.

Update window

To update a resource window (after modifying an icon with the editor, for example), you can use the "Update" command from the "Resource" menu.

11.6 Create a New Resource

To create a resource file, use "Resource/Create". The rules for naming the resource file apply here as well. Click on the asterisk, then enter a name for your new resource.

11.7 The Snapshot Utility

The snapshot function of Studio allows you to import icons from other graphics programs.

You install the memory resident snapshot program with the command "Install snapshot" from the "Snapshot" menu or by calling "SCANPIC.EXE" outside of Studio. Once it is loaded, it remains in the memory until you shut down the computer or reboot it.

Making screen shots

To capture a screen shot, bring the image you want to grab icons from on the screen and press (Prt Sc). The current screen content will be saved in the file "SCAN.PIC" in Studio's directory. Notice that the screen format has to be EGA or VGA (640 pixel columns), the mode in which you operate Tempest.

Grabbing icons from the screen shot

Return to Studio and select the function "Snapshot/Frame icons" or press (F4). The snap shot will appear on the screen, along with an icon-size cursor. Notice that the palette of Studio will be used, regardless of the colors that were on the screen when you took the snapshot. You can move the cursor with the mouse or the keyboard (the cursor keys move it in pixel steps, (PgUp) and (PgDn) move it in steps of 10 vertically, (Home) and (End) do the same horizontally). When the desired icon is focused, press (Enter) or the left mouse button. You can go on selecting more icons in the same way. As soon as you quit this process by pressing (Esc) or the right mouse button, icon editor windows with all grabbed icons appear on the screen, from where you can either process them or save them directly to a resource file.

Selecting background color

The function "Snapshot/Background color..." allows you to select a color that will appear transparent in the icon editor window. The default color is black.

11.8 Graphics Programs on the Desktop

It is often useful to switch directly between Studio and another graphics program to transfer large amounts of icons or to call it in an easier way. The command "Install graphics prg." from the "Snapshot" menu allows you to place frequently used programs as icons on the desktop. Just enter the full file name (with drive, path and extension) and select an icon via the "Icon..." button (the Tempest home resource is always used). The file icon will appear in the lower left-hand corner of the screen, like iconized windows. You call the program by selecting the icon and pressing (Enter) or performing a double click.

You remove a file icon with the "Close" command from the "Windows" menu.

11.9 Change Color Palette

"Studio/Colors" allows you to customize the screen colors.

11.10 Developing Icon Resources for TIM Files

One of the main purposes of Studio is to create icon libraries for TIM files easily. If you're a programmer, you may want to supply your own icons with your program. For example, you can keep all your icons in a main library, and create individual libraries in which you copy the required icons from the main library. It is also a good idea to agree on one color palette for all your icons so you can use it throughout the library. If you mix up icons that were drawn using different palettes, the color adaptation routine of Iconize might not be able to work properly.

For more details on TIM files, refer to Chapter 9, "The Iconize Utility".

12. Additional Utilities

Tempest includes two additional utilities, "CLEANRES.EXE" and "MAKEPAL.EXE". These two programs are for more advanced users of Tempest and are used for resource file handling.

12.1 CLEANRES.EXE

"CLEANRES.EXE" removes unnecessary spaces from resource files that are created when a resource is extensively used. This process will make the resource file more compact and more efficient to access.

The format is:

```
CLEANRES <resource file name>
```

12.2 MAKEPAL.EXE

You can create your own palette files with "MAKEPAL". The actual color settings of Tempest are always used. Its calling format is:

```
MAKEPAL <file name> <palette name>
```

<File name> is the name the palette is saved under; <palette name> is a name, which can consist of up to 16 characters, containing its real name. If <palette name> contains spaces, they must be replaced by underlines ('_').

Example:

```
MAKEPAL MYPAL.VGA My_VGA_palette
```

saves the currently used palette as "MYPAL.VGA", with the name "My VGA palette". When you place this file in Tempest's "PAL" directory, this is the name that will appear in the dialog box "Load color set" of the color configuration section of the CONFIG program.

Appendix A: Keyboard Reference

All of the function keys and their actions are listed here:

Key	Action
F1	Help
Shift + F1	Tempest Info
F2	Notepad
F3	View file
F4	Edit text file
Shift + F4	Create text file
Alt + F4	Change to parent directory
F5	Copy files
Ctrl + F5	Place program in Icon bar
Alt + F5	Zoom window
F6	Move files
F7	Make directory
Alt + F7	Search for files
F8	Delete files
F9	File Information
Ctrl + F9	Select files
F10	Enable menu bar
Shift + F10	Tree on/off
Ctrl + F10	Arrange windows

Appendix B: Files Of Tempest

Here is a list of the files that Tempest copies to your hard drive, as well as the files created during your work in Tempest, along with a description of each file.

CLEANRES.EXE	Resource cleanup utility
CONFIG.EXE	Configuration Setup Utility program
CONFIG.TED	Configuration file (of TED)
CONFIG.TID	Configuration file (of Tempest Desktop)
CONFIG.TST	Configuration file (of Tempest Studio)
DEFAULTS.TID	File for defaults
HELP.TED	Help file for TED text editor
HELP_RES.TID	Help file
ICONIZE.EXE	Iconize utility
ICON_LIB.TID	Icon library (used by Iconize, located in TIM directory)
MAKEPAL.EXE	Palette generator
NOTES.TID	Note file (of Tempest Desktop)
NOTES.TIS	Note file (of TED)
STUDIO.COM	Tempest Studio
STUDIO.EXE	Tempest Studio (main program)
TED.EXE	External text editor program
TEMPEST.COM	Resident startup program
TMAIN.EXE	Main program
*.EGA	EGA color sets (in PAL directory)
*.TIM	Tempest Icon Map files for various software packages (in TIM directory)
*.VGA	VGA color sets (in PAL directory)

Index

Abacus

pc catalog

Order Toll Free 1-800-451-4319

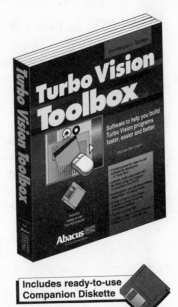

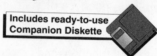

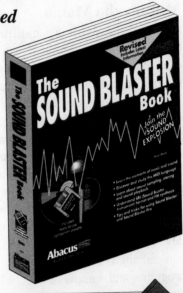

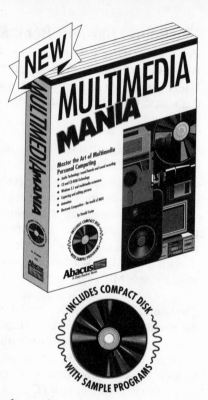

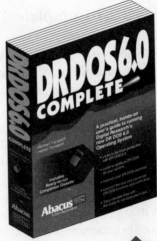

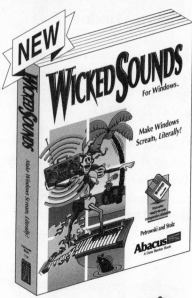

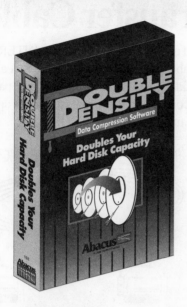

Universal Data Transfer Cables

Universal data transfer cables for parallel or serial use with INTERLNK and INTERSVR are available directly from Abacus. The serial cable is a multiple head cable that allows serial transfer through most IBM compatible desktop and laptop computers. The parallel cable allows parallel transfer through most IBM compatible systems. Both cables operate with the INTERLNK and INTERSVR software included with MS-DOS 6.0.

Universal Serial Data Transfer cable   *Universal Parallel Data Transfer cable*

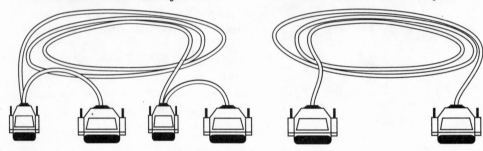

These cables allow INTERLNK/INTERSVR transfer between any two IBM compatible PCs with matching parallel, 9 pin serial or 25 pin serial ports.

ON THE DISKETTE...

This book is a complete reference and practical users guide to learning and using DOS 6.0. **DOS 6.0 Complete** contains numerous examples and tips for getting the most out of DOS 6.0. **Tempest** (a $29.95 value), the graphic shell for MS-DOS 6.0 is included with this book.

The companion diskette included with this book saves you time because you don't have to type in the examples or program listings presented in the book. It also enables you to start using the many programs and tips and tricks immediately. So you can quickly become a DOS 6.0 expert. The following directories are included on the diskette:

TEMPEST

- As an added BONUS to this book is the complete Graphic User Interface for DOS 6.0, TEMPEST. TEMPEST is a complete independent software package included with this book. The complete TEMPEST manual is the last section of this book.

  TEMPEST is an intuitive shell for DOS 6.0 that allows you to graphically display all of the program and files on your hard drive. Using Tempest anyone can easily master complex DOS computer commands with a simple point and click of the mouse.

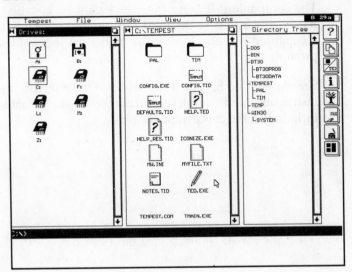

DOS6CPLT directory

This contains the directories with the examples and program listings presented in the book. The INSTALL program will easily copy these to your hard drive. After running INSTALL, your hard drive will contain the following directories:

BASIC directory

- Contains program listings for QBasic, DOS 6.0's programming language. QBasic, which stands for Quick Beginners All Purpose Symbolic Instruction Code, is included with DOS 6.0. With QBasic you can write your own computer applications. This directory includes programs that will show you how to start programming in QBasic. See Chapter 17, Using QBasic for complete information about the files contained in this directory.

TOOLS directory

- Contains ready-to-run programs that speed up your work with DOS 6.0. Includes programs that configure screen colors, find files, display function key assignments, safely format diskettes (doesn't endanger hard drive), configure your printer and much more.

Easy Installation

The companion diskette files can easily be installed on your hard drive by using the INSTALL program. Simply insert the companion diskette in drive A: and type INSTALL at the A: prompt.

See Appendix E, The Companion Diskette for installation instructions and complete information on the valuable utilities included on the companion diskette.

Book/Diskette Packages:

• • • • Save hours of typing in source listings from the book.

• • • • Provide complete ready-to-run batch file listings and multiple examples; help avoid printing and typing mistakes.

• • • • This diskette contains the QBasic programs and batch files presented in the text along with many examples to make you an MS-DOS 6.0 expert now. This *Special Edition* also includes **Tempest**, an intuitive DOS 6.0 Shell.

If you bought this book without the diskette, call us Toll Free **1-800-451-4319** to order our economical companion diskette and save yourself valuable time.

Abacus  5370 52nd Street SE • Grand Rapids, MI 49512

DOS 6.0 Complete Special Edition Companion Diskette:

TEMPEST directory
As an added BONUS to this *Special Edition* is the complete Graphic User Interface for DOS 6.0, **Tempest**. **Tempest** is an intuitive shell for DOS 6.0 that allows you to graphically display all of the programs and files on your hard drive. Using **Tempest** anyone can easily master complex DOS commands with a simple point and click of the mouse.

DOS6CPLT directory
This contains archived files of the examples and program listings presented in the book. The INSTALL program will easily copy these to your hard drive. After running INSTALL your hard drive will contain the following directories:

• • • • The BASIC directory contains all the QBasic program listings from Chapter 17 (Using QBasic).

• • • • The TOOLS directory contains a group of new, ready-to-run programs to streamline your sessions with DOS 6.0.

• • • • The companion diskette allows you to start using the program, tips, hints and tricks presented in the book immediately.

Turn Back for More Information on the Companion Diskette!

DOS 6 has many new features
...except one – and it's HERE!

ON THE DISKETTE ...

Tempest is a full featured graphical shell that makes working with DOS 6 a breeze.

So in addition to all the inside info that you need to know about using DOS 6, you'll also get a super graphical shell that makes DOS 6 even more user friendly.

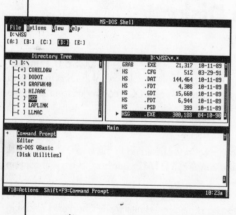

Compare Tempest... ▼

Tempest

▲ ...to the MS-DOS Shell

...and See for Yourself how much Easier Tempest is to Use!

◄ **Turn Back for More Information on the Companion Diskette!**